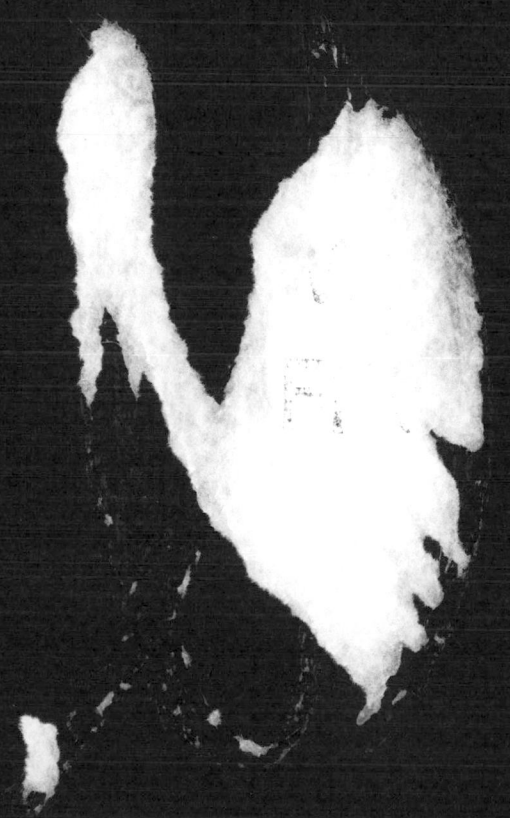

Treasures *from* Budapest

EUROPEAN MASTERPIECES FROM LEONARDO TO SCHIELE

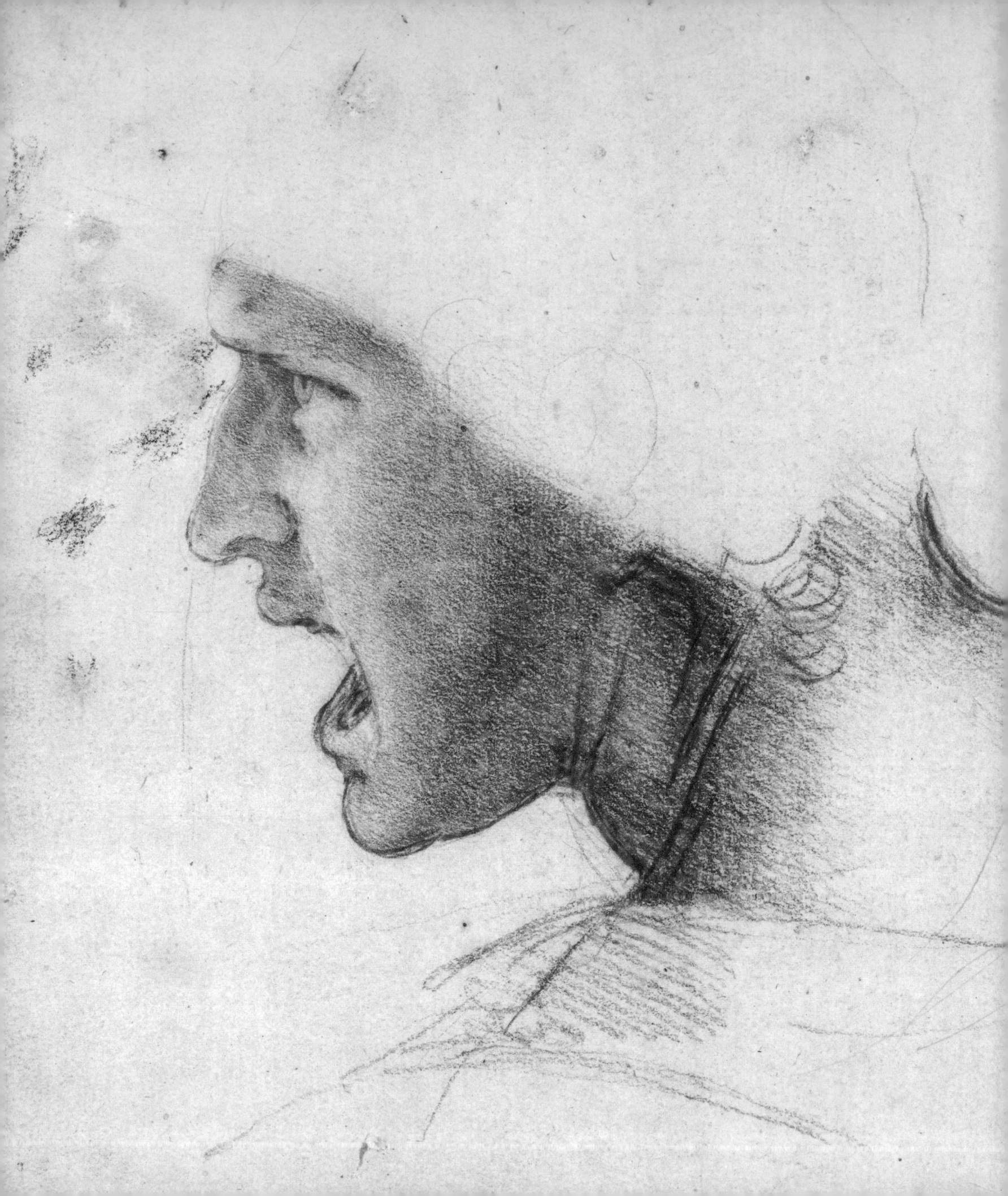

Treasures *from* Budapest

EUROPEAN MASTERPIECES FROM LEONARDO TO SCHIELE

Edited by
David Ekserdjian

ROYAL ACADEMY OF ARTS

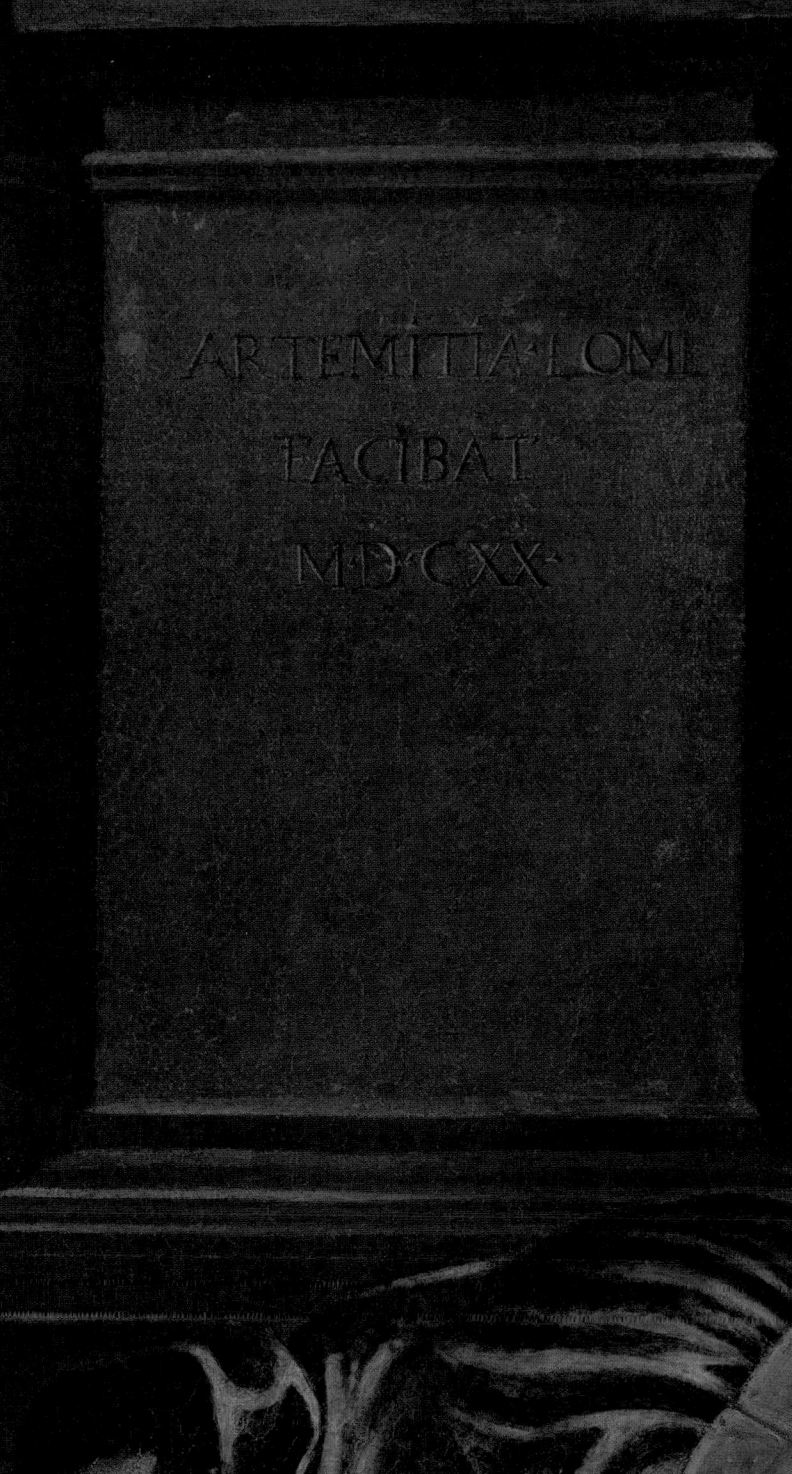

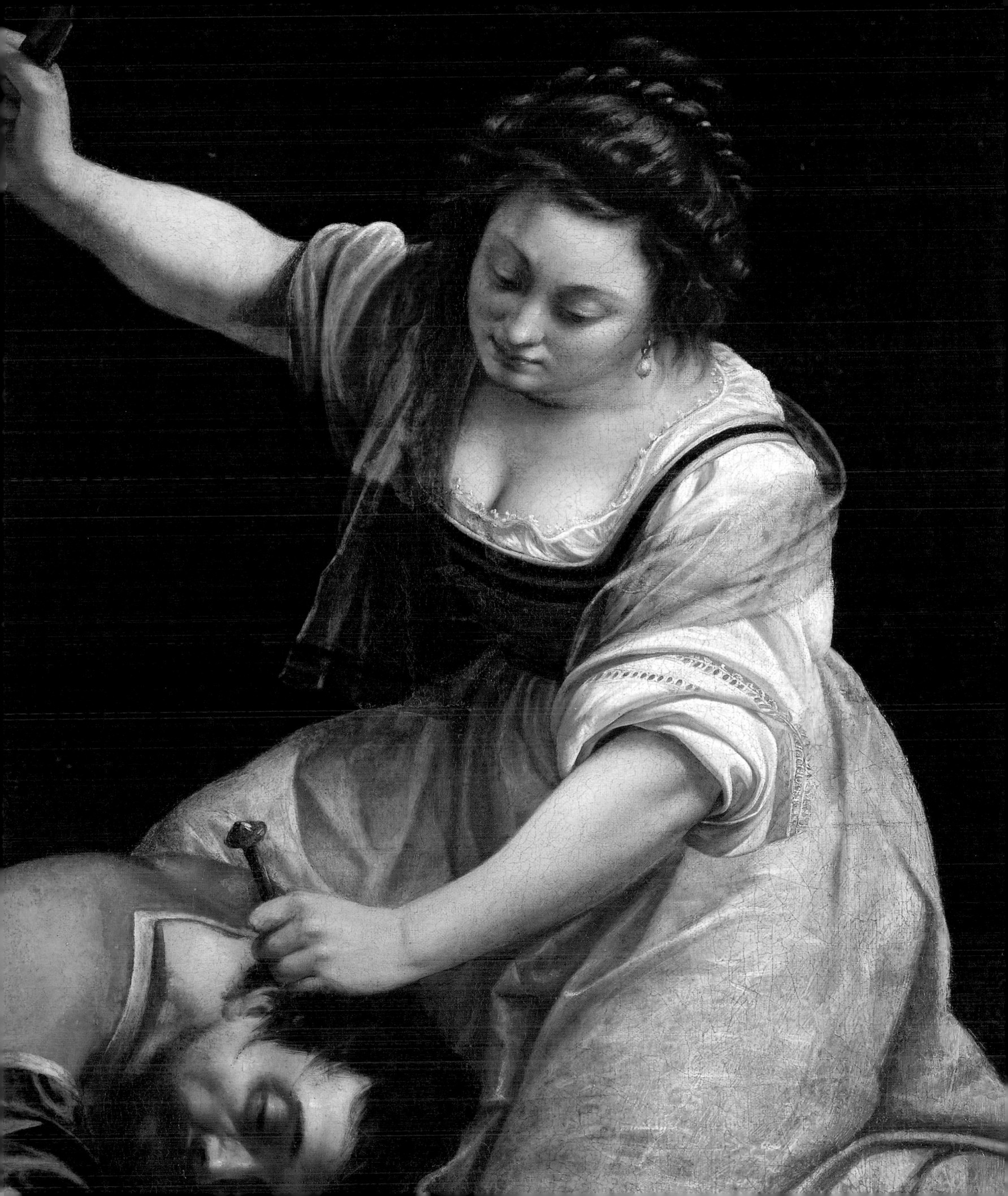

First published on the
occasion of the exhibition
'Treasures from Budapest:
European Masterpieces from
Leonardo to Schiele'

Royal Academy of Arts, London
25 September – 12 December 2010

Supported by

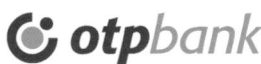 otpbank

Travel Partner

COX & KINGS

The Royal Academy of Arts
is grateful to Her Majesty's
Government for agreeing to
indemnify this exhibition under
the National Heritage Act 1980,
and to Resource, The Council for
Museums, Archives and Libraries, for
its help in arranging the indemnity.

EXHIBITION CURATORS
David Ekserdjian
Joanna Norman
assisted by Sarah Lea

EXHIBITION MANAGEMENT
Idoya Beitia
assisted by Ana B. Martínez

PHOTOGRAPHIC AND
COPYRIGHT CO-ORDINATION
Trine Lyngby Hougaard

CATALOGUE
Royal Academy Publications
David Breuer
Beatrice Gullström
Carola Krueger
Sophie Oliver
Peter Sawbridge
Nick Tite

Copy-editing and proofreading: Kate Bell
Design: Isambard Thomas
Colour origination: DawkinsColour
Printed by Graphicom

EDITORIAL NOTE

All works have been generously
lent by the Museum of Fine
Arts, Budapest, except where
otherwise stated. All measurements
are given height before width (and
before depth in the case of sculpture).

ILLUSTRATIONS
PAGE 2: detail of cat. 12
PAGES 4–5: detail of cat. 79
PAGES 8–9: detail of cat. 78
PAGES 12–13: detail of cat. 73
PAGES 30–31: detail of cat. 54
PAGE 33: detail of cat. 4
PAGE 45: detail of cat. 67
PAGE 103: detail of cat. 97
PAGE 157: detail of cat. 158
PAGE 191: detail of cat. 221
PAGES 280–81: detail of cat. 77

PHOTOGRAPHIC
ACKNOWLEDGEMENTS
All images of works of art are
supplied and reproduced by kind
permission of the Museum of Fine
Arts and the Hungarian National
Gallery, Budapest. We are grateful to
the photographers, Zsuzsa Bokor,
Dénes Józsa, Tibor Mester, András
Rázsó and Csanád Sesztay for their
images. The infrared reflectography
on page 227 is reproduced by kind
permission of Erwin Emmerling.

COPYRIGHT ACKNOWLEDGEMENTS
Cats 194, 220 © ADAGP, Paris,
and DACS, London 2010; cat. 212
© ADAGP, Paris, and DACS,
London 2010 (FULL CONSULT);
cat. 218 © Fondation Oskar
Kokoschka/DACS 2010; cat. 219
© Succession Picasso 2010

ACKNOWLEDGEMENTS

The curators of the exhibition would
like to express their gratitude to the
following individuals for their
invaluable assistance during the
realisation of this exhibition: Zsuzsa
Bakó, Eszter Bakonyi, Ilona Balogh,
Gábor Bellák, Zsuzsanna Boda,
Szilvia Bodnár, Nicholas Bodóczky,
Kata Bodor, Judit Boros, Enikő
Buzási, Andrea Czére, Zsuzsanna
Dobos, Kinga Dornacher, Anna
Ecsedy, Margit Eisenmayer, Ildikó
Ember, Melinda Erdőháti, András
Fáy, Krisztián Fonyódi, Henrietta
Galambos, Andrew T. Gane,
Mariann Gergely, Teréz Gerszi,
Judit Geskó, Zsuzsanna Gila, László
Gippert, Zsuzsa Gonda, Annamária
Gosztola, Anna Jávor, Enikő Jigl,
István Juhász, Emese Kádár, Zoltán
Kárpáti, Zoltán Kiss, Zsófia Kovács,
Sára Kulcsár-Szabó, Mónika Kumin,
József Lakatos, Adriána Lantos,
Ferenc Magyari, Magdi Máté, Árpád
Mikó, Amy Módly, Eszter Molnár
Aczél, Erzsébet Mózer, Márton
Orosz, Miklós Pataky, Manga
Pattantyús, Judit Nagy, Melinda
Nagy, Imre Nemcsics, Gábor
Németh, István Pankaszi, Edit
Ploennivy, Györgyi Poszler, Barbara
Potzner, Orsolya Radványi, Dávid
János Rátonyi, Tünde Réti, Richard
Robinson, Eszter Seres, Dávid Szabó,
Marianne Szabó, Eszter Szász, Edit
Szentgyörgyi, Miklós Szentkirályi,
Miriam Szőcs, György Szücs, Kinga
Tarcsai, Vilmos Tátrai, Ferenc Tóth,
Gyöngyi Török, József Varga, Axel
Vécsey, Orsolya Zsámboki

Catalogue *plates*

Catalogue *entries*

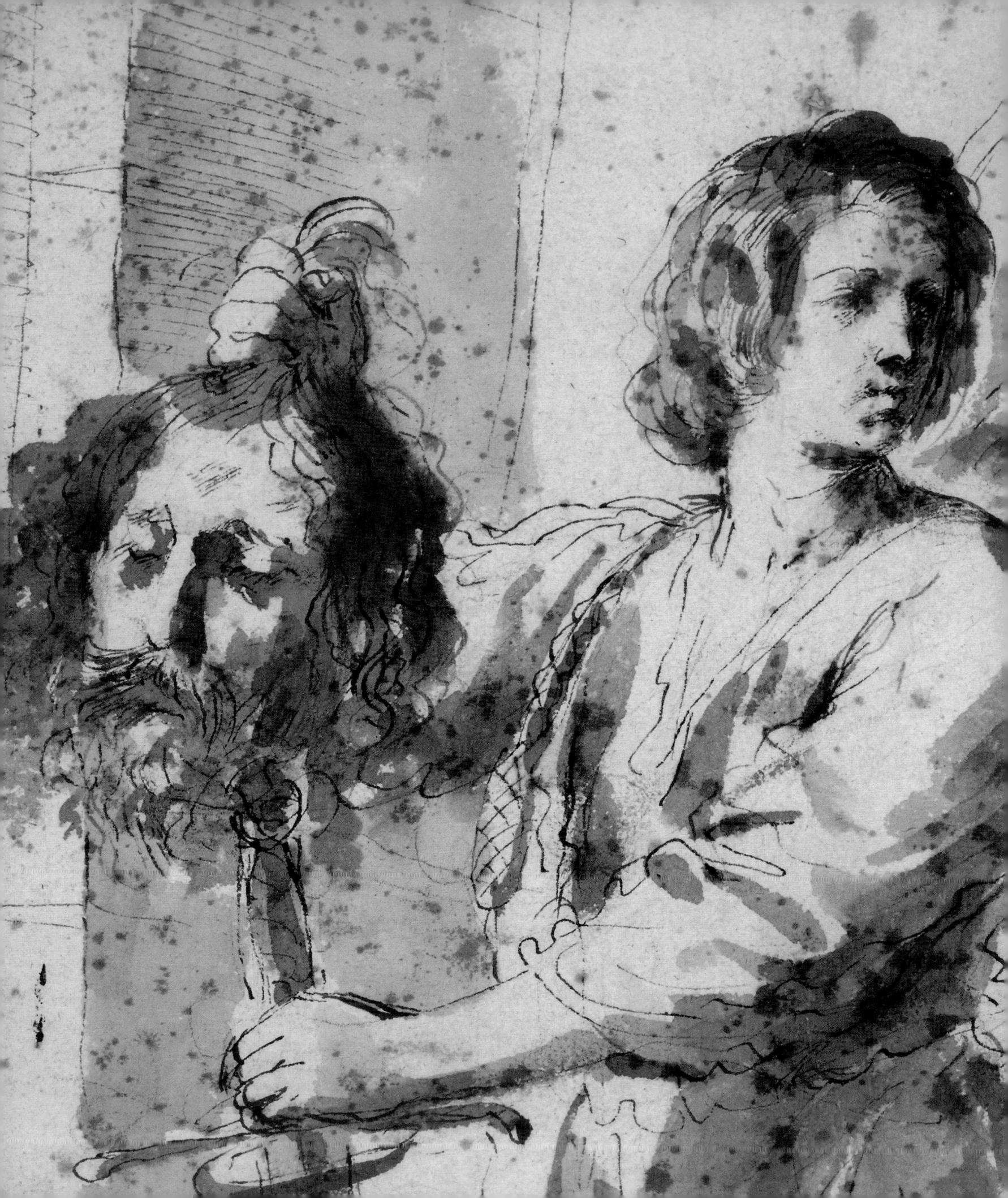

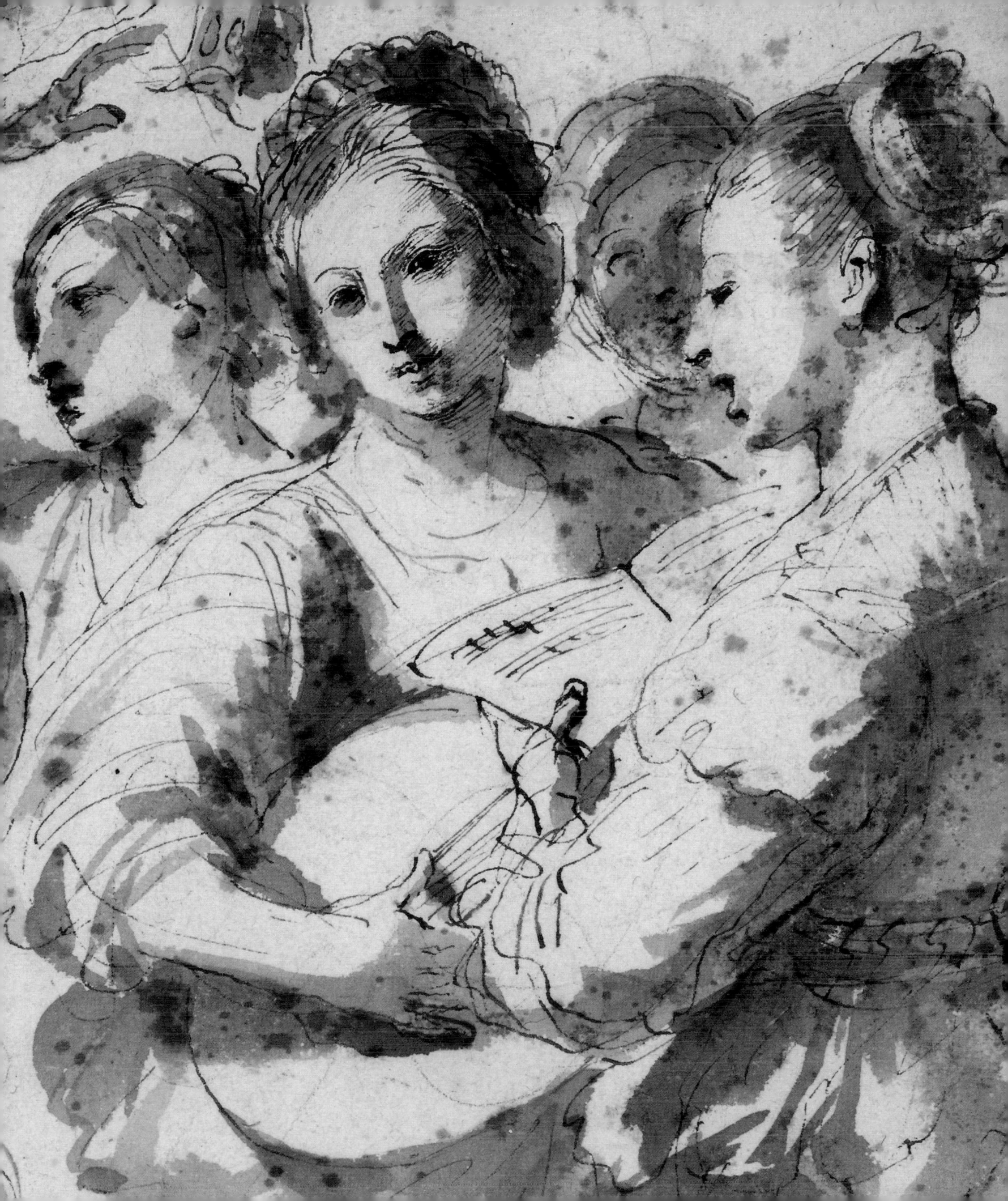

President's Foreword

The Royal Academy is delighted to be presenting 'Treasures from Budapest' at the moment when Hungary is about to take up the mantle of the presidency of the European Union. Between them, the Museum of Fine Arts and the Hungarian National Gallery hold one of the finest art collections in Central Europe. This has hitherto not been accorded the recognition it deserves, a fact which this exhibition aims to rectify. 'Treasures from Budapest' is the largest single loan ever made by the museums and the first major showcase of the collections in the United Kingdom. It reveals the breadth, richness and quality of the treasures to be found in Budapest.

Since its foundation in 1896 (the millennium of Hungarian statehood) the Museum of Fine Arts has established itself as a historical and contemporary art collection for the Hungarian people. With the acquisition by the Hungarian state of the Esterházy Collection, the nucleus of the collection of Old Master paintings and drawings was formed, with an outstanding selection of works ranging from Leonardo da Vinci to Goya. Later acquisitions, as well as important bequests and donations of works from Hungarian benefactors, built on the riches of the Esterházy holdings to create a comprehensive collection of European art of the highest quality. From its inception, the museum also acquired historical and contemporary Hungarian art, which is now housed in the Hungarian National Gallery. Much of this wonderful collection is on show here for the first time outside Hungary.

The Royal Academy wishes to express its sincere thanks to the directors of the two Budapest institutions: Dr László Baán of the Museum of Fine Arts and Ferenc Csák of the Hungarian National Gallery. Their extraordinary generosity in agreeing to lend so many of their finest works has enabled the exhibition to reveal the exceptional quality of the collections. We are profoundly grateful to them and to the curators from the two museums for their commitment to the project and for the contribution of their scholarship to this exhibition catalogue. We extend our thanks to their colleagues in the Exhibitions Department at the Museum of Fine Arts, particularly Henrietta Galambos, Zsófia Kovács and Eszter Szász, for their support in realising the practical organisation of the exhibition and catalogue. At the Hungarian National Gallery thanks are also due in particular to Mariann Gergely, Chief Curator. At the Royal Academy we are grateful to the exhibition's chief curator, Professor David Ekserdjian, for his commitment to the project. We would also like to thank the exhibition designers, PearsonDooney, for their splendid presentation of the works within the beautiful spaces of the Royal Academy's main galleries.

This exhibition would not have been possible without the generous sponsorship of OTP Bank, with additional support from Daniel Katz Gallery. We would also like to thank Borbála Czakó, Hungarian Ambassador to the United Kingdom, and Ildikó Takács, Director of the Hungarian Cultural Centre in London, for all their assistance with the project.

Inevitably, the exhibition can only offer a taste of the riches held within these two institutions. We hope that our visitors will be inspired to visit Budapest to discover further treasures of the collections for themselves.

Sir Nicholas Grimshaw CBE
President, Royal Academy of Arts

Director's Foreword

I am delighted and proud that the Museum of Fine Arts, Budapest, has been given the opportunity to present the highlights of its collections at such an illustrious institution as the Royal Academy of Arts, London.

Although many individual works of art from our collections have appeared in Britain, 'Treasures from Budapest' is the first entire exhibition we have sent to the United Kingdom, and the selection of works that it contains is greater in value than any previously sent abroad from Hungary. As a complement to our loans, the Hungarian National Gallery, with whose early history our institution has much in common, has lent some of the most spectacular pieces from its own collection, thereby giving visitors a representative sample of Hungarian masterpieces within an international art-historical context.

The paintings, drawings and sculptures shown here – over two hundred works – encompass the art of more than five centuries, from the fifteenth century to the twentieth, from Leonardo da Vinci to Egon Schiele. We hope that art historians and museum visitors alike will appreciate the completeness of the selection, comprising as it does a cross-section of the four most important holdings of the museum: the Gallery of Old Masters, the Department of Prints and Drawings, the Collection of Art after 1800, and the Department of Old Sculptures.

This handsome catalogue is a permanent record of an exceptional showing of masterpieces from one of the most significant Central European museums. Although the museum itself was founded on the occasion of the millennial celebration of Hungarian statehood in 1896, the collections that it was created to display can trace their history back to the seventeenth century, as is explained in the introductory essay.

I would like to express my heartfelt thanks to my British colleagues: Professor David Ekserdjian of the University of Leicester, curator of the exhibition with Joanna Norman of the Royal Academy; Charles Saumarez Smith, Secretary and Chief Executive of the Royal Academy; Sir Nicholas Grimshaw, President of the Royal Academy; Kathleen Soriano, Director of Exhibitions; Sarah Lea, Curatorial Assistant; Idoya Beitia, Exhibitions Manager; Peter Sawbridge, Managing Editor; and all those who have taken part in the organisation of the exhibition and the creation of its catalogue.

I hope the London public will receive 'Treasures from Budapest' with interest and enthusiasm.

László Baán
General Director, Museum of Fine Arts, Budapest

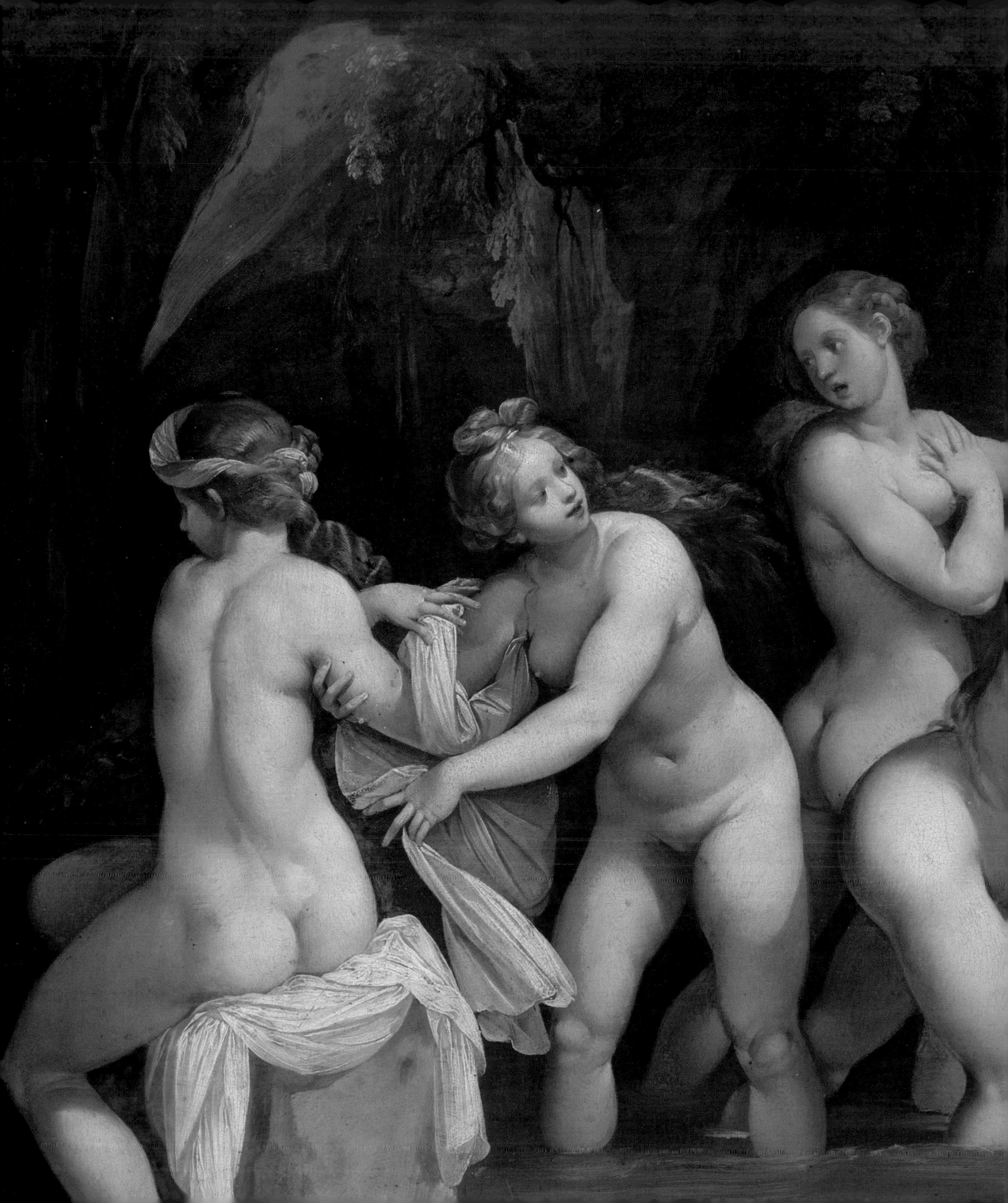

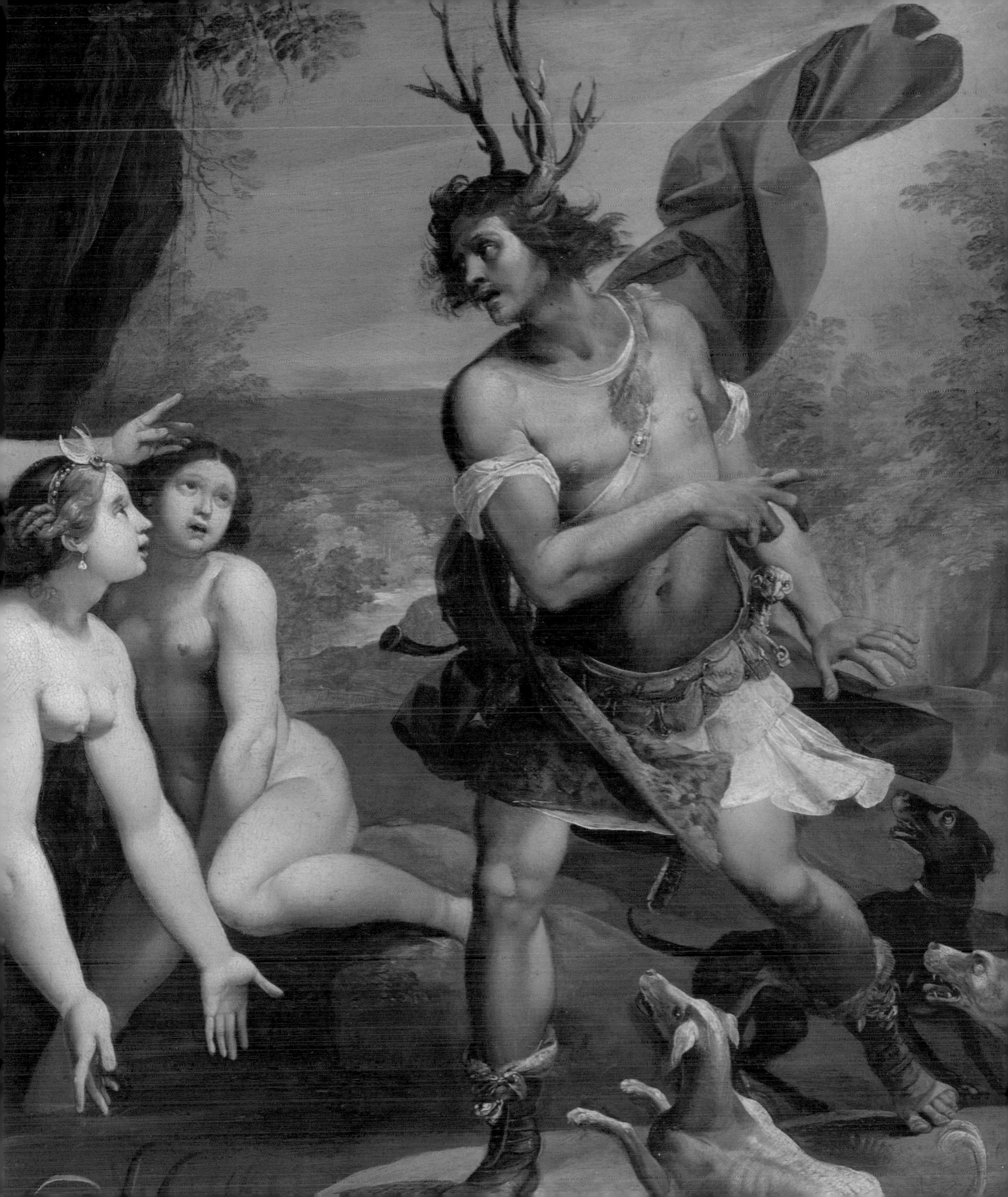

The Museum of Fine Arts, Budapest: Past and Present

ANDREA CZÉRE

The Museum of Fine Arts (fig. 1) opened its doors in 1906, and is today considered the most important art museum in Central Europe, after the Kunsthistorisches Museum in Vienna. The establishment of the Budapest museum was neither facilitated by monarchical resolution, nor based on a royal collection. The museum's existence was indebted to the consolidation of prior institutions formed from the collections of the Hungarian nobility and intellectual élite, and its collections are derived from two main sources. Firstly the fund of Hungarian and international painting, sculpture, drawings and prints, and antiquities of the Hungarian National Museum, augmented over a century by donations and acquisitions. Secondly the collections of the National Picture Gallery, established in 1871 when the European paintings, drawings and prints collected by the leading family of the Hungarian aristocracy, the Esterházy, were purchased by the state,[1] and subsequently further expanded.

The Formation of the Esterházy Collection

The Esterházy family initiated their art patronage and collecting activities at the beginning of the seventeenth century. Count Nikolaus Esterházy (1582–1645) advanced from his line of lesser nobility to the Palatinate of Hungary by election, and later built Schloss Esterházy in Forchtenstein (Austria). According to the evidence of his last will and testament (1641), at that time he already had at his disposal significant riches. His son Paul Esterházy (1635–1713) was likewise elected Palatine, and in 1687 received the title of Prince of the Holy Roman Empire; he was soon to become the lord of vast lands as a reward for his loyalty to the Habsburg rulers. The prince was a poet, composer and painter, the builder of Schloss Eisenstadt (Austria), and at the same time a passionate collector. He donated a library to the Franciscans, and in Schloss Forchtenstein he accumulated his collection of portraits, weapons and the items in his *Wunderkammer* – the famous Esterházy treasures. Sub-

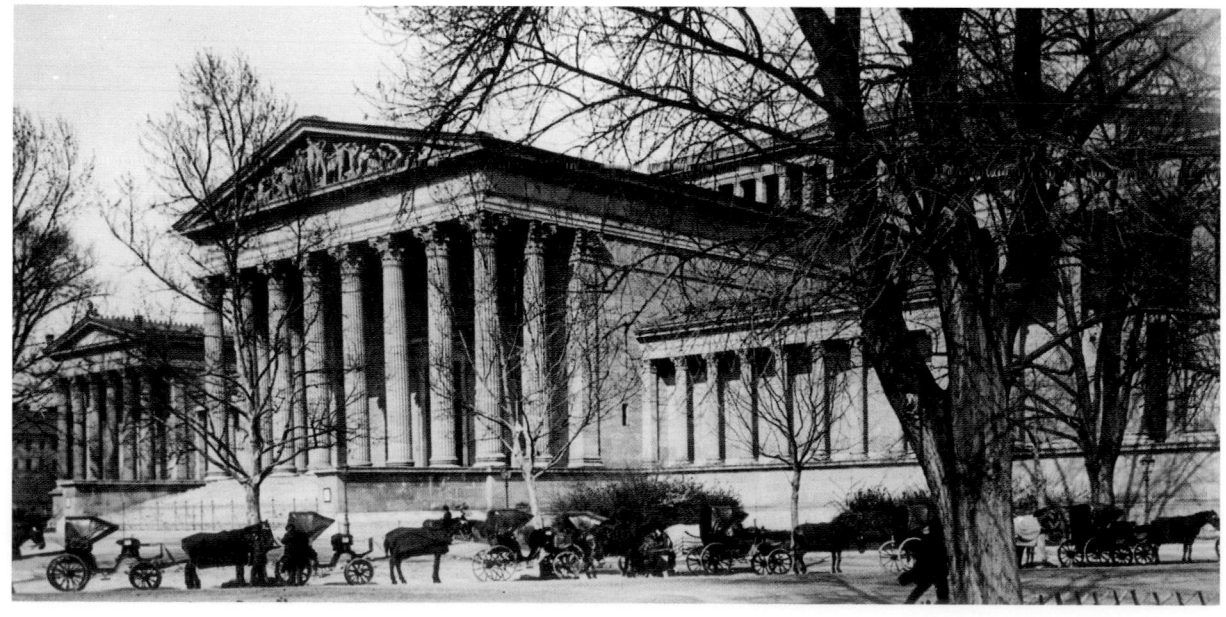

Fig. 1
The Museum of Fine Arts, Budapest, 1906

sequent descendants of the family continued to collect on an increasingly expansive scale, encouraged by their studies abroad. One of the sons of Paul the Palatine, Prince Joseph (1687–1721), built a hunting lodge near Süttör (Hungary) on the banks of Lake Fertő, which became a favoured residence of his first son, Prince Paul Anton (1711–1762), a cavalry general and envoy extraordinary to Naples, and founder of the princely library and music archives. The second son of Prince Joseph, Nikolaus (1714–1790), colonel, then general, and from 1765 Captain of the Hungarian Guards, expanded the Süttör lodge into a luxurious palace (fig. 2) modelled on Versailles, receiving guests of princely rank in its 126 rooms, opera house, puppet theatre, and sumptuous garden and park. He was fittingly named Nikolaus 'the Magnificent' owing to his taste for memorable festivities and patronage of the arts. From descriptions we know that he gathered in the palace some 348 paintings – primarily Italian, Netherlandish and Austrian – though the majority were decorative rather than works of any great artistic distinction.

Following Anton Esterházy, his son Nikolaus II (1765–1833) (fig. 3) inherited the estate, and it is his name that is most strongly connected with the true development of the Esterházy Collection. Nikolaus purchased more than one thousand pictures and assembled a magnificent collection of drawings and prints in the first three decades of the nineteenth century. He remodelled his primary residence, Schloss Eisenstadt, in the classical style. A legion of art connoisseurs and specialists from home and abroad assisted his passionate collecting – including the Prefect of the Royal Museum in Naples, Mattia Zarullo. Among the artists entrusted with administering the collection, the Viennese engraver Joseph Fischer (1769–1822) (fig. 4) was the most significant, aiding in classification and acquisition. Fischer became the prince's gallery inspector from 1804, and from 1811 director of the collection of paintings and prints. His role expanded, especially from 1814, when, following the setting up of the galleries at Pottendorf and then Laxenburg, the collections were transferred to Vienna. During his two decades of work,

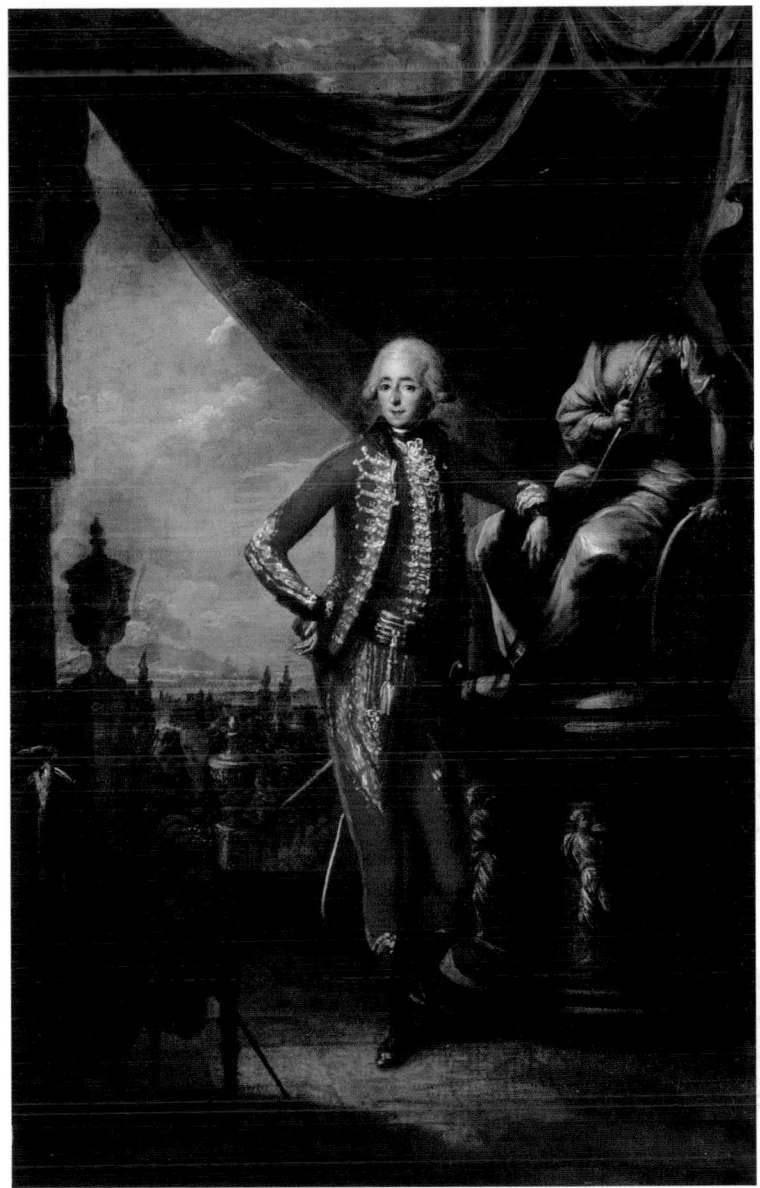

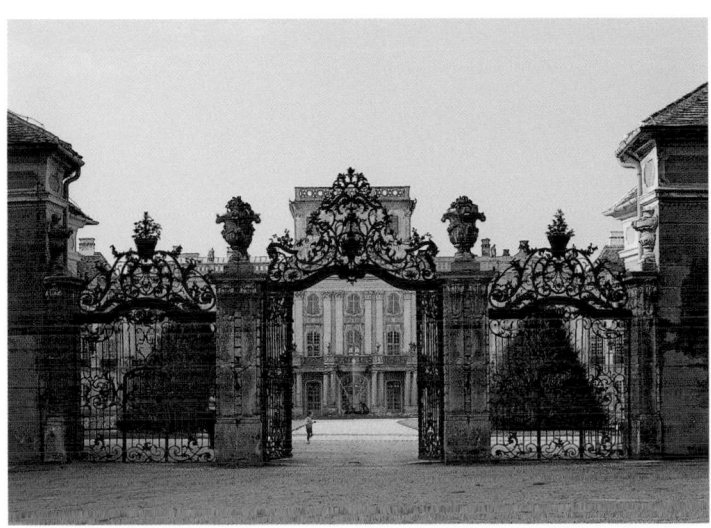

Fig. 2
Entrance to the Esterházy Palace, Fertőd

Fig. 3
Martin Knoller, *Portrait of Prince Nikolaus II Esterházy*, 1792–93.
Oil on canvas, 59 × 37 cm. Hungarian National Gallery, Budapest

Fig. 4
Joseph Fischer, *Self-portrait*, 1794.
Etching and aquatint, 233 × 154 mm. Museum of Fine Arts, Budapest

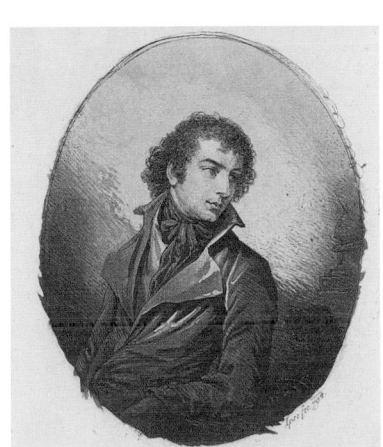

the collection of drawings and prints grew enormously in renown, becoming the third most important collection of graphic art in Vienna after the Hofbibliothek and the Albertina. In the first catalogue of the gallery's holdings, prepared in 1812 on the occasion of the Laxenburg installation, from approximately one thousand pictures, 528 were on display, arranged by nationality. In 1814 Prince Nikolaus II purchased the Viennese summer palace of Prince Kaunitz in Mariahilf (fig. 5) – in conjuction with many of his paintings – and brought all his collections together there. Comprising major works from many previously well-known galleries and drawings collections – among them the Borghese, the Doria-Pamphilj, the Barberini and the Bourke collections, as well as the Parisian Poggi drawings collection, the Prague Nowohratzky-Kollowrath collection of drawings and prints, and the Praun Collection of Nuremberg – this was one of the most celebrated groups of treasures in Vienna for half a century. From 27 April 1815, the gallery was open to visitors twice a week. However, following the death of Prince Nikolaus II in 1833, financial constraints prevented significant further growth of the collection.

With the rise of nationalist movements during the era of reform, as early as 1836, there emerged an ambition to bring home to Hungary the renowned Esterházy Gallery. In keeping with the demands of public opinion seeking to shift cultural development to Hungary, Prince Paul Anton III (1786–1866) transported his family collection from Vienna to Pest in 1865, where its contents were shown from 12 December in the second- and third-floor rooms of the palace recently built for the Hungarian Academy of Sciences (fig. 6).

The name of Nikolaus Esterházy III (1817–1894), son of Paul, is linked with the sale of the gallery to the Hungarian state, which was motivated by financial difficulties. The administrator of the princely property offered the collection to the President of the Hungarian Academy of Sciences, the Minister of Culture, József Eötvös, and the purchase agreement was signed in December 1870. Accordingly, the gallery of 637 paintings was purchased for 1.1 million forints, and the collection of 3,535 drawings, 51,301 prints and 305 volumes of illustrated books for an additional 200,000 forints. Although there were more advantageous offers, Prince Nikolaus was happy to sell the collection to the Hungarian state, and in 1871 donated to the nation a further six paintings from his palace in Vienna. It is this collection that still represents the core of the Museum of Fine Arts's holdings of Old Master paintings and graphic works. More than a third of the paintings in the current exhibition come from the Esterházy Collection, among them numerous outstanding works, including Raphael's *Esterházy Madonna* (cat. 23), Jan Brueghel the Elder's *Entry of the Animals into the Ark* (cat. 75), Jusepe de Ribera's *Martyrdom of St Andrew* (cat. 97), Goya's *Water-carrier* (cat. 178), Anthony van Dyck's *Married Couple* (cat. 127), Claude Lorrain's *Villa in the Roman Campagna* (cat. 84) and Salomon van Ruysdael's *'After the Rain'* (cat. 132). The most beautiful drawings also originated in the Esterházy Collection, including Leonardo's *Studies for the Heads of Two Soldiers* (cat. 11), Raphael's *Study for a Temporary Decoration* (cat. 22), Veronese's *Peter of Amiens Exhorts Doge Vitale Michiel* (cat. 54), Daniele Crespi's *St Cecilia* (cat. 77) and Rembrandt's *Saskia* (cat. 120). Another sheet shown here, Fra Bartolommeo's *Studies of Dominican Friars* (cat. 27), exemplifies the distinction of the provenance of many of the Esterházy drawings, since it was once part of the collection of Giorgio Vasari, which was later taken over by Pierre Crozat, Pierre-Jean Mariette and Antonio Cesare Poggi.

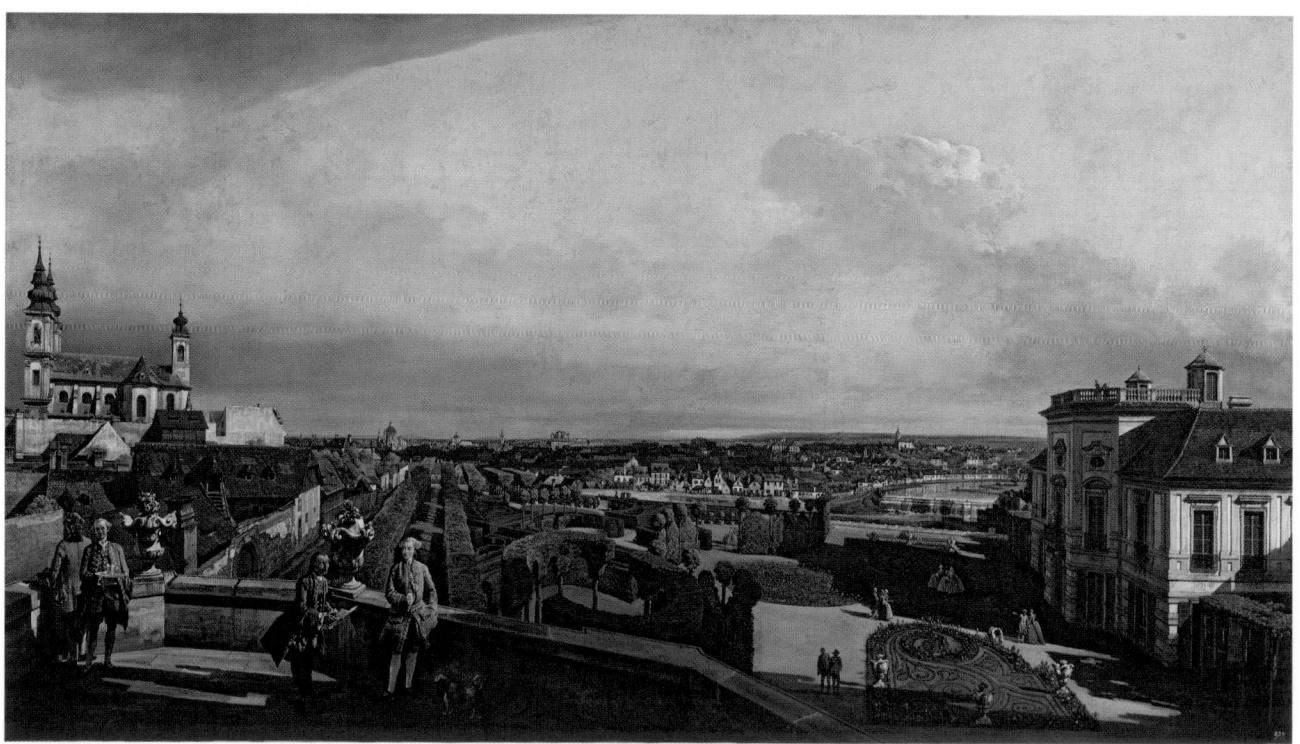

Fig. 5
Bernardo Bellotto, *Kaunitz Palace and Garden in Vienna*, c.1759.
Oil on canvas, 134 × 237 cm. Museum of Fine Arts, Budapest

Fig. 6
Design for the Hungarian Academy of Sciences, 1861

Fig. 7
Gyula Háry, *A Room in the National Picture Gallery*, 1904.
Watercolour, 350 × 455 mm. Museum of Fine Arts, Budapest

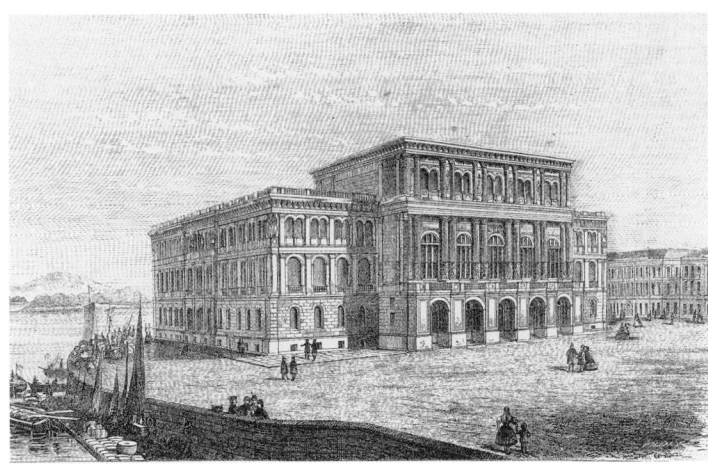

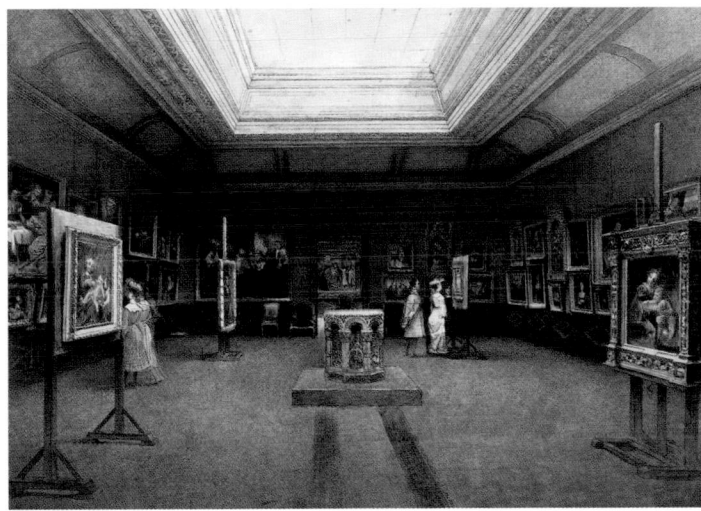

With the purchase of the Esterházy Gallery the most valuable Hungarian art collection was placed in public hands and existed under the name of the National Picture Gallery (Országos Képtár) for 34 years within the Academy of Sciences. Gyula Háry's watercolours executed in 1904 documented the arrangement of the galleries (fig. 7). In 1872 Bishop Arnold Ipolyi, director of the seminary in Pest and one of the first Hungarian art historians, enriched the holdings of the National Picture Gallery with a gift comprising 64 paintings. His collection, with its early Italian paintings, consciously complemented the predominantly later paintings of the Esterházy Gallery.

The Collections of the Hungarian National Museum

Besides the Esterházy Collection, the other main source of works in the future Museum of Fine Arts was the Hungarian National Museum. The first Hungarian public collection, the Széchényi Library and National Museum had been established by Count Ferenc Széchényi (1754–1820) in 1802, and its development commenced during the Parliamentary sessions of the Reform period between 1832 and 1836. The institution, which was founded for the collection of literary and historical relics of the Hungarian past, initially possessed only a few works of art – mainly portraits – but the gallery and collection of drawings and prints soon grew through bequests and gifts. In 1836, with the aid of the Palatine Joseph (1776–1847), the collection of the lawyer and scholar Miklós Jankovich (1772–1846) was purchased. Jankovich had begun to collect in the 1790s, mainly jewellery and archival and library material, but he also acquired several Hungarian and foreign paintings and sculptures. Almost simultaneously with Jankovich's collection, the National Museum obtained 192 paintings from the estate of the Archbishop of Eger, János László Pyrker (1772–1847), rich chiefly in Italian works of art, since Pyrker was Patriarch of Venice. This outstanding collection of paintings included such masterpieces as Giambattista Tiepolo's *Virgin in Glory with Six Saints* (cat. 136).

In 1875 and 1877, on the recommendation of the National Museum's director Ferenc Pulszky (1814–1897), a man with a far-sighted, European outlook, exchanges of Old Masters and modern paintings took place between the National Museum and the National Picture Gallery. With this clarification of their respective remits, the basis for the two most important departments of the later Museum of Fine Arts – the Old Master Paintings and the Department of Art after 1800 – began to take form. Thus, in the newly available rooms of the Academy of Sciences, 726 paintings could be displayed in a hang enriched by the works of the Jankovich and Pyrker Galleries, now amalgamated into the National Picture Gallery. Three paintings in the present exhibition arrived at the Museum of Fine Arts through the National Museum and the National Picture Gallery: Lorenzo Lotto's *Apollo and the Muses with Fame* (cat. 47), and Salvator Rosa's two landscapes, *Harbour with Ruins* (cat. 102) and *Rocky Landscape with Waterfall* (cat. 103). The series of alabaster medallions by Franz Xaver Messerschmidt (cats 151, 152) also originate from the National Museum.

From the National Picture Gallery to the Museum of Fine Arts

The art historian Károly Pulszky (1853–1899), Ferenc Pulszky's son, worked as a museum guard from 1880 at the National Picture Gallery, and then from 1884 as director of the institution. Having had the pictures restored, he swiftly addressed the issue of their scientific cataloguing and proposed many new attributions, as well as making attempts to popularise the collection. By the last years of the nineteenth century the gallery was becoming overcrowded, and since this hindered

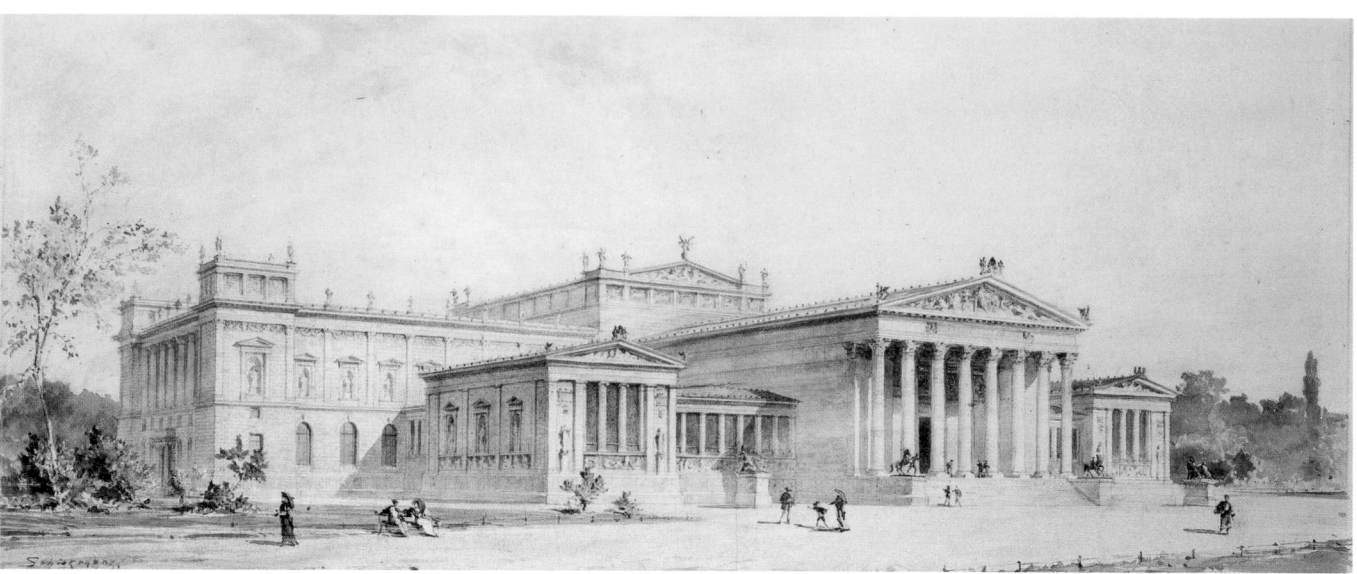

Fig.8
Albert Schickedanz, *Design for the Museum of Fine Arts, Budapest*, 1899.
Watercolour, 515 × 835 mm.
Museum of Fine Arts, Budapest

further growth, the idea arose of establishing a new, independent institution, the Museum of Fine Arts. This museum, whose foundation was entrusted to Pulszky, would merge the country's collections of Hungarian and international art. Indeed the government had already transferred 400,000 forints in 1894 for the expansion of the collections. The director of the National Picture Gallery played a prominent role in this, purchasing a number of works from abroad between 1894 and 1895, and establishing two new categories within the collection: Old Sculptures and Frescoes. As a result of Pulszky's efforts the gallery was enriched with several masterpieces, including Domenico Rosselli's stone relief representing the *Virgin and Child*, acquired in 1895 (cat.3), the tempera panel of *St James the Greater with a Living and a Dead Pilgrim*, now recognised as by Luca Signorelli (cat.35), and the *Portrait of Paul Randon de Boisset* by Jean-Baptiste Greuze (cat.145), an oil painting acquired on the art market in Cologne in 1894.

In 1896 the country celebrated the millennium of Hungarian statehood. The Seventh Legal Statute of Parliament in 1896 – the Millennium Law – provided for the institution of the Museum of Fine Arts. The state appropriated 3.2 million forints for the new museum, of which 1.2 million forints were allotted to its construction. The foundation of the Museum of Fine Arts set as its aim both the collection and the display of works of art, providing visitors with a chronological overview of developments in Hungarian and European painting, sculpture and graphic art, with an emphasis on promoting Hungarian art.

In 1898, in a design competition for the new museum building judged by an international jury, Albert Schickedanz and Fülöp Herzog won second prize (fig.8). Nevertheless, the practicality of their plan in both masterfully fulfilling the requirements of a museum and assimilating the building harmoniously within its surroundings meant that they were commissioned to carry out the project. Construction took place between 1900 and 1906.

In the meantime, in 1901, the painter and restorer István Delhaes (1843–1901) left to the nation the works of art he had collected in Austria, primarily in Vienna. This legacy comprised antique objects as well as works of graphic art, including more than 2,500 drawings and 14,500 prints. The Delhaes Collection, rich in eighteenth- and nineteenth-century Austrian, German and Italian drawings, was a perfect complement to the chiefly earlier sheets from the Esterházy Collection, and included the *Landscape with Waterfall* by Adrian Zingg (cat.170). During the years of preparation for the opening of the Museum of Fine Arts, from the end of the nineteenth century onwards, the state made purchases to fill gaps that had been identified in an attempt to achieve an art-historical continuity. Many nineteenth- and twentieth-century works were acquired during the first decades of the twentieth century to supplement those in the modern collection, which were more modest in number, including Camille Corot's *Nest-robbers* (cat.186), Pierre Puvis de Chavannes's *Magdalene* (cat.191) and Camille Pissarro's *Pont Neuf*, (cat.197). The emerging museum regarded the study of European models and a living connection with contemporary art as being of the foremost importance; an example of this is the acquisition of Auguste Rodin's bronze *Sirens* (cat.193), purchased directly from the artist in 1900, only twelve years after its creation. The 1934 donation by Pál Majovszky of more than 250 works acquired mainly in Paris was a significant enrichment of the museum's nineteenth-century drawings collection.

Past and Present Activity of the Museum of Fine Arts

By the intensive acquisition of Hungarian art and presentation of its development in magnificent exhibitions, the museum's second director, Elek Petrovics (1873–1945), made Hungarian art accessible to a wider public. In the first half of the twentieth century, the museum's staff made great progress in mapping the art of Hungary, and this resulted in substantial and authoritative works published at mid-century that are considered the foundation stones of Hungarian art history.

The structure of the museum, first conceived by the director of the National Picture Gallery, Károly Pulszky, and followed by the first scientific director of the Museum of Fine Arts, Gábor Térey, has undergone numerous changes in the 114 years since its foundation. In the chronology that follows this introduction, the gradual expansion of the collections can be traced, as can the establishment of new departments and the opening of a series of permanent displays.[2] The social role and state subsidy of the institution have also changed a great deal over the past century. Signs of a reduction in the strong state support that had characterised the decades around the museum's foundation appear in the years following the First World War, when, due to the financial difficulties of the truncated country defeated in the war, collections could not be increased by purchases in foreign art markets. During this period, the management of the museum concentrated on the acquisition and presentation of Hungarian art. In the history of the museum, the period surrounding the Second World War was the nadir, when the majority of the collections were evacuated, but fortunately survived without great losses. In the decades following the war – until the political changes of 1989 – there was similarly no possibility for the enrichment of the European collections through purchases abroad. Nevertheless the museum was able significantly to augment its holdings through acquisitions from Hungarian collections. This is illustrated by the list of acquisitions from between 1964 and 1984, when, under the directorship of Klára Garas, the Gallery of Old Master Paintings was enhanced by the addition of 330 pictures.

In 1957 a change in policy brought a fundamental modification to the aims of the institution: Hungarian and European art were divided, and the Hungarian National Gallery was established. It was precisely the fortunate growth of the collections that had made this decision necessary, since the building of the Museum of Fine Arts was no longer able to accommodate the quantity of works of art that it had accumulated over the previous half century. From this time on, the activities of the museum were concentrated on the collection, presentation and cataloguing of European artworks, from ancient times to the present day.

Until recently, the primary emphasis has been on permanent displays at the museum, with the arrangement of the Egyptian, Greek and Roman works and the hang of the Old Master Paintings and Modern Paintings and Sculpture collections in some cases remaining unchanged for years on end. Temporary exhibitions tended to present various artistic movements and genres separately from one another, rather than as collective groupings. Since the 1980s, however, a revolution has occurred in the exhibition activities of museums, motivated by transformed audience expectations. This change is also evident in the exhibition policies of the Museum of Fine Arts in recent years. The permanent displays are extended and renewed more often, and temporary shows have acquired a greater significance than ever before.

Despite increasing economic difficulties and a decline in state support, the political changes of 1989 also brought a fresh spirit to the museum and allowed it to align itself with Western European museum practice. Subsequently this has been further reinforced by the 2004 accession of Hungary to the European Union. At the same time, the increase in visitor numbers indicates a growing interest in art. In 1907, the year following the opening of the Museum of Fine Arts, the number of visitors totalled 198,837, whereas in 2004 their number was more than 500,000, and in 2007 it rose to 763,349. With this figure, the Museum of Fine Arts succeeded in joining the 50 most visited art museums in the world that year. In recent years the institution has received an average of between 400,000 and 500,000 visitors per annum, in contrast to a former average of 250,000, making it the most visited museum in Hungary.

The museum's recent attempt to provide visitors with an enjoyable experience as well as presenting them with information is playing a role in the renewal of interest. The demand for spectacular presentation is not an entirely new phenomenon, neither is the expectation for comprehensive explanatory material. Although it did not occur within the walls of a museum, the Great Exhibition of 1851 in London nevertheless made a considerable impact through ingenious groupings of objects. The goal of the Crystal Palace constructed in Hyde Park was not merely to be a shopping paradise, but also to provide an attractive location for exhibitions and entertainment: a multi-faceted series of events.[3] There are earlier examples of detailed explanation and frequent lectures in connection with exhibited objects in Hungary, not only from the 1950s, when, in line with the cultural policy expectations of the Socialist government, the museum attempted to bring art closer to the mass of the workers who had until then been neglected, but also in late nineteenth-century Europe and America.[4] It is clear, however, that satisfying the public's hunger for information and demand for spectacle, a phenomenon we experience in the present day, calls for increased material support. The museum depends upon the support of sponsors in ever greater measure. Increased attention towards visitors has necessitated new methods of encouraging interest. As of 2005, new departments have been established within the Museum of Fine Arts:

the Exhibitions, Communications, Legal, Registrar's and IT departments have all been called upon to assist in the preparation and realisation of exhibitions. Within the Department of Communications, the Museum Education Department continues to build a wide range of contacts with schools.

Over the past hundred years or so, the individual collections have grown to several times their original size. Measured against the increase in acquisitions that occurred until the 1950s, accessions have not waned in the succeeding half-century or so. Between 1956 and 2006, 627 newly acquired paintings were added to the collection of Old Master paintings, the majority of them from the seventeenth and eighteenth centuries; collecting of works from these epochs had not been to the fore in the preceding period, due to previous lack of knowledge. Today the museum possesses 2,989 Old Master paintings. The individual schools – the Spanish, Italian and Dutch, which make up the strength of the collections just as much as the lesser groupings – were enriched with important works (fig. 9). Many were purchased from collections in Hungary, and these became part of the permanent display. Among them are Artemisia Gentileschi's *Jael and Sisera*, bought in 1975 (cat. 79), and Nicolas Poussin's *Holy Family* (cat. 80), acquired from a private owner in 1957. In the years following the political changes of 1989, purchases abroad also began to become possible.

The Department of Old Sculptures was significantly enhanced in 1914, when the bequest of a nineteenth-century Hungarian sculptor, István Ferenczy, was acquired. This collection consisted of nearly 100 works, including important Italian Renaissance small bronzes, such as the *Mounted Warrior* attributed to Leonardo (cat. 14) and the *Rape of Europa* (cat. 13), attributed to Andrea Riccio. The superlative pair of German Baroque sculptures attributed to Georg Raphael Donner – *Venus in the Forge of Vulcan* and *Judgement of Paris* (cats 165.1, 165.2) – also originated from the Ferenczy Collection. The Department of Old Sculptures was further enlarged with 218 acquisitions over the course of the past 50 years, bringing its current total to 800. Among its newer treasures are Damiano Capelli's bronze sculptures of a *Rider Pursuing a Boar* and a *Rider Killing a Bull* (cats 89.1, 89.2).

During the past 50 years, the collections of the Department of Prints and Drawings have been augmented by 1,301 drawings and 5,959 prints, the majority of them works of modern art, since previously the collection of twentieth-century art did not receive its proper due. Marc Chagall's gouache *Donkey on the Roof* (cat. 220) was acquired in 1969. The Hungarian art market, traditionally poor in Old Master drawings, seems in recent years to have been still further depleted, and there has been only one instance of foreign acquisition: a purchase in 2001 of five significant pieces at the art fair 'Master Drawings London' filled gaps in the collection. The collection of Old Master prints has been in-

creased modestly but steadily with the purchase of sheets in antique shops. The collection of modern graphics, however, grew significantly: among others, twelve sheets by Picasso were received as a donation from the art dealer Daniel-Henry Kahnweiler, who had also provided the museum's early etchings by Picasso. In 1968 Victor Vasarely gave the museum a large group of his own series of silkscreen prints, as well as works by his contemporaries. The Professor of Medicine Péter Véghelyi contributed in large measure to the acquisition of modern graphics through his twentieth-century foundation, established in 1985. The works of art received from the collection of Maria Marghescu were a valuable addition: many twentieth-century graphic works came to the museum in 1999 and in 2001, among them works by Antoni Tàpies and Joan Miró.

The museum's Department of Art after 1800 is one of the oldest of its kind, and yet from the start the emphasis was on the acquisition of Hungarian works, and hence – alongside conservative taste – it did not grow appropriately. In the groupings of works of art inherited from previous collections, only the Biedermeier and the art of the turn of the twentieth century – Symbolism and Secession – were well represented. Although in the first half of the twentieth century, due to gradually rising prices, it was difficult to enhance the holdings of previously neglected art-historical periods, the museum's holdings of the French and Northern European schools, Barbizon Realism, Impressionism and Post-Impressionism are due for the most part to purchases made in the first half of the century. The Department of Art after 1800 has been enlarged over the past 50 years with 643 works. The acquisition of twentieth-century works had greater momentum in the 1960s, thanks not least to the generosity and intervention of Hungarian artists living

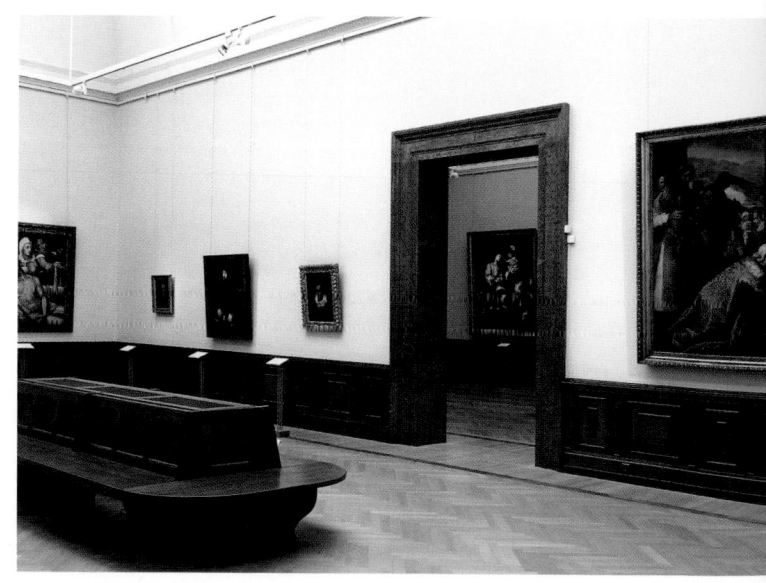

abroad.[5] Many works came to the museum in the 1980s, either donated by artists exhibiting in Budapest or coming to us following purchase. Once again, the Hungarian-born artist Victor Vasarely played a great part in the enrichment of the collection. To house these works, the museum established an exhibition space at Zichy Castle in Óbuda in 1983. The artist Zoltán Kemény likewise lived abroad, and his estate gave 50 paintings and reliefs, two sculptures and more than 300 drawings to the museum in 1984. A group of 150 contemporary paintings, sculptures and graphic works – primarily by British artists – was donated to the museum in 1991 by the London collector Bryan Montgomery.[6] The department is now responsible for 1,843 works of art.

An enduring, methodical growth characterises the collection of antiquities, which became independent late on in the history of the museum. The department was separated from the Sculpture Collection in 1935, and subsequently divided in two in 1957 as the Egyptian, and Greek and Roman Collections. The Department of Classical Antiquities has been expanded by 2,785 objects over the past half-century, and today contains 5,884 items (fig. 10). With the proceeds of the sale of plaster copies of statues in its own collection, even in the most difficult of times, it was able to make foreign purchases, while more recently support from sponsorship has become increasingly important.

The Department of Egyptian Art has also been enlarged with new acquisitions whose quality allows them to be on permanent display. Among nearly 1,000 works of art and objects for personal use accumulated over the past 50 years, around half were collected in the course of the 1964 rescue excavations in Nubia, and are thus a significant group. The Department of Egyptian Art, which possessed 2,256 pieces in 1956, now has more than 3,300.

The growth of the collections and new developments in archaeology and art history, as well as the accelerated demand for interpretative materials, necessitate ever deeper and broader research for the scholarly processing of individual works. Over the last half century, the attention of museum staff has been directed towards the acquisition of works of European art and scholarly research on this topic, and, accordingly, countless scholarly catalogues, monographs, catalogues of Hungarian and international exhibitions have been published, in both domestic and foreign editions.[7] The value of art objects cannot be judged, their purchase cannot be determined, nor can they be placed in an exhibition context without identification and scientific definition and by determining the identity of their creator, the place where they were created, age and function. None of this is possible, however, without knowledge of foreign collections and international specialised literature. To this end, the museum's library furnishes indispensable aid, as it is also the largest specialised art library in Hungary. The foundation of this collection of books was the reference library of the National Picture Gallery and the Esterházy Collection, but while in 1908 this consisted of just 4,334 volumes, by 1956 it had grown to 30,114, and today it holds nearly 200,000 items, including books, periodicals, exhibition catalogues and other publications. In terms of quantity, the accession of private libraries from inside and outside Hungary as purchases or publications has brought about especially significant enrichment. In more recent acquisitions of specialised literature, the support of the American J. Paul Getty Trust has been invaluable.[8] As a basis for exchange of periodicals and books the specialised journal of the museum, the *Bulletin* (fig. 11) plays an important role, as do other publications, such as scholarly catalogues, systematic catalogues, exhibition cata-

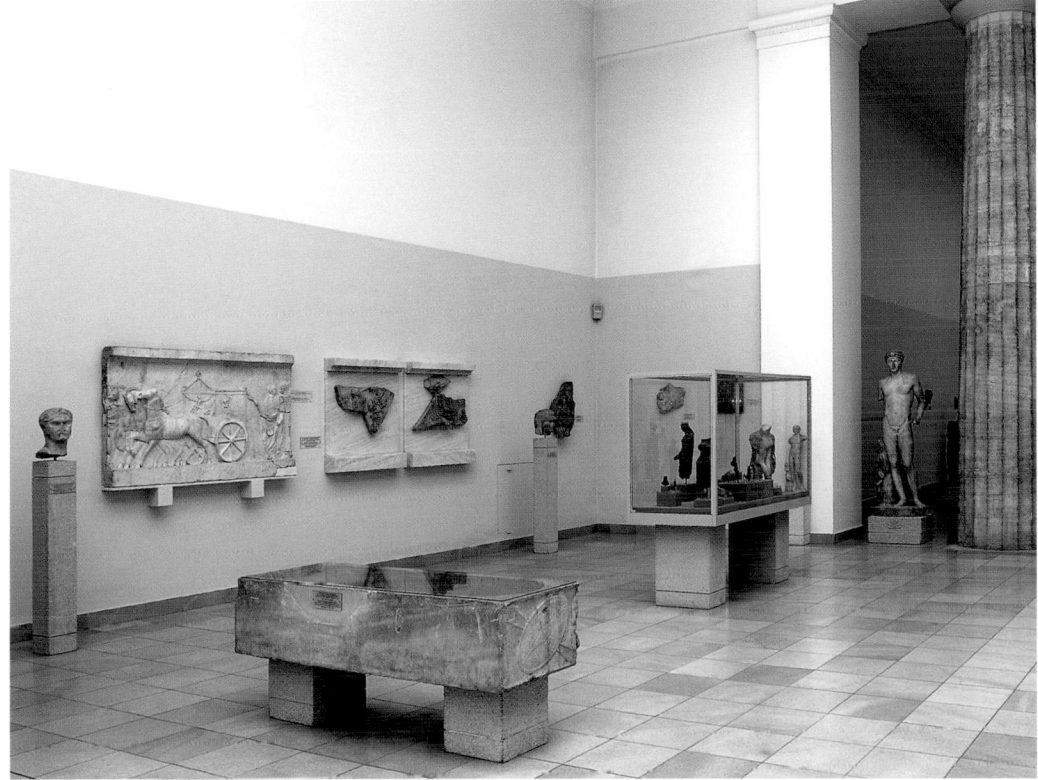

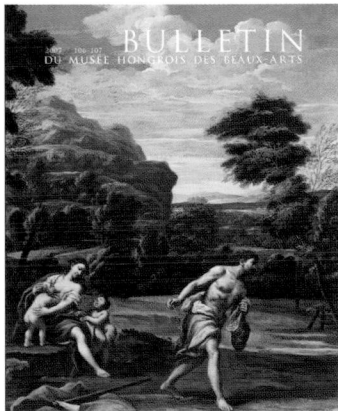

Fig. 9
The Spanish Galleries,
Museum of Fine Arts, Budapest

Fig. 10
View of the Greek and Roman
permanent display in the Museum
of Fine Arts, Budapest

Fig. 11
Front cover of the *Bulletin* of the
Museum of Fine Arts, Budapest,
106–07

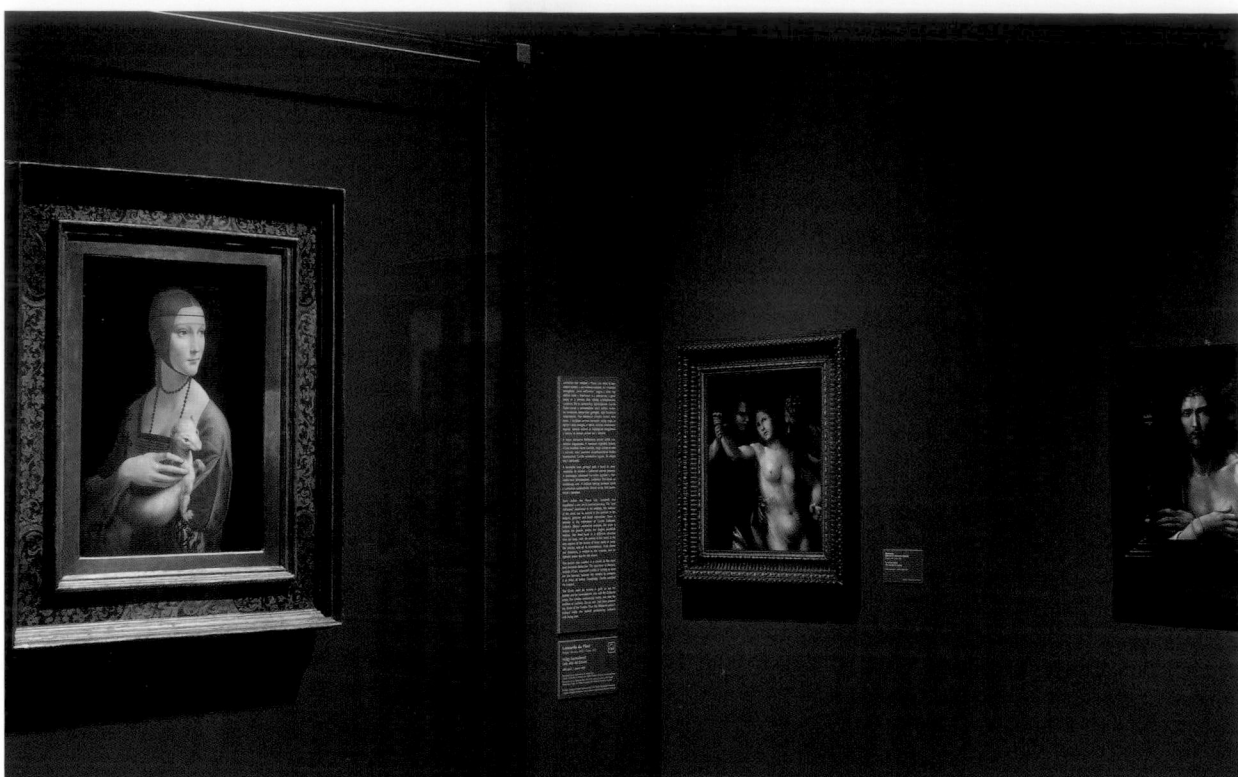

Fig. 12
View of the exhibition
*Botticelli to Titian: Two
Centuries of Italian
Masterpieces*, 2009

logues and books written and edited by museum staff. The library organises transactions of publication exchange with 100 Hungarian and 600 foreign partner institutions and art libraries. The reference library is open to art historians, collectors and art lovers.

Although today an increasing number of publications and art collections can be studied online, first-hand experience of original works of art will never lose its significance. Similarly, study trips abroad can influence positively the building of professional contacts. As a means for the ex-Socialist-era countries to join forces, large-scale exhibitions had already been successfully staged in the 1950s and 1960s.[9] As international relations relaxed, in accordance with the endeavours of Hungarian cultural policy, exhibitions from the museum toured to Western European countries from the 1960s onward, for example in Italy,[10] and France,[11] as well as America[12] and Japan.[13] Since 1956 the Museum of Fine Arts, Budapest, has organised some 35 autonomous exhibitions in foreign museums, and numerous additional shows in collaboration with the Hungarian National Gallery. Among the museum's staff there have always been distinguished professionals whose work has received

international recognition. Through information gained from our publications, an ever-increasing number of works from the museum appear in foreign exhibitions.[14] Moreover, individual staff members also take part in the realisation of international exhibitions abroad, and in the scientific classification of the collections.[15] Over the past few decades, our international co-operation has grown significantly. Not only has the museum arranged numerous independent exhibitions in various locations around the world, but it has also received a series of successful visiting exhibitions within its own walls, and more recently, it has been organising large-scale shows with a significant number of loans from abroad. Exhibitions such as *Monet and His Friends* (2003–04), *Van Gogh in Budapest* (2006), *El Greco, Velázquez, Goya: Five Centuries of Spanish Painting* (2006), *The Splendour of the Medici: Art and Life in Renaissance Florence* (2008) and *Botticelli to Titian: Two Centuries of Italian Masterpieces* (2009; fig. 12) have proved very popular. The realisation of loan exhibitions of this kind can only be achieved through intensive building of international contacts and a broad base of professional and scientific collaboration.

Notes

1 Jakob Perschy et al., *Die Fürsten Esterházy, Magnaten, Diplomaten & Mäzene*, Eisenstadt, 1995; Géza Galavics and Gerda Mraz et al., *Von Bildern und anderen Schätzen: Die Sammlungen der Fürsten Esterházy*, 1999; István Barkóczi et al., *Von Raffael bis Tiepolo: Italienische Kunst aus der Sammlung des Fürstenhauses Esterházy*, Schirn Kunsthalle, Frankfurt, 1999; Andrea Czére, *L'Eredità Esterházy: Disegni italiani del Seicento dal Museo di Belle Arti di Budapest*, exh.cat., Istituto Nazionale per la Grafica, Palazzo di Fontana di Trevi, Rome, 2002.

2 A detailed description of the museum and its six collections can be found in Ildikó Ember and Klára Garas et al., *Szépművészeti Múzeum*, 2nd edition, Budapest, 1998.

3 Randolph Starn, 'How the Museum Never Became Modern: A Postmodern Tale', in Gábor Klaniczay and Ernő Marosi (eds), *The Nineteenth-Century Process of 'Musealization' in Hungary and Europe*, Collegium Budapest Workshop Series no.17, Budapest, 2006, p.33.

4 As early as 1891, the Secretary of the Smithsonian Institution considered that from a didactic perspective, the most effective means of disseminating information was to provide a great number of explanatory texts, illustrated by a well-chosen object. George Brown Goode, 'The Museum of the Future', in *Annual Report of the Board of Regents of the Smithsonian Institute for the Year Ending June 30, 1889*, Washington DC, 1891, p.433.

5 Krisztina Passuth, at the time head of the Department of Modern Art, made contact with Hungarian artists living abroad, arranging an exhibition of their works at the Műcsarnok/Kunsthalle Budapest. These works, as well as contemporary pieces in their possession, comprised the first large group of twentieth-century acquisitions.

6 Ferenc Tóth, *The Bryan Montgomery Collection: The Collections of the Museum of Fine Arts*, 3, Budapest, 1999.

7 A selection of these publications is listed below.

8 In 1991, the library received support worth $50,000, and in 1994, $100,000, for new acquisitions.

9 The first highly successful loan exhibition was held in the Dresden Gallery in 1959, curated by Marianne Haraszti-Takács and Klára Garas.

10 Iván Fenyő curated an exhibition of the Venetian drawings in 1965 at the Fondazione Giorgio Cini in Venice.

11 The first large exhibition of works from the Museum of Fine Arts, Budapest in the West was *Trésors du Musée de Budapest*, which opened at the Musée des Beaux-Arts, Bordeaux, in 1972, under the direction of Klára Garas.

12 The museum's first American exhibition opened in 1985, under the direction of Teréz Gerszi, and was presented in three museums: *Leonardo to Van Gogh: Master Drawings from Budapest*, National Gallery of Art, Washington DC, The Art Institute of Chicago, and Los Angeles County Museum of Art.

13 The museum's first exhibition in Japan was organised in 1979, jointly with the Hungarian National Gallery, under the direction of Klára Garas, and was presented in three Japanese museums: *Exhibition of Famed Paintings Owned by the Budapest Museum of Fine Arts and the Hungarian National Gallery*, Isetan, Shinjuku, Tokyo, The Kitakyushu City Museum of Art, and Nara Prefectural Museum of Art.

14 The annual average number of loans over the past ten years – including complete exhibitions – totals around 180 works.

15 Miklós Mojzer catalogued the pictures of an American private collection: *The Warshaw Collection: Los Angeles, California*, Budapest, 1971; Klára Garas, among others, organised an exhibition in Langenargen: *Franz Anton Maulbertsch und sein Kreis in Ungarn aus den Beständen des Museums der Bildenden Künste Budapest, der Ungarischen Nationalgalerie Budapest und dem Museum für Christliche Kunst in Esztergom*, exh. cat., Langenargen am Bodensee, 1984; Teréz Gerszi, among others, selected the drawings and prints included in the Rudolph II exhibition in Essen and Vienna: *Prag um 1600: Kunst und Kultur am Hofe Rudolfs II*, Freren, 1988; János György Szilágyi, among others, participated in the cataloguing of the Antique Collection of Giacinto Guglielmi, which the collector had donated to the Vatican, where it was exhibited: *Raccolta di Giacinto Guglielmi*, I, Rome, 1997; Andrea Czére, among others, took part in the scientific cataloguing of a drawing collection in Avignon: *Disegni della Donazione Marcel Puech al Museo Calvet di Avignone*, Naples, 1998; Vilmos Tátrai, among others, was invited to join the advisory committee for the 2008 Sebastiano del Piombo exhibition in Rome and Berlin.

Further Reading

MUSEUM OF FINE ARTS, BUDAPEST

Klára Garas (ed.), *Museum of Fine Arts*, 2nd revised and expanded edition, Budapest, 1998

Szilvia Bodnár (ed.), *Museum of Fine Arts, Budapest*, 1995, 3rd revised edition, Budapest, 2006

Andrea Czére (ed.), *Museum of Fine Arts, Budapest: Masterpieces from the Collection*, Budapest, 2006

EGYPTIAN ART

István Nagy, *Guide to the Egyptian Collection: The Collections of the Museum of Fine Arts*, 2, Budapest, 1999

CLASSICAL ANTIQUITIES

Tihamér Szentléleky, *Ancient Lamps: Monumenta Antiquitatis Extra Fines Hungariae Reperta quae in Museo Artium Hungarico Aliisque Museis et Collectionibus Hungaricis Conservantur*, 1, Budapest, 1969

János György Szilágyi, *Corpus Vasorum Antiquorum: Budapest 1 (Hongrie 1), Budapest Musée des Beaux-Arts*, 1, Bonn and Budapest, 1981

László Török, *Coptic Antiquities I – Stone Sculpture, Bronze Objects, Ceramic Coffin Lids and Vessels, Terracotta Statuettes, Bone and Glass Artefacts: Monumenta Antiquitatis Extra Fines Hungariae Reperta quae in Museo Artium Hungarico Aliisque Museis et Collectionibus Hungaricis Conservantur*, 2, (Bibliotheca Archaeologica 11), Rome, 1993

László Török, *Coptic Antiquities II – Textiles: Monumenta Antiquitatis Extra Fines Hungariae Reperta quae in Museo Artium Hungarico Aliisque Museis et Collectionibus Hungaricis Conservantur*, 5, (Bibliotheca Archaeologica 12), Rome, 1993

László Török, *Hellenistic and Roman Terracottas from Egypt: Monumenta Antiquitatis Extra Fines Hungariae Reperta quae in Museo Artium Hungarico Aliisque Museis et Collectionibus Hungaricis Conservantur*, 4, (Bibliotheca Archaeologica 15), Rome, 1995

László Barkóczi, *Antike Gläser: Monumenta Antiquitatis Extra Fines Hungariae Reperta quae in Museo Artium Hungarico Aliisque Museis et Collectionibus Hungaricis Conservantur*, 5, (Bibliotheca Archaeologica 19), Rome, 1996

Boldizsár Csornay-Caprez, *Cypriote Antiquities: Monumenta Antiquitatis Extra Fines Hungariae Reperta quae in Museo Artium Hungarico Aliisque Museis et Collectionibus Hungaricis Conservantur*, 6, (Bibliotheca Archaeologica 30), Rome, 2000

János György Szilágyi, *Ancient Art: Department of Antiquities: Handbook of the Permanent Exhibition: Collections of the Museum of Fine Arts*, 5, Budapest, 2003

OLD MASTER PAINTINGS

Andor Pigler, *Katalog der Galerie Alter Meister*, 2 vols, Budapest, 1967

Klára Garas, *Paintings in the Budapest Museum of Fine Arts*, London, 1973

Vilmos Tátrai (ed.), *Old Masters' Gallery: Summary Catalogue 1: Italian, French, Spanish and Greek Paintings*, London and Budapest, 1991

Ildikó Ember and Zsuzsa Urbach (eds), *Old Masters' Gallery: Summary Catalogue 2: Early Netherlandish, Dutch and Flemish Paintings*, Budapest, 2000

Ildikó Ember and Imre Takács (eds), *Old Masters' Gallery: Summary Catalogue 3: German, Austrian, Bohemian and British Paintings*, Budapest, 2003

Ágnes Szigethi, *Old French Painting: Sixteenth to Eighteenth Centuries: The Collections of the Museum of Fine Arts*, 6, Budapest, 2004

Nyerges, Éva, *Spanish Paintings: The Collections of the Museum of Fine Arts*, Budapest, 2008

OLD SCULPTURES

Paul Schubring, *Katalog der Bildwerke der italienischen Renaissance des Museums der Bildenden Künste: Bildwerke der italienischen Renaissance in Marmor, Ton, Stucco, Holz und Leder aus den toscanischen, römischen und oberitalienischen Schulen*, Budapest, 1913

Jolán Balogh, *Katalog der Ausländischen Bildwerke des Museums der Bildenden Künste in Budapest, IV–XVIII Jahrhundert*, 2 vols, Budapest, 1975

Mária G. Aggházy, *Leonardo's Equestrian Statuette*, Budapest, 1989

Jolán Balogh and Éva Szmodis-Eszláry, *Katalog der Ausländischen Bildwerke des Museums der Bildenden Künste in Budapest*, 3, Budapest, 1994

Éva Szmodis-Eszláry, *The Treasures of the Old Sculpture Collection*, Budapest, 1994

PRINTS AND DRAWINGS

Teréz Gerszi, *Netherlandish Drawings in the Budapest Museum: Sixteenth-century Drawings: An Illustrated Catalogue*, 2 vols, Amsterdam and New York, 1971

Teréz Gerszi, *Zwei Jahrhunderte niederländischer Zeichenkunst: Meisterzeichnungen aus dem Museum der Bildenden Künste in Budapest*, 1, Budapest, 1976

Klára Garas, *Deutsche und österreichische Zeichnungen des 18. Jahrhunderts: Meisterzeichnungen aus dem Museum der Bildenden Künste in Budapest*, 2, Budapest, 1980

Andrea Czére, *Italienische Barockzeichnungen: Meisterzeichnungen aus dem Museum der Bildenden Künste in Budapest*, 3, Budapest, 1990

Andrea Czére, *Seventeenth-century Italian Drawings in the Budapest Museum of Fine Arts: A Complete Catalogue*, Budapest, 2004

Teréz Gerszi, *Seventeenth-century Dutch and Flemish Drawings in the Budapest Museum of Fine Arts: A Complete Catalogue*, Budapest, 2005

MODERN ART

Krisztina Passuth and Dénes Pataky, *Twentieth-century Art: Museum of Fine Arts Budapest*, Budapest, 1978

Brigitta Cifka (ed.), *Victor Vasarely*, exh.cat., Museum of Fine Arts, Budapest, 1982

Ferenc Tóth, *The Bryan Montgomery Collection: The Collections of the Museum of Fine Arts*, 3, Budapest, 1999

Mária Illyés, *Oeuvres français du XIXe siècle: Les collections de Musée des Beaux-Arts Budapest*, 4, Budapest, 2001

Principal Events in the History of the Museum of Fine Arts, Budapest

1906

The Museum of Fine Arts opened on 1 December, in the presence of the Emperor Franz Joseph. In the fashion of the age, its monumental building amalgamated the features of various historical styles and was designed in accordance with foreign models of museums. The Hungarian and foreign works of art of the Old Masters Gallery and Modern Gallery were placed on the upper floor. A gallery specially suited to both the exhibition and storage of the collection of prints and drawings was constructed in the North Wing, on the ground-floor level. Large galleries were also made ready on the ground floor for plaster casts, representing the universal development of sculpture, but this section was to open two years later, in 1908. The new museum, which aspired to present both Hungarian and international works of art, received the collections of sculpture, painting and graphic works preserved in the National Museum and the National Picture Gallery, and the plaster copies held in the Department of Antiquities of the National Museum.

1908, 1913

The purchase in these years of 135 antique marble sculptures from the German archaeologist and collector Paul Arndt (1865–1937), as well as a quarter (650 pieces) of his terracotta collection, took place on the recommendation of Antal Hekler. This laid the foundation for the museum's antiquities collection, which until then had comprised only plaster casts.

1912

A significant new private collection arrived at the museum in the form of a bequest. The collection of Count János Pálffy, which had been assembled in the second half of the nineteenth century, comprised 121 Old Master and 56 nineteenth-century paintings, and was considered one of the most important private holdings in the country. Many of the museum's masterpieces came from Pálffy, including Veronese's *Portrait of a Man* (cat.48).

1914

The museum purchased the estate of the sculptor István Ferenczy (1792–1856) from his heirs. This distinguished figure of Hungarian classicist sculpture had created a collection of small Italian Renaissance bronzes, consisting of 83 pieces purchased during his study trip to Italy between 1818 and 1824. With this fortunate acquisition, the principal works of the sculpture collection arrived at the Museum of Fine Arts, among them, such outstanding masterpieces as the *Mounted Warrior* later attributed to Leonardo (cat.14), which the museum has long employed as its emblem.

Elek Petrovics (1873–1945) took office as director in 1914, a post in which he served until 1935. Even in the difficult post-war years he managed to direct and enrich the museum scrupulously with remarkable acumen and great success. He created a forum to communicate the results of research in connection with the works in the collections. These *Yearbooks* appeared first in 1918, and ten volumes had been published by 1940. Thus a medium to communicate new scholarly research came into being, which also provided a means to obtain foreign periodicals for the museum library through international exchange.

1921

Marcell Nemes (1866–1930), a Hungarian collector living in Munich, enriched the Spanish collection of the Old Masters Gallery with an extremely significant donation: El Greco's *St Mary Magdalene* (cat. 69). Many other pictures in the museum, among them other works by El Greco, also come from his collection. Moreover, he had supported the concerns of the museum at an earlier date: a gift of fourteen antique vases in 1917 represented a foundation for the important collection of ancient ceramics that subsequently came into being.

1934

A law passed in 1934 centrally regulated the domain of collecting for museums. Consequently, the mutual exchange between museums of pieces began. The collections of the Museum of Fine Arts were increased through this act; it was at this time that the collection of 1,200 Egyptian pieces was established through the transfer of items belonging to the Ethnographic Museum, the National Museum and the Museum of Applied Arts. From 1934, the Collection of Hungarian Old Masters functioned as an independent department. In the same year, the collection of the Department of Prints and Drawings was also expanded, as the nineteenth- and twentieth-century collection of the ministerial advisor Pál Majovszky (1871–1935), comprising 259 drawings, was given to the museum. He had acquired the bulk of his collection in Paris, intending it for the museum from the outset. This collection, established with the assistance and advice of Simon Meller, head of the Department of Prints and Drawings, contains works of great quality such as Richard Parkes Bonington's *View of the South Coast* (cat. 184). Earlier, in 1914, Majovszky had already featured in the history of the museum with the gift of his collection of prints.

1935

In 1935 the Antique Collections broke away from the Department of Sculpture, and gained their independence under the name of the Egyptian Collection and the Collection of Antique Sculpture.

1944–47

During the Second World War the director sent the hastily packed works of art to bomb-ravaged Germany. As a direct consequence, many were damaged, and some were lost, but fortunately the collections suffered no serious losses. After peace agreements, and with the co-operation of the American authorities, the works of art returned home in 1946 and 1947. Their restoration, as well as the reconstruction of the damaged building, took many years to complete. From 1947 the *Yearbook* started up again in Hungarian and French, under the title *Bulletin du Musée Hongrois des Beaux-Arts* (*Szépművészeti Múzeum Közleményei*); in a multilingual version and a renewed format, the periodical remains an important forum for publishing the results of research by the curatorial staff.

1949–50

Beginning in 1949, and through the early 1950s, the new permanent displays of the Museum of Fine Arts opened in sequence. First were the Gallery of Old Masters, the New Hungarian Gallery and the Egyptian Collection, followed by the displays of the Department of Old Sculptures on the second floor of the building (sculpture), in the stairway (carved stone fragments), and in the Renaissance Hall (Venetian fountains). The sculpture displays remained unchanged until the start of reconstruction work on the museum in 1985; currently only the fountains of the Renaissance Hall are visible in their former arrangement. In the interest of implementing the permanent displays of Antiquities, including Greek and Roman works, the exhibition galleries were reconstructed from 1950, and were opened in two phases – in 1951 and 1953.

1951, 1953

As a consequence of the new, centralised arrangements for organising museum collections, the holdings of the György Ráth Collection, which until then had been handled by the

Museum of Applied Arts, were absorbed into the collections. Alongside paintings, it was at this time that a group of antique cameos that had formerly been part of the renowned Fejérváry-Pulszky Collection arrived at the museum, as did some important Egyptian bronze statues. Likewise, as the result of another rearrangement, the Zichy Gallery, formerly managed by Budapest City Council, was taken over, thereby enriching the museum's collections of Netherlandish, German, and Austrian Baroque paintings.

1957

The profile of the Museum of Fine Arts changed, since a new institution was founded for the collection of Hungarian art. The Hungarian National Gallery was initially housed in the former Supreme Court in Kossuth Square, and subsequently, from 1973, was given a place in the Royal Buda Palace. From this time onwards, the Museum of Fine Arts became engaged in the collection, preservation, study and presentation of European, non-Hungarian art.

A corollary effect of this development was that the Department of Egyptian Art broke away from the Collections of Antiquity and became an independent unit within the Museum of Fine Arts.

1964–72

Hungarian participation in the 1964 Nubian excavations resulted in the large-scale growth of the Egyptian collections, with an additional 469 pieces. From 1972 the Egyptian permanent collection was on view in the so-called Doric Hall, and from 1983, in the same location, but in a rearranged display.

In the 1960s expansion of the museum's previously rather modest twentieth-century collection took place with greater momentum, due to the activities and bequests of Hungarian artists living abroad.

1983

On 6 November seven valuable paintings were stolen from the museum, among them two works by Raphael. With the aid of Interpol the pictures were soon found, and the case drew the attention of the Ministry and the Government to the financial difficulties that the museum was facing. As a result more security personnel were employed and security systems improved, and a decision was taken on the refurbishment of the building.

1985

The Professor of Medicine and art collector Péter Véghelyi established a foundation for the enrichment of the museum's international twentieth-century holdings. From this moment, interest on the invested capital, and the exchange of Hungarian works of art bequeathed to the museum, permitted the acquisition of modern drawings and prints on a regular basis.

1987

In 1983 a foundation had been established to present the paintings and graphic works of Victor Vasarely (1908–1997). These were housed in Zichy Castle at Óbuda, as a branch of the Museum of Fine Arts, and the collection opened in 1987 as the Vasarely Museum.

In the same year, refurbishment of the Museum of Fine Arts building began. The first phase included the entrance wing, under which new, lower level galleries were established.

1990–2004

Many of the museum's galleries underwent reconstruction (the Doric, Ionic, Pergamon, Marble, Baroque Hall and the Old Masters Gallery) in the course of which numerous areas of the permanent display of the Old Masters Gallery (German and Austrian, Flemish, Spanish and Dutch Old Masters) were also refurbished, in addition to a renewal of the Departments of Classical Antiquities, Egyptian Art and Art after 1800. New facilities and further galleries for both temporary and permanent exhibitions were built on the basement level, and a new building was opened near the museum to house its library and conservation workshops.

1991

A bequest from the London collector Bryan Montgomery enriched the Modern Collection of the museum with 150 contemporary British paintings, sculptures and graphic works.

2003

The opening of the exhibition *Monet and His Friends* was a turning point in the history of the museum. With its enormous attendance in comparison with previous years, it drew the attention of the public, the media and the government to museums in general.

2006

The Museum of Fine Arts celebrated the centenary of its inauguration. As part of the building's refurbishment programme, the façade was completely cleaned and restored. A new, expanded permanent display of Italian Old Masters opened. The museum organised a splendid series of temporary exhibitions unprecedented in its history: more than 25 shows were mounted within its walls in provincial museums in Hungary and abroad. Visitor numbers reached 600,000. From this year on the Museum of Fine Arts became the most visited museum in Hungary.

2007

Exhibitions in the museum such as '… and the Incas Arrived' and *Van Gogh in Budapest*, attracted over 750,000 visitors, the highest number so far in its history. The institution joined the list of the 50 most visited art museums in the world for the year.

2009

For the first time in its history the Museum of Fine Arts organised excavations in Egypt at El-Lahun, in order to take a greater part in international archaeological activity and scientific research.

2010

The Swiss Stiftung Franz Larese und Jörg Janett presented a large collection of contemporary prints to the Department of Prints and Drawings, comprising 309 lithographs and woodcuts, 41 litho-posters, 40 illustrated art books and 17 albums with lithographs; among the artists represented were Antoni Tàpies, Hans Hartung, Günther Uecker, Eduardo Chillida and Max Bill.

Directors of the Museum of Fine Arts, Budapest

1906–14	Ernő Kammerer
1914–35	Elek Petrovics
1935–44	Dénes Csánky
1945–49	István Genthon
1949–52	Imre Oltványi
1952–55	Ferenc Redő
1956–64	Andor Pigler
1964–84	Klára Garas
1984–89	Ferenc Merényi
1989–2004	Miklós Mojzer
2004–	László Baán

The Hungarian National Gallery

ANNA JÁVOR

The Hungarian National Gallery is an independent, state-run museum dedicated to the Hungarian fine arts. Although it was officially only established in 1957, the gallery dates its early history from 1802, along with the National Museum and most other national museums in Hungary.[1]

By 1913 the Museum of Fine Arts was already treating Hungarian modern art as a separate category. Its director Elek Petrovics expanded the Hungarian contemporary art collection significantly as well as aiming to rediscover surviving vestiges of Hungarian Old Master painting. The New Hungarian Gallery, established in 1928, was a permanent exhibition staged in the Old Palace of Arts on Andrássy út (Andrássy Avenue) until 1934 (today the University of Fine Arts).[2]

After 1945, under the post-war Soviet occupation, the cultural education of the general public came to the fore in the museum world, and a politically oriented perspective took hold. In the course of nationalisation, museum art collections expanded further. In 1953 the Municipal Gallery was annexed to the Museum of Fine Arts, which had been the official institution in Budapest for the acquisition of fine art since 1933, and these additions were displayed at the Károlyi Palace (today the Petőfi Literary Museum).

The idea of establishing an independent National Gallery had already surfaced by this time and came to fruition in the spring of 1957. The former Supreme Court, an eclectic building constructed by Alajos Hauszmann in Kossuth Square in 1891–96, was chosen to house it (today it is home to the Ethnographic Museum). The collection of the new gallery came from the modern Hungarian collection of the Museum of Fine Arts, following the example set by the Nationalgalerie in Berlin, Leningrad's Russian Museum and the State Tretyakov Gallery in Moscow, as well as the newly restructured Österreichische Galerie (Belvedere) in Vienna. The Ministry of Culture and Education appointed Gábor Ö. Pogány, deputy director of the Museum of Fine Arts, as the new gallery's first director; his successor Lóránd Bereczky held the position from 1982 to the beginning of 2010.

In the spirit of the prevailing sentiment of the time, which focused on 'progressive traditions', the Hungarian National Gallery in Kossuth Square presented only a century and a half of Hungarian art. The paintings and sculptures were displayed chronologically from 1800 in an enduring classical arrangement in the elegant galleries of the imposing building, with a separate room for paintings by Mihály Munkácsy. The gallery enjoyed exceptional attendance. In an era of limited cultural opportunities it became deservedly the leading edge, welcoming on a regular basis groups of schoolchildren, workers' brigades, envoys and tourists from the Socialist Bloc. In addition to the permanent displays, lively temporary exhibitions and activities took place in the building. The gallery was also the official location for the preparation of touring exhibitions around the country, accompanied by modest catalogues and brochures for the cultural education of the public. Furthermore, the former National Gallery was the centre of important academic work, as a result of which the institution remains the base for research into Hungary's fine arts in the nineteenth century to this day.

A new location for the gallery in the former Royal Buda Palace – at the time in need of reconstruction – was made possible through a government act in 1959 (fig. 13). During the early Middle Ages a fortress had stood at the edge of Castle Hill in Buda above the Danube. Sigismund of Luxembourg (1387–1437) was the first to move the royal court to Buda at the beginning of the fifteenth century. It was at this time that development of the grand palace complex began; during the reigns of Matthias Corvinus (1458–1490) and Wladislaw II (1490–1526) this was expanded still further in the late Gothic and Renaissance styles. In the aftermath of the Turkish defeat of the Hungarian forces at the Battle of Mohács in 1526, the Ottomans occupied Buda in 1541. During their 145-year rule the palace fell into disrepair but it was not until the siege for repossession in 1686 and the ensuing construction of fortifications that the palace was completely destroyed. At the initiative of the Hungarian nobility, construction of a new Baroque royal palace came about from 1750 during the era of Maria Theresa. The plans were by her chief court architect Jean Nicholas Jadot, and the palace was built under the direction of Ignác Oracsek. Jadot was replaced in 1753 by Nicolas Pacassi, and its late Baroque construction is associated with the name of Franz Anton Hillebrandt.

The capital of Hungary at this time was Pozsony (now Bratislava, Slovakia); in any event, Maria Theresa resided in Vienna and never used the palace there. In 1777 she had the university moved to Buda from Nagyszombat (now Trnava, Slovakia), and an astronomical observatory was built in front of the cupola.

In the wake of the 1848–49 War of Independence, during which the buildings were damaged, necessary renovations were completed in 1856. Large-scale alterations began after the compromise with the Habsburg Court and the coronation of Franz Joseph as King of Hungary in 1867. Miklós Ybl planned a new row of buildings on the western side, and from 1893 Alajos Hauszmann expanded the palace complex with a symmetrical wing to the north. The impressive interior space with its neo-baroque ornamentation was used by the Regent, Miklós Horthy, after 1919.

The palace suffered tremendous damage during the Second World War. Reconstruction began in 1949 and continued for several decades.[3] The group of buildings, based on plans by István Janáky (1901–1966), were reconstructed and completely modernised for the purpose of a museum complex. The Budapest History Museum was the first to open its doors in the south wing of the building and has on display archaeological remains and architectural fragments from the Middle Ages and the Renaissance that were unearthed in the course of digging through the rubble. The National Gallery was able to move into three adjoining blocks facing the Danube in 1974. Remodelling of the western Ybl Wing to house the National Széchényi Library was completed in 1985.

The gallery's relocation to the palace occurred at the same time as the expansion of the collection. It was at this time that the Museum of Fine Arts transferred to the National Gallery its collection of Hungarian Old Masters from the Middle Ages and the Baroque period that had been created within the territory of historic Hungary, as well as celebrated works by Hungarian seventeenth- and eighteenth-century artists, even those living abroad. In 1974, the Contemporary Collection was established with the aim of creating a comprehensive foundation for a permanent collection that would present post-1945 Hungarian art. With the addition of these two categories the Hungarian National Gallery's collection extends from the country's establishment as a nation in the eleventh century to the present, and contains over 100,000 works of art.[4]

The new Hungarian National Gallery opened its doors in the Buda Palace on 12 October 1975. The first installation emphasised art from the past, and included a visually stimulating introduction to its historical context, although this latter display was soon restructured. Installing air-conditioning became a necessity, while restoration and the

Fig. 13
The Hungarian National Gallery,
Budapest

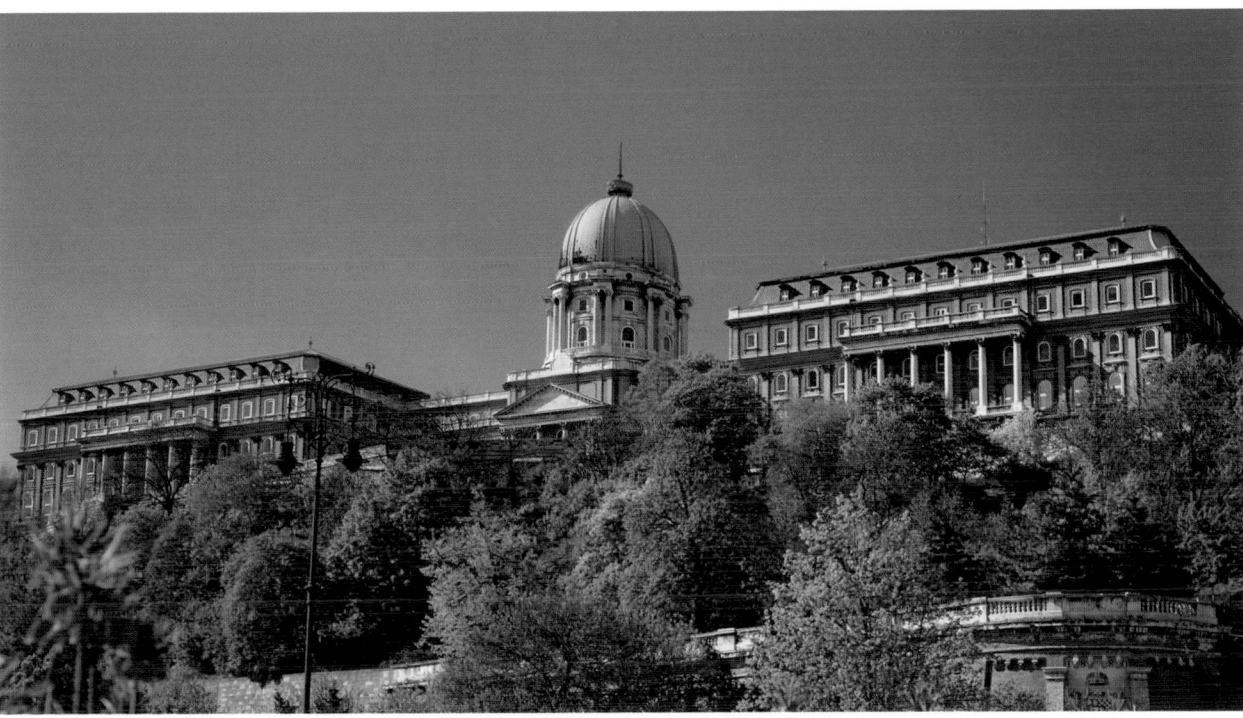

reassembling of the medieval winged altars took on tremendous momentum. Thanks to the successful acquisitions policy of the head of the Hungarian Old Masters Collection, Miklós Mojzer (director of the Museum of Fine Arts, 1989–2004), and the increased number of Baroque artworks, a separate workshop was established for their restoration. The permanent exhibition of medieval panels and wooden sculptures opened in 1979 on the ground floor and the permanent Baroque display above it on the first floor.[5] The unique collection of winged altars from the late Gothic period has been on view since 1982 in the former Throne Room;[6] the arrangement of Medieval and Renaissance sculpture and carvings in the entrance hall was completed in 1985.[7] The displays have been developing ever since, becoming more modern, although the essential design of the gallery's permanent displays has retained its original chronological arrangement.

We advance in time to the nineteenth century in the exhibition galleries on the first floor and the first half of the twentieth century on the second floor.[8] Most of the displays show sculptures and medals alongside the paintings (fig. 14); the twentieth-century display also offers selections from its collection of works on paper. A comprehensive exhibition of works dating from after 1945 opened on the third floor in 1983; since its reorganisation in 2002 it has dedicated increasing space to contemporary trends.

The Hungarian National Gallery was expanded in 2005 when it took possession of the vacated north wing as a result of the move of the Ludwig Museum to the newly constructed Palace of Arts on the banks of the Danube.[9] In addition to offices, storerooms and a restaurant, it also acquired two large areas of exhibition space: the rooms on the first floor serve as locations for highly prized temporary exhibitions, while on the second floor a long-term display opened, under the name

of 'Akali', presenting Hungarian contemporary works of art arranged thematically.[10]

Temporary exhibitions are significant in the life of the gallery as public demand for these has always been great. Since the 1980s they have been presented increasingly with scientific apparatus and regularly win the Opus Mirabile Award of the Hungarian Academy of Sciences. High-calibre adult and children's education programmes accompany these projects in which higher education, in the form of the Hungarian National Gallery Free University, plays an important part. Monographic exhibitions of specific artists display a wide range of contemporary artists and styles, accompanied by lavishly illustrated scholarly catalogues.

Pannonia Regia: Art in Transdanubia 1000–1541 (1994–95) was a tremendous undertaking, followed by *Gold Medals, Silver Wreaths: The Cult of Artists and Art Patronage in Nineteenth-century Hungary* (1994–95). An all-encompassing exhibition in 1996 dedicated to the centenary of the artists' colony at Nagybánya (Baia Mare, today in Transylvania) was followed in 1997 by the dossier exhibition entitled *Magnificat anima mea*, which focused on the main altarpiece from 1506 by Master MS of Selmecbánya (Banská tiavnica, today in Slovakia).[11] The 1998 exhibition of works by József Rippl-Rónai was also shown in France, Belgium and Germany the following year.[12] To mark the new millennium the gallery covered a serious subject in an exhibition entitled *History – Image*, an overview of the relationship between the past and art in Hungary.

The monographic exhibitions on Ádám Mányoki and later László Mednyánszky (1852–1919) were organised with significant foreign participation in 2003 and 2004 respectively. More recently the gallery has mounted retrospective exhibitions for János Vaszary (2007) and Mihály Zichy (1827–1906) (2008)[13] and is planning shows for Károly Markó and Károly Ferenczy (2011). Several international partners contributed by lending works to the major project of 2006, *Hungarian Fauves from Paris to Nagybánya, 1904–1914*. As a sign of recognition, the exhibition toured to three museums in France in 2008.[14]

The Hungarian National Gallery's international contacts are fortunately long-standing. In 1975, in conjunction with the Belvedere in Vienna, an exhibition on August von Pettenkofen (1822–1889) and the history of the Szolnok School founded on the Great Hungarian Plain was organised at two Hungarian and two Austrian locations in succession. In 1979, on a French initiative, an exhibition was mounted from the Hungarian National Gallery's collection at the Musée d'art moderne de la Ville de Paris under the title *L'Art en Hongrie, 1905–1930*.[15] On commission from Austria, the gallery facilitated the opening of *Matthias Corvinus und die Renaissance in Ungarn* at Schallaburg in Lower Austria in 1982, which was subsequently shown in Hungary as well, where it enjoyed unparalleled success.[16]

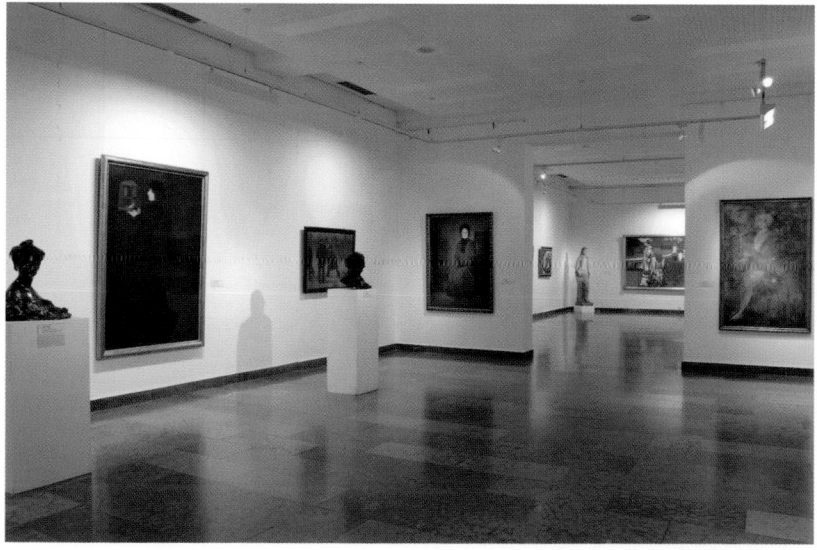

Fig. 14
The twentieth-century
permanent collection

The Musée des Beaux-Arts de Dijon approached various institutions in Central Europe in 1995 with an unusual proposal involving the presentation of an important exhibition under the title *Budapest 1869–1914: modernité hongroise et peinture européenne*, a project which would have been impossible without the co-operation of the Museum of Fine Arts. The same was true for a joint undertaking by the Hungarian National Gallery and the Stuttgart Staatsgalerie for an exchange exhibition of works on paper entitled *Modernisms 1900–1930* (2004–05).[17]

Our co-operative endeavours with museums in neighbouring countries are developing ever more fruitfully. We have collaborated by lending works and providing expertise for the Slovak National Gallery's major exhibitions on the Gothic (2003–04) and Renaissance eras (2009–10), as well as relying on loans from their collections. A similar exchange occurred with the museum in Marosvásárhely (now Targu Mures, Romania) for our recent temporary exhibition *Munich in Hungarian: Hungarian Artists in Munich 1850–1914* (2009). Hungarian paintings are regularly on view in the exhibition programmes in Csíkszereda (now Miercurea Ciuc, Romania).[18] Hungarian works also appear in their own right at large international exhibitions (for example *Le Fauvisme ou l'épreuve de feu'* in Paris in 1999 and *Künstlerkolonien in Europa* in Nuremberg in 2001).[19] We have paintings that are seemingly always on the road. In contrast, certain works – because of their fragility or size, others because of their symbolic significance – may never leave the gallery. These include Master MS's painting *The Visitation* (1506), Ádám Mányoki's portrait of Ferenc Rákóczi II (1712), and Pál Szinyei Merse's *Picnic in May* (1872–73), all of which receive local and foreign visitors in their home in the Buda Palace.[20]

Notes

1   The history of the gallery was compiled by Katalin Sinkó based on original sources, taking into account institutional predecessors and political references: Katalin Sinkó, 'Nemzeti Képtár: "Emlékezet és történelem között" ', in *A Magyar Nemzeti Galéria Évkönyve / Annales de la Galerie Nationale Hongroise 2008*, 26, 11, special edition, Budapest, 2009; condensed English version: Katalin Sinkó, 'The Making of an Independent National Gallery: Between Memory and History', in *A Magyar Nemzeti Galéria Évkönyve / Annales de la Galerie Nationale Hongroise 2005 2007*, 25, 10, Budapest, 2008, pp.9–20.

2   See Béla Bacher and Gábor Ö. Pogány (eds), *The Museum of Fine Arts 1906–1956*, Budapest, 1956, and the current catalogue.

3   Gizella Szatmári and Anna Szinyei Merse (eds.), *The Hungarian National Gallery*, Budapest, 1993, pp.16–19; József Sisa and Dora Wiebenson, *Architecture of Historic Hungary*, Cambridge, Mass., and London, 1998, pp.55, 66–67, 142–43, 231–32; *Un château pour un royaume: Histoire du château de Budapest*, ed. A., Musée Carnavalet, Paris, 2001; Gizella Szatmári in Szilvia Cseh and Ferenc Gosztonyi (eds), *Hungarian National Gallery: The Collections, Guide*, Budapest, 2007, pp. 7–8.

4   Sinkó op. cit., 2009, pp.95–160.

5   Miklós Mojzer (ed.), *The Hungarian National Gallery: The Old Collection*, Budapest, 1984; Gyöngyi Török, *Gothic Panel Paintings and Wood Carvings in Hungary: Permanent Exhibition of the Hungarian National Gallery*, Budapest, 2005.

6   Gyöngyi Török, *Gótikus szárnyasoltárok a középkori Magyarországon: Állandó kiállítás a Magyar Nemzeti Galériában*, Budapest, 2005.

7   Sándor Tóth, *Catalogue of Stoneworks from the Romanesque Period*, Budapest, 2010 (forthcoming).

8   István Solymár (ed.), *Collections of the Hungarian National Gallery*, Budapest, 1976; Géza Csorba (ed.), *The Collections of the Hungarian National Gallery*, Budapest, 1987; Anna Szinyei Merse, 'Periods, Masters, Styles, Themes: Nineteenth-Century Painting in the National Gallery', in *A Magyar Nemzeti Galéria Évkönyve / Annales de la Galerie Nationale Hongroise 2005–2007*, 25, 10, Budapest, 2008, pp.21–31.

9   Astrid Becker and Éva Rubovszky (eds), *Válogatás a Ludwig Gy jtemény modern m vészeti anyagából / Internationale Kunst heute aus der Sammlung Ludwig*, exh. cat., Hungarian National Gallery, Budapest, 1987. The collection donated to Hungary in 1989 was originally part of the Gallery; the independent Ludwig Museum was established in 1996 in the Buda Palace's 'A' building, location of the former Workers' Movement Museum, which was later integrated into the Hungarian National Museum's history collection.

10   See: www.HNG.hu/kiállítások; www.HNG.hu/collections; and Gábor Andrási, Gábor Pataki, György Szücs and András Zwickl, *The History of Hungarian Art in the Twentieth Century*, Budapest, 1999.

11   Árpád Mikó and Imre Takács (eds), *Pannonia Regia, Művészet a Dunántúlon 1000–1541*, exh. cat., Hungarian National Gallery, Budapest, 1994; Ildikó Nagy and Katalin Sinkó (eds), *Aranyérmek, ezüstkoszorúk: Művészkultusz és műpártolás Magyarországon a 19. században*, exh. cat., Hungarian National Gallery, Budapest, 1995; Géza Csorba and György Szücs (eds), *Nagybánya művészete (The Art of Nagybánya: Centennial Exhibition in Commemoration of the Artist's Colony in Nagybánya)*, exh.cat., Hungarian National Gallery, Budapest, 1996; Árpád Mikó and Györgyi Poszler (eds), *'Magnificat anima mea dominum', MS mester Vizitáció-képe és egykori selmecbányai főoltára ('The Visitation' by Master MS, and his Former High Altar at Selmecbánya)*, exh.cat., Hungarian National Gallery, Budapest, 1997.

12   Mária Bernáth and Ildikó Nagy (eds), *Rippl-Rónai József gyűjteményes kiállítása (József Rippl-Rónai's Collected Works)*, exh.cat., Hungarian National Gallery, Budapest, 1998; Anna Szinyei Merse, Anna Jávor and Agnès Delannoy (eds), *József Rippl-Rónai: Le Nabi hongrois*, exh. cat., Saint-Germain-en-Laye, Musée départemental Maurice Denis le Prieuré, Paris, 1998, Anna Jávor and Bettina-Martine Wolter (eds), *Ein Ungar in Paris: József Rippl-Rónai 1861 bis 1927*, exh.cat., Schirn Kunsthalle, Frankfurt, 1999.

13   Árpád Mikó and Katalin Sinkó (eds), *Történelem – kép: Szemelvények múlt és művészet kapcsolatából Magyarországon*, exh.cat., Hungarian National Gallery, Budapest, 2000; Enikő Buzási (ed.), *In Europe's Princely Courts: Ádám Mányoki, Actors and Venues of a Portraitist's Career*, exh.cat., Hungarian National Gallery, Budapest, 2003; Csilla Markója (ed.), *László Mednyánszky 1852–1919*, exh.cat., Hungarian National Gallery, Budapest, 2003; Nóra Veszprémi (ed.), *Vaszary János (1867–1939): gyűjteményes kiállítása*, exh.cat., Hungarian National Gallery, Budapest, 2007; Enikő Róka (ed.), *Zichy Mihály: a 'rajzoló fejedelem'*, exh.cat., Hungarian National Gallery, Budapest, 2007.

14   Krisztina Passuth and György Szücs (eds), *Hungarian Fauves from Paris to Nagybánya 1904–1914*, exh.cat., Hungarian National Gallery, Budapest, 2006; Krisztina Passuth et al. (eds), *Fauves hongrois 1904–1914*, exh.cat., Musée d'art moderne de la Ville de Paris, and Musée d'art moderne de Céret, 2008, p.66; *Fauves hongrois 1904–1914: La leçon de Matisse*, exh.cat., Musée des Beaux-Arts de Dijon, 2009.

15   Hans Aurenhammer and Éva Bodnár, *A szolnoki festőiskola – Die Szolnoker Malerschule*, exh.cat., Österreichische Galerie, Vienna, 1975; Charles Dautrey and Jean-Claude Guerlain (eds), *L'art en Hongrie 1905–1930*, exh.cat., Paris, 1979.

16   Tibor Klaniczay, Gottfried Stangler and Gyöngyi Török (eds), *Matthias Corvinus und die Renaissance in Ungarn 1458–1541*, Vienna, 1982; Gyöngyi Török (ed.), *Mátyás király és a magyarországi reneszánsz 1458–1541*, exh.cat., Hungarian National Gallery, Budapest, 1983.

17   Emmanuel Starcky and László Beke (eds), *Budapest 1869–1914: Modernité hongroise et peinture européenne*, exh.cat., Musée des Beaux-Arts de Dijon, Paris, 1995; Katalin Bakos, Enikő Róka and Ulrike Gauss (eds), *Modernizmusok: Európai grafika 1900–1930 / Modernisms / Graphik in Europa 1900–1930*, exh.cat., Staatsgalerie, Stuttgart, 2004; in addition to popular introductions showcasing Impressionist tendencies in Hungarian painting (Düsseldorf, The Hague, Krakow) important modern exhibitions with catalogues in English-speaking regions: S.A. Mansbach (ed.), *Standing in the Tempest: Painters of the Hungarian Avant-Garde 1908–1930*, exh.cat., Santa Barbara Museum of Art, California, 1991; Mariann Gergely (ed.), *A Storm in Europe: Béla Kádár, Hugó Scheiber and Der Sturm Gallery in Berlin*, exh.cat., Ben Uri Gallery, The London Jewish Museum of Art, London, 2003.

18   Du an Buran (ed.), *Gotika*, exh. cat., Slovenská národná galéria, Bratislava, 2003; Zuzana Ludiková (ed.), *Renesancia*, exh.cat., Slovenská národná galéria, Bratislava, 2009; Orsolya Hessky, Petra Kárai and Nóra Veszprémi (eds), *München magyarul: Magyar művészek Münchenben 1850–1914*, exh.cat., Hungarian National Gallery, Budapest, 2009; Zsuzsanna Bakó, *Munkácsy-képek Erdélyben*, exh.cat., Székelyudvarhely, 2007; Judit Boros and György Szücs, *A nagybányai művésztelep*, exh.cat., Székelyudvarhely, 2008; Zsuzsanna Bakó and Beatrix Basics, *Barabas, Munkácsy, Szinyei és kortársaik: Remekművek a 19. századi magyar festészetből*, exh.cat., Csiki Székely Múzeum, Csíkszereda, 2010.

19   Suzanne Pagé (ed.), *Le fauvisme ou l'épreuve du feu': Éruption de la modernité en Europe*, exh.cat., Musée d'art moderne de la Ville de Paris, 1999; Claus Pese (ed.), *Künstlerkolonien in Europa: Im Zeichen der Ebene und des Himmels*, exh.cat., Germanisches Nationalmuseum, Nuremberg, 2001.

20   See Miklós Mojzer, 'Der historische Meister MS sive Martin Swarcz seu Martinus Niger alias Marcin Czarny, der Maler des Krakauer Hochaltars von Veit Stoss, II. Teil: Krakau und Nürnberg im Jahr 1477 und davor', in *A Magyar Nemzeti Galéria Évkönyve / Annales de la Galerie Nationale Hongroise 2005–2007*, 25, 10, Budapest, 2008, pp.90–141; Enikő Buzási, *Ádám Mányoki (1673–1757): Monographie und Oeuvrekatalog*, Hungarian National Gallery, Budapest, 2003; Anna Szinyei Merse, *Szinyei Merse Pál élete és művészete*, Hungarian National Gallery, Budapest, 1990; similar unmovable masterpieces include, among others: István Ferenczy's sculpture, *Shepherd Girl (The Origins of Painting)* (1820 22) and Tivadar Csontváry Kosztka's monumental painting, *Ruins of the Greek Theatre in Taormina* (1904–05). See Anna Szinyei Merse (ed.), *The Hungarian National Gallery*, Budapest, 1993, pp.66, 131.

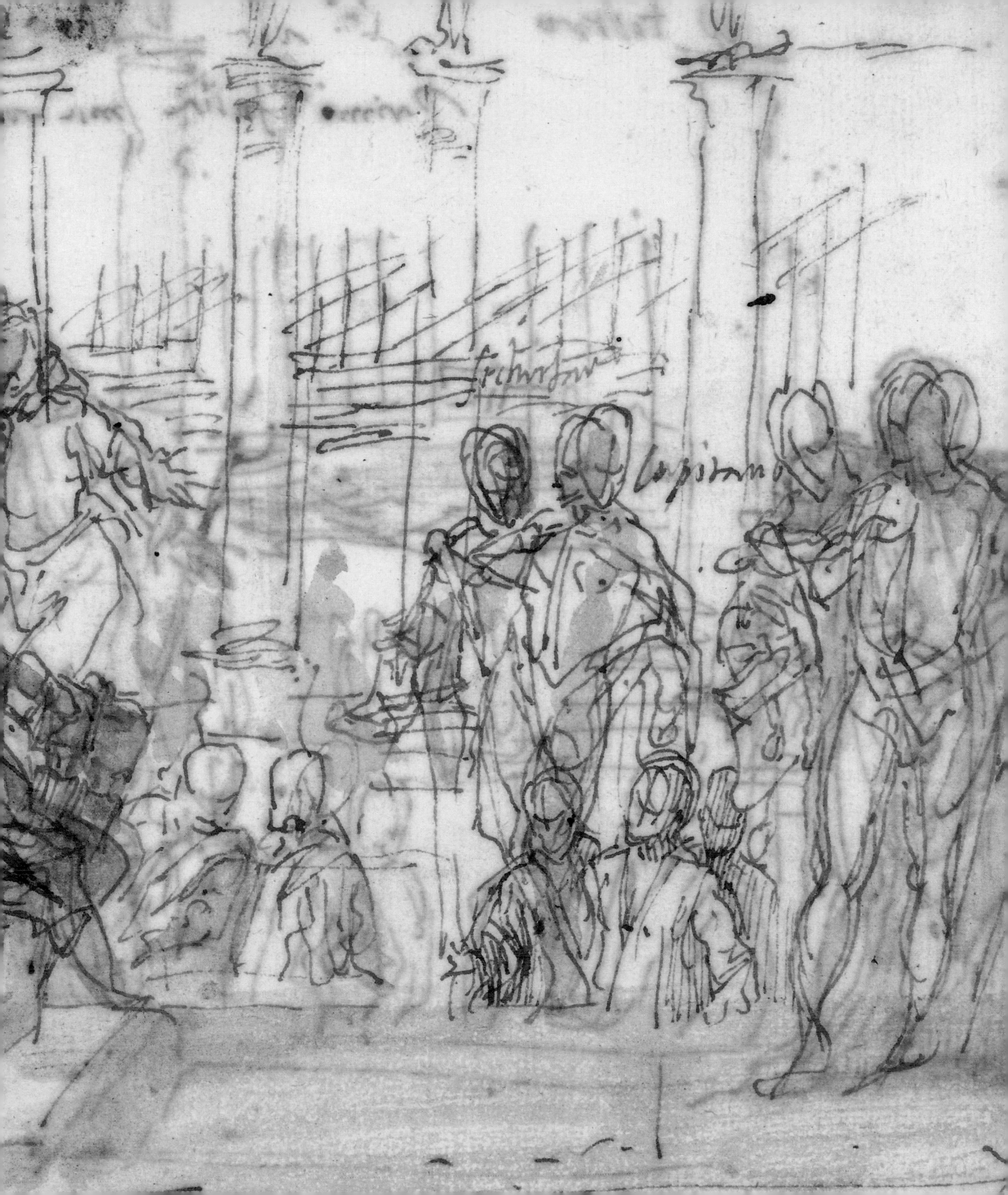

I

FOURTEENTH AND FIFTEENTH
centuries

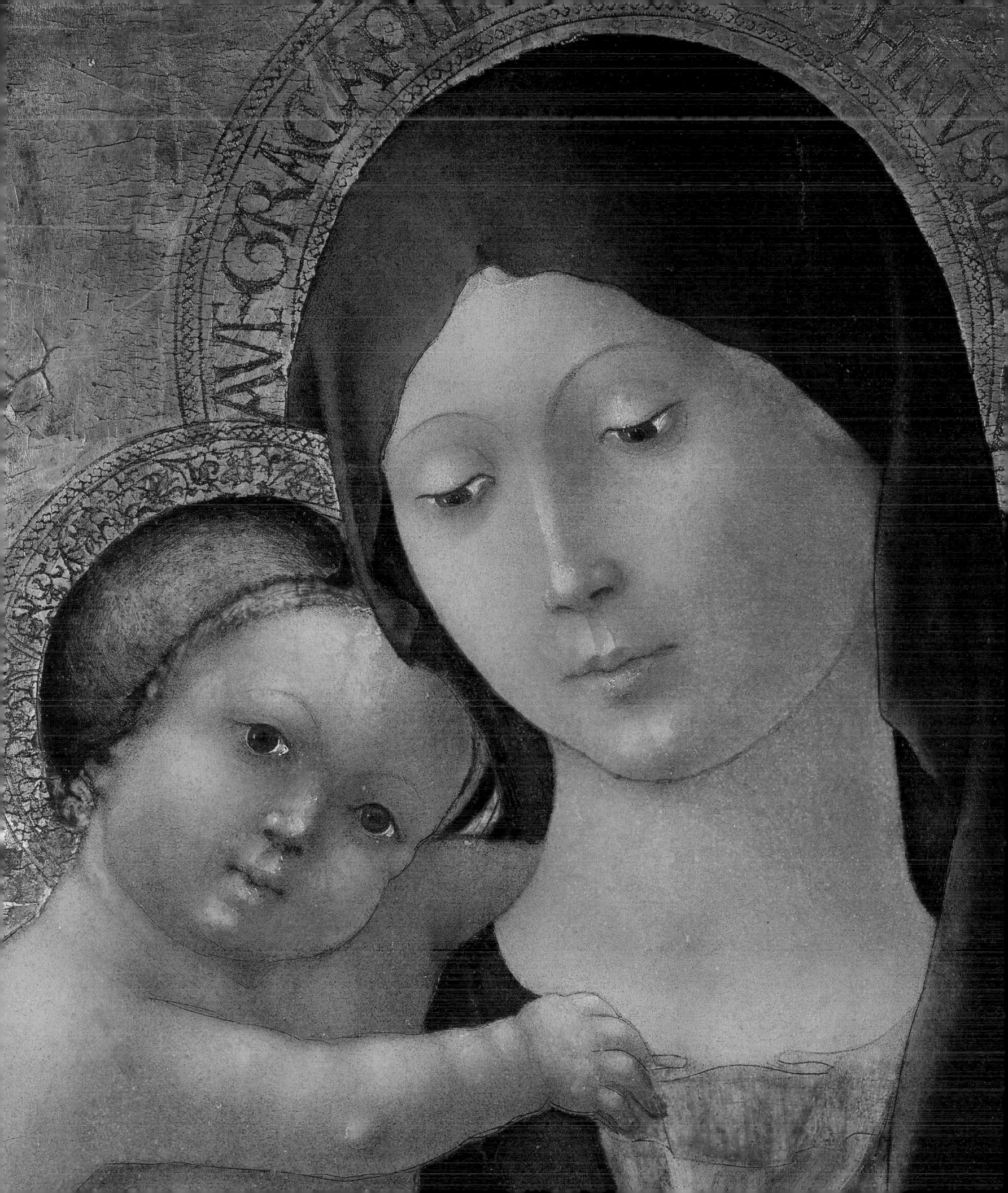

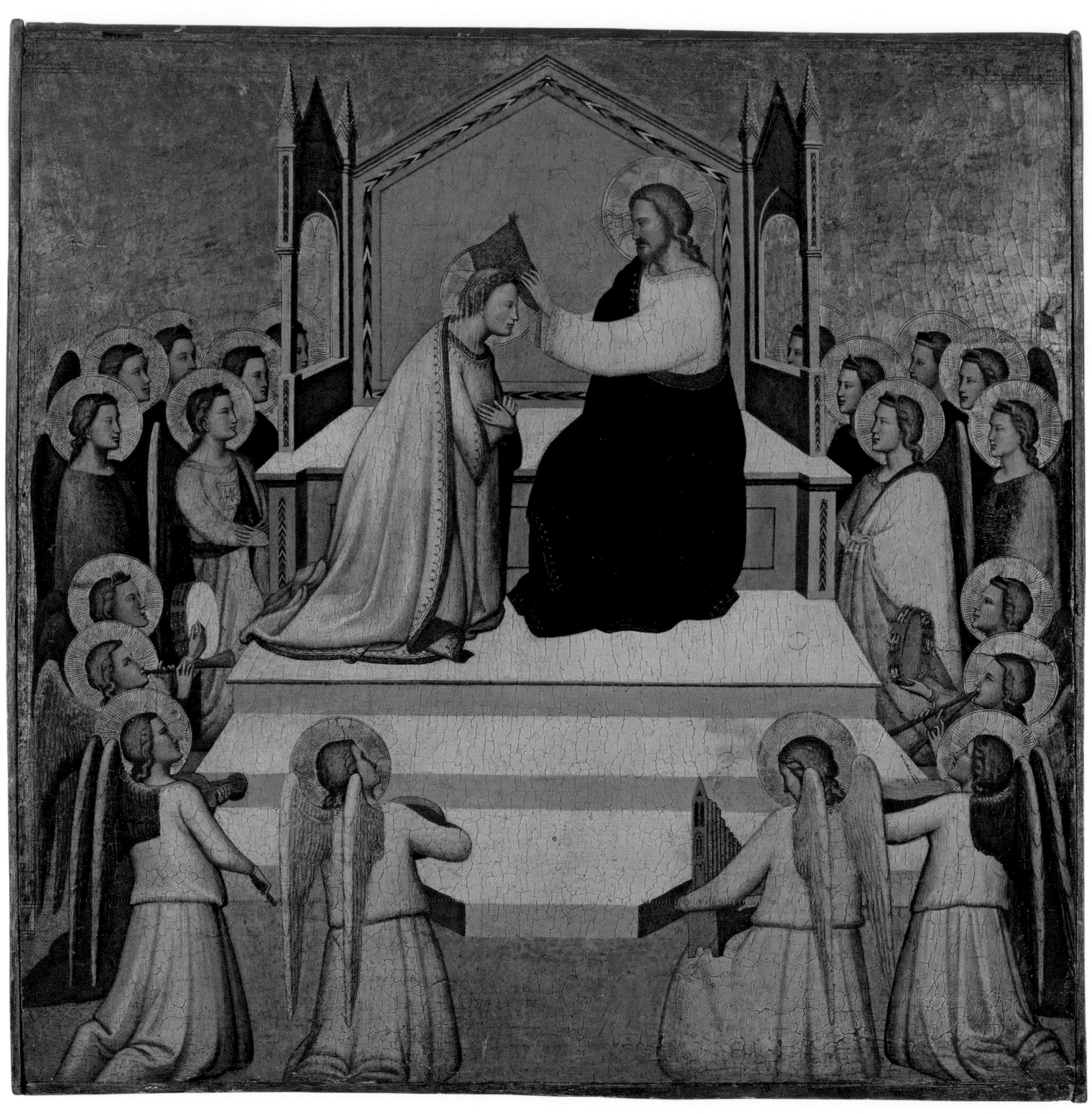

1   Maso di Banco, *Coronation of the Virgin*

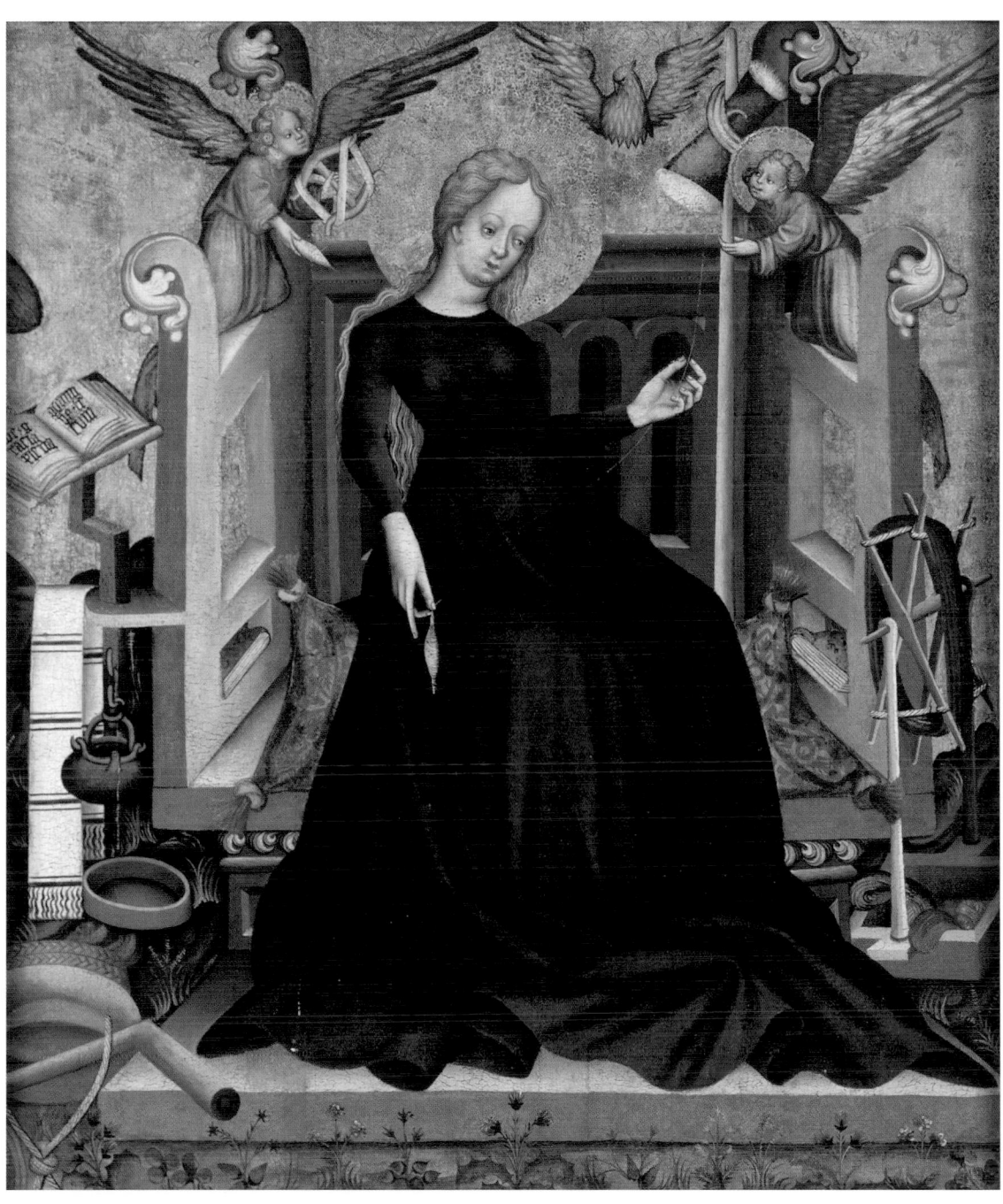

2　Artist active in Vienna, early fifteenth century, *Pregnant Virgin*

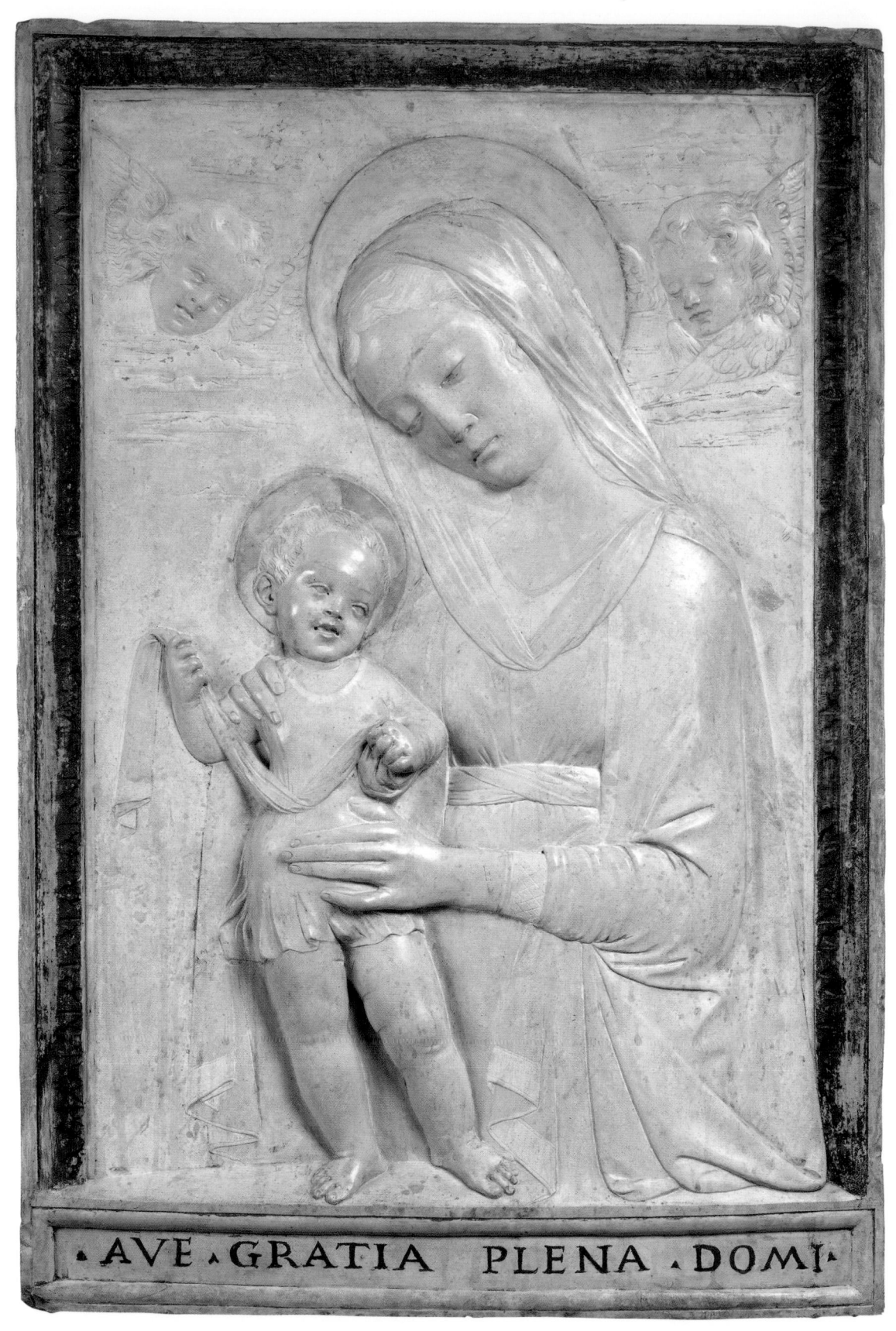

·AVE·GRATIA PLENA·DOMI·

3   Domenico (di Giovanni) Rosselli, *Virgin and Child*

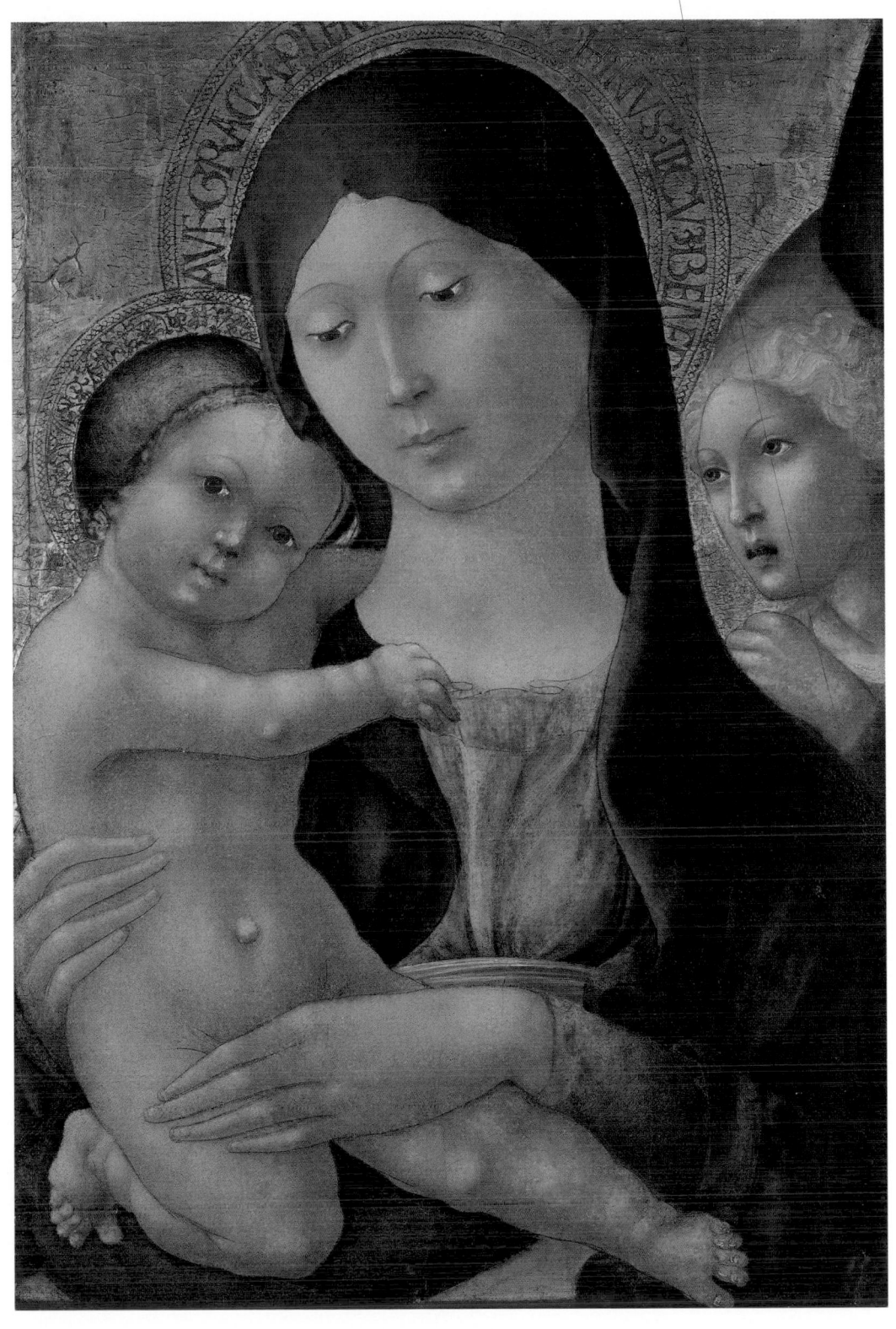

4   Liberale da Verona, *Virgin and Child with an Angel*

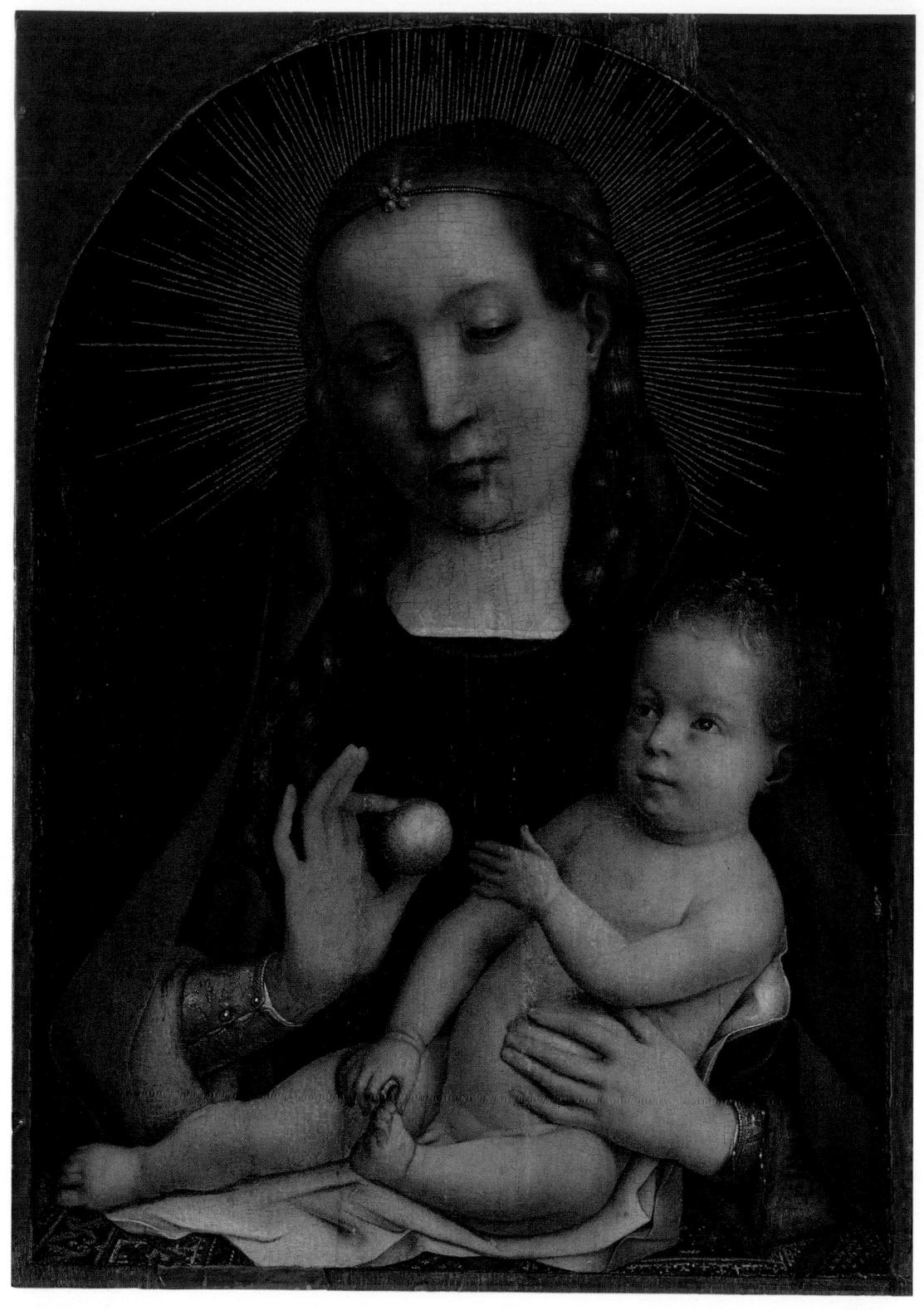

5   Michel Sittow, *Virgin and Child*

6   Hungarian master, early fifteenth century, *Virgin and Child from Toporc*

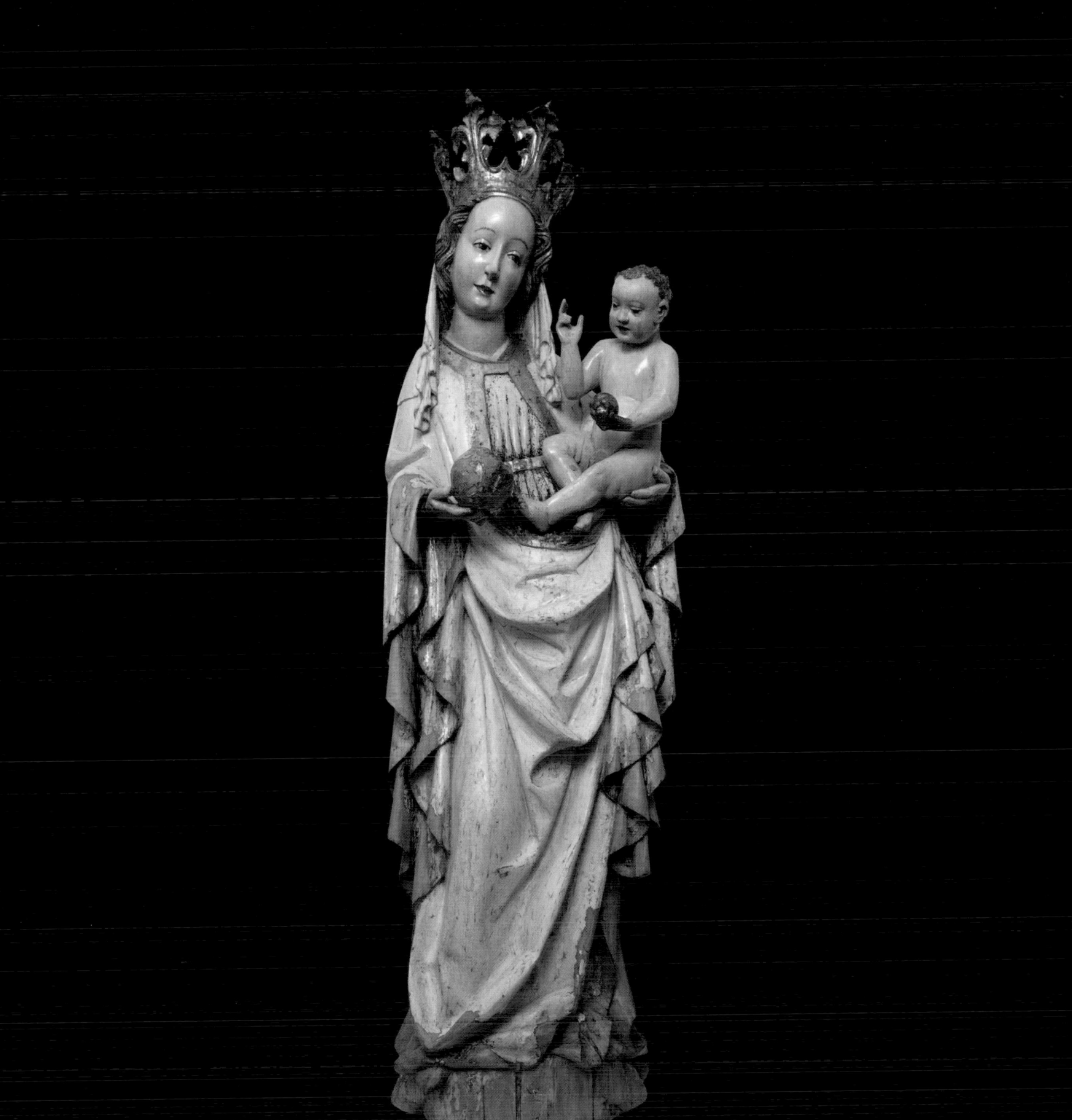

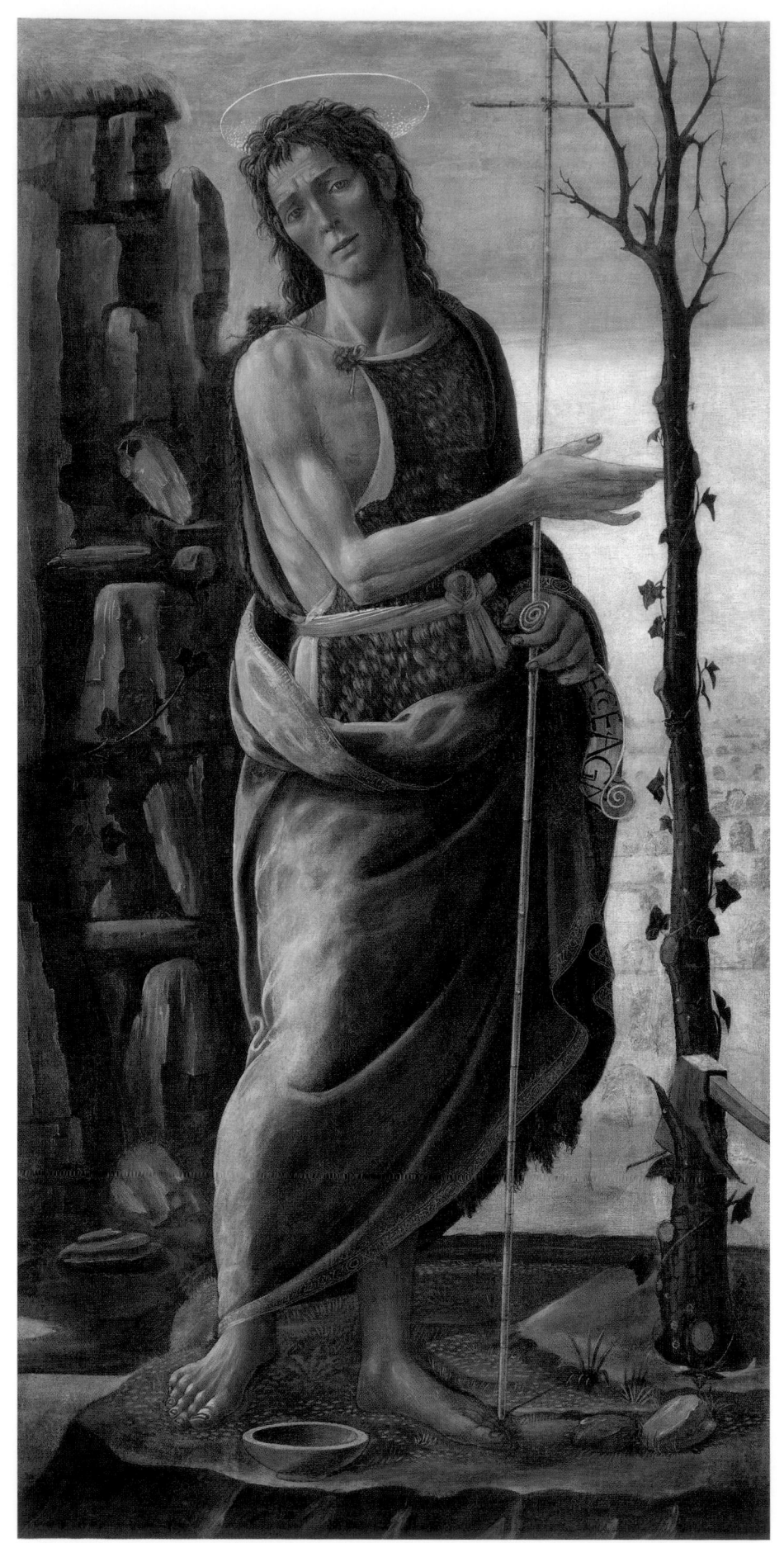

7   Jacopo del Sellaio, *St John the Baptist*

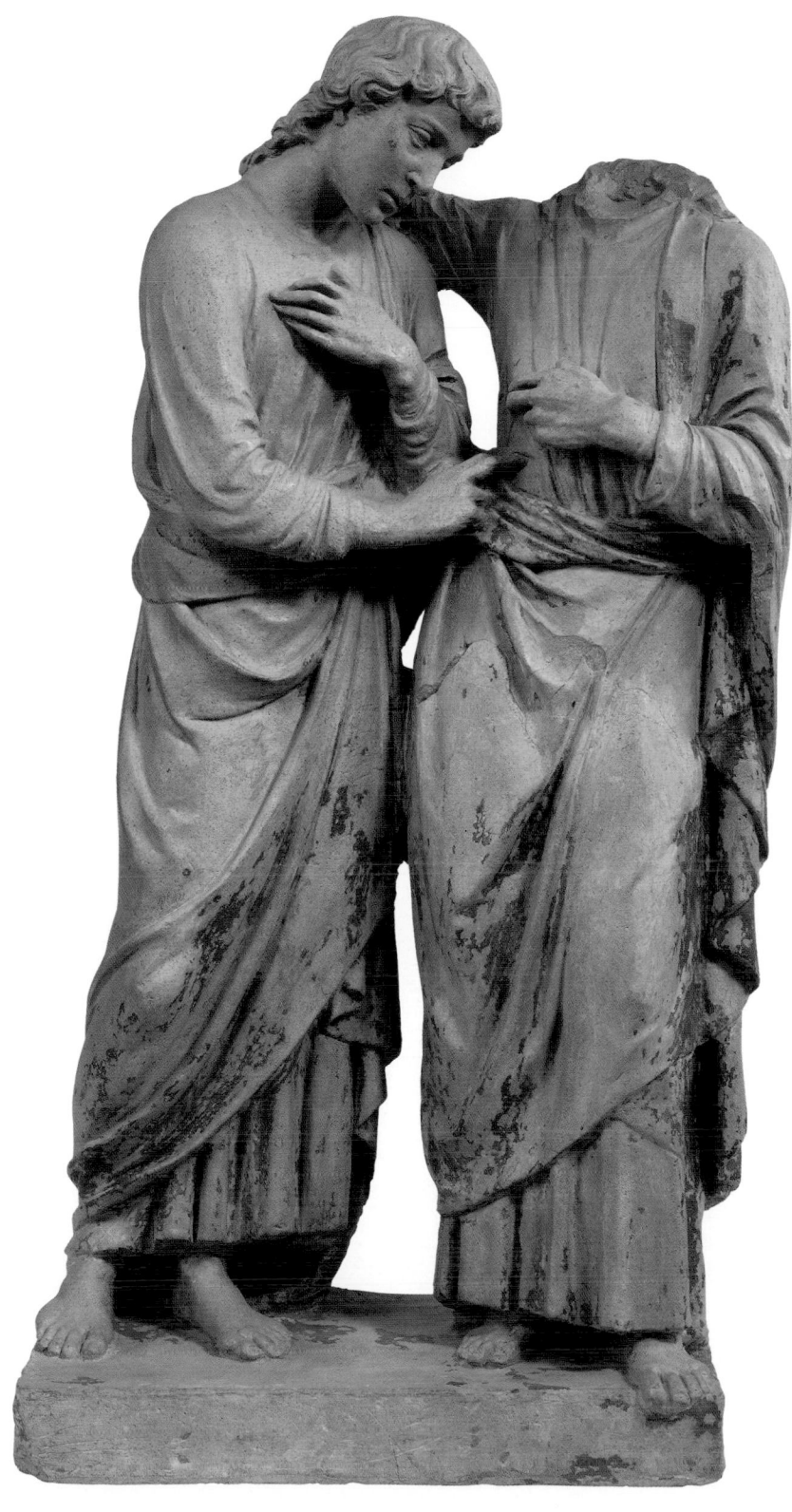

8   Luca della Robbia, *Christ and St Thomas*

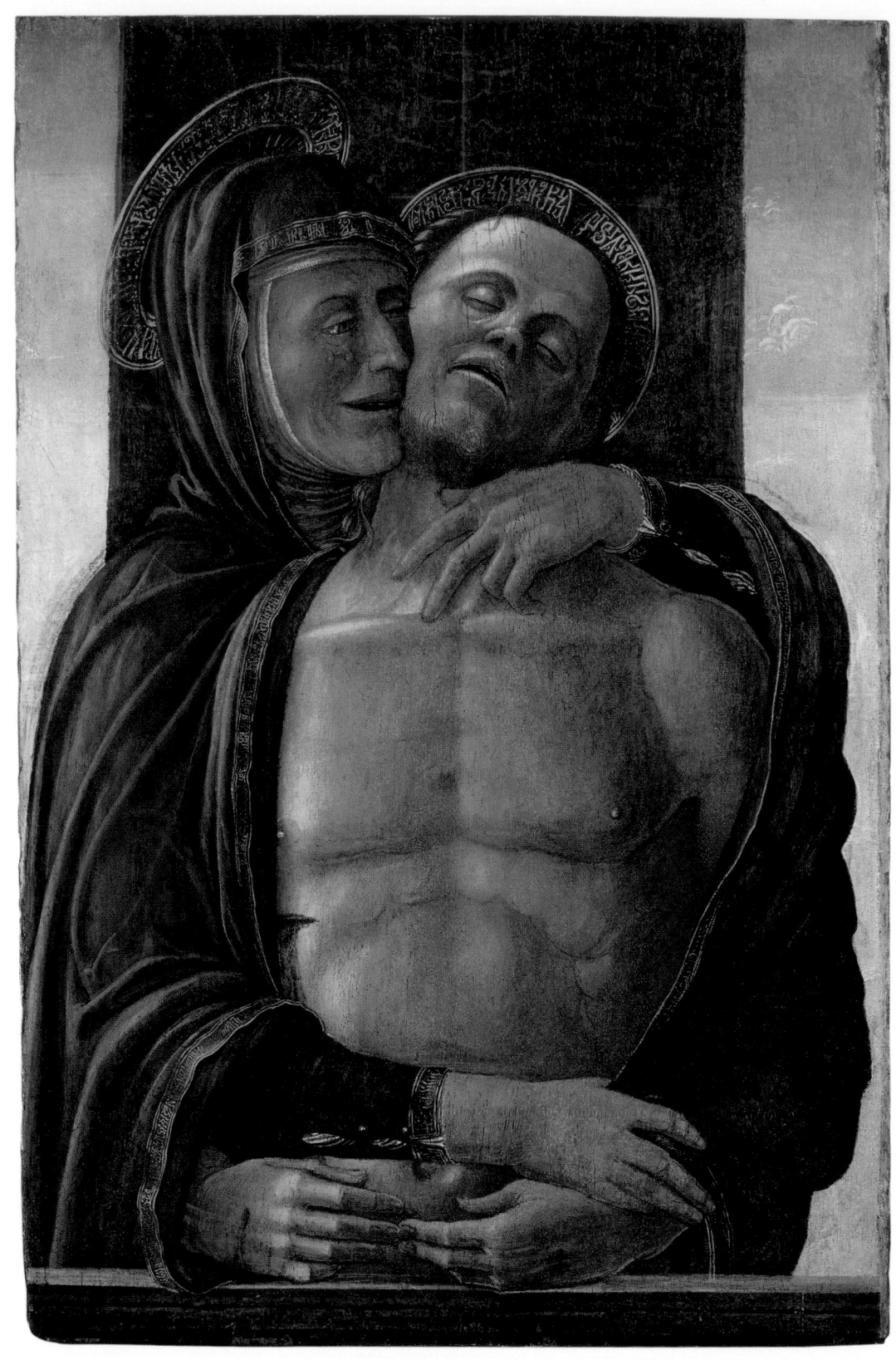

9 Jacopo Parisati da Montagnana, *Pietà*

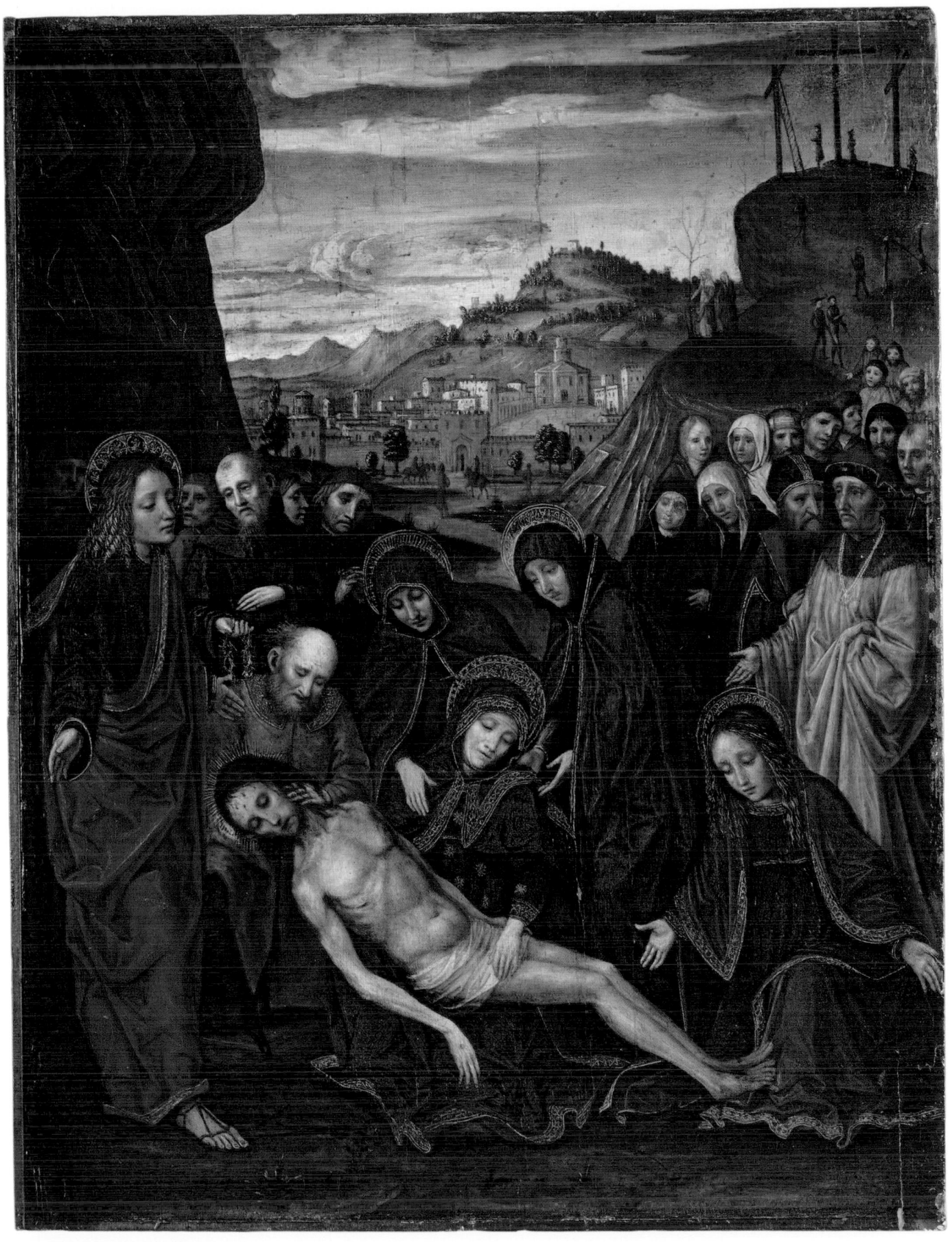

10 Bergognone, *Lamentation*

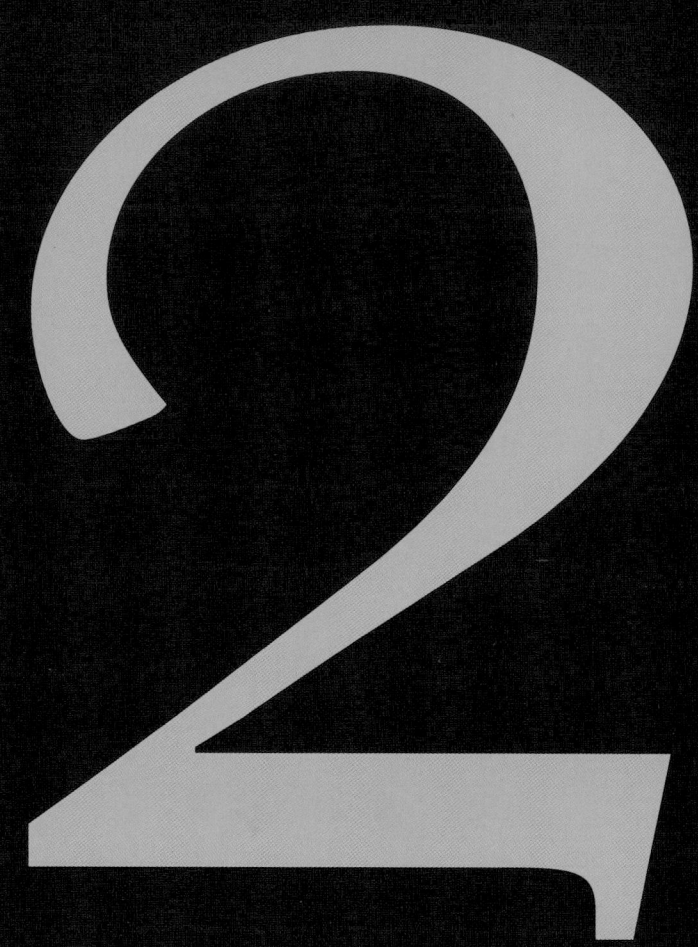

2

SIXTEENTH
century

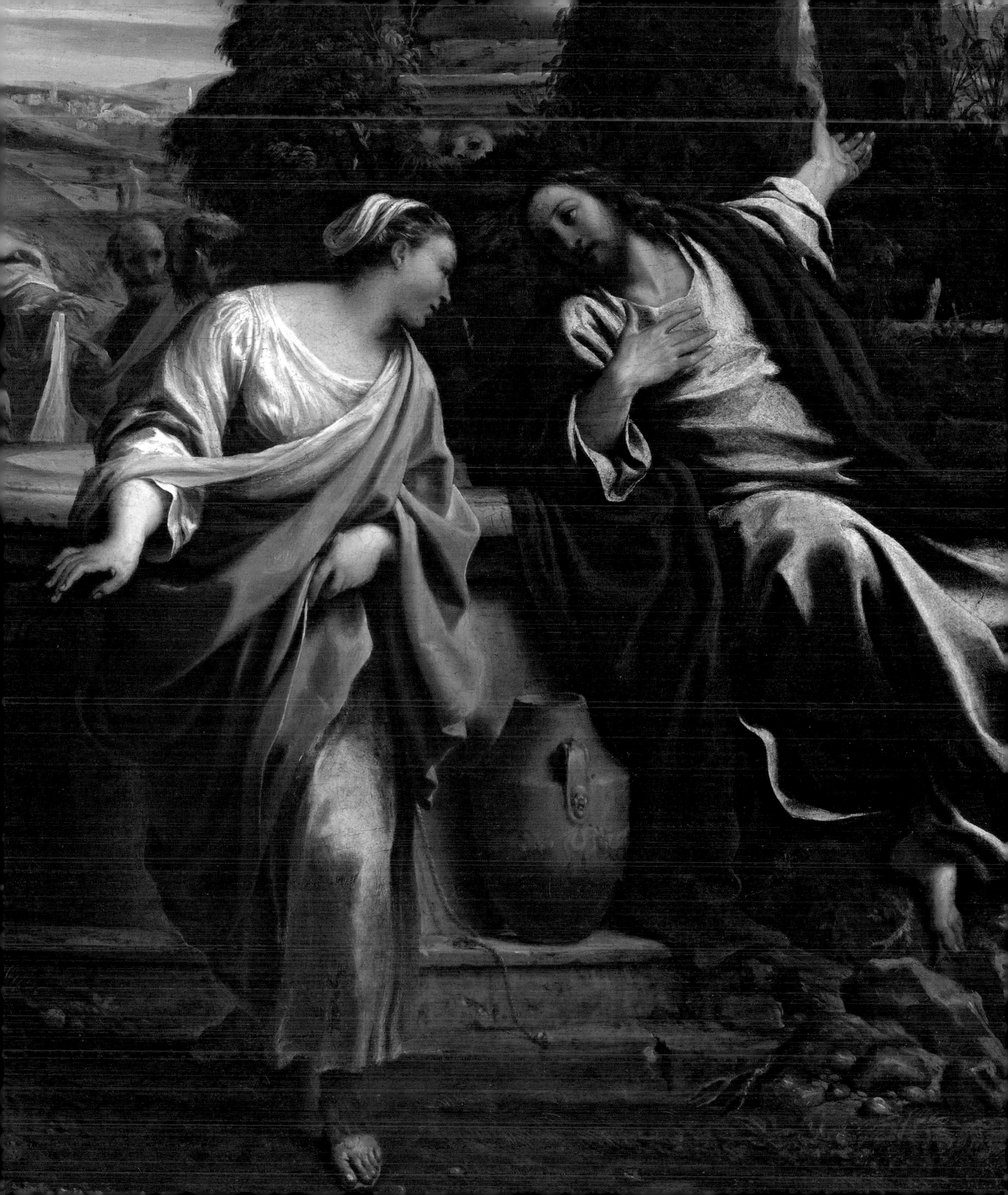

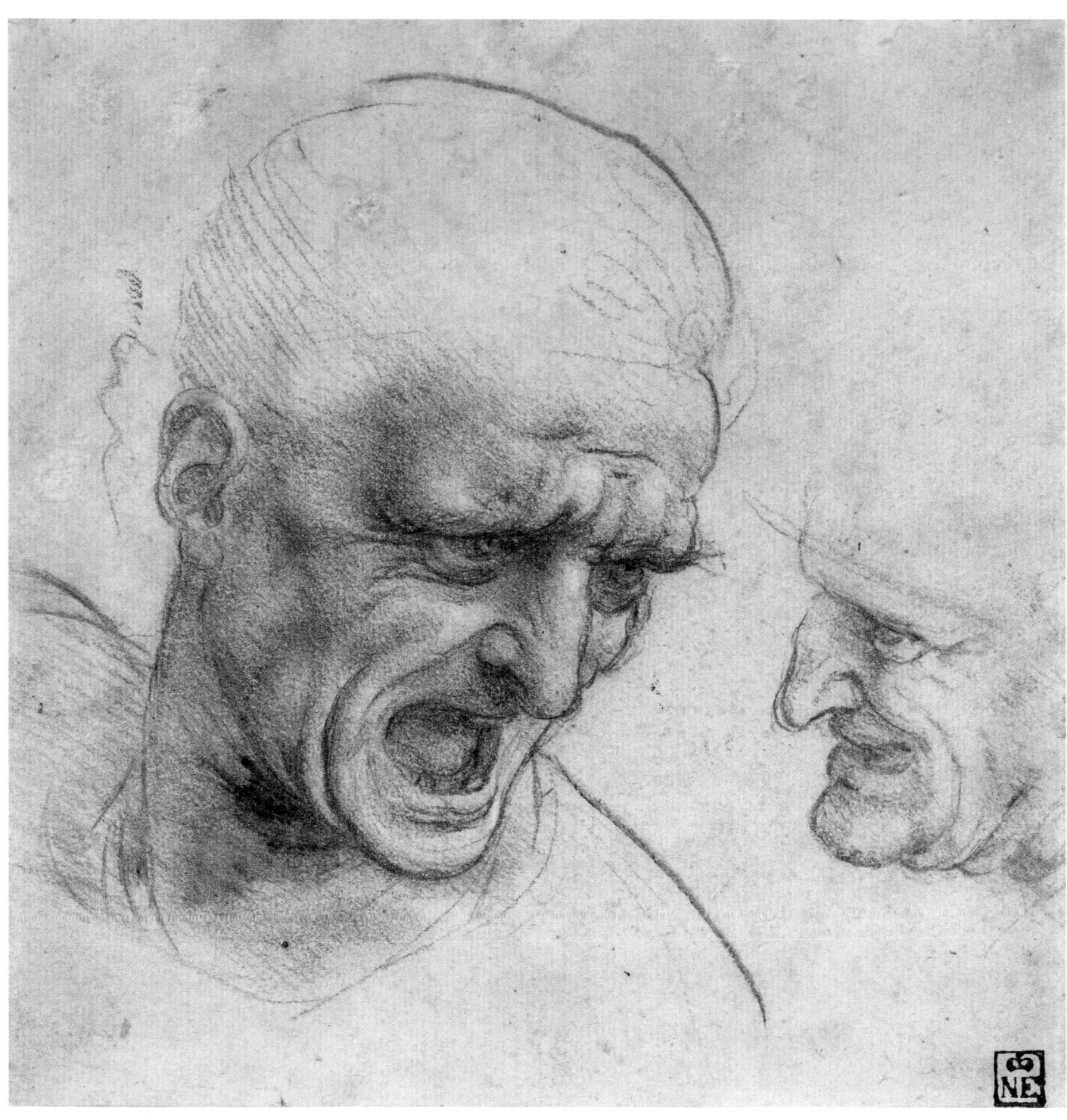

11   Leonardo da Vinci, *Studies for the Heads of Two Soldiers in the Battle of Anghiari*

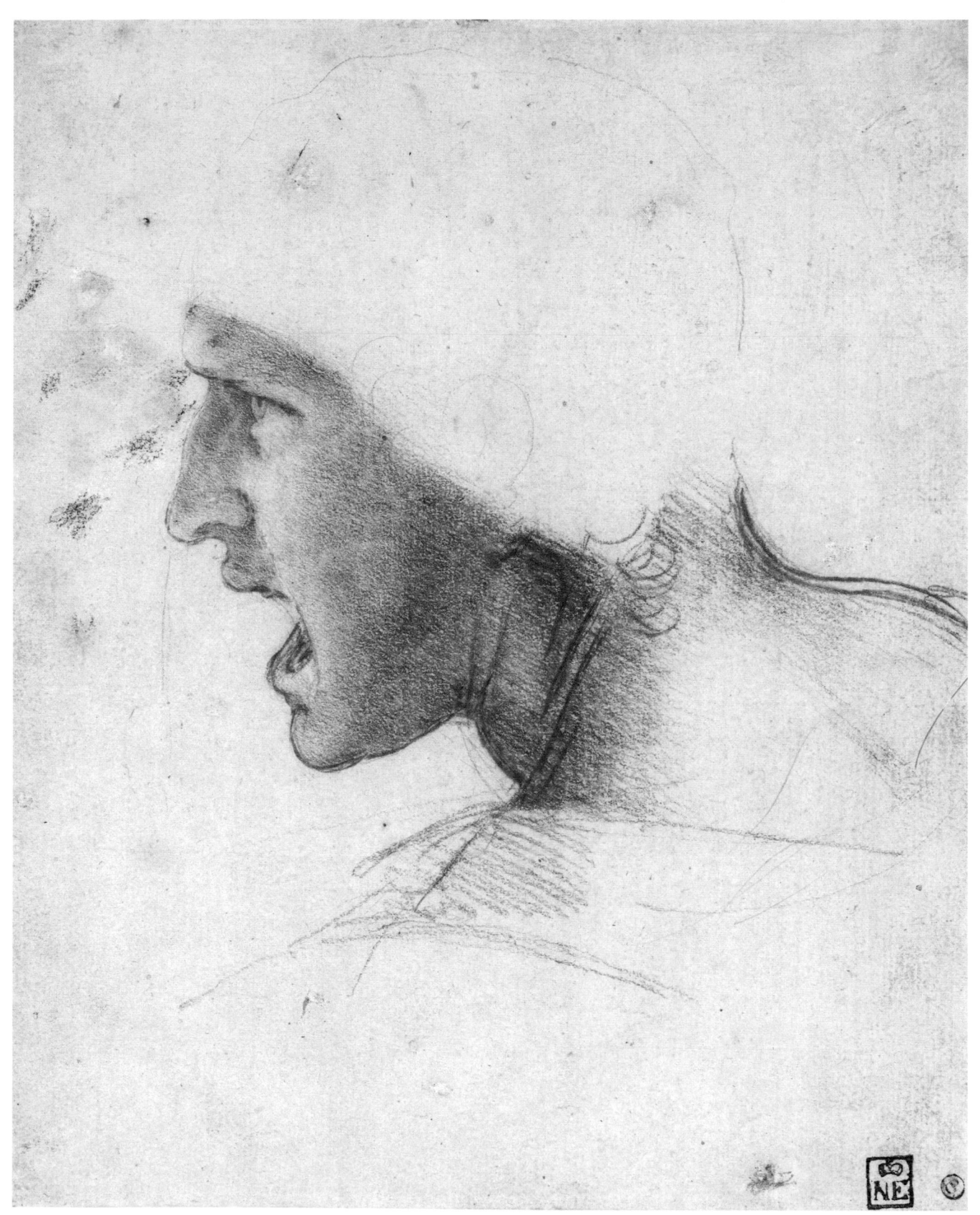

12   Leonardo da Vinci, *Study for the Head of a Soldier in the Battle of Anghiari*

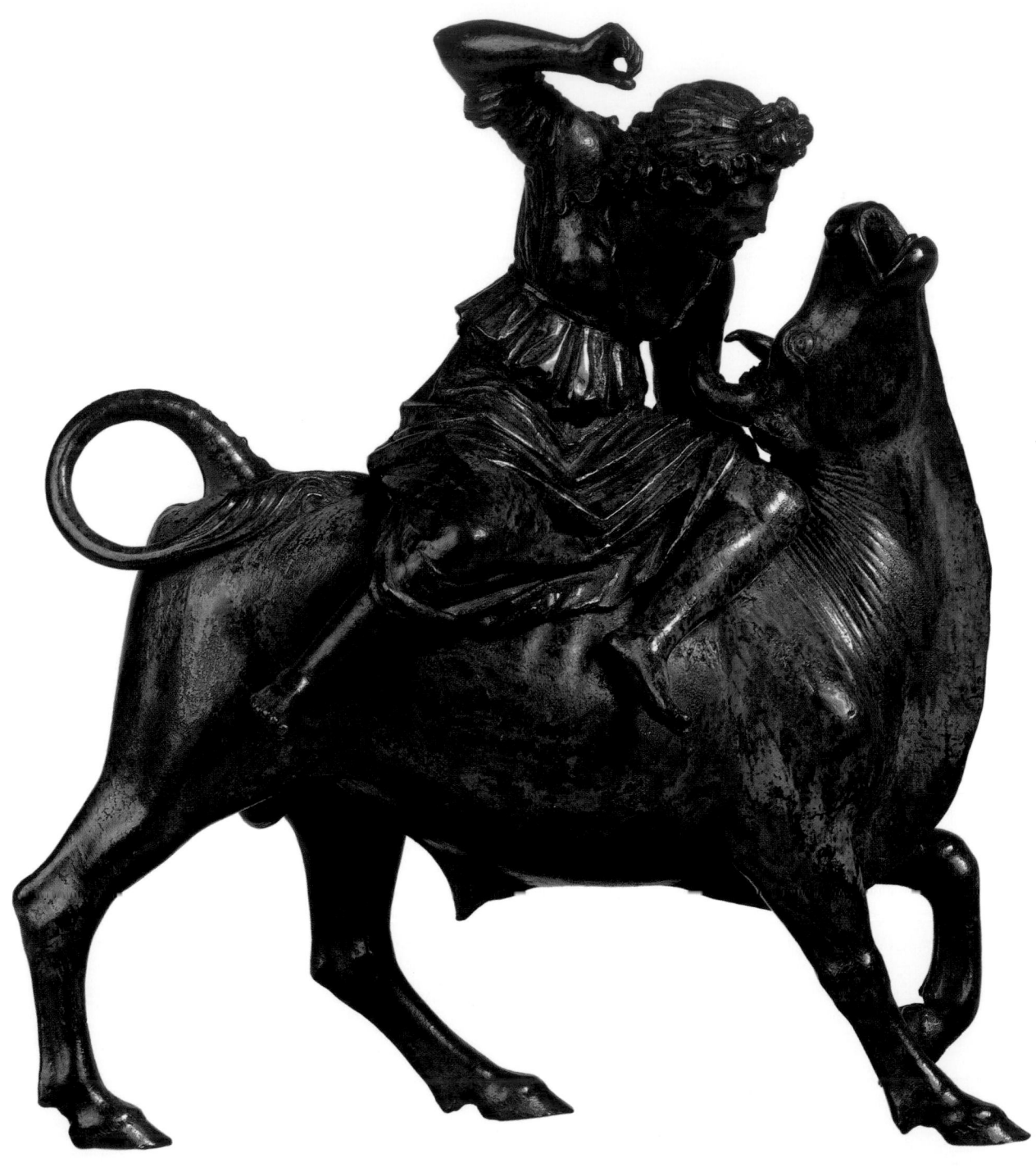

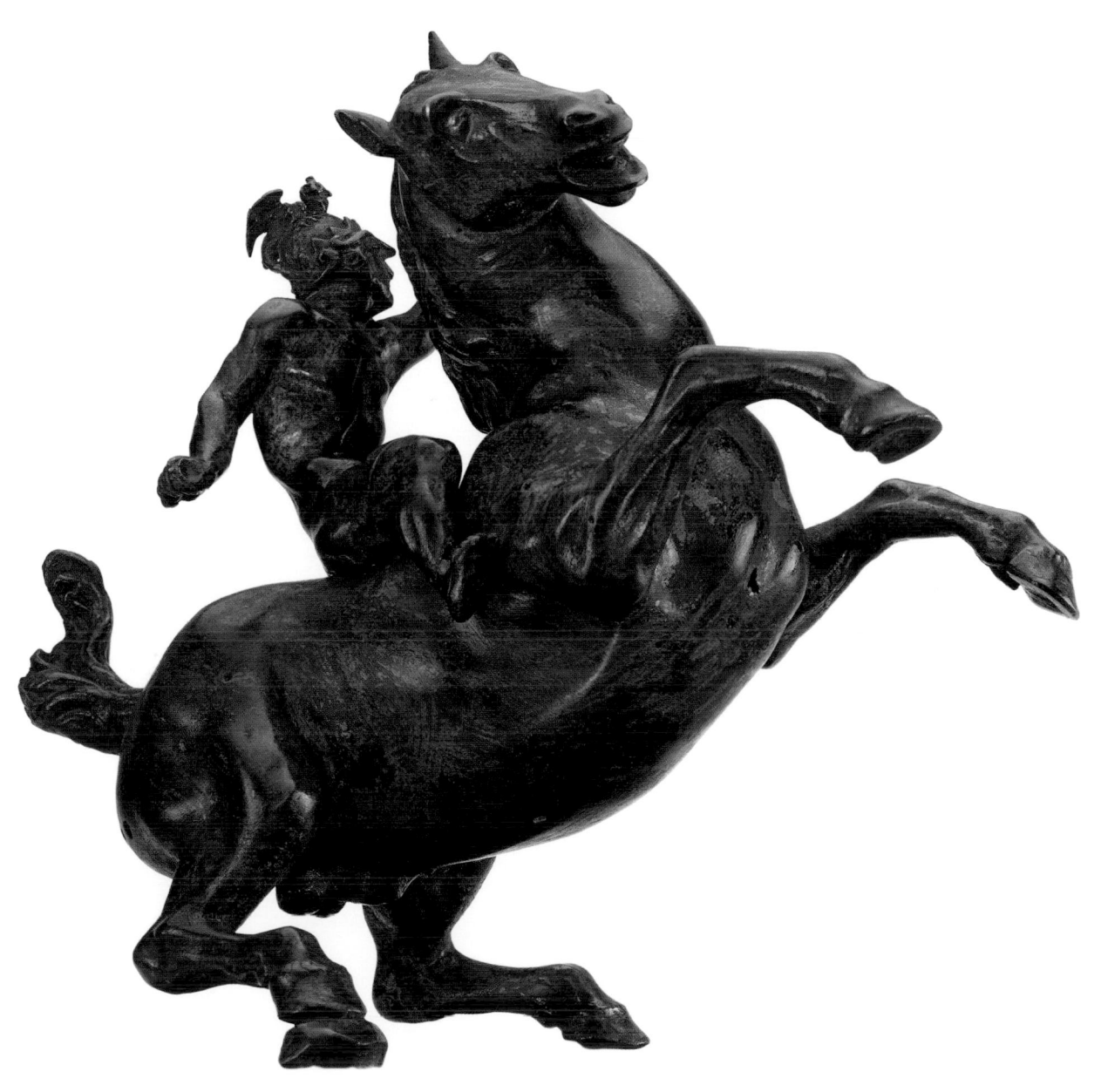

14   Attributed to Leonardo da Vinci, *Mounted Warrior*

13   Attributed to Riccio, *Rape of Europa*

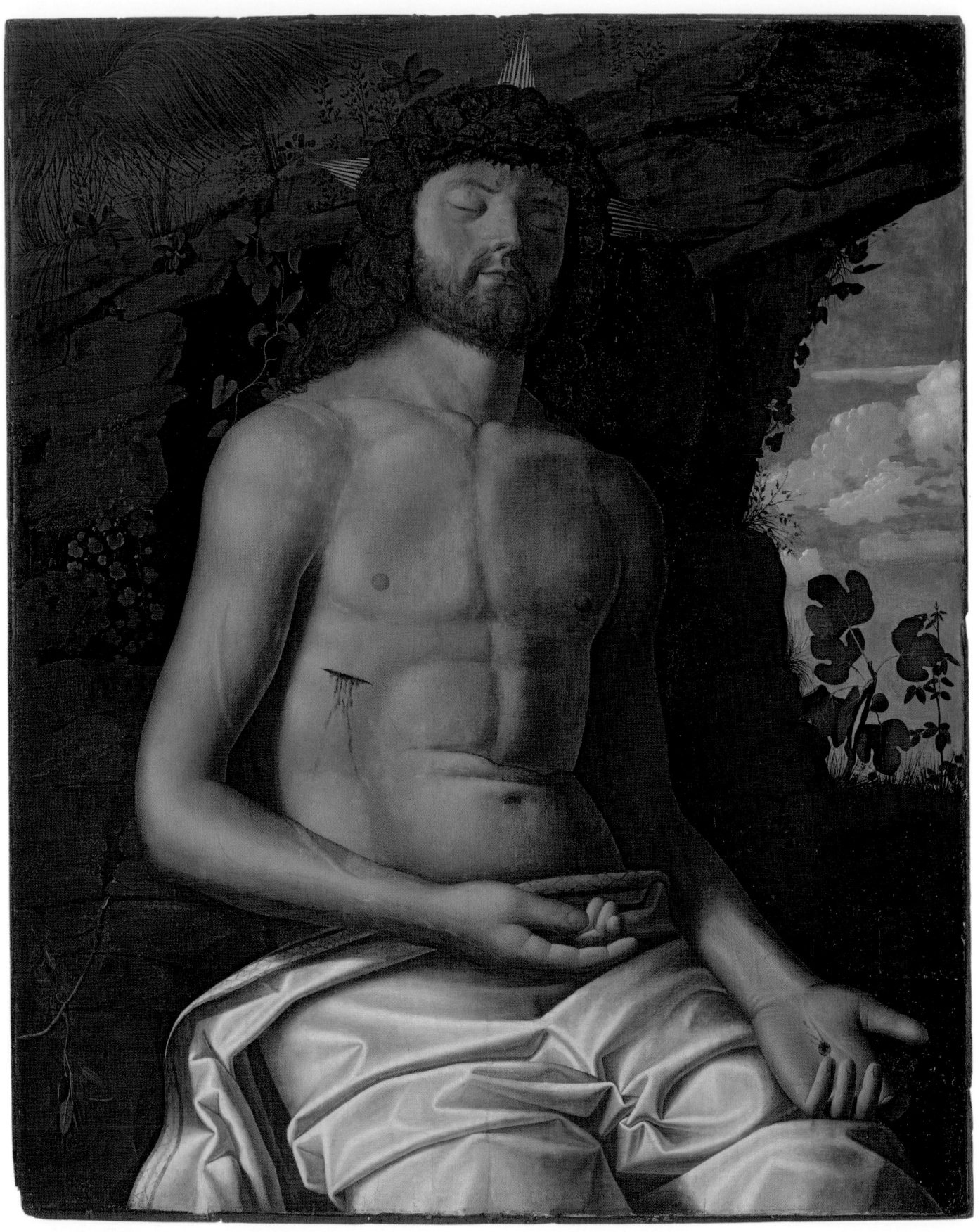

15   Marco Basaiti, *Dead Christ*

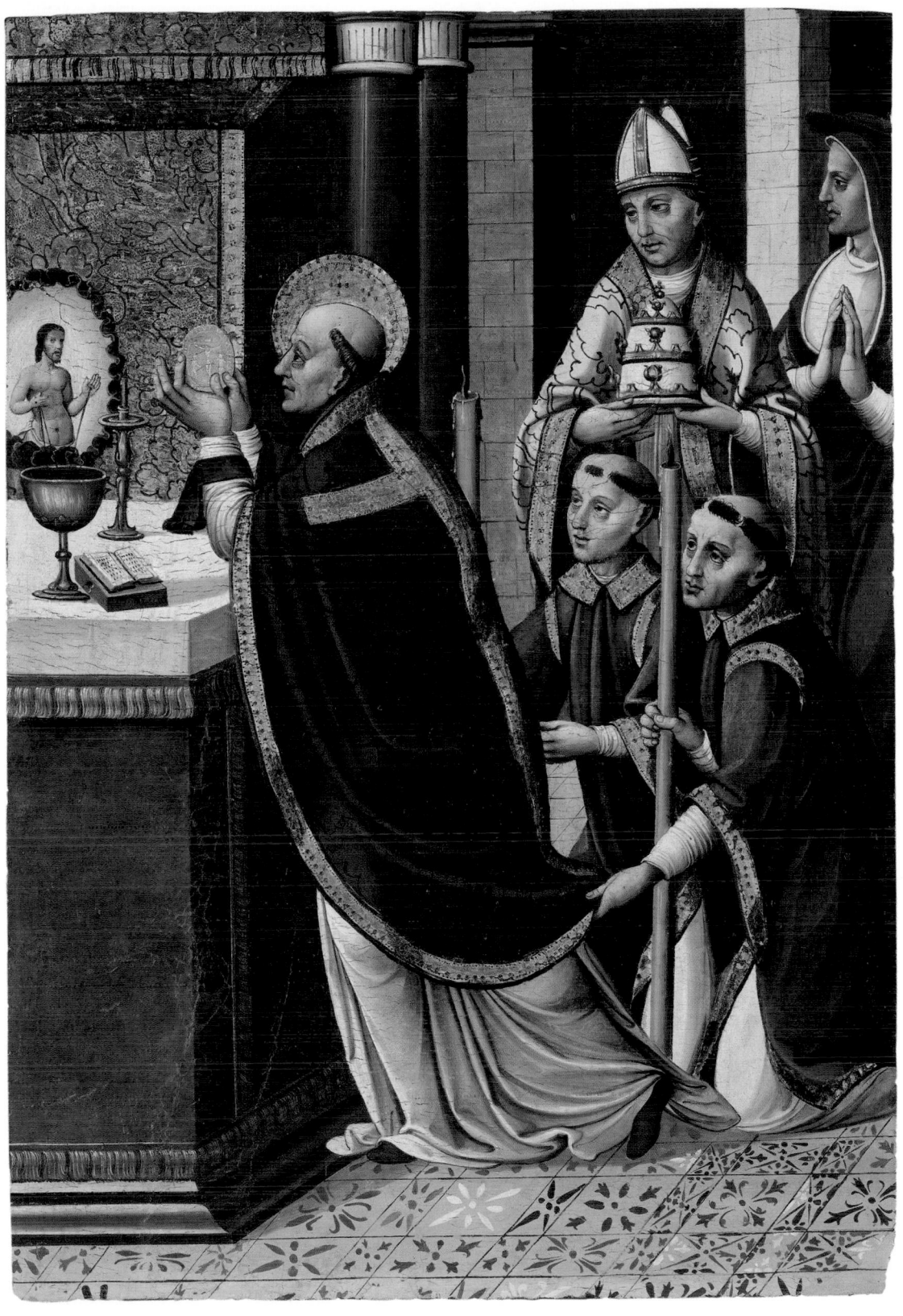

16   Master of Portillo, *Mass of St Gregory*

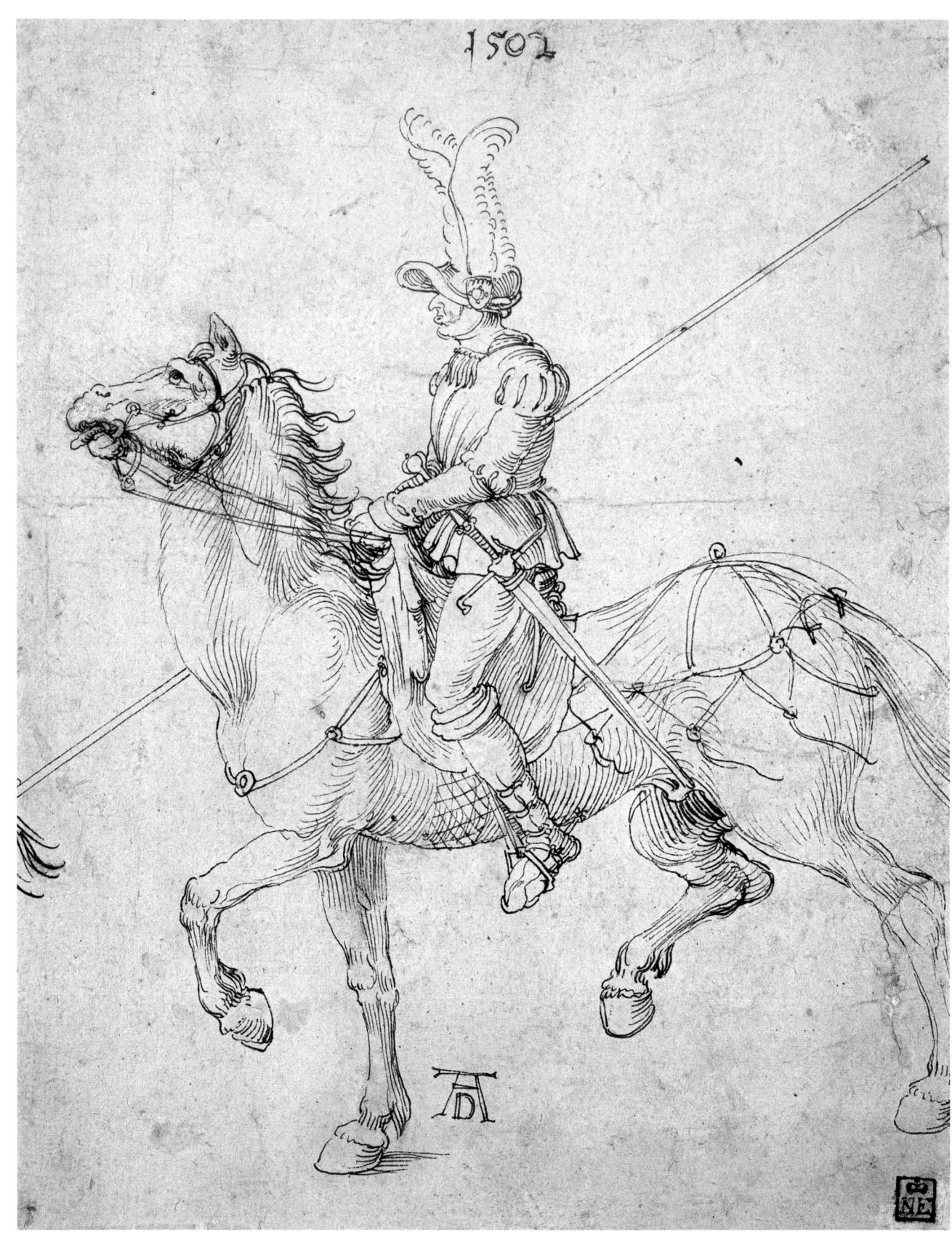

17   Albrecht Dürer, *Lancer on Horseback*

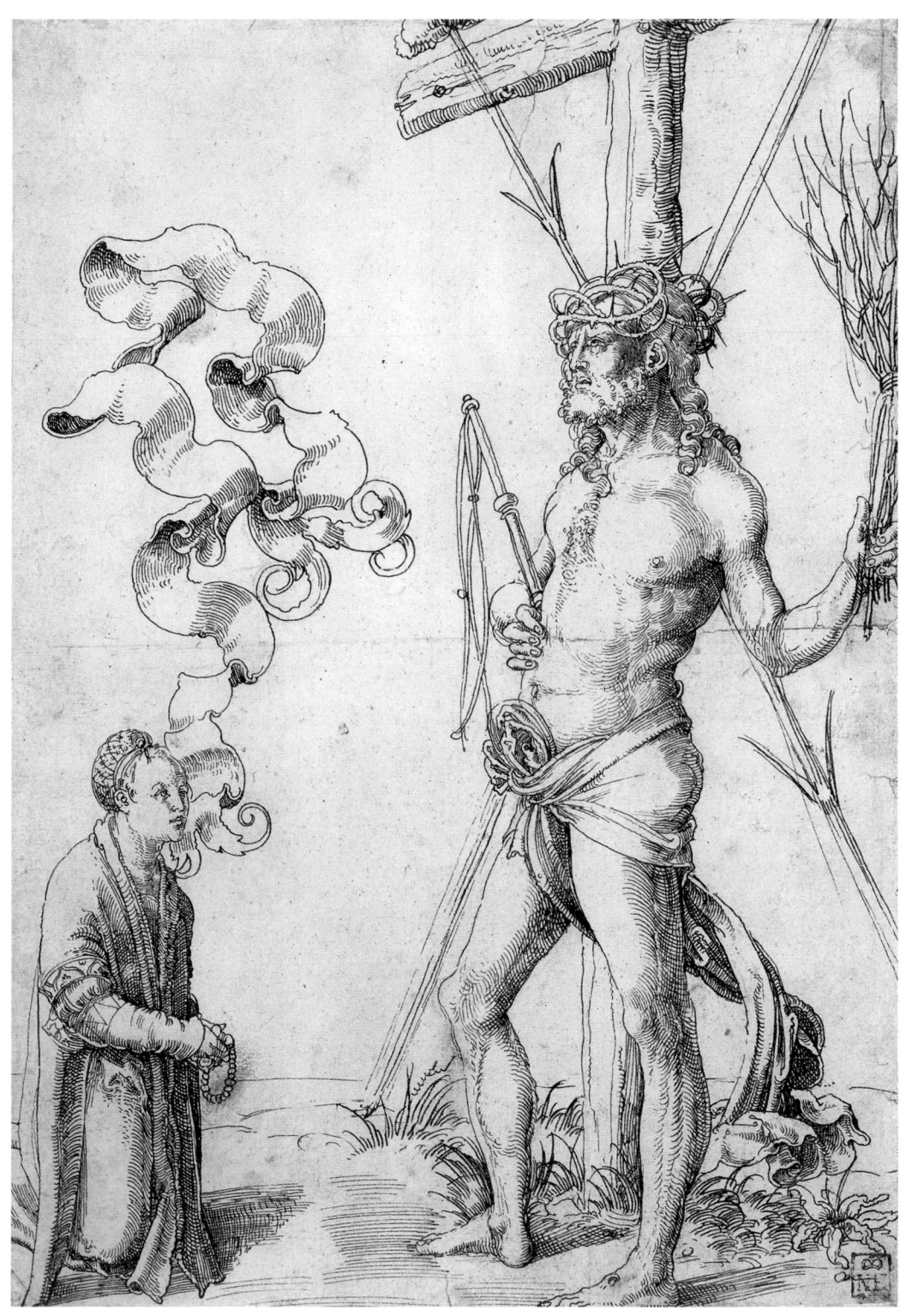

18　Hans Baldung Grien, *Christ with the Instruments of the Passion and a Donor*

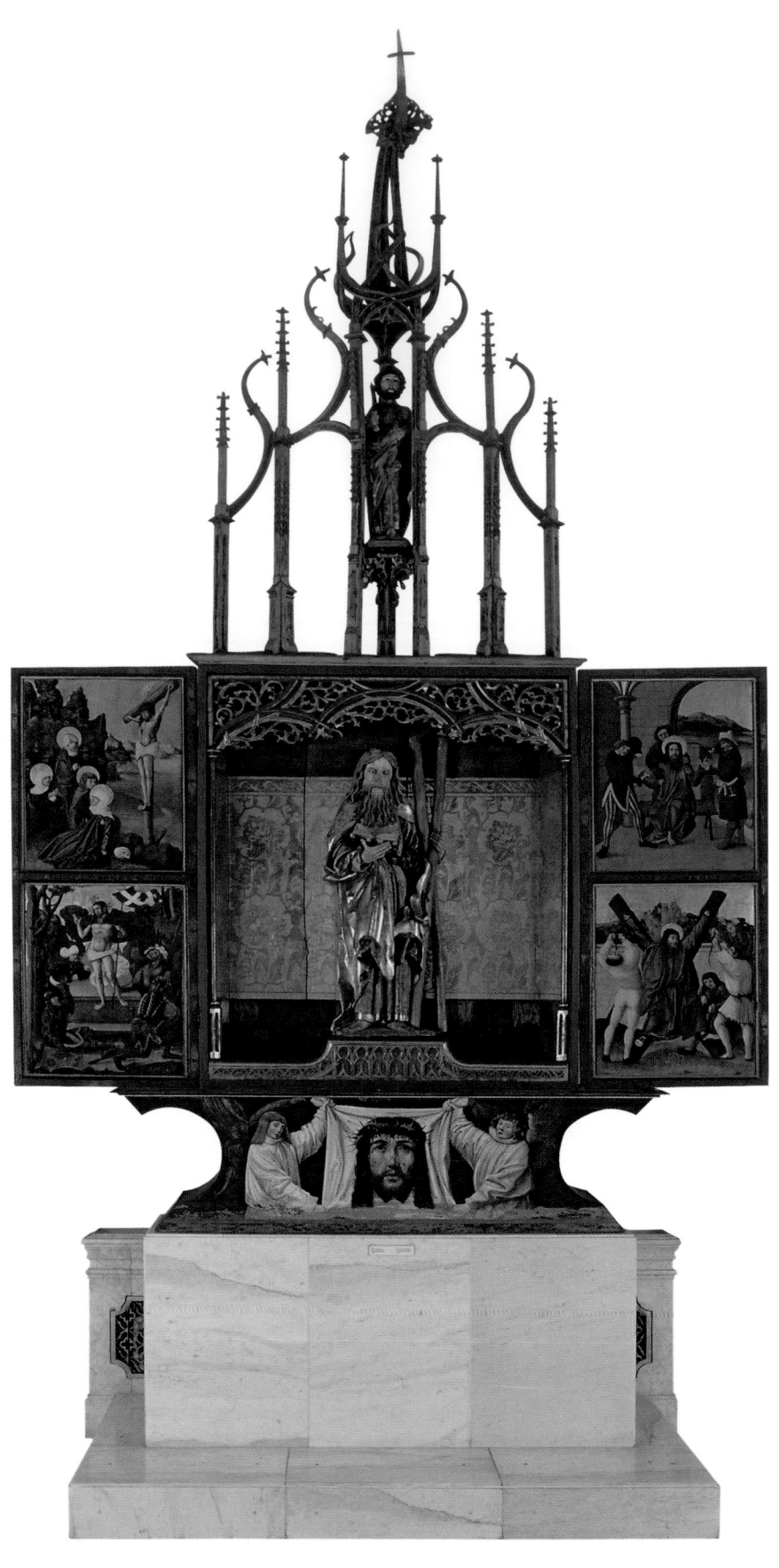

19   Hungarian master, early sixteenth century, *St Andrew Altarpiece*

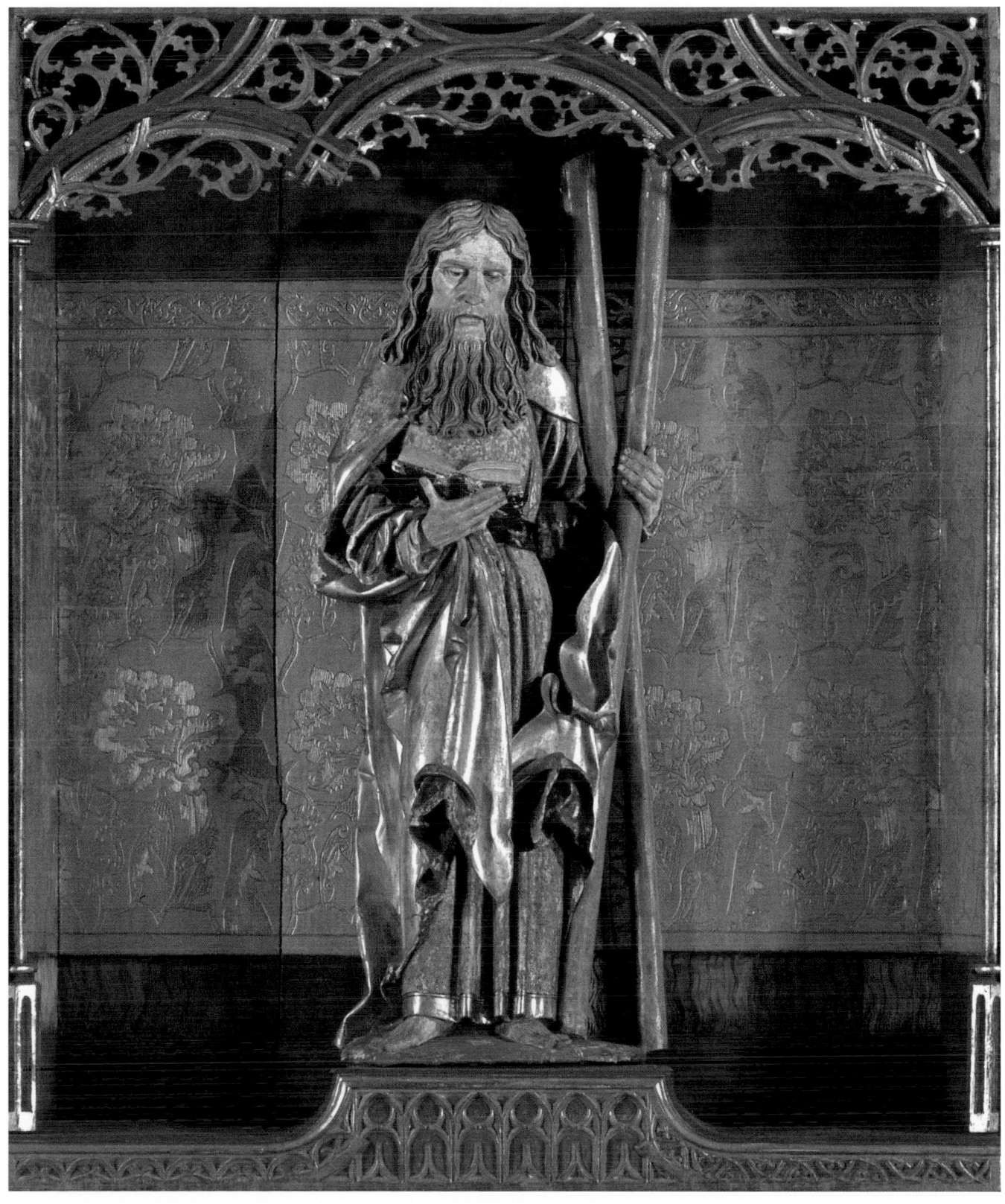

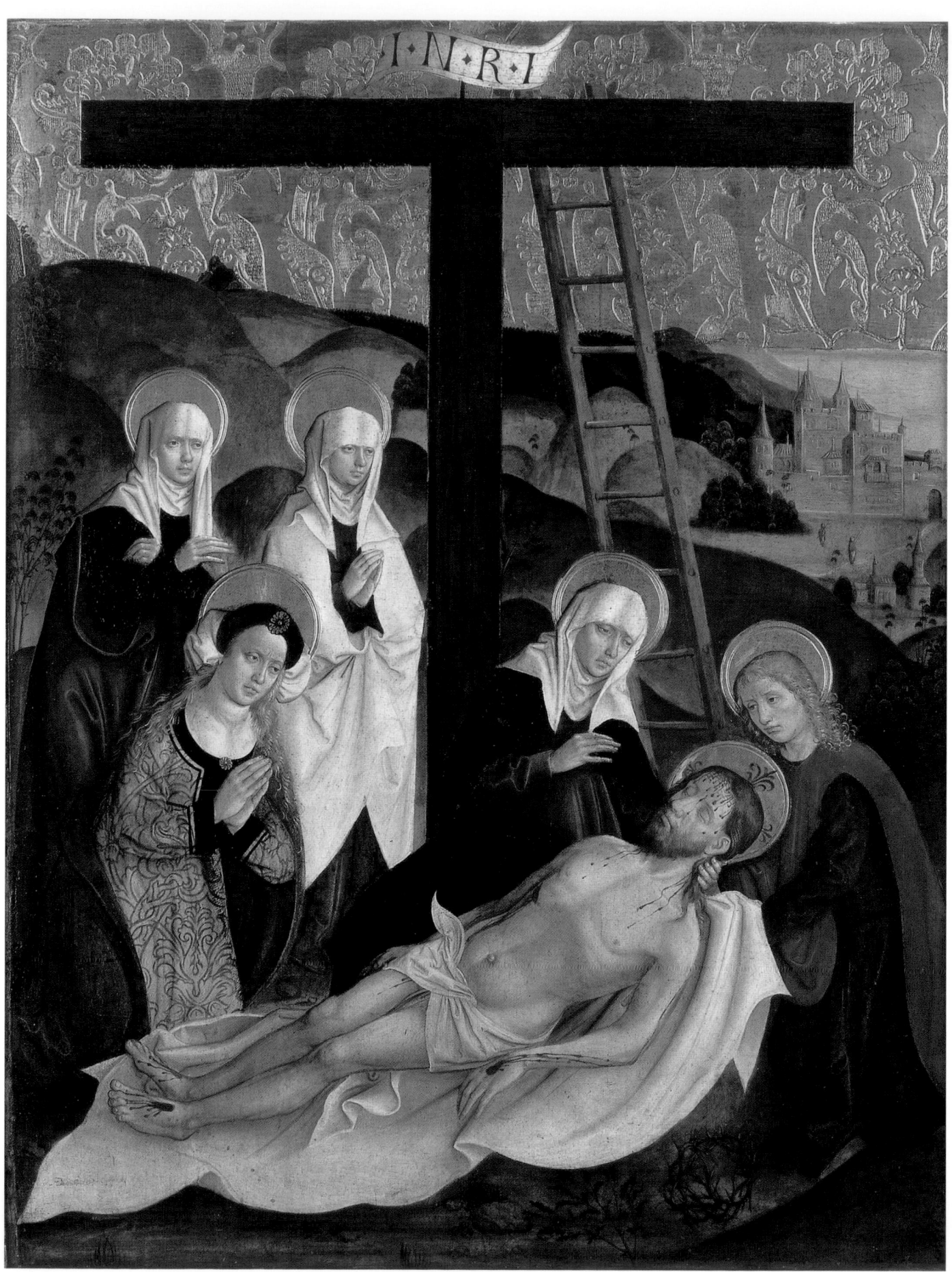

20 Master of Okolicsnó, *Lamentation*

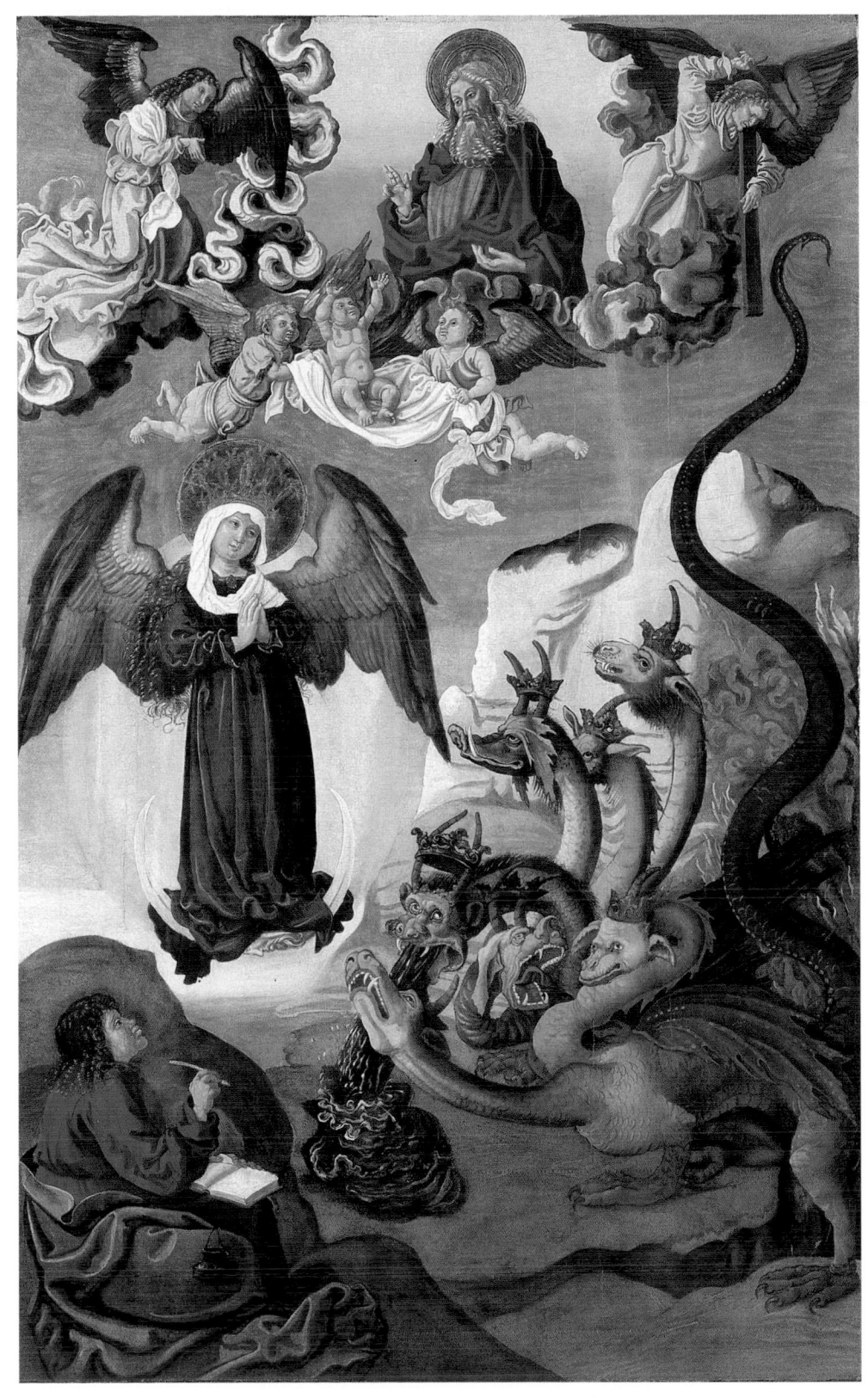

21　Hungarian(?) master, early sixteenth century, *Woman of the Apocalypse Clothed with the Sun and the Dragon*

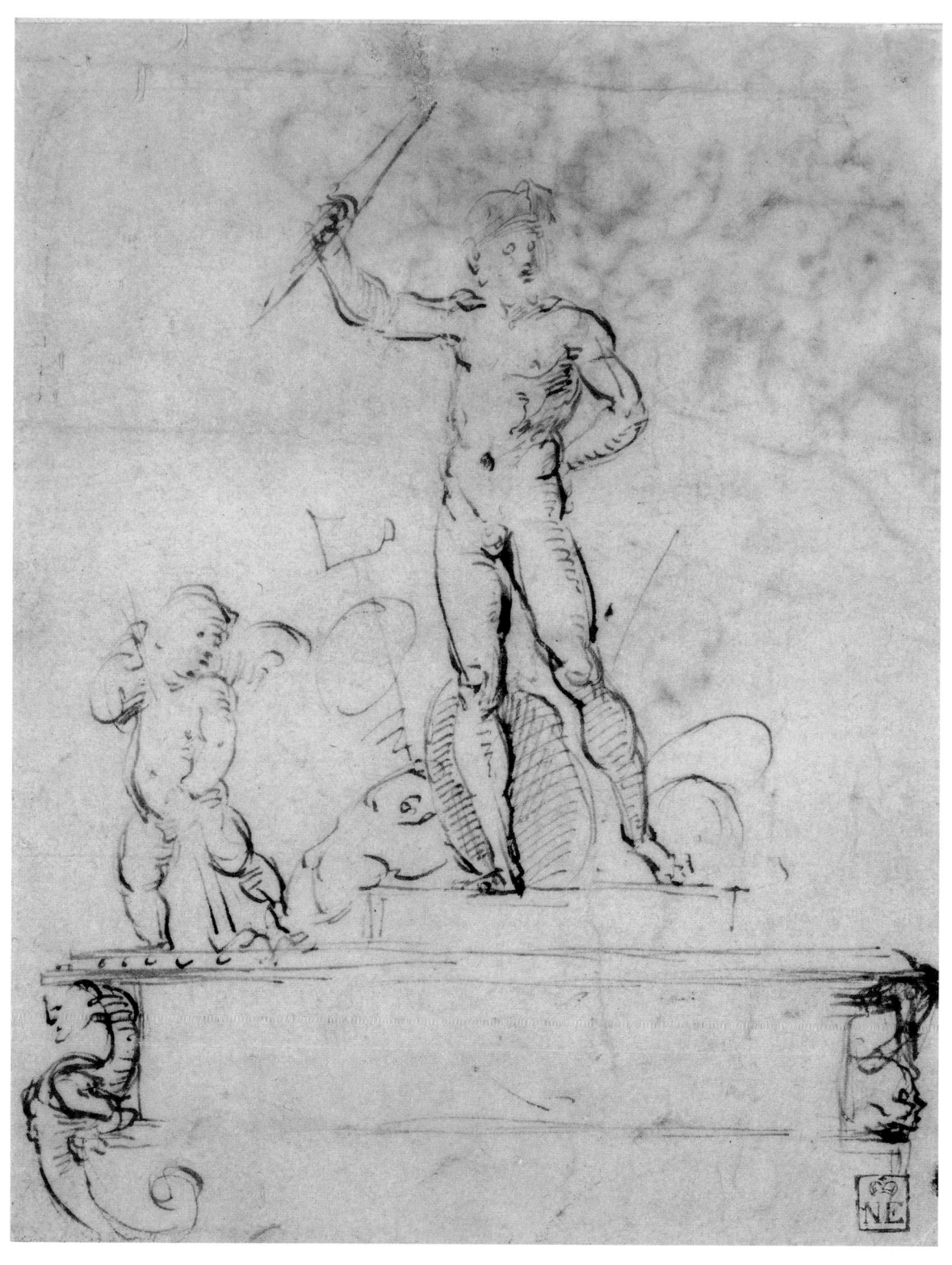

22 Raphael, *Study for a Temporary Decoration*

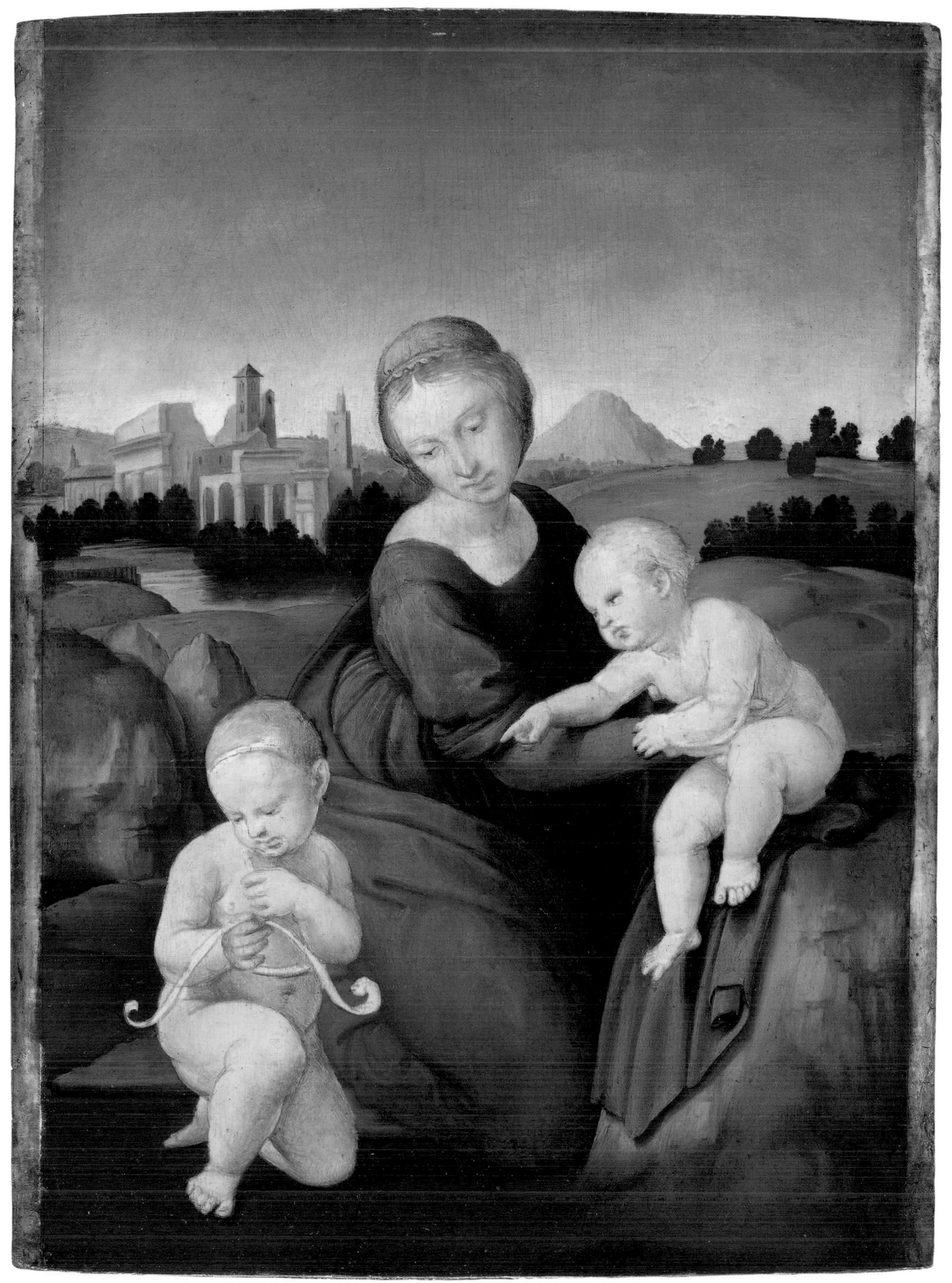

23 Raphael, *Esterházy Madonna*

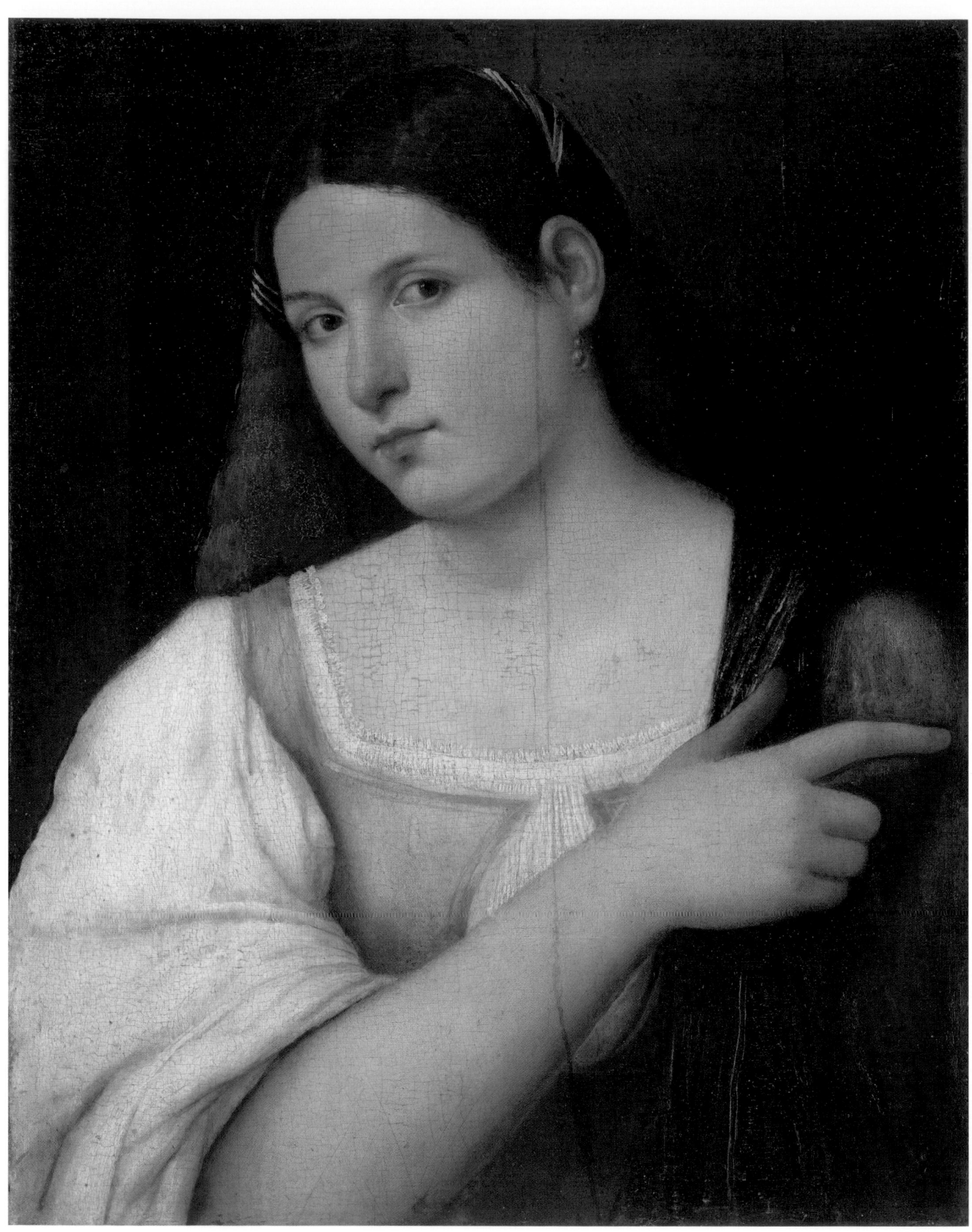

24 Sebastiano del Piombo, *Girl Pointing*

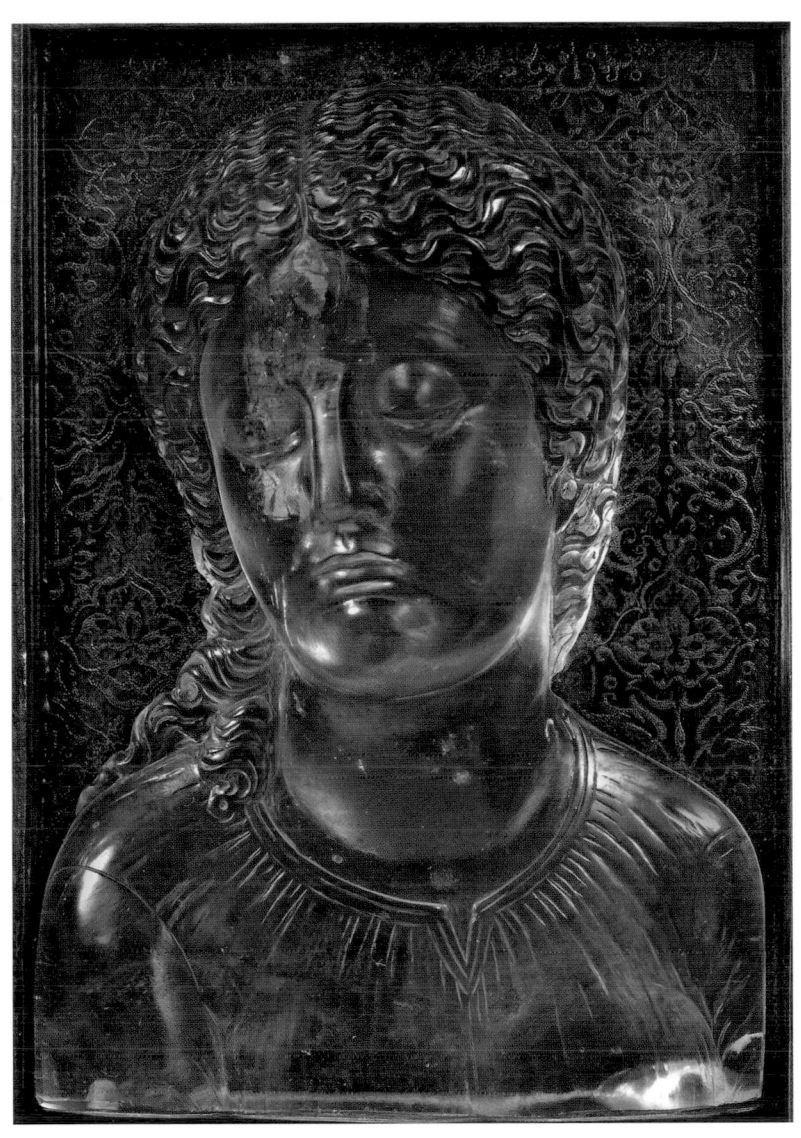

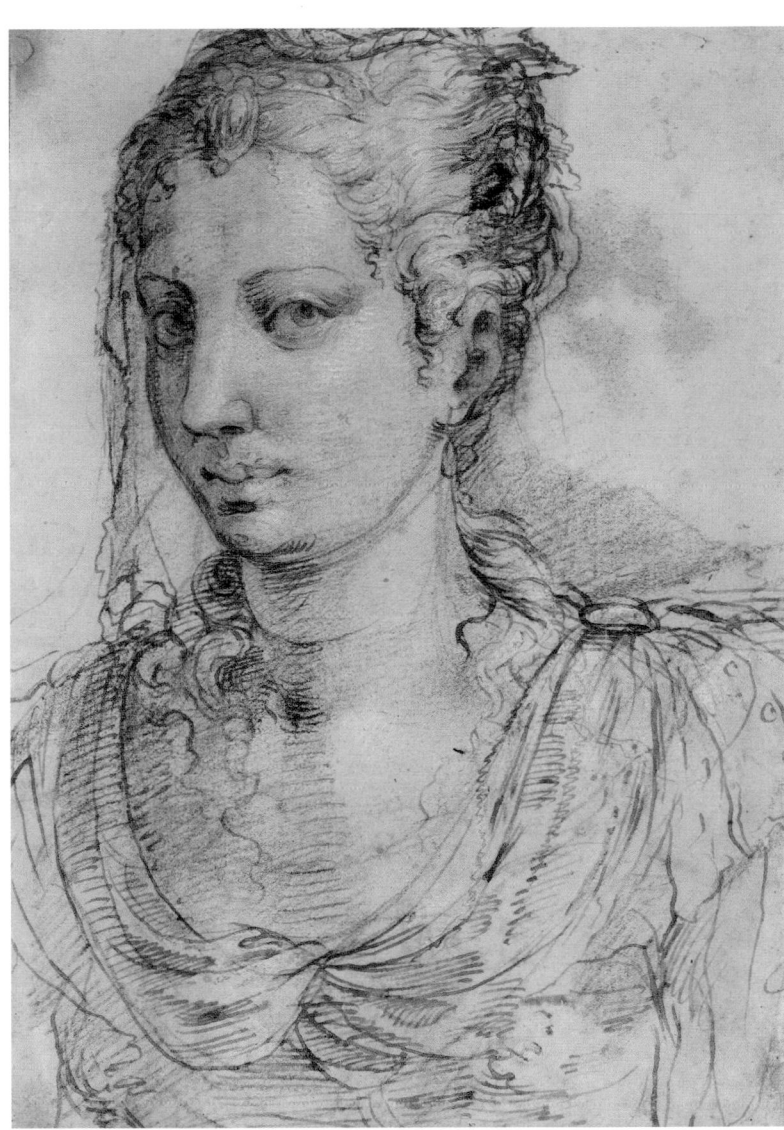

25 Pyrgoteles, *Bust of a Woman*

26 Nicolò dell'Abate, *Bust of a Woman*

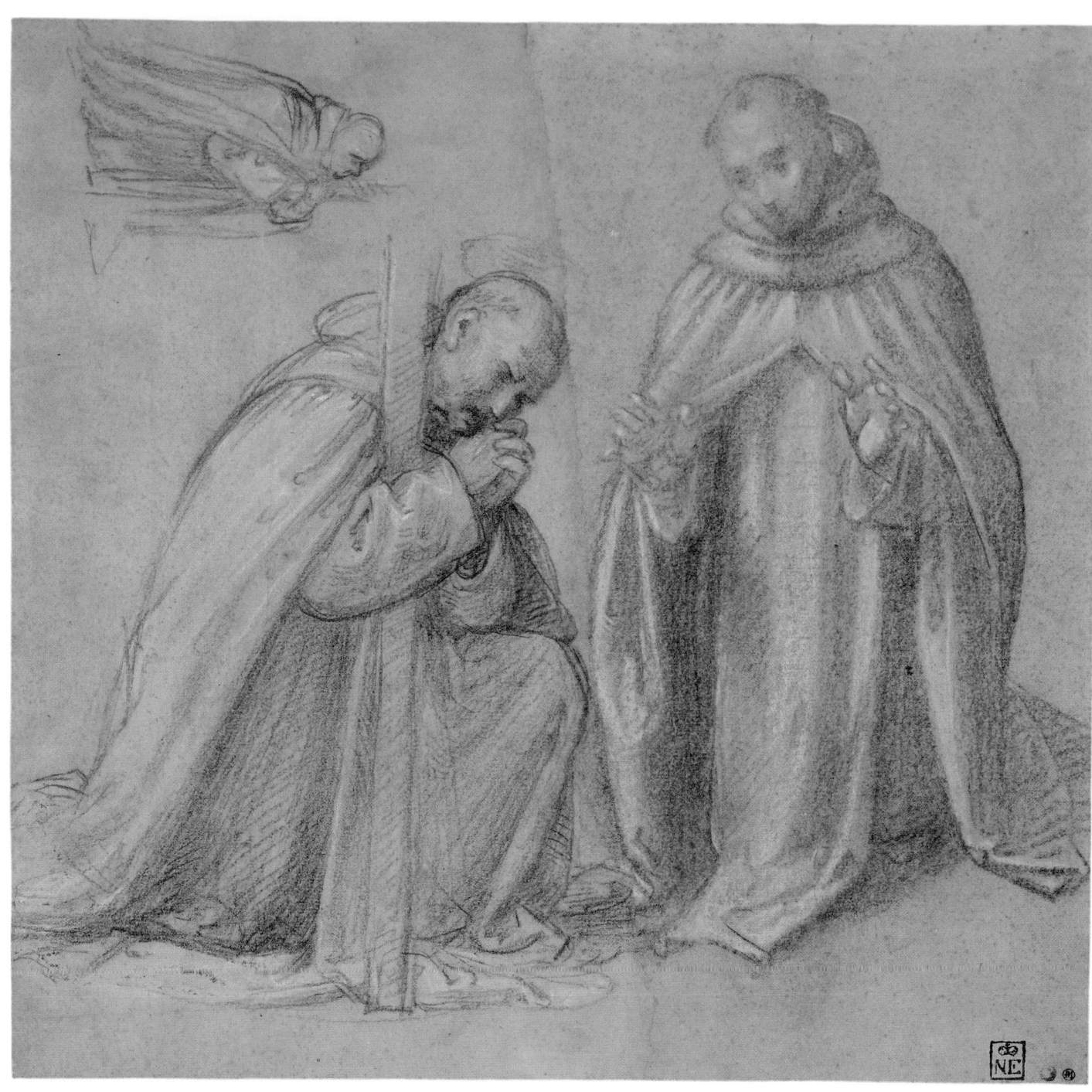

27   Fra Bartolommeo, *Three Studies of Dominican Friars*

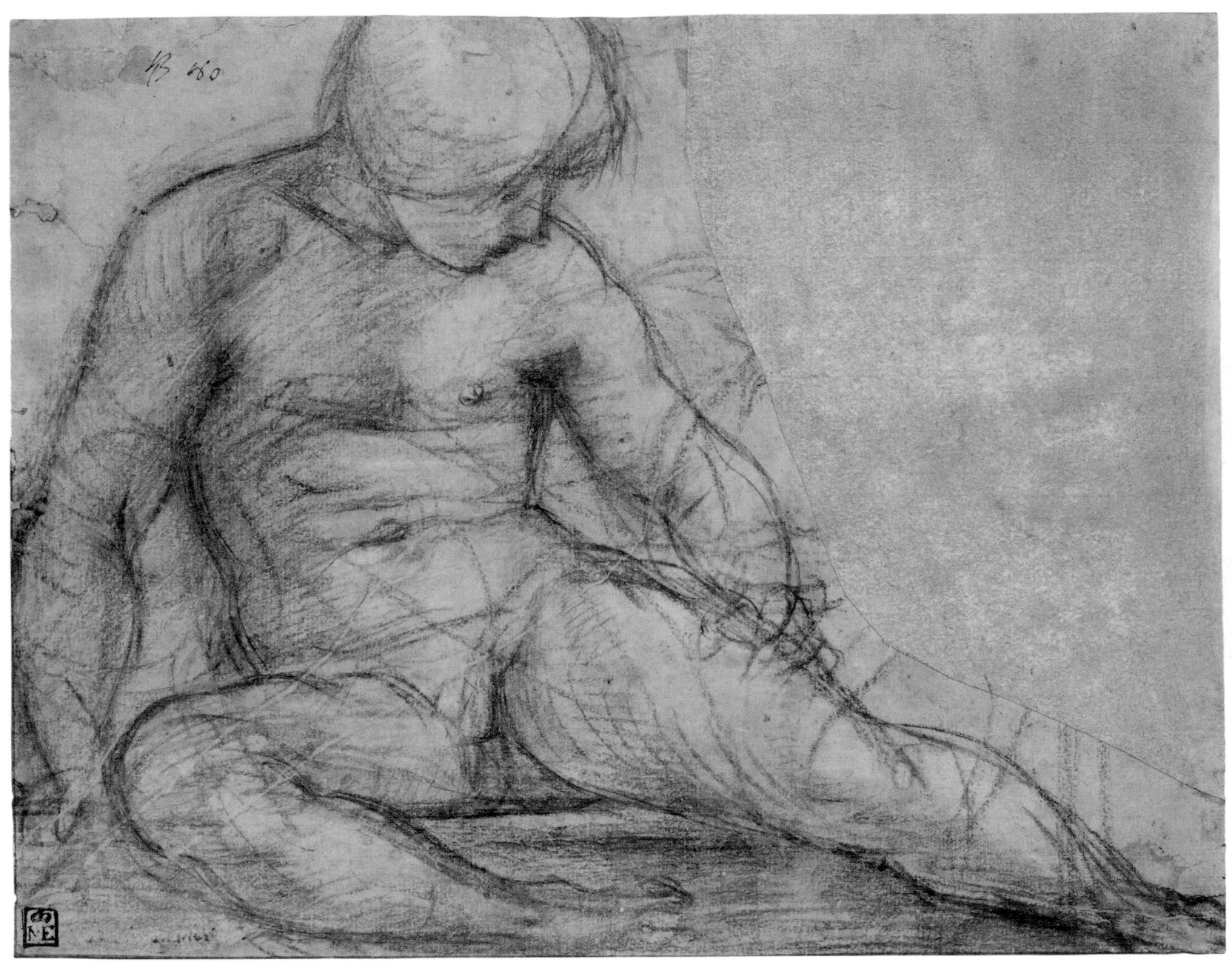

28   Pontormo, *Study for a Seated Youth*

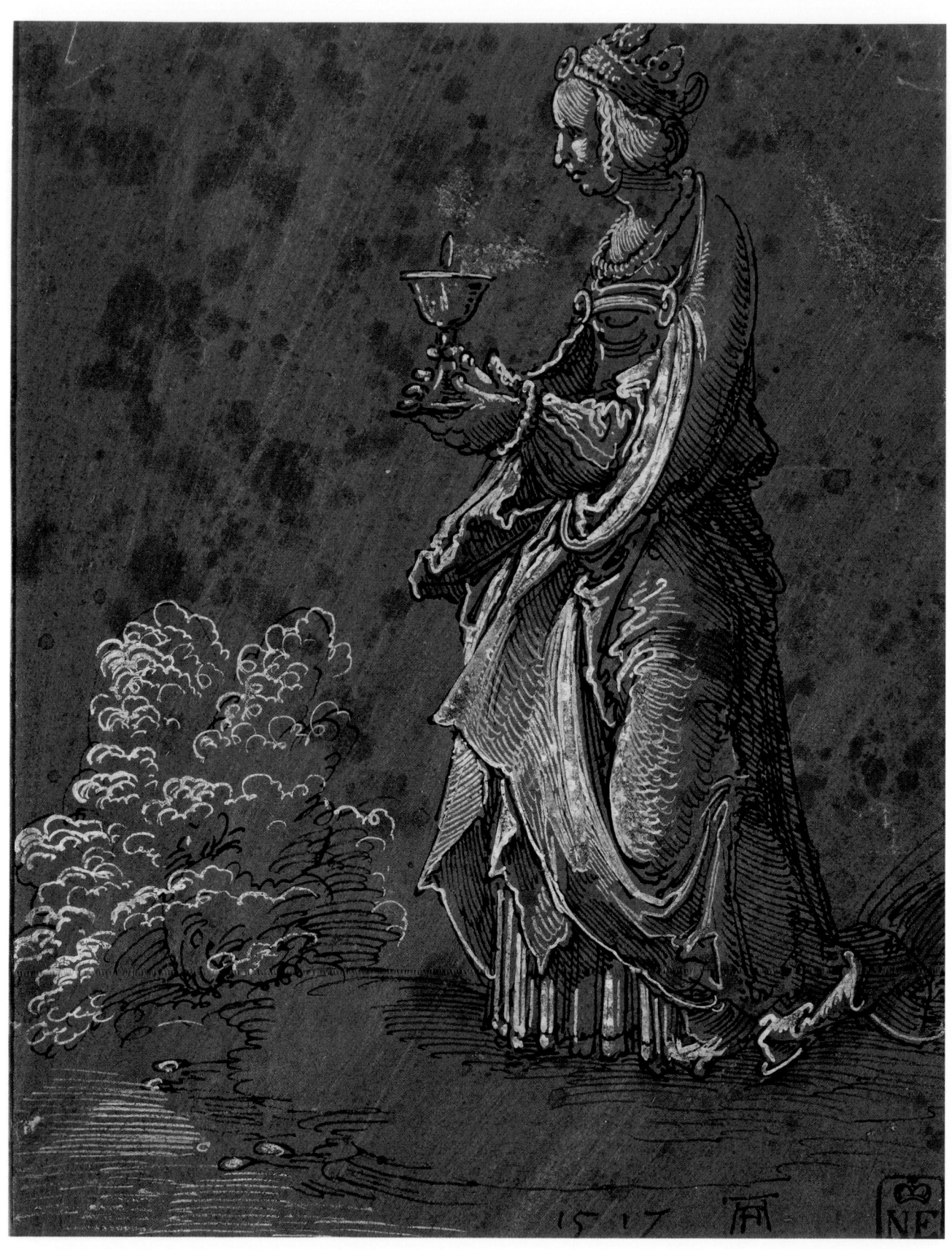

29   Albrecht Altdorfer, *St Barbara*

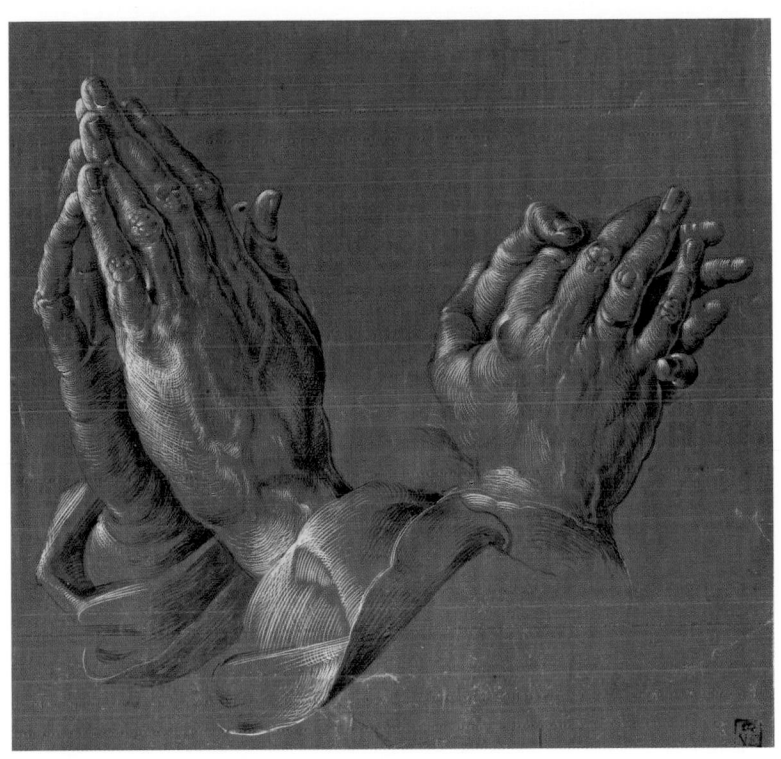

30   Hans Hoffmann, *Two Studies of Hands*

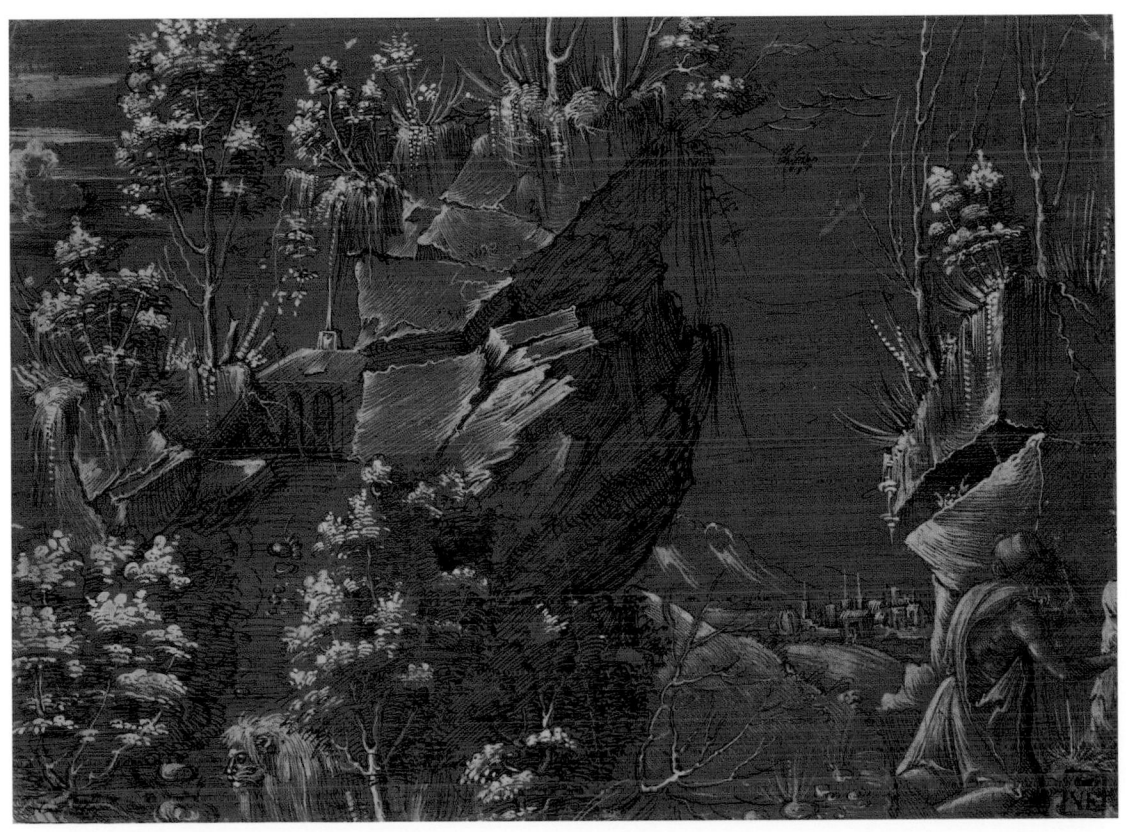

31   Hans Leu the Younger, *St Jerome*

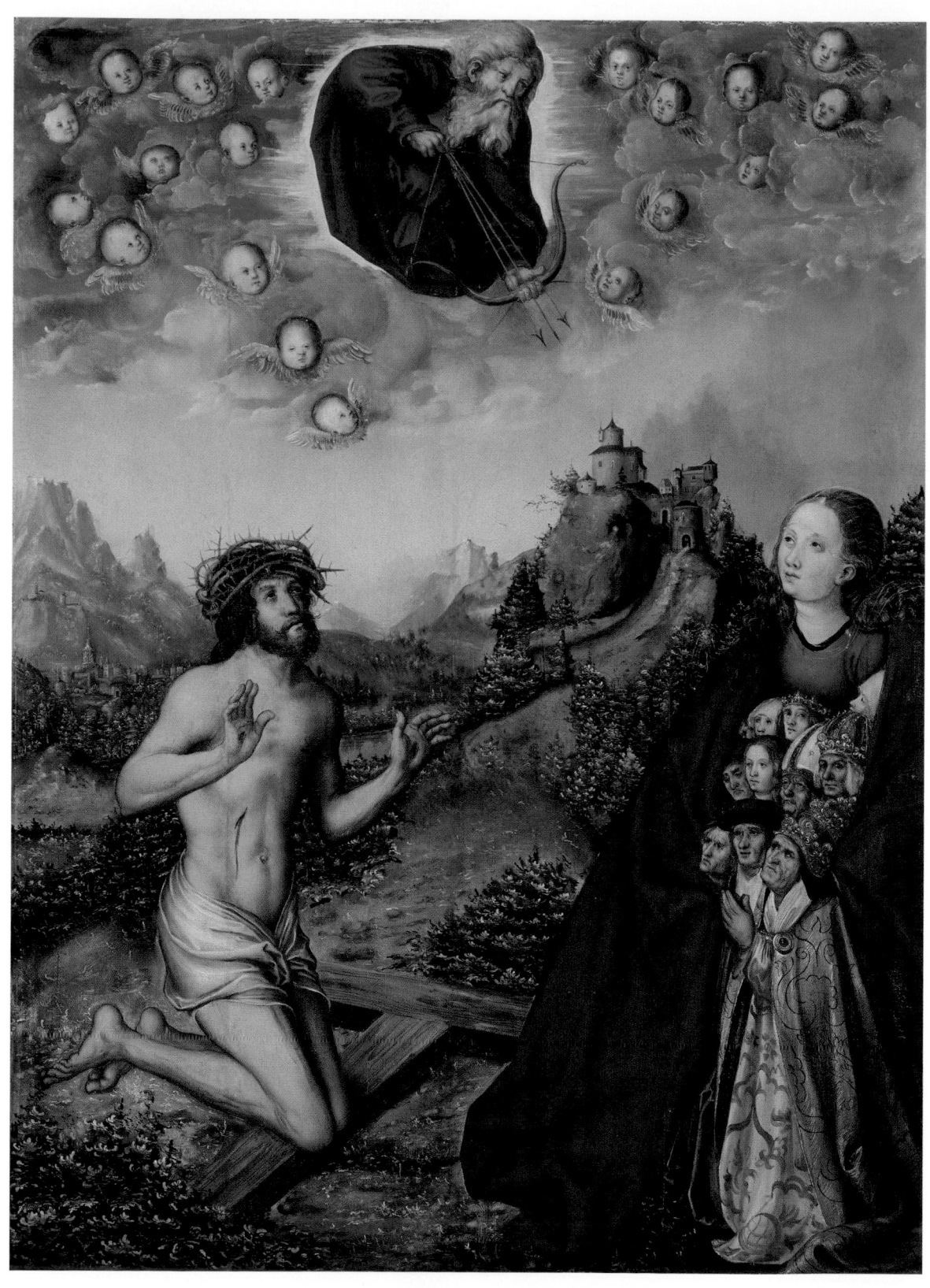

32   Lucas Cranach the Elder, *Christ and the Virgin Interceding for Humanity before God the Father*

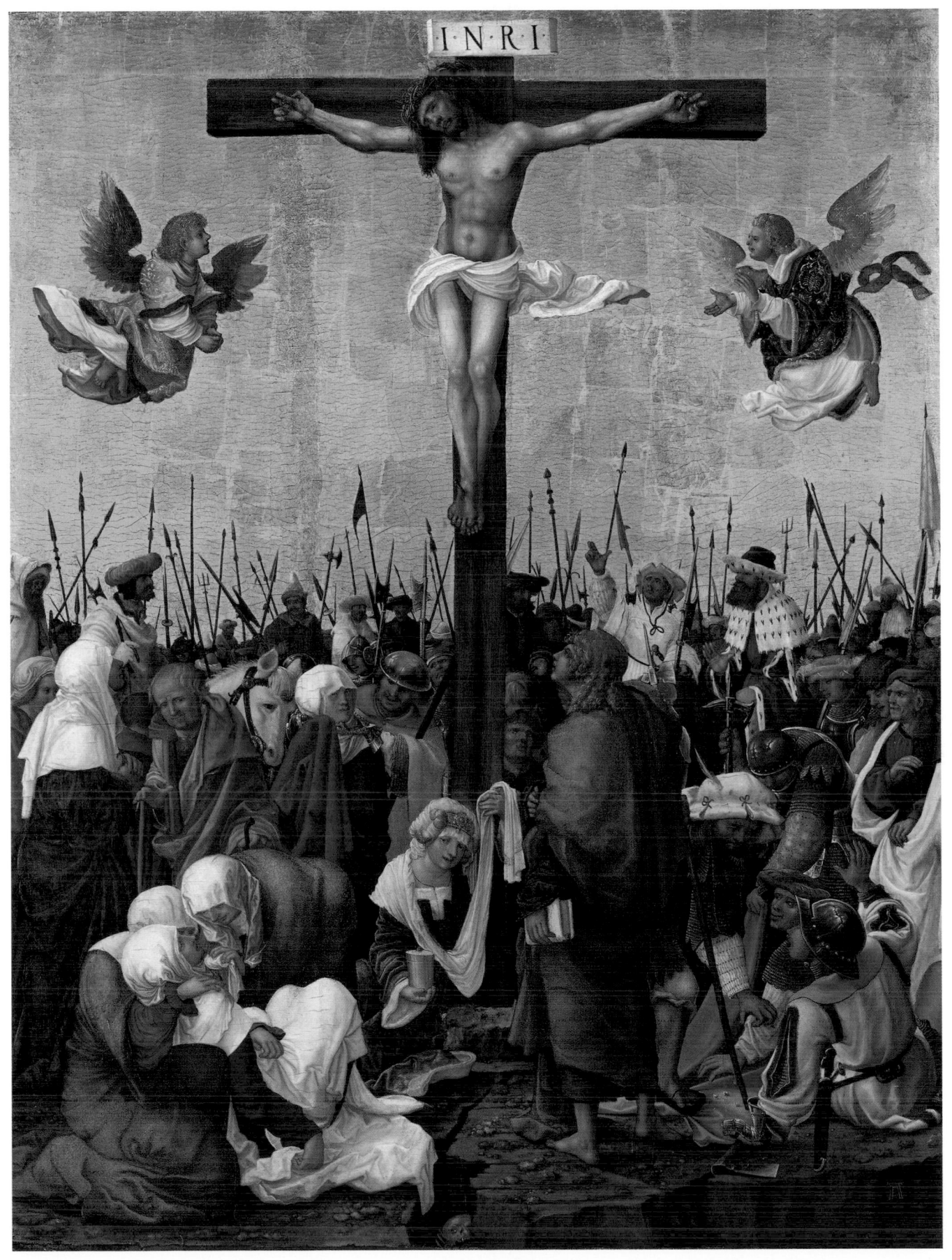

33 Albrecht Altdorfer, *Crucifixion*

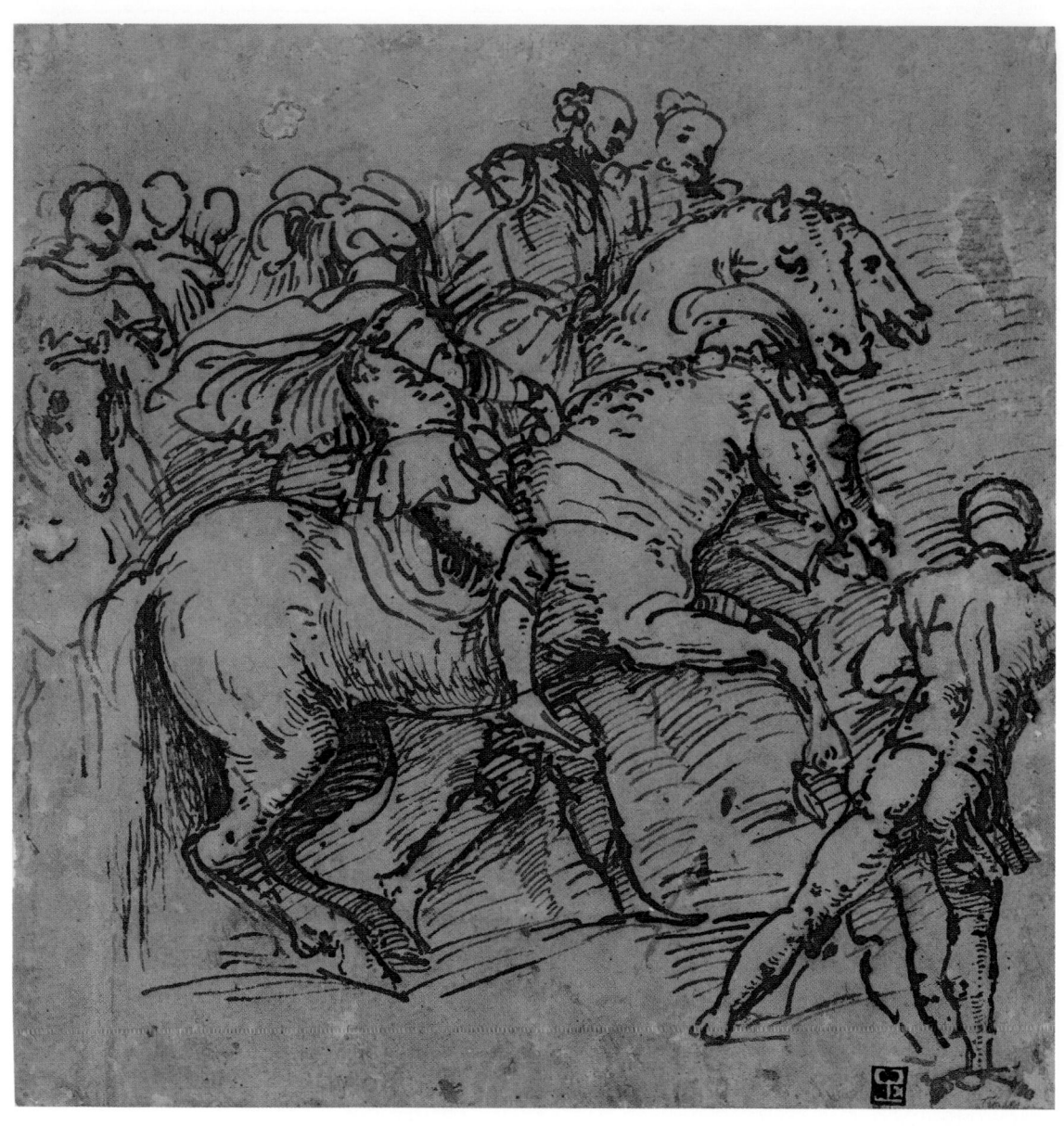

34   Girolamo Romanino, *Men on Horseback Riding to the Right*

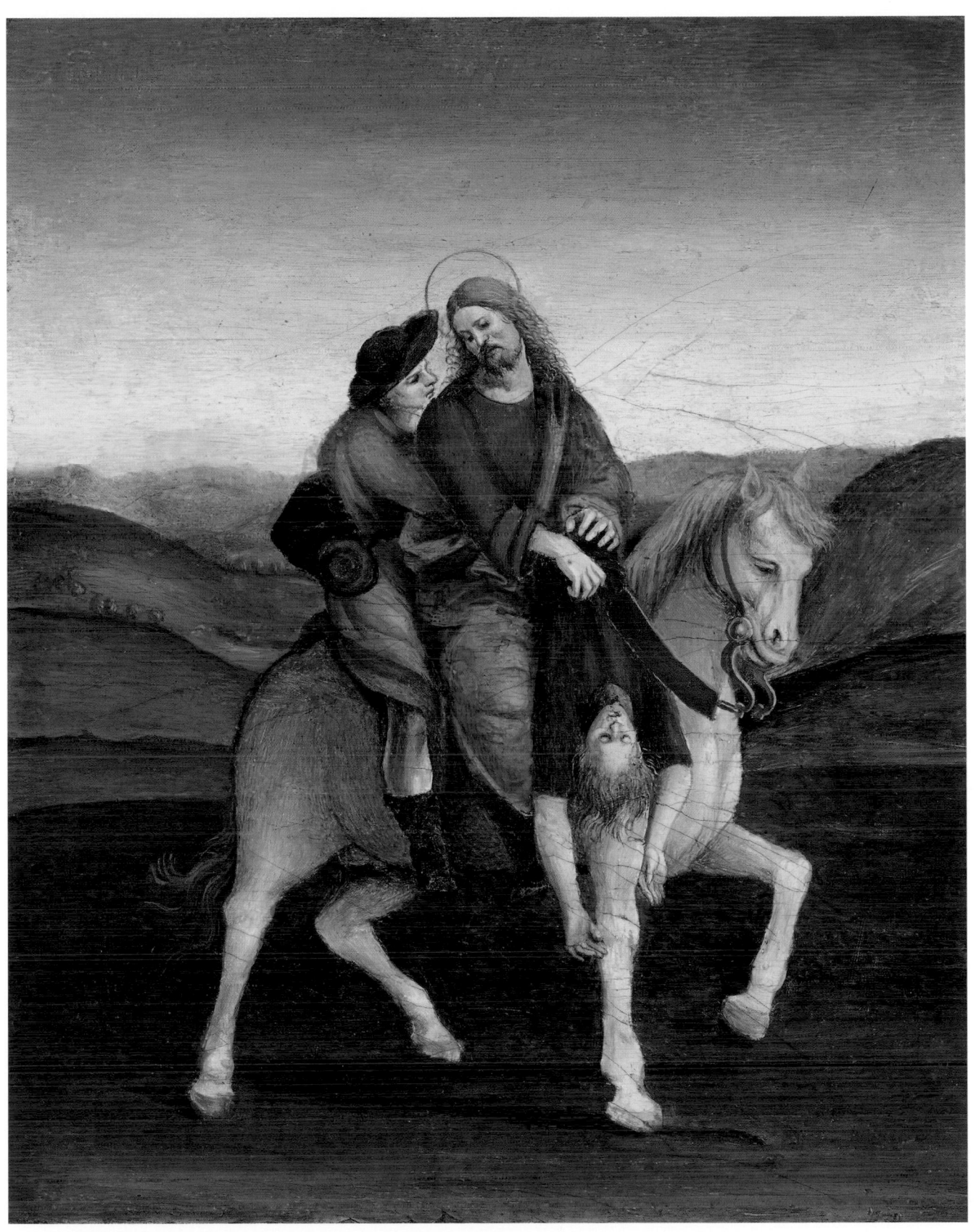

35   Luca Signorelli, *St James the Greater with a Living and a Dead Pilgrim*

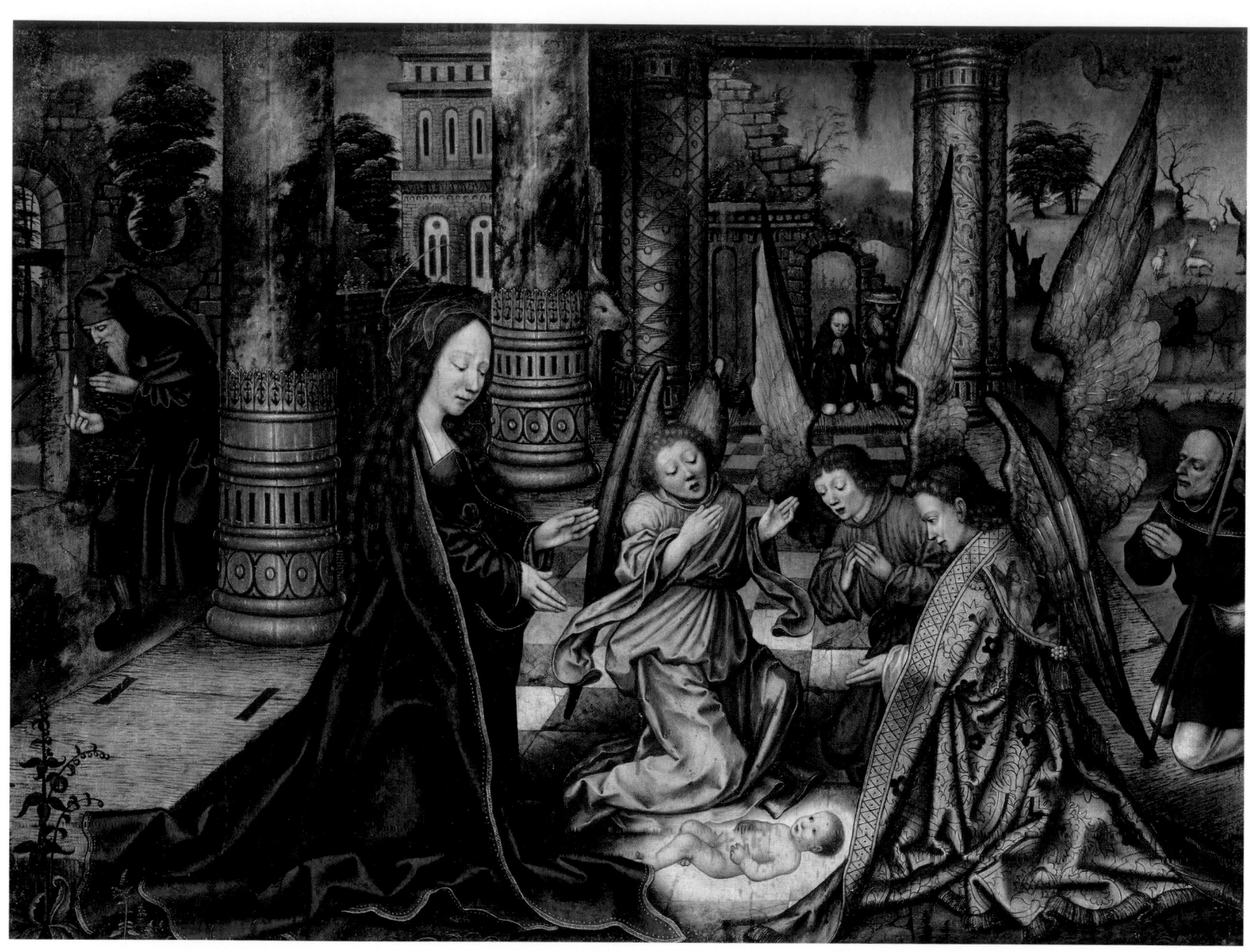

36 Master of Frankfurt, *Nativity*

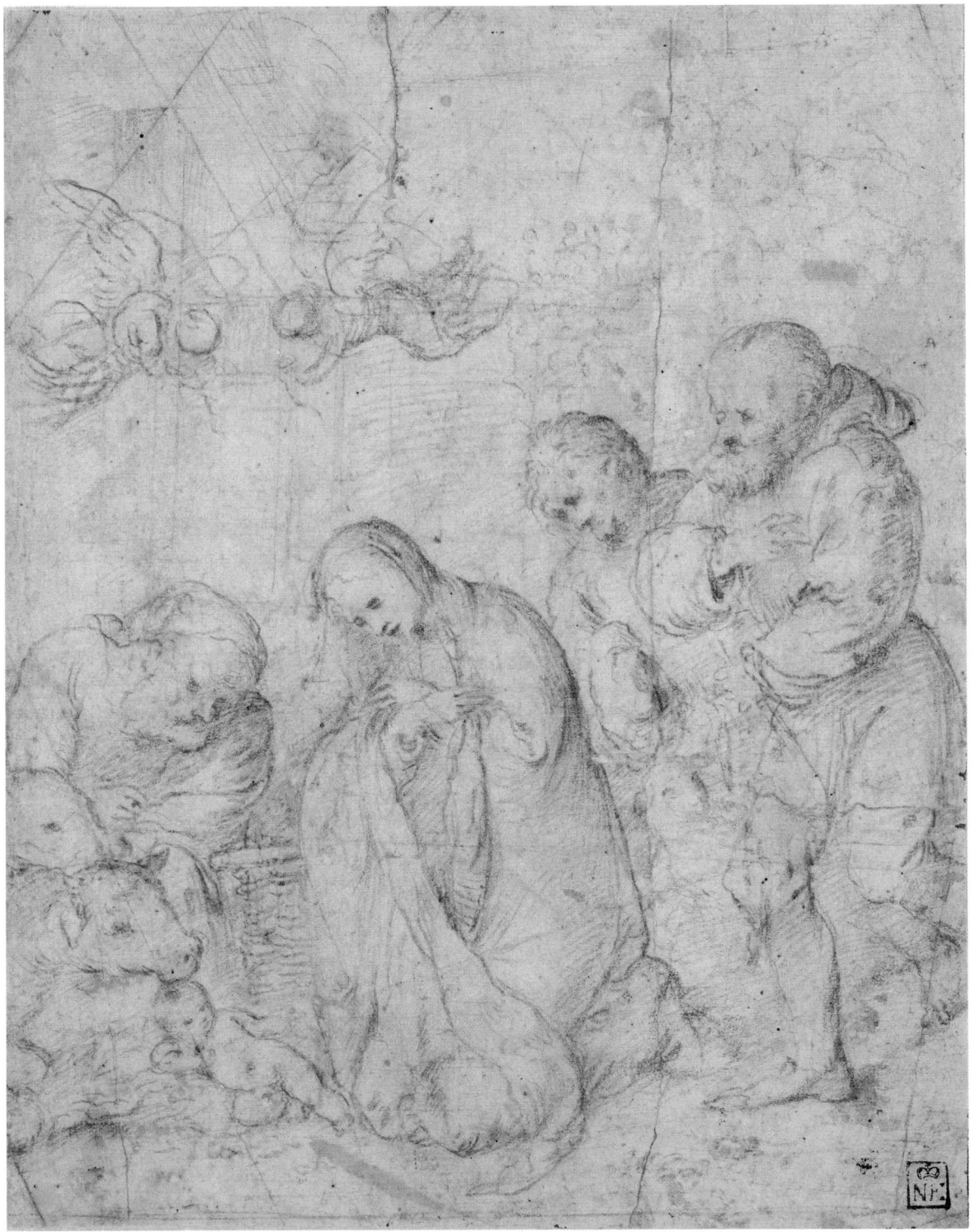

37   Girolamo Romanino, *Adoration of the Shepherds*

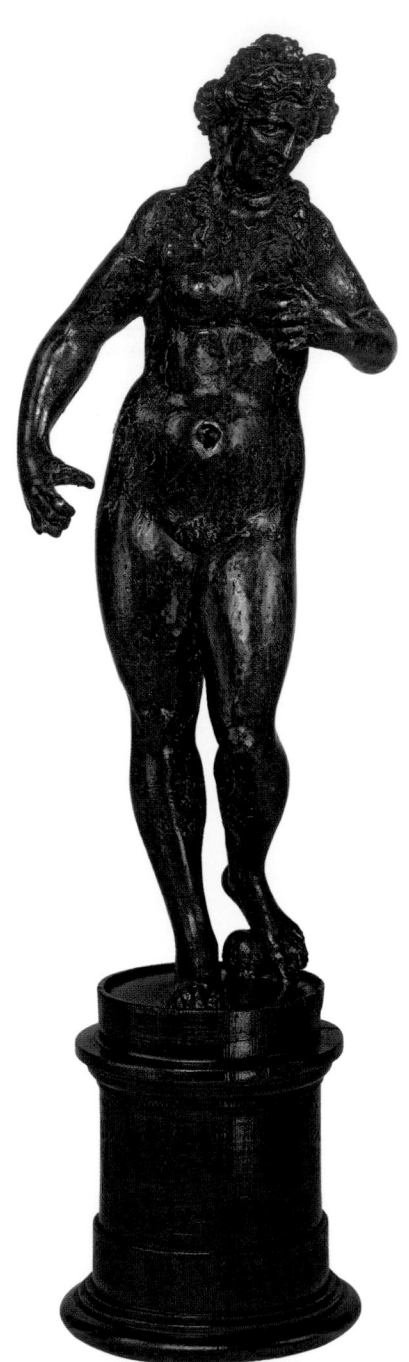

38   Master of the Budapest Abundance, *Abundance*

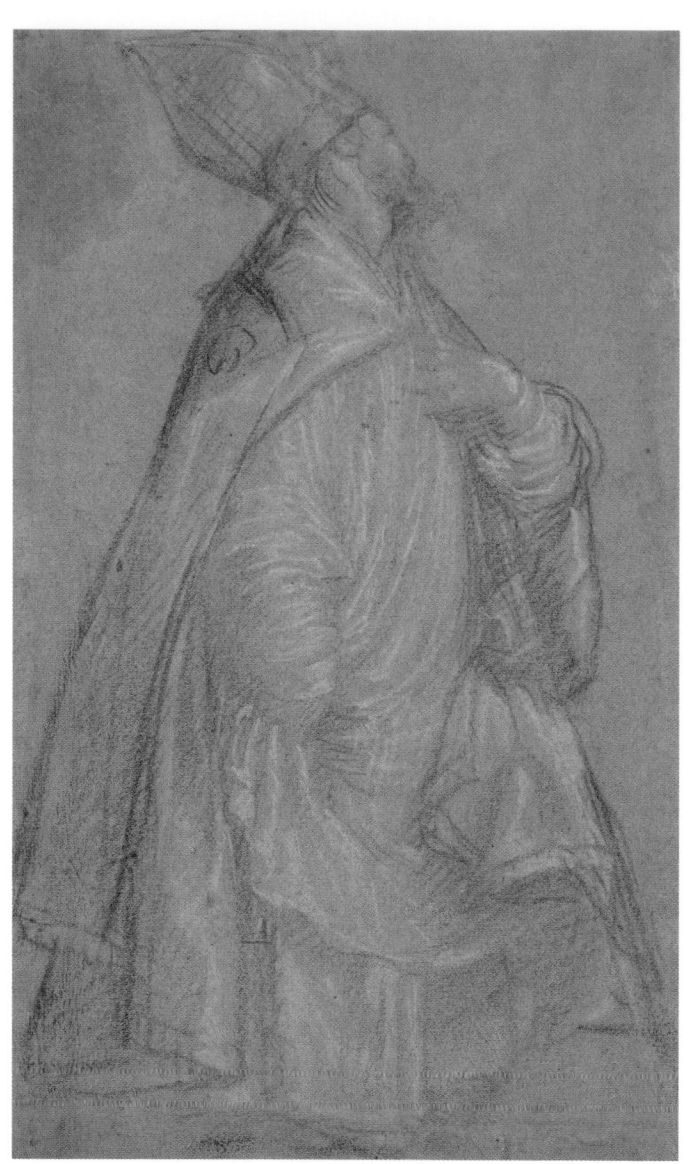

39   Camillo Boccaccino, *St Bernard*

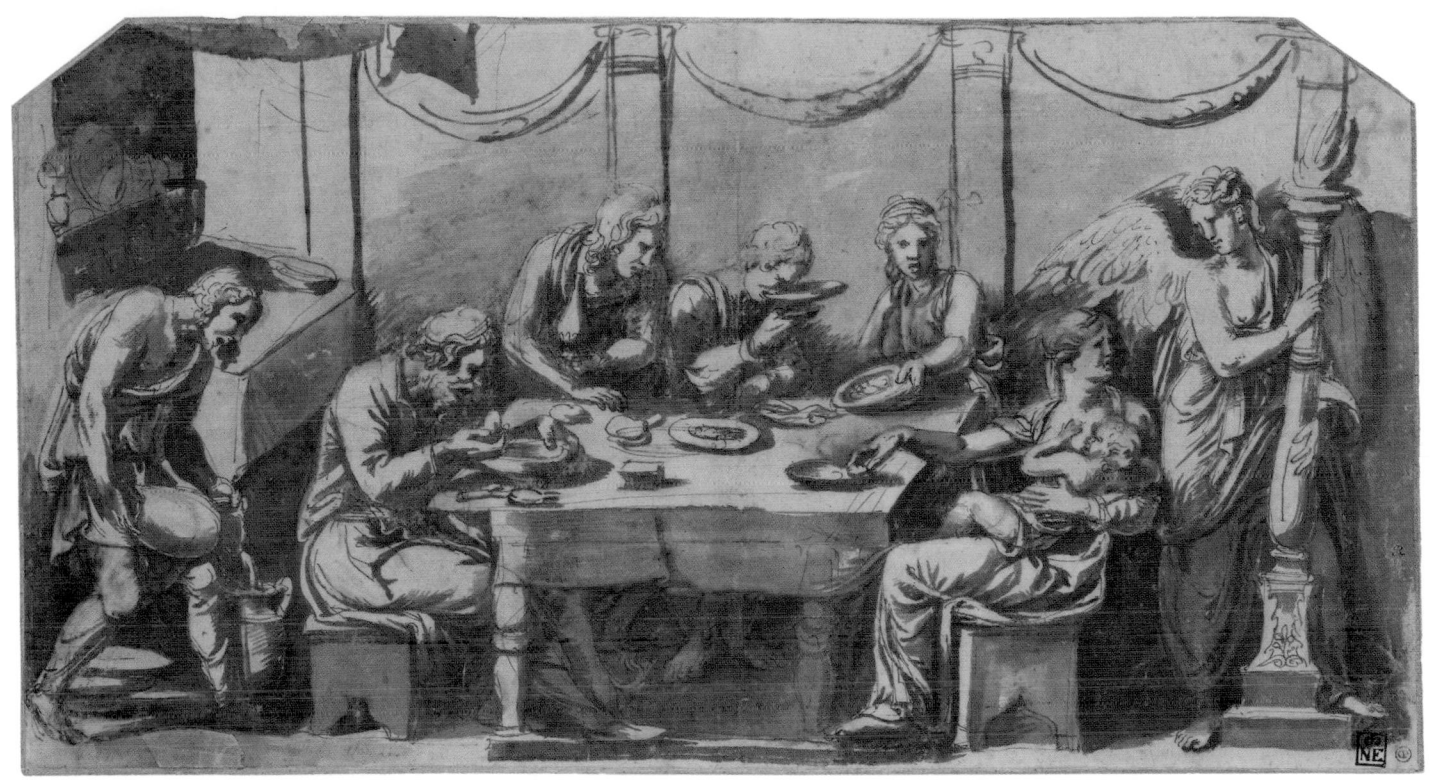

40   Giulio Romano, *Family Meal*

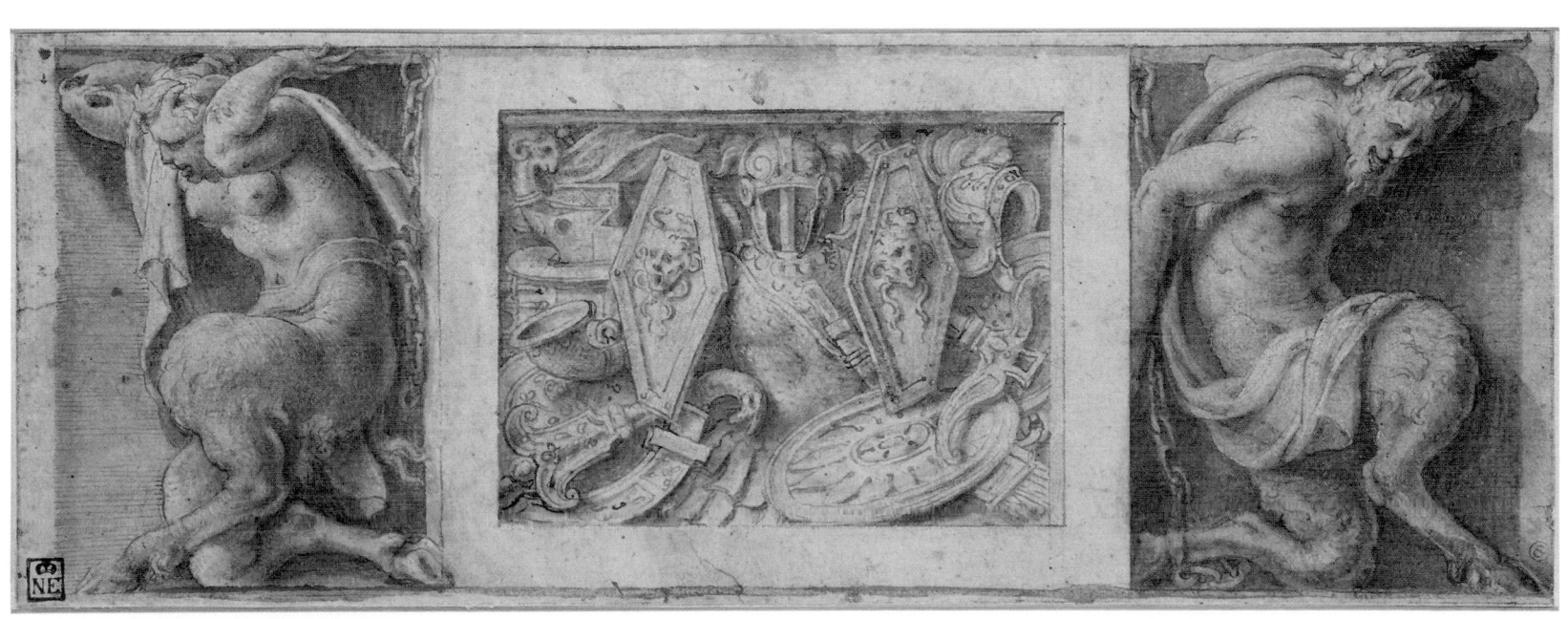

41   Giulio Campi, *Design for a Frieze*

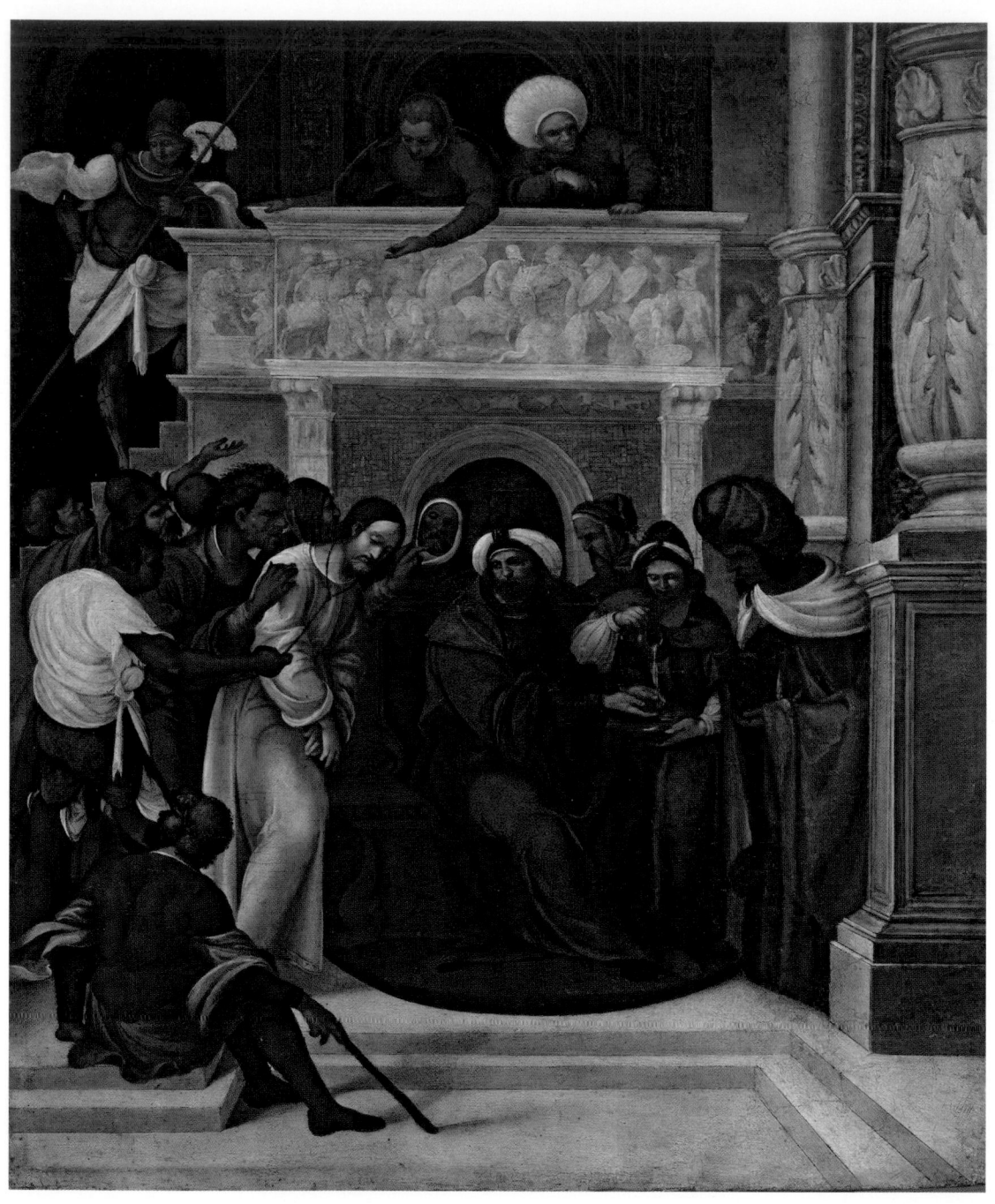

42   Ludovico Mazzolino, *Christ before Pilate*

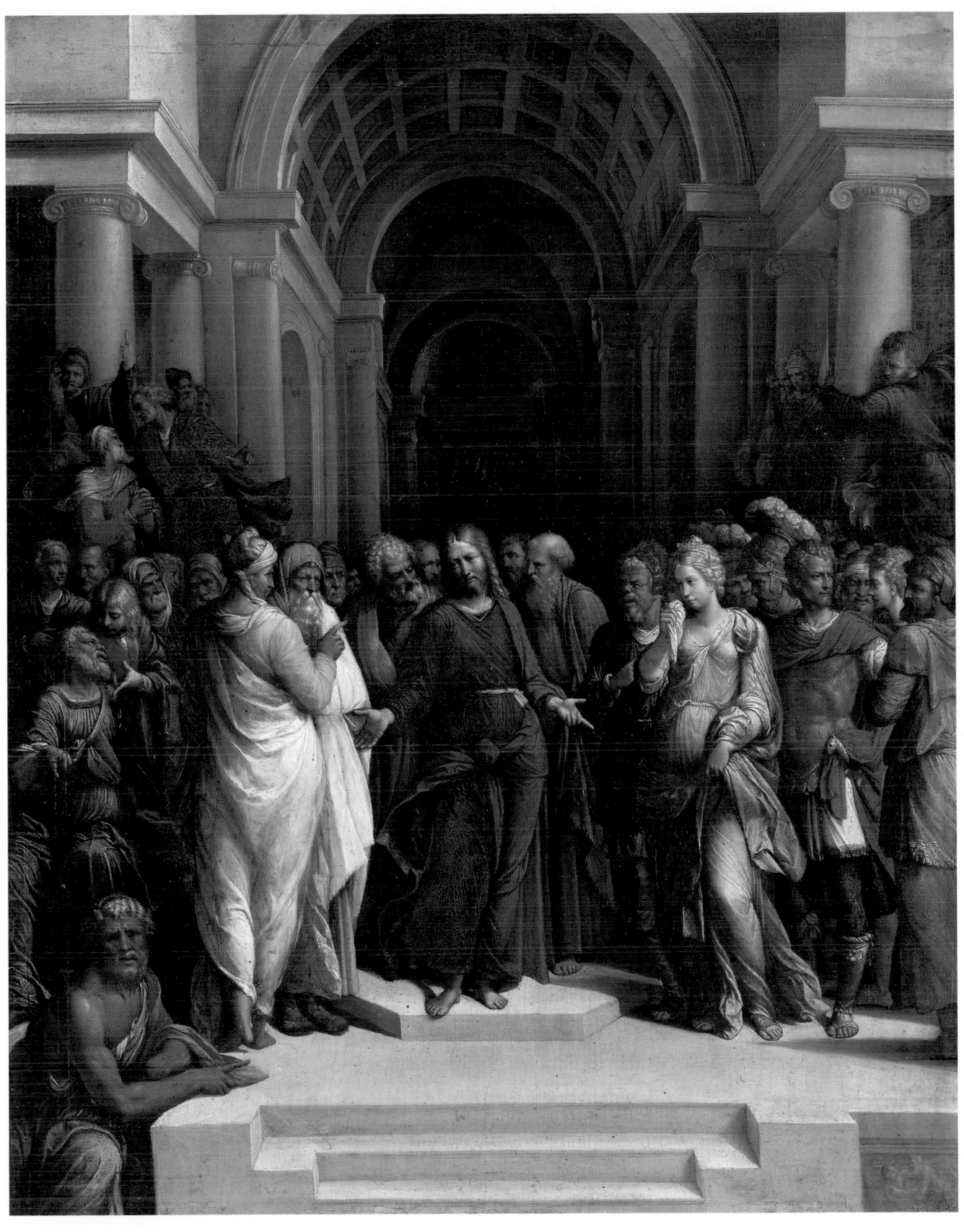

43   Garofalo, *Christ and the Woman Taken in Adultery*

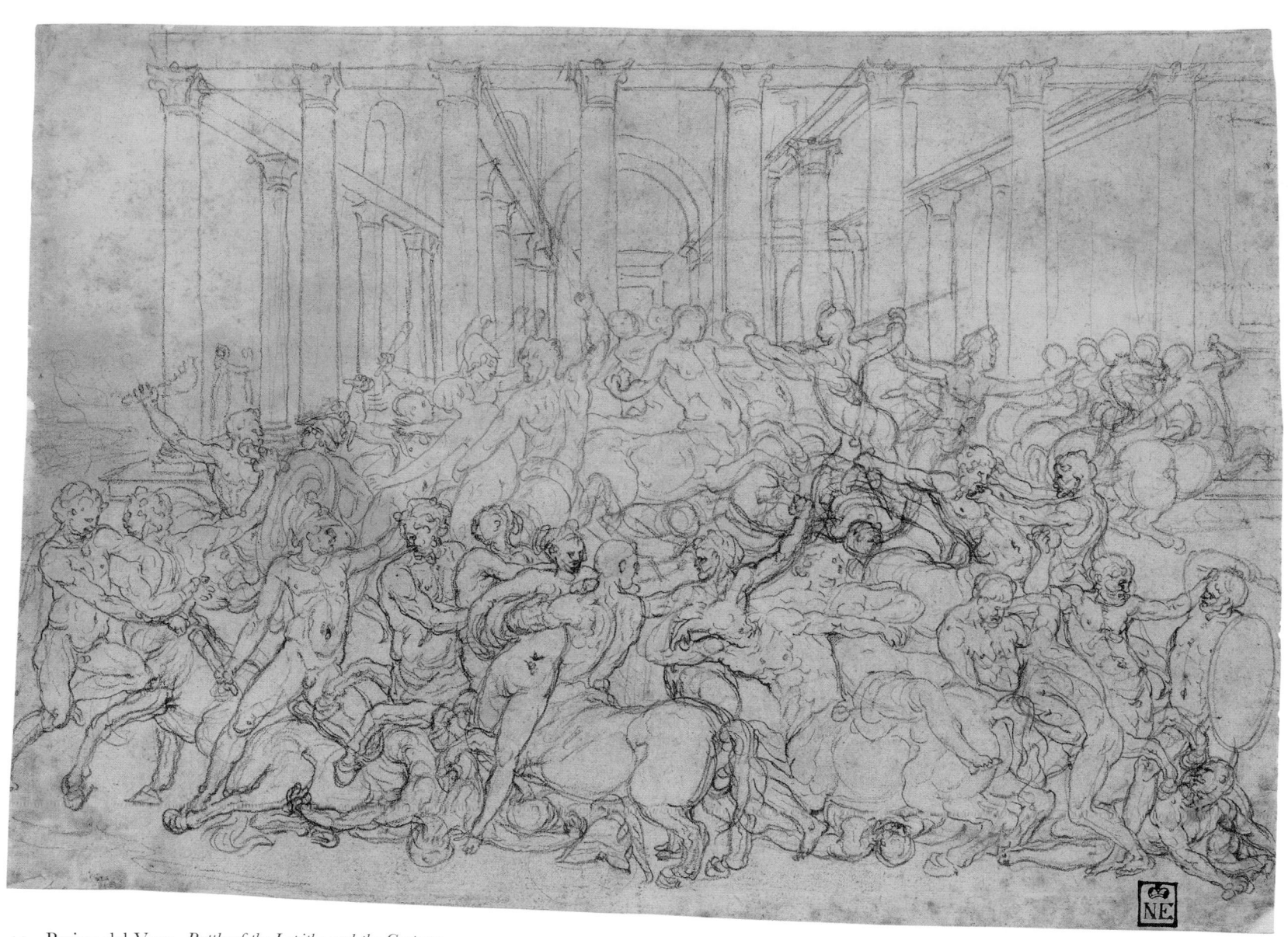

44   Perino del Vaga, *Battle of the Lapiths and the Centaurs*

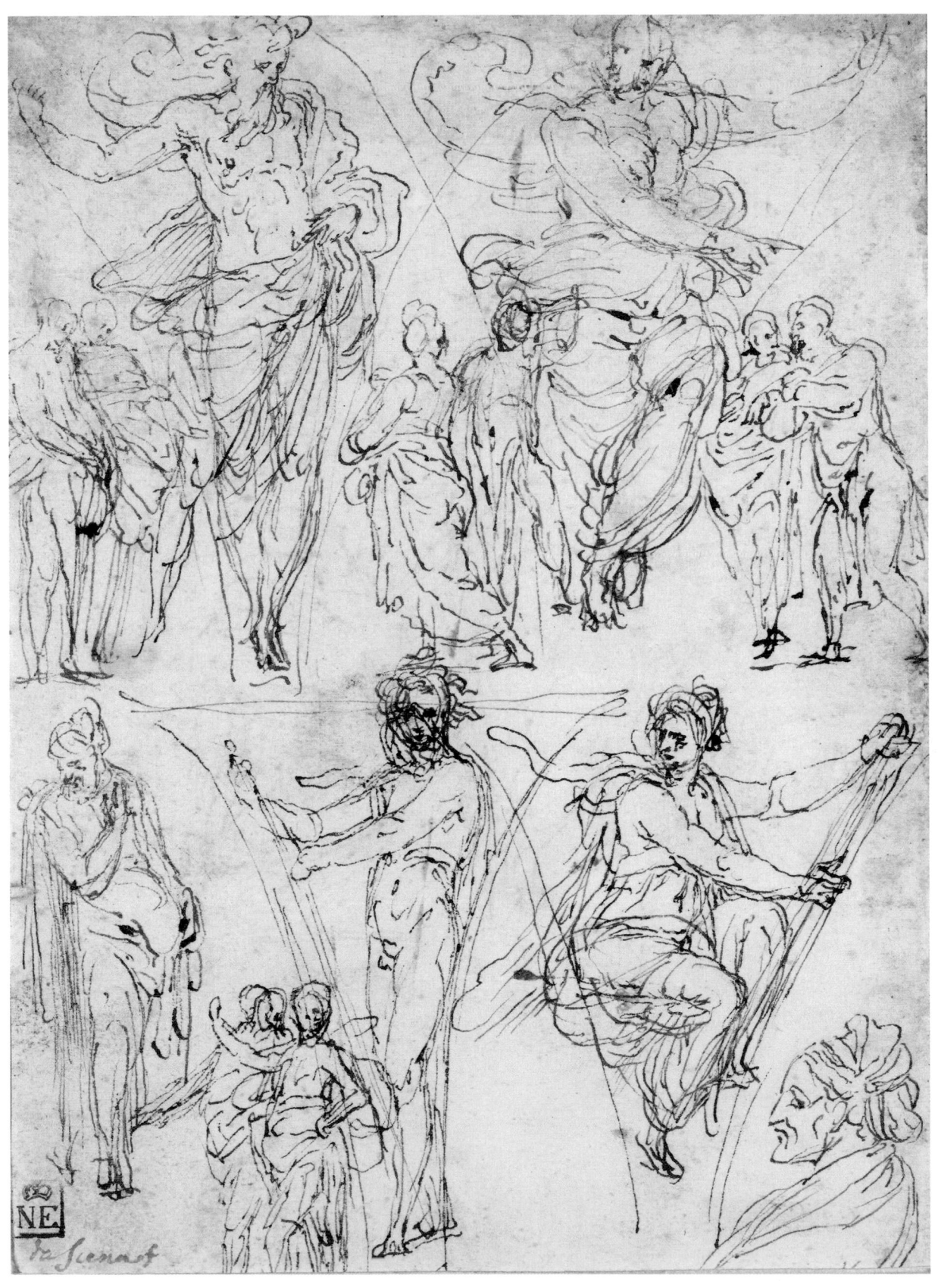

45   Perino del Vaga, *Studies for the Ceiling of the Entrance Hall in the Palazzo Doria*

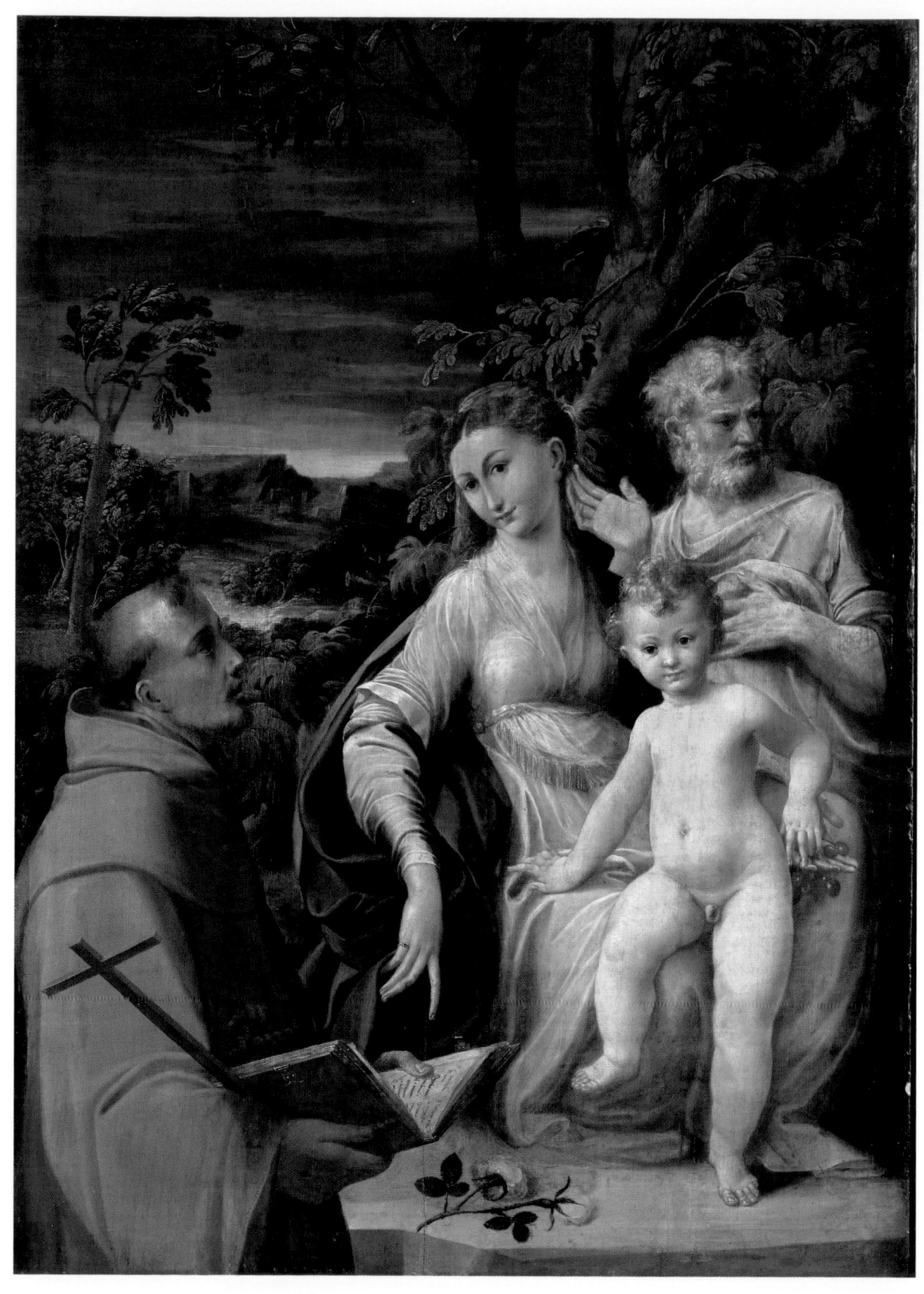

46 Girolamo Mazzola Bedoli, *Holy Family with St Francis*

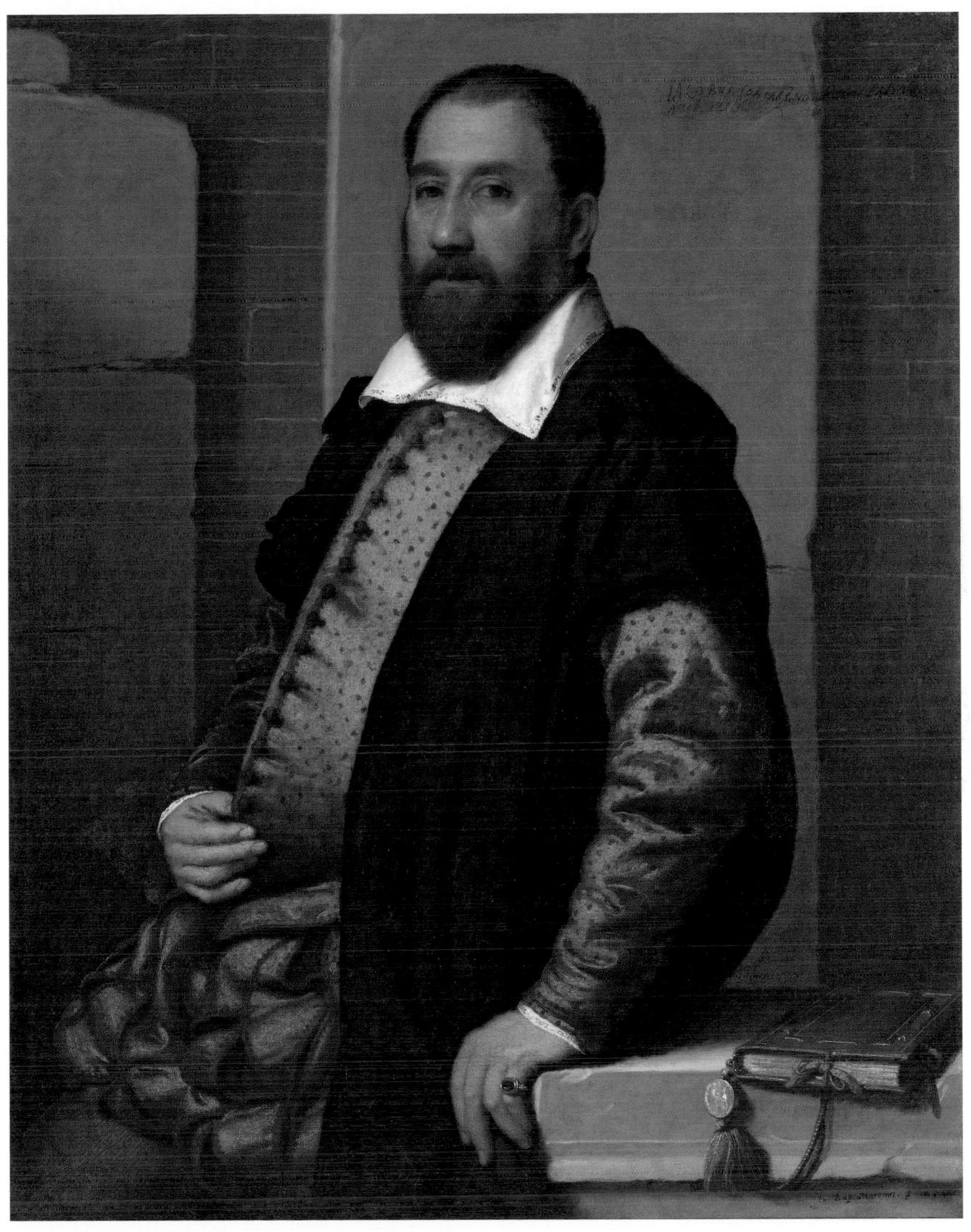

49   Giovanni Battista Moroni, *Portrait of Jacopo Foscarini*

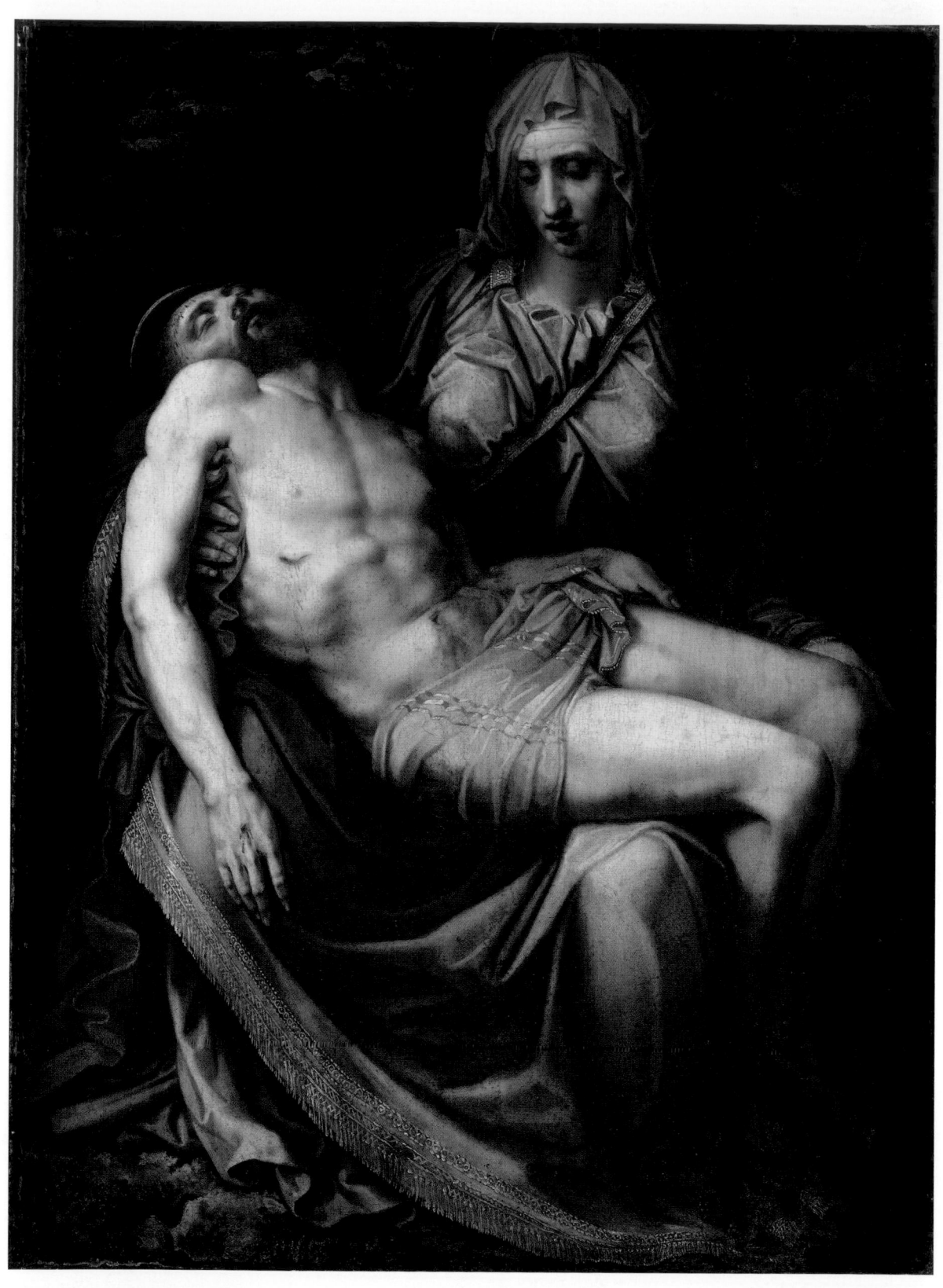

50   Michele di Ridolfo, *Pietà*

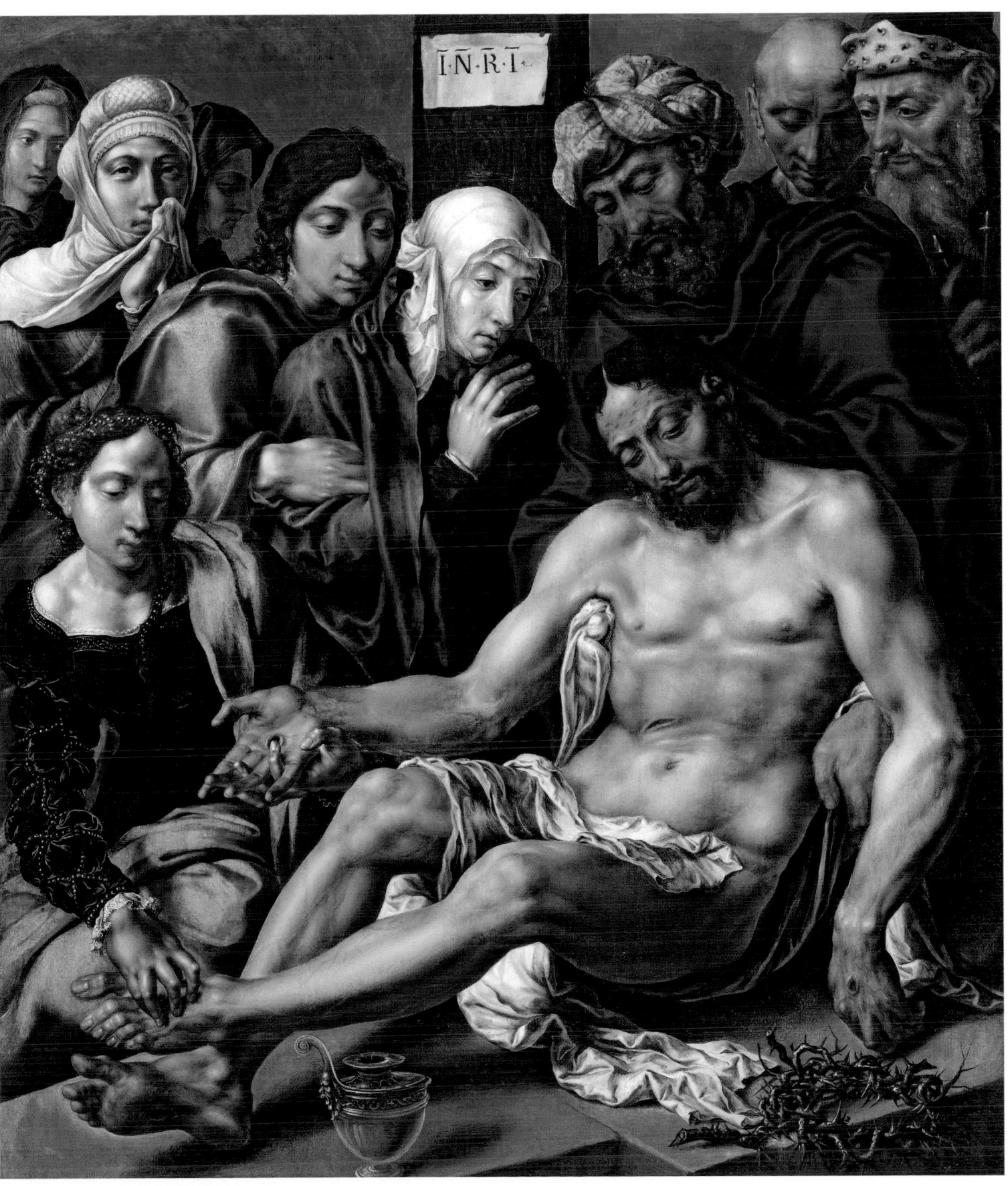

51 Maerten van Heemskerck, *Lamentation*

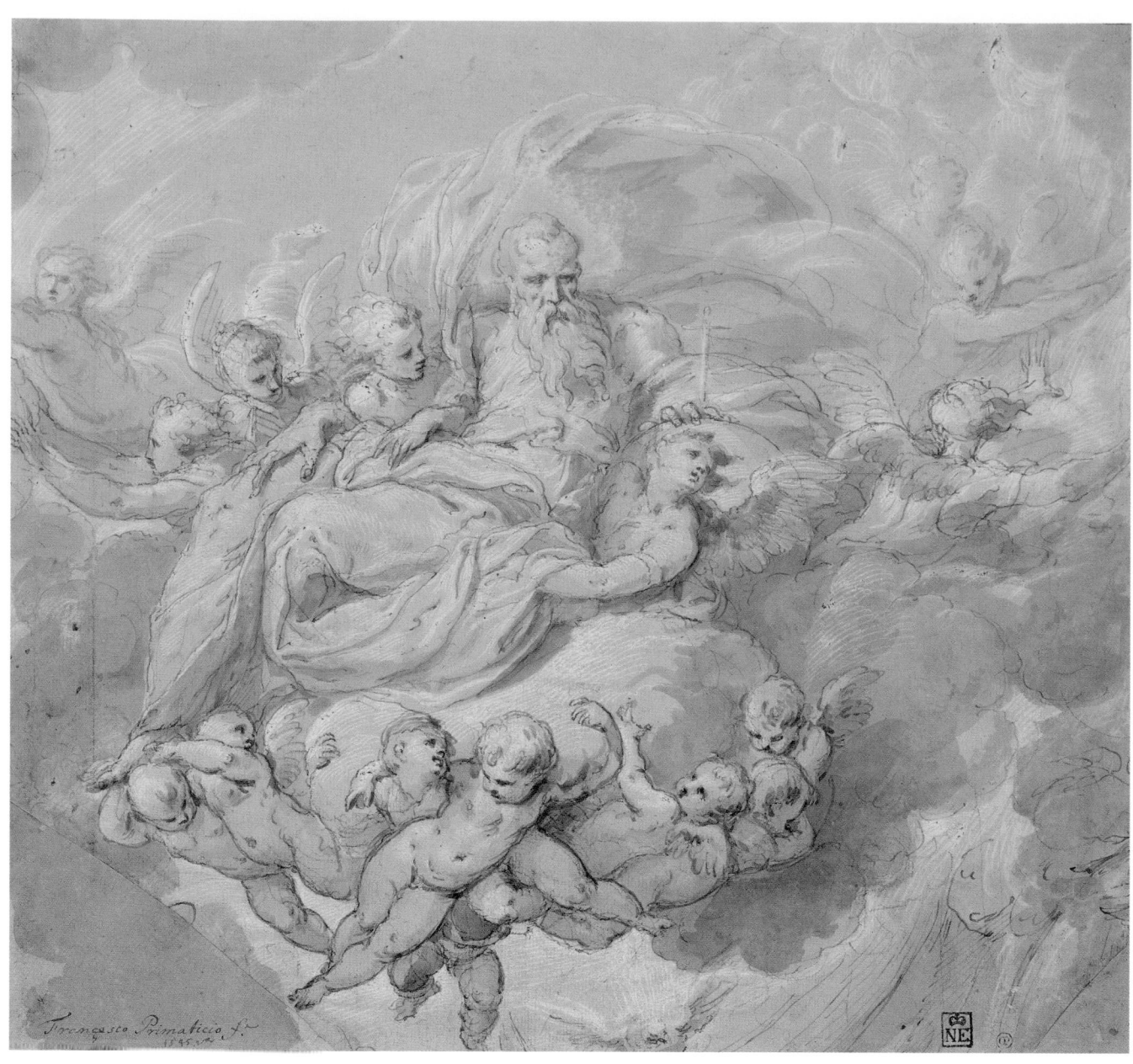

52   Nicolò dell'Abate, *God the Father with Angels*

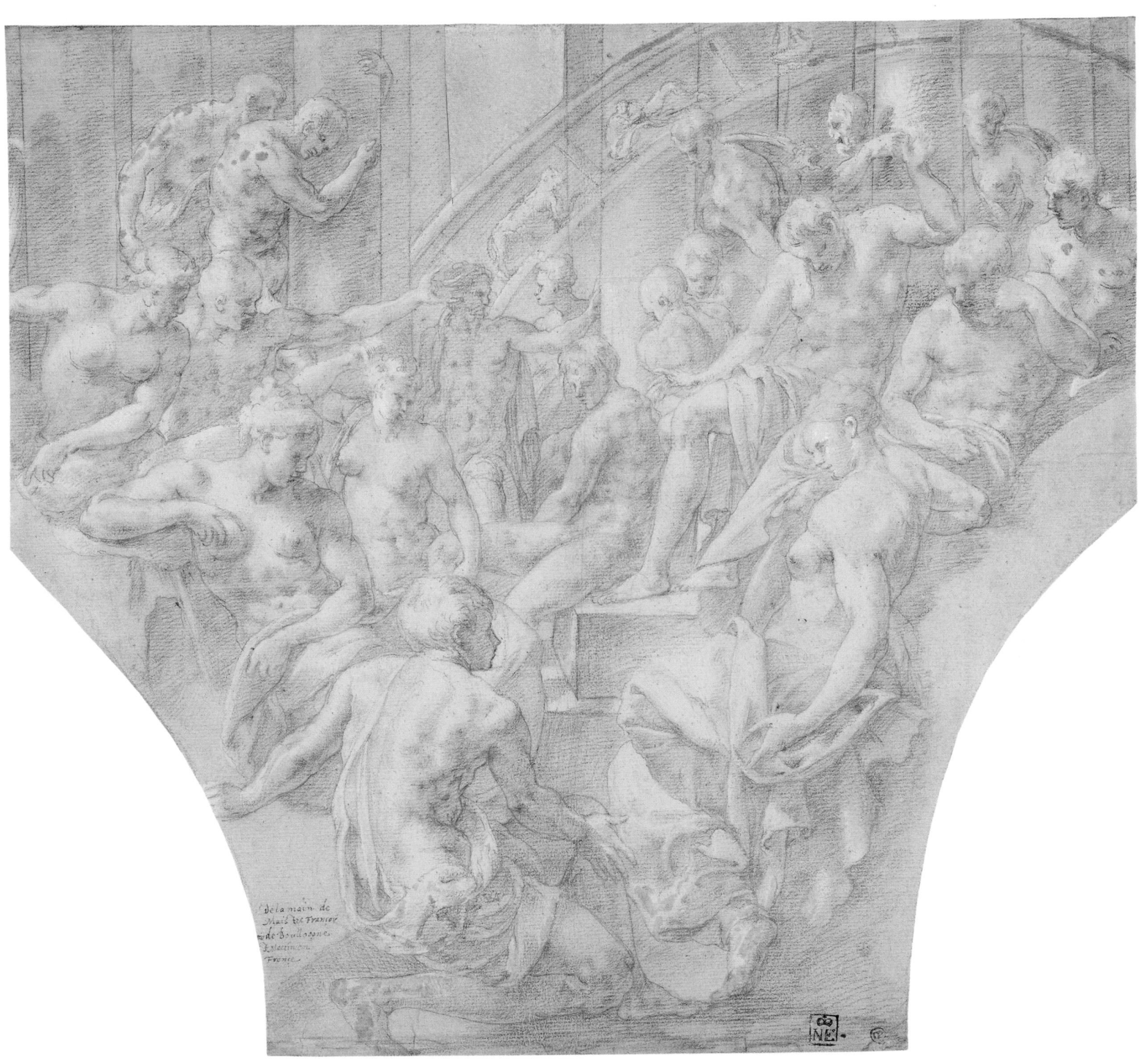

53   Francesco Primaticcio, *Phaeton Begging Apollo to Let Him Drive His Chariot*

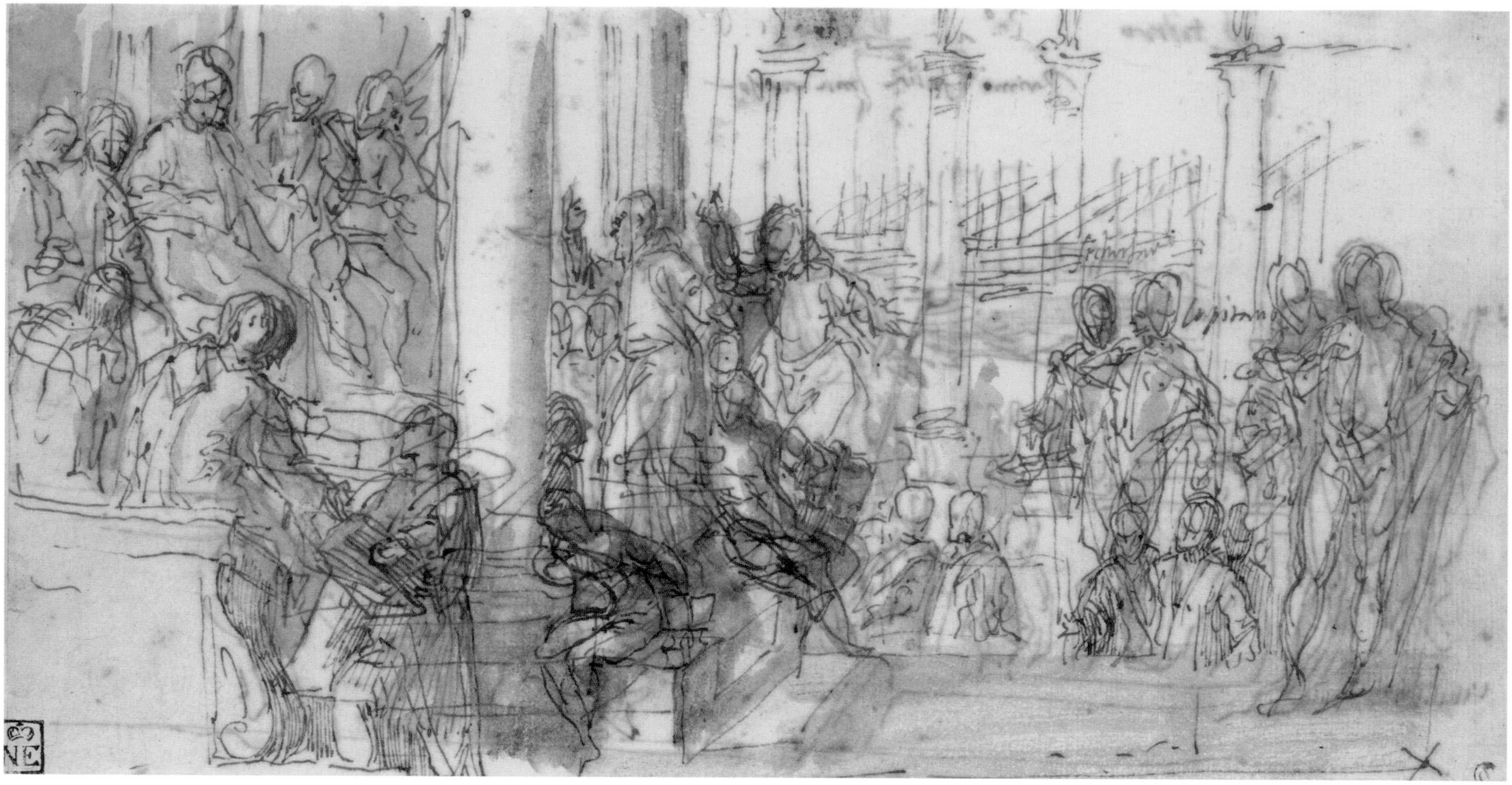

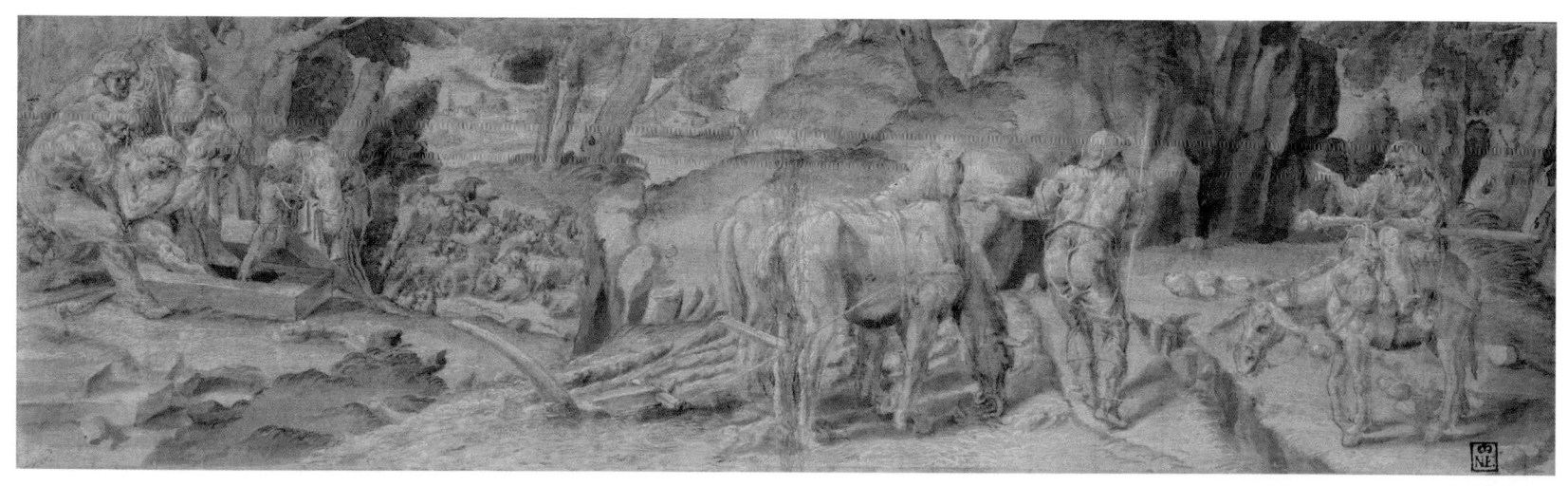

54 Veronese, *Peter of Amiens Exhorts Doge Vitale Michiel*

55 Lelio Orsi, *Joseph Cast into the Pit by His Brothers*

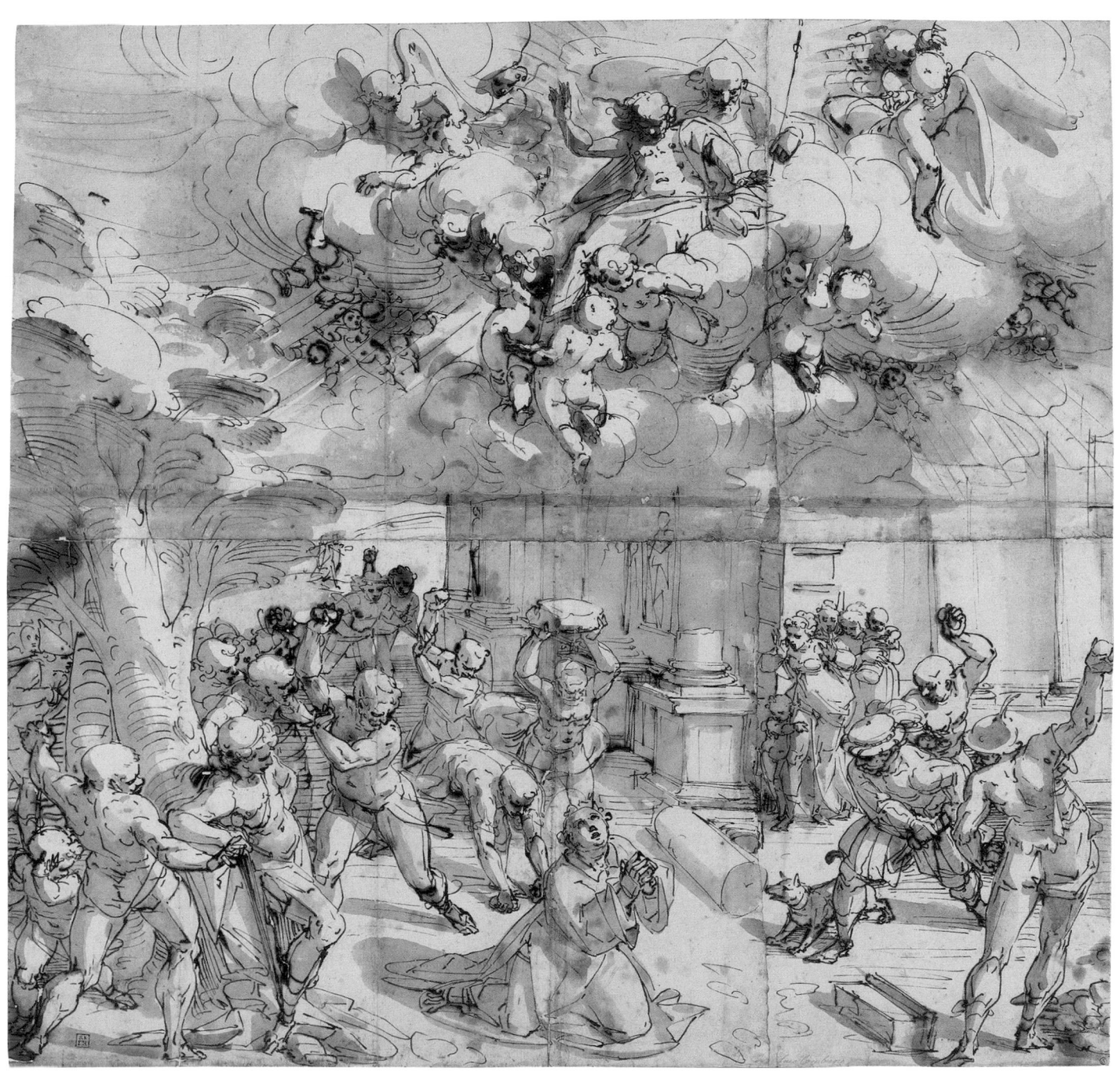

56   Luca Cambiaso, *Stoning of St Stephen*

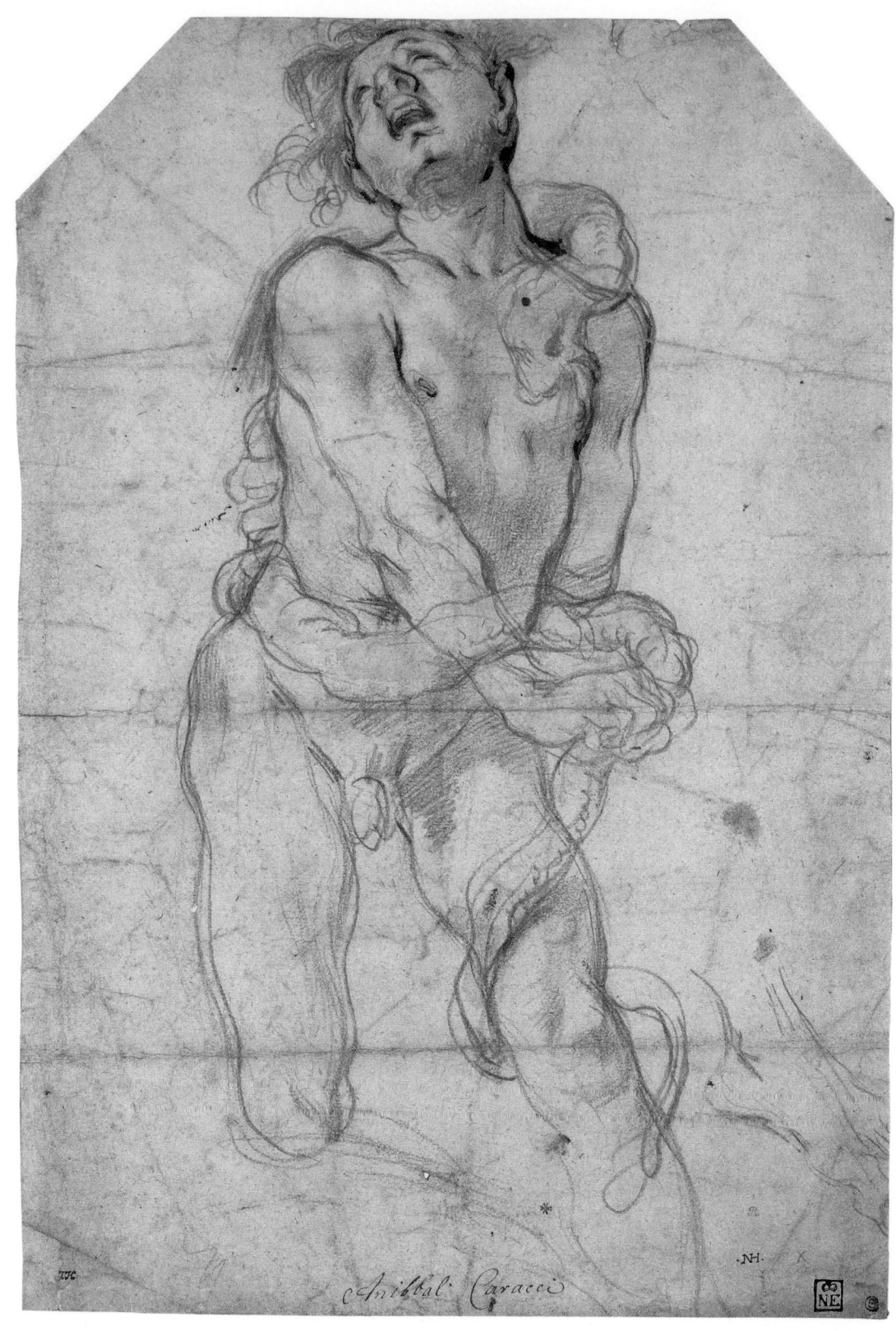

57   Ferraù Fenzoni, *Study of a Male Nude Entwined by a Serpent*

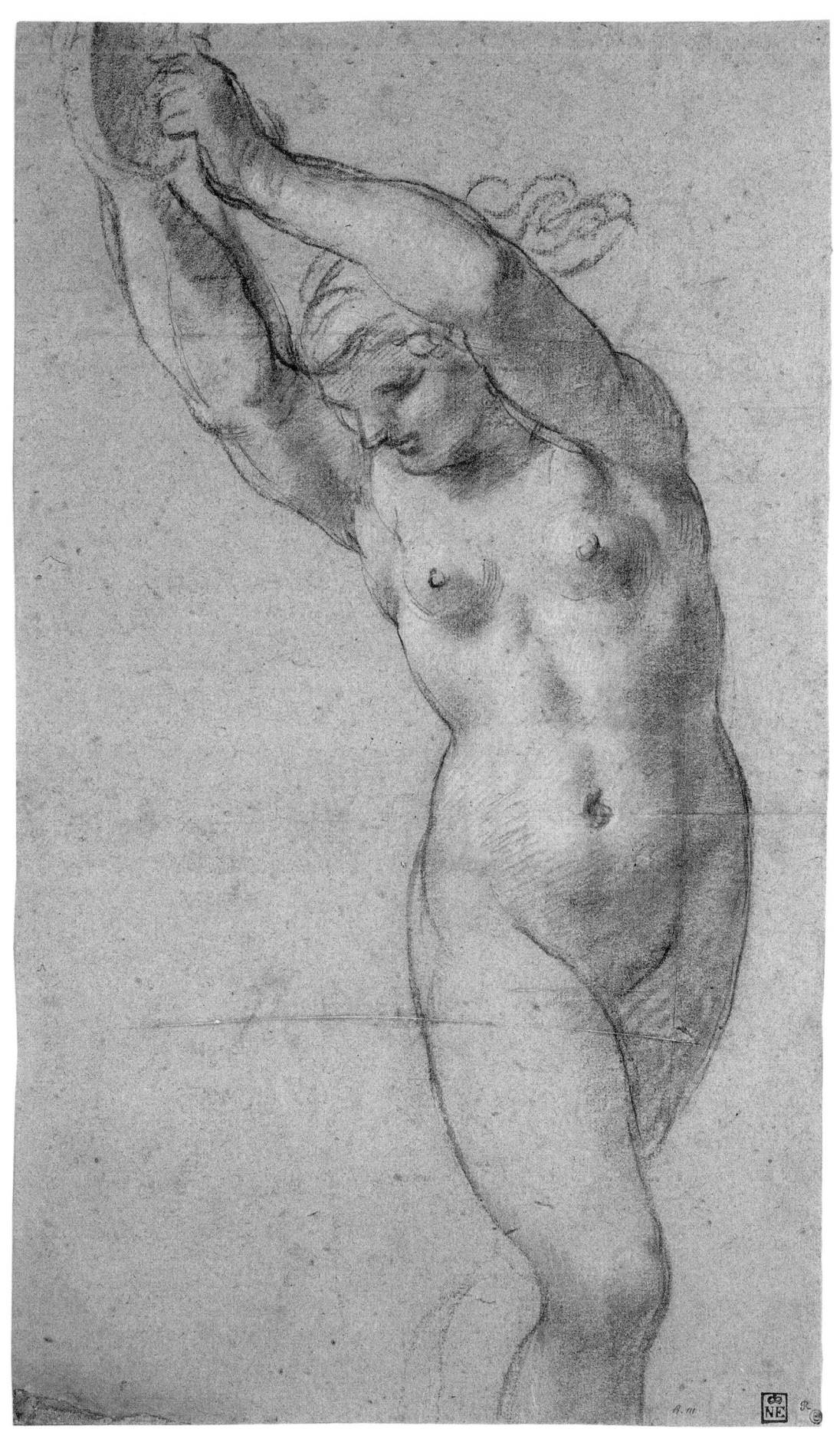

58   Annibale Carracci, *Study for a Bacchante*

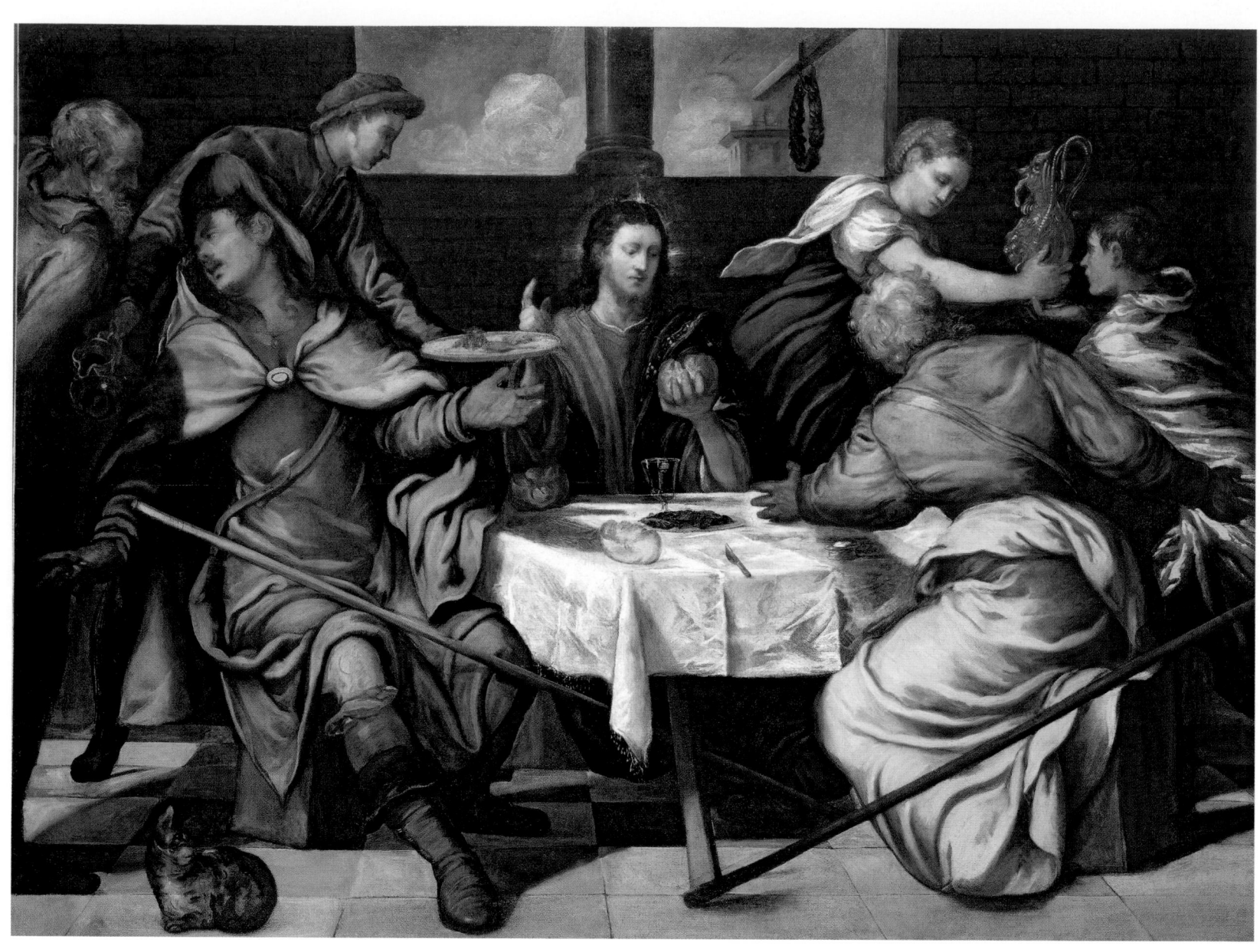

59 Tintoretto, *Supper at Emmaus*

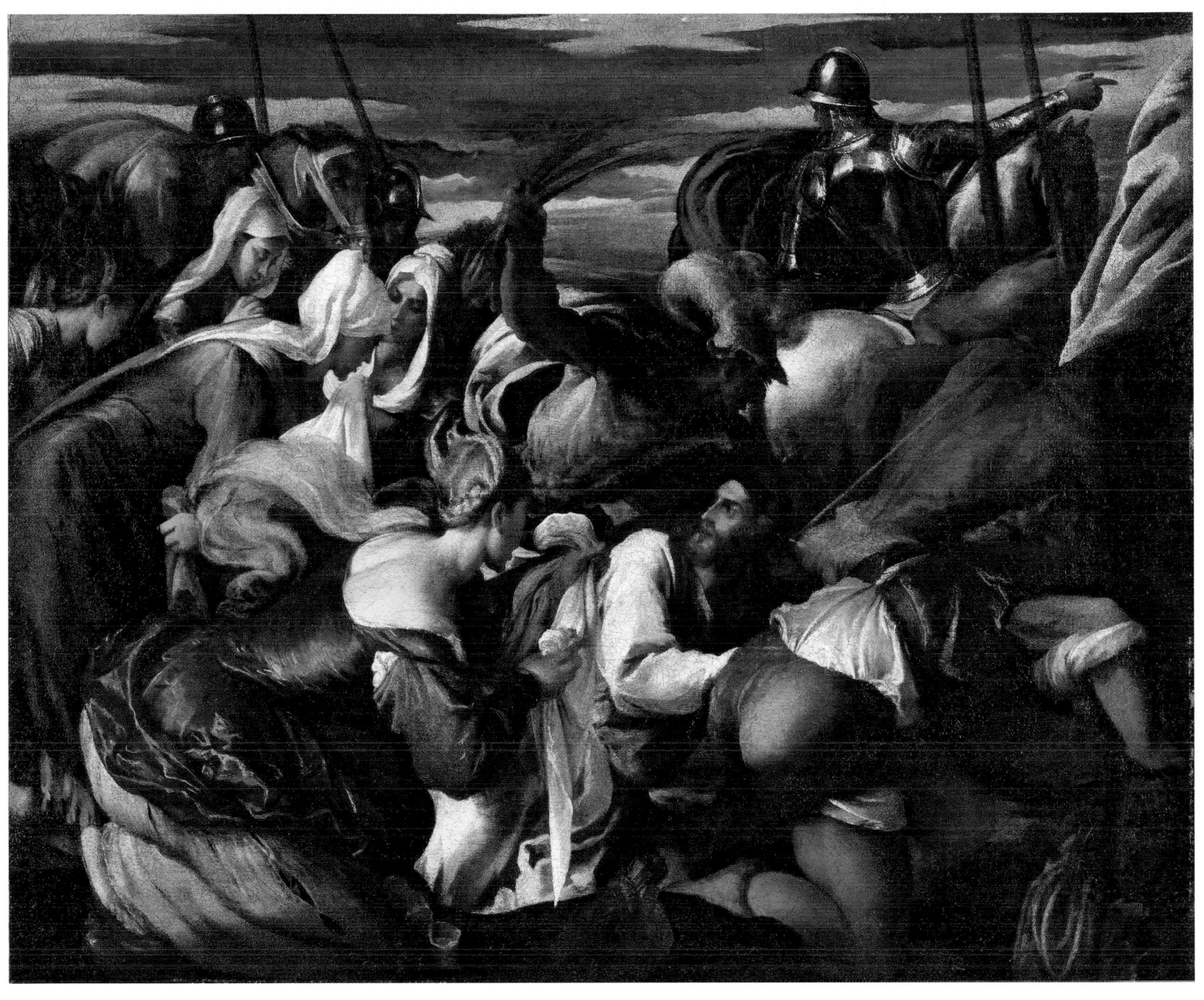

60   Bassano, *Way to Calvary*

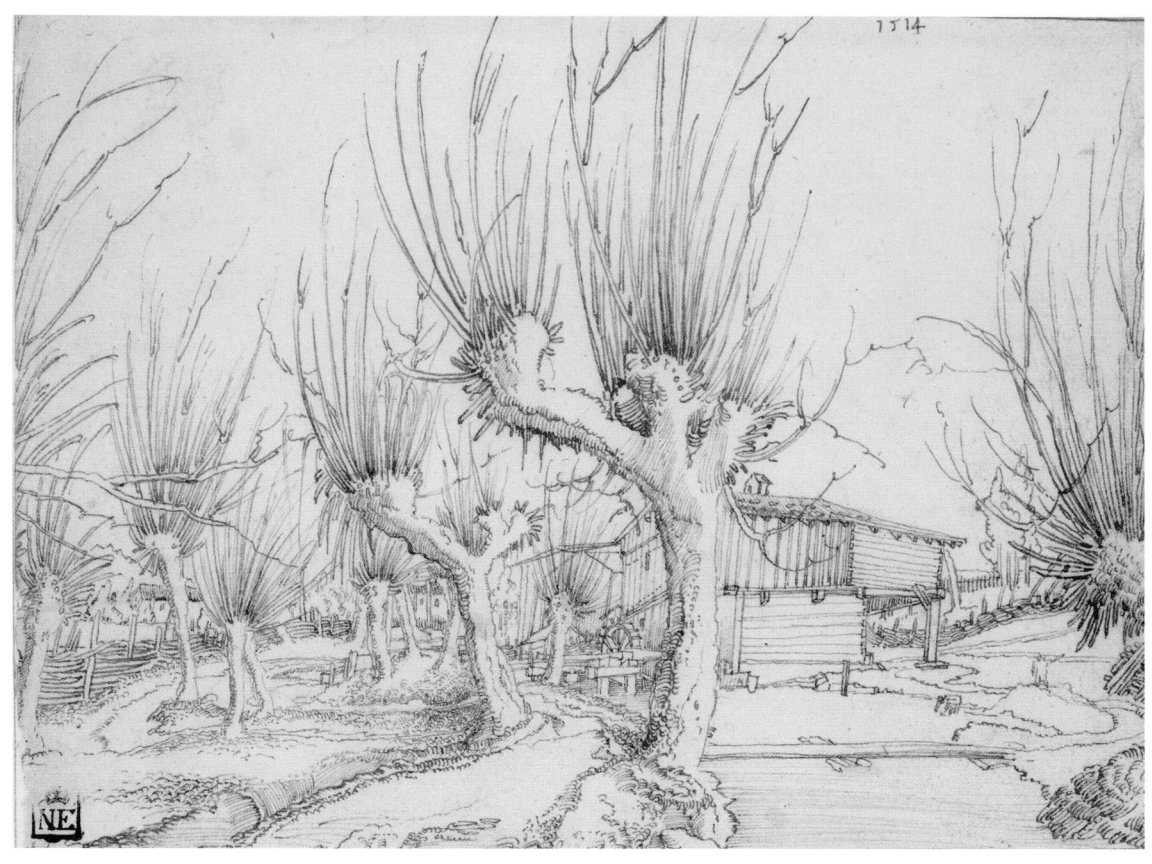

61   Wolf Huber, *Landscape with Willows and a Mill*

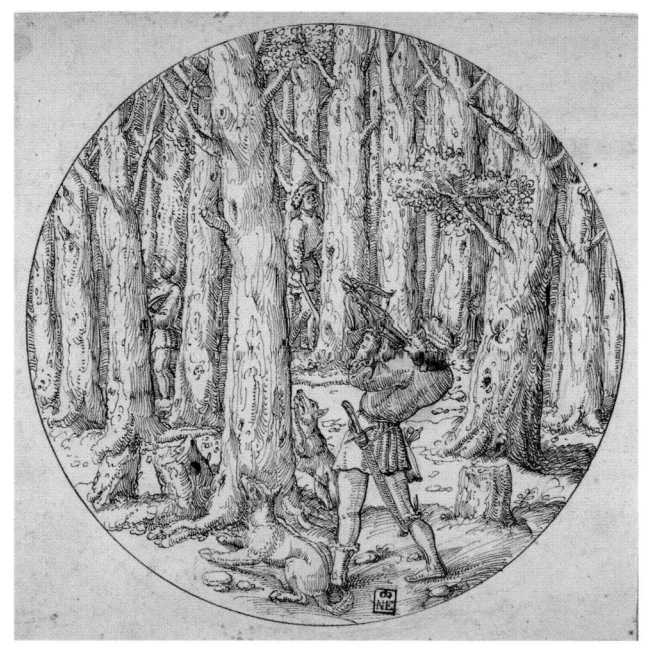

62.1   Augustin Hirschvogel, *Squirrel Hunt*

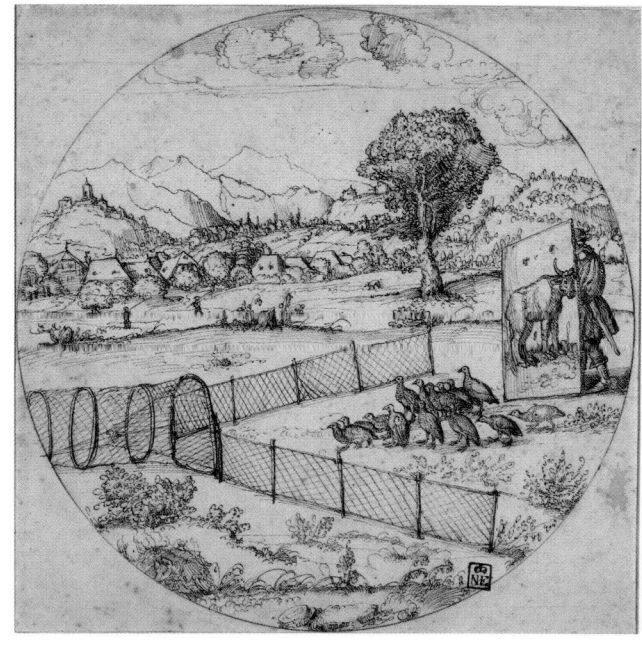

62.2   Augustin Hirschvogel, *Stalking Partridges into a Tunnel-net*

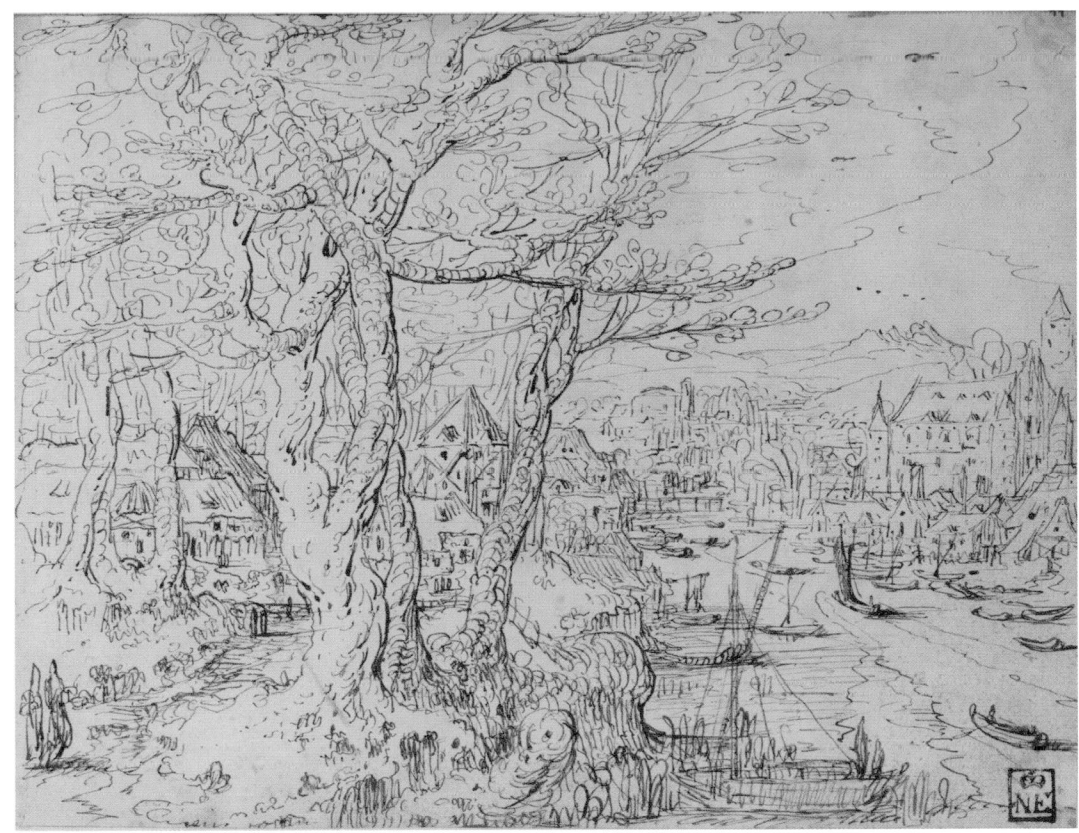

63.1 Master of the Budapest Sketchbook, *River with Houses on either Side*

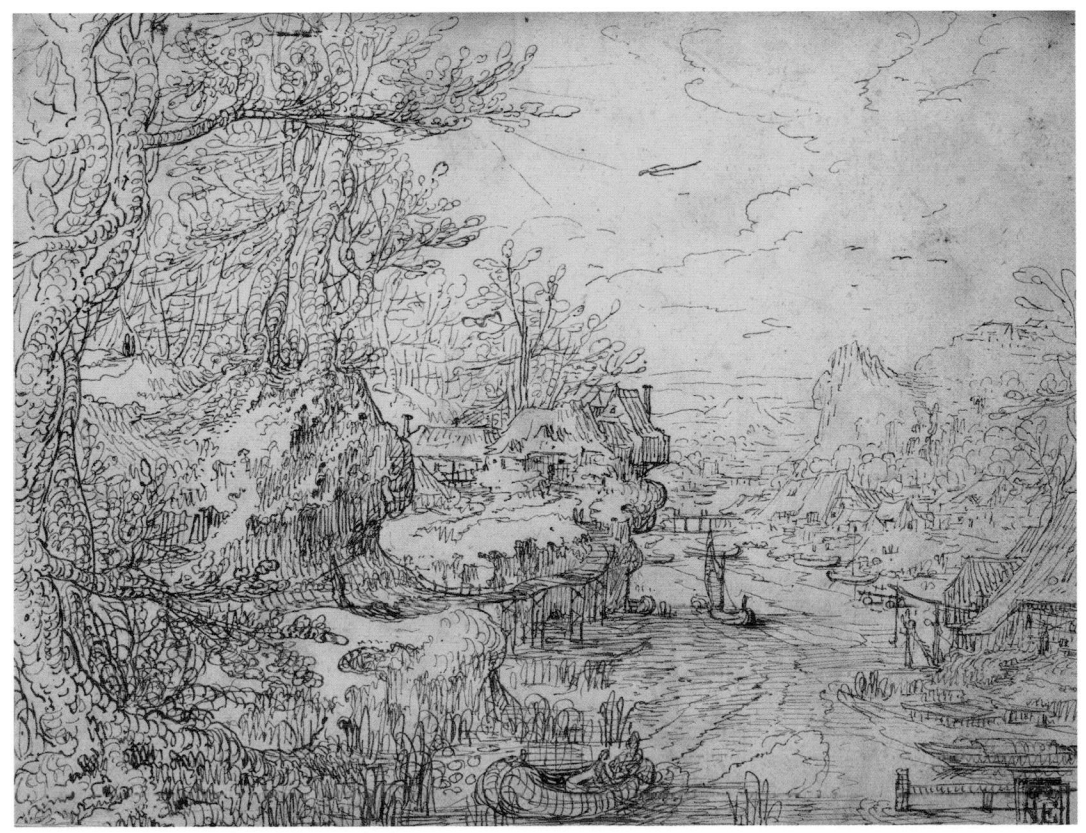

63.2 Master of the Budapest Sketchbook, *Town with Jetty*

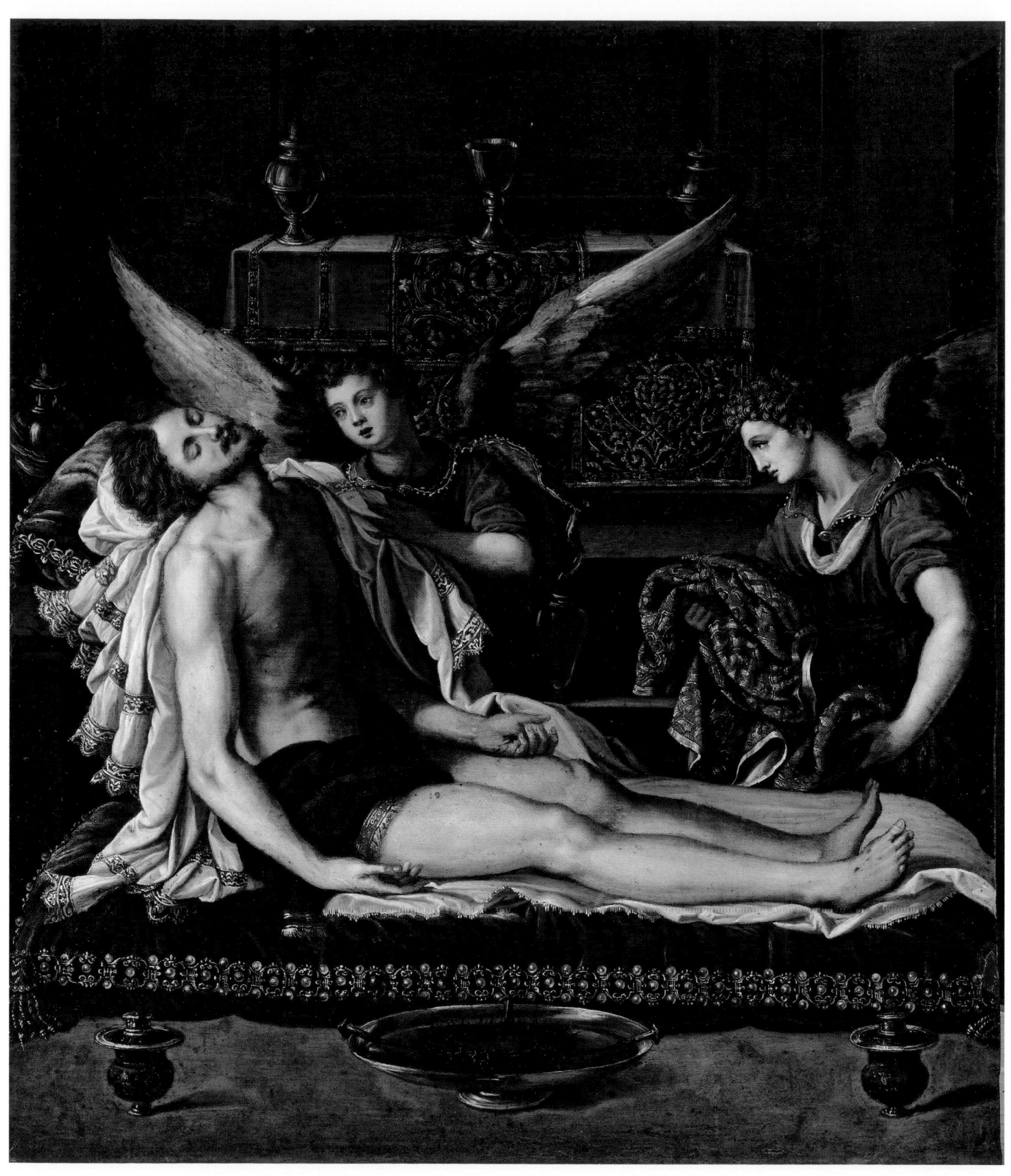

64   Alessandro Allori, *Dead Christ with Two Angels*

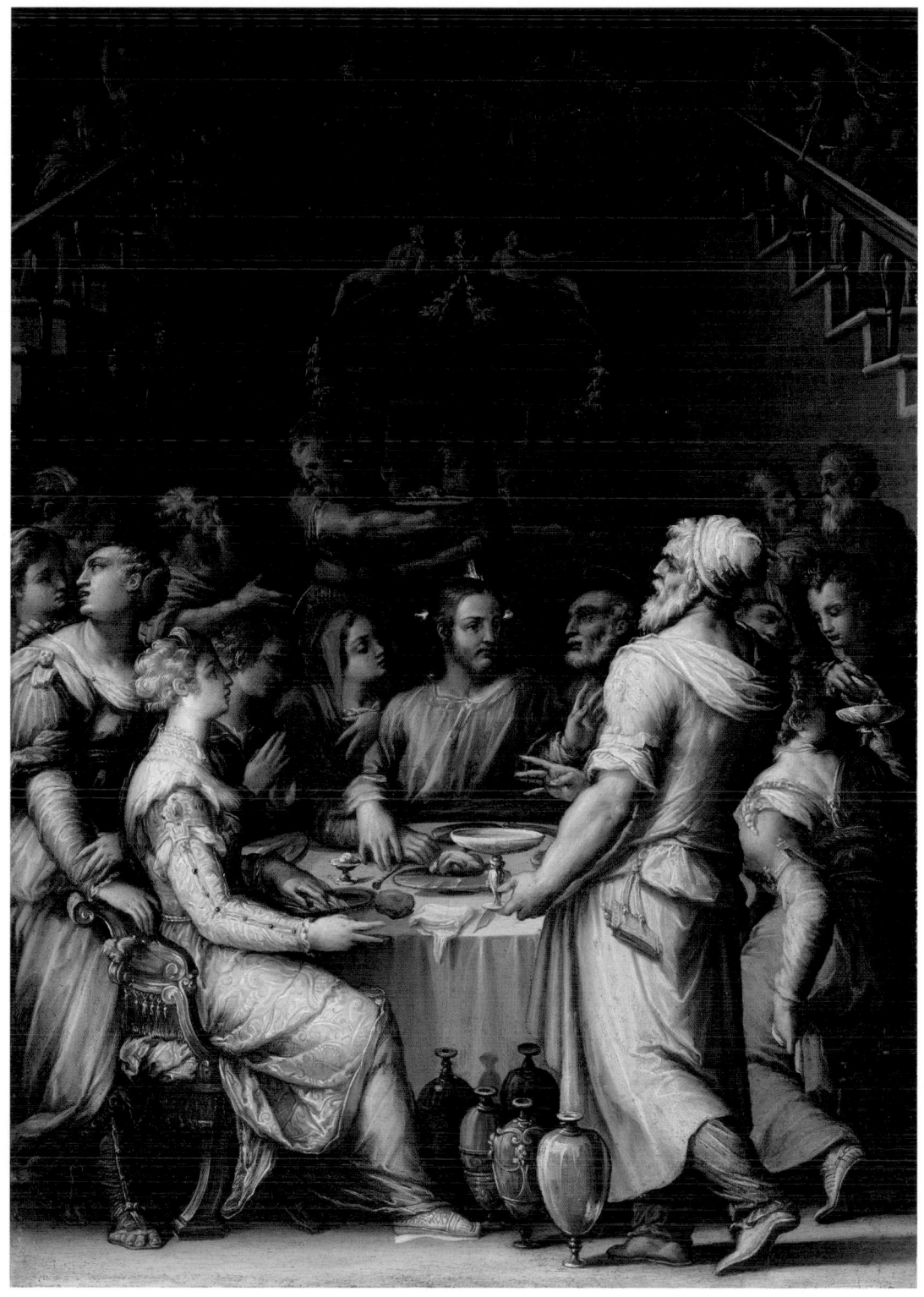

65   Giorgio Vasari, *Marriage at Cana*

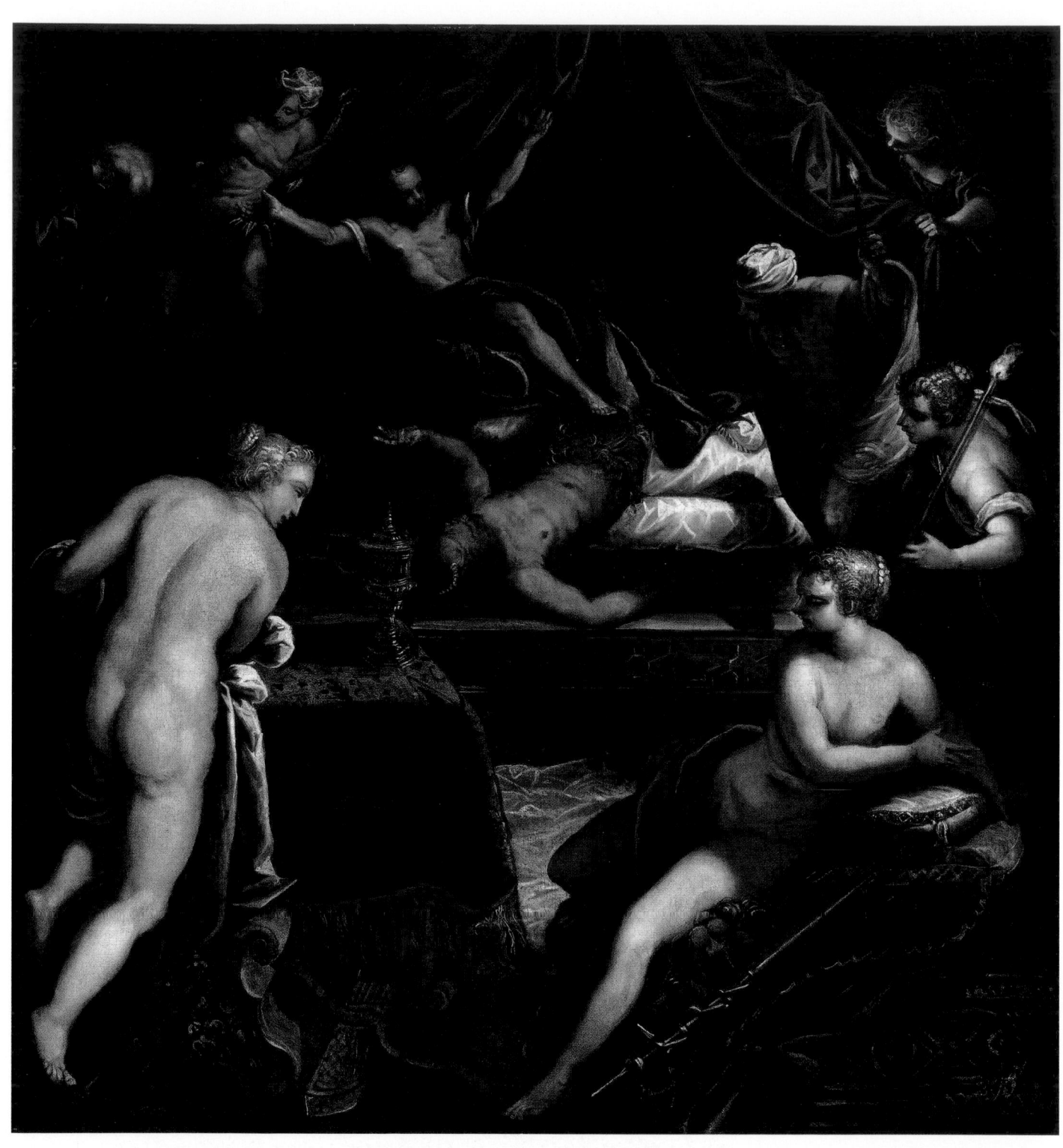

66   Tintoretto, *Hercules Expelling Faunus from Omphale's Bed*

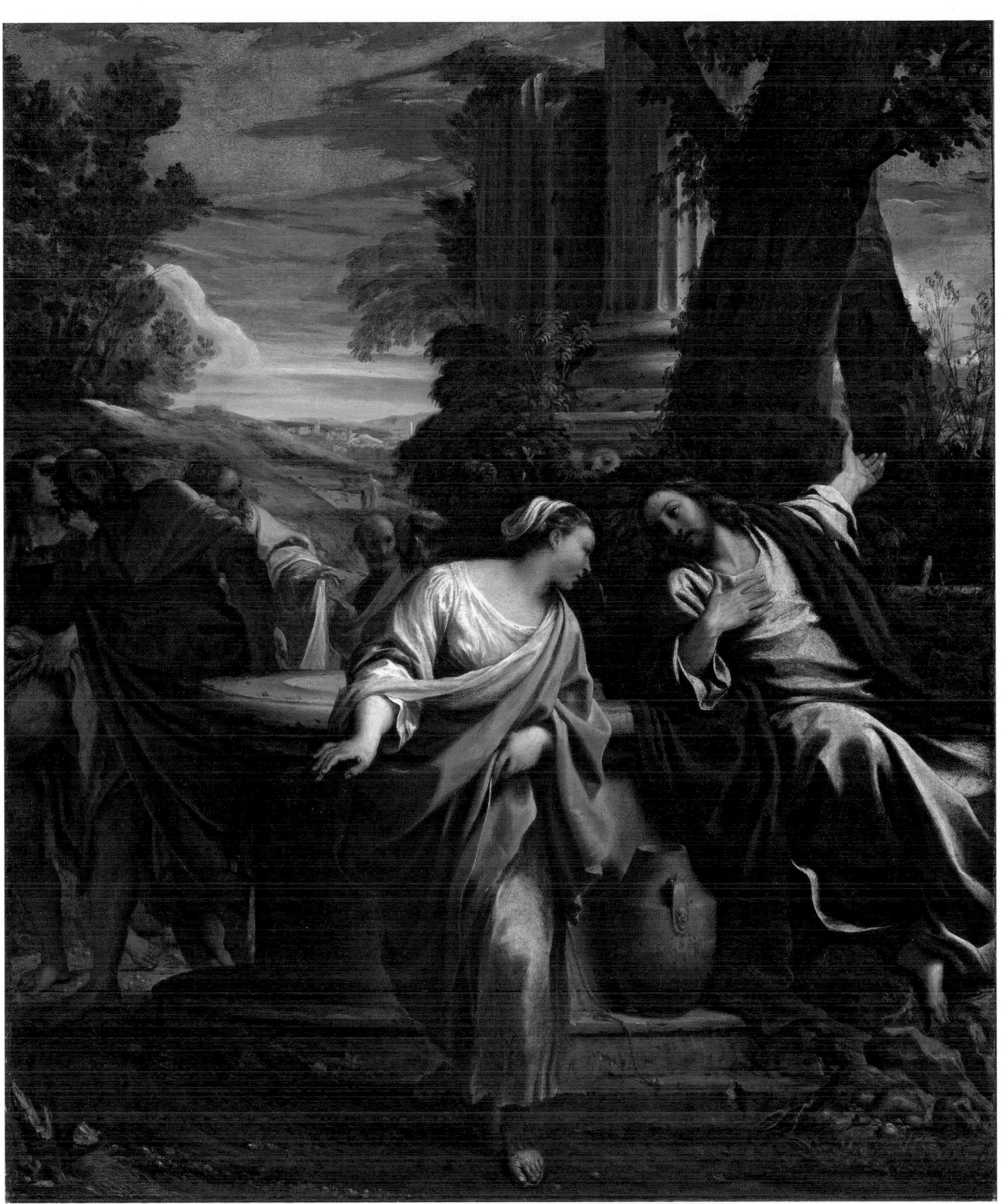

67   Annibale Carracci, *Christ and the Woman of Samaria*

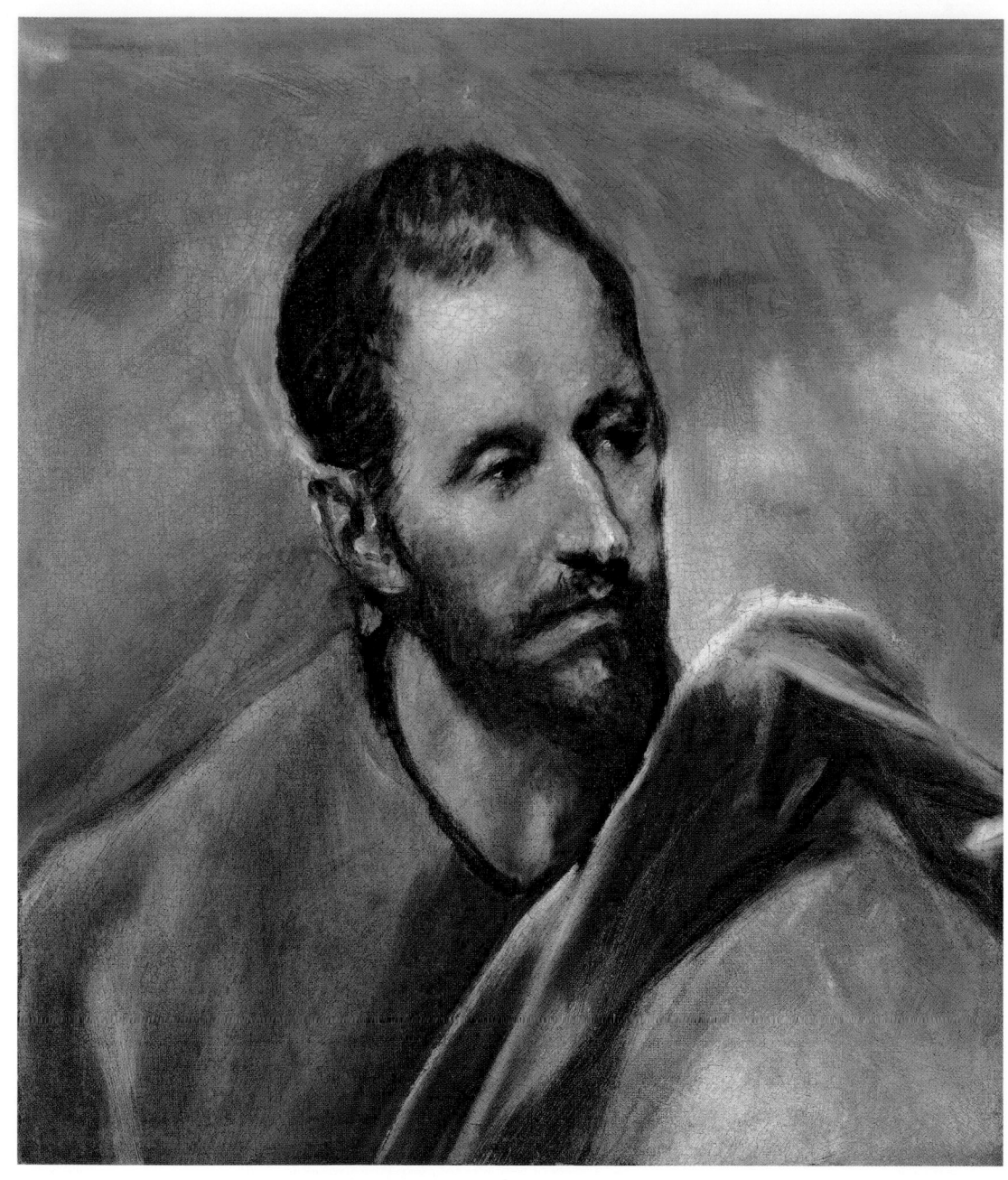

68　El Greco, *St James the Less*

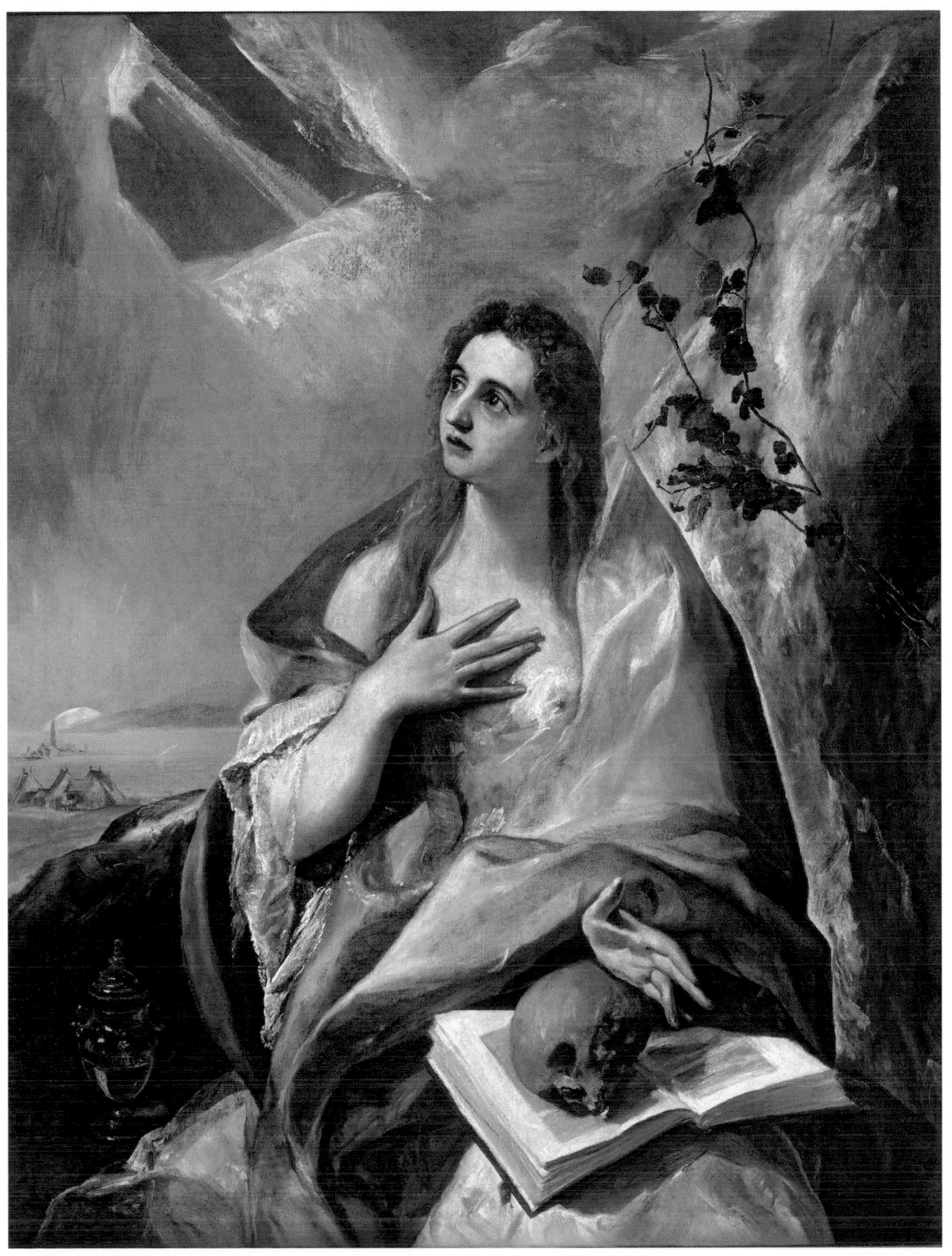

69   El Greco, *St Mary Magdalene*

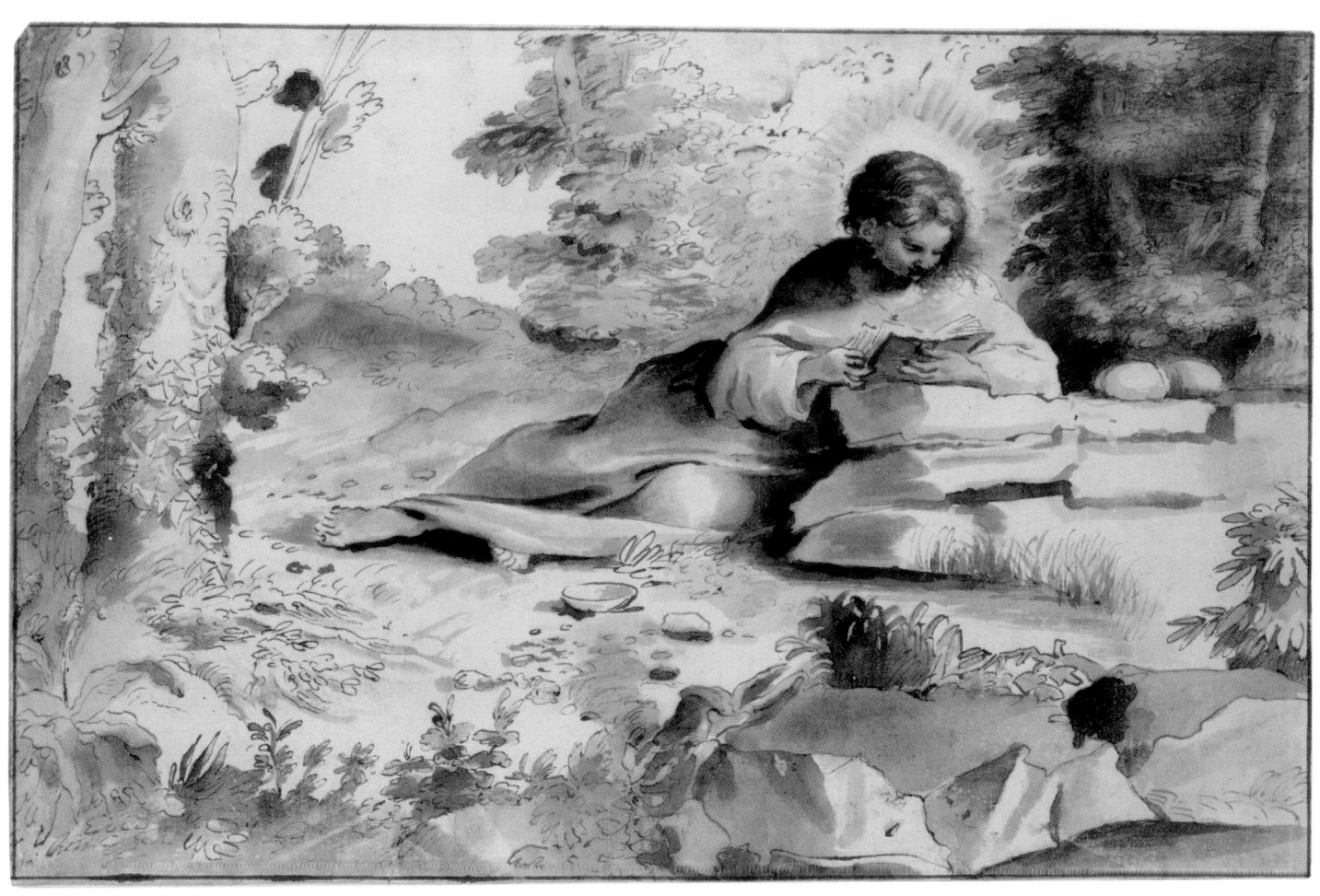

70   Pietro Faccini, *St Mary of Egypt*

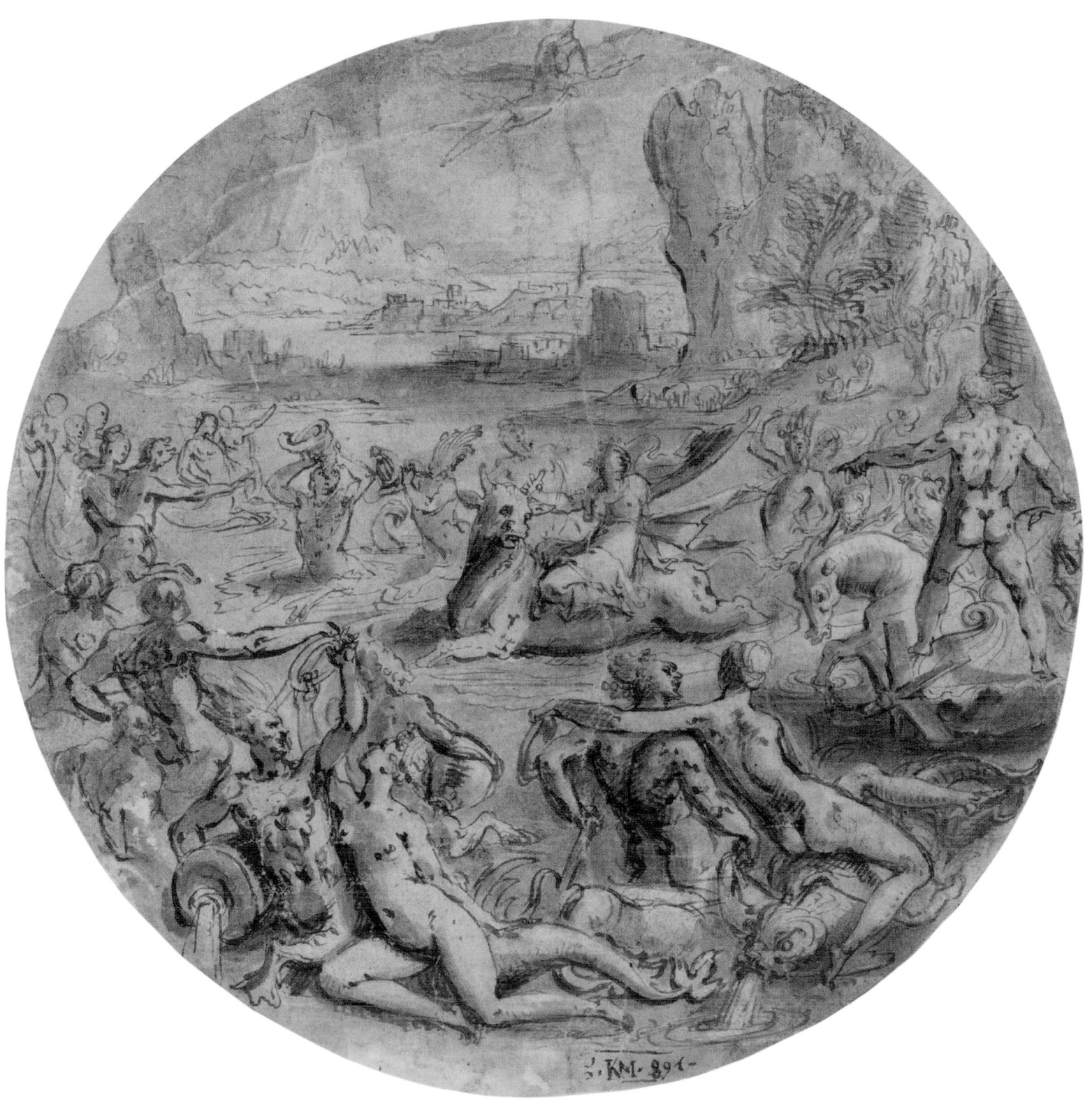

71　Karel van Mander, *Rape of Europa*

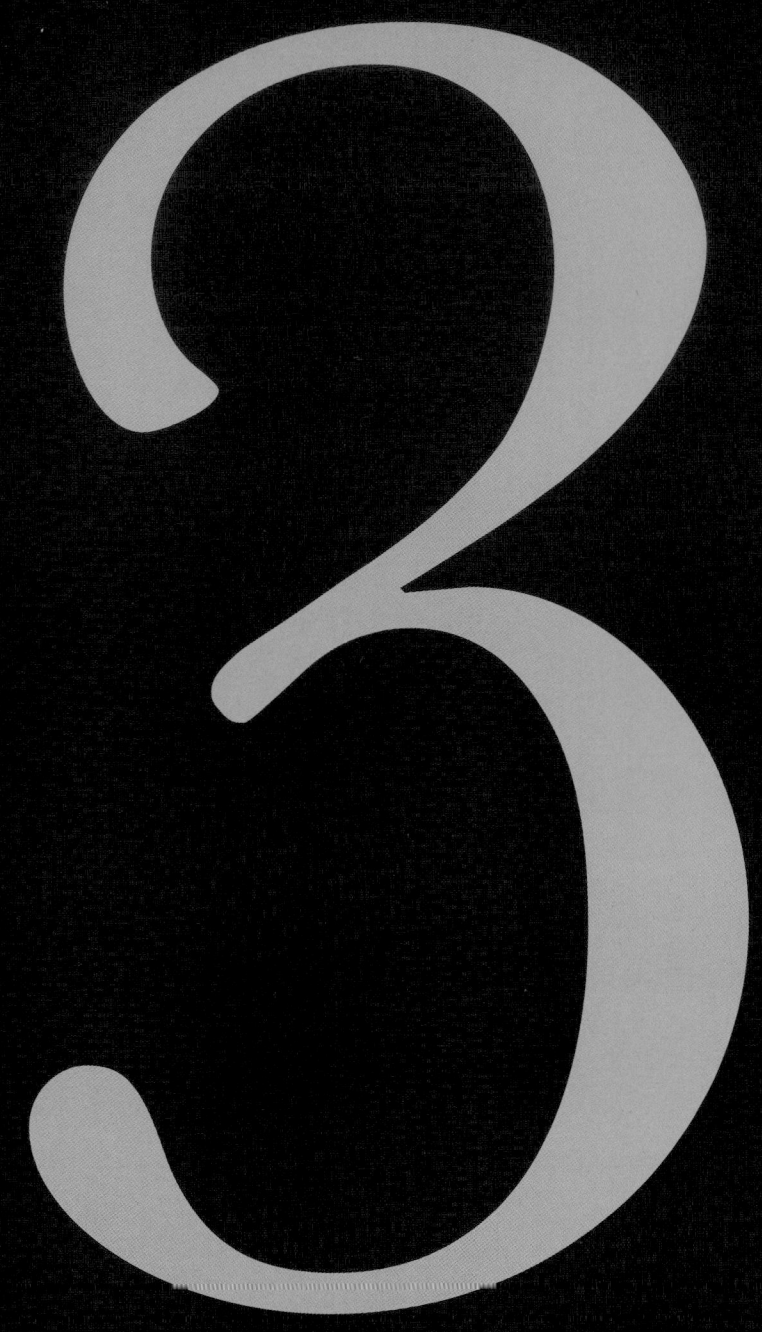

3

SEVENTEENTH
century

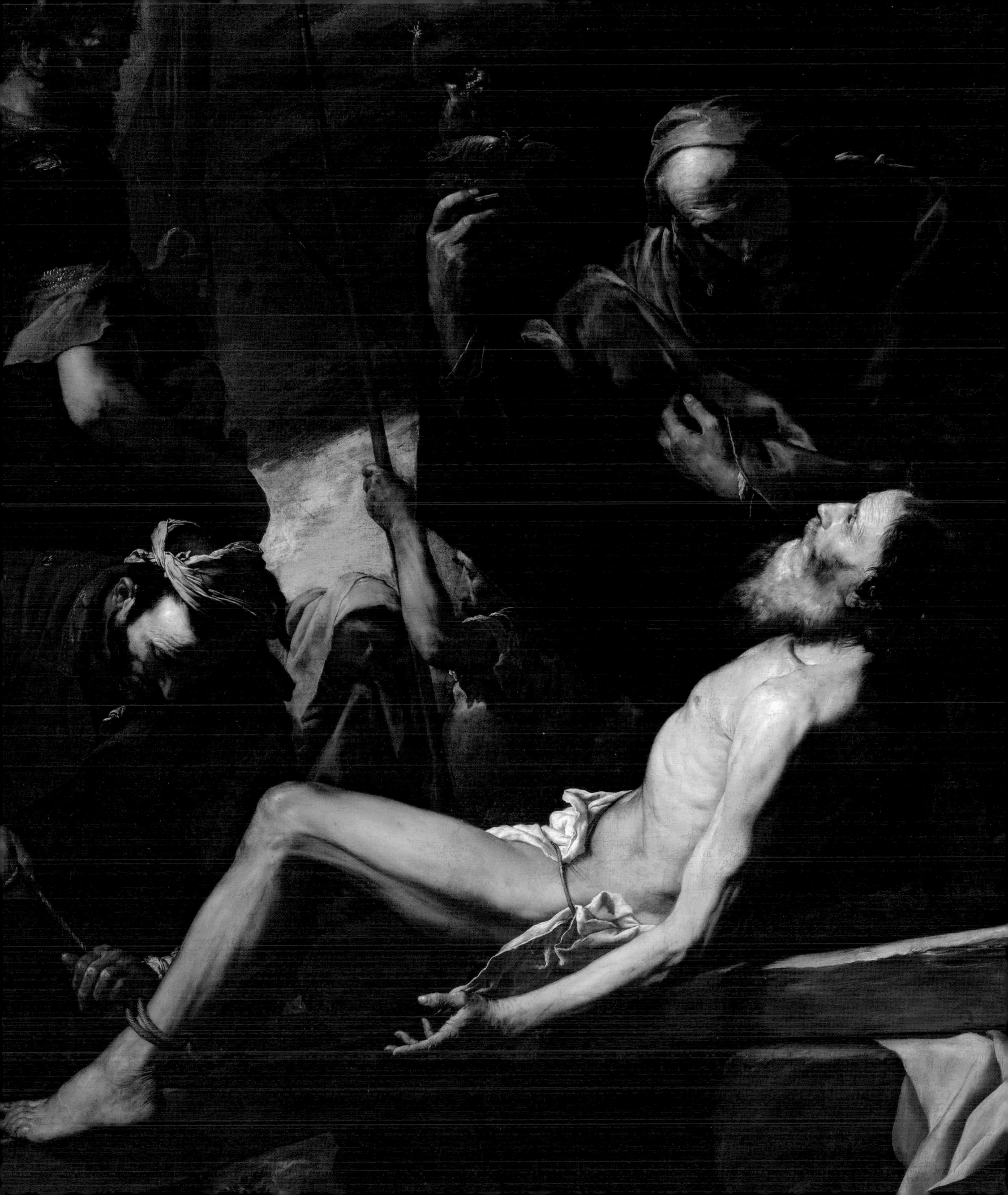

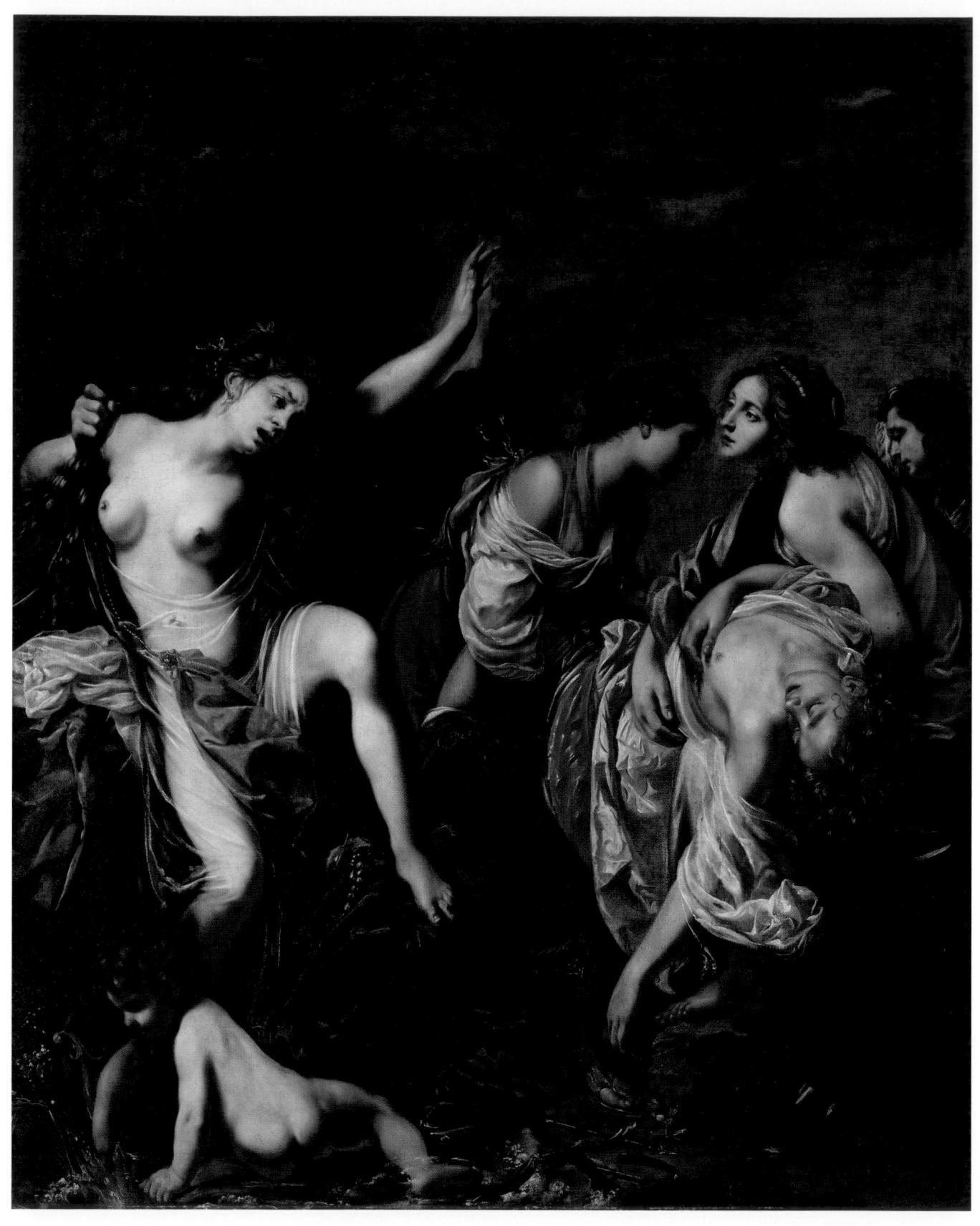

72   Francesco Furini, *Venus Lamenting the Death of Adonis*

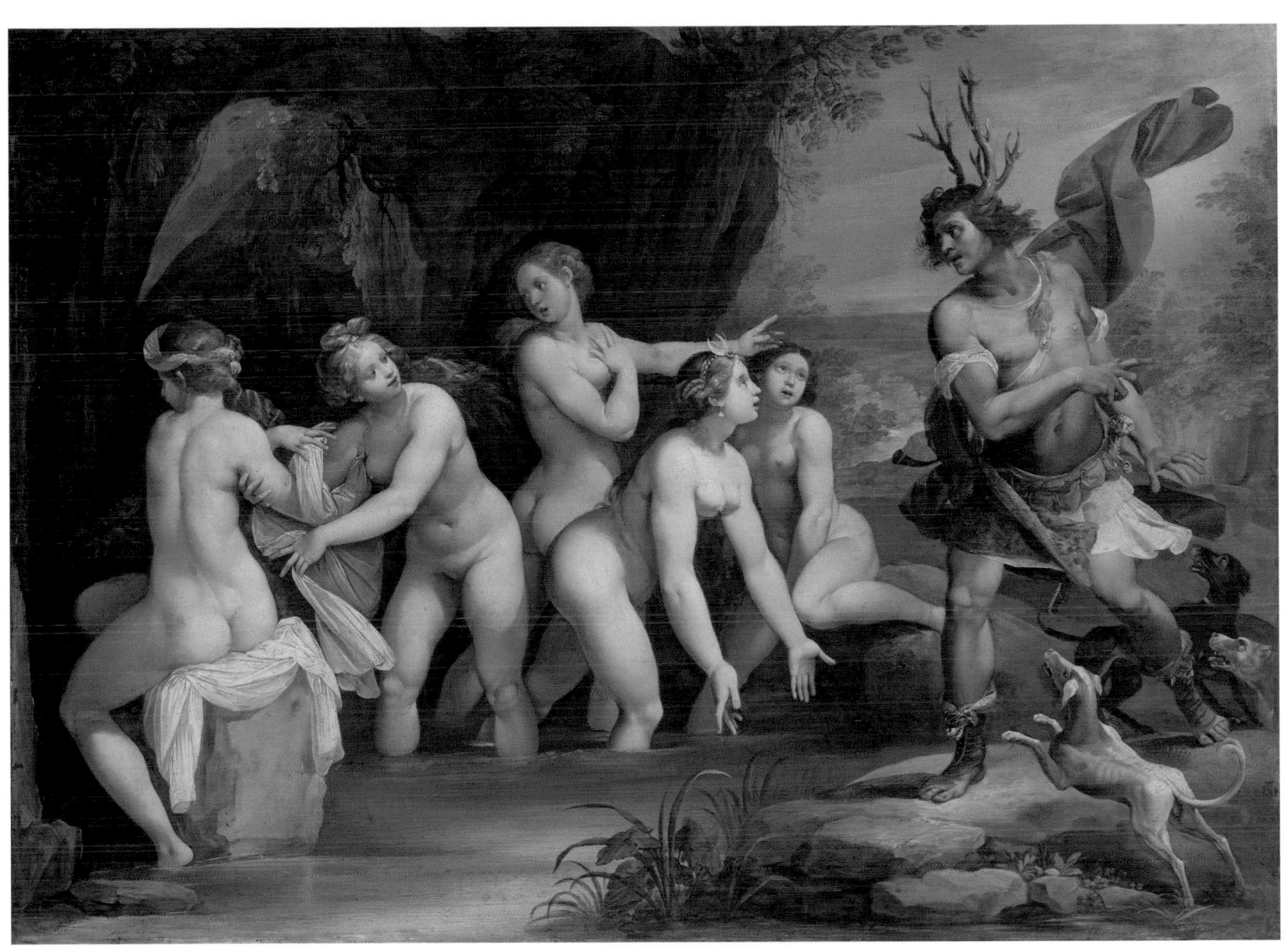

73   Cavaliere d'Arpino, *Diana and Actaeon*

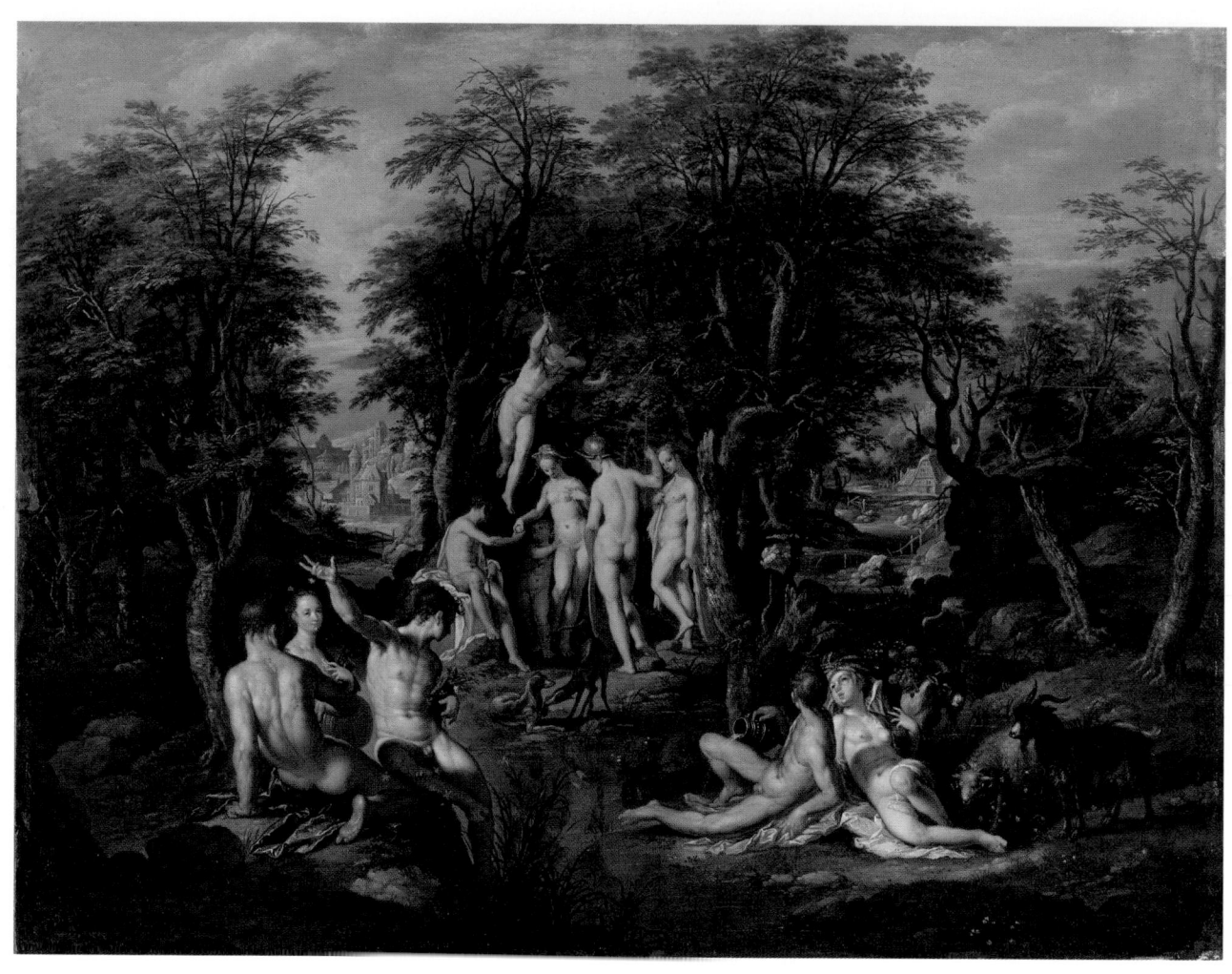

74   Joachim Wtewael, *Judgement of Paris*

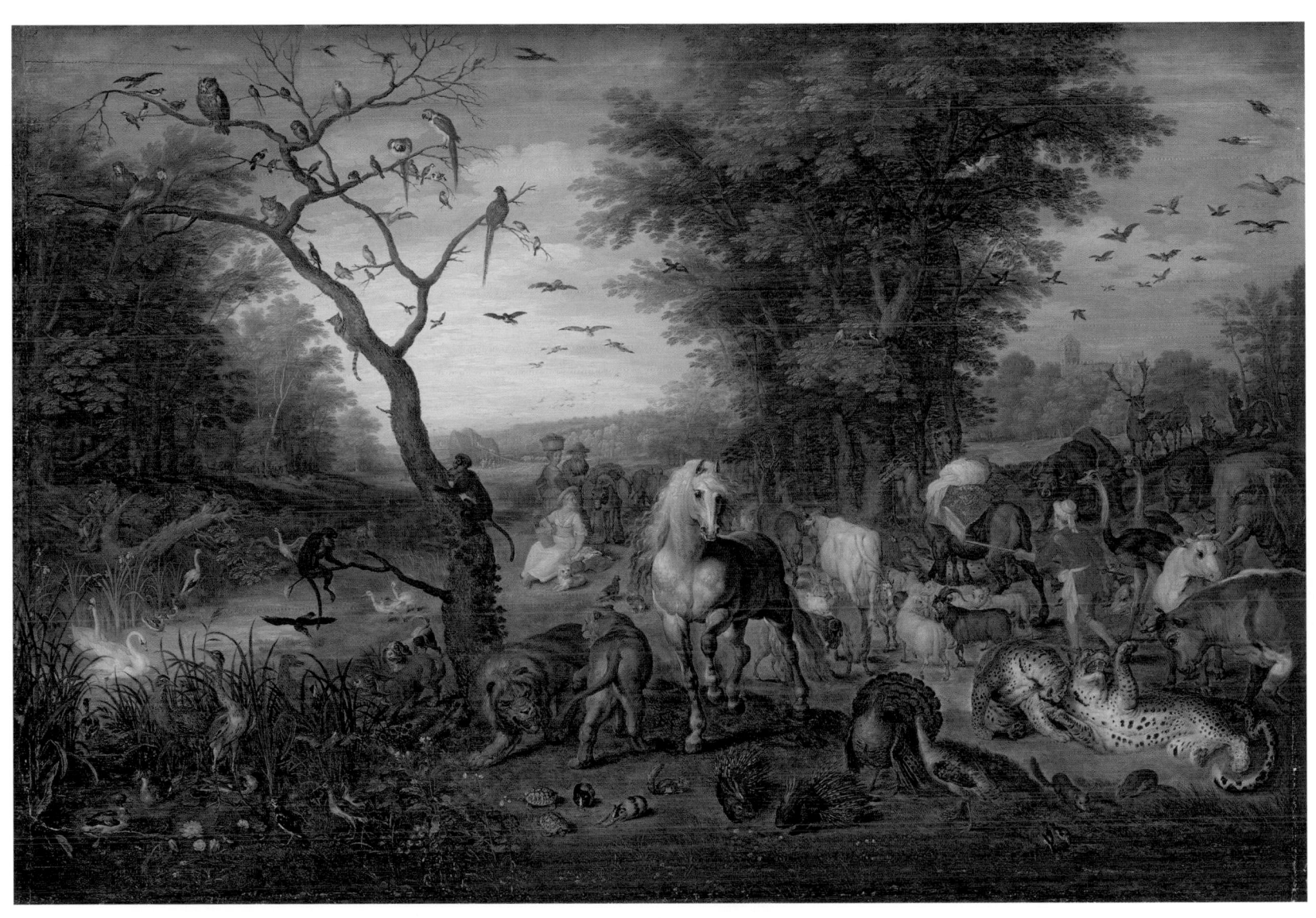

75   Jan Brueghel the Elder, *Entry of the Animals into the Ark*

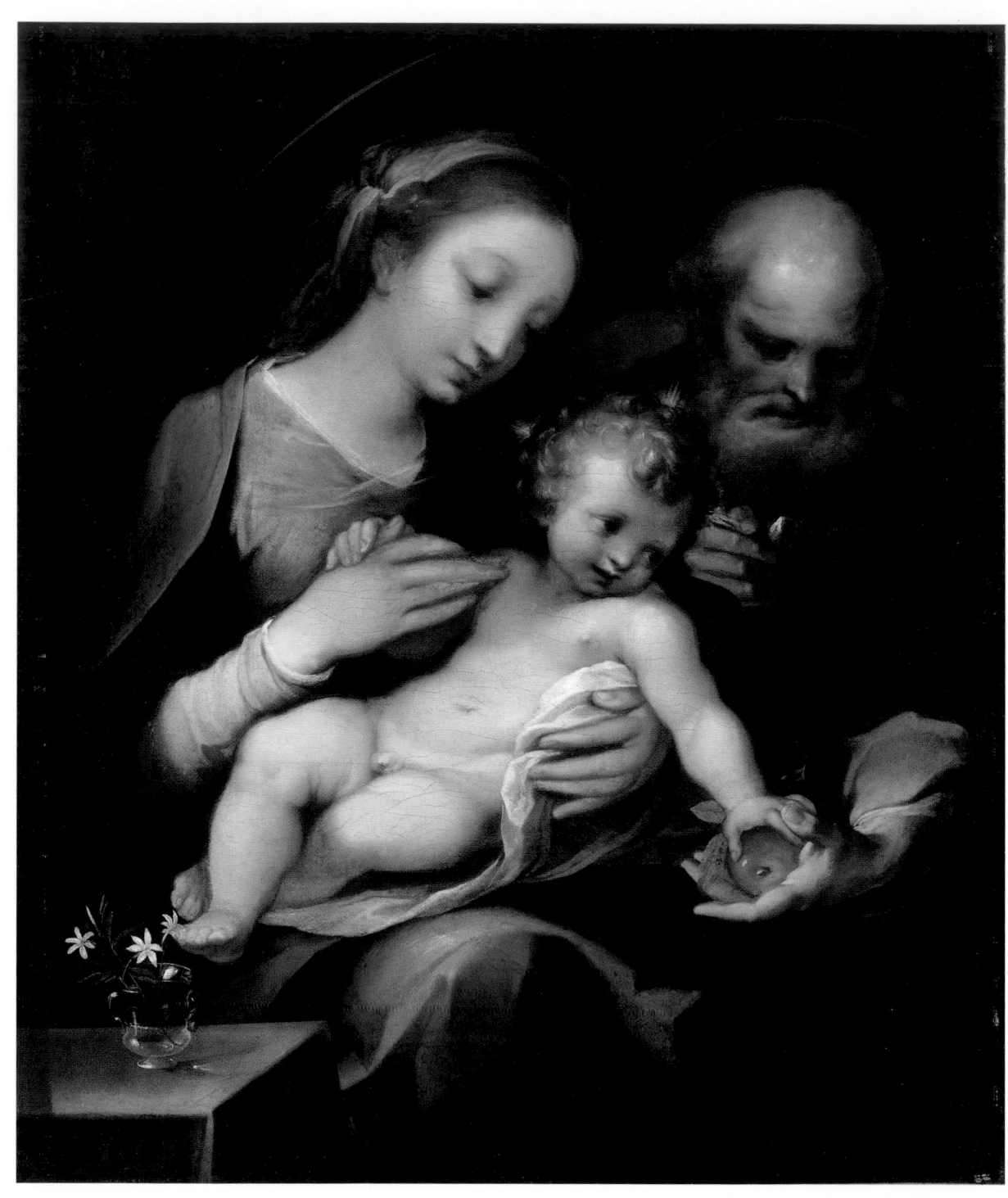

76   Francesco Vanni, *Holy Family*

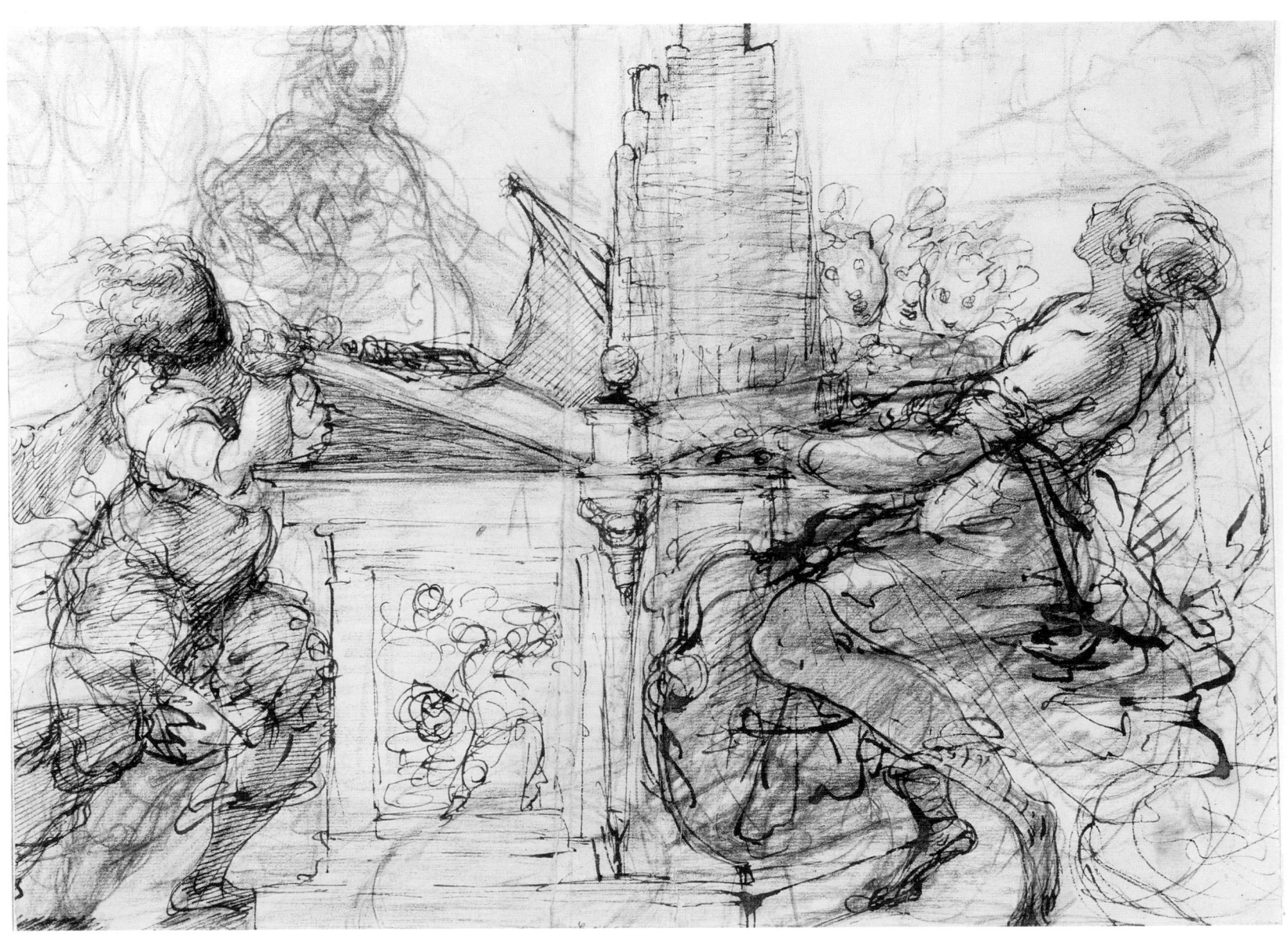

77 Daniele Crespi, *St Cecilia at the Organ*

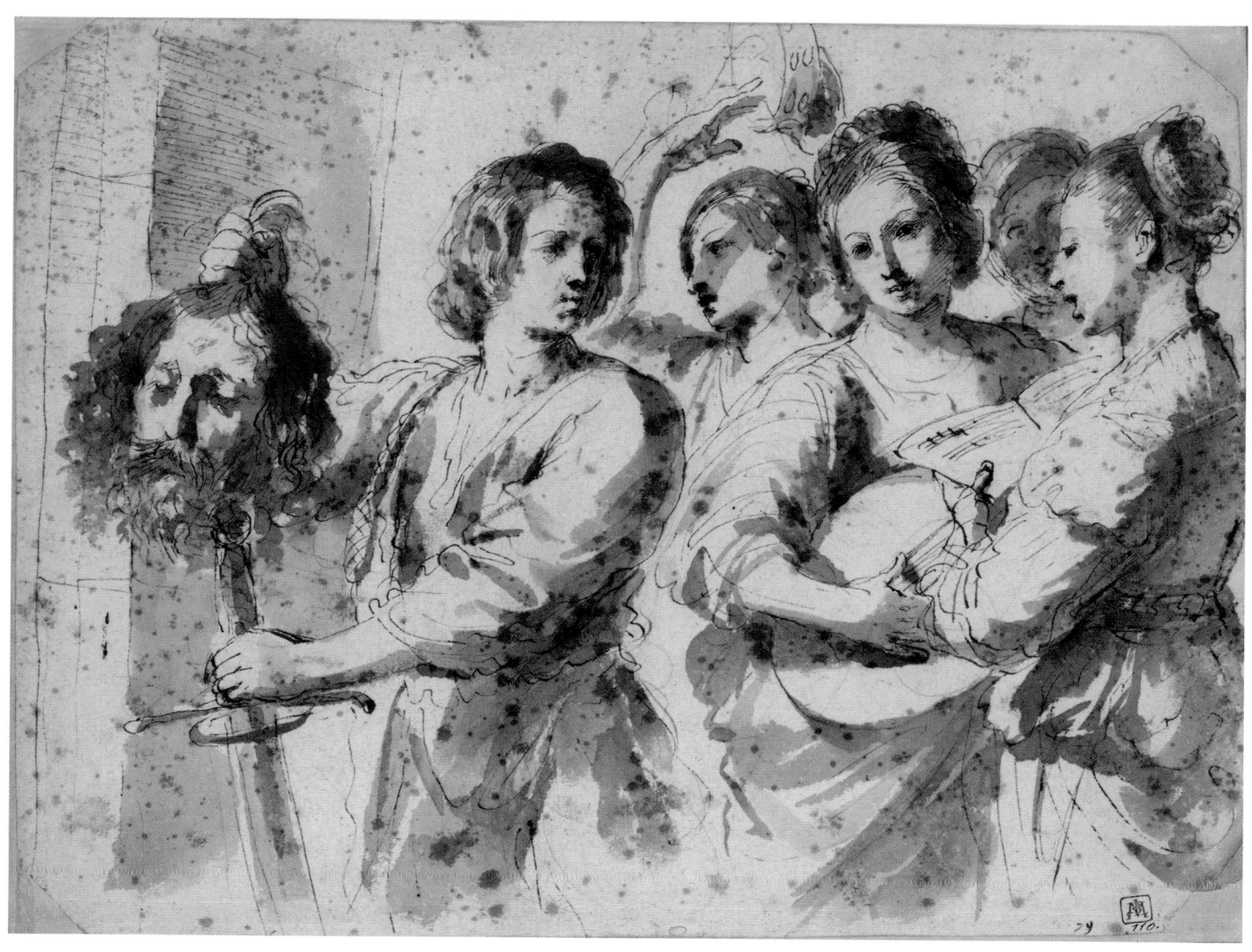

78   Guercino, *Triumph of David*

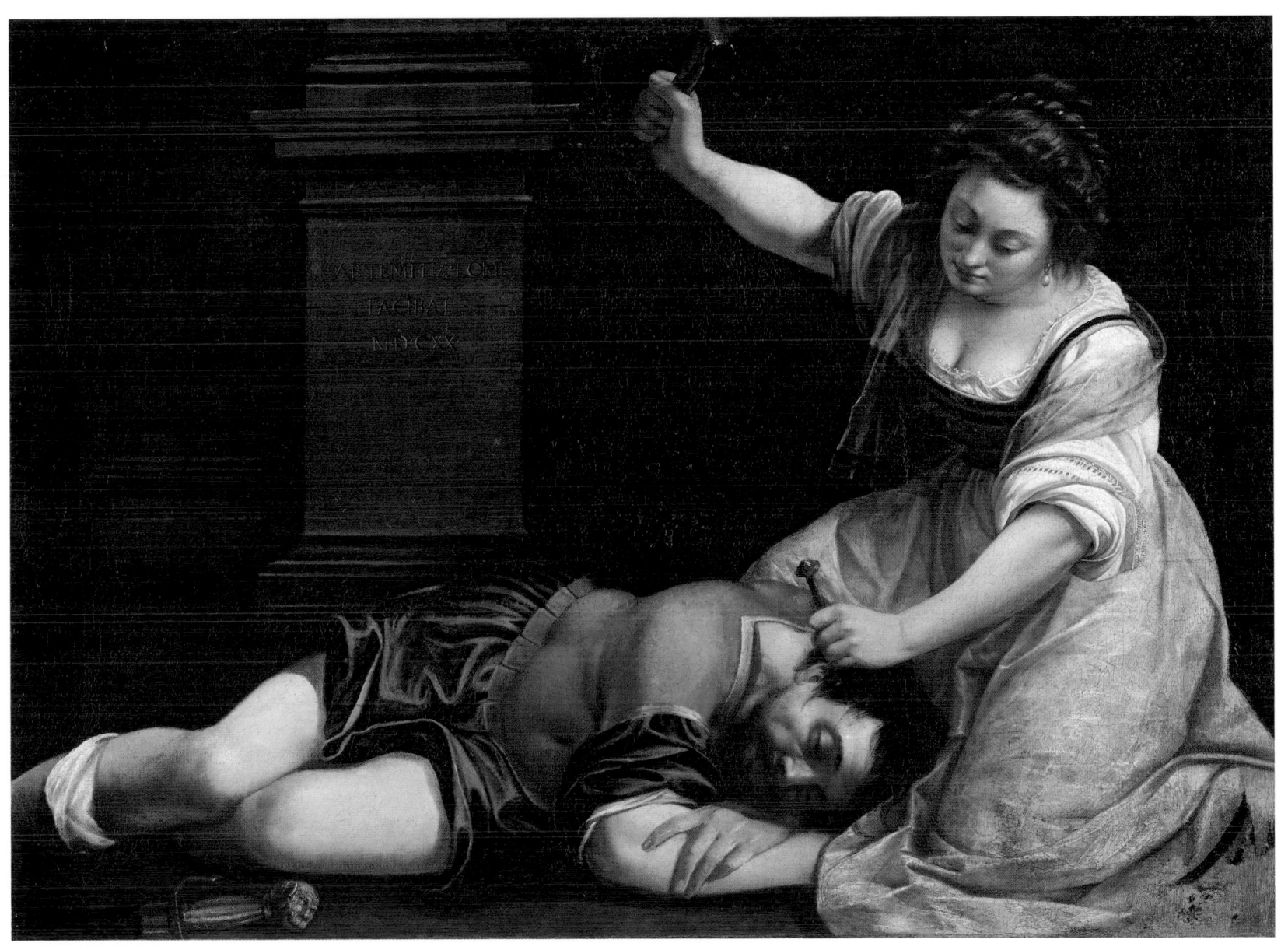

79 Artemisia Gentileschi, *Jael and Sisera*

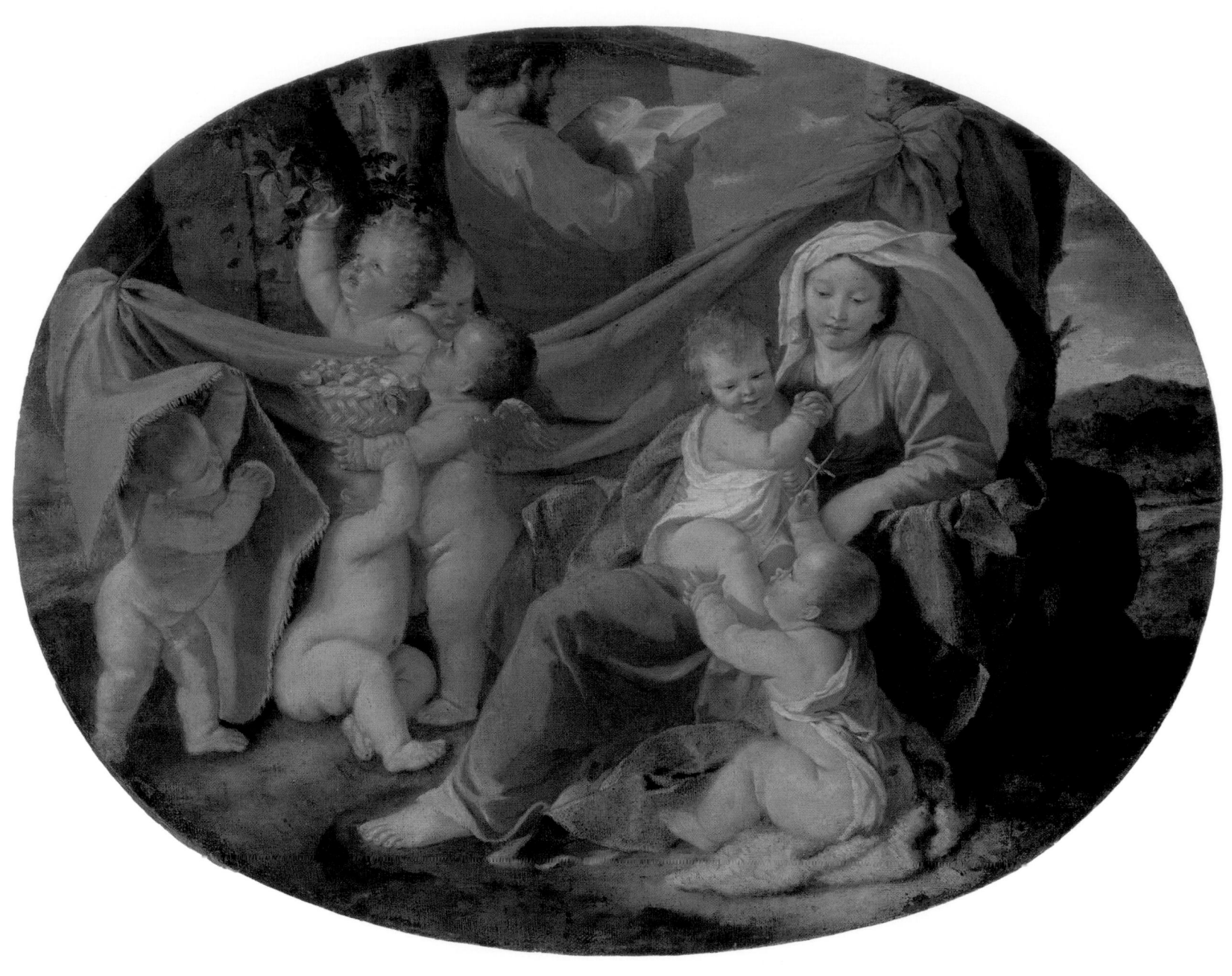

80 Nicolas Poussin, *Holy Family with the Infant St John the Baptist and Putti*

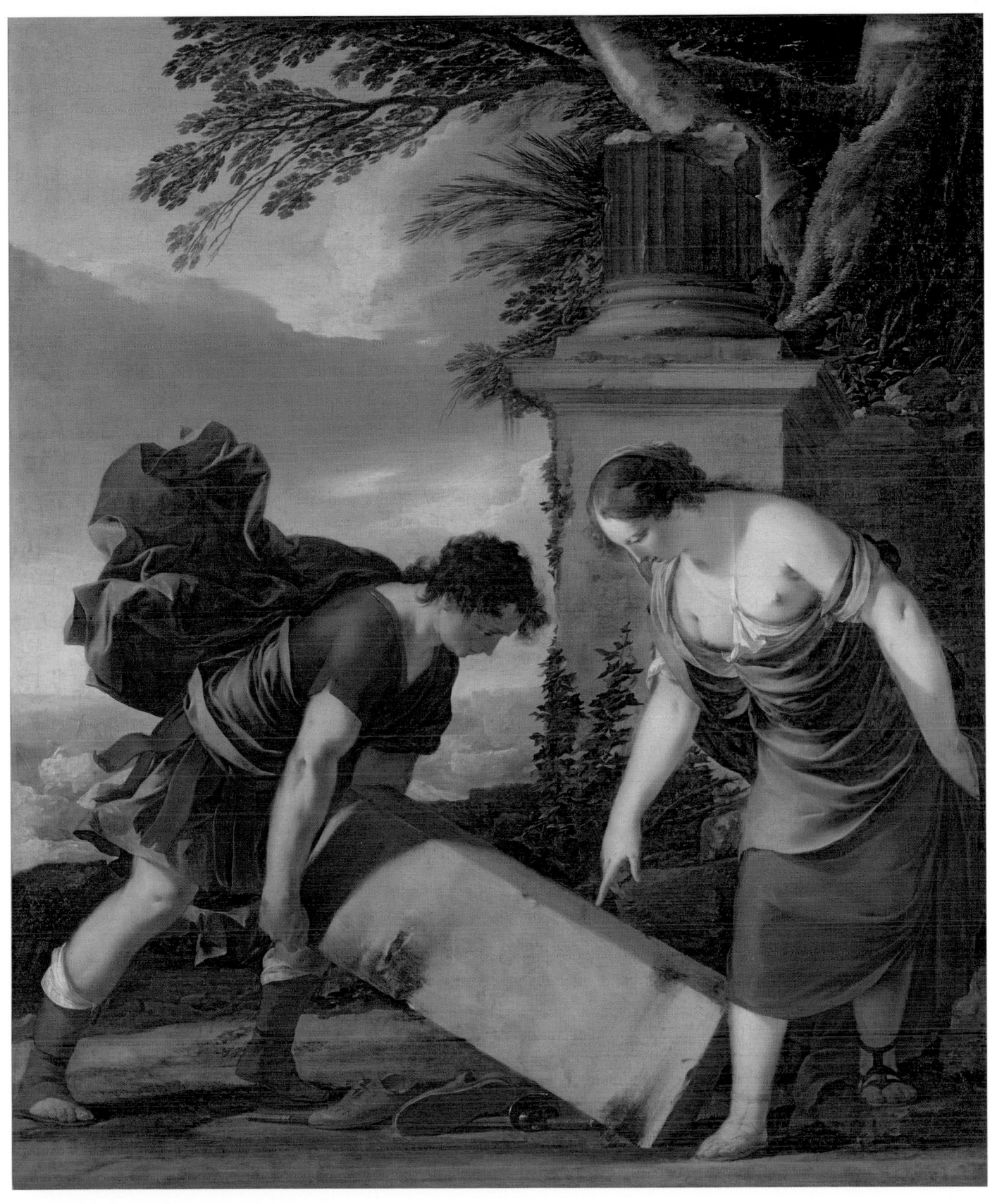

81   Laurent de La Hyre, *Theseus and Aethra*

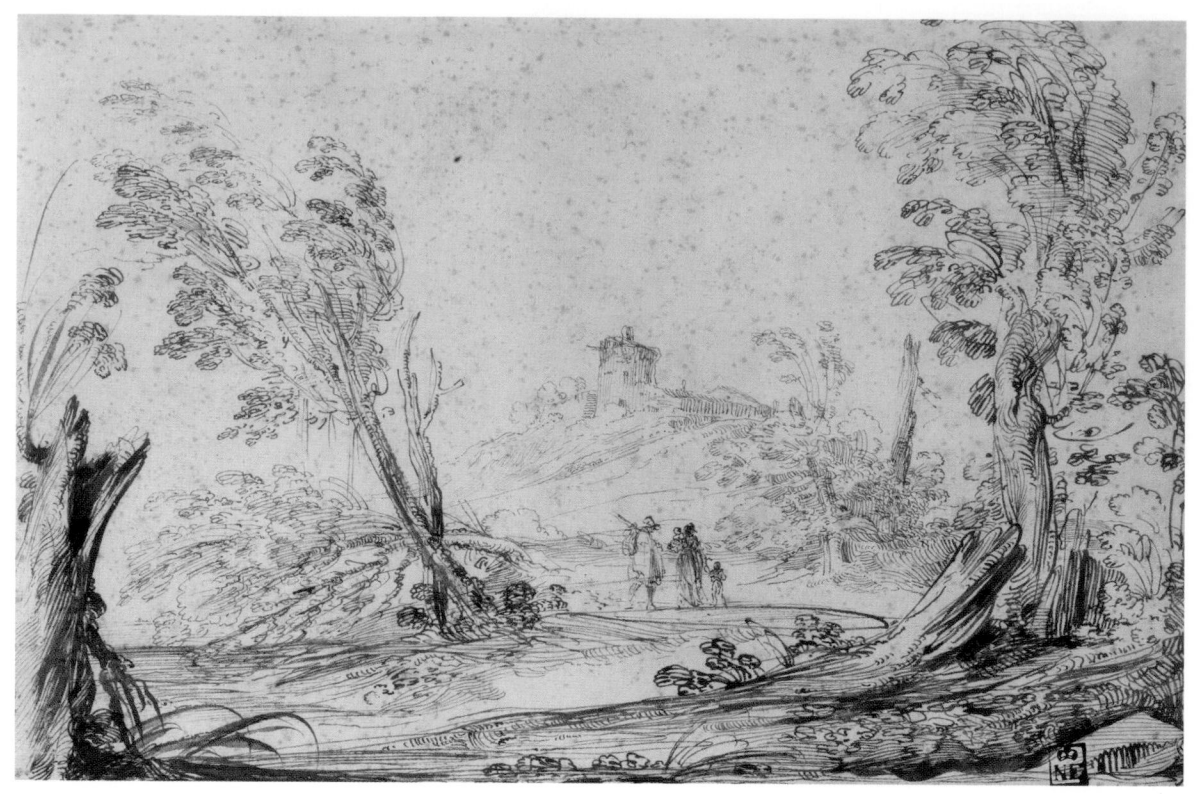

82   Guercino, *Landscape with Travellers*

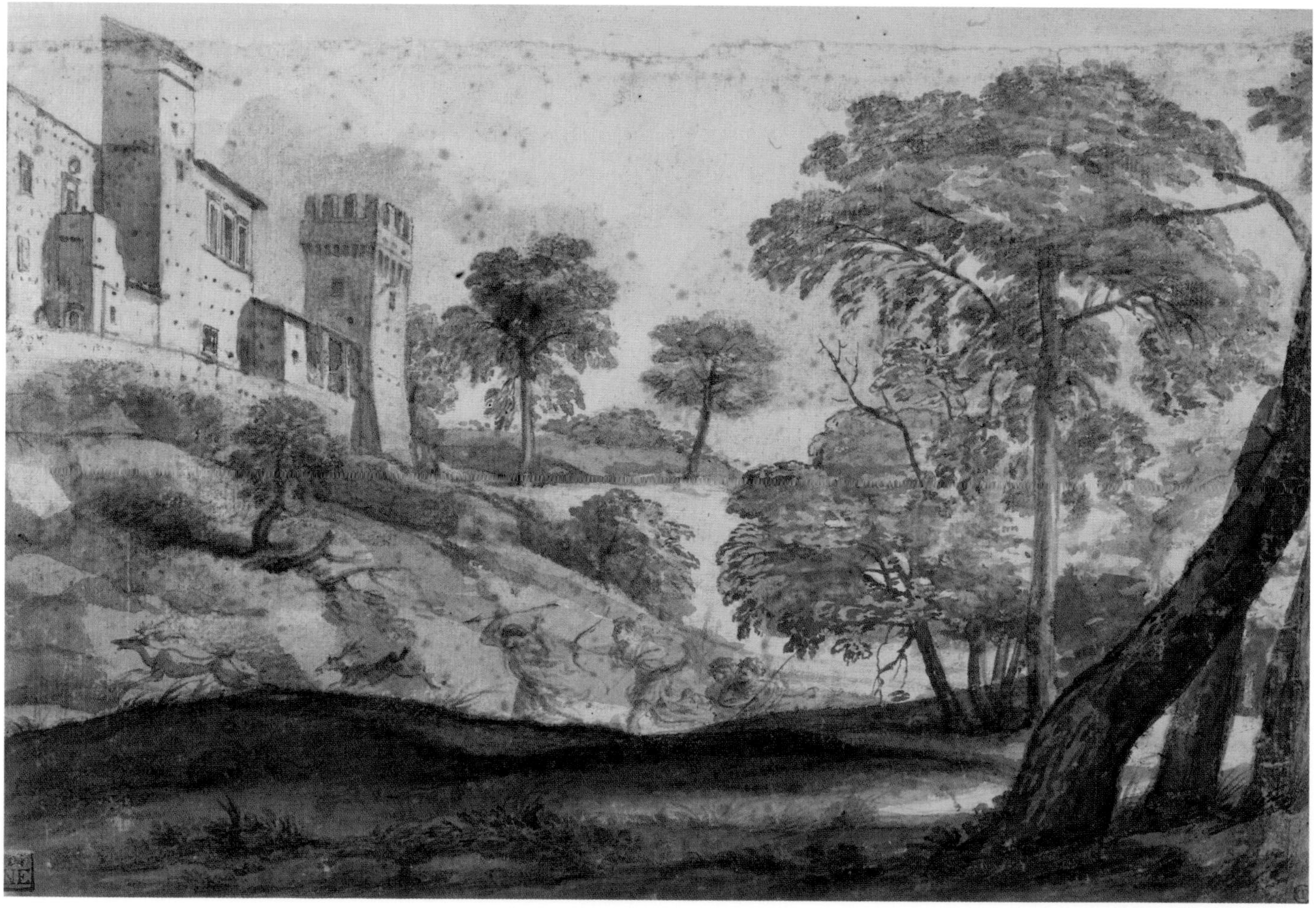

83   Claude Lorrain, *Deer Hunt*

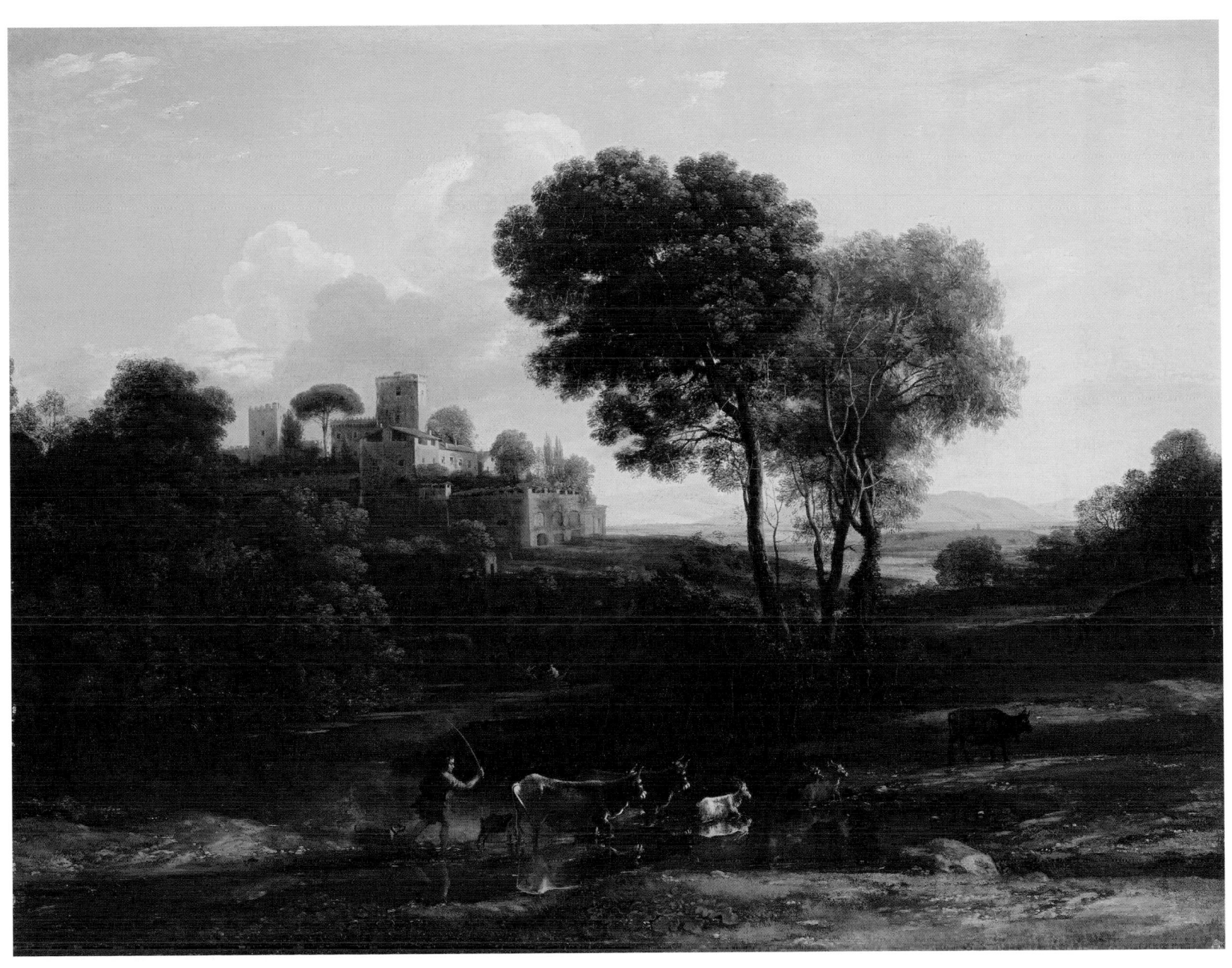

84   Claude Lorrain, *Villa in the Roman Campagna*

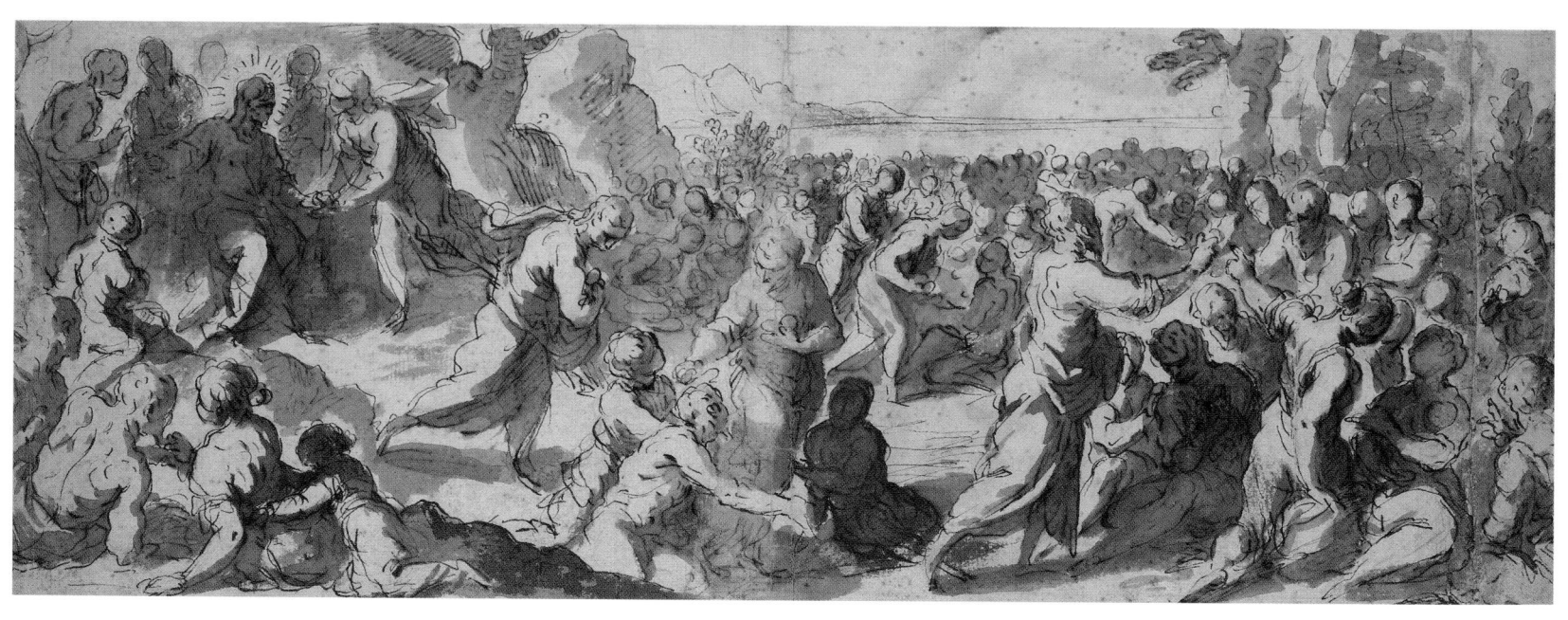

85 Jacopo Palma il Giovane, *Miracle of the Loaves and Fishes*

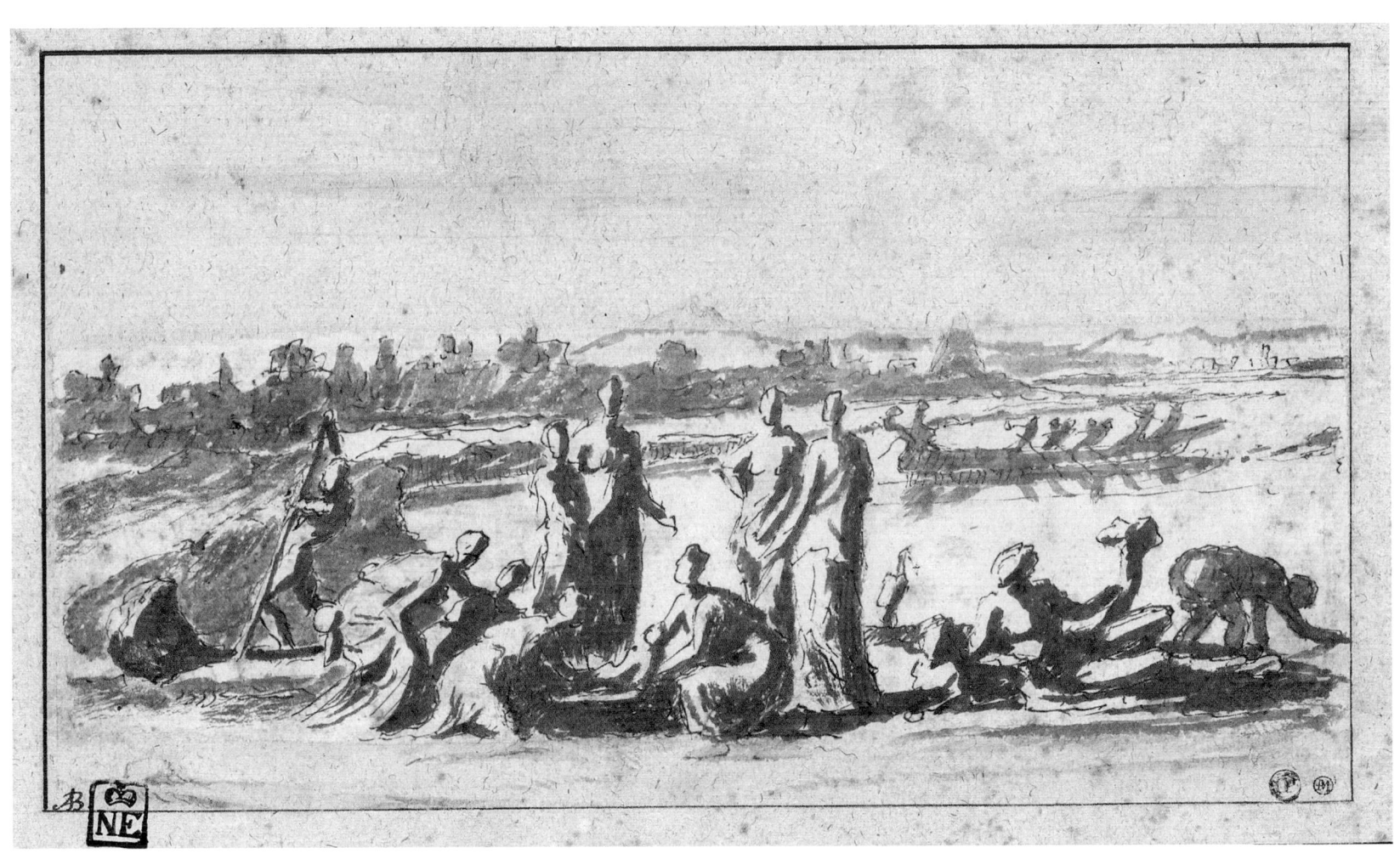

86 Nicolas Poussin, *Finding of Moses*

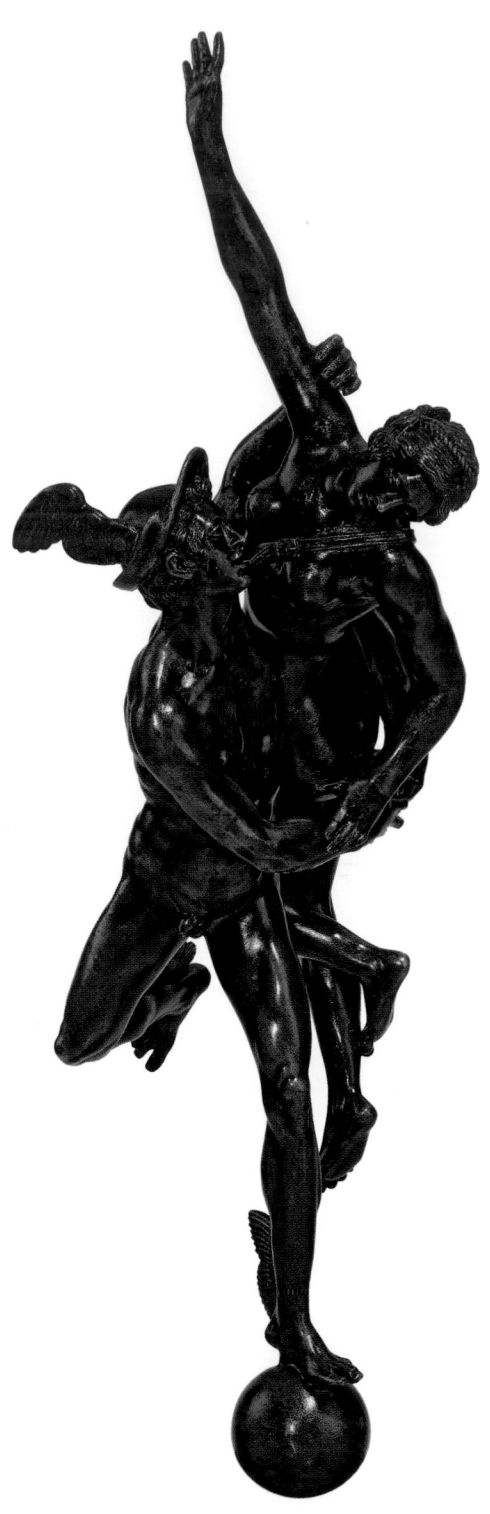

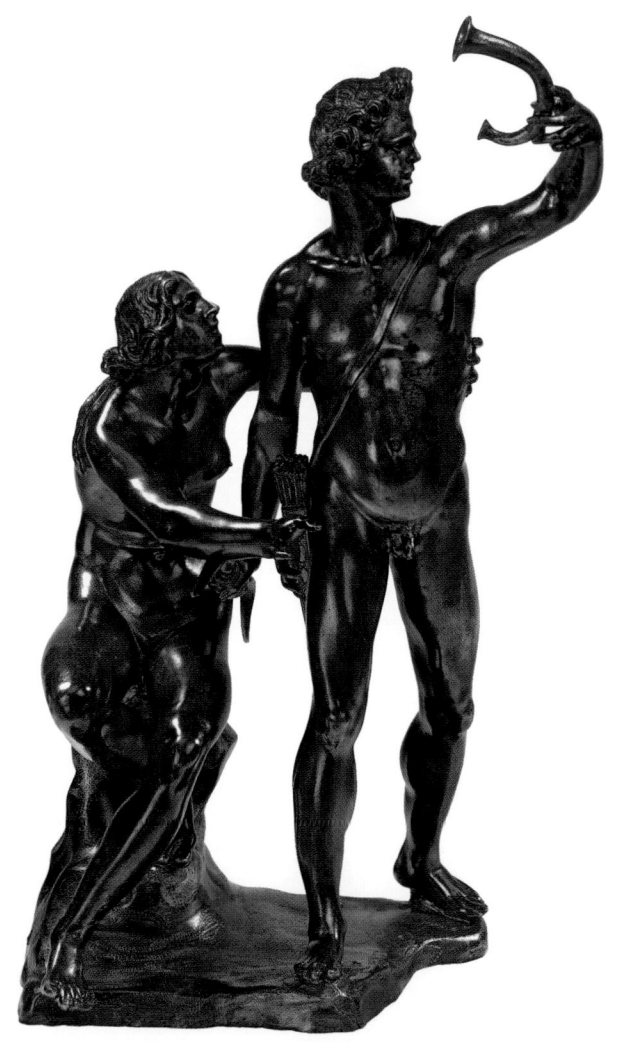

87   Caspar Gras, *Mercury and Psyche*

88   Ferdinando Tacca, *Venus and Adonis*

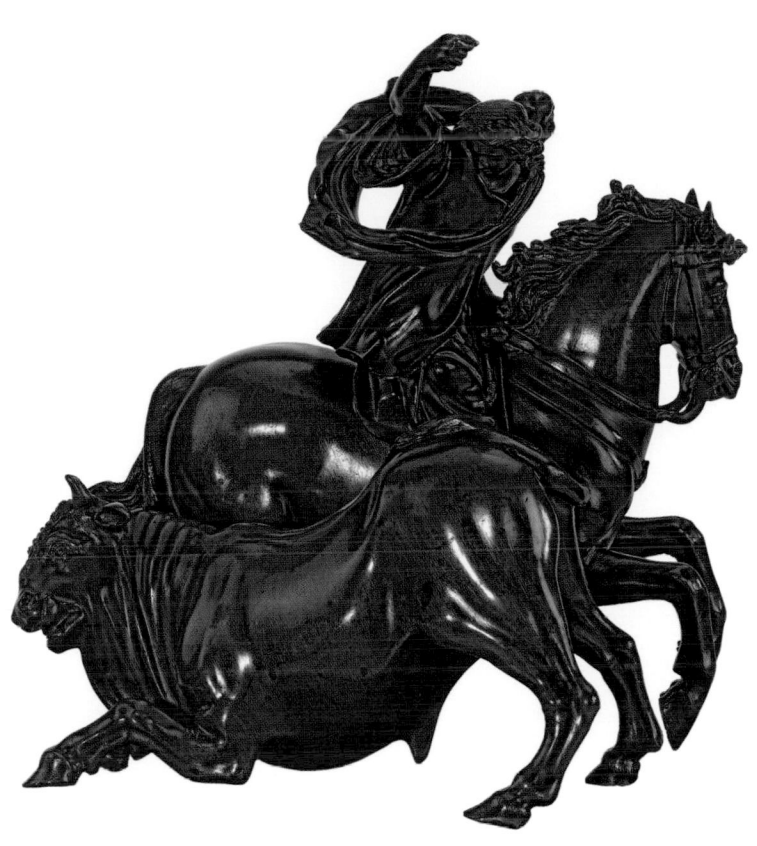

89.1   Damiano Capelli, *Rider Killing a Bull*

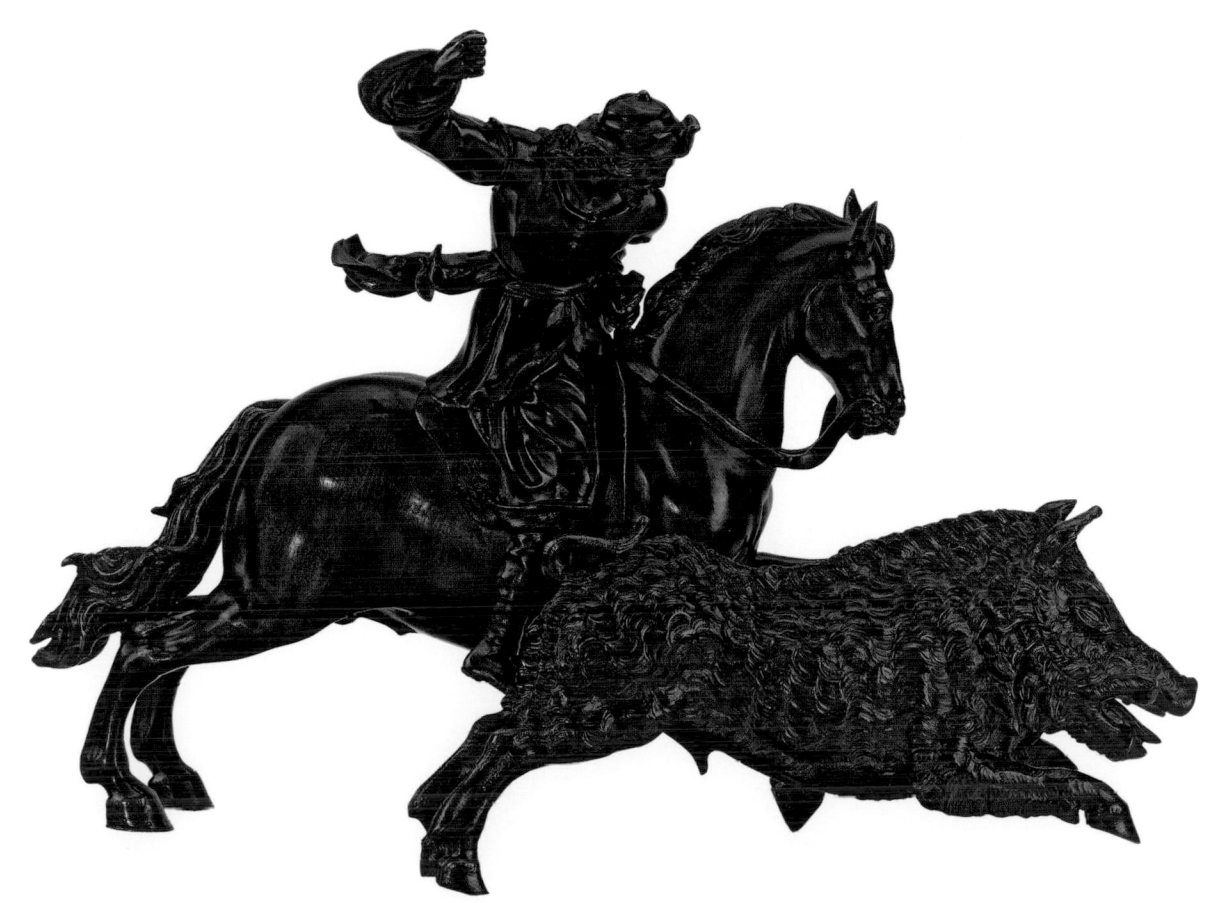

89.2   Damiano Capelli, *Rider Pursuing a Boar*

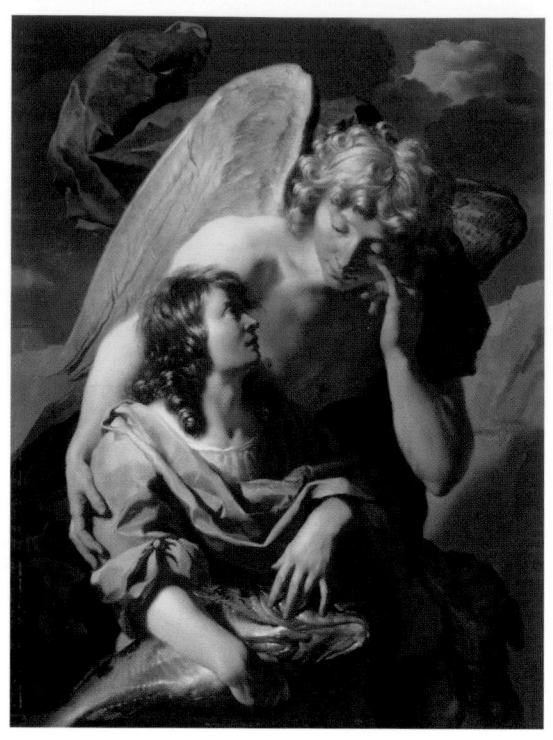

90   Karel Dujardin, *Tobias and the Angel*

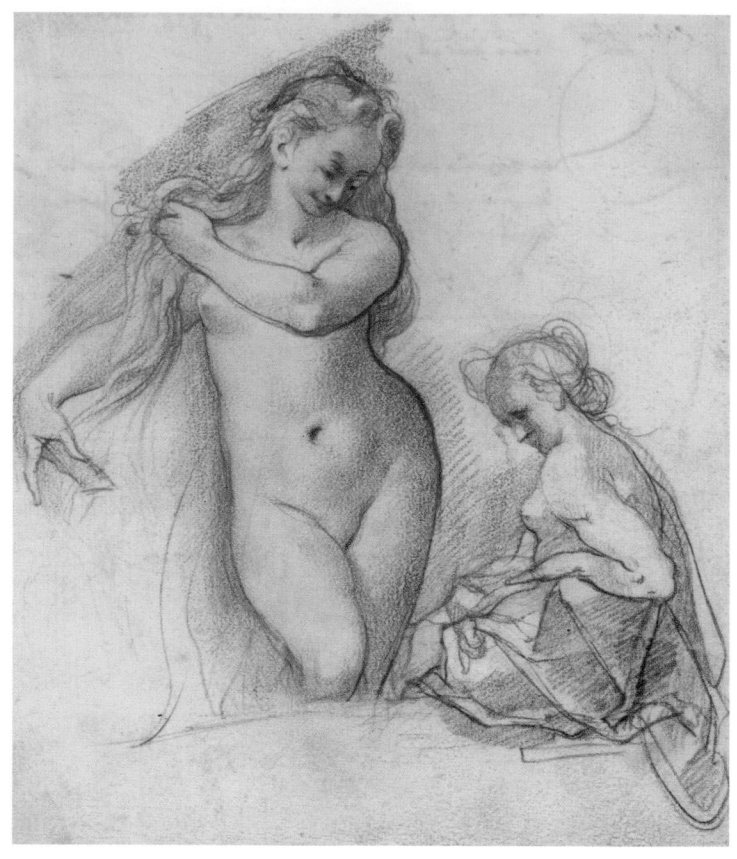

91   Joseph Heintz the Elder, *Study of Two Nymphs*

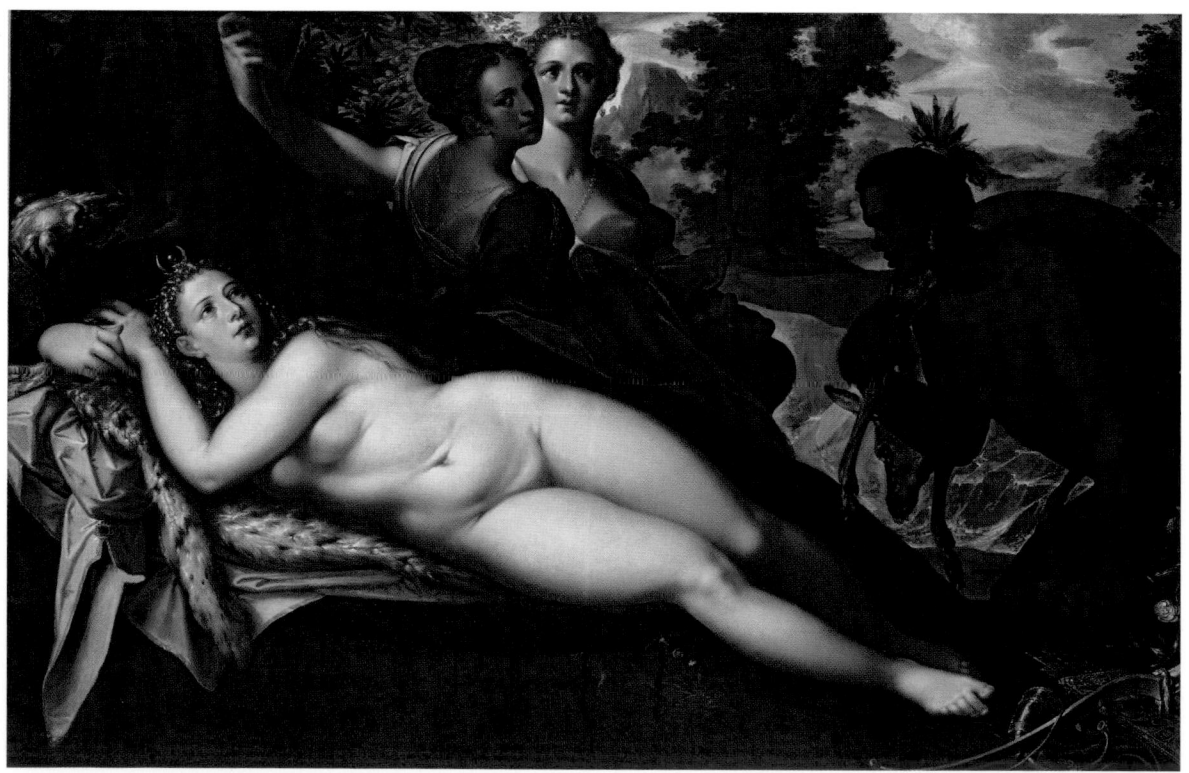

92   Bartholomäus Spranger, *Diana and Her Nymphs*

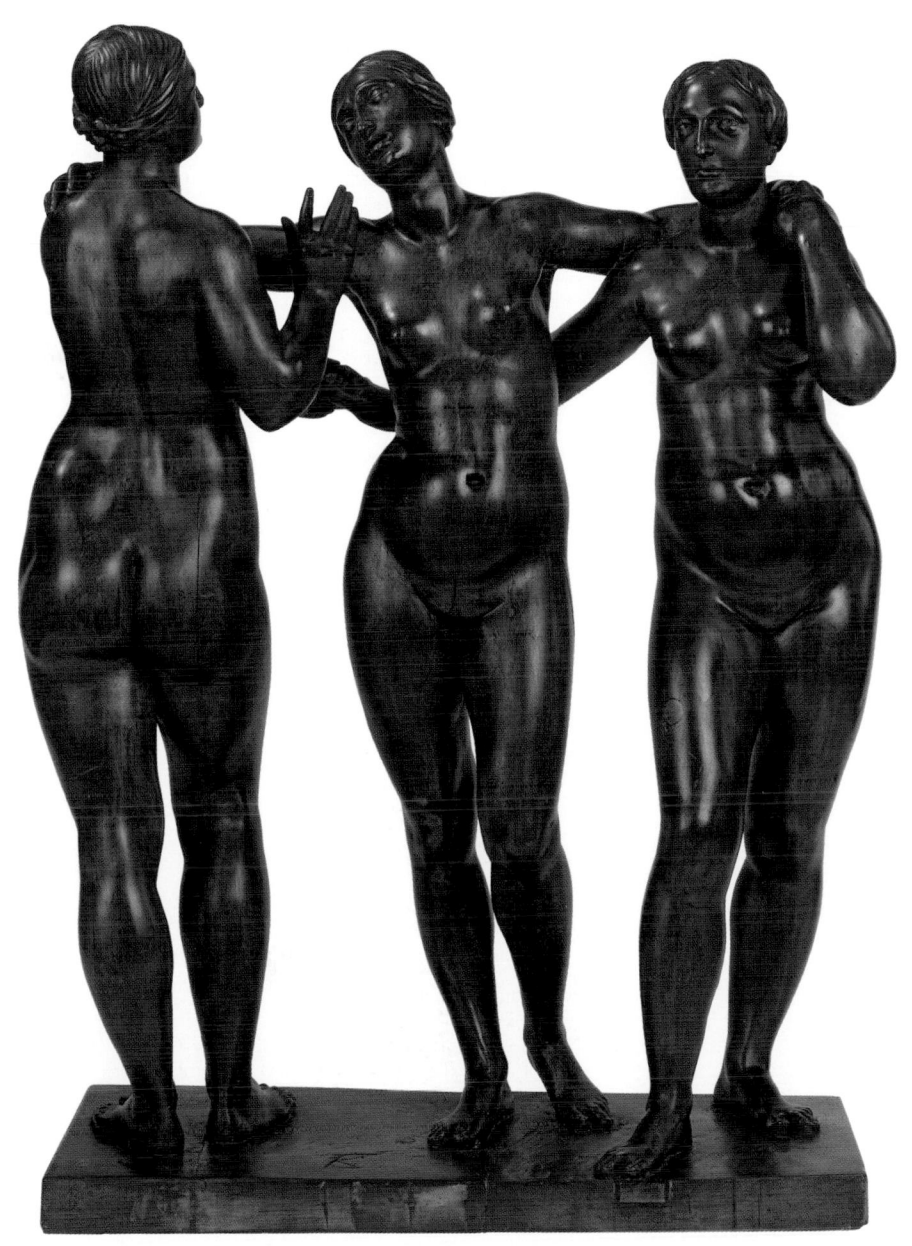

93   Leonhard Kern, *Three Graces*

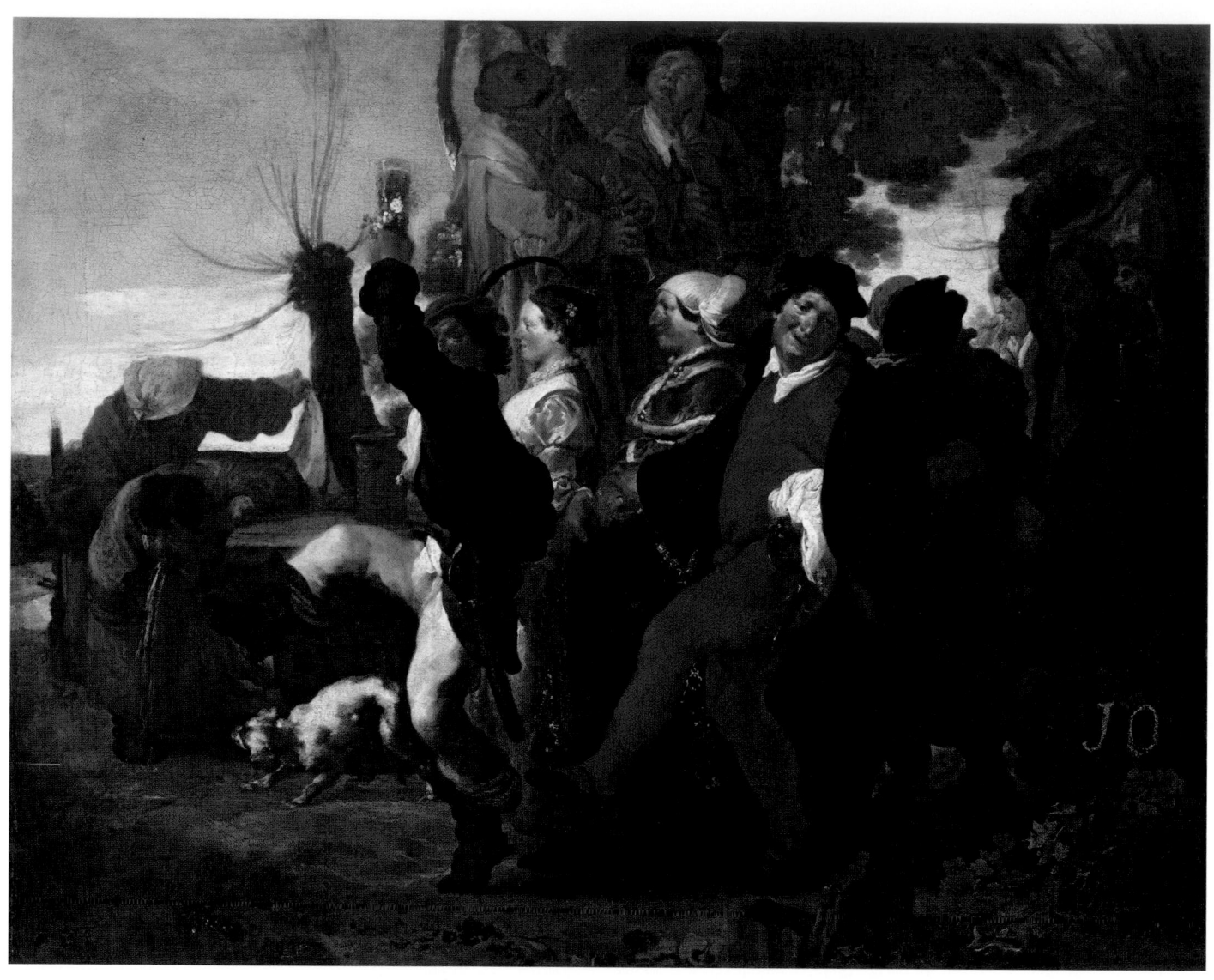

94   Johann Liss, *Peasant Wedding*

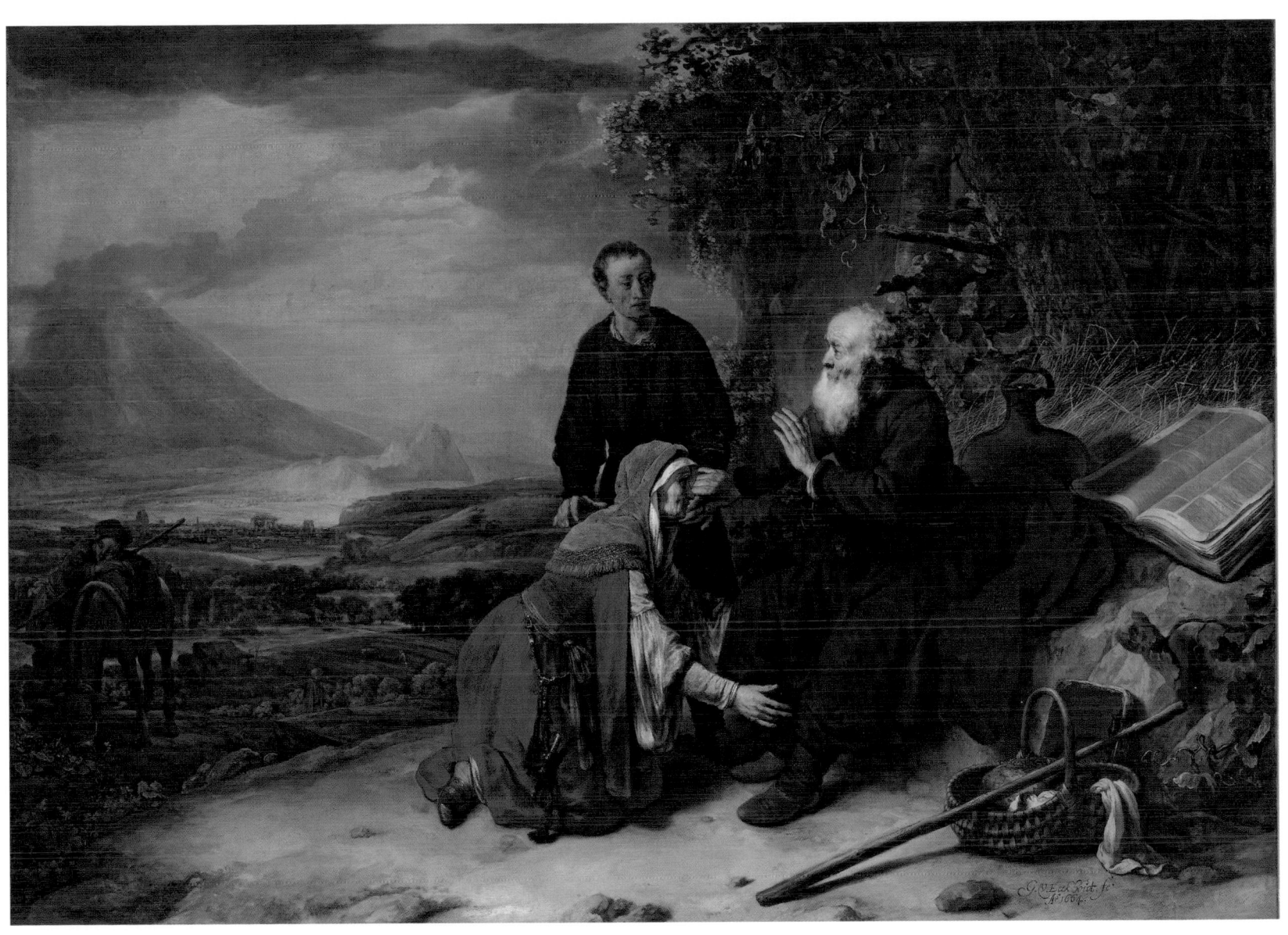

95   Gerbrandt van den Eeckhout, *Elisha and the Shunammite Woman*

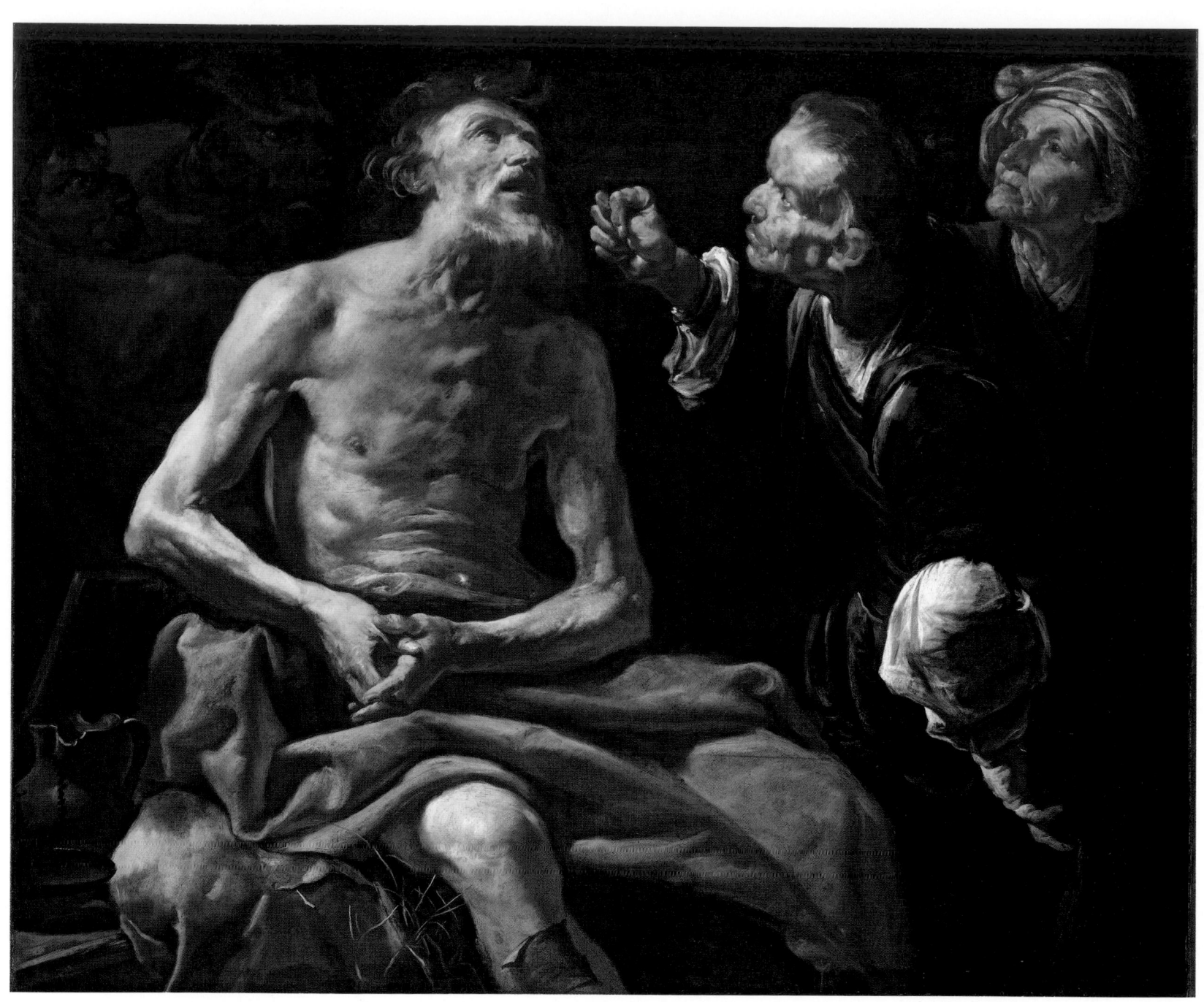

96   Gioacchino Assereto, *Mocking of Job*

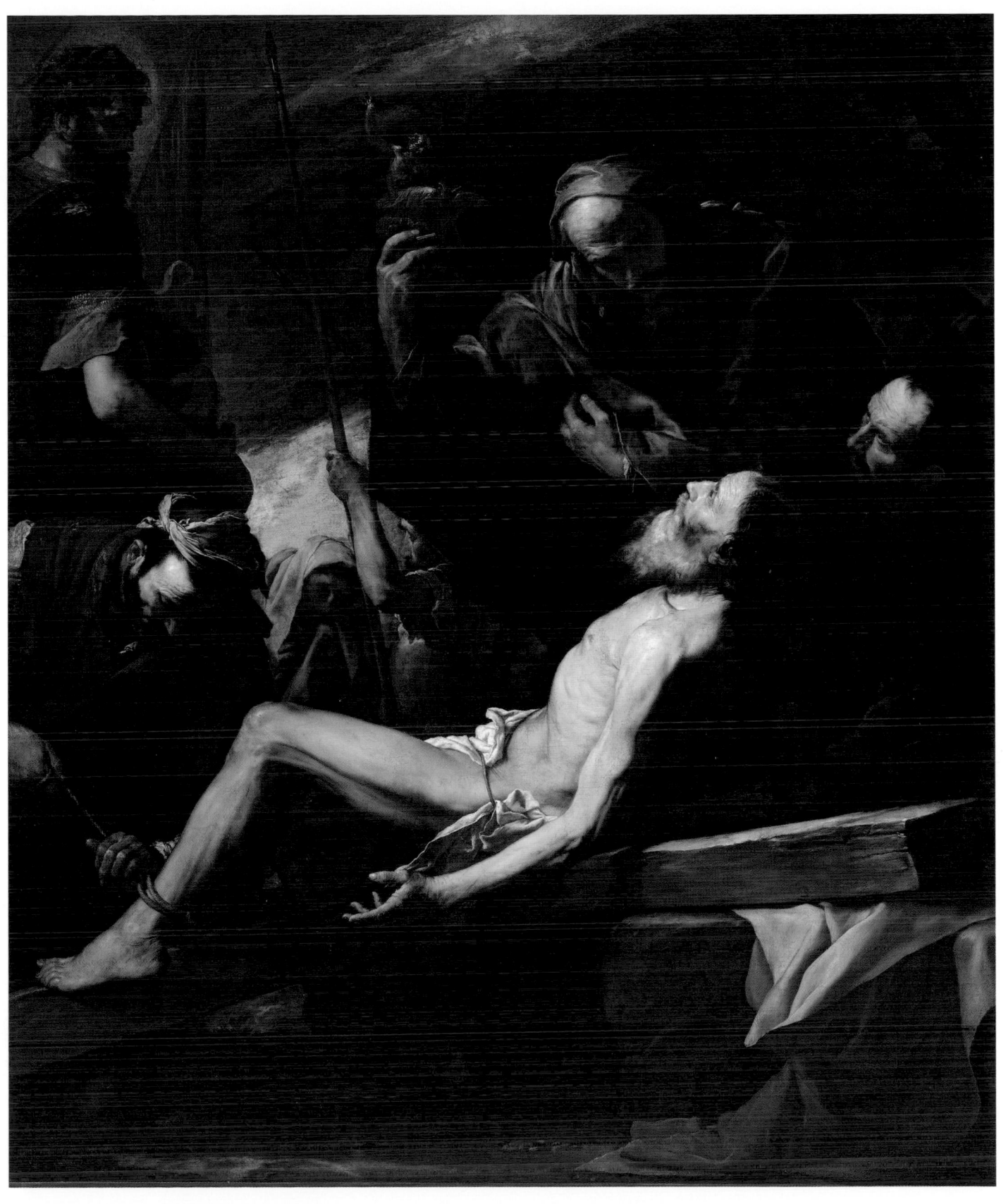

97   Jusepe de Ribera, *Martyrdom of St Andrew*

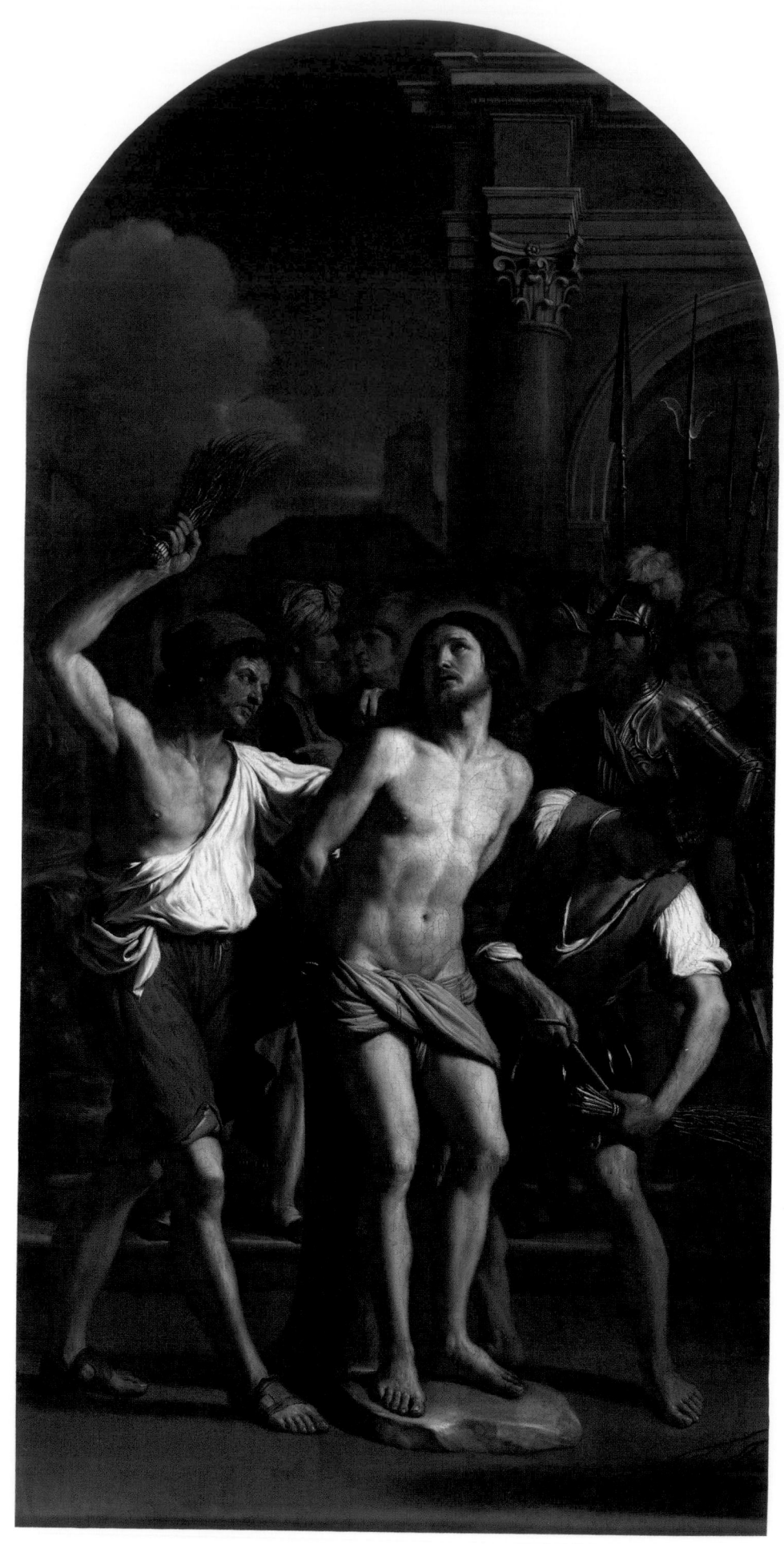

98   Guercino, *Flagellation of Christ*

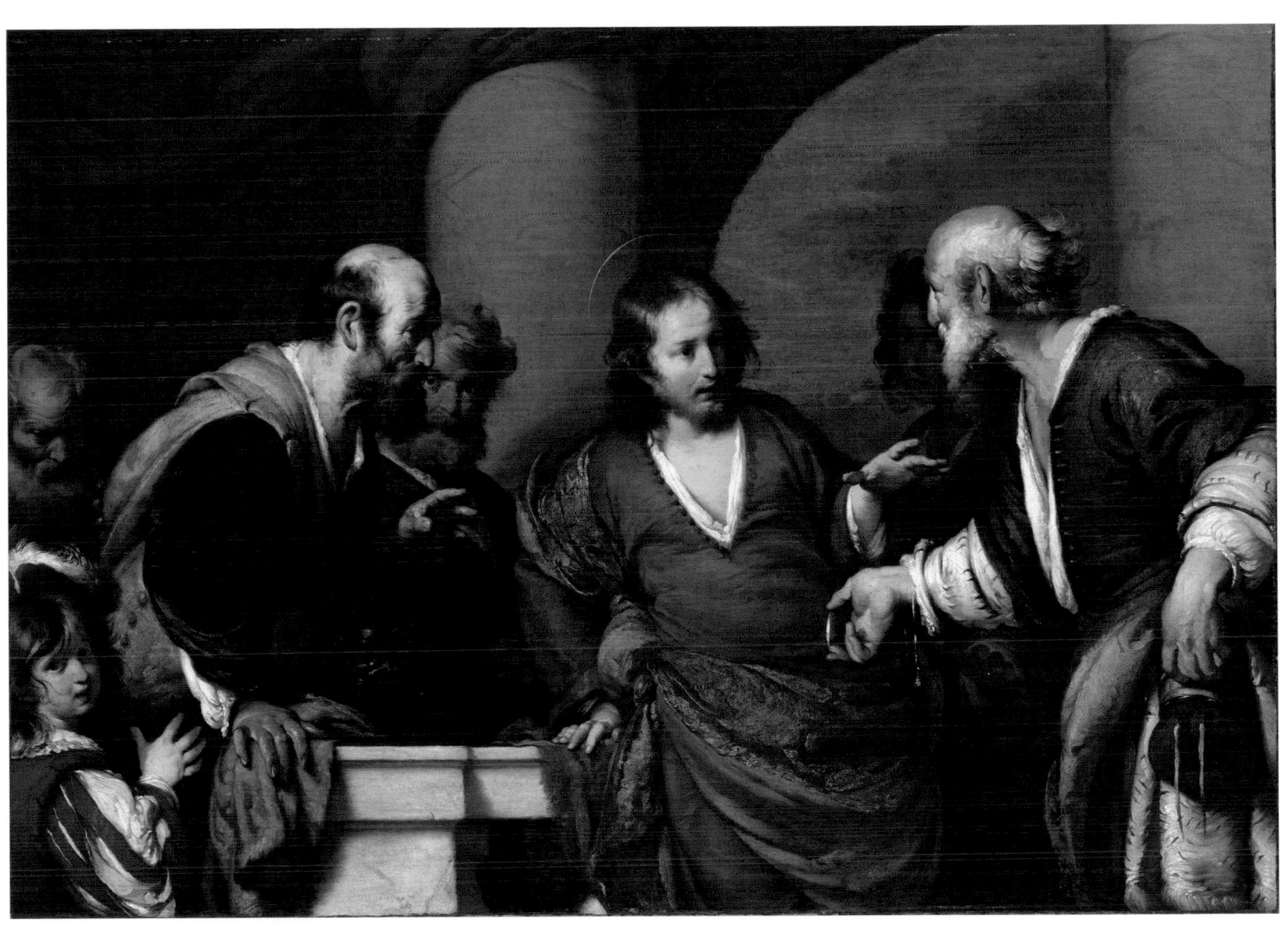

99   Bernardo Strozzi, *Tribute Money*

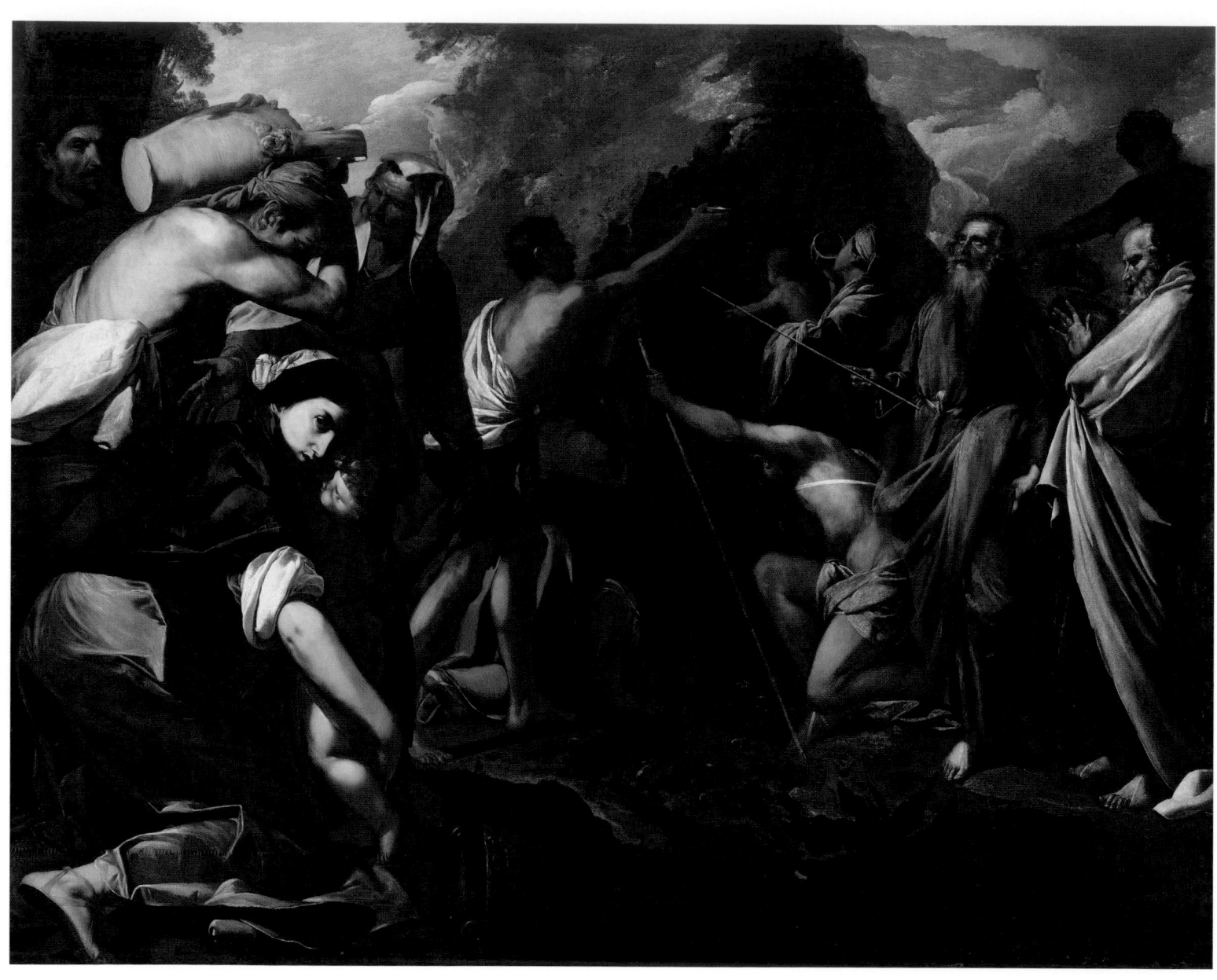

100   Antonio de Bellis, *Moses Striking Water from the Rock*

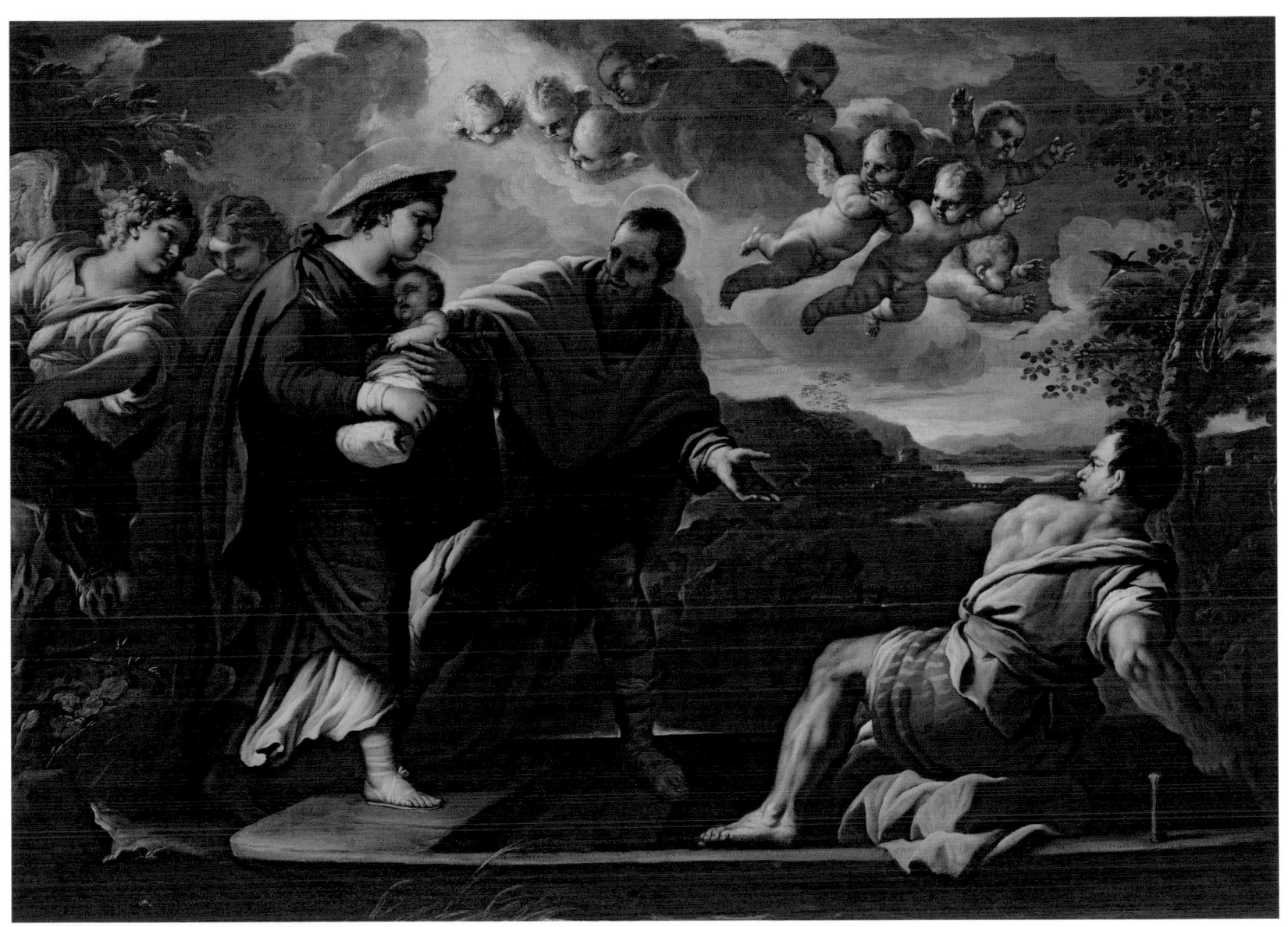

101 Luca Giordano, *Flight into Egypt*

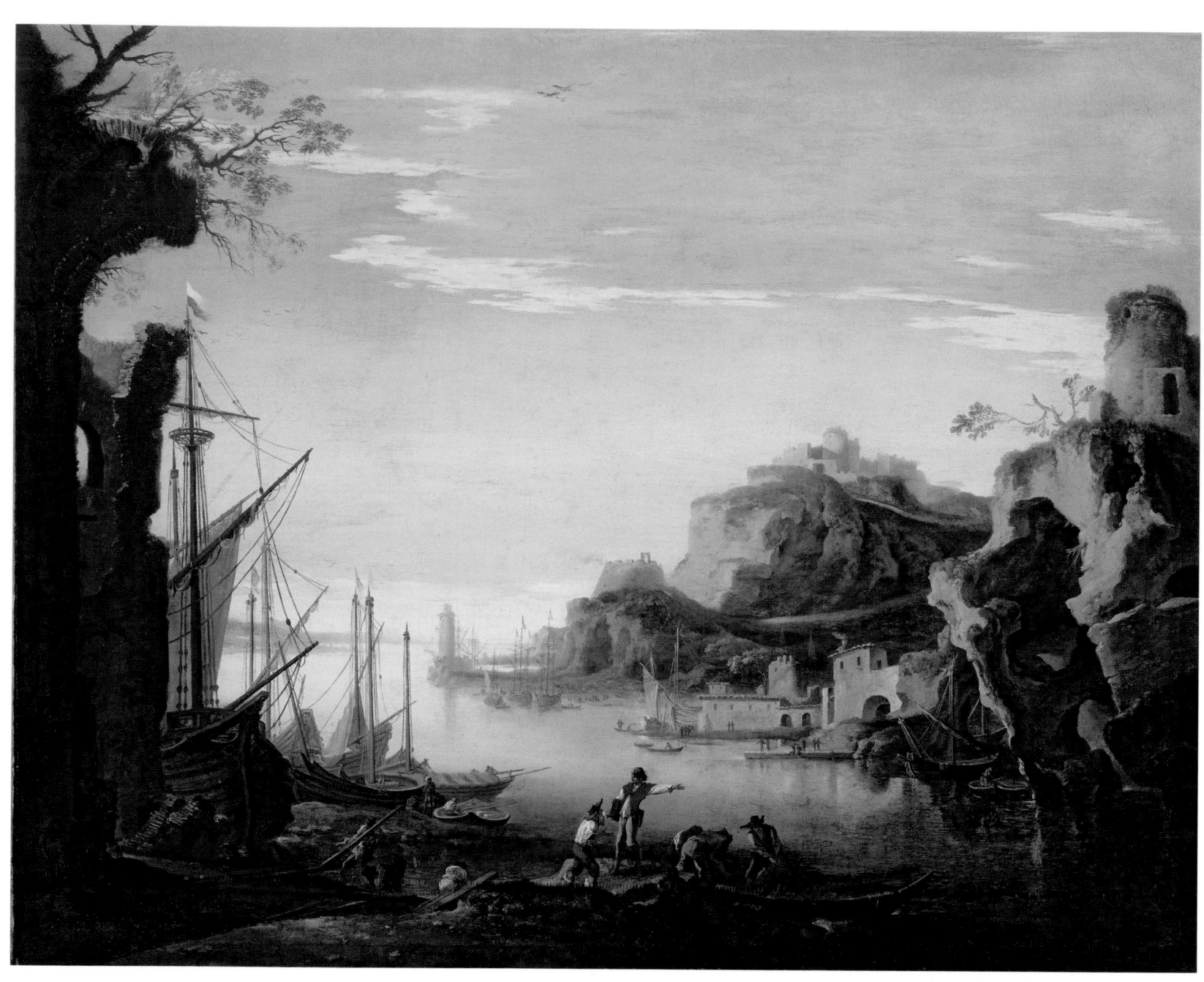

102 Salvator Rosa, *Harbour with Ruins*

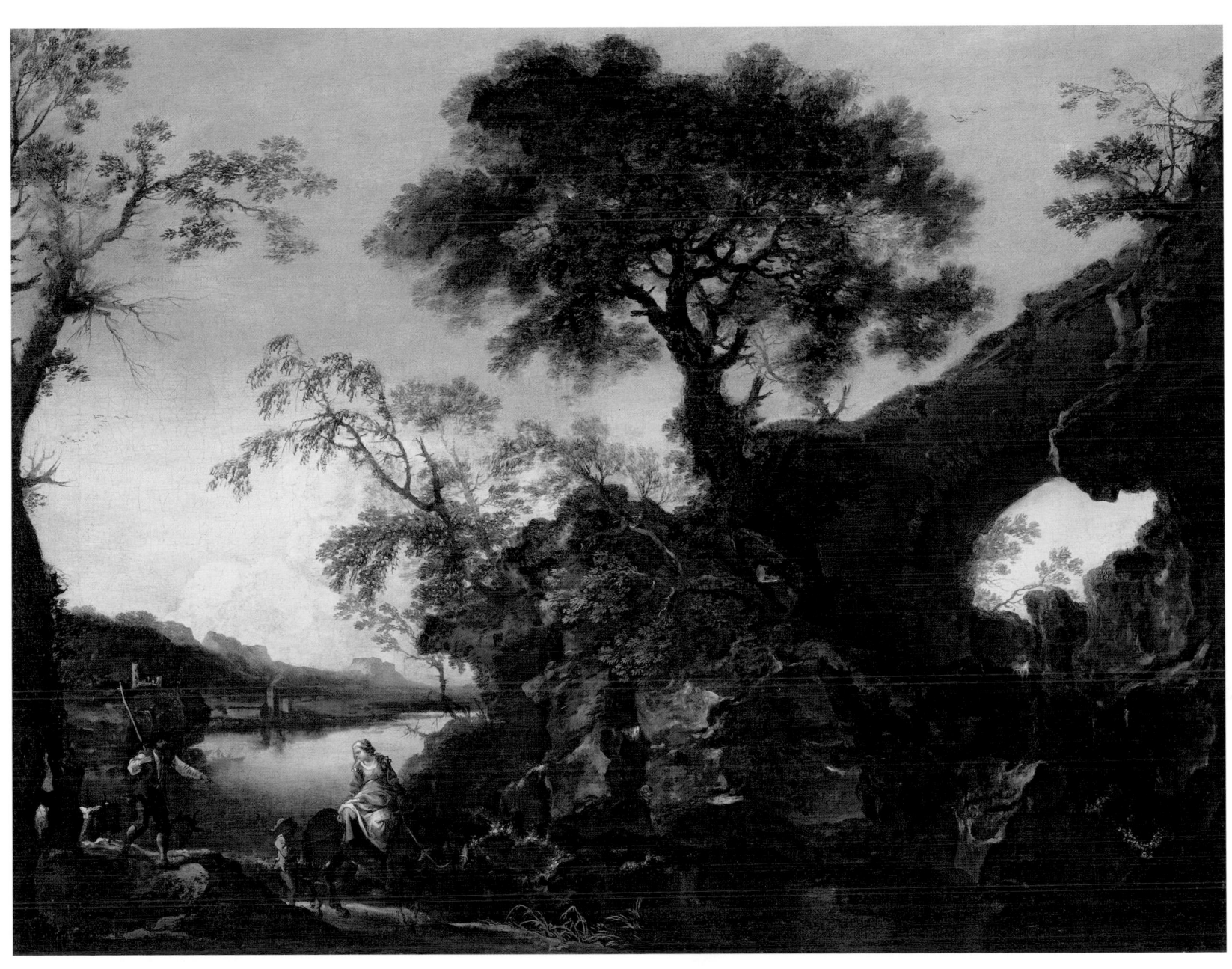

103   Salvator Rosa, *Rocky Landscape with Waterfall*

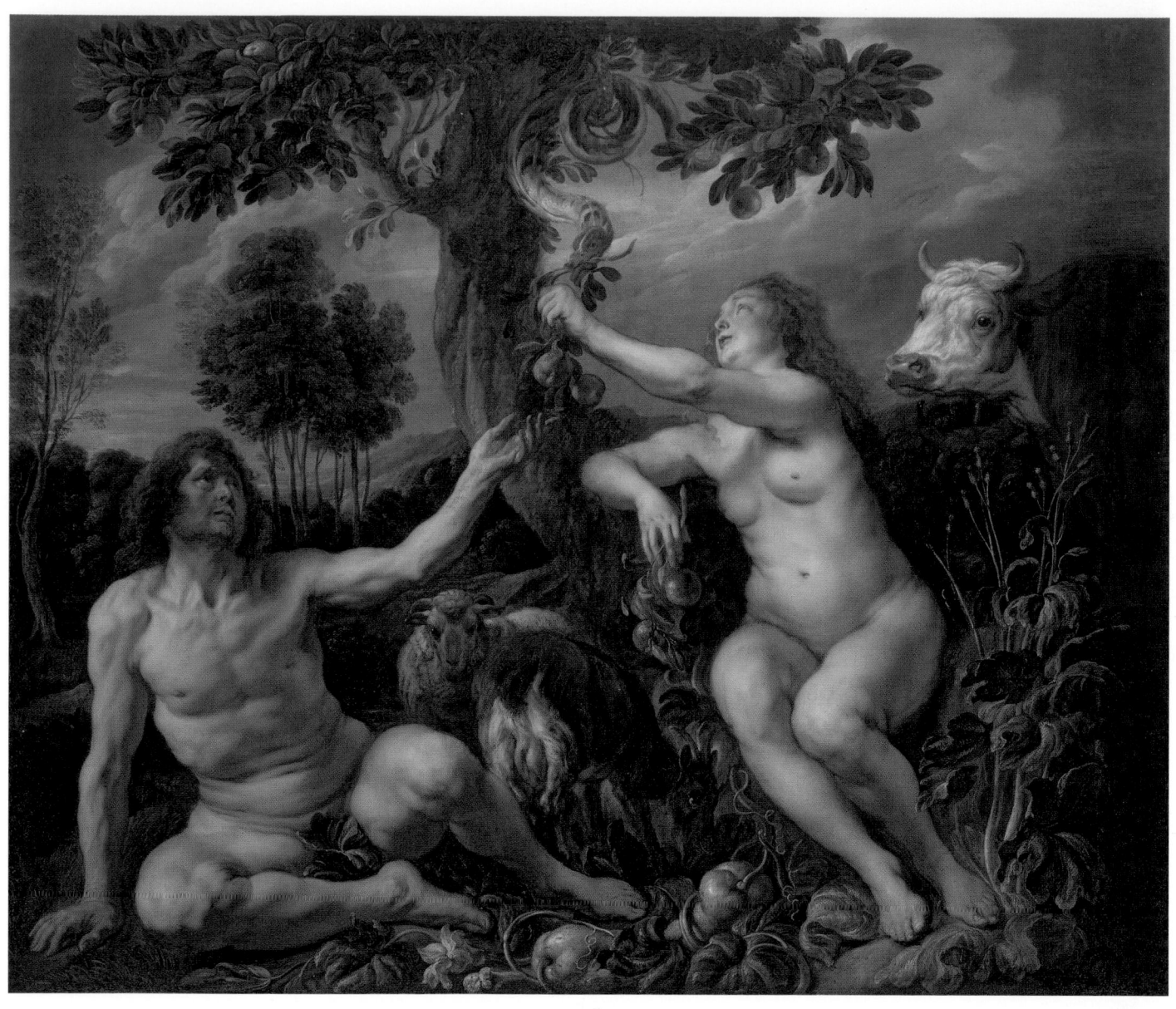

104 Jacob Jordaens, *Fall of Man*

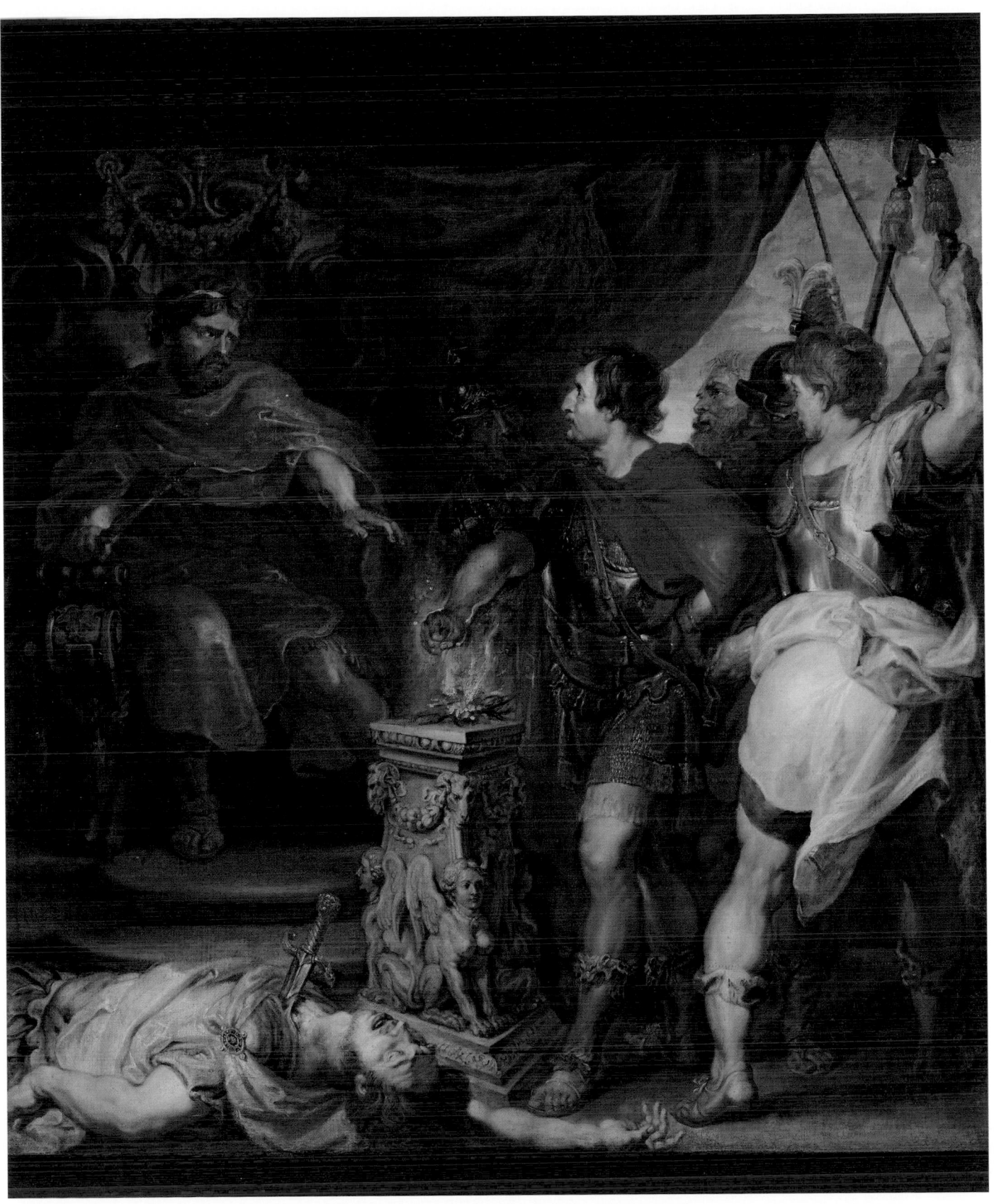

105 Peter Paul Rubens, possibly assisted by Anthony van Dyck, *Mucius Scaevola before Lars Porsena*

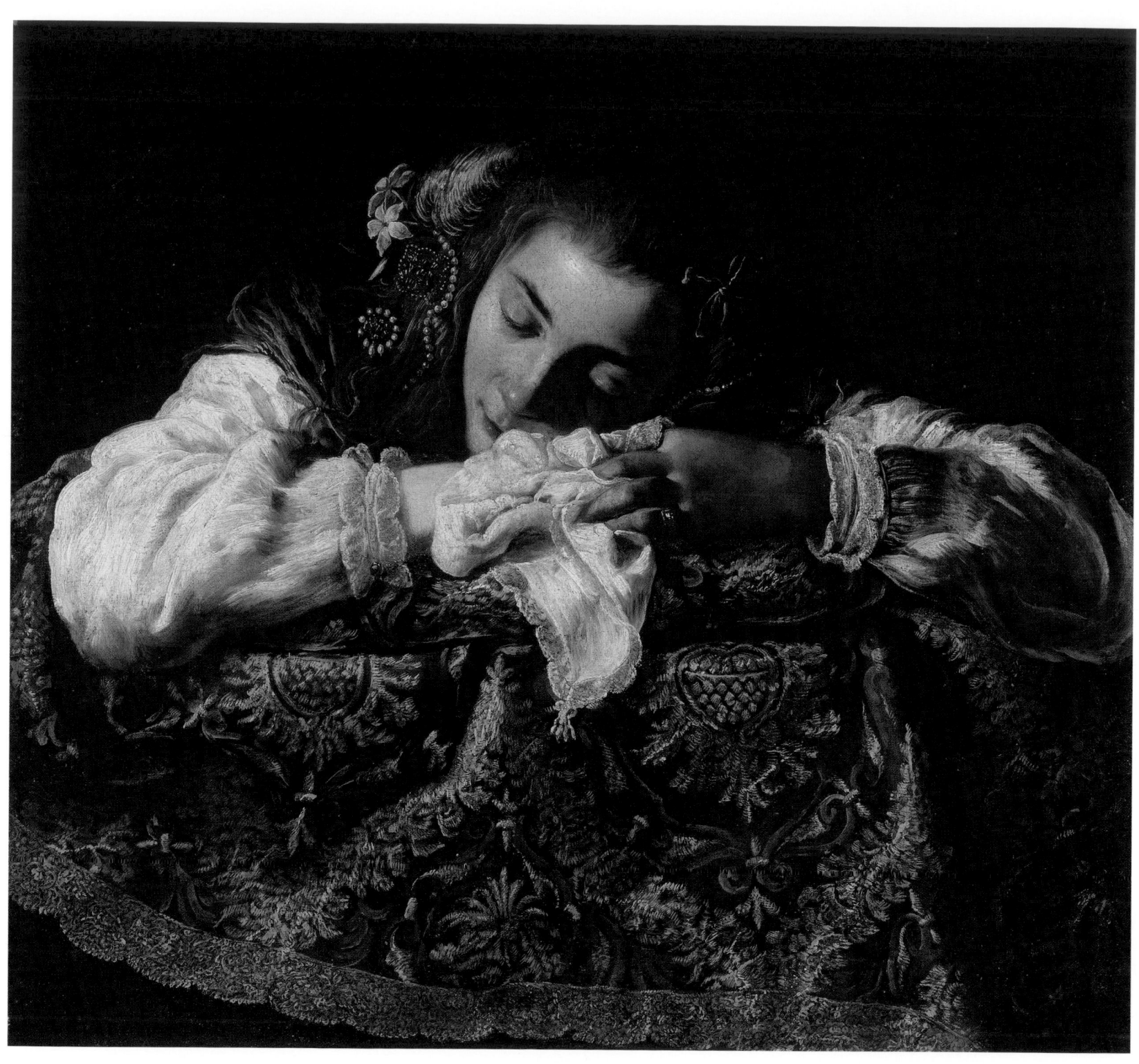

106   Unidentified painter active in Rome, first half of the seventeenth century, *Sleeping Girl*

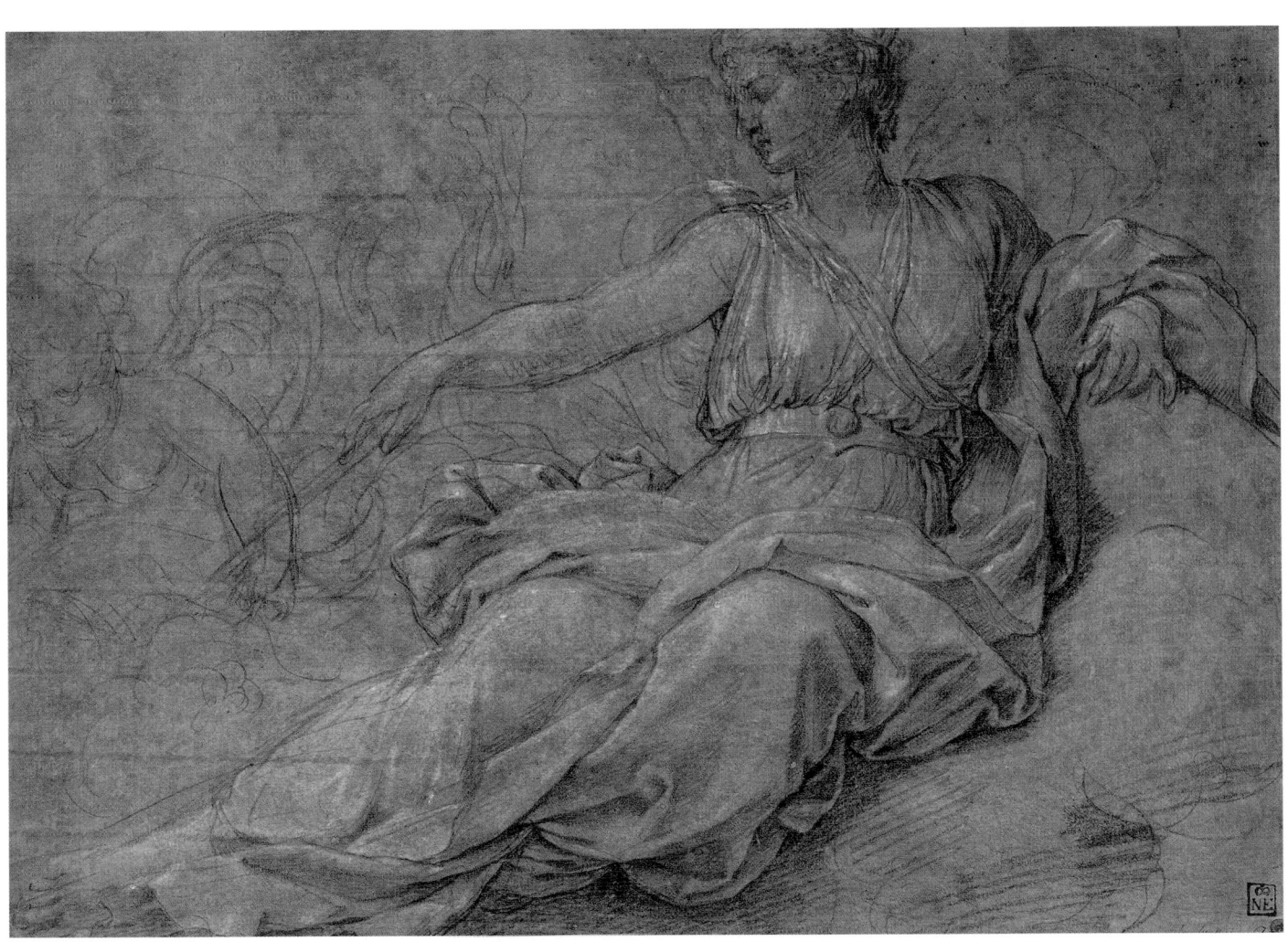

107   Eustache Le Sueur, *Study of Juno Distributing Riches to Carthage*

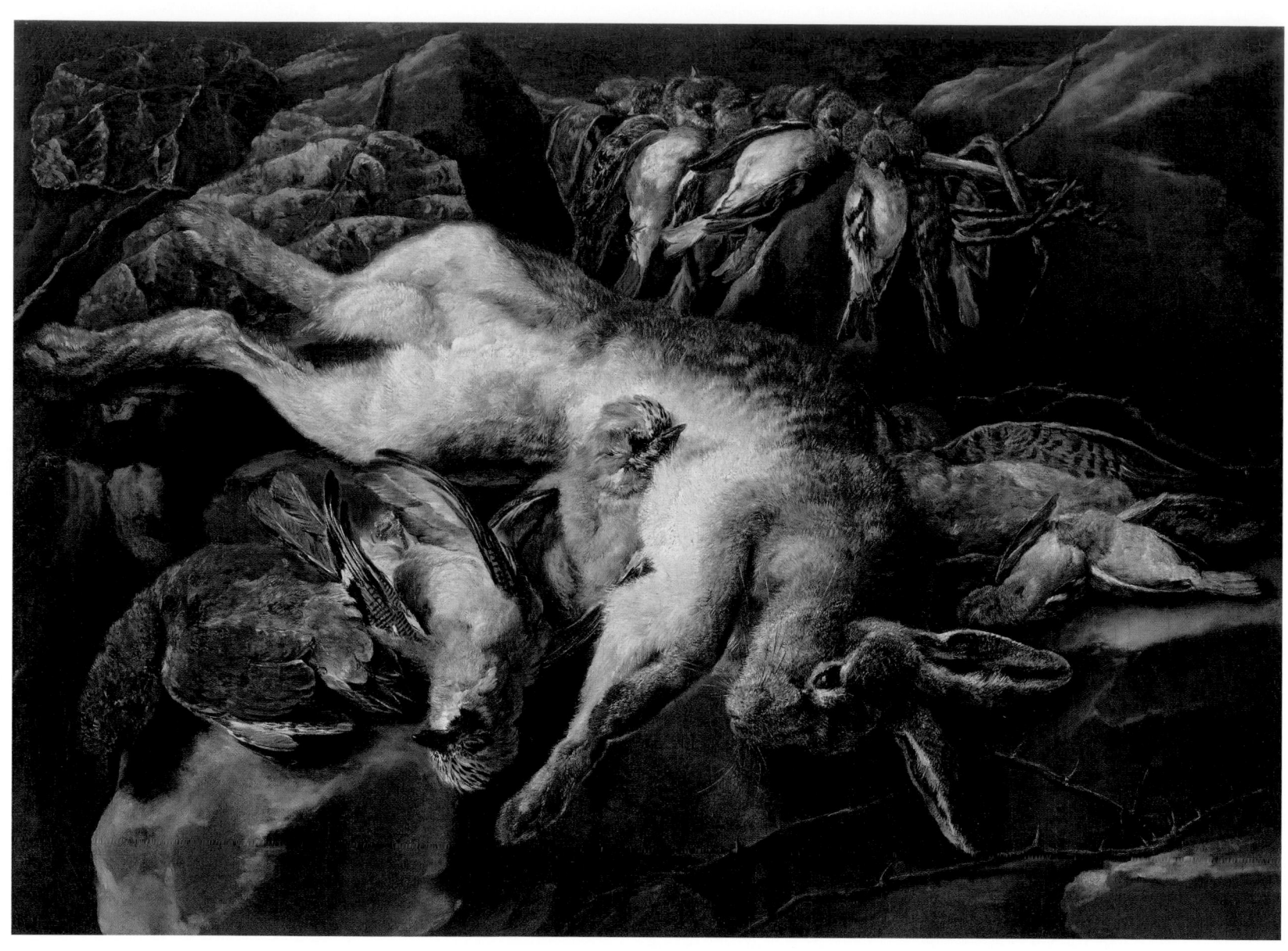

108 Jan Fyt, *Still-life with Dead Hare and Birds*

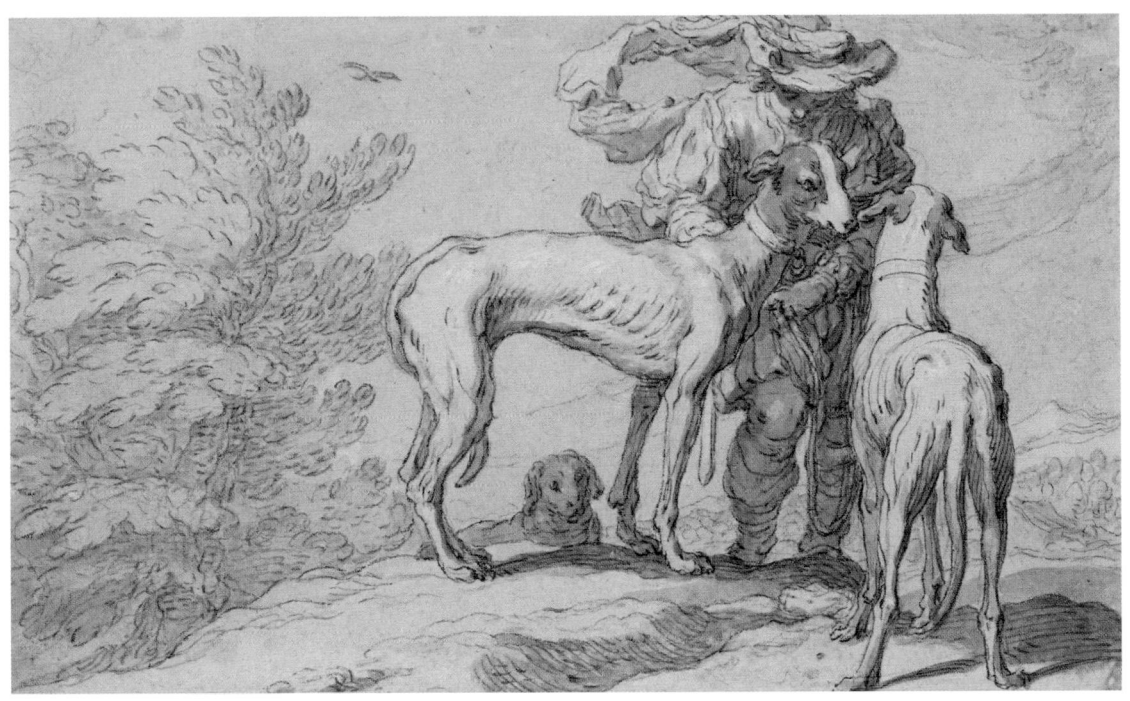

109   Abraham Bloemaert, *Huntsman with Dogs*

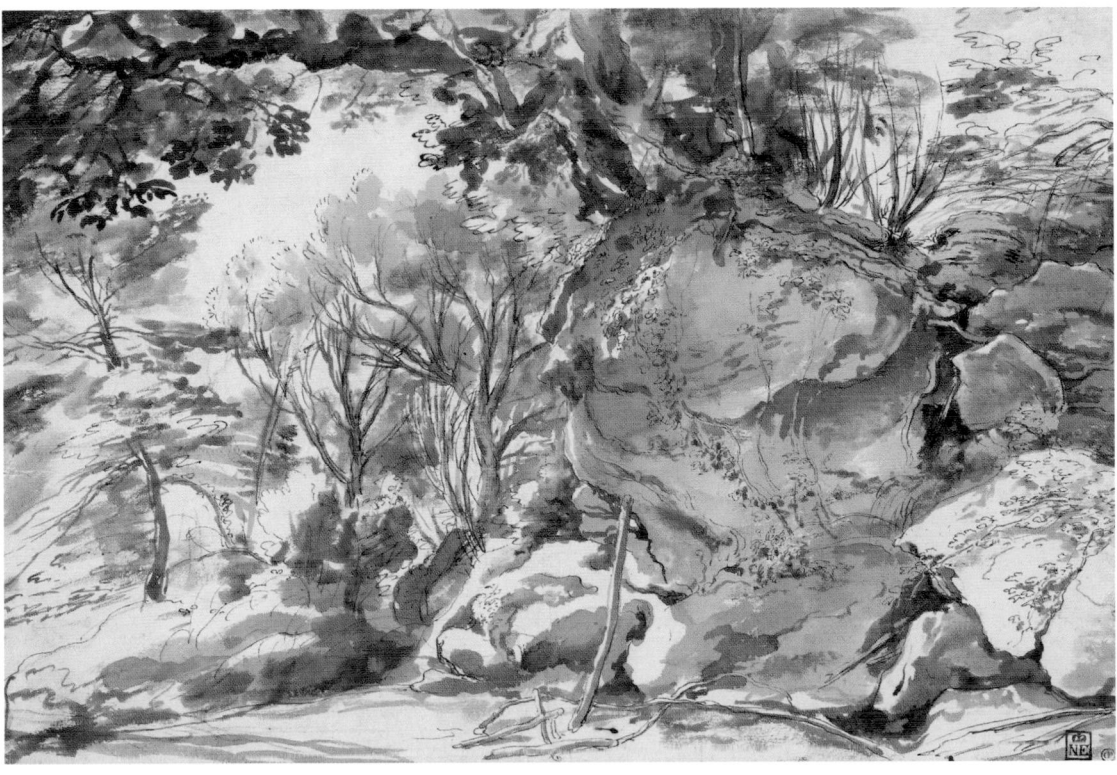

110   Herman van Swanevelt, *Rocks and Trees*

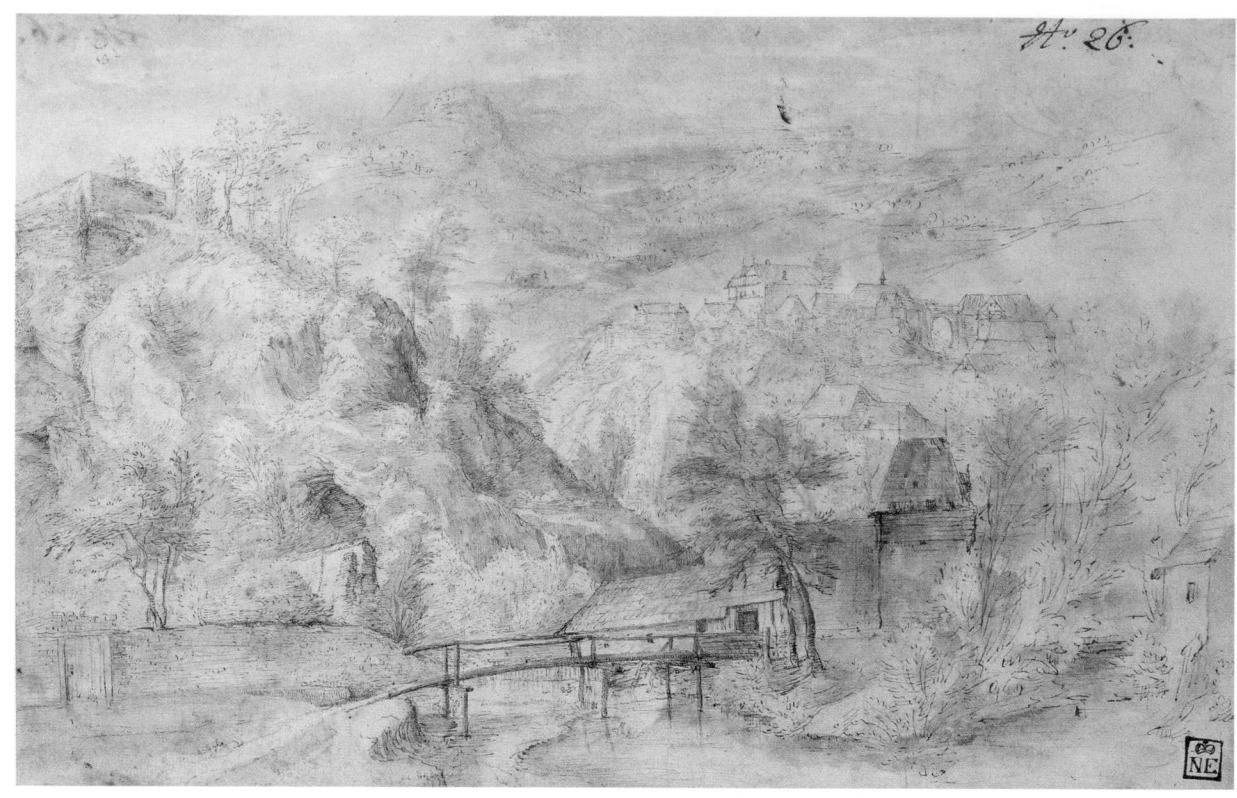

111   Paulus van Vianen, *River Landscape with Bridge*

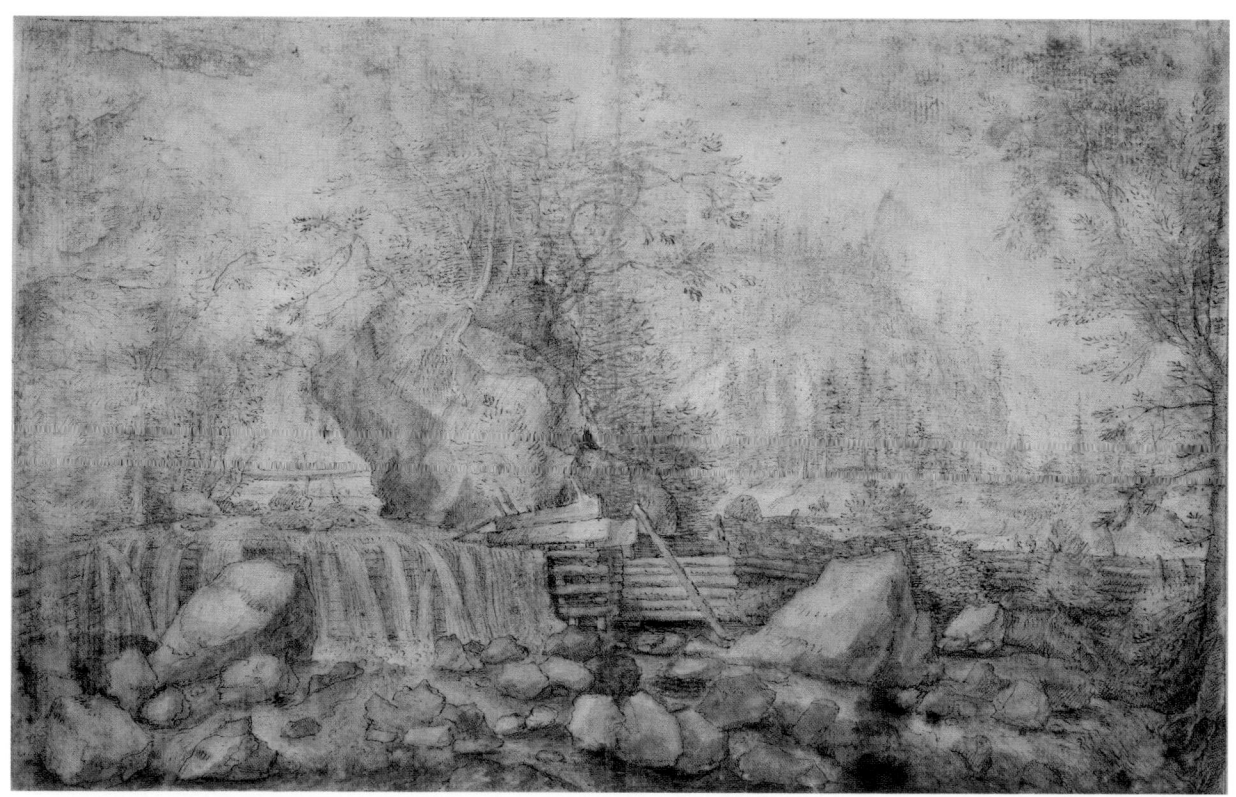

112   Pieter Stevens the Younger, *Landscape with a Weir*

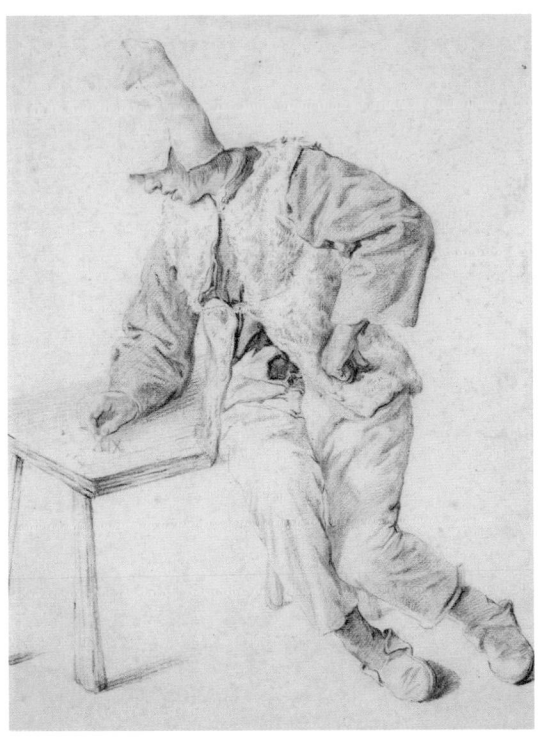

113   Cornelis Dusart, *Peasant Counting*

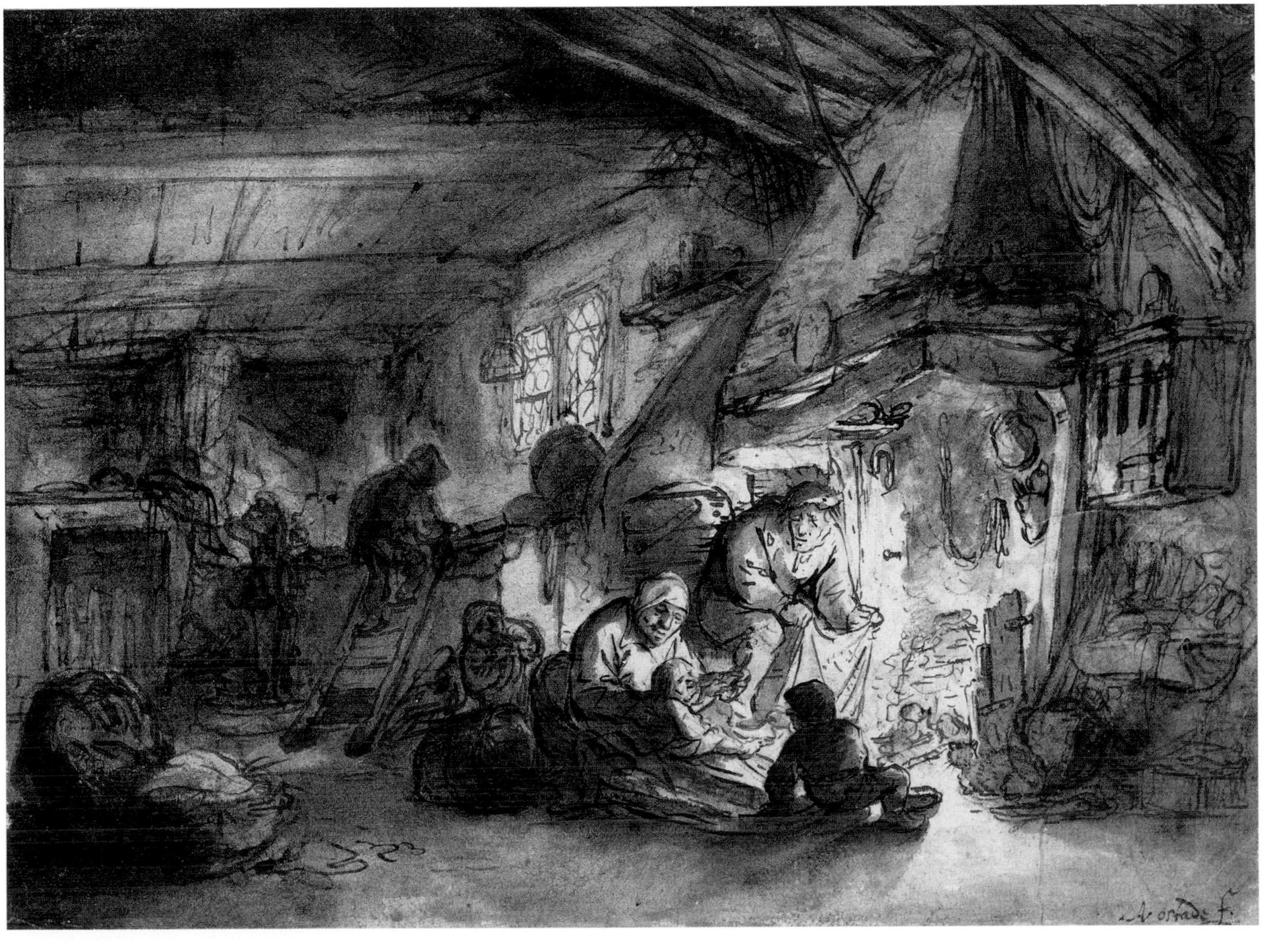

114   Adriaen van Ostade, *Family Group at the Fireplace*

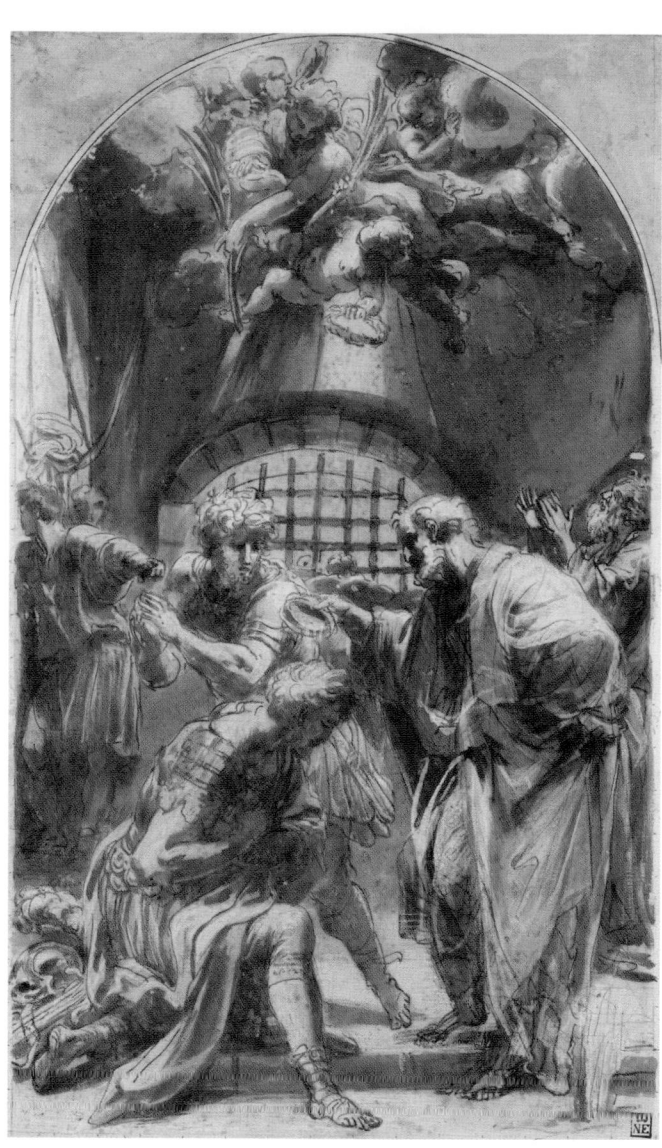

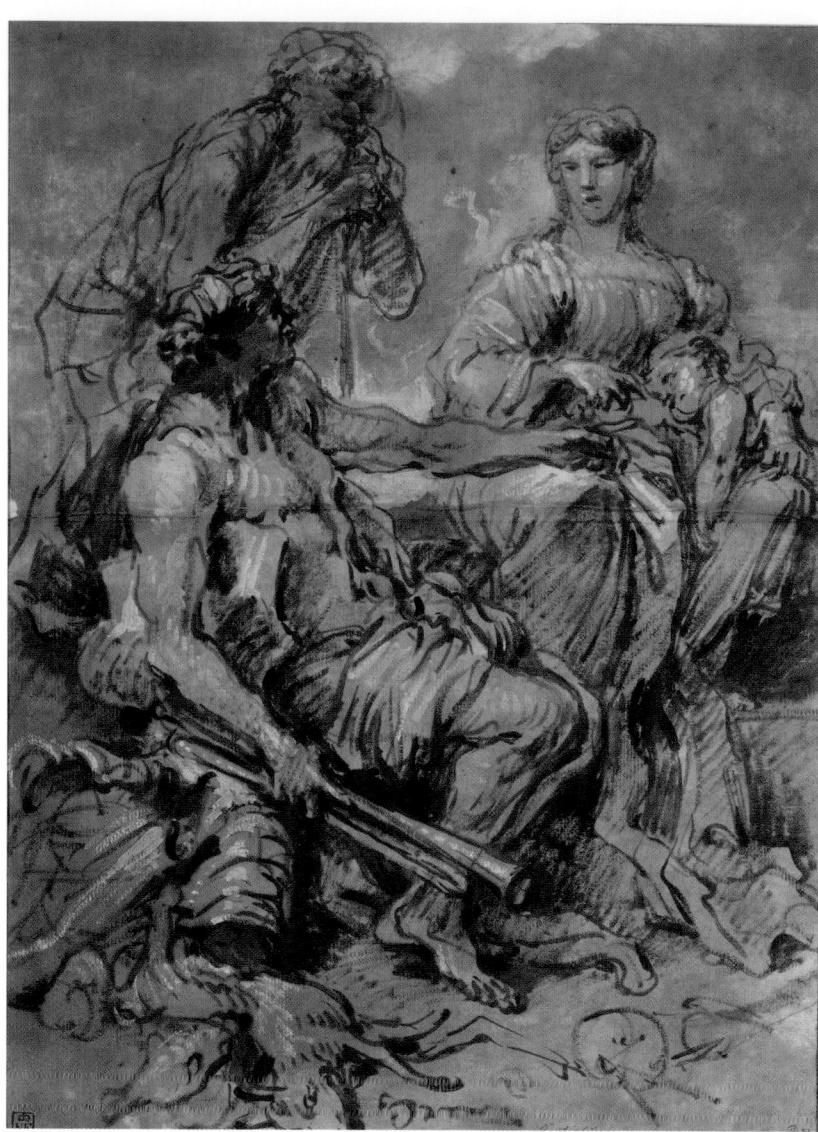

115   Carlo Maratta, *St Peter Baptises SS. Processus and Martinian in the Mamertine Prison*

116   Giovanni Benedetto Castiglione, *Allegory in Honour of the Ruling Couple of Mantua*

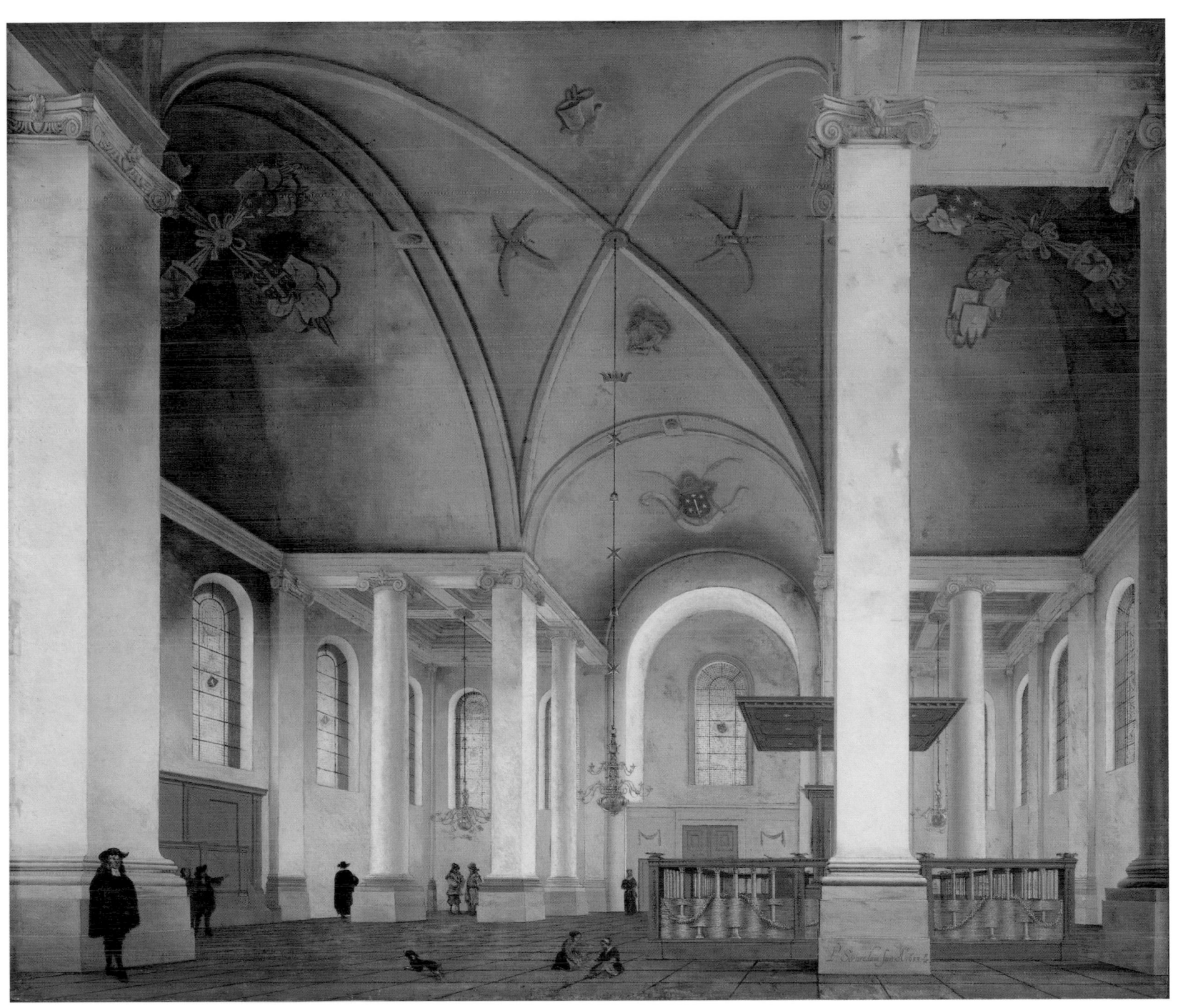

117 Pieter Jansz. Saenredam, *Interior of the Nieuwe Kerk at Haarlem*

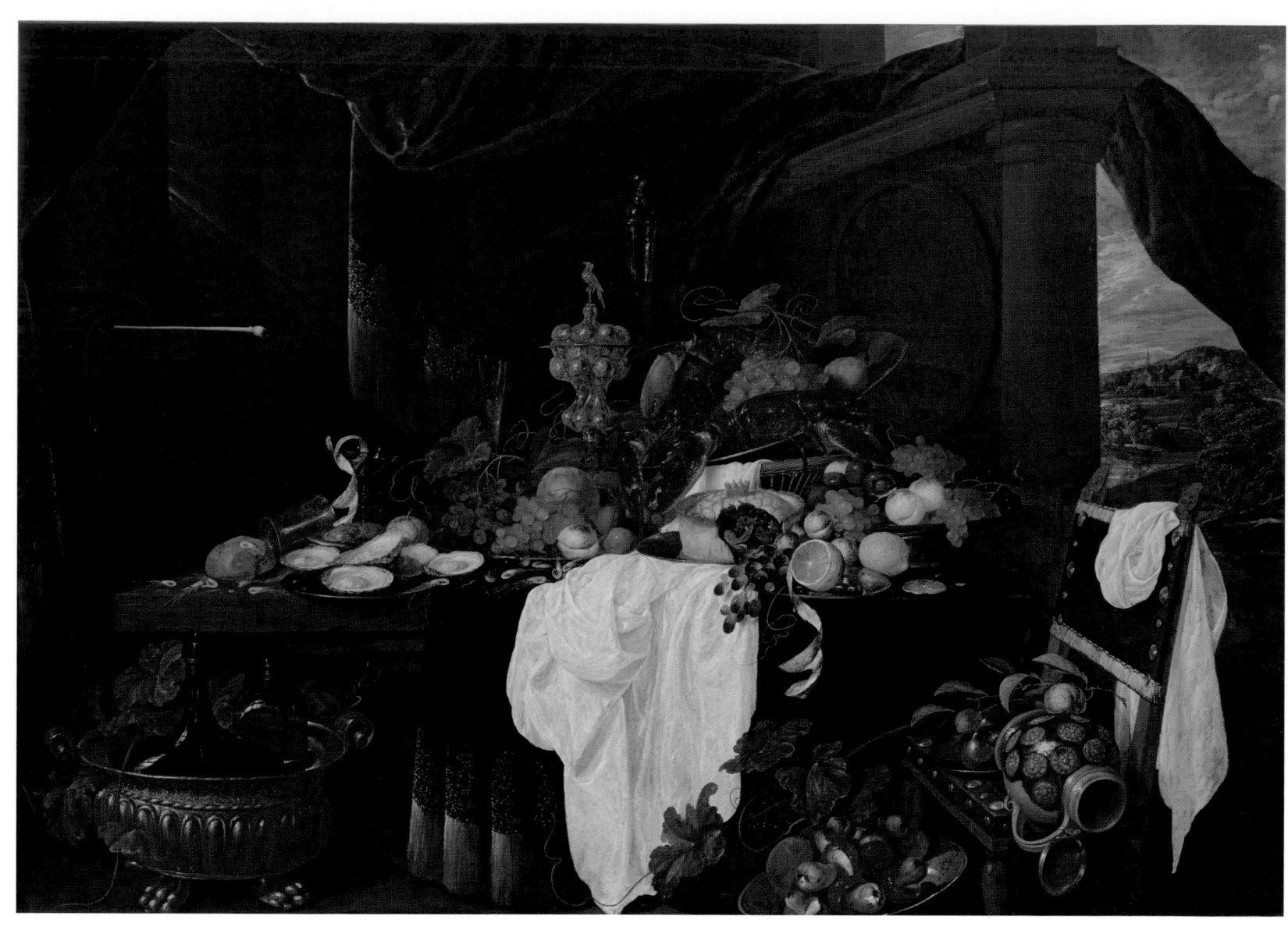

118   Andries Benedetti, *Still-life with Fruit, Oysters and Lobsters*

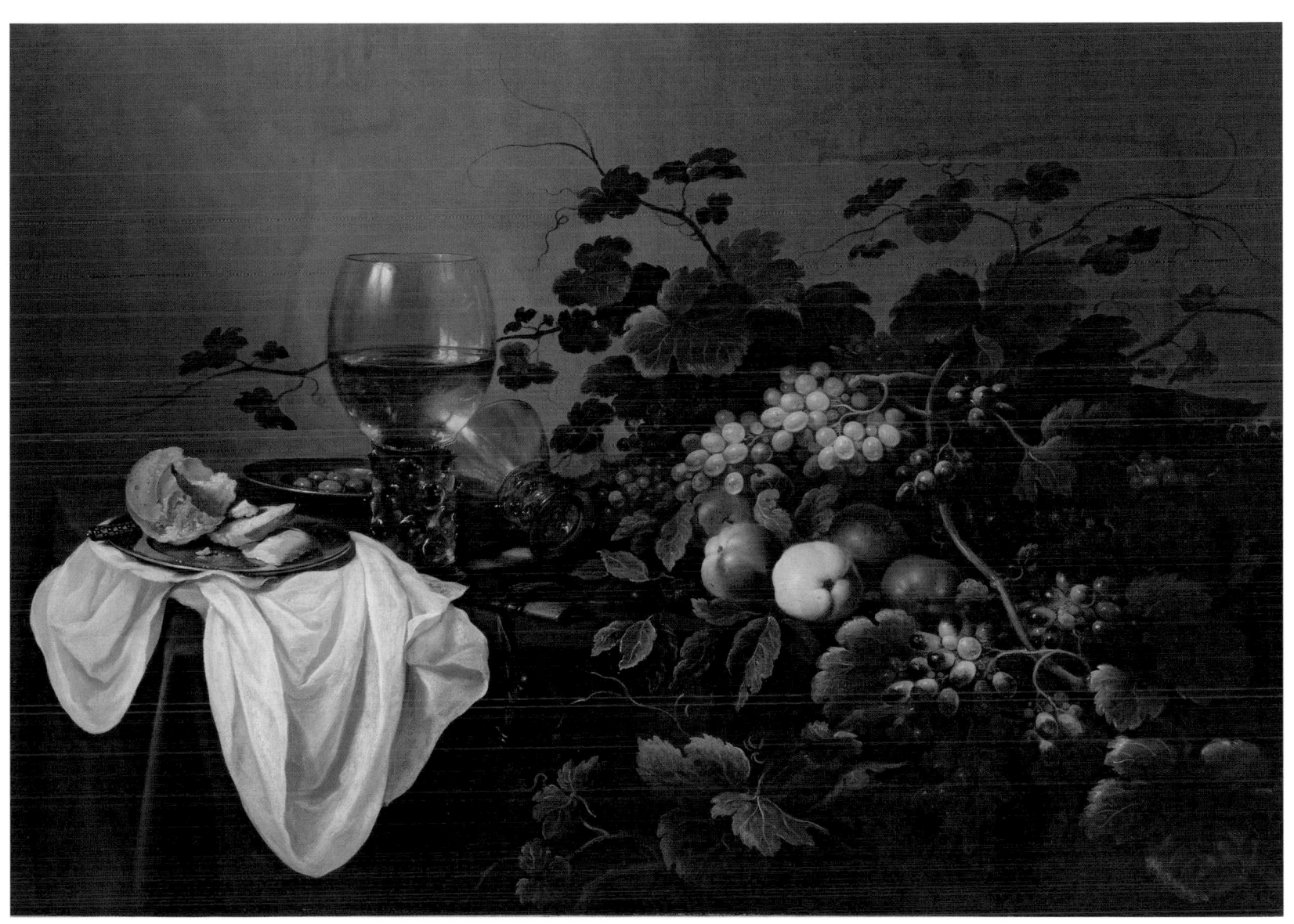

119   Pieter Claesz. and Roelof Koets, *Still-life with a Large Rummer and Fruit*

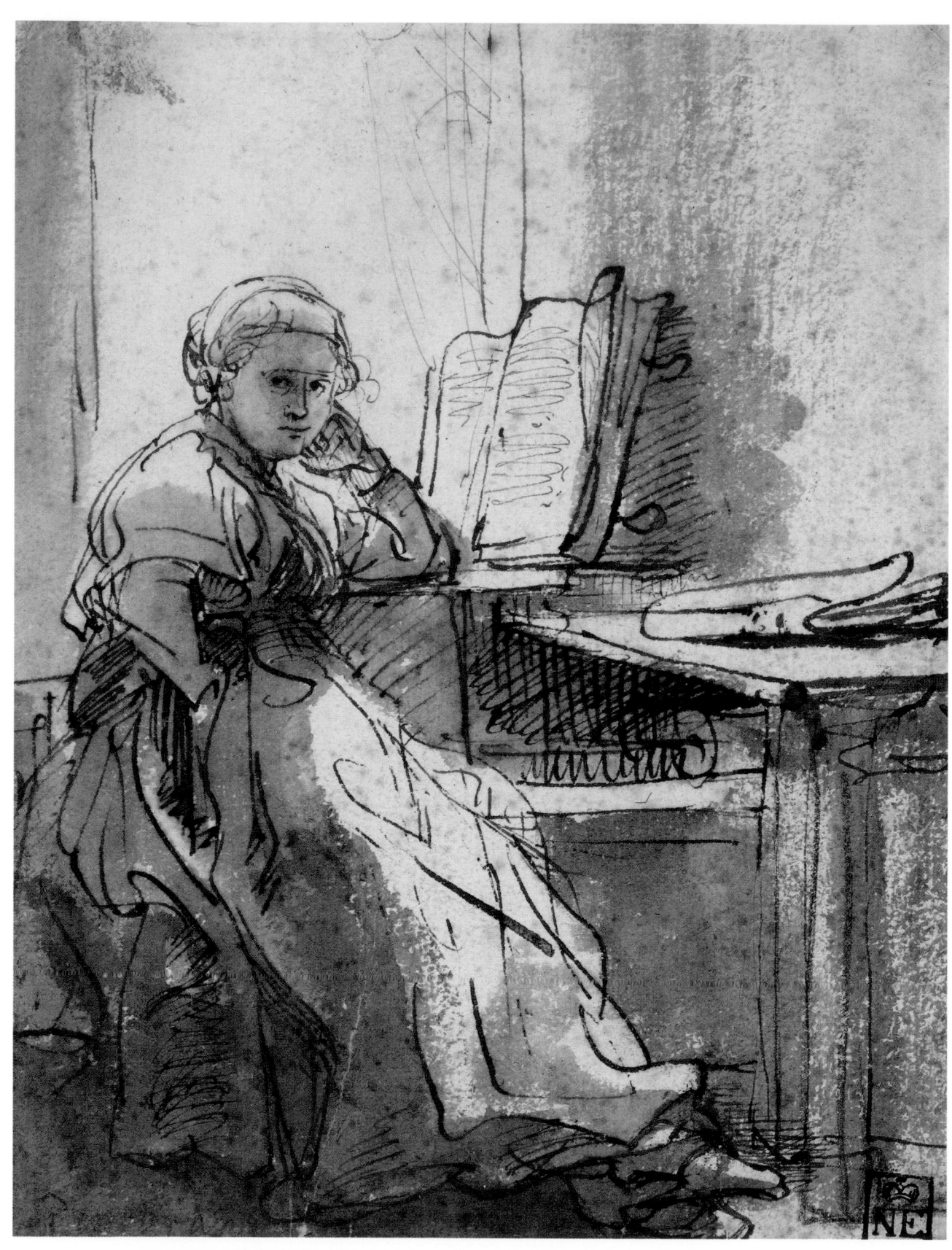

120   Rembrandt Harmensz. van Rijn, *Saskia van Uylenburgh Sitting by a Window*

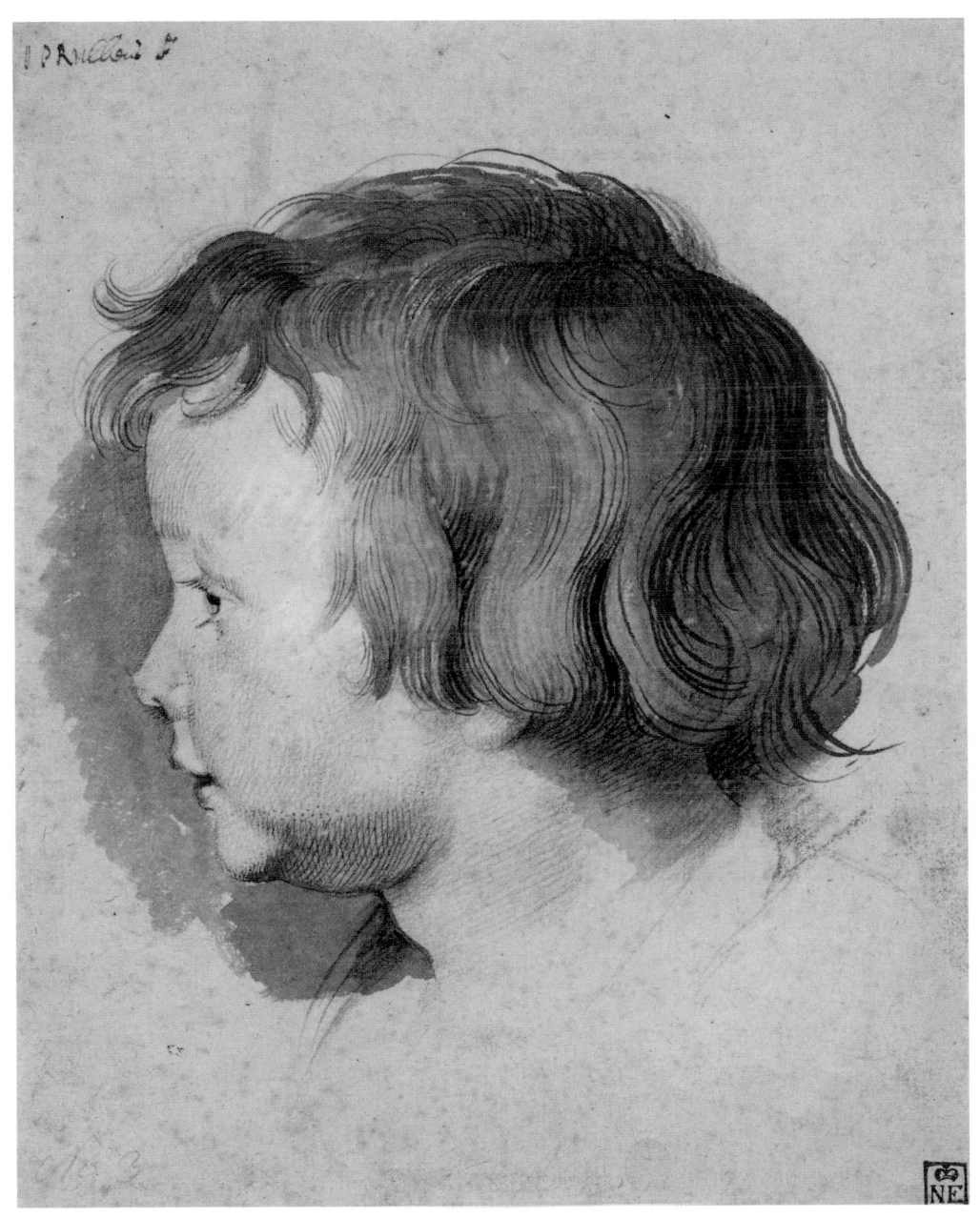

121   Peter Paul Rubens, *Portrait of Albert Rubens, Son of the Artist, in Profile*

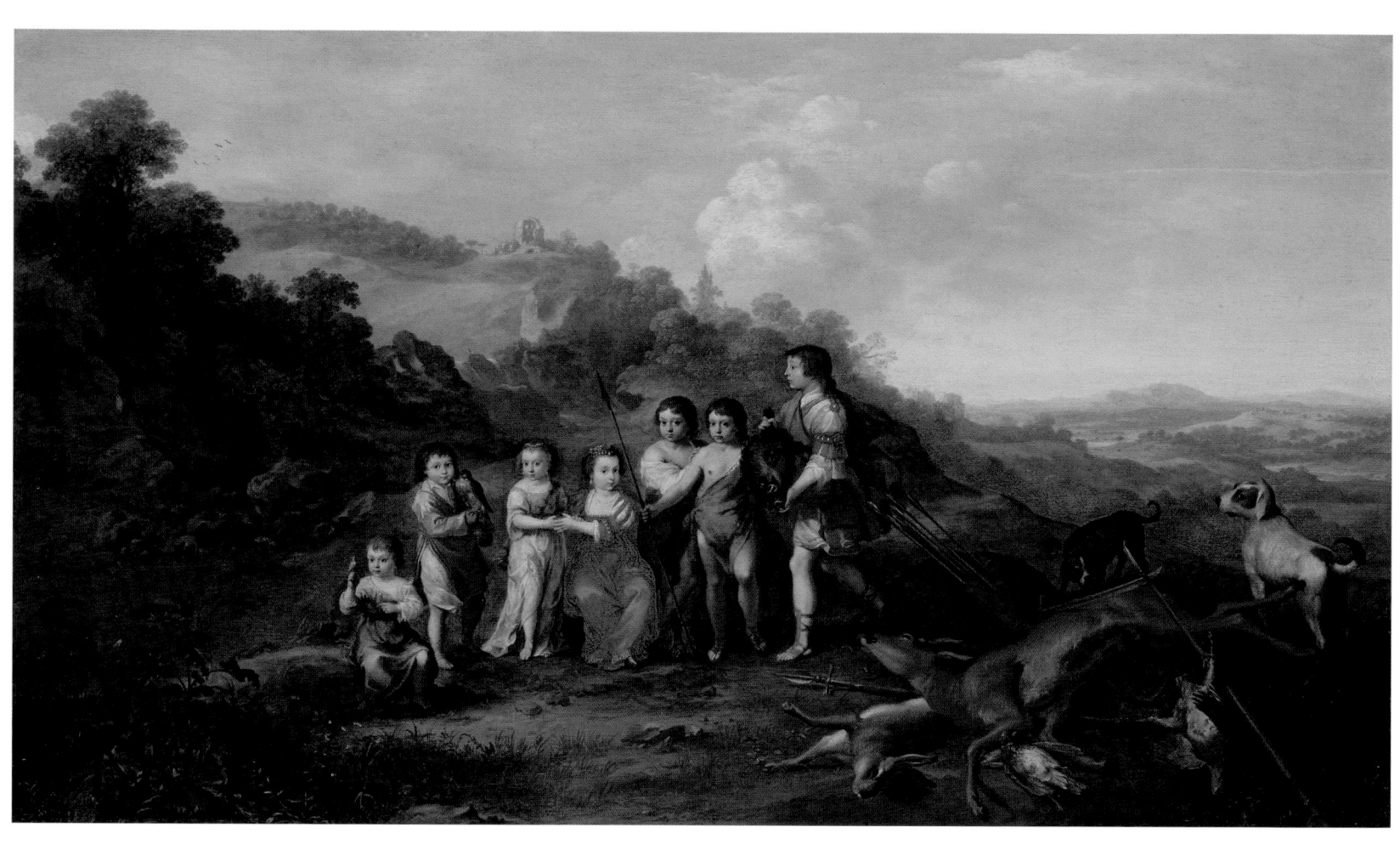

122　Cornelis van Poelenburgh, *Children of the Elector Palatine Frederick V, King of Bohemia*

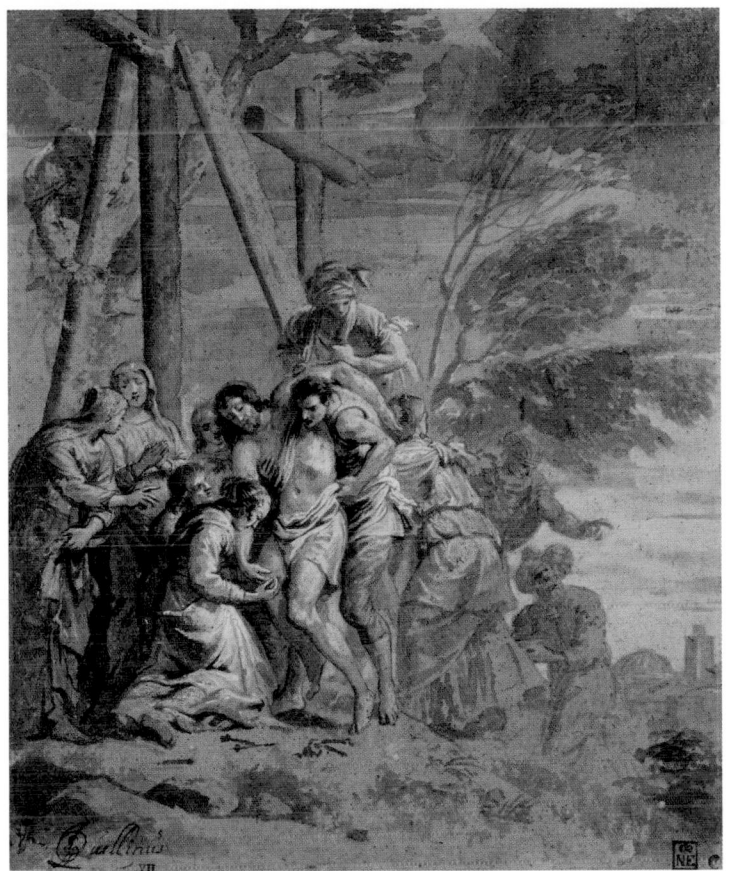

123   Jan-Erasmus Quellinus, *Lamentation at the Foot of the Cross*

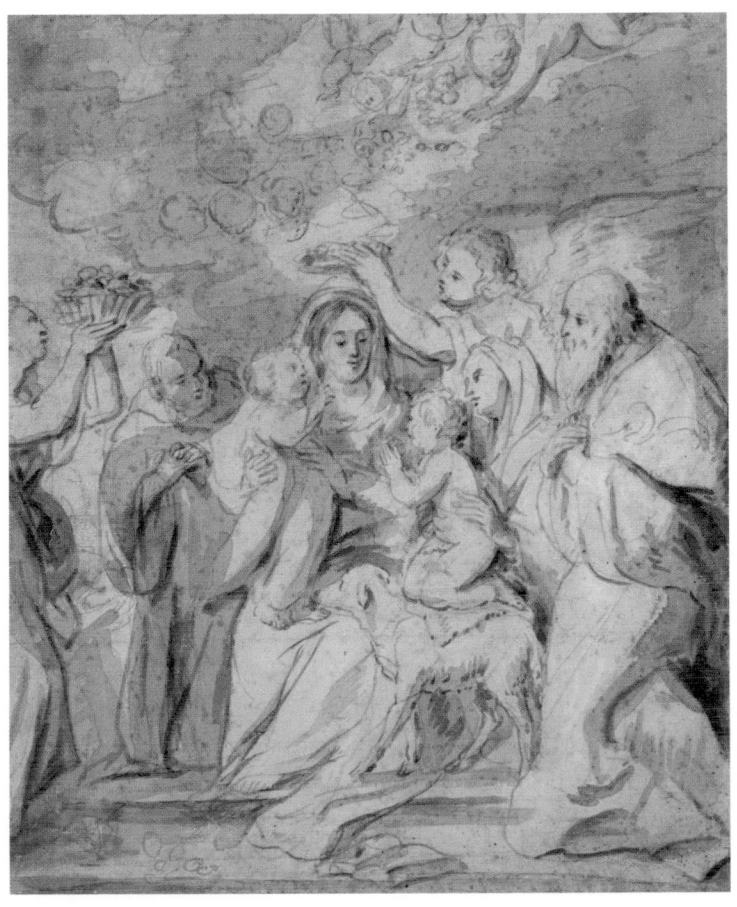

124   Jacob Jordaens, *Holy Family with St John the Baptist, His Parents and Angels*

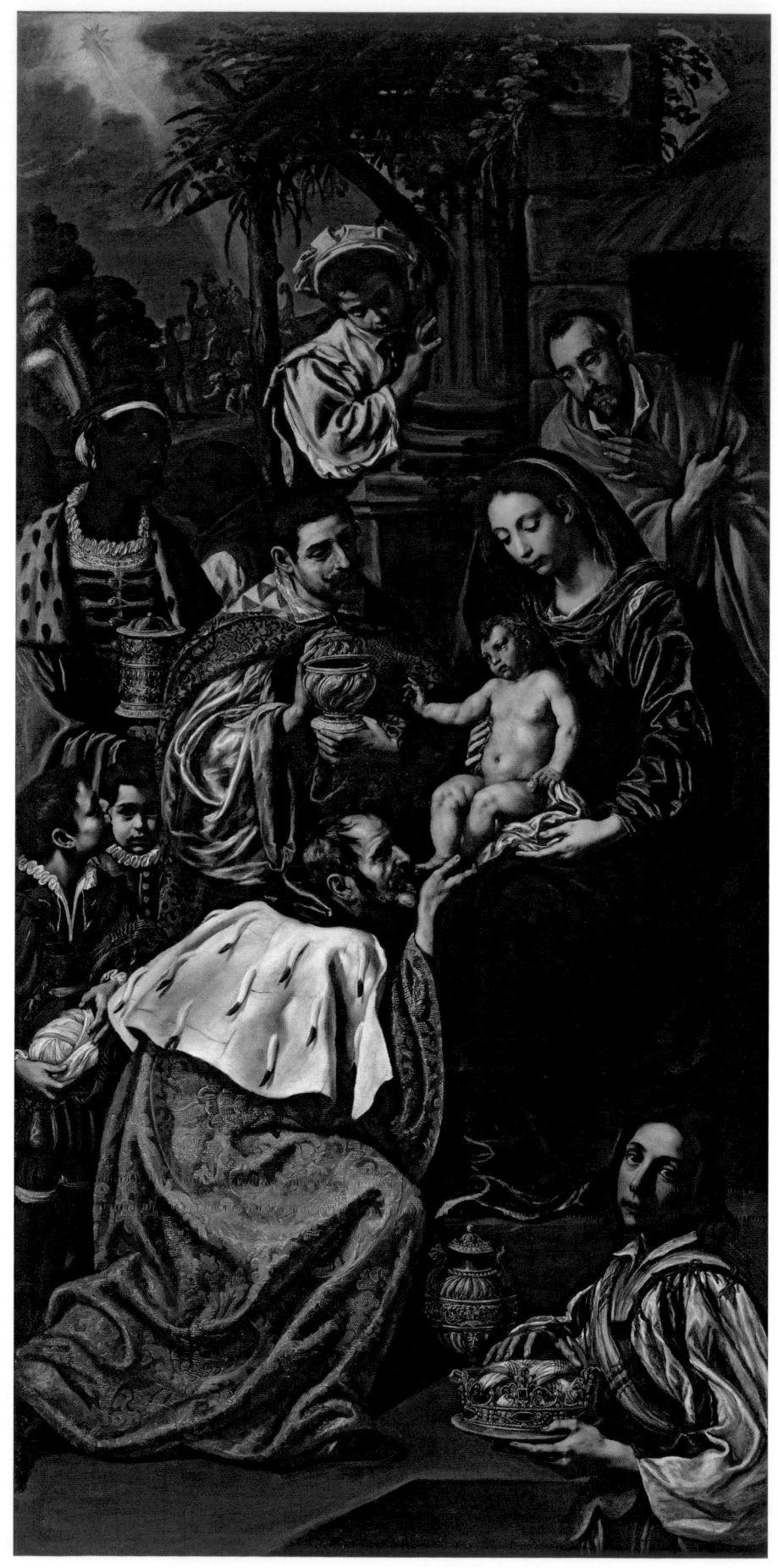

125   Luis Tristán de Escamilla, *Adoration of the Magi*

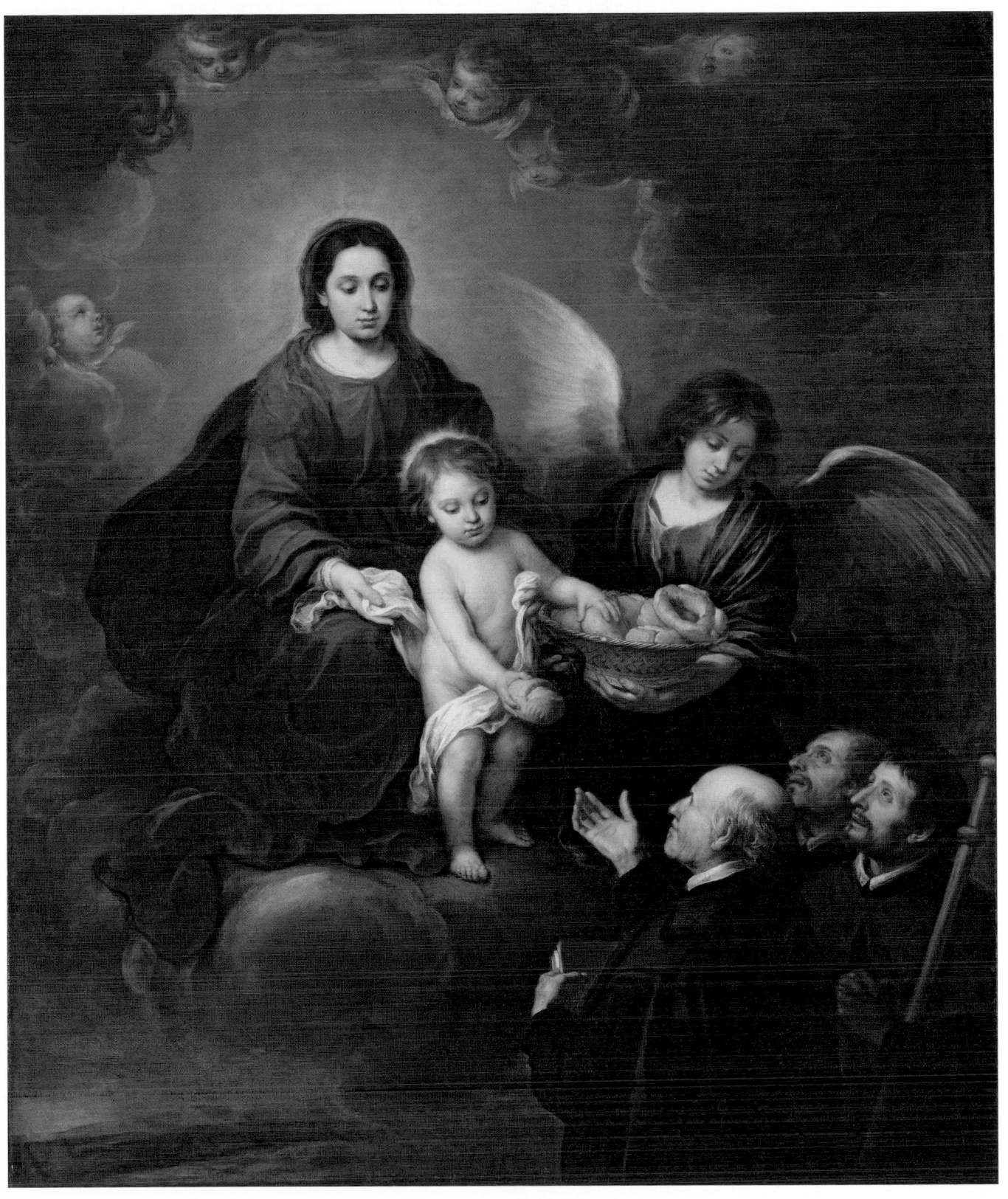

126   Bartolomé Esteban Murillo, *Virgin with the Infant Christ Distributing Bread to Pilgrims*

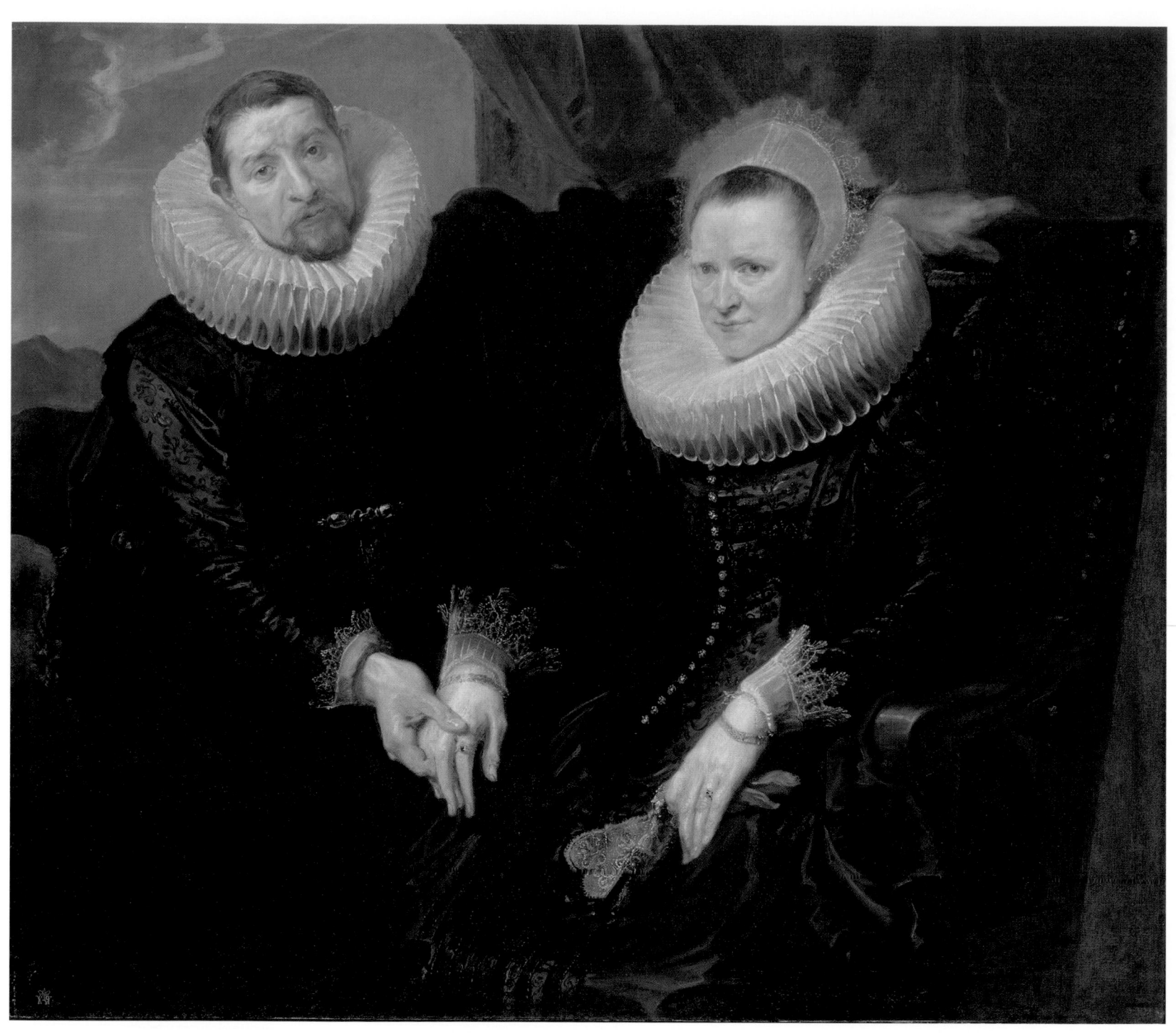

127   Anthony van Dyck, *Married Couple*

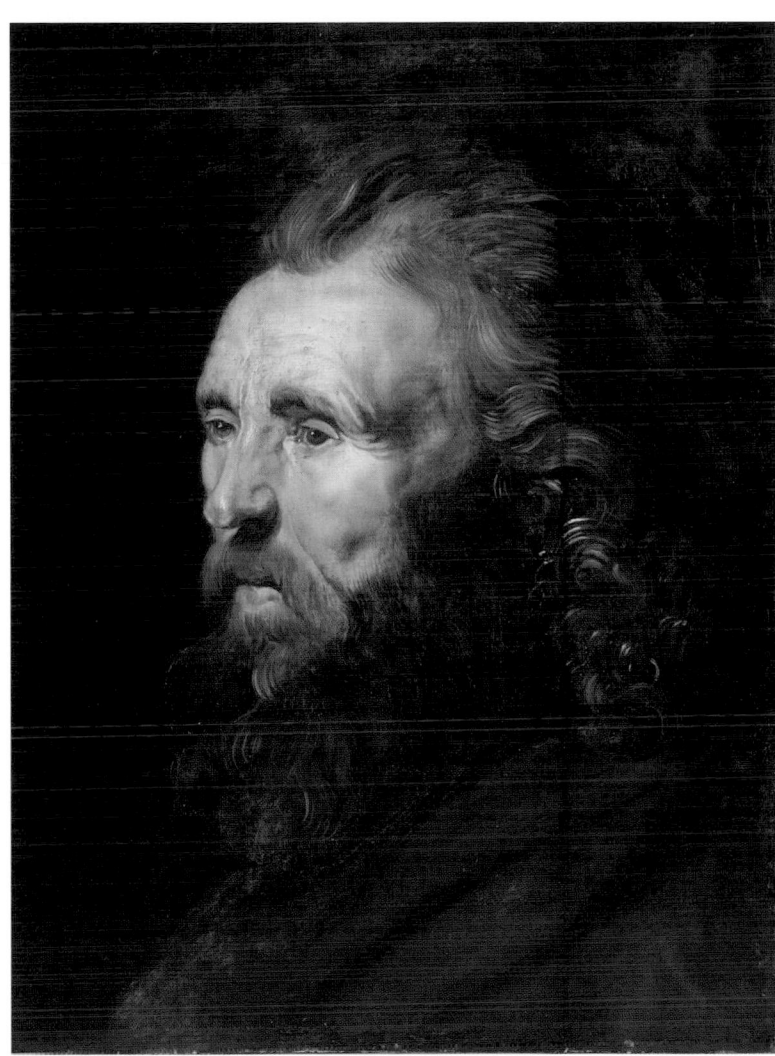

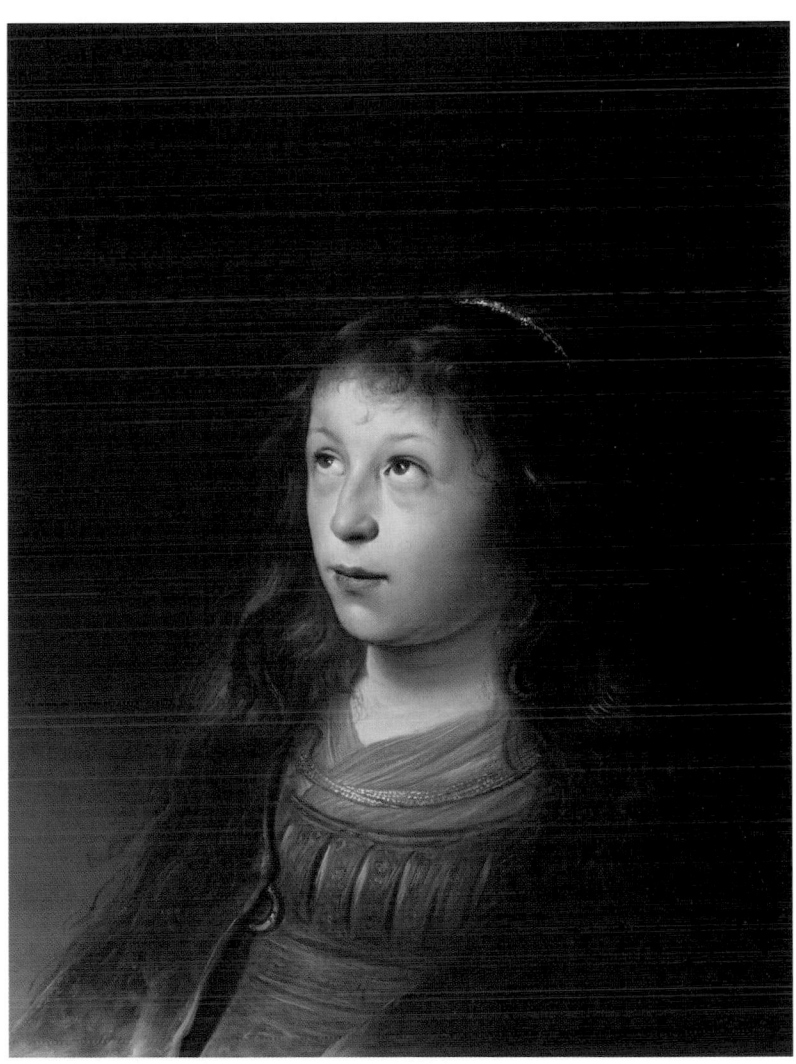

128   Peter Paul Rubens, *Head of a Bearded Man*

129   Jan Lievens, *Half-length of a Girl*

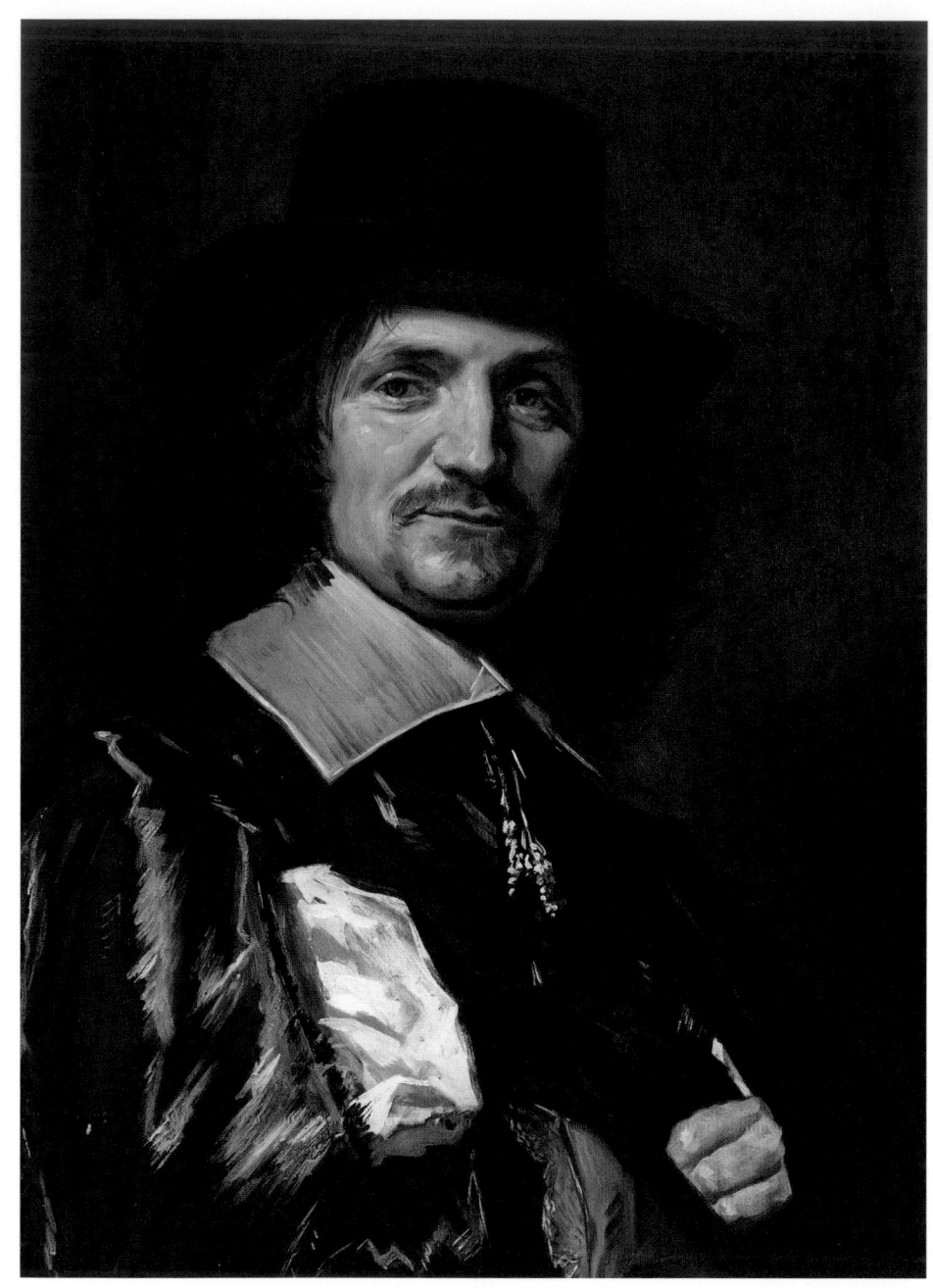

130   Frans Hals, *Portrait of a Man*

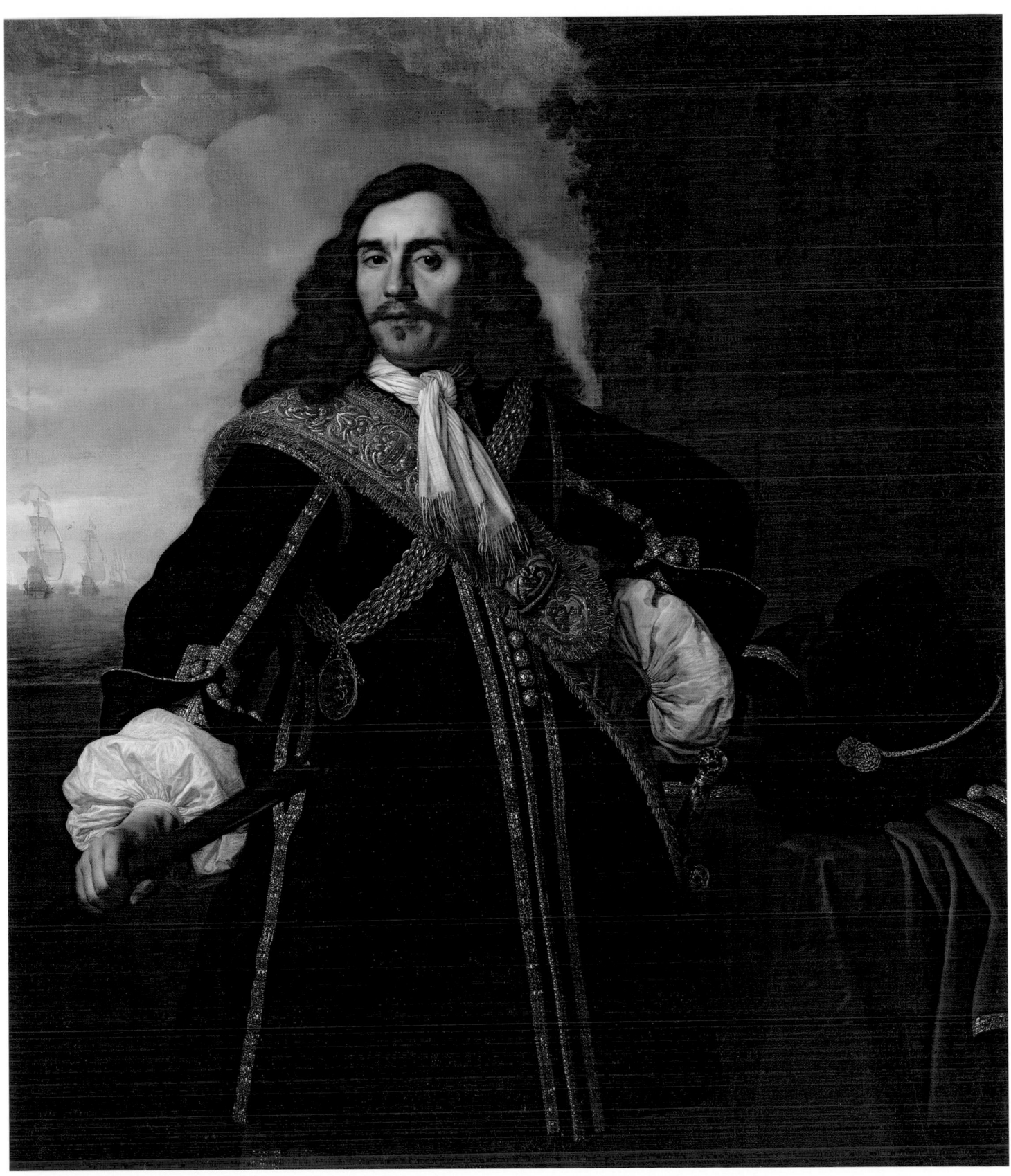

131   Bartholomeus van der Helst, *Portrait of Gideon de Wildt*

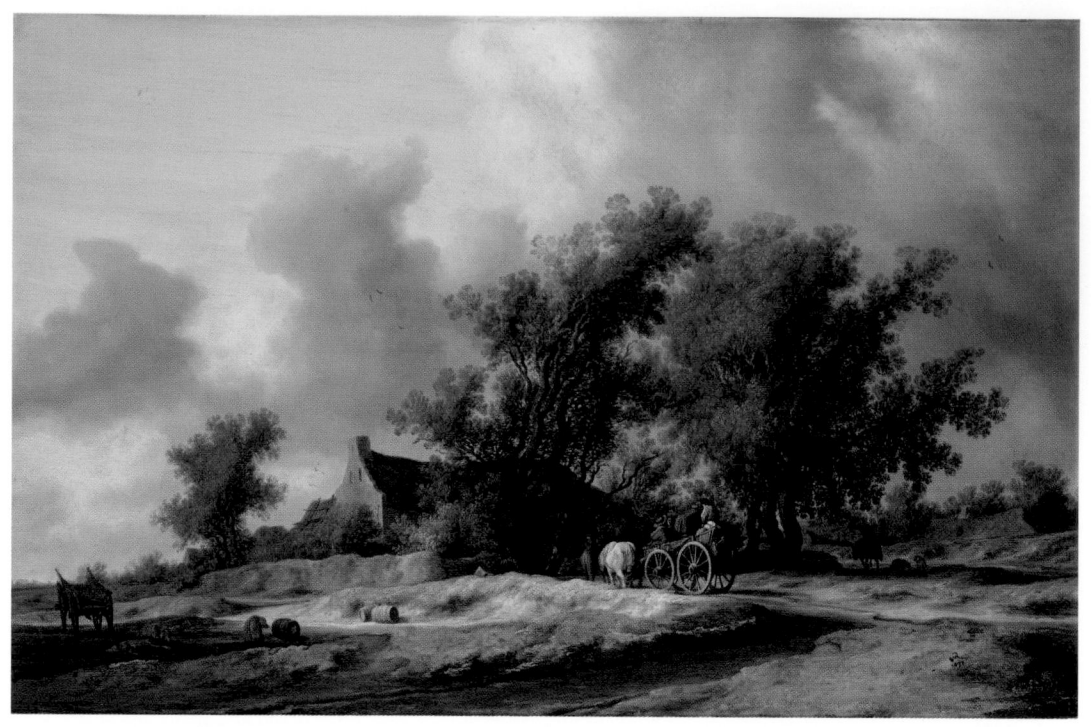

132   Salomon van Ruysdael, *Road among the Dunes with a Wagon ('After the Rain')*

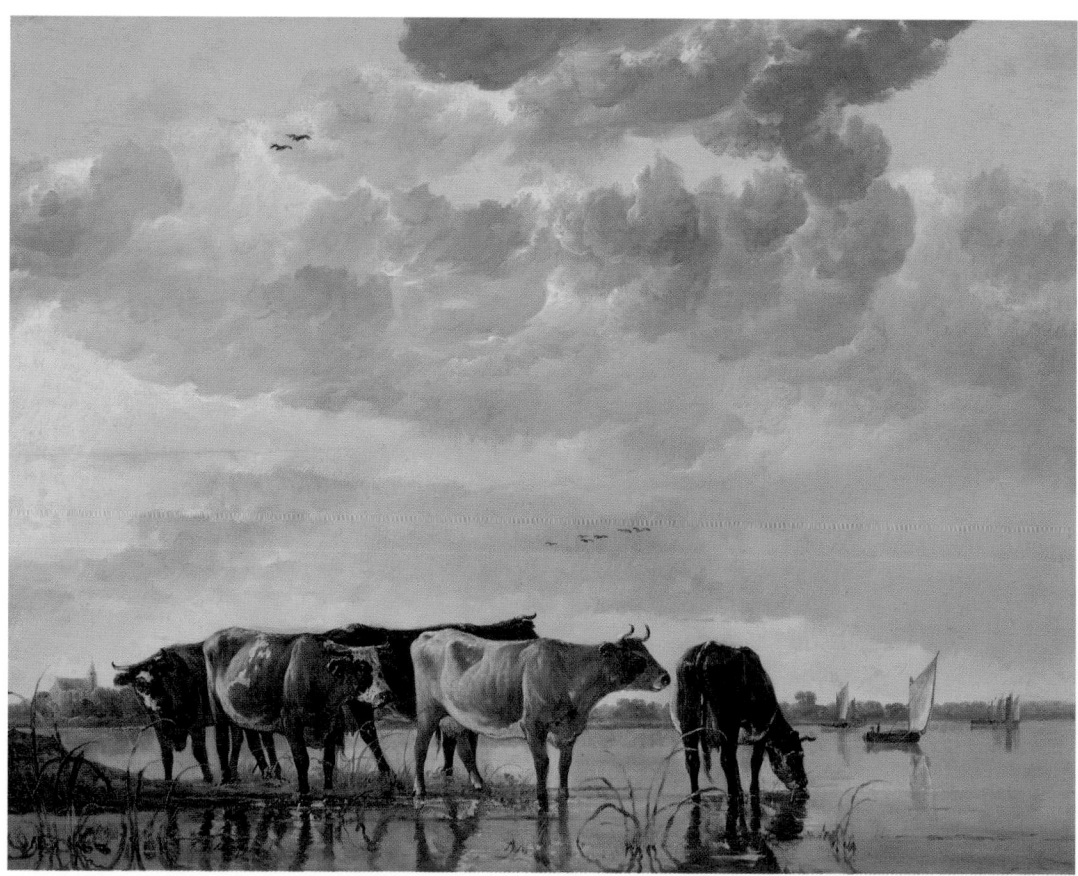

133   Aelbert Cuyp, *Cows in a River*

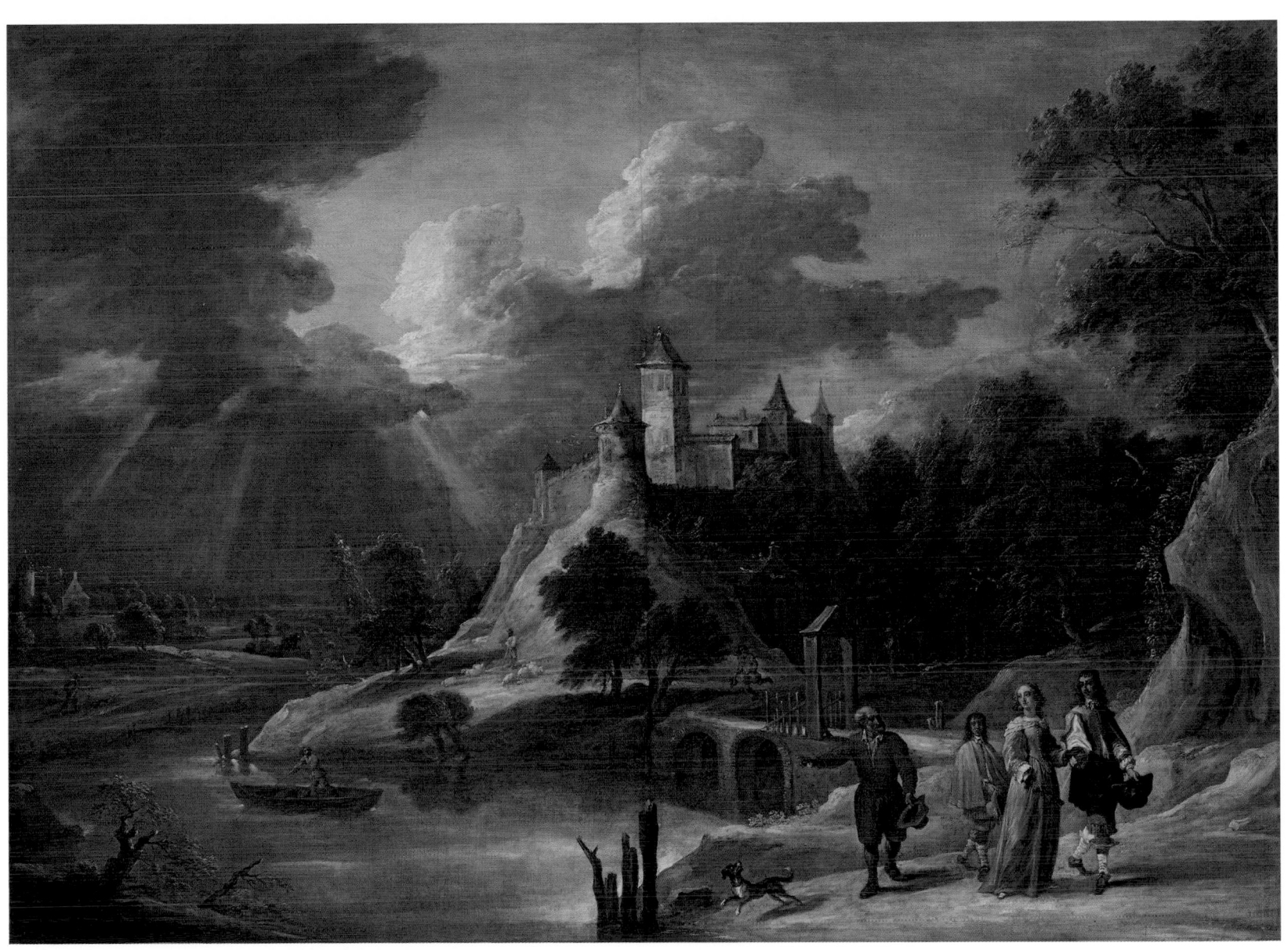

134   David Teniers the Younger, *Landscape with a Castle*

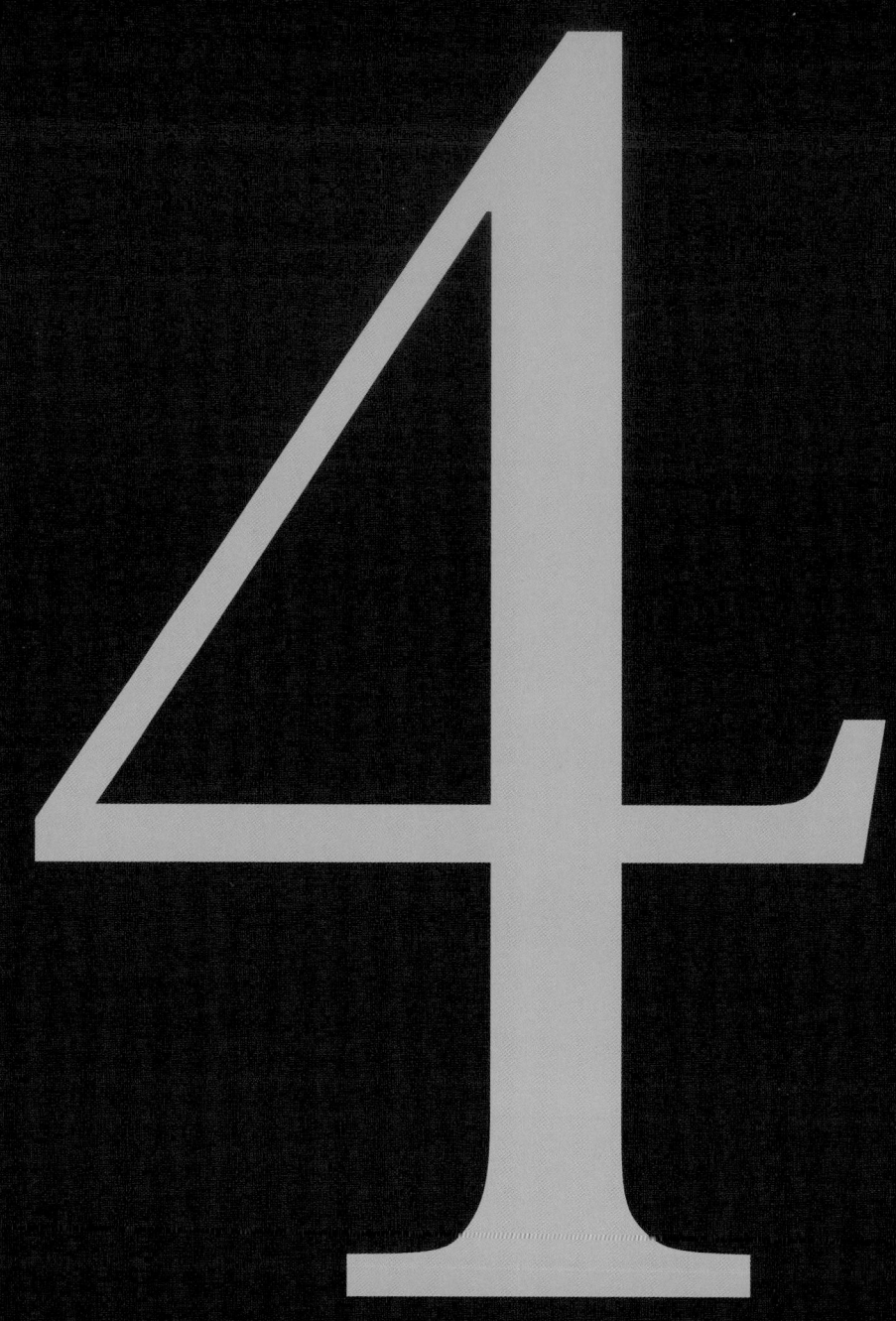

EIGHTEENTH
century

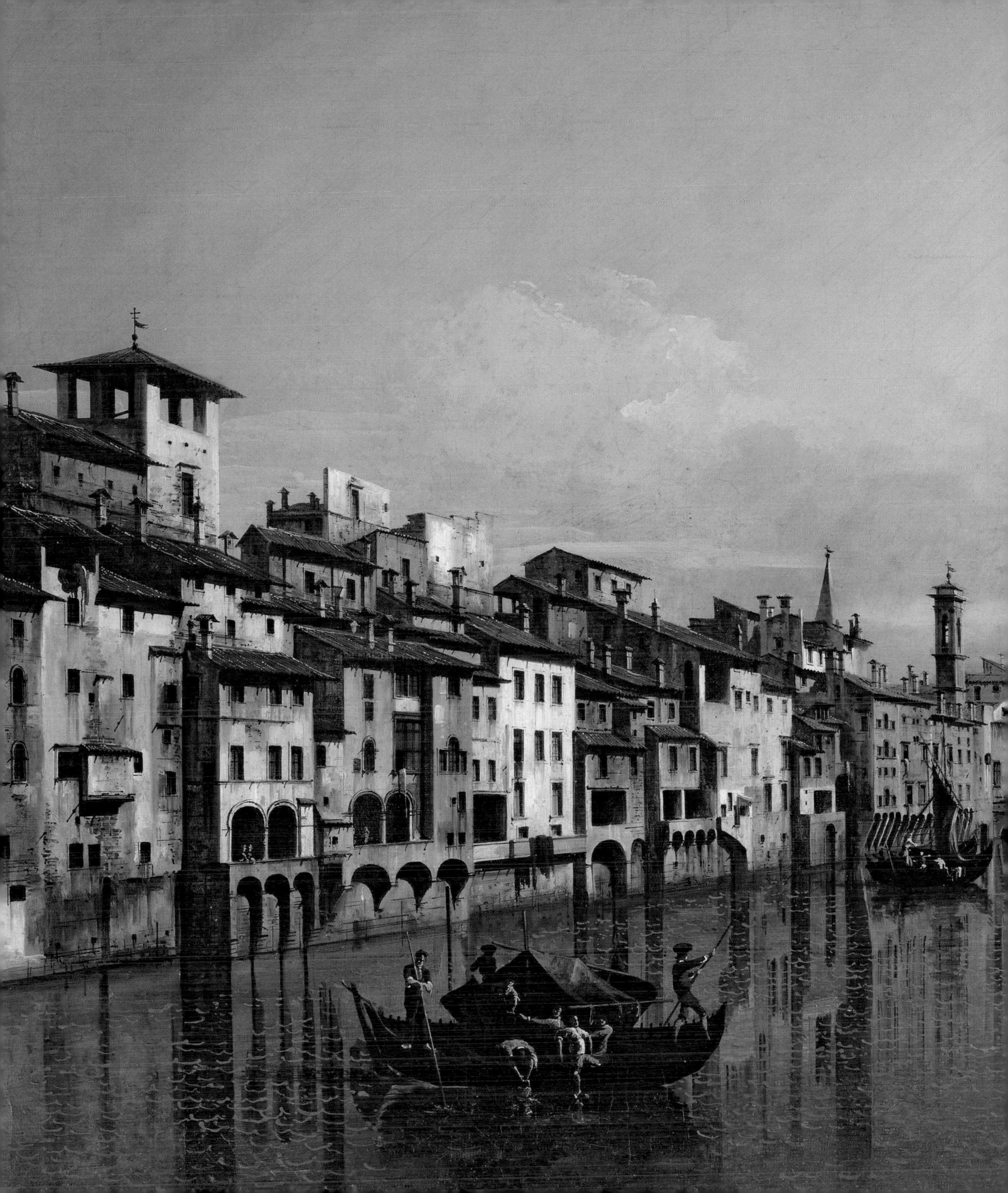

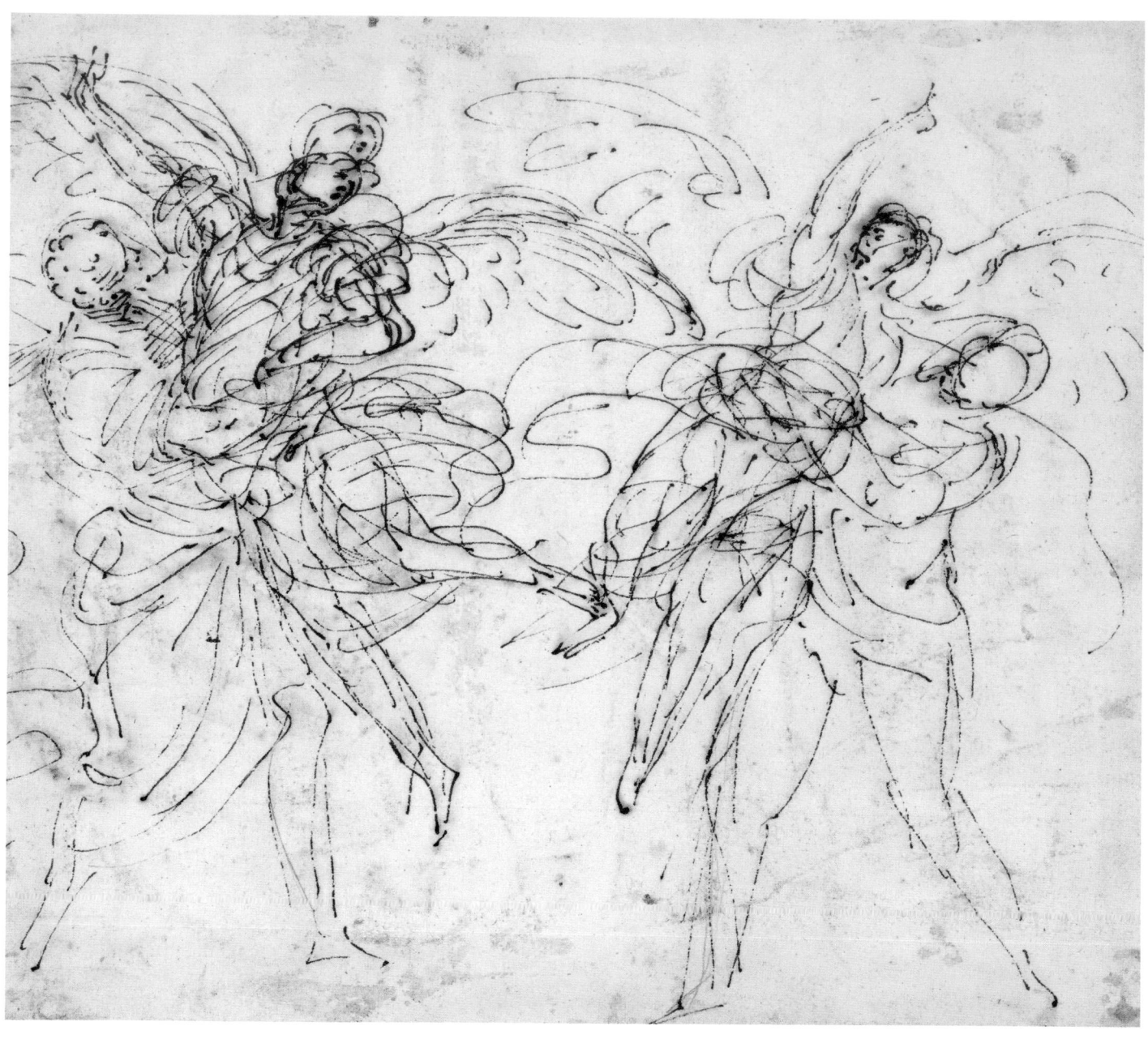

135   Donato Creti, *Studies of Jacob Wrestling with the Angel*

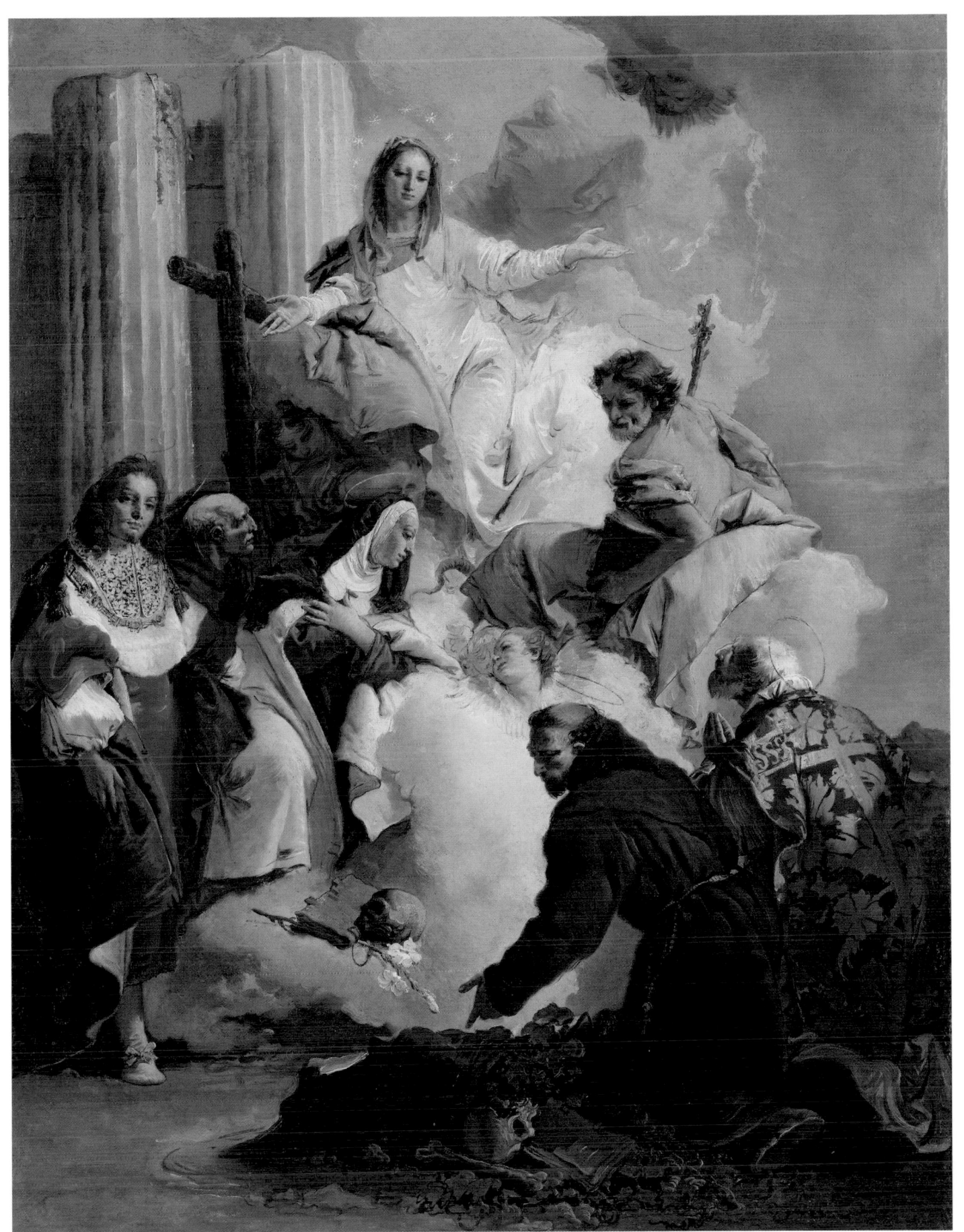

136   Giambattista Tiepolo, *Virgin in Glory with Six Saints*

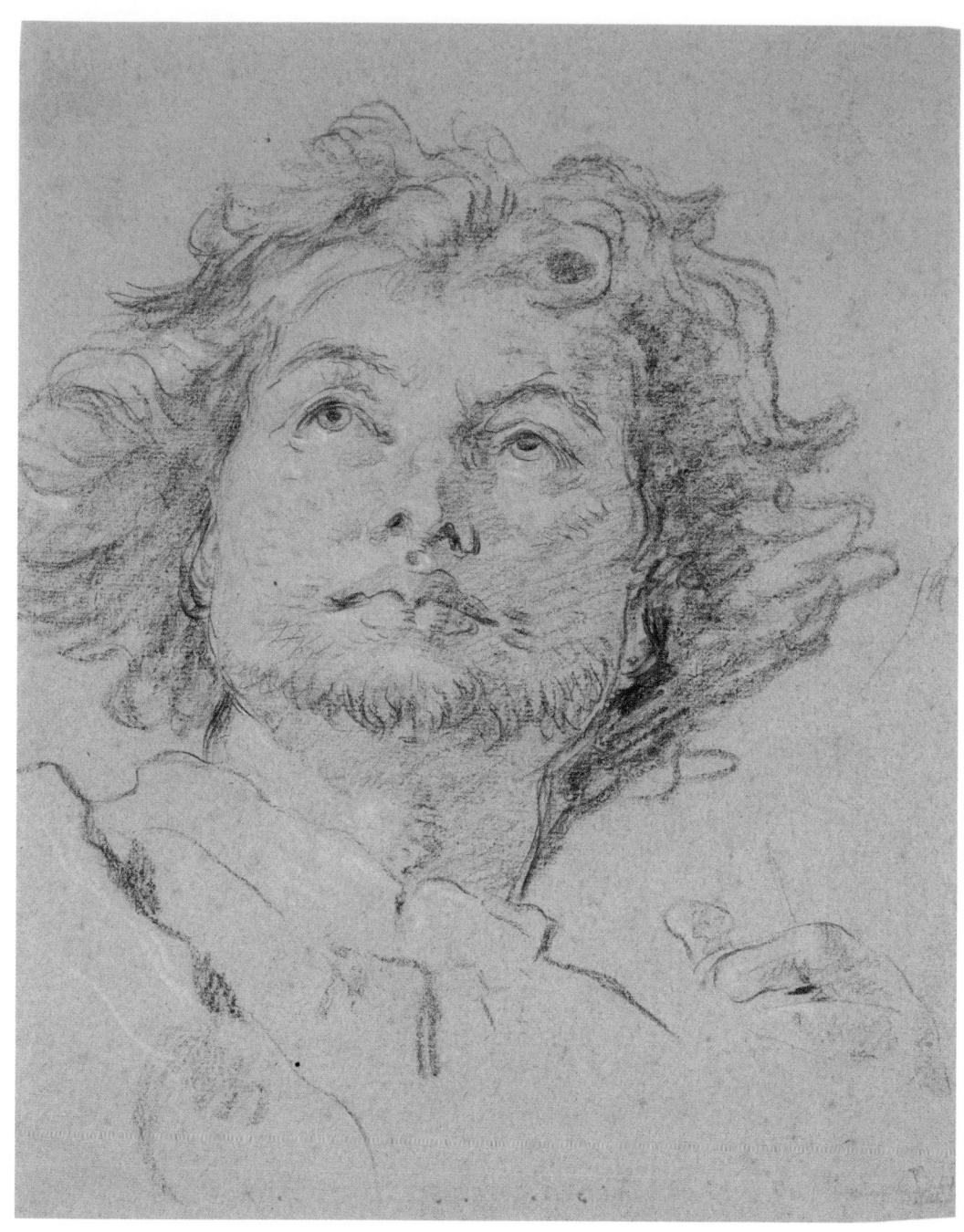

137   Giandomenico Tiepolo, *Head Study of St James*

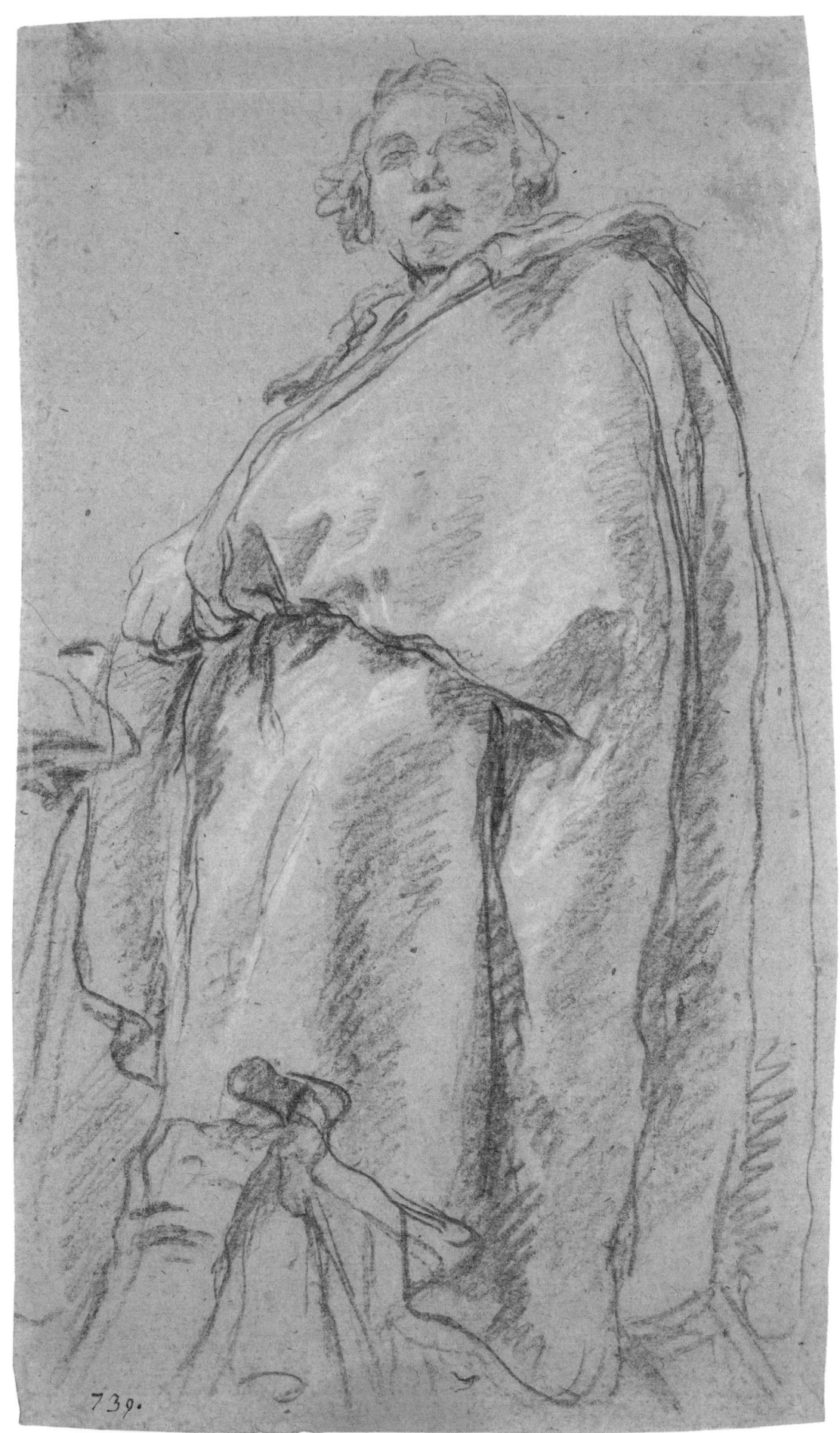

739.

138   Giambattista Tiepolo, *Figure Study*

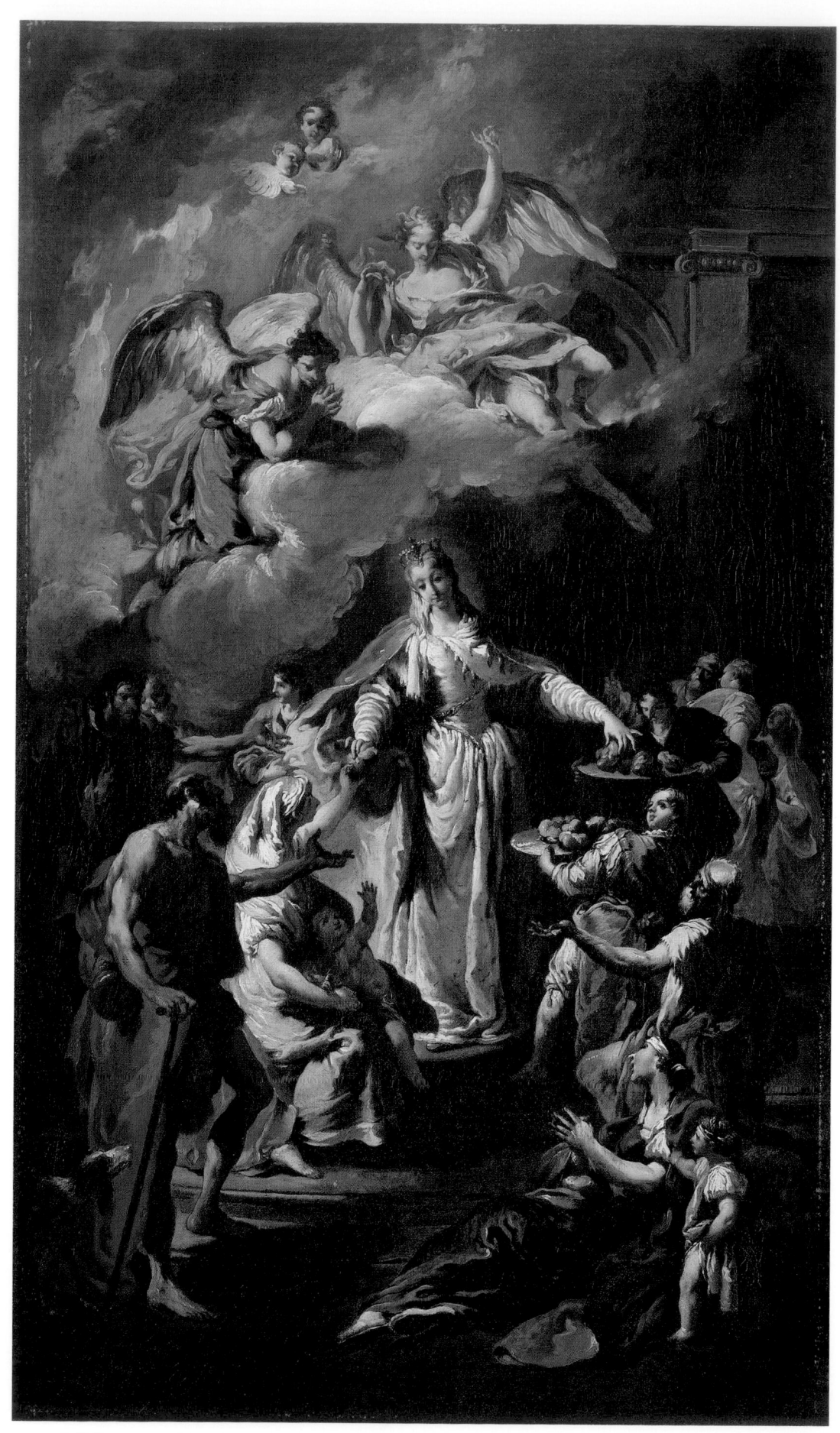

139   Giambattista Pittoni, *St Elizabeth of Hungary Distributing Alms*

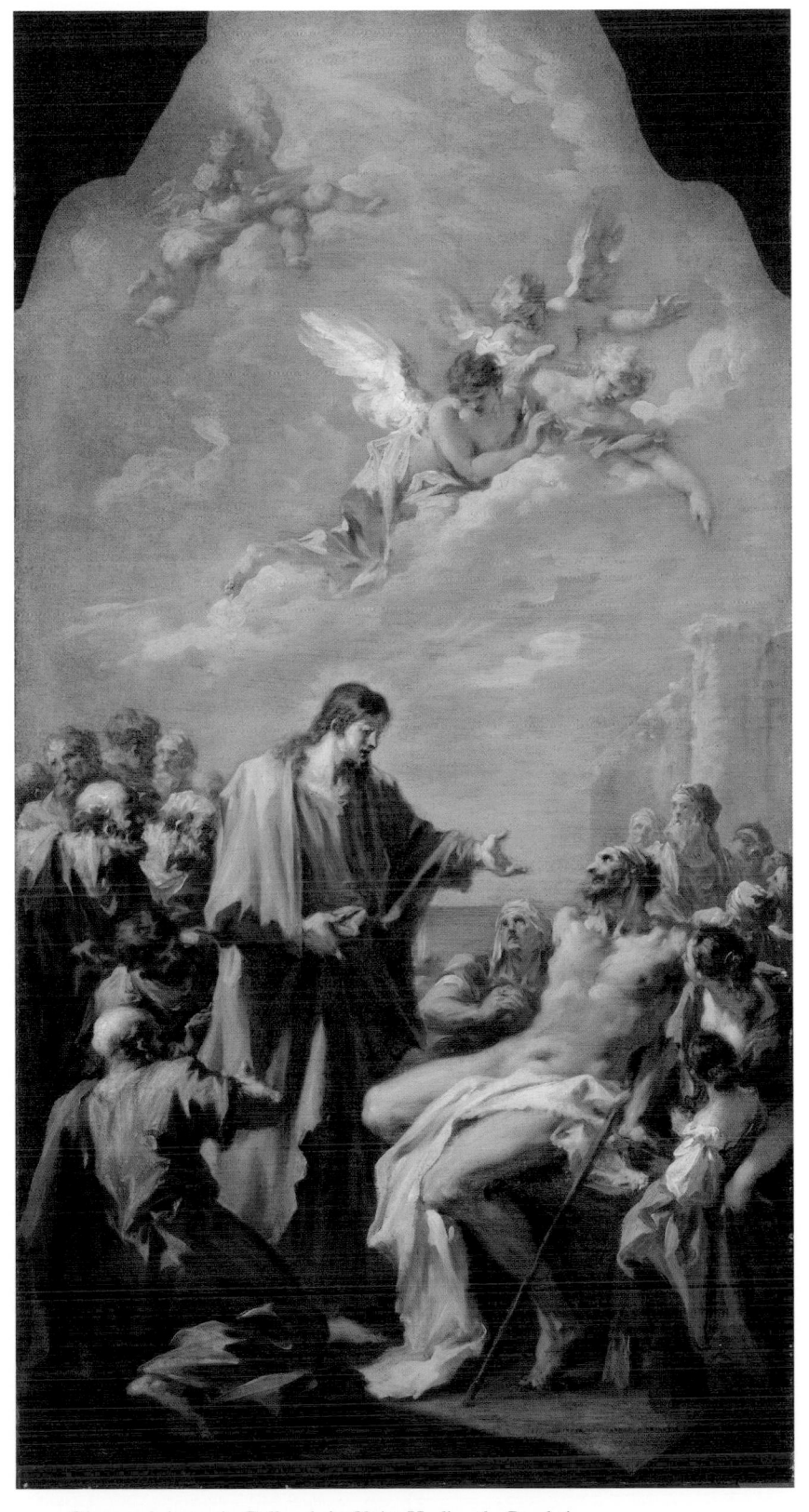

140   Giovanni Antonio Pellegrini, *Christ Healing the Paralytic*

141, 142 *overleaf* Philipp Jakob Straub, *St Roch, St Sebastian*

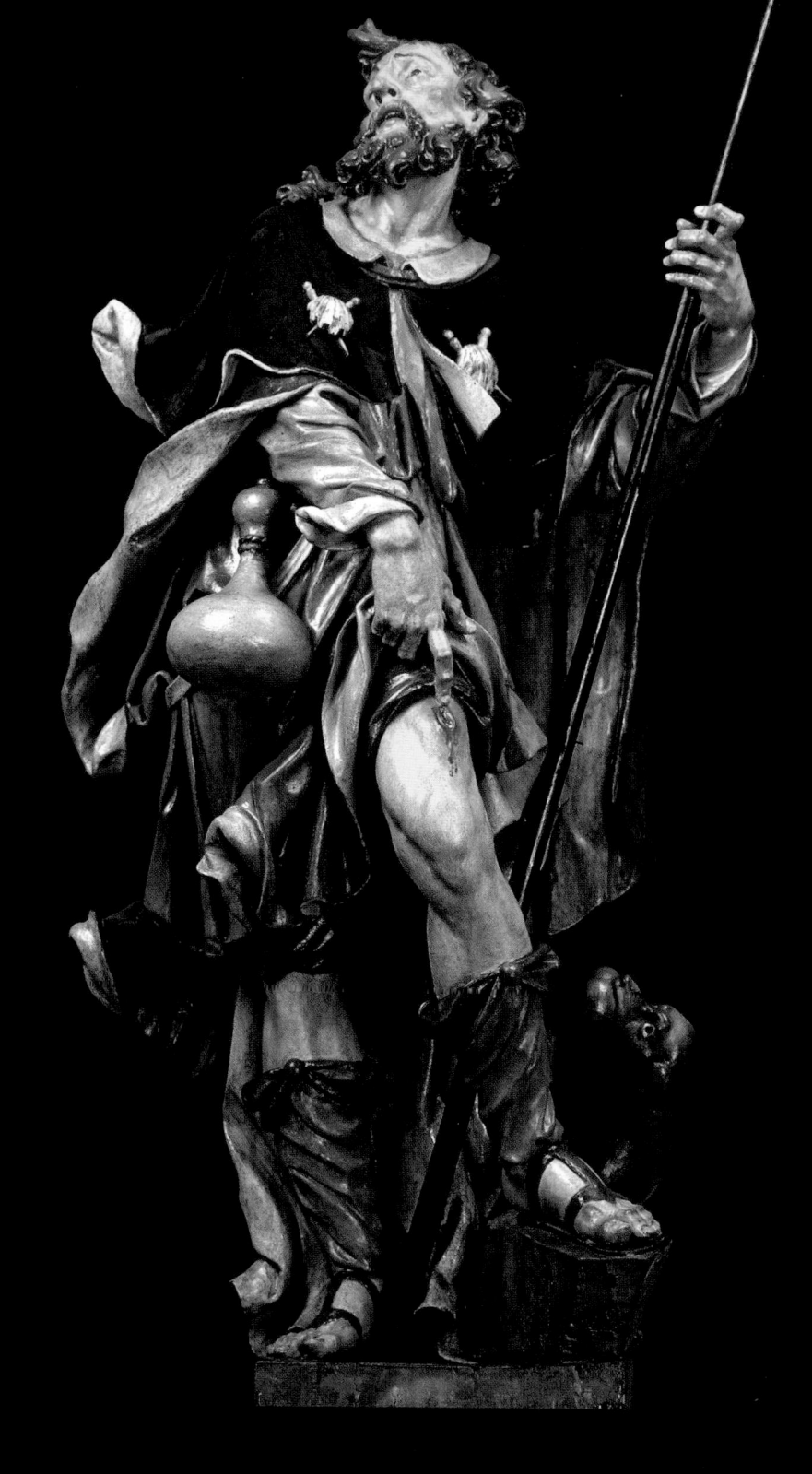

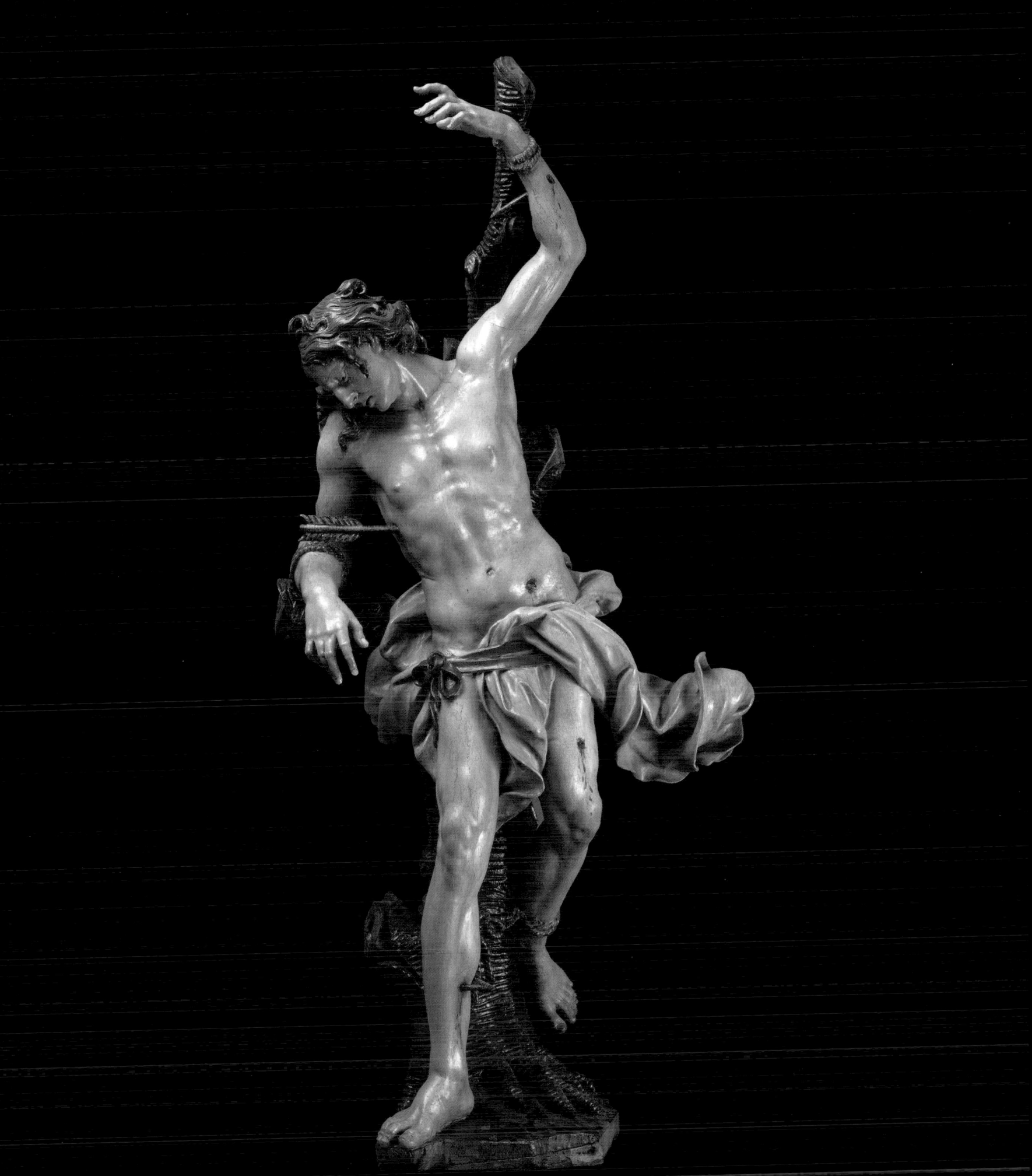

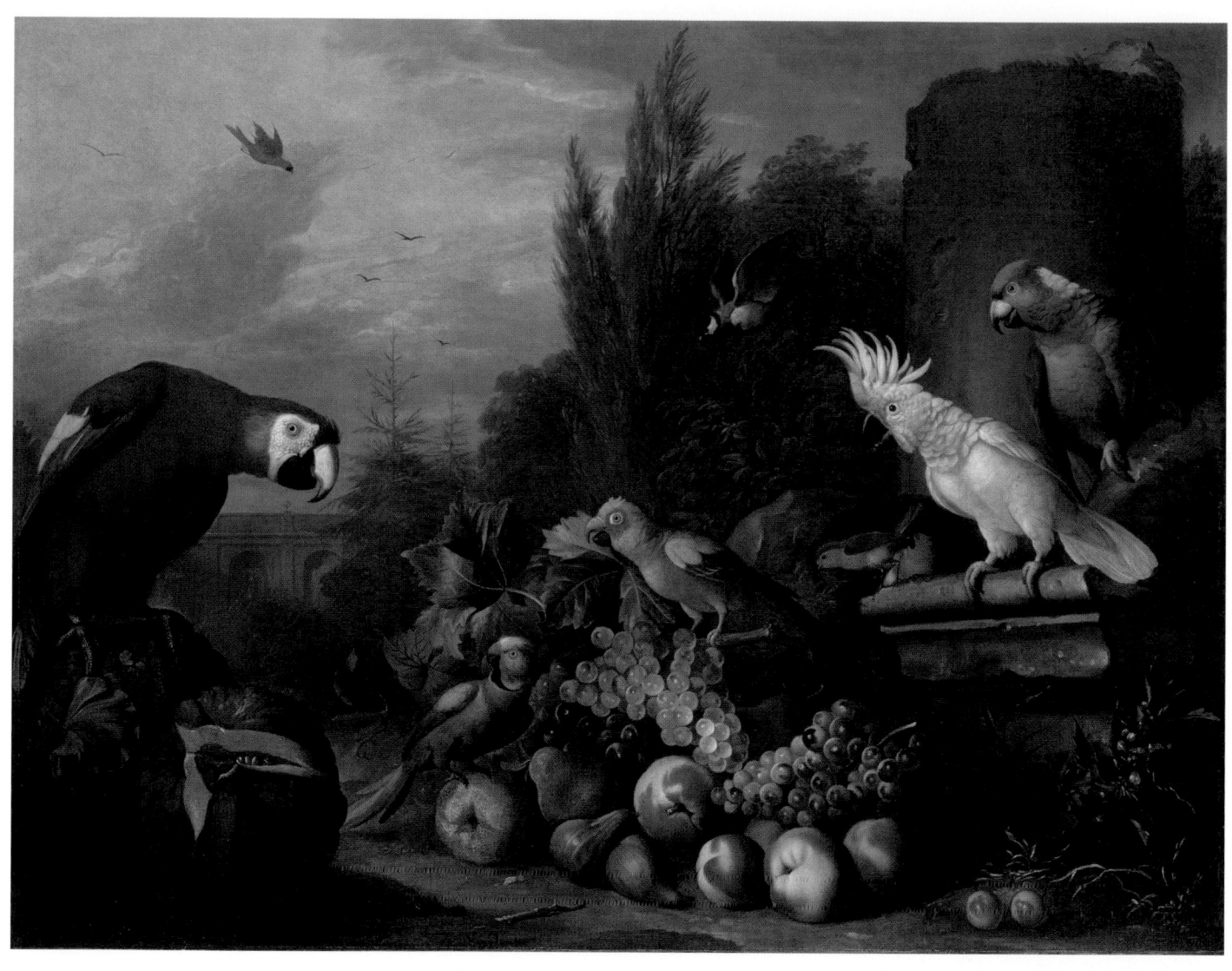

143   Jakob Bogdány, *Still-life with Fruit, Parrots and White Cockatoo*

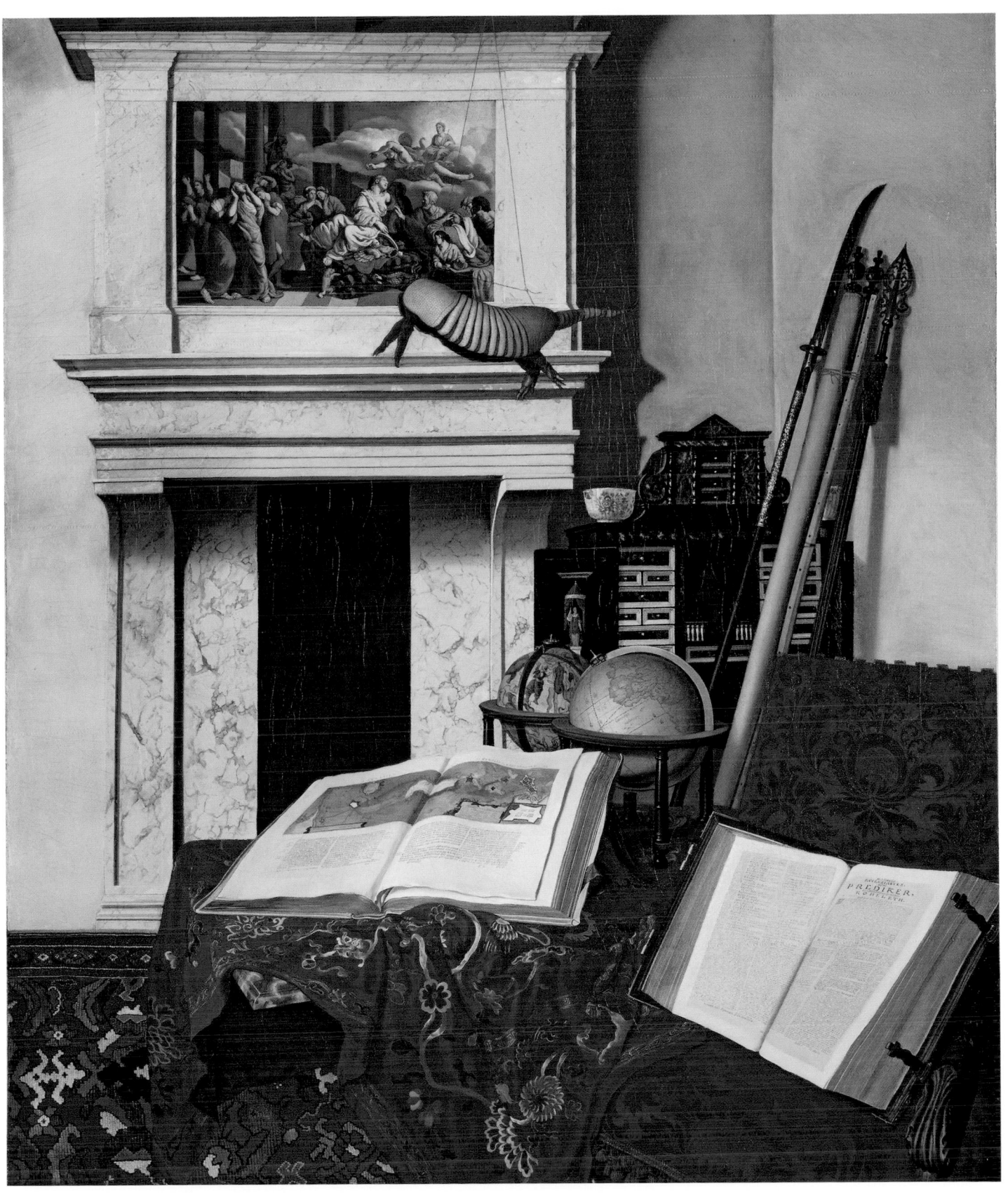

144   Jan van der Heyden, *Corner of a Room*

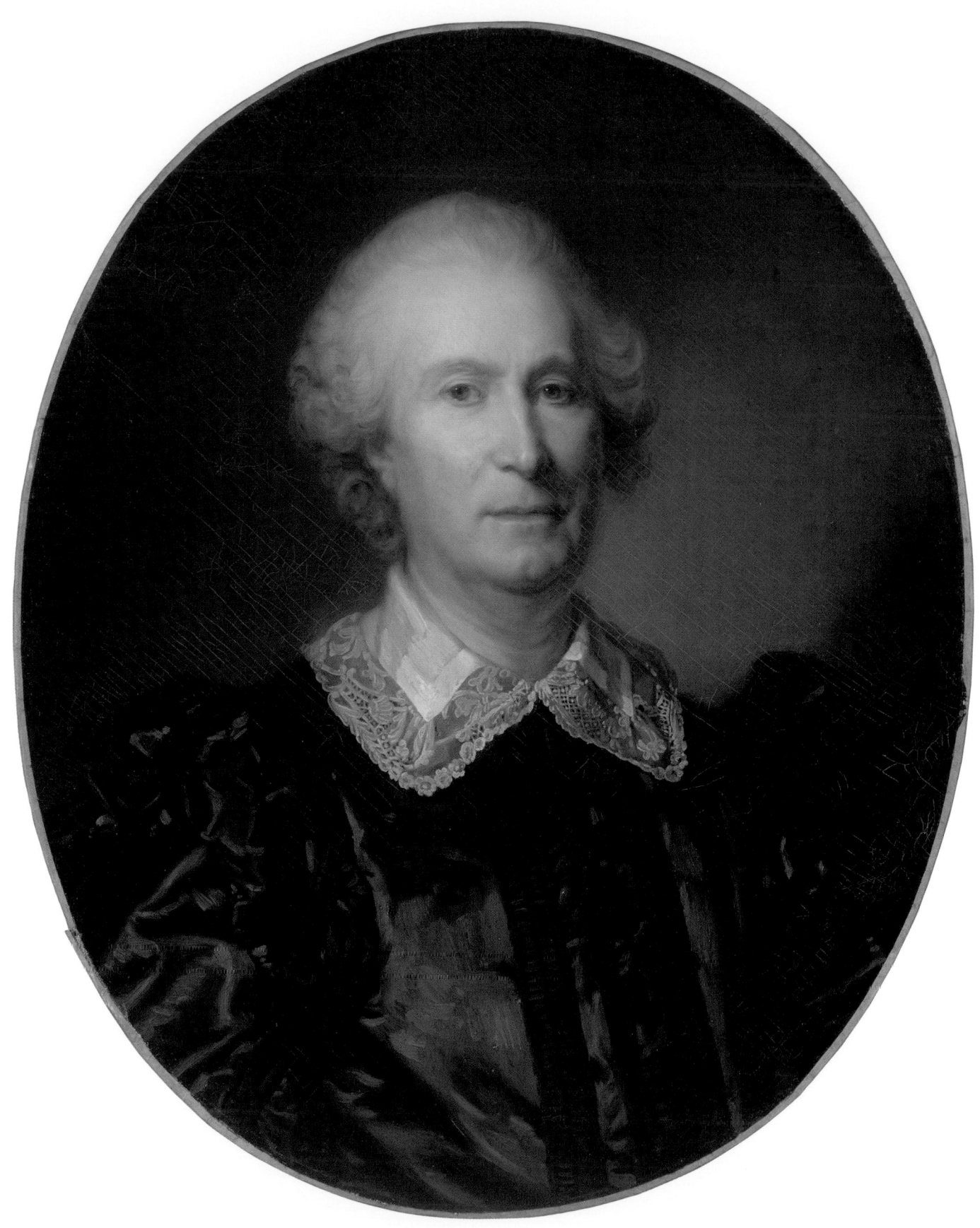

145   Jean-Baptiste Greuze, *Portrait of Paul Randon de Boisset*

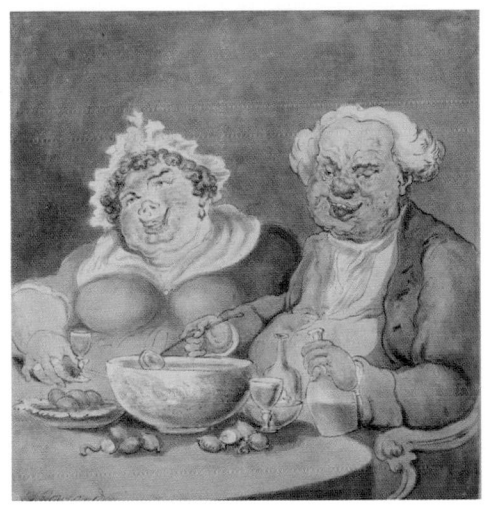

146   Thomas Rowlandson, *Gluttons*

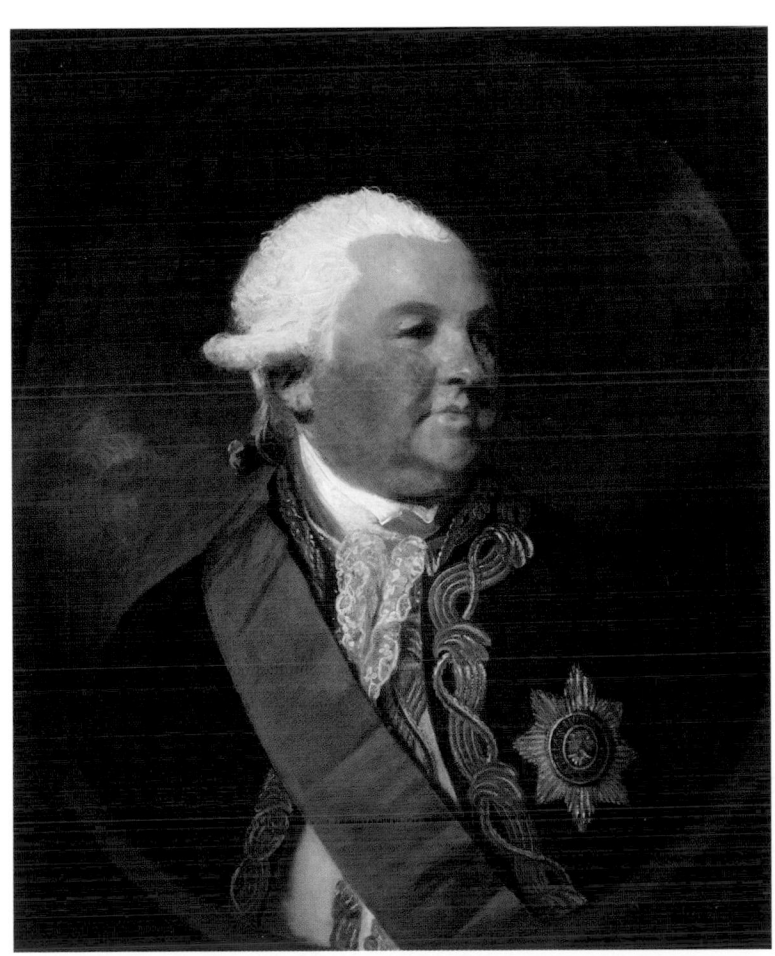

147   Sir Joshua Reynolds PRA, *Portrait of Admiral Sir Edward Hughes*

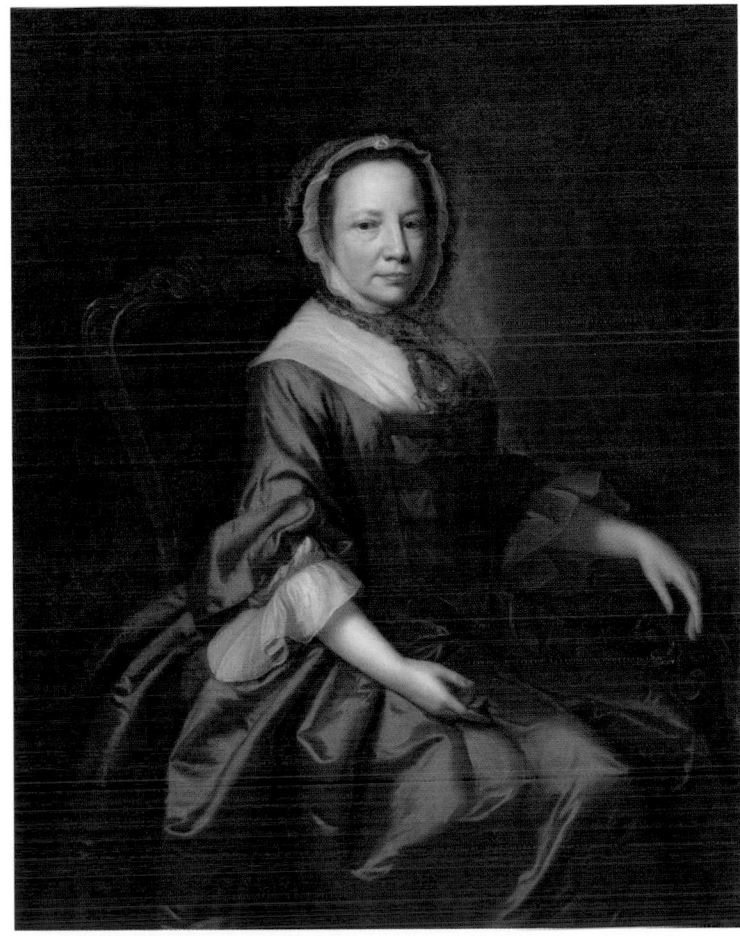

148   Thomas Hudson, *Portrait of a Lady*

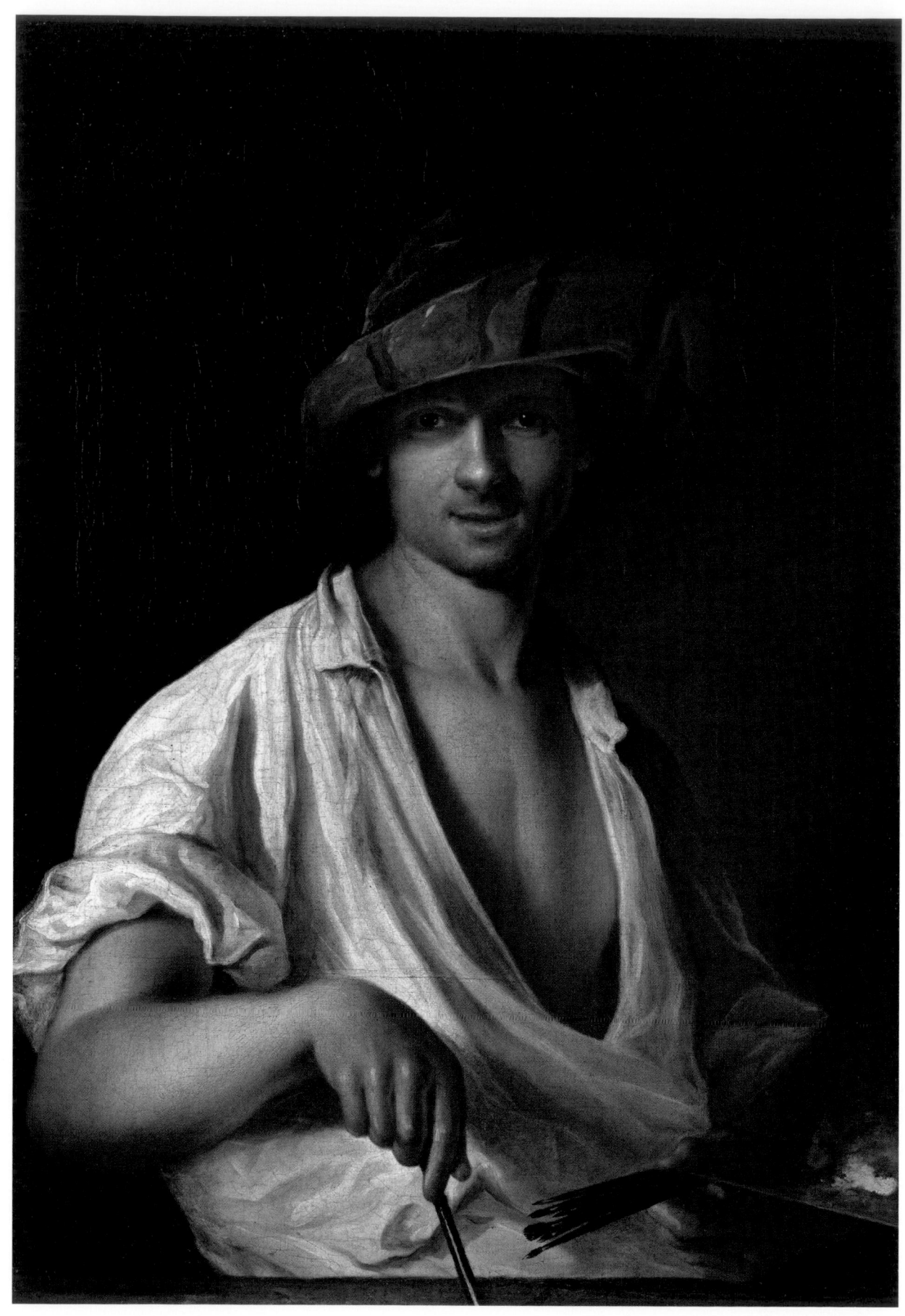

149   Ádám Mányoki, *Self-portrait*

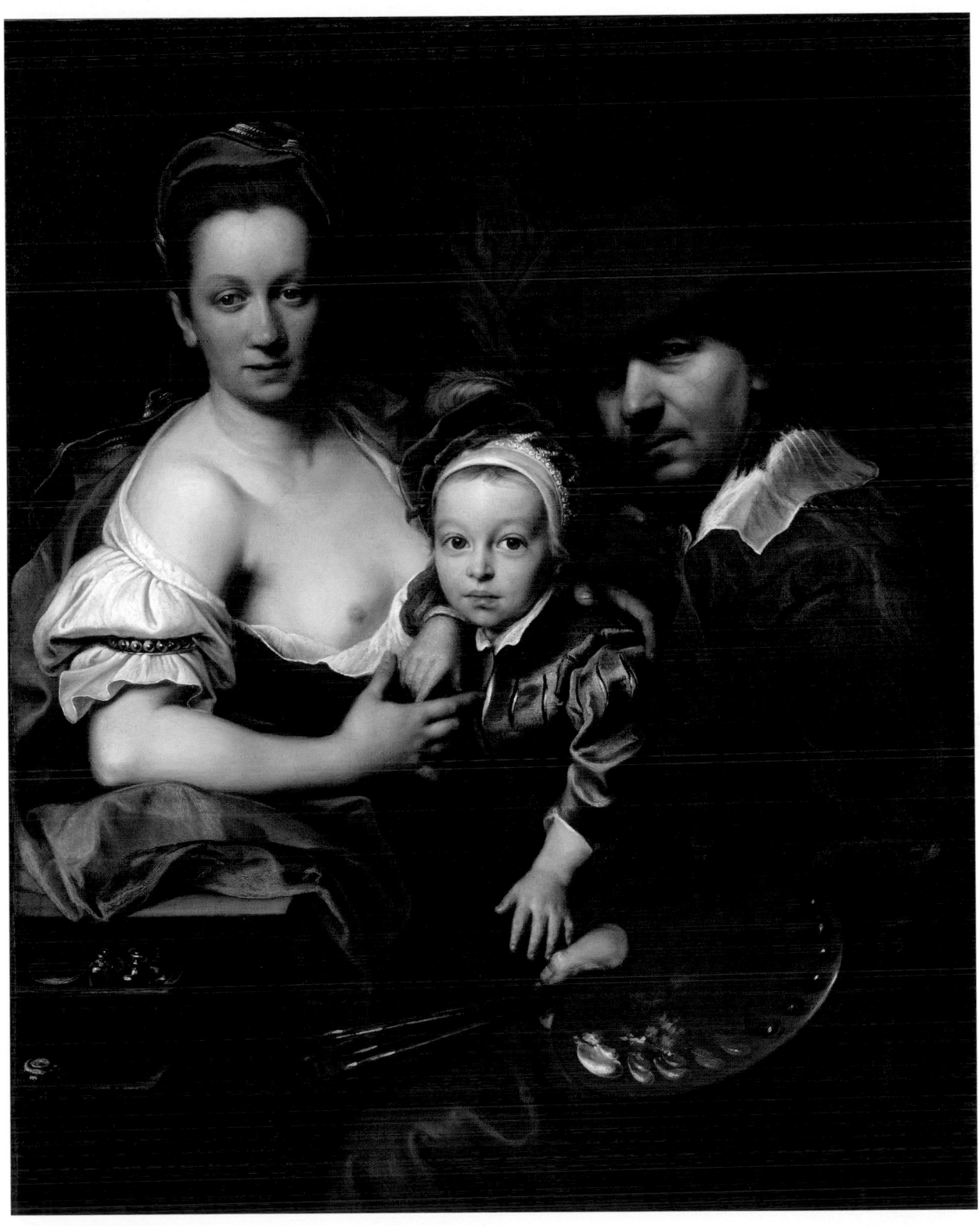

150   Jan Kupecký, *Self-portrait of the Artist with His Wife and Son*

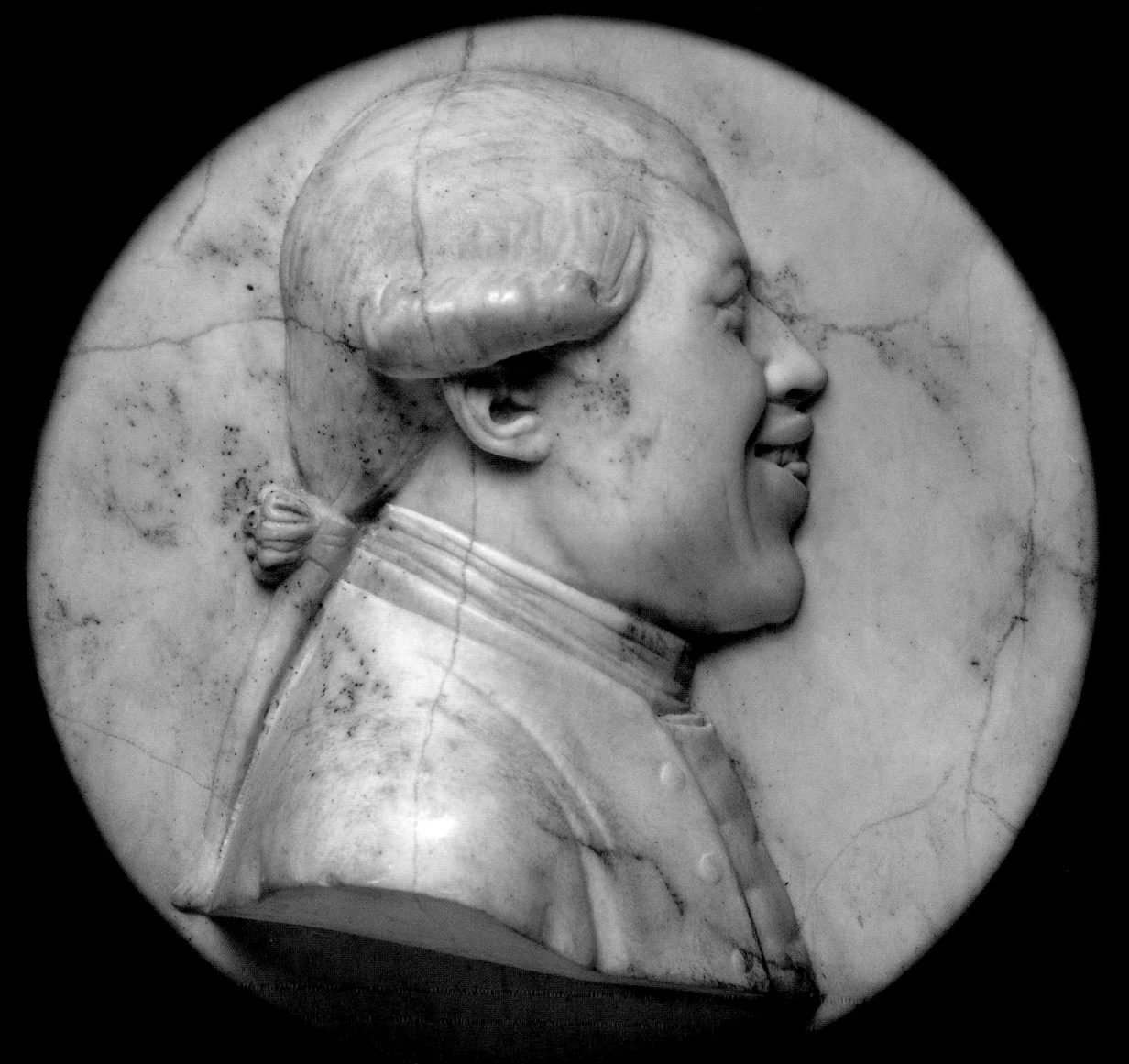

151.1   Franz Xaver Messerschmidt, *Self-portrait, Laughing*

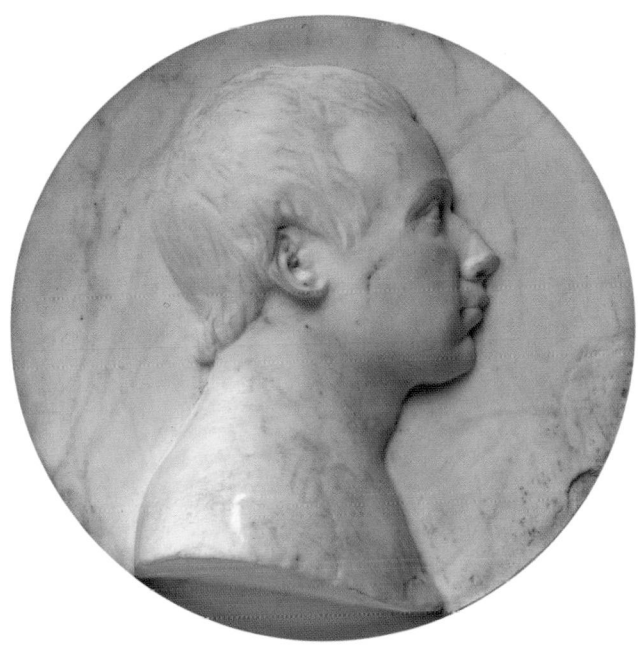

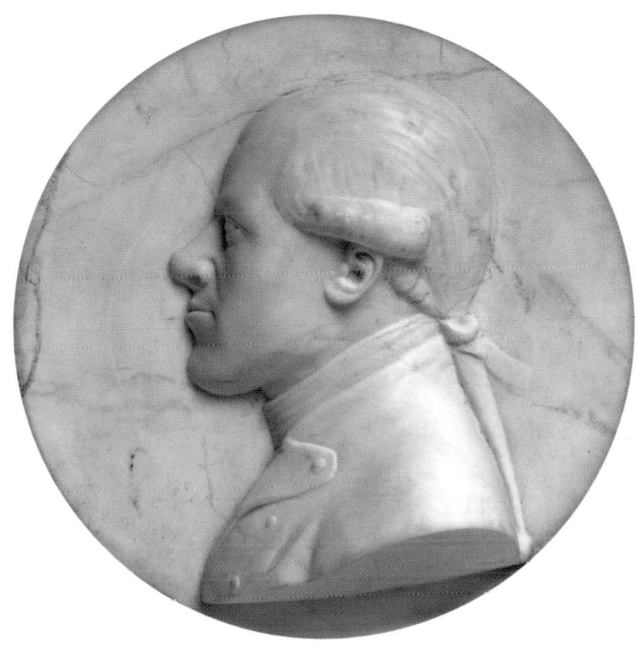

151.2   Franz Xaver Messerschmidt, *Self-portrait, Serious*

151.3   Franz Xaver Messerschmidt, *Self-portrait with Wig*

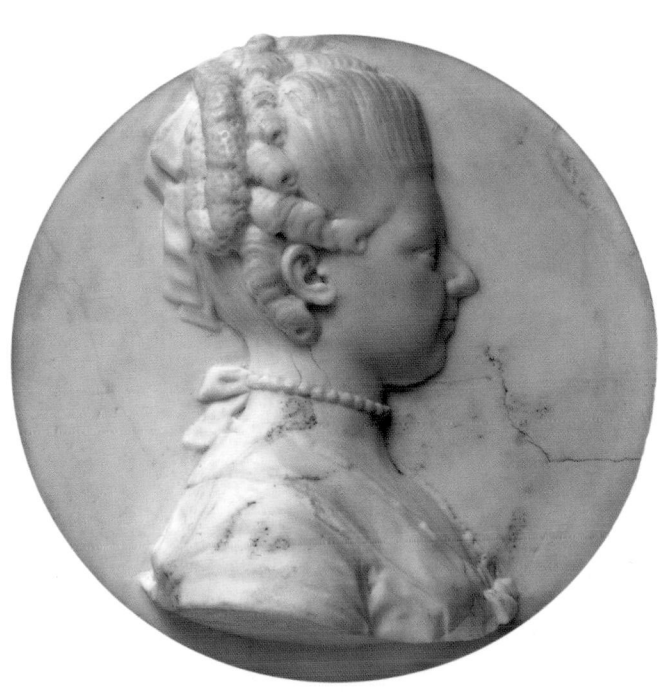

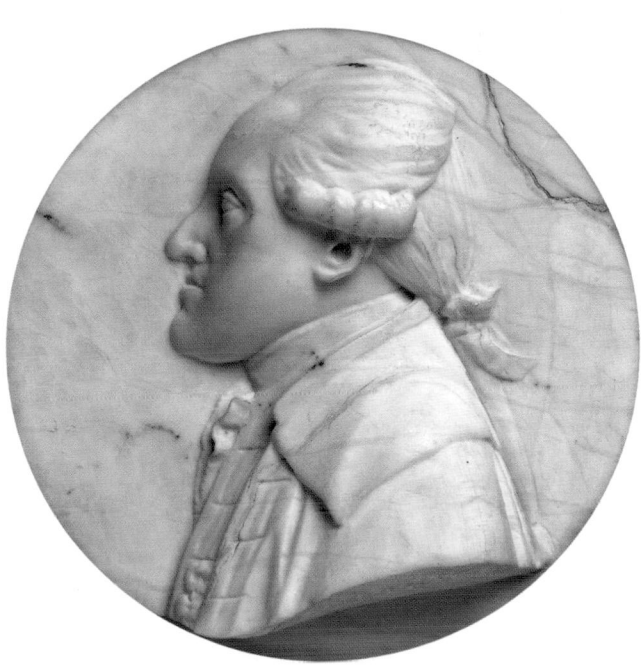

152.1   Franz Xaver Messerschmidt, *Archduchess Maria Christina*

152.2   Franz Xaver Messerschmidt, *Duke Albert of Sachsen-Teschen*

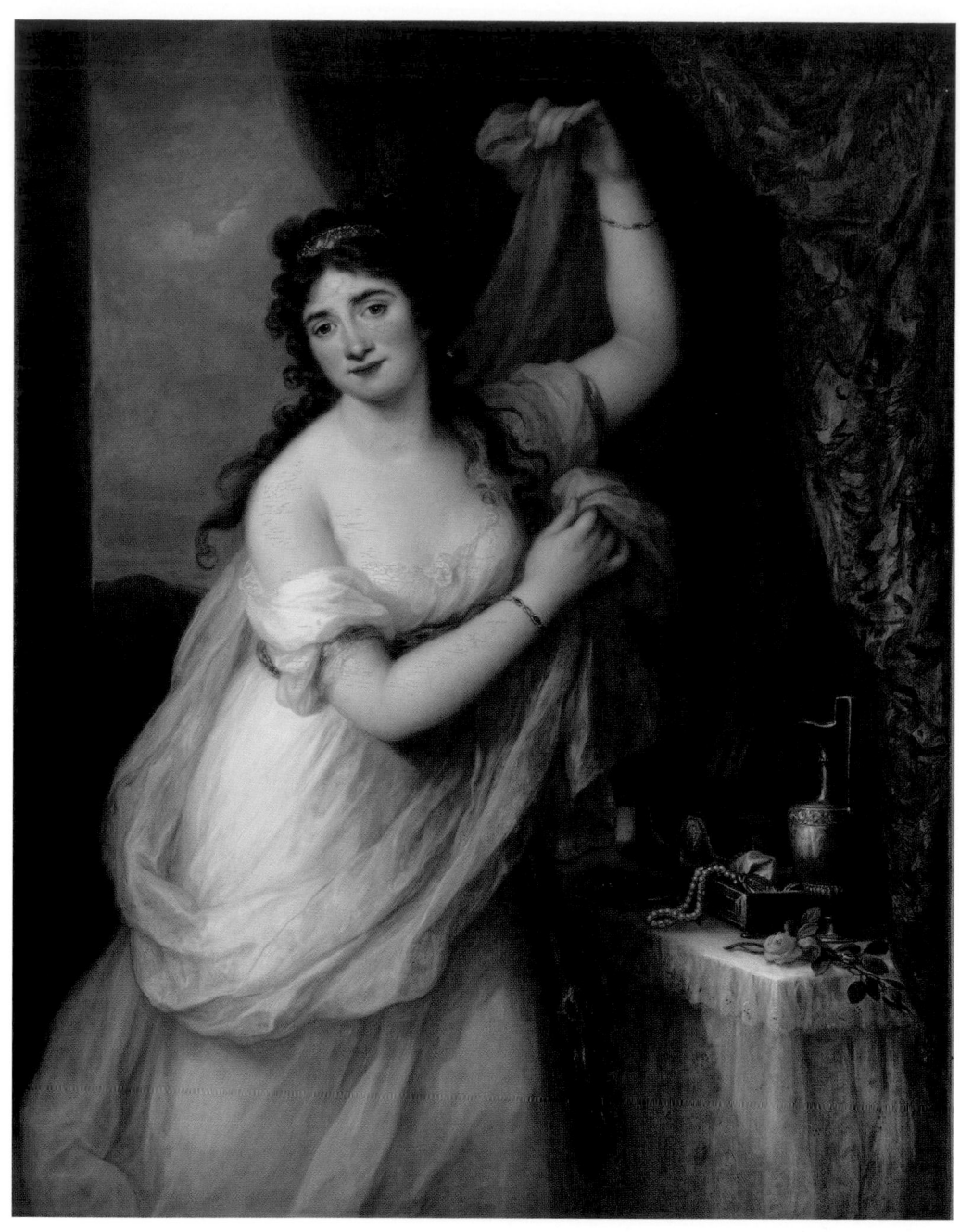

153   Angelica Kauffmann RA, *Portrait of a Woman at Her Toilet*

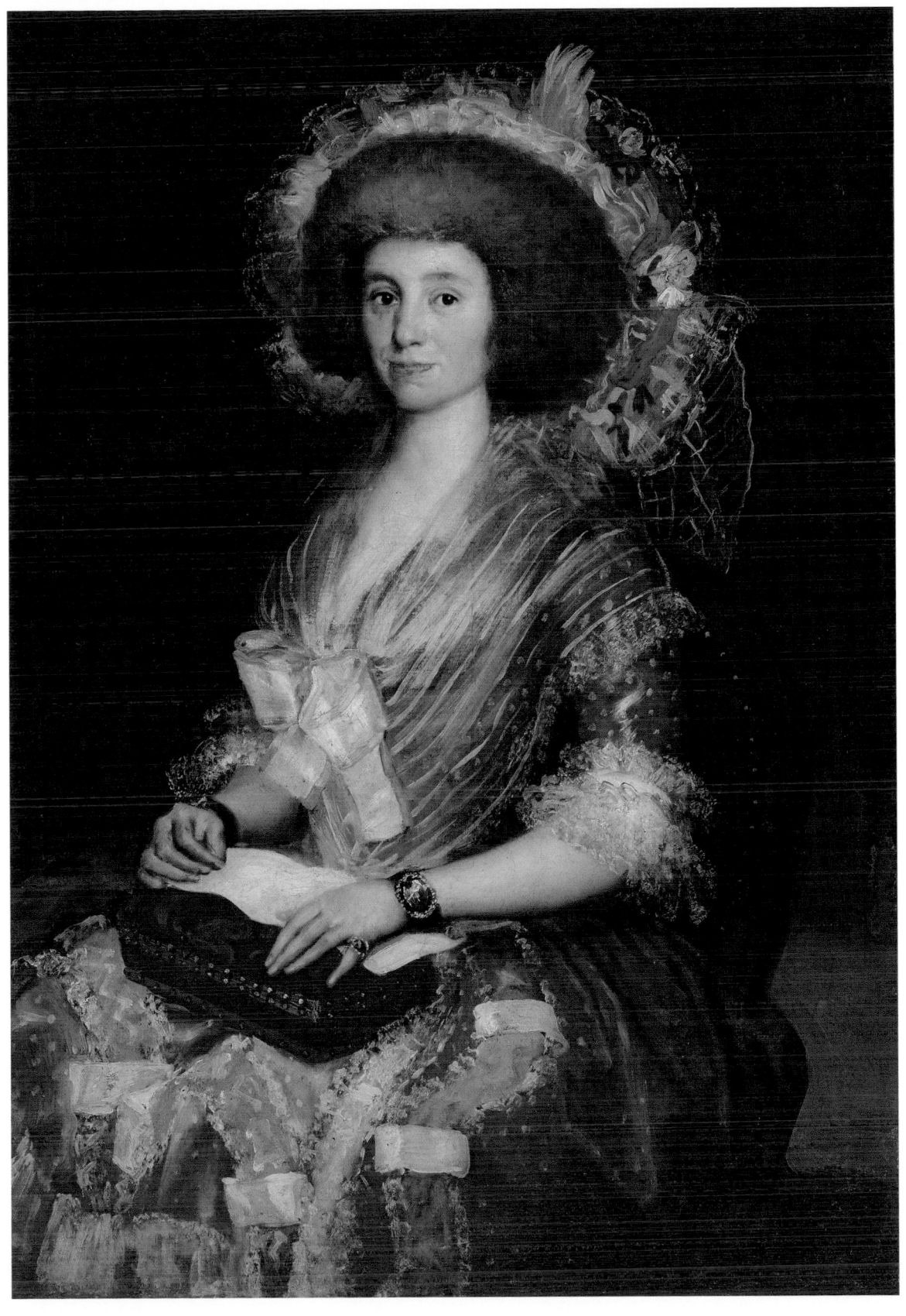

154   Francisco José de Goya y Lucientes, *Portrait of Manuela de Ceán Bermúdez*

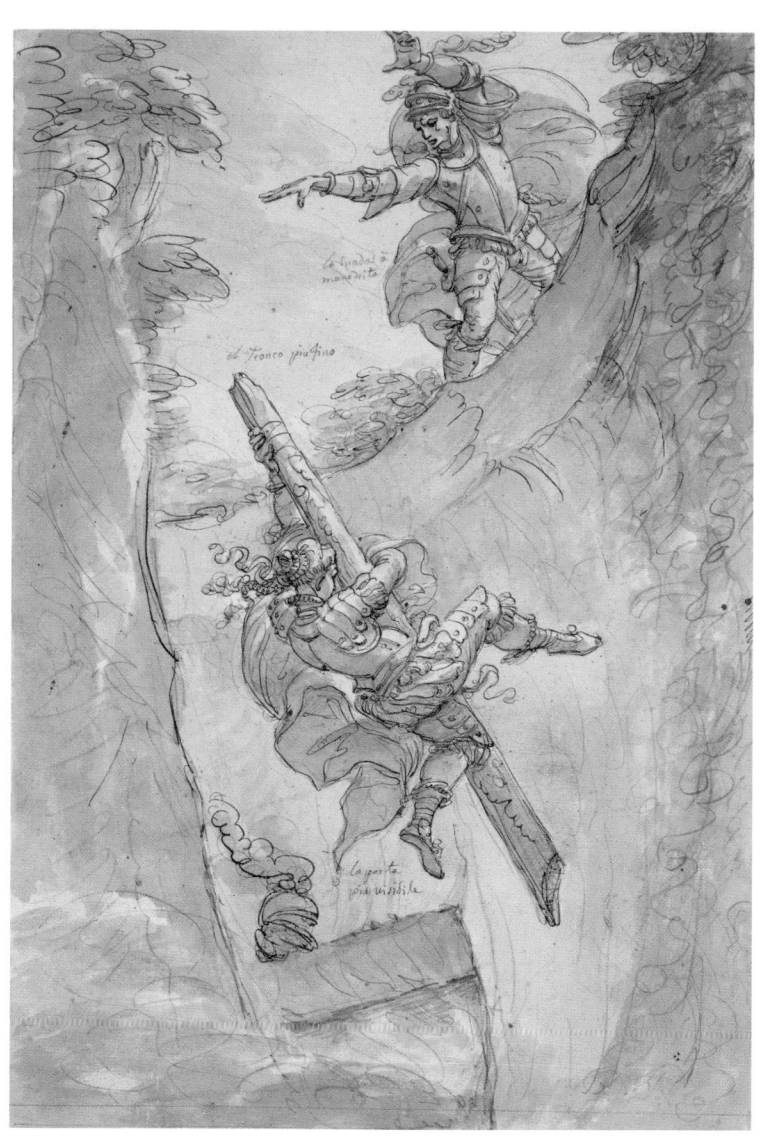

155.1   Giuseppe Cades, *Pinabello Pushes Bradamante into a Ravine*

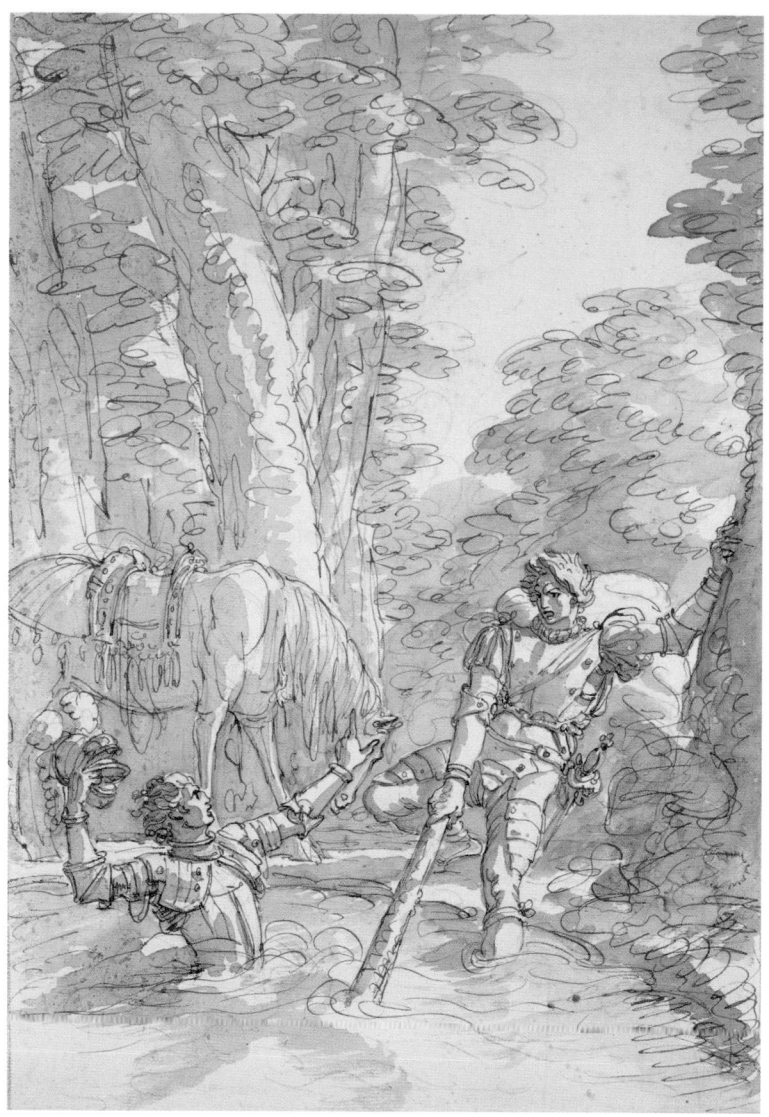

155.2   Giuseppe Cades, *Argalia's Spirit Appears to Ferragù*

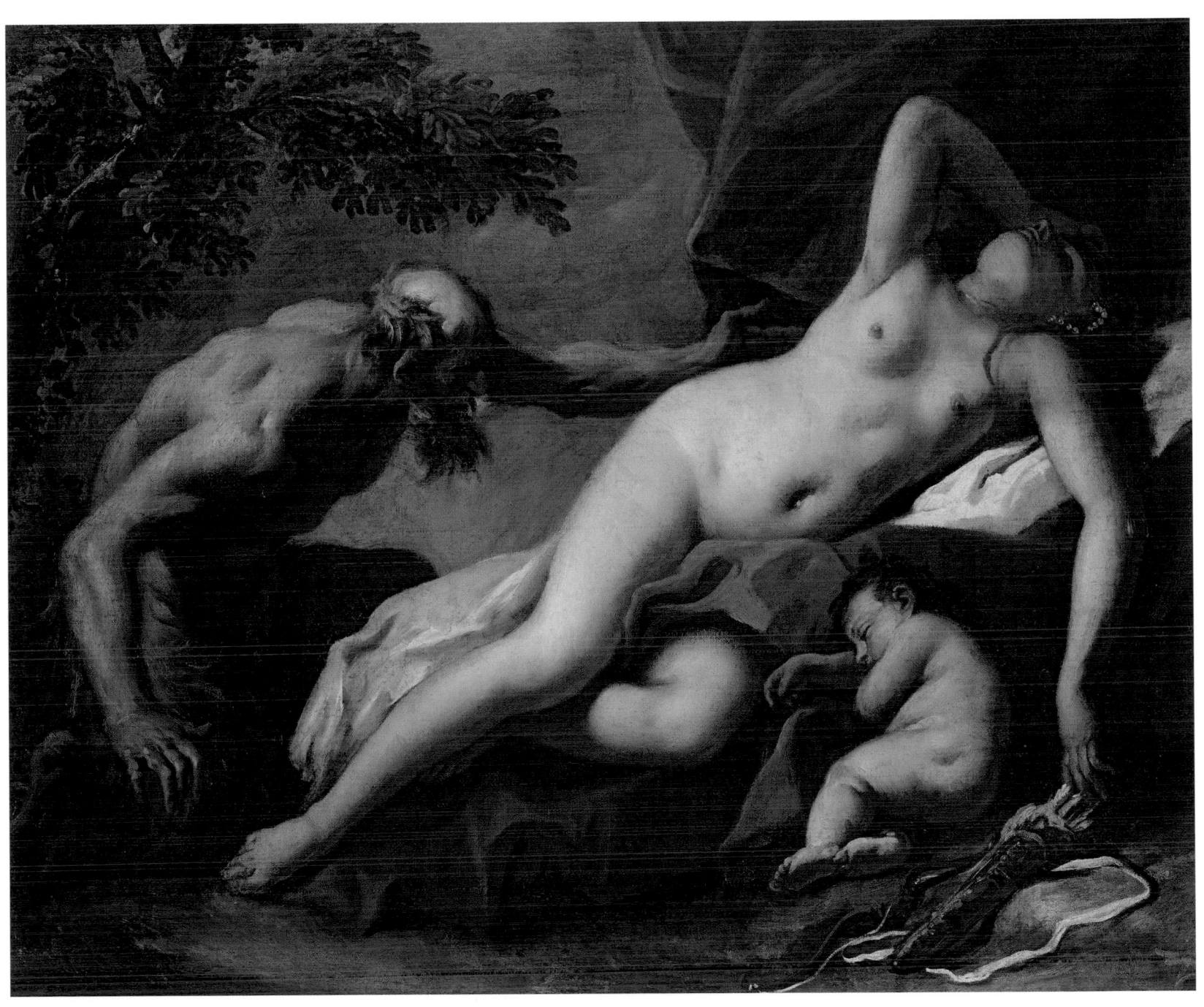

156   Sebastiano Ricci, *Venus and Cupid with a Satyr*

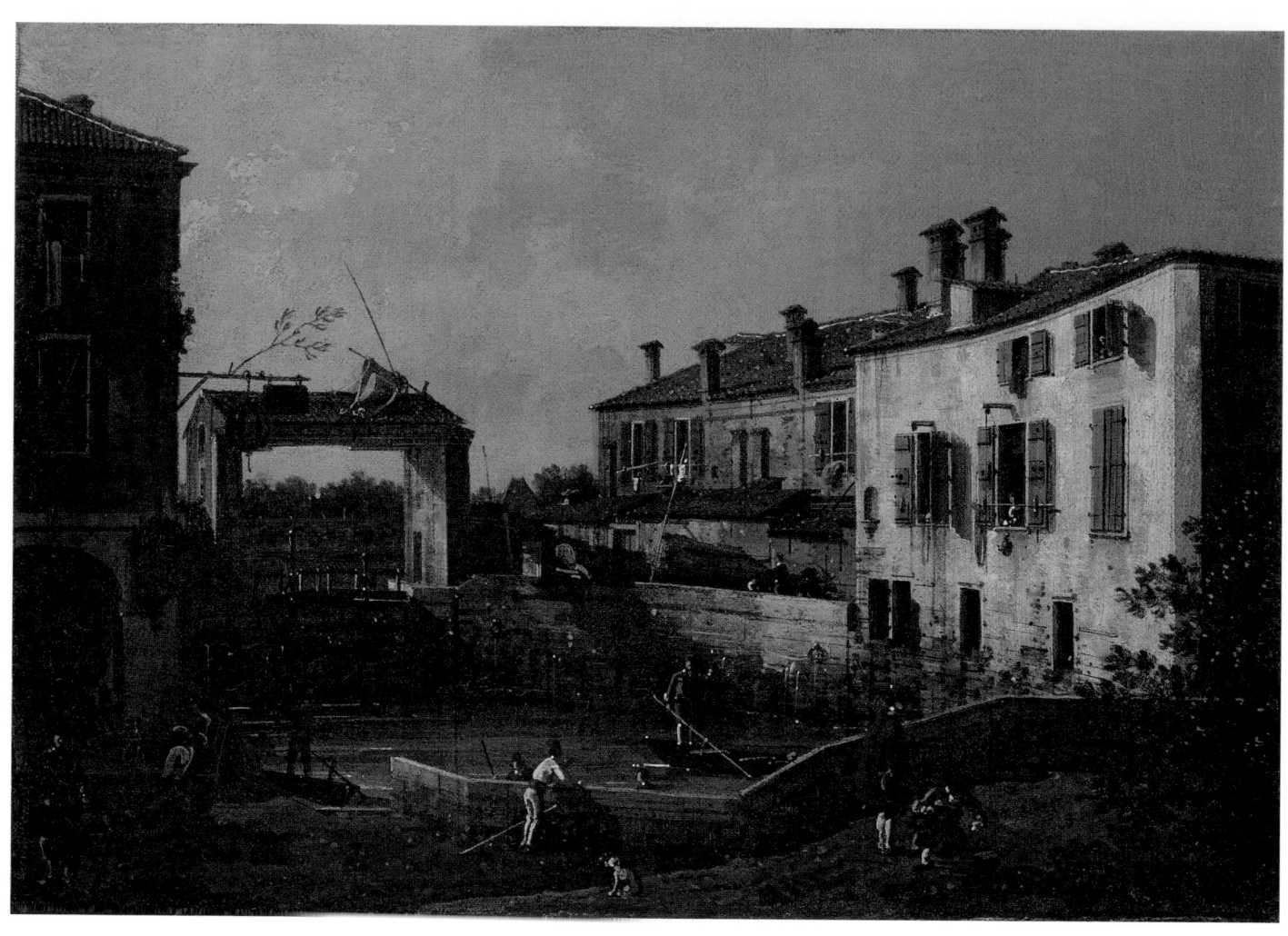

157   Canaletto, *Lock at Dolo*

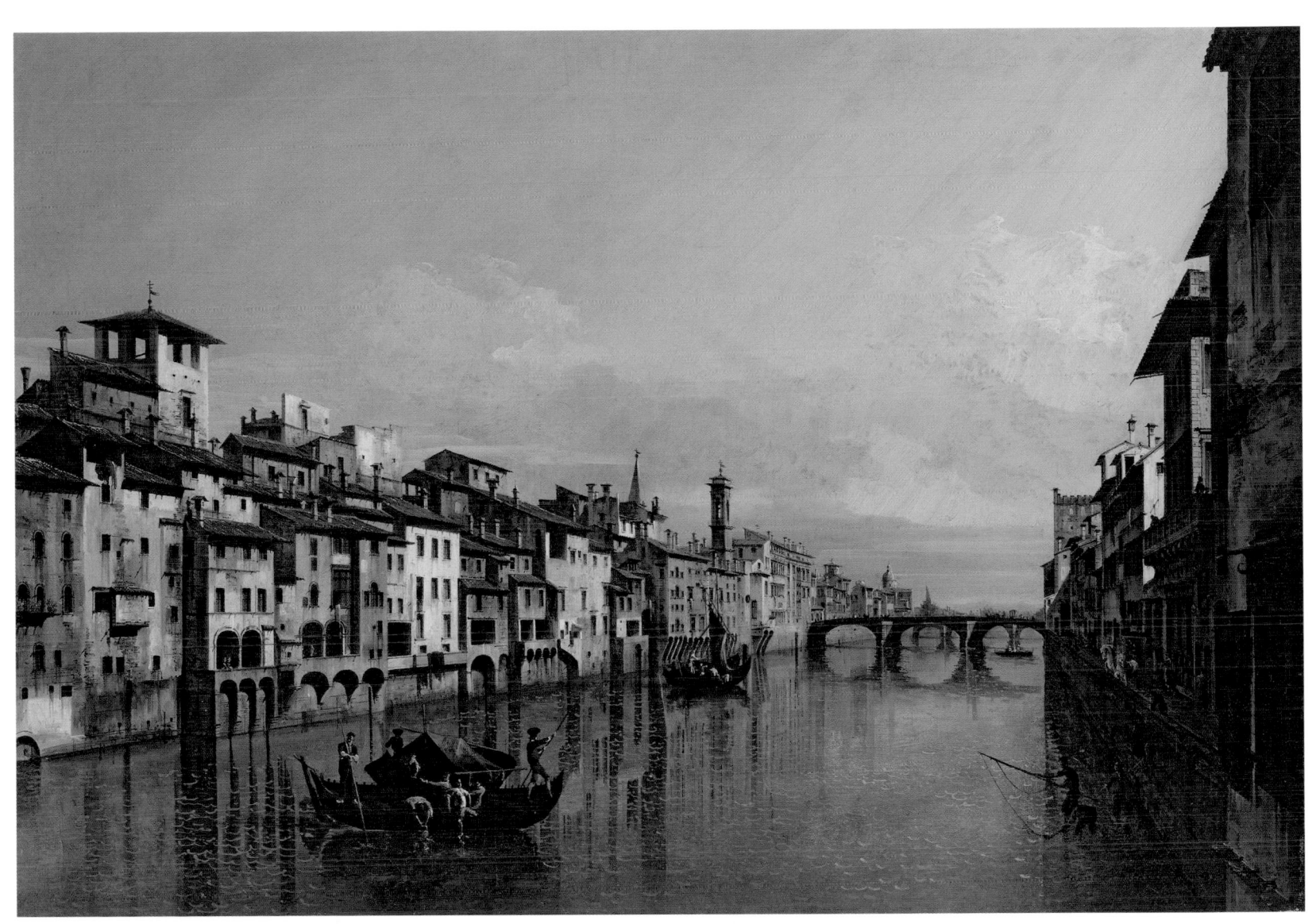

158   Bernardo Bellotto, *The Arno towards the Ponte Santa Trinita, Florence*

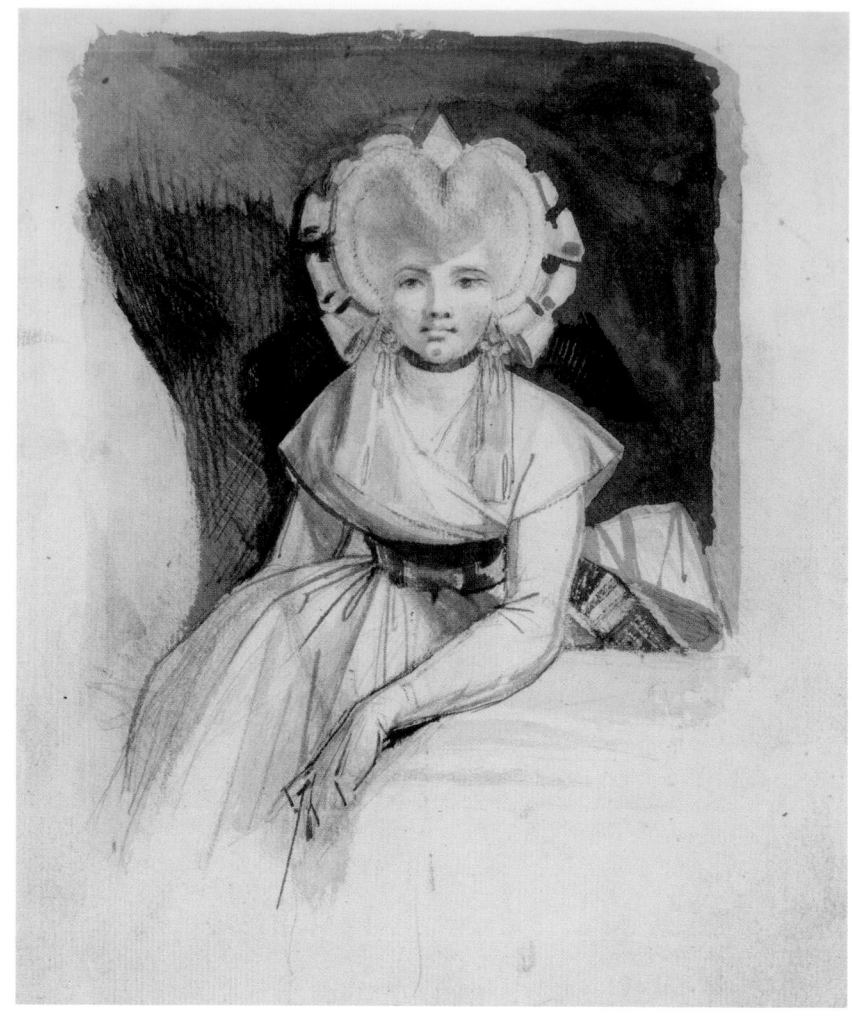

159   Henry Fuseli RA, *Portrait of the Artist's Wife*

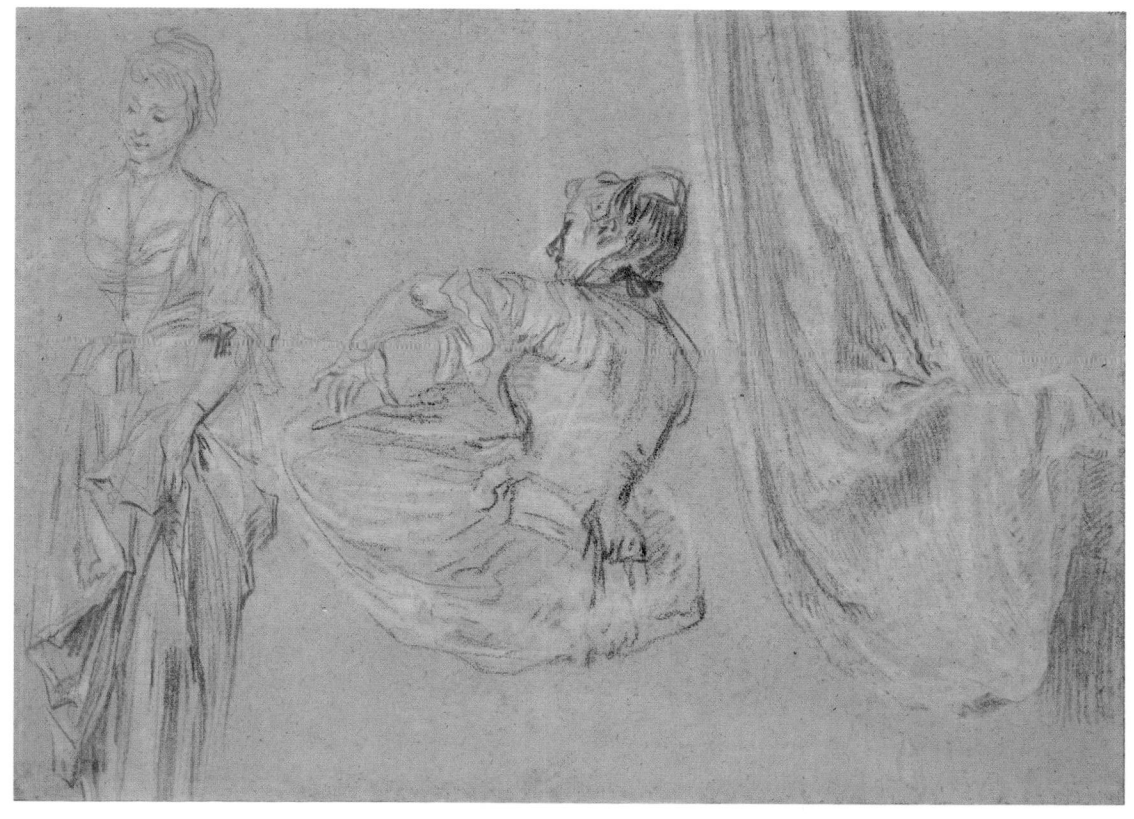

160   Jean-Antoine Watteau, *Studies of Women and Drapery*

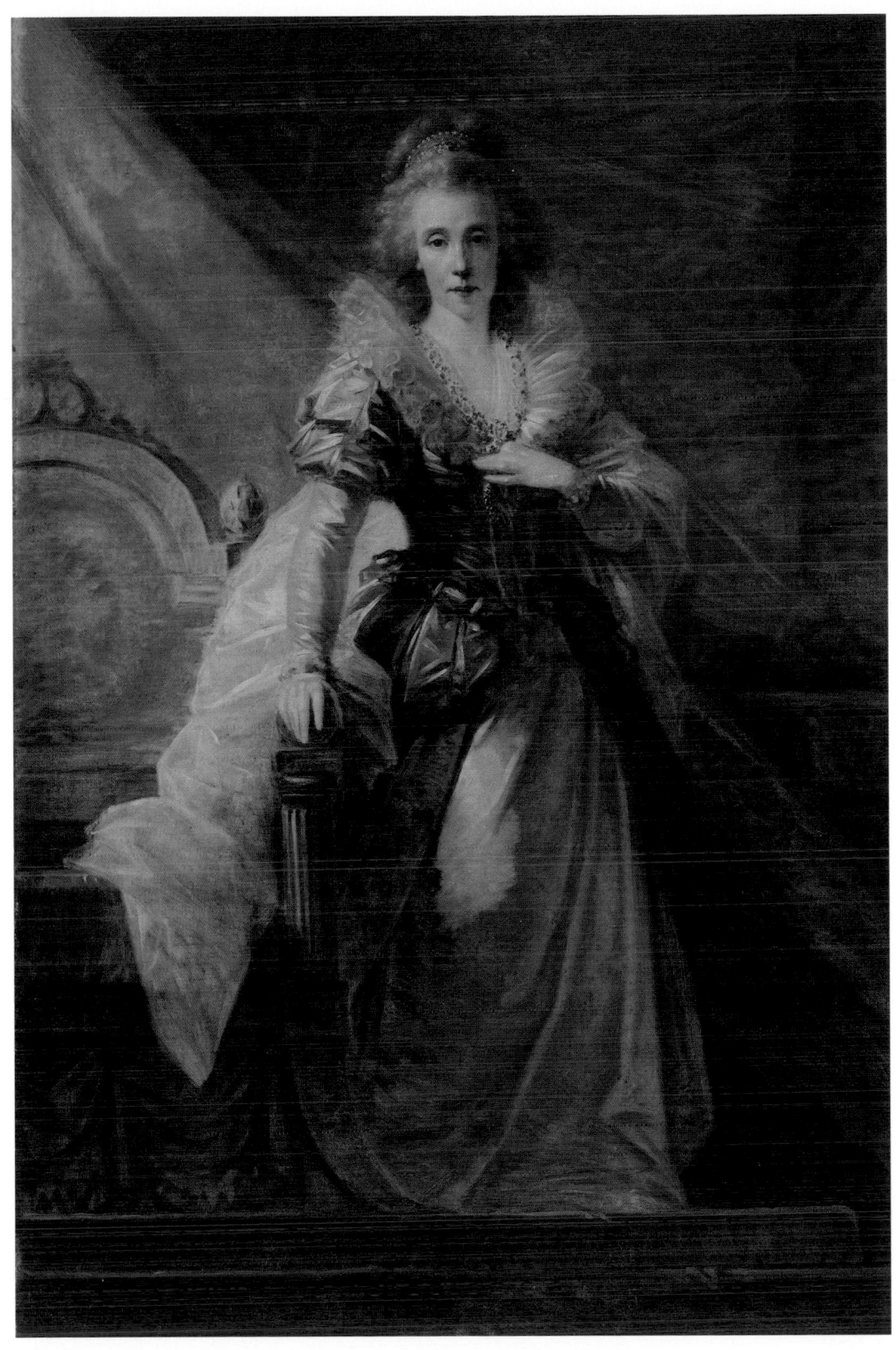

161   Friedrich Heinrich Füger, *Portrait of the Empress Maria Luisa*

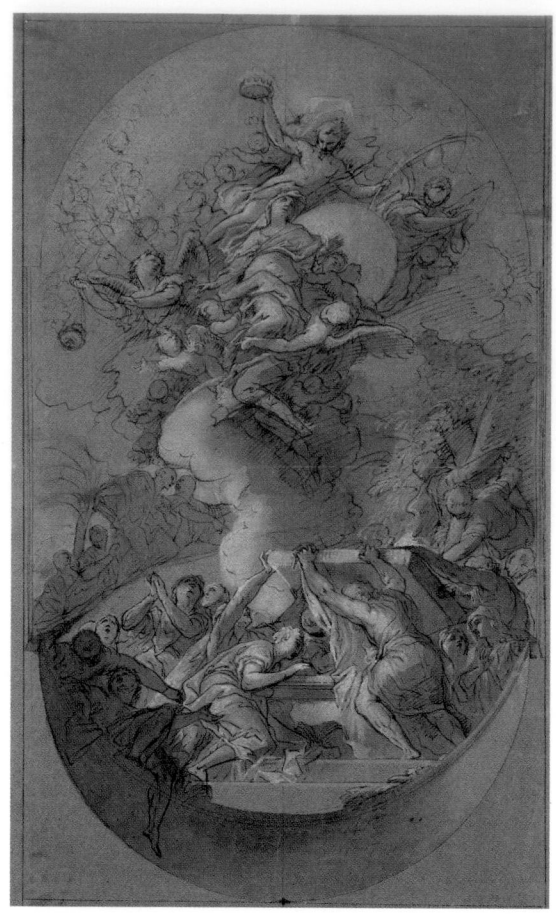

162 Melchior Steidl, *Assumption of the Virgin*

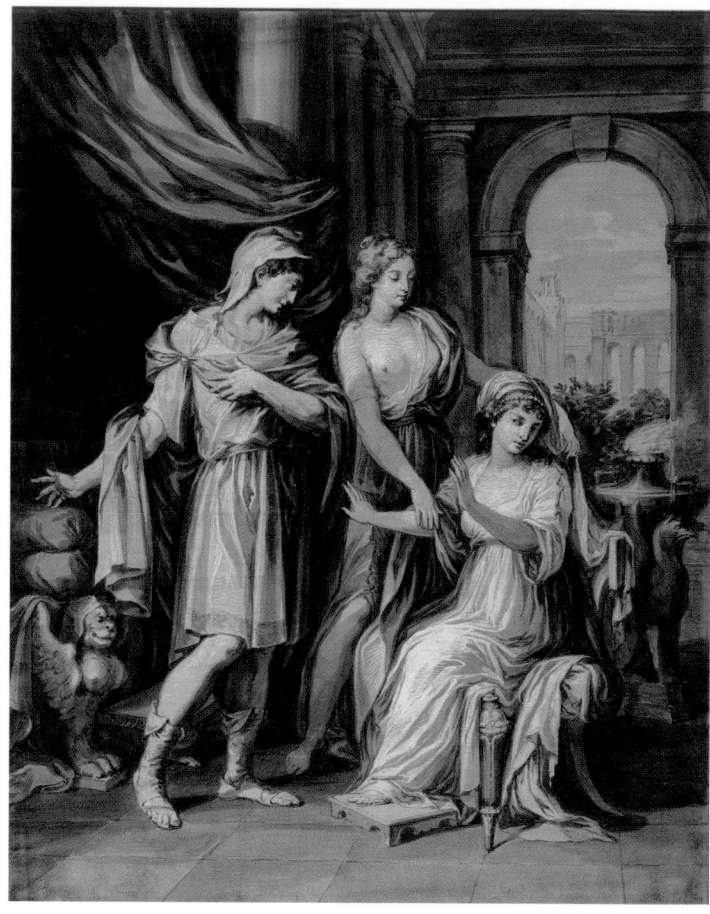

164 Joseph Bergler, *Venus Persuading Helen to Love Paris*

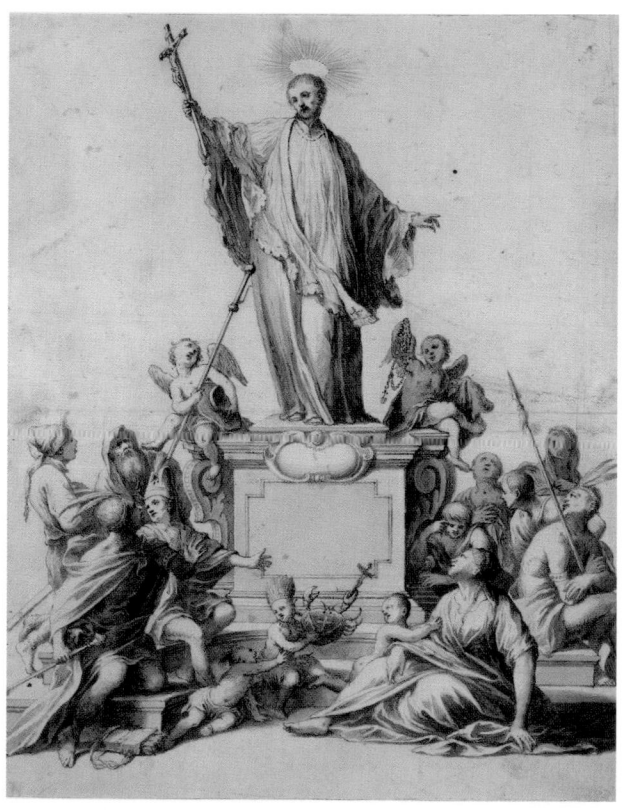

163 Johann Georg Heintsch, *Design for the St Francis Xavier Group on the Charles Bridge in Prague*

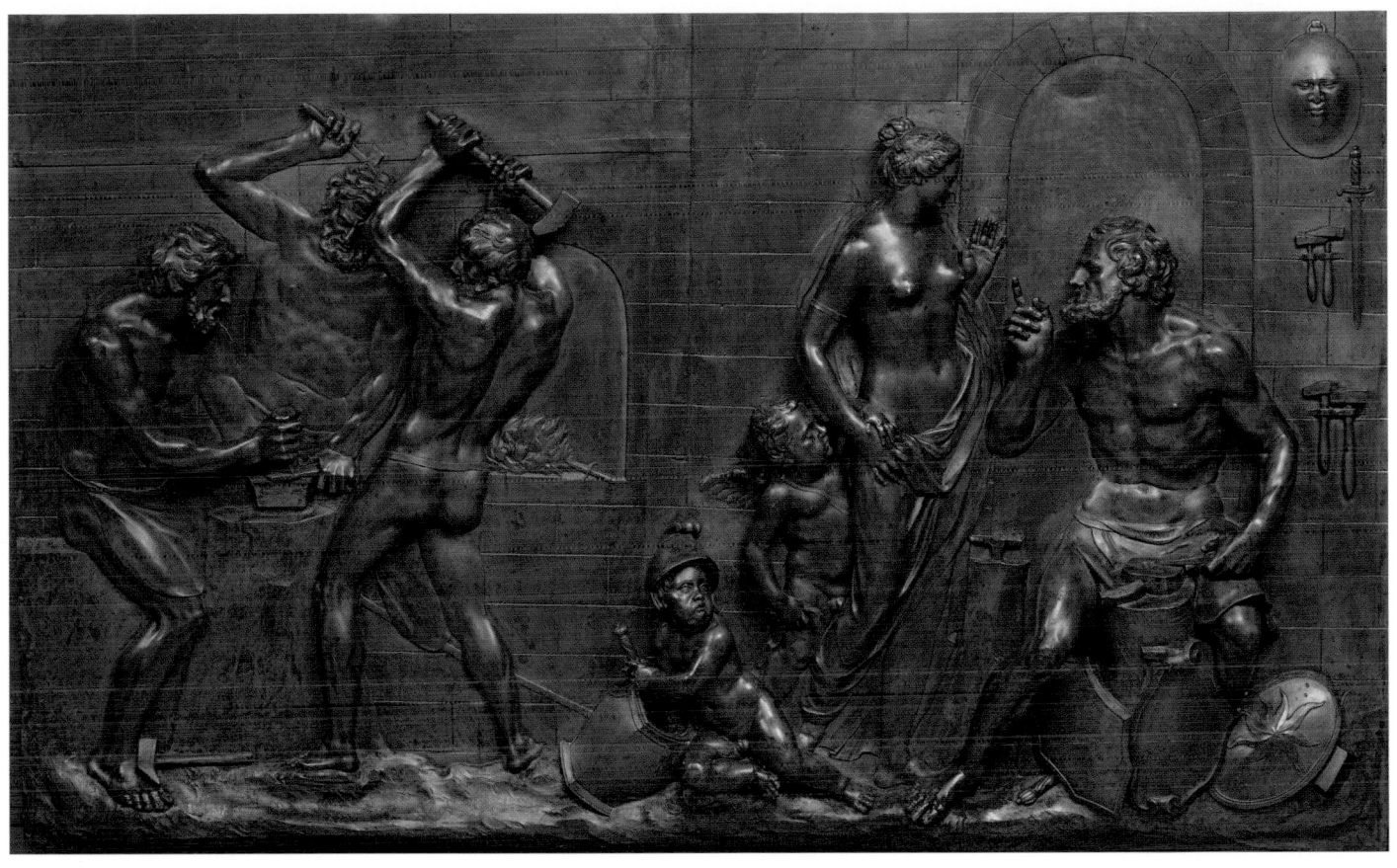

165.1, 165.2 Attributed to Georg Raphael Donner, *Venus in the Forge of Vulcan, Judgement of Paris*

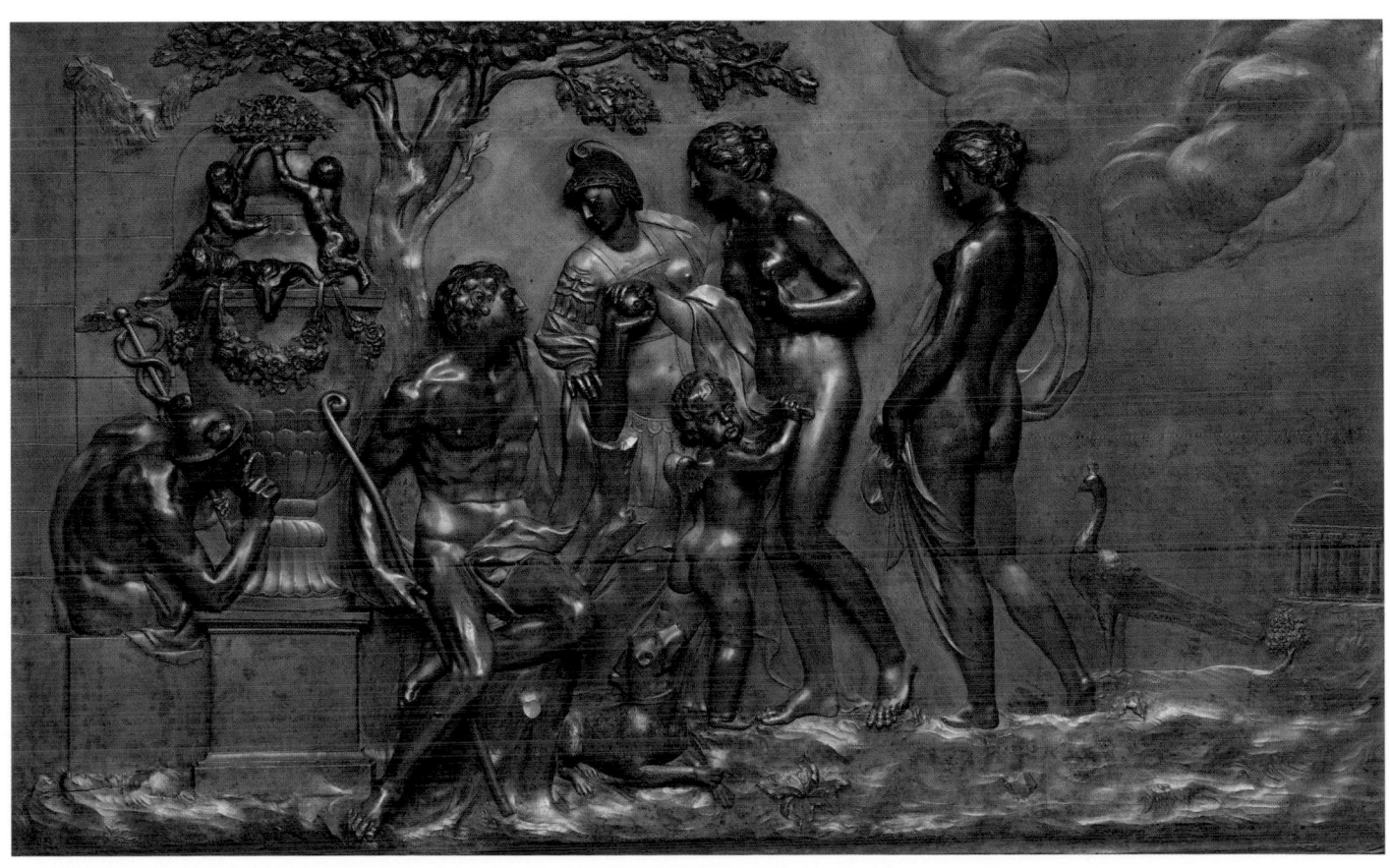

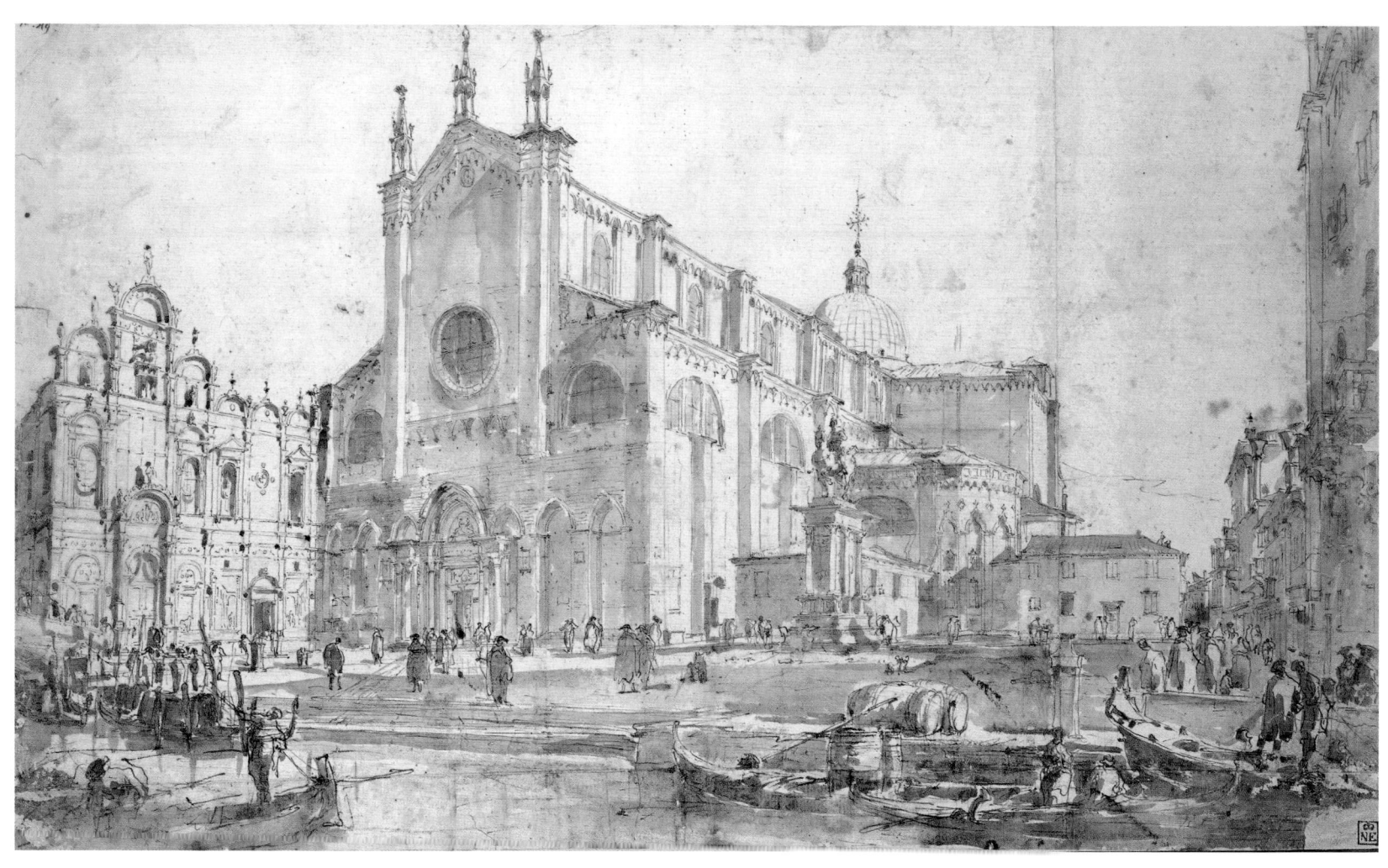

166   Francesco Guardi, *Campo San Zanipolo in Venice*

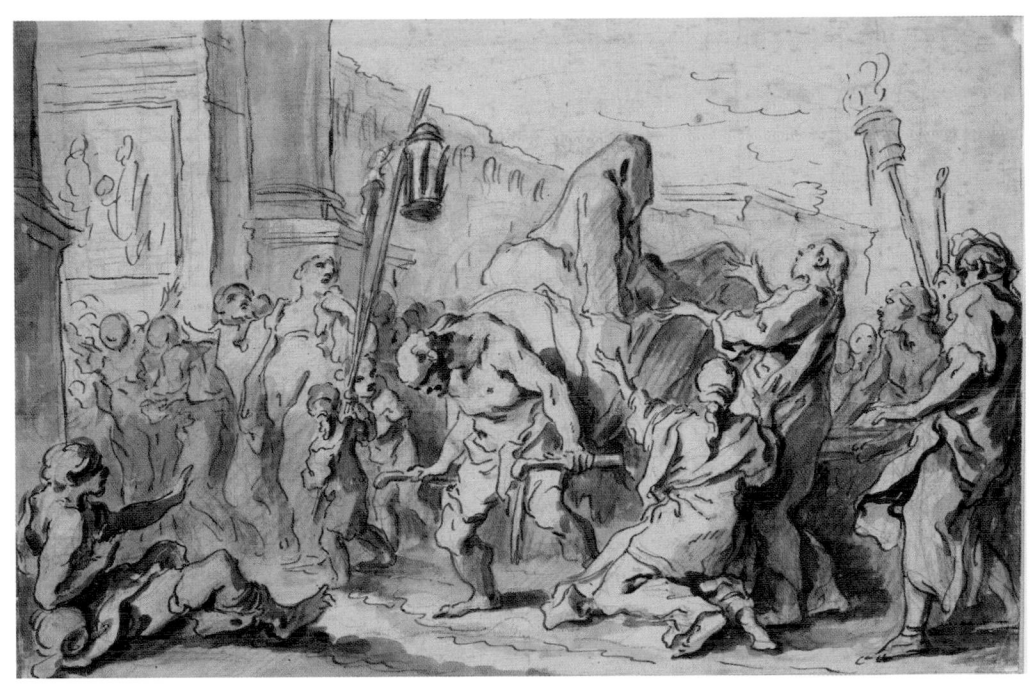

167   François Boucher, *Resurrection of the Son of the Widow of Nain*

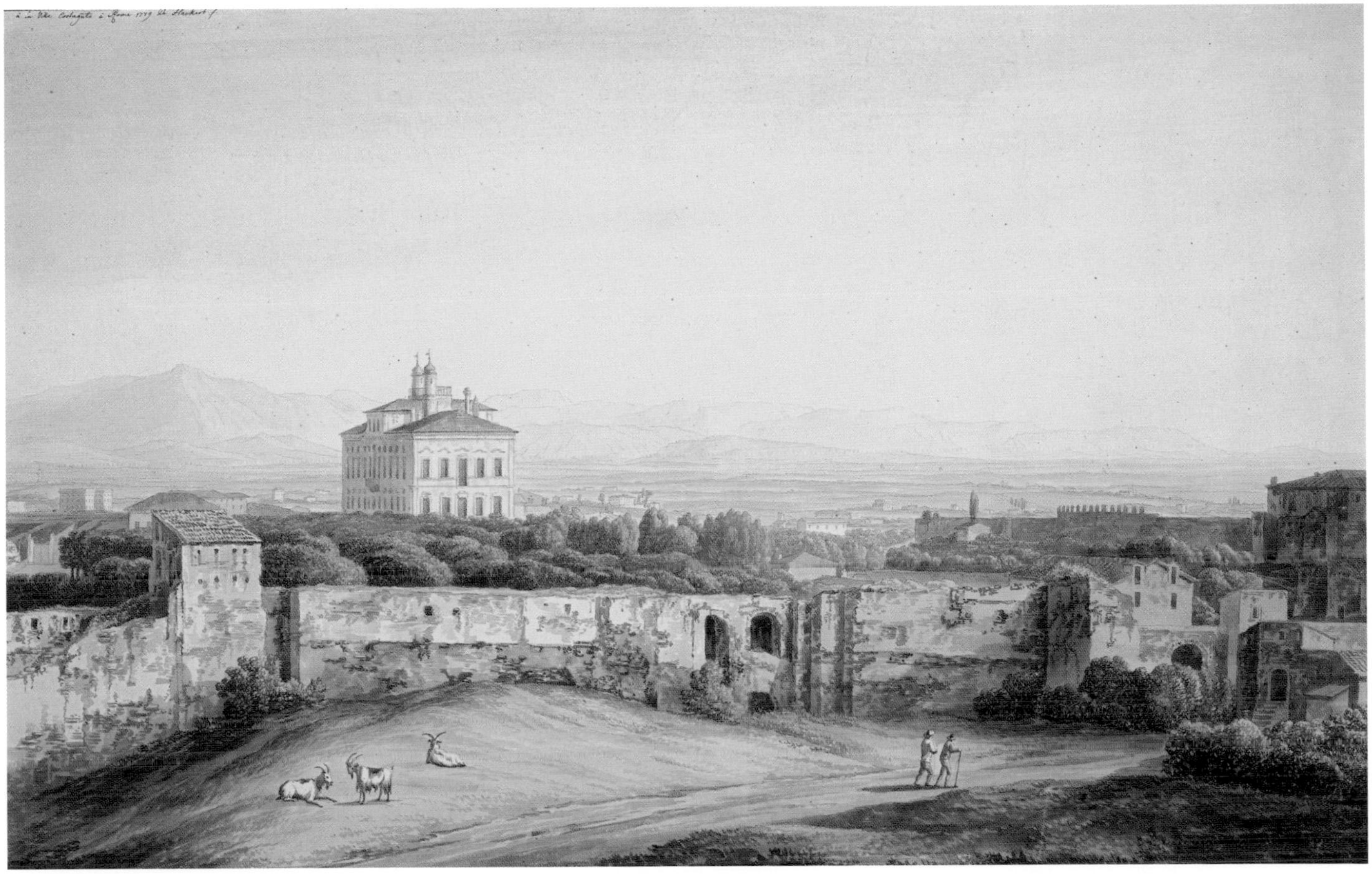

168   Jacob Philipp Hackert, *View of the Villa Patrizi from the Villa Costaguti, Rome*

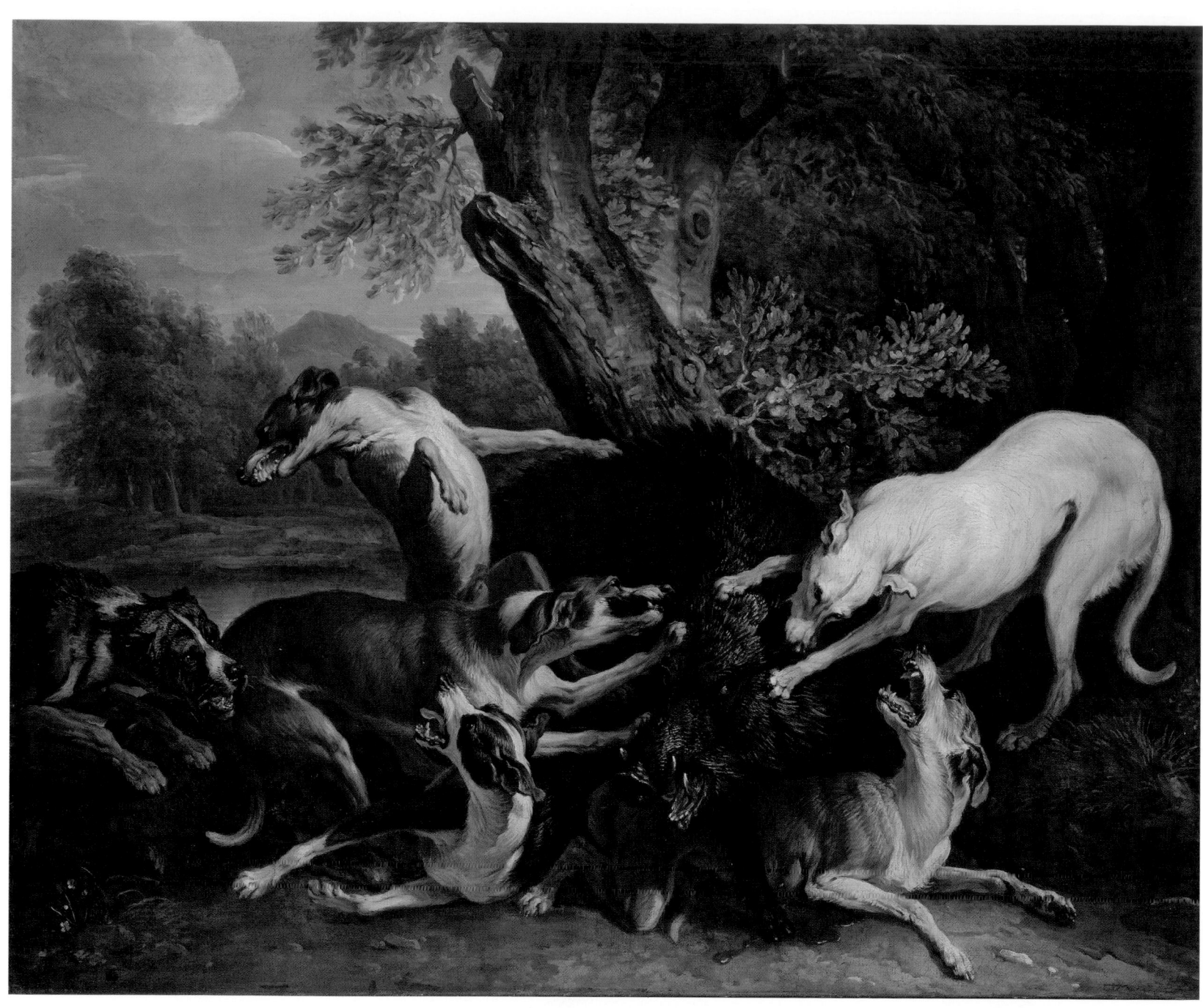

169   Jean-Baptiste Oudry, *Boar Hunt*

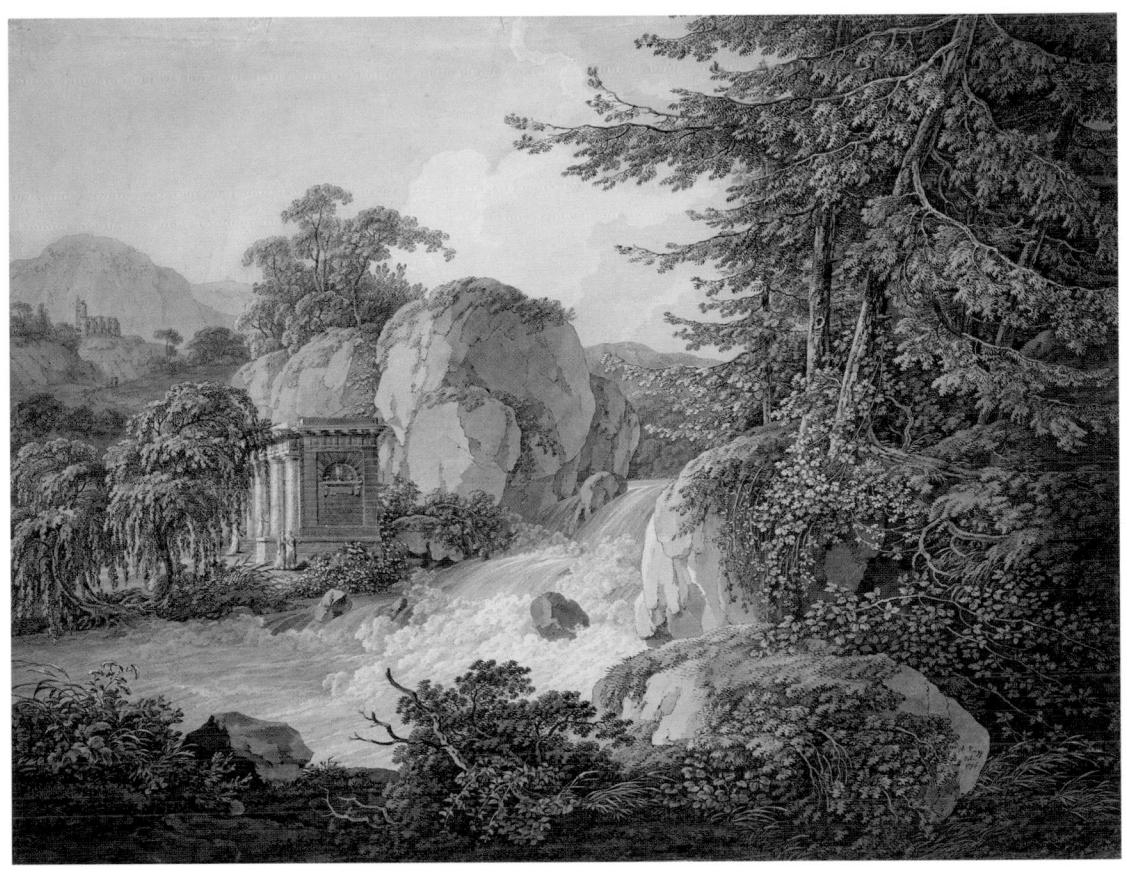

170   Adrian Zingg, *Landscape with Waterfall*

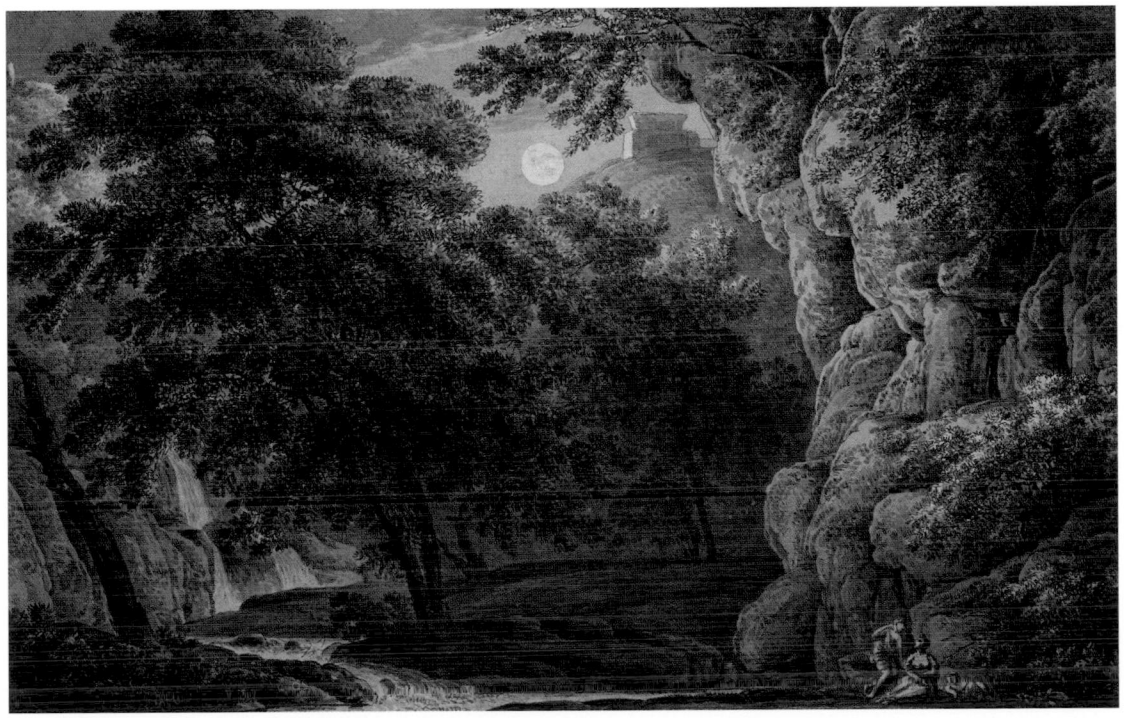

171   Franz Kobell, *Rocky Landscape by Moonlight*

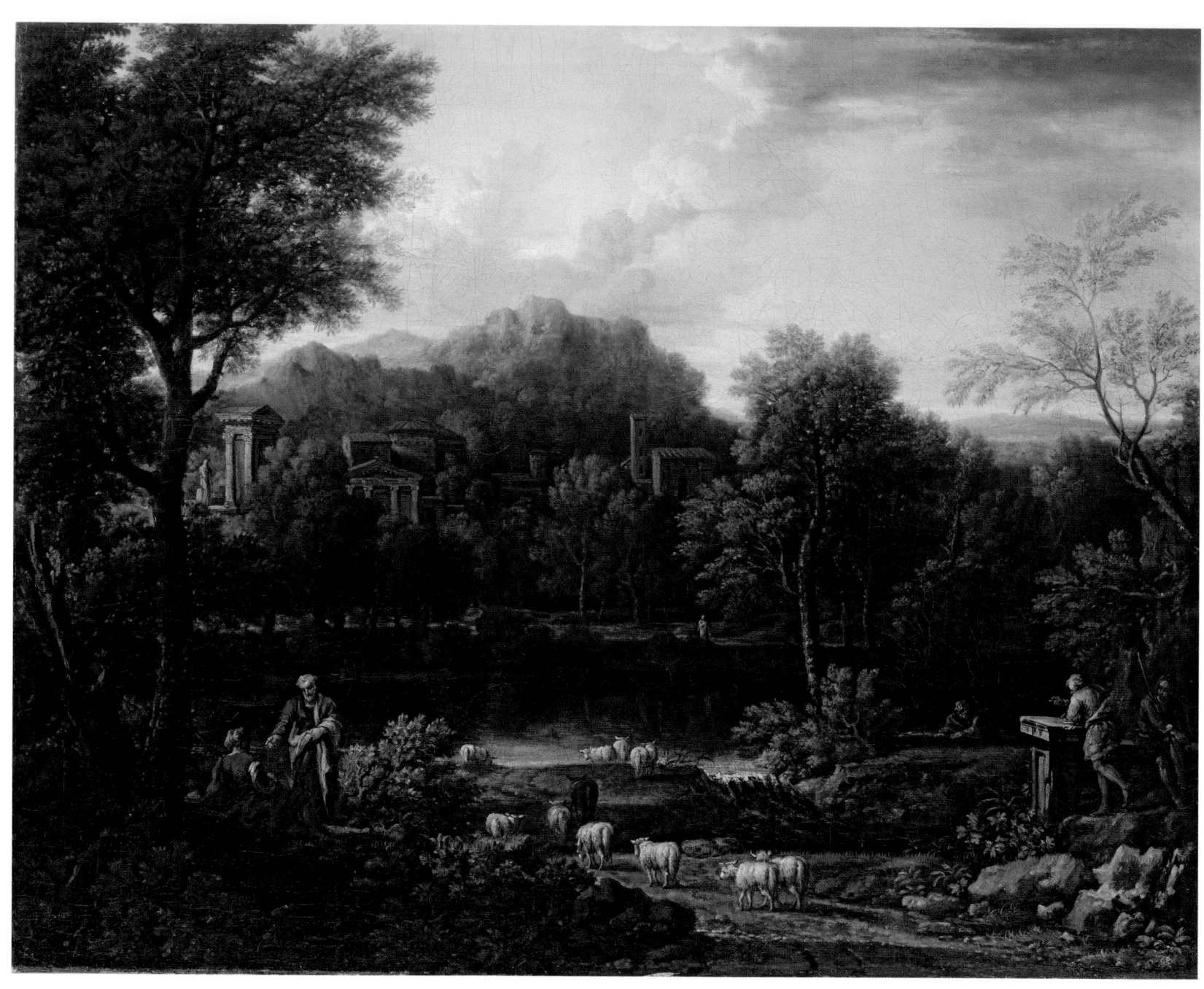

172   John Wootton, *Classical Landscape*

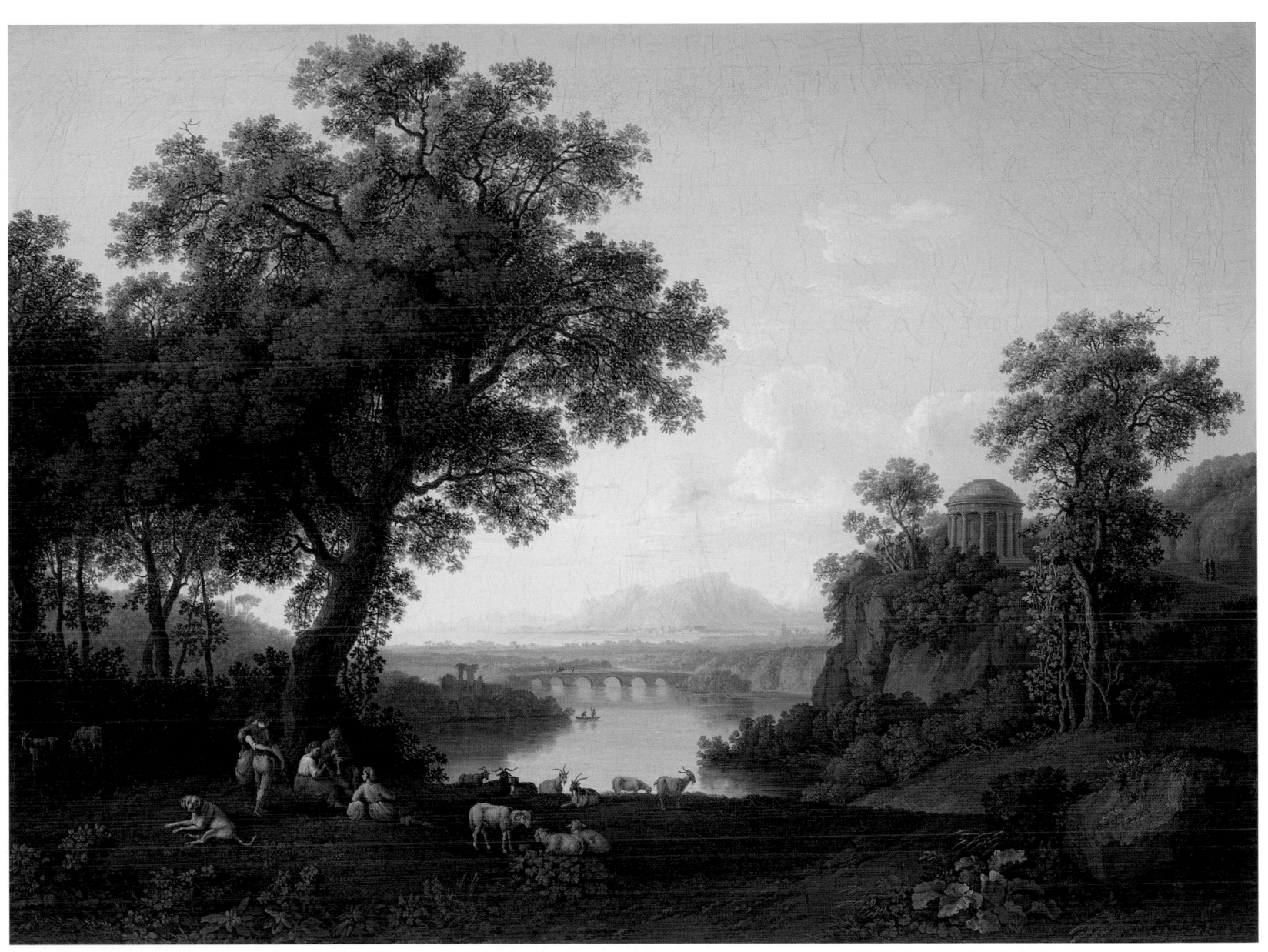

173   Jacob Philipp Hackert, *Landscape with River*

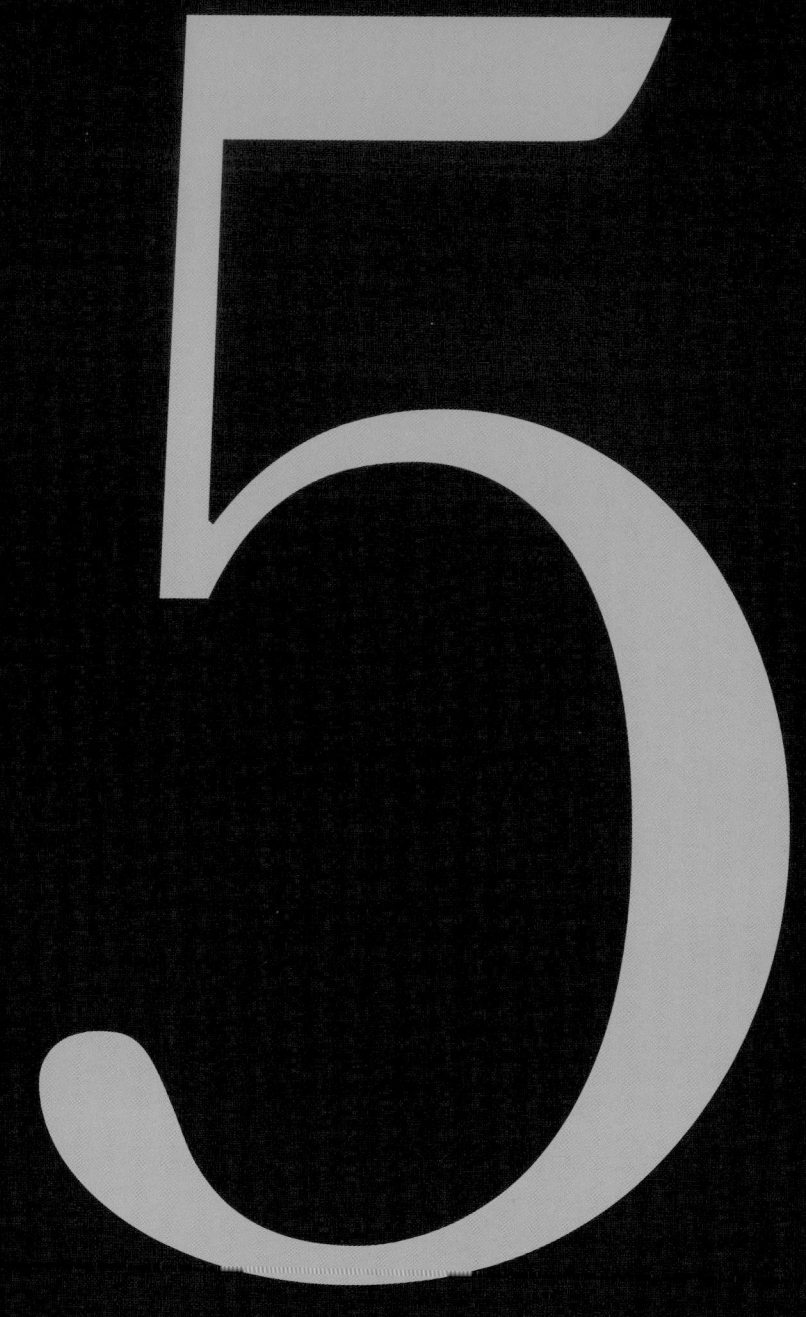

5

NINETEENTH AND TWENTIETH
centuries

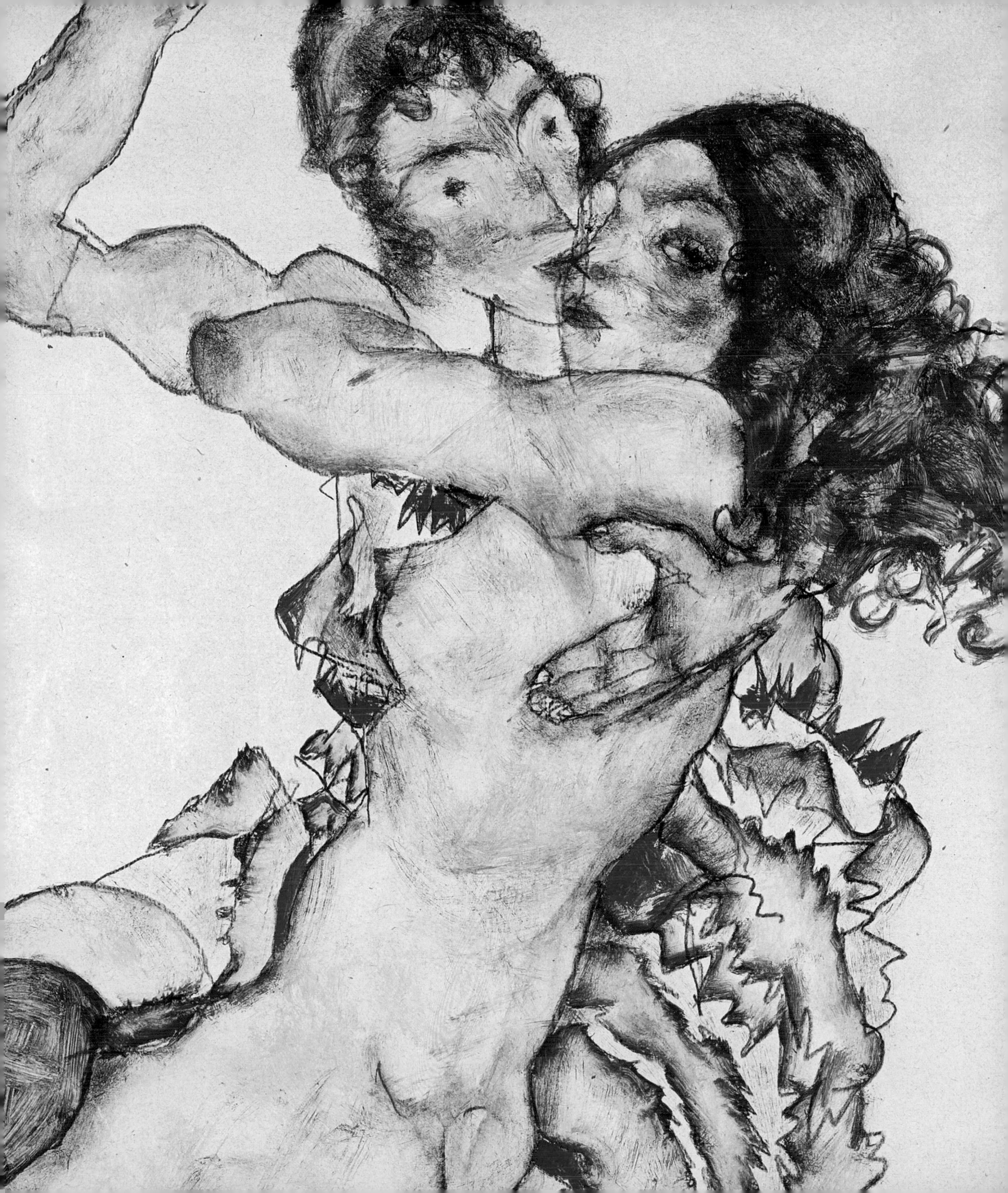

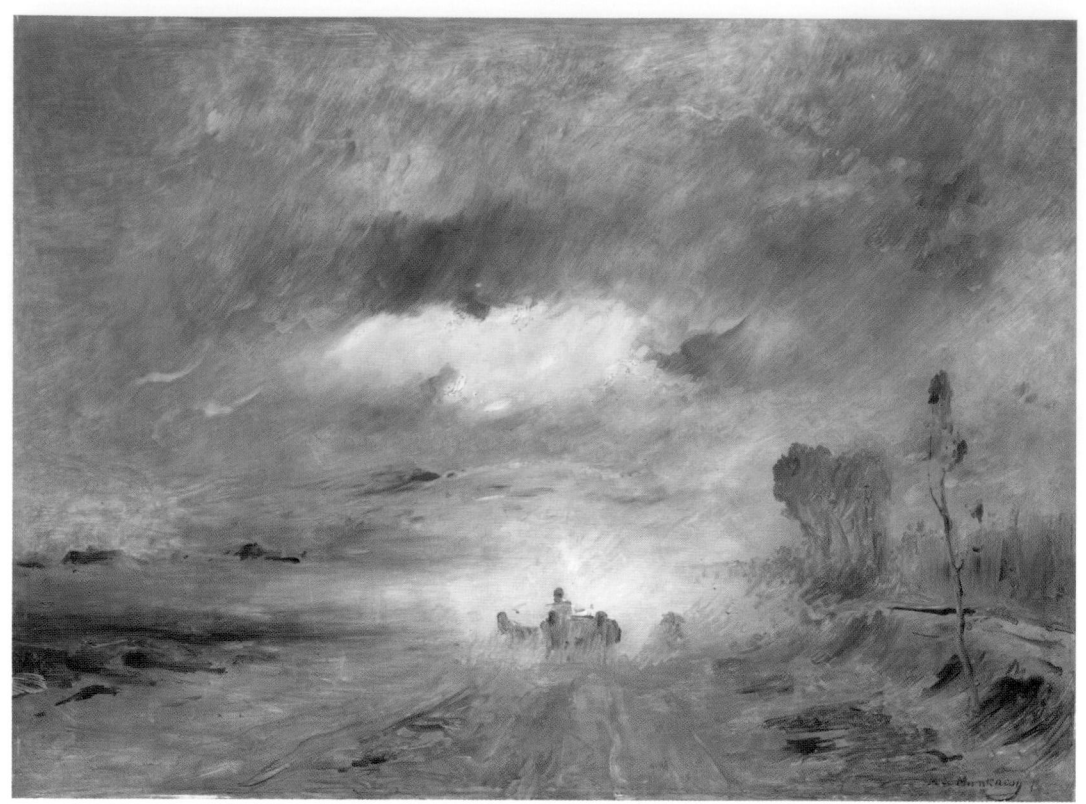

174   Mihály Munkácsy, *Dusty Road II*

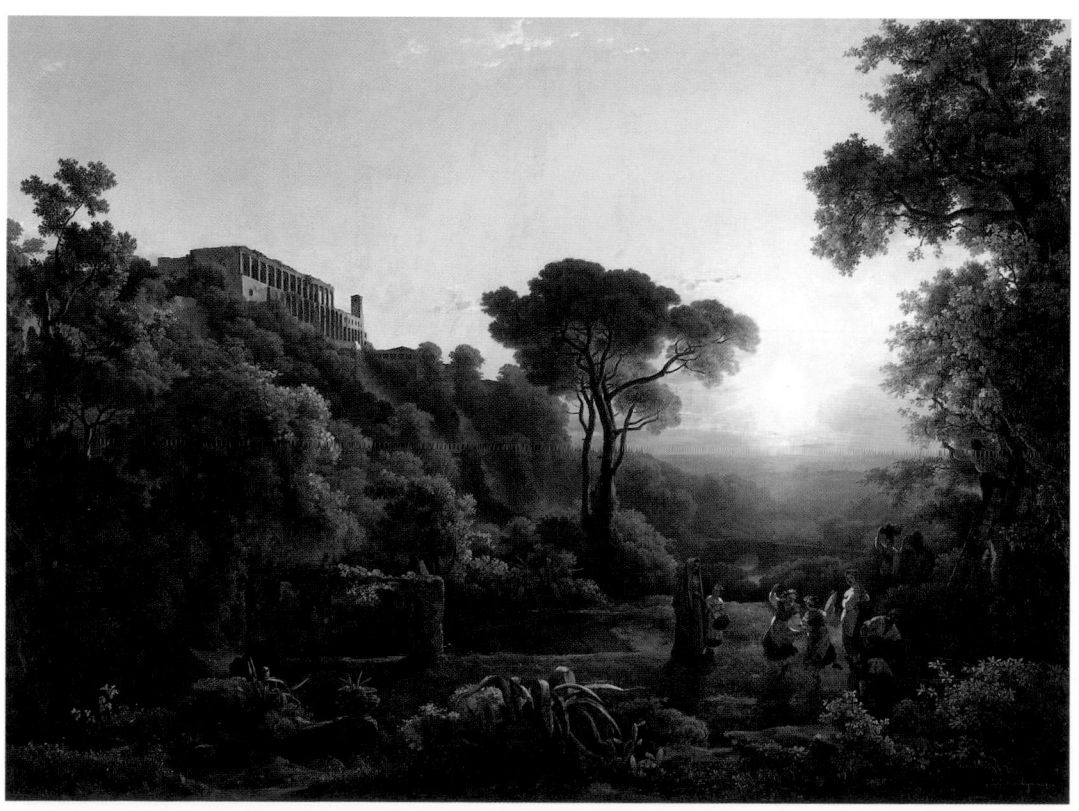

175   Károly Markó the Elder, *Landscape with a Vintage Scene near Tivoli*

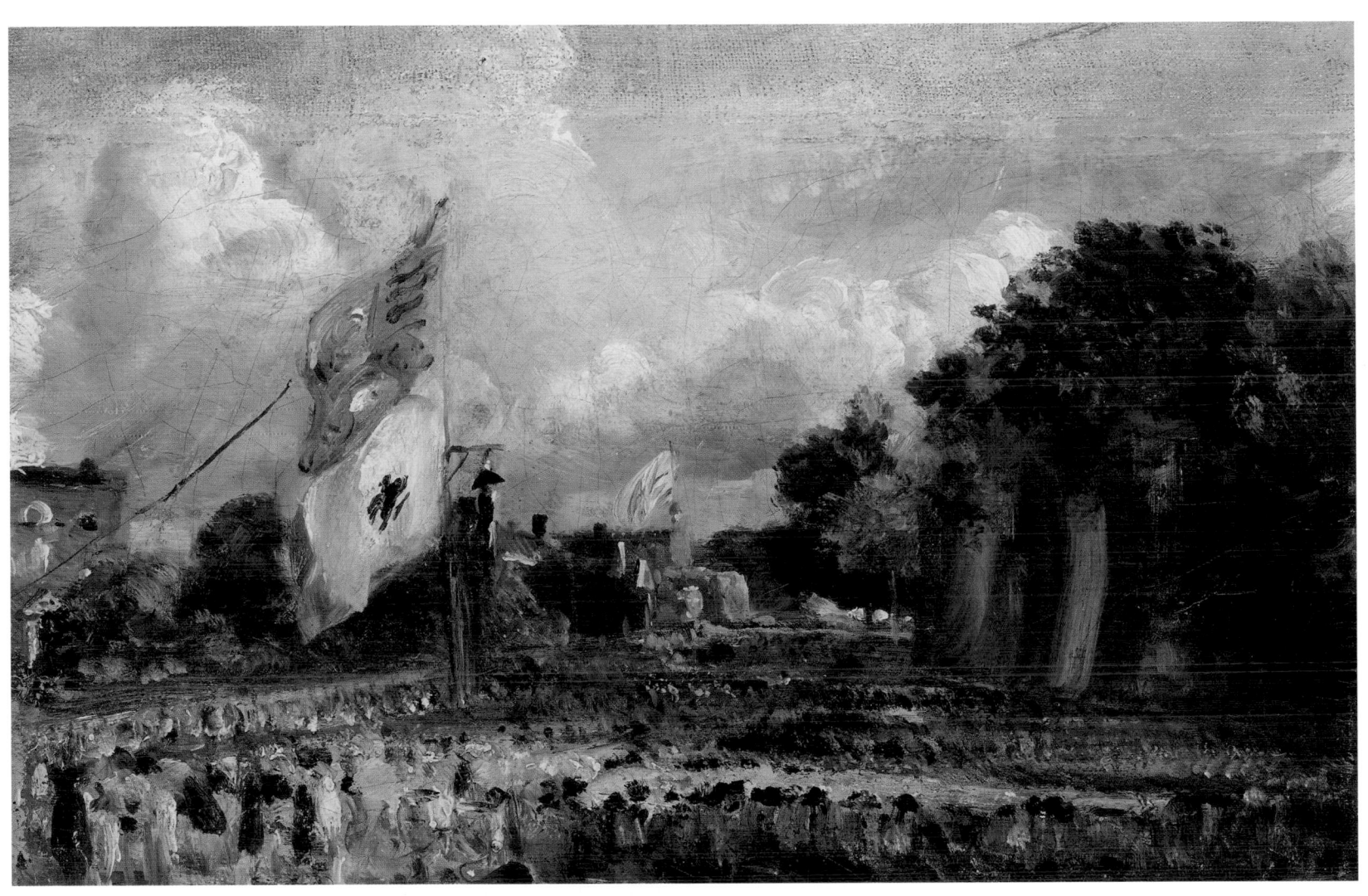

176   John Constable RA, *Celebration of the General Peace of 1814 in East Bergholt*

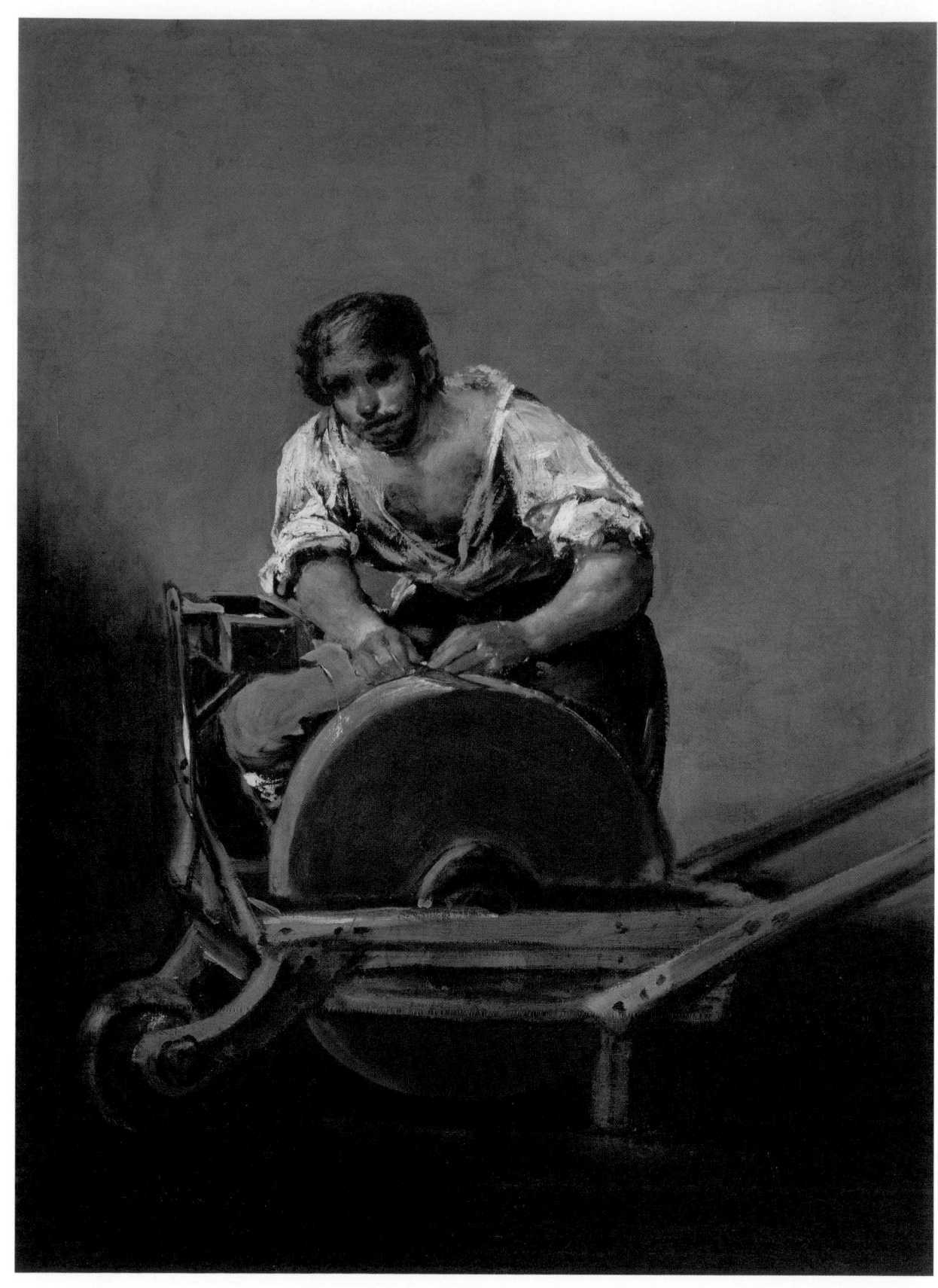

177 Francisco José de Goya y Lucientes, *Knife-grinder*

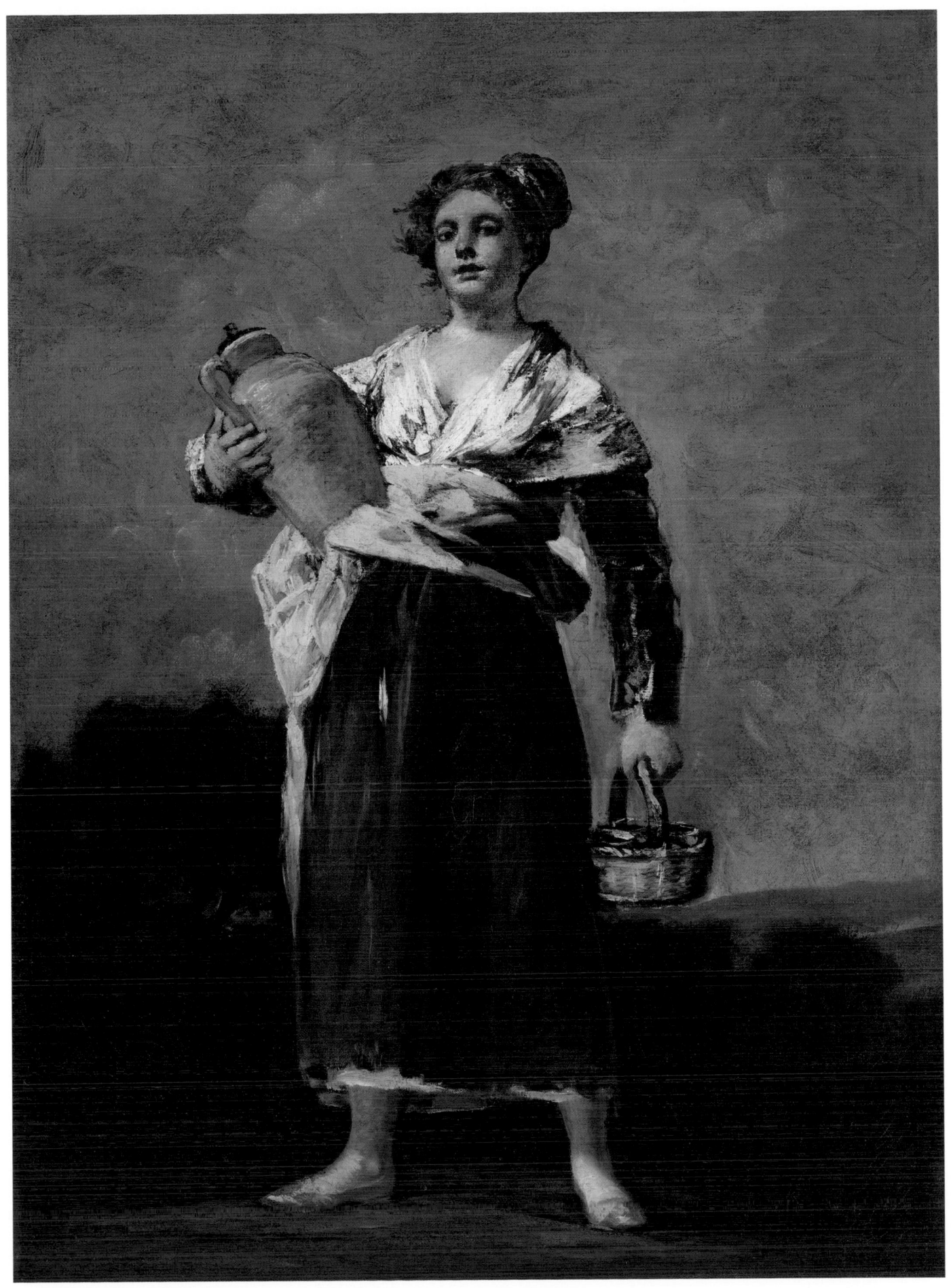

178 Francisco José de Goya y Lucientes, *Water-carrier*

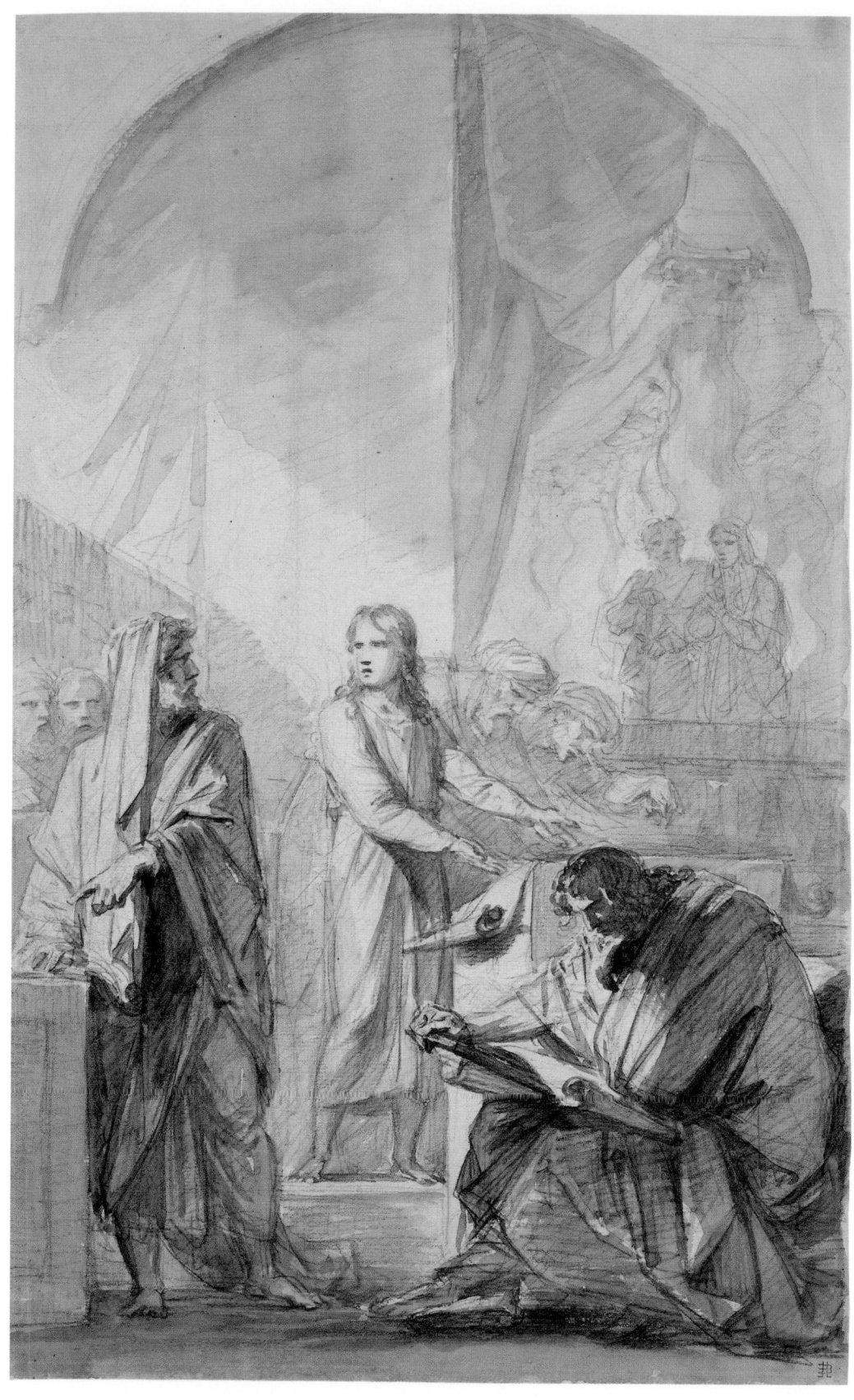

179   Friedrich Heinrich Füger, *Christ among the Doctors*

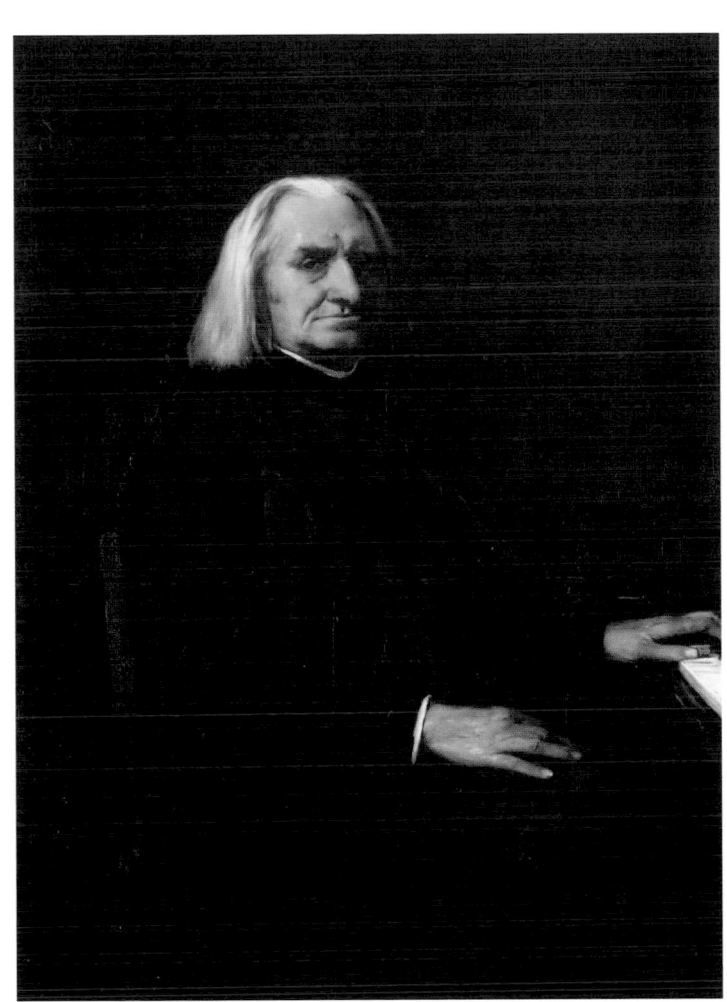

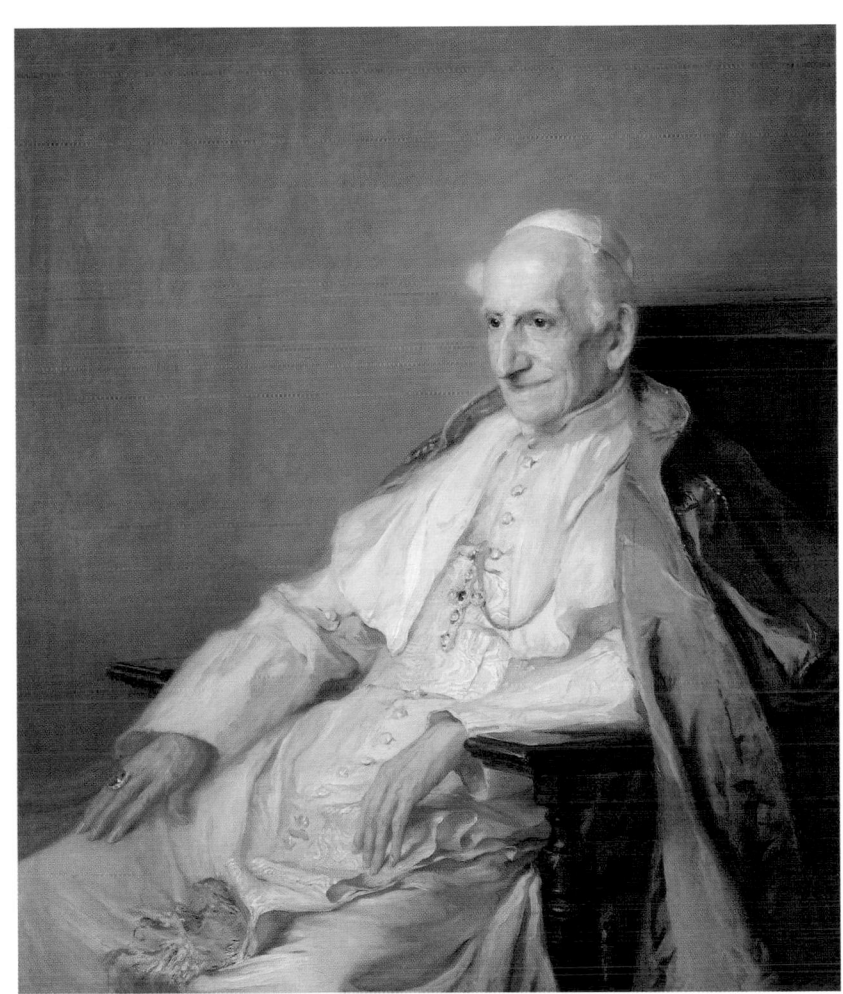

180   Mihály Munkácsy, *Portrait of Franz Liszt*   181   Philip de László, *Portrait of Pope Leo XIII*

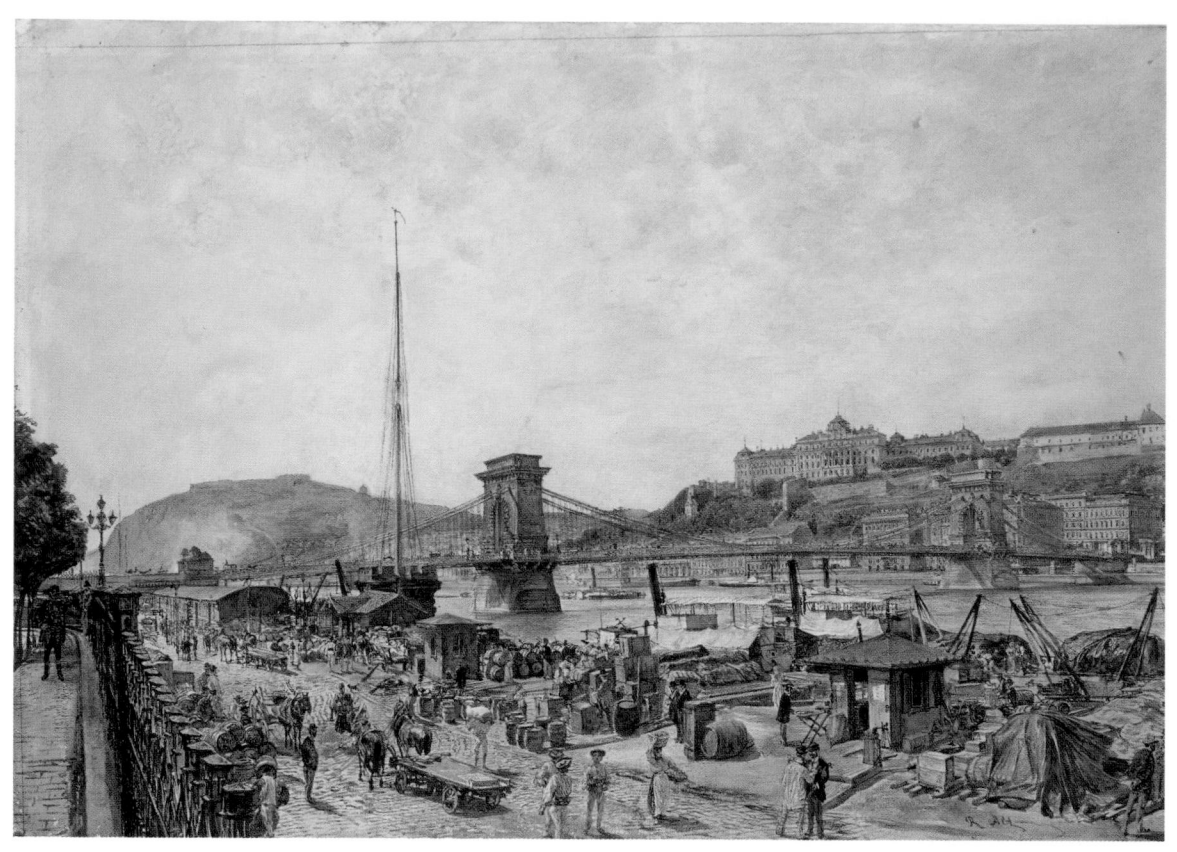

182   Rudolf von Alt, *View of Budapest with the Chain Bridge and the Royal Palace*

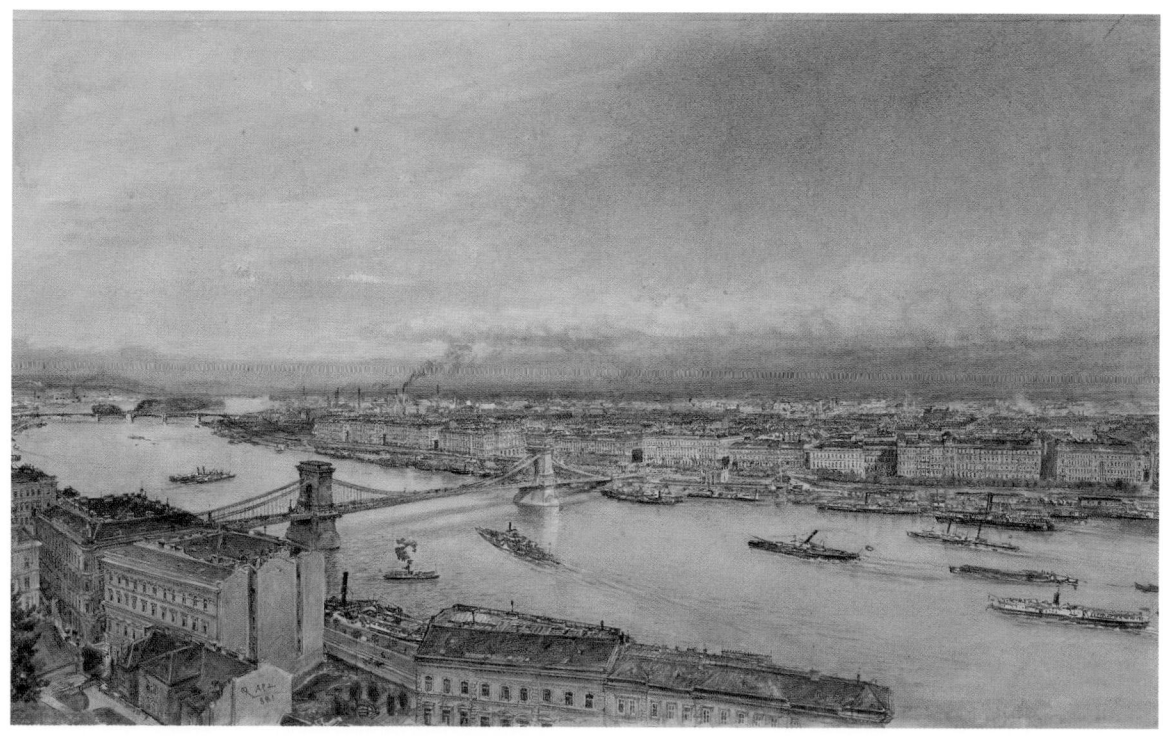

183   Rudolf von Alt, *View of Budapest from Castle Hill*

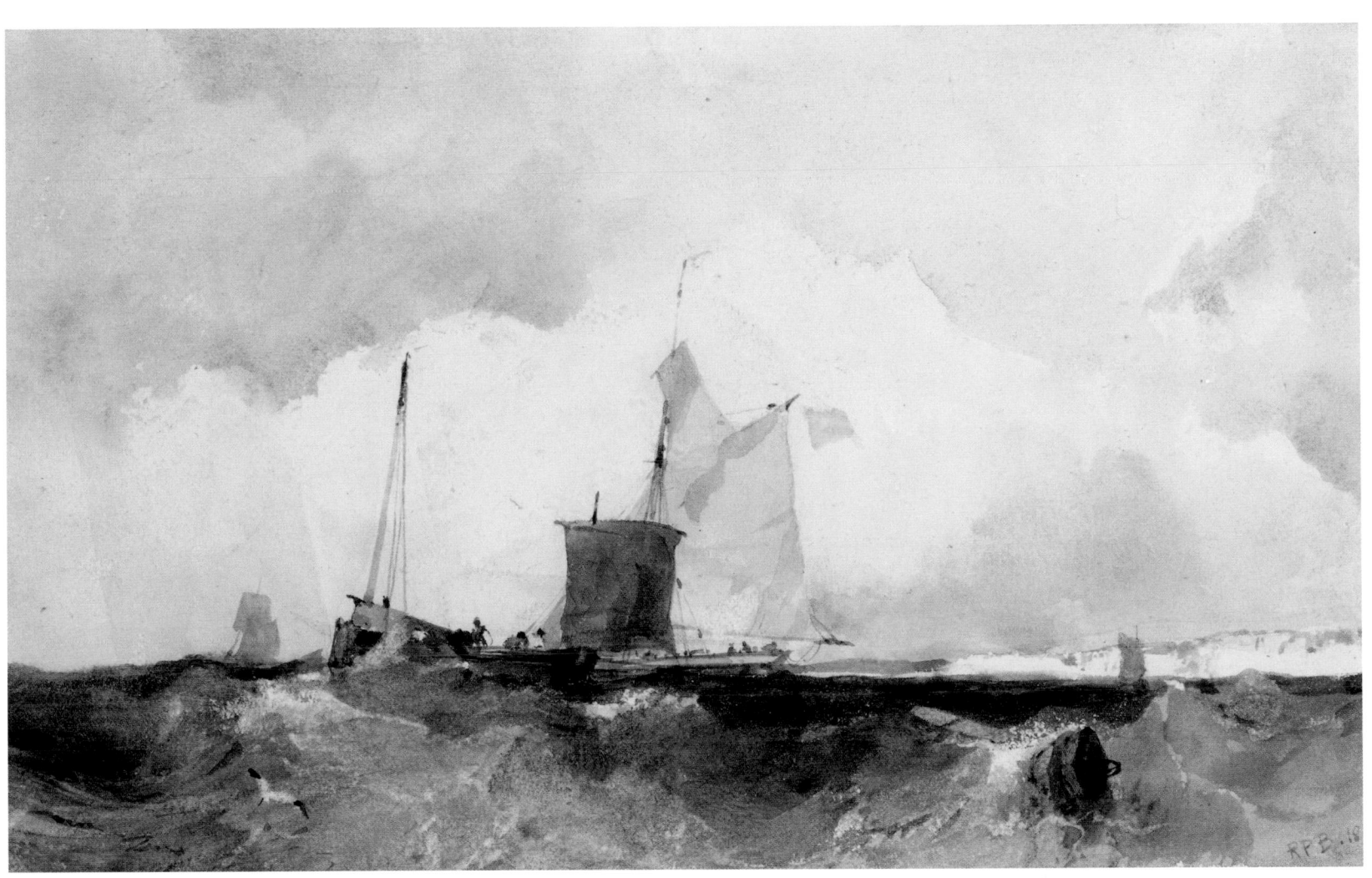

184   Richard Parkes Bonington, *View of the South Coast*

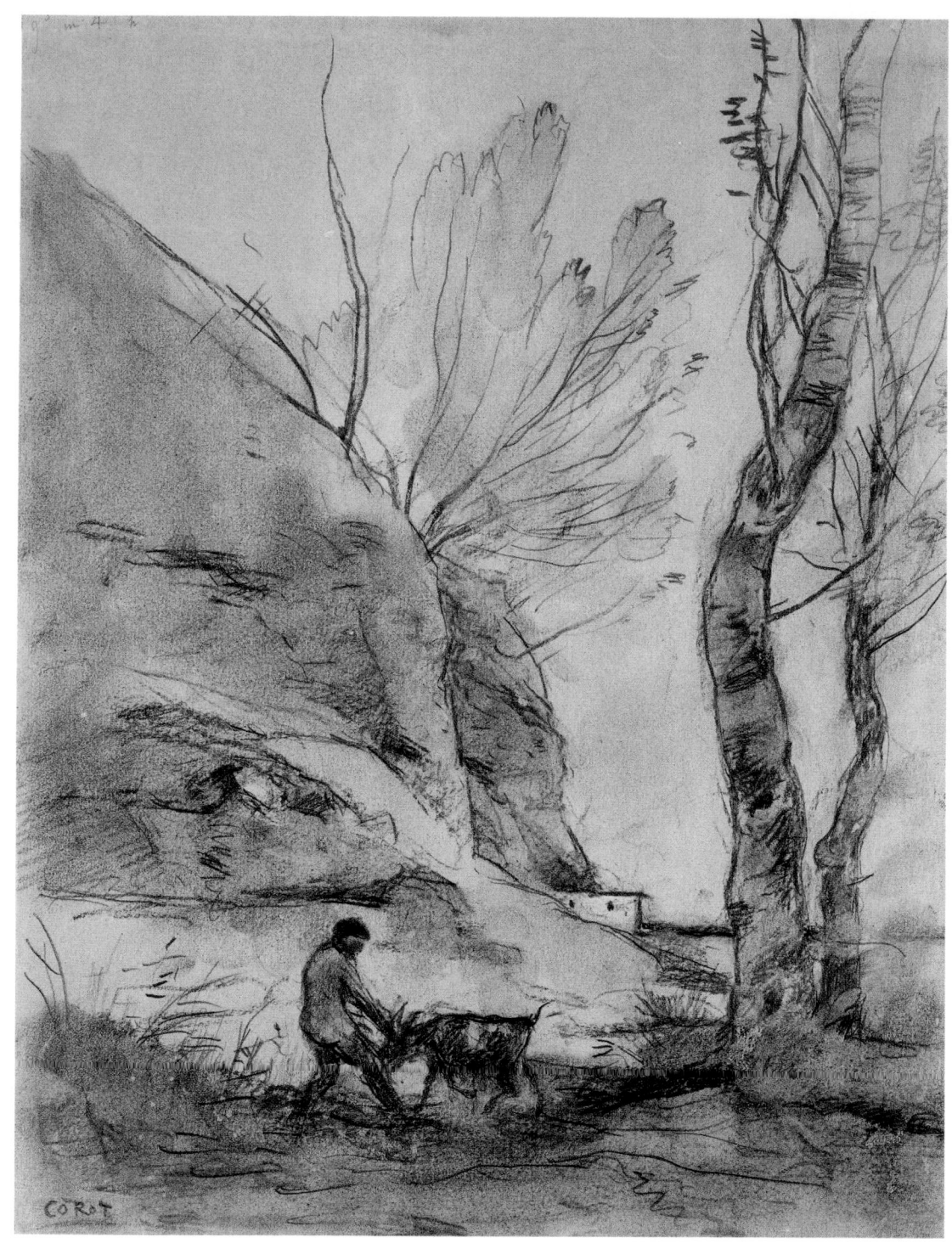

185   Jean-Baptiste-Camille Corot, *Shepherd Wrestling with a Goat*

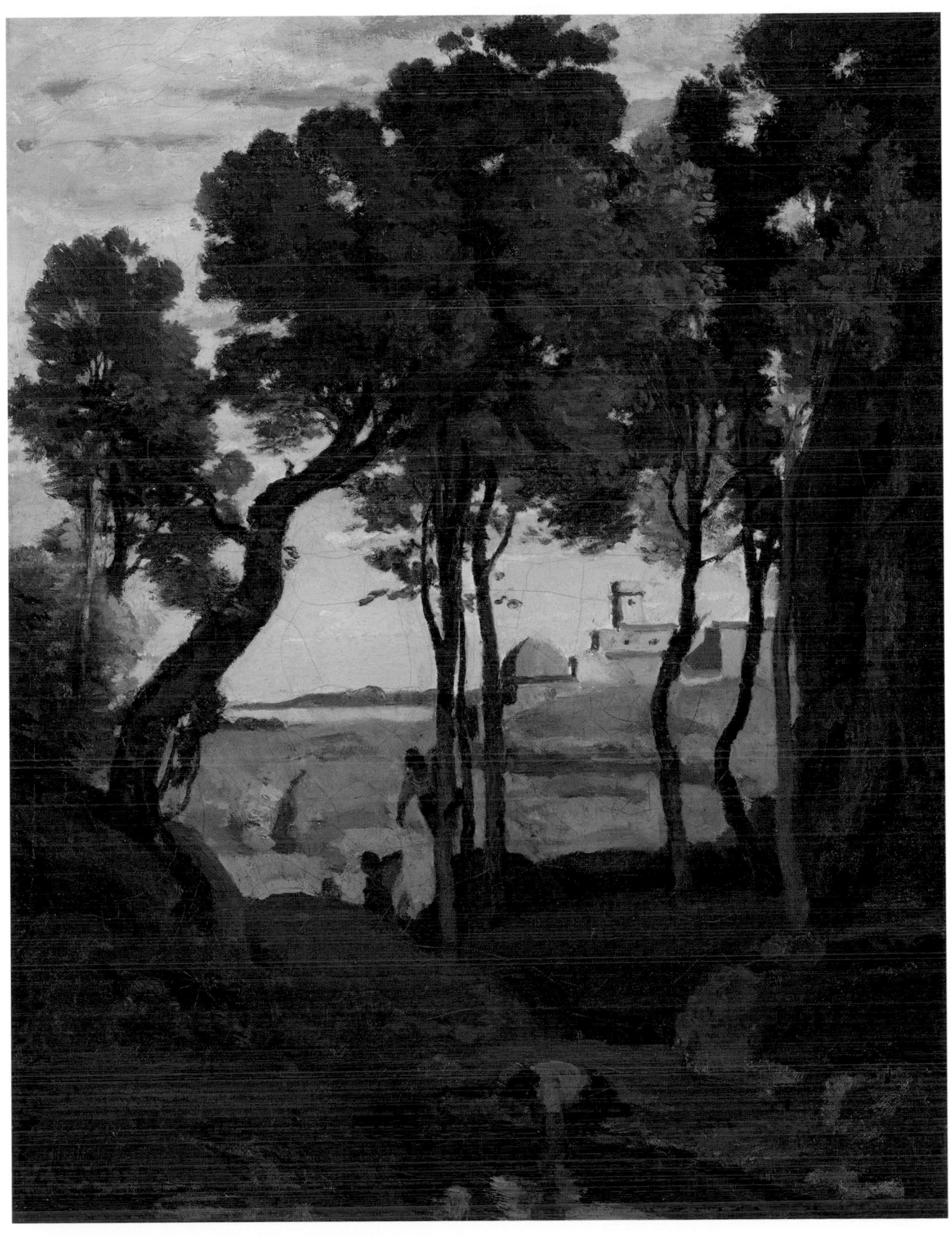

186 Jean-Baptiste-Camille Corot, *Nest-robbers (Italian Landscape)*

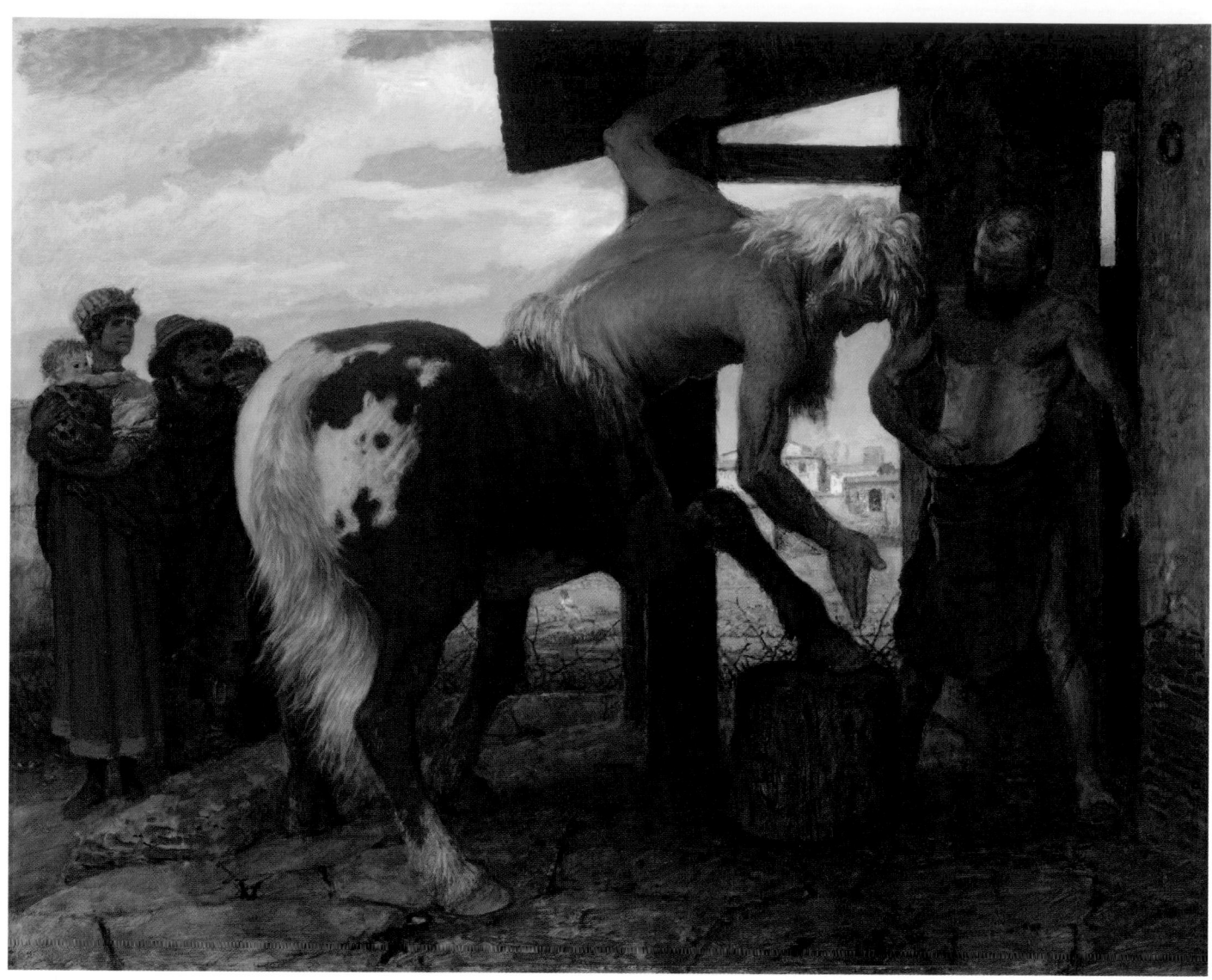

187   Arnold Böcklin, *Centaur at the Village Blacksmith's Shop*

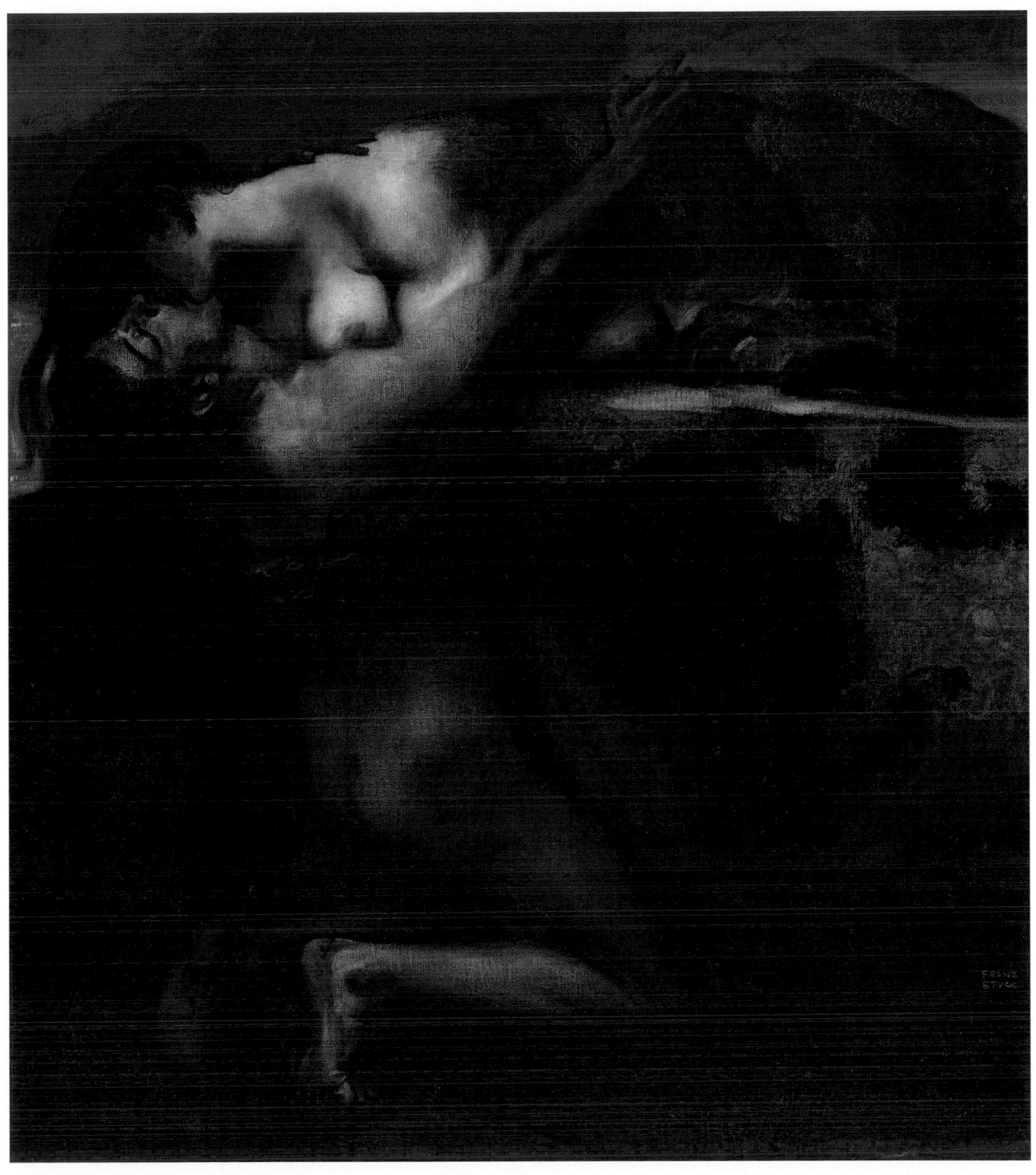

188 Franz von Stuck, *Kiss of the Sphinx*

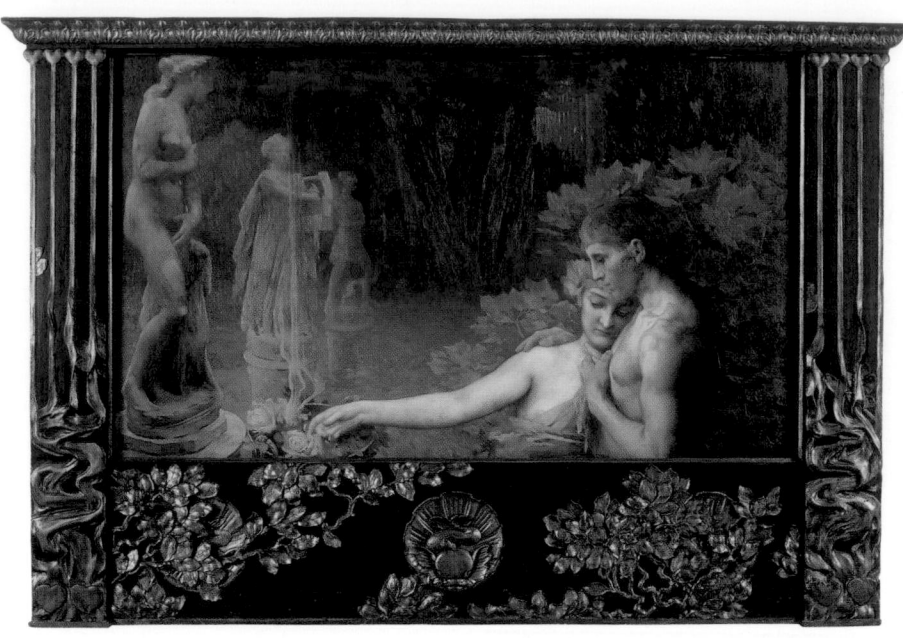

189   János Vaszary, *Golden Age*

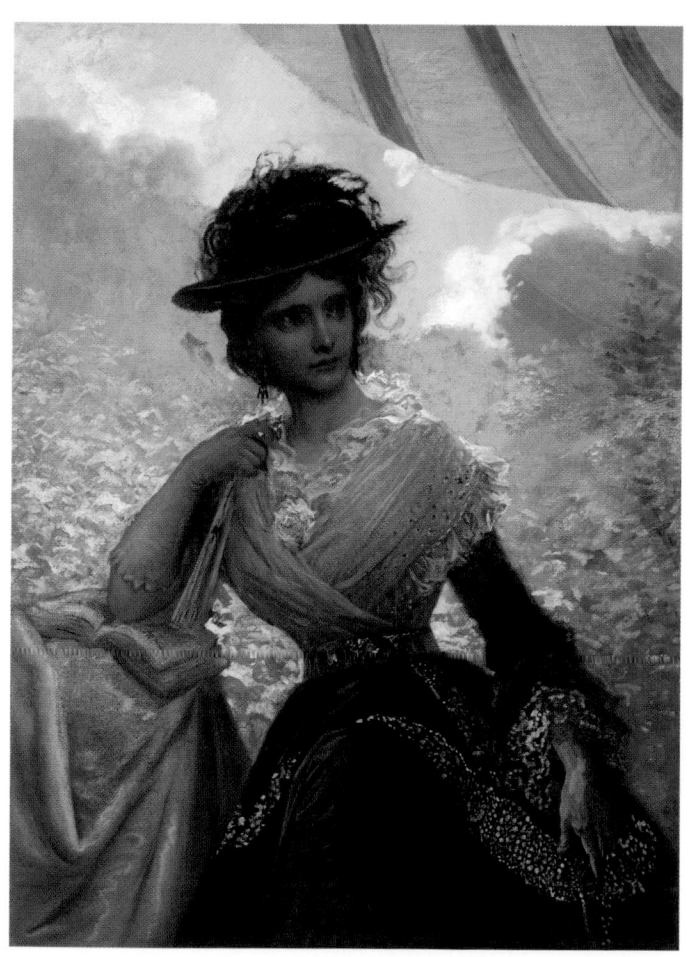

190   Gustave Doré, *Young Woman with a White Scarf*

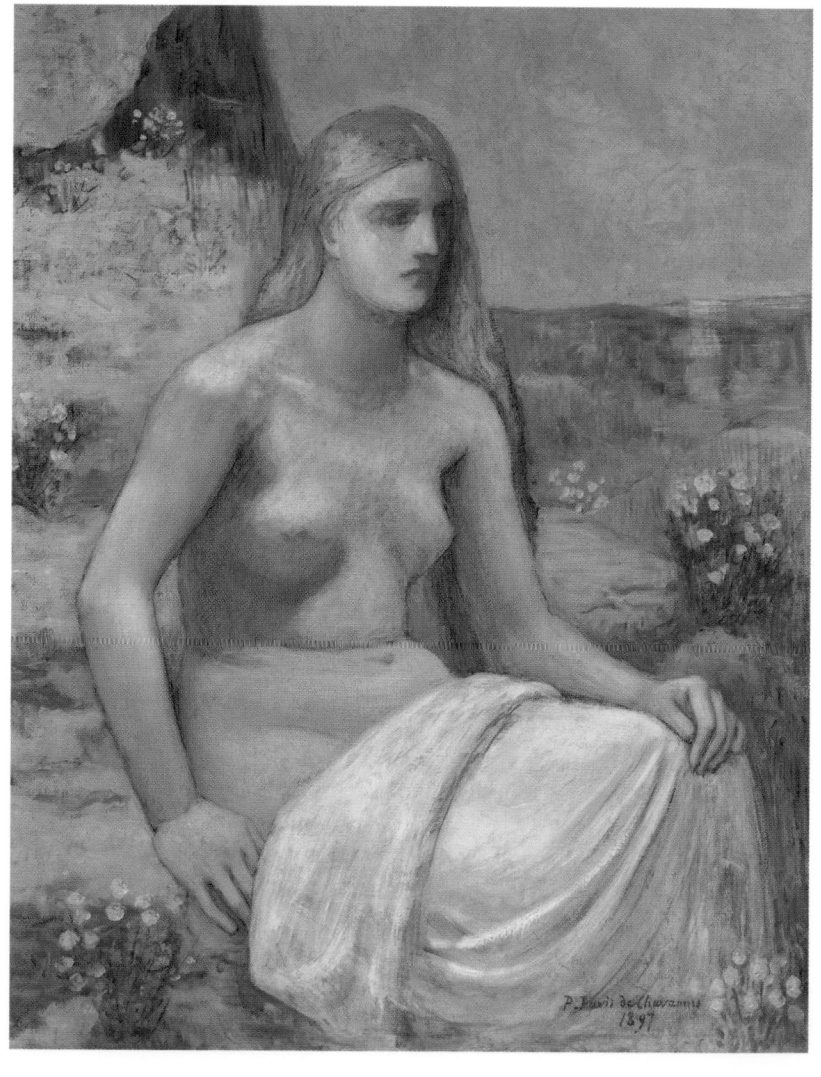

191   Pierre Puvis de Chavannes, *Magdalene*

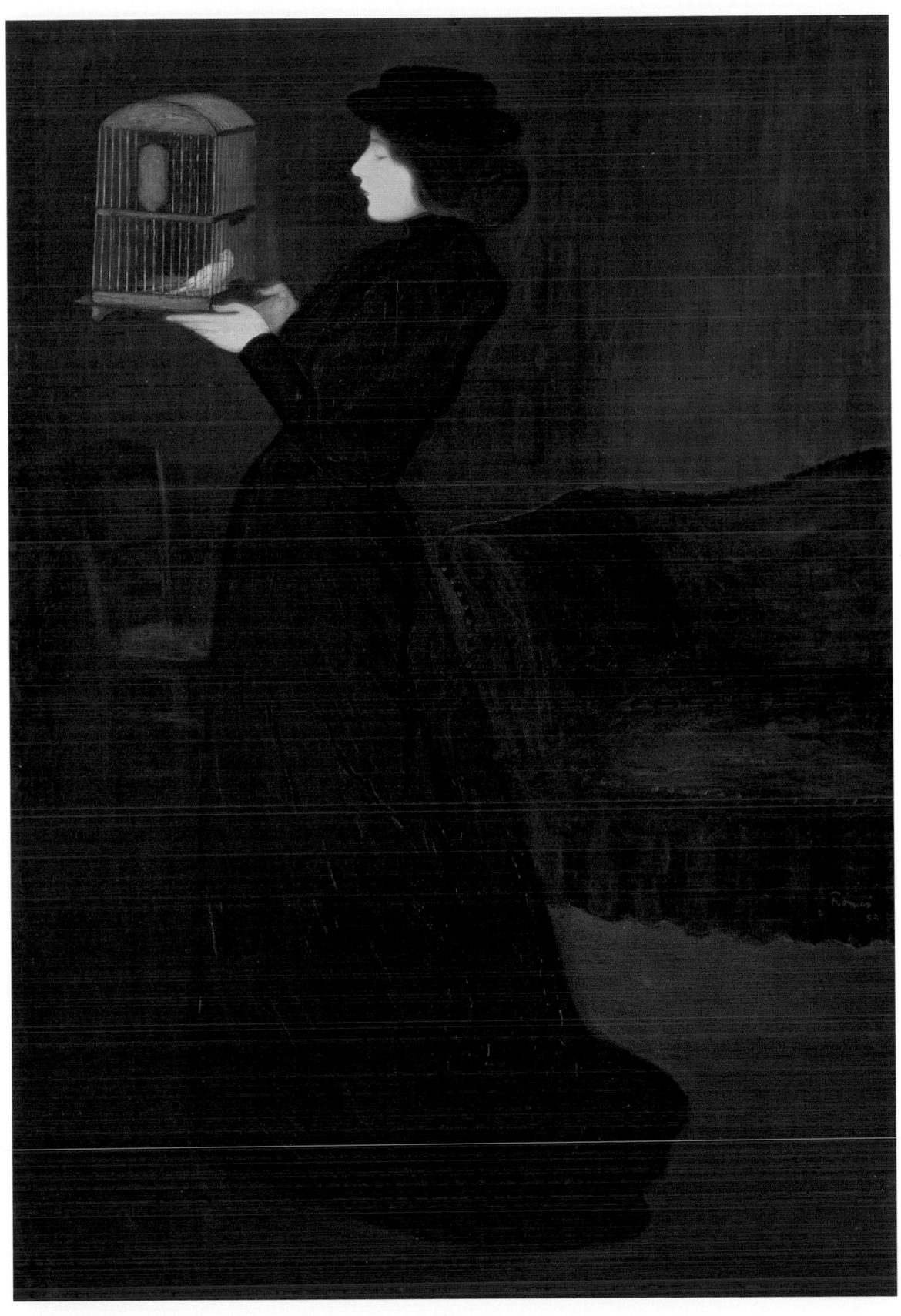

192   József Rippl-Rónai, *Woman with Birdcage*

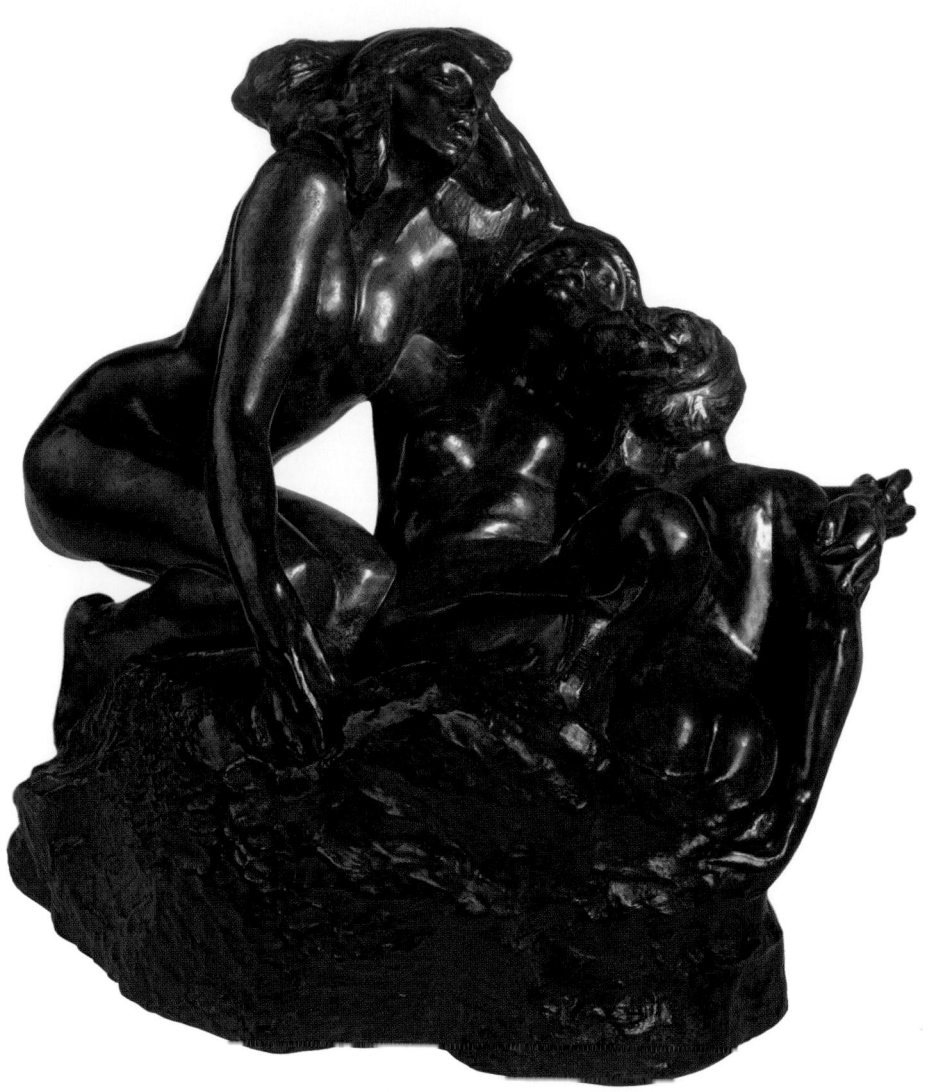

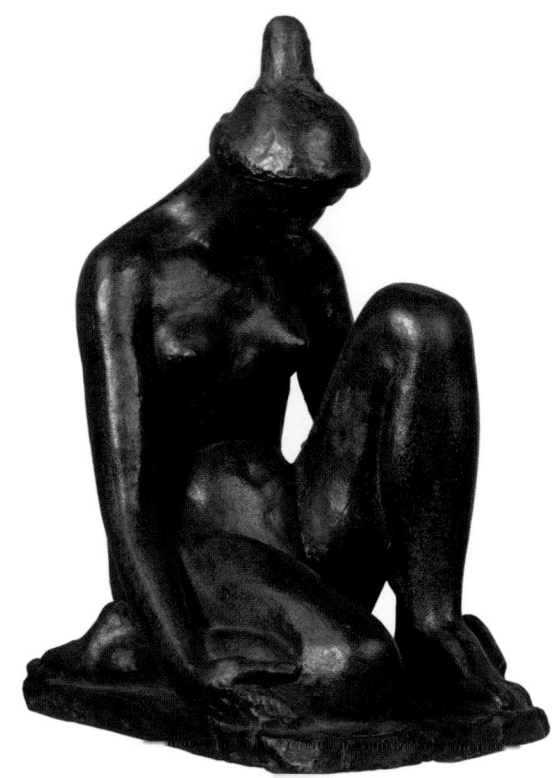

193   Auguste Rodin, *Sirens*

194   Aristide Maillol, *Crouching Girl with Peaked Hairknot*

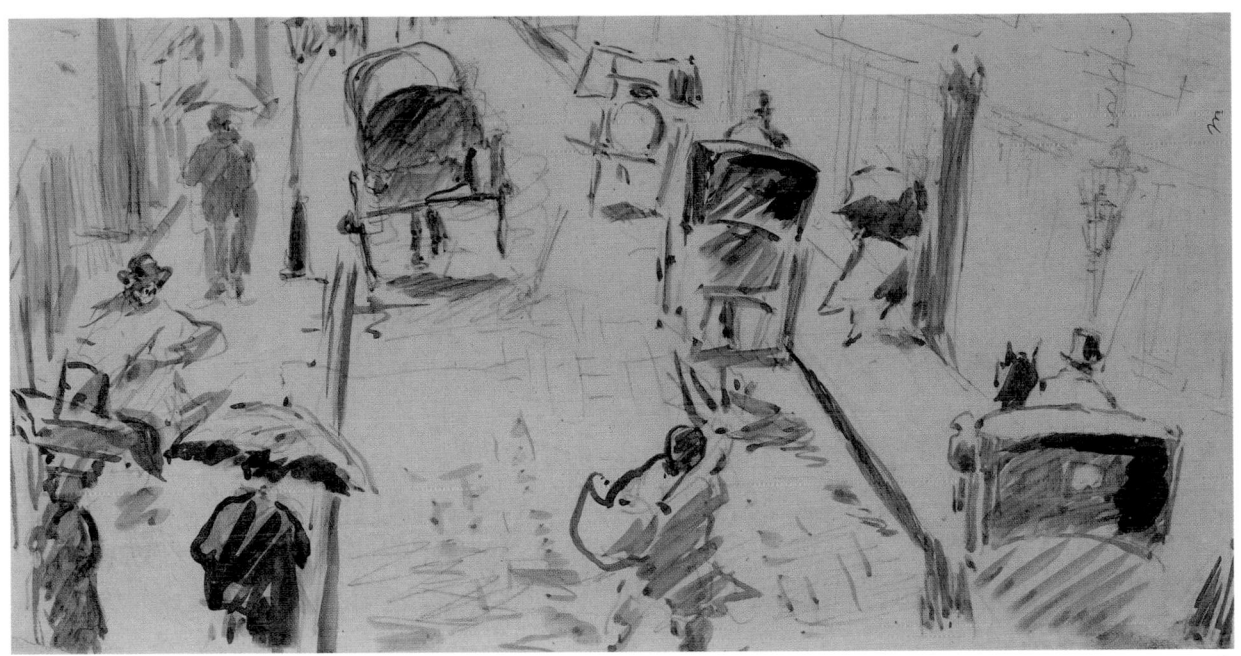

195　Edouard Manet, *Rue Mosnier in the Rain*

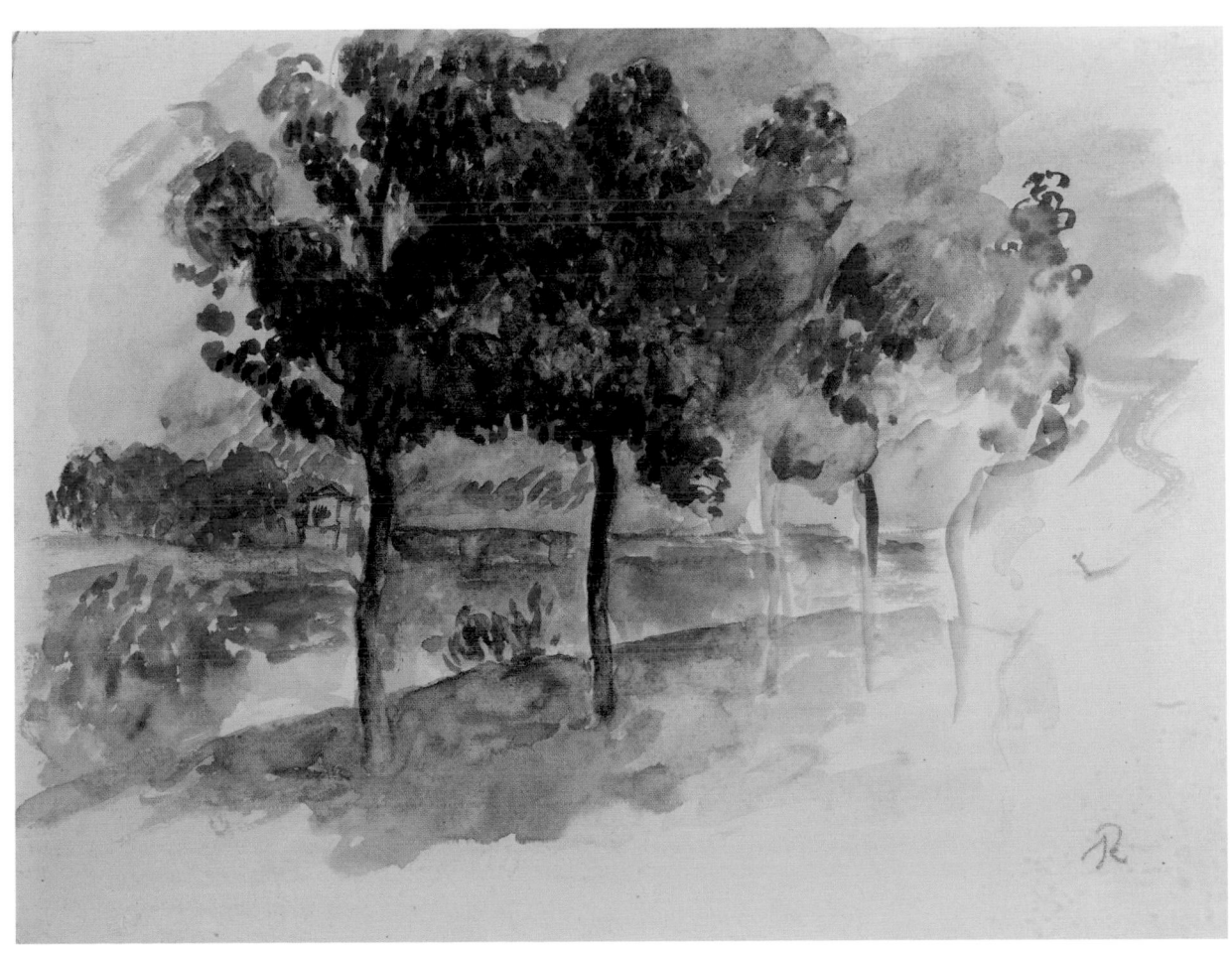

196　Pierre-Auguste Renoir, *Bridge at Argenteuil*

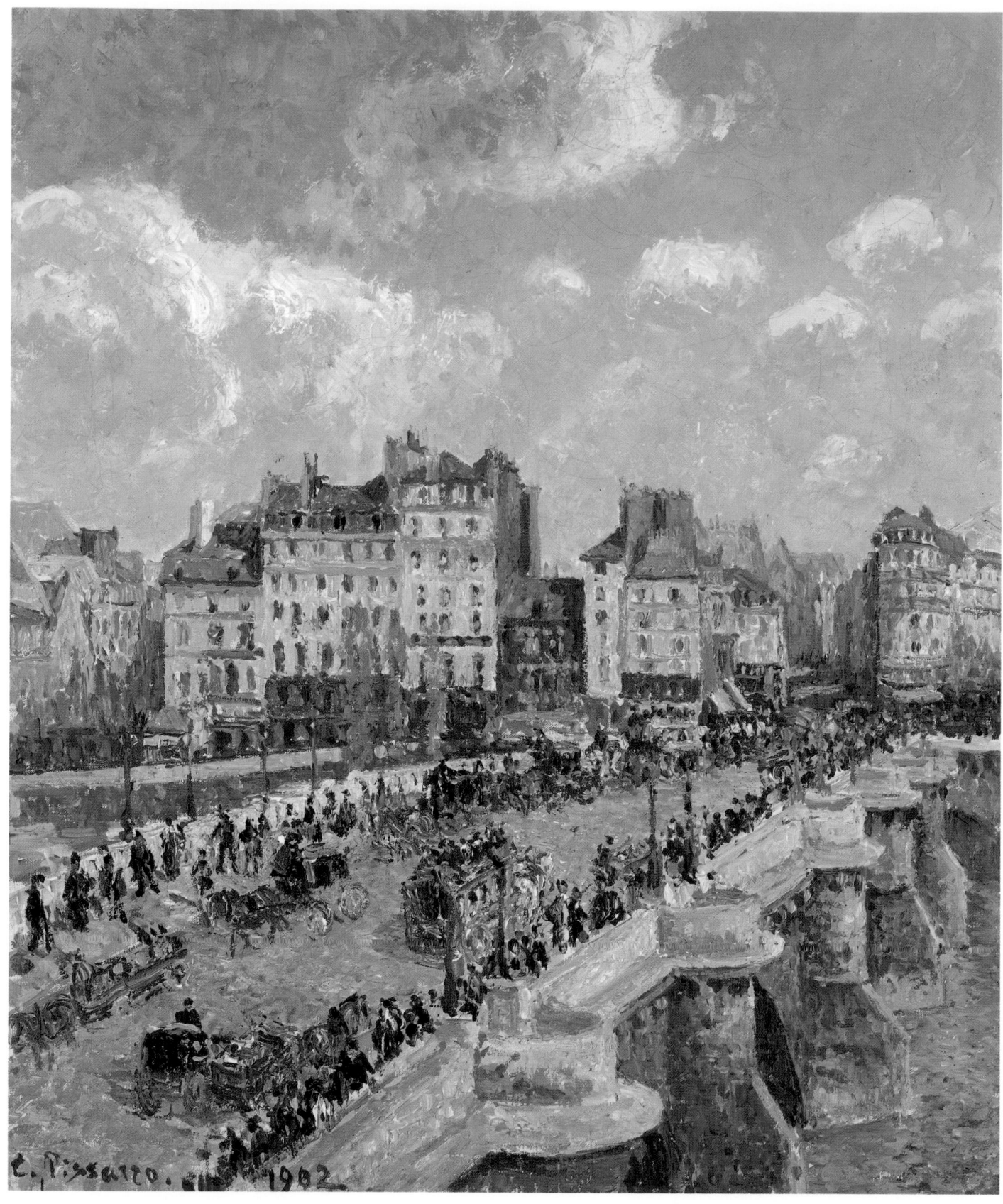

197   Camille Pissarro, *Pont Neuf*

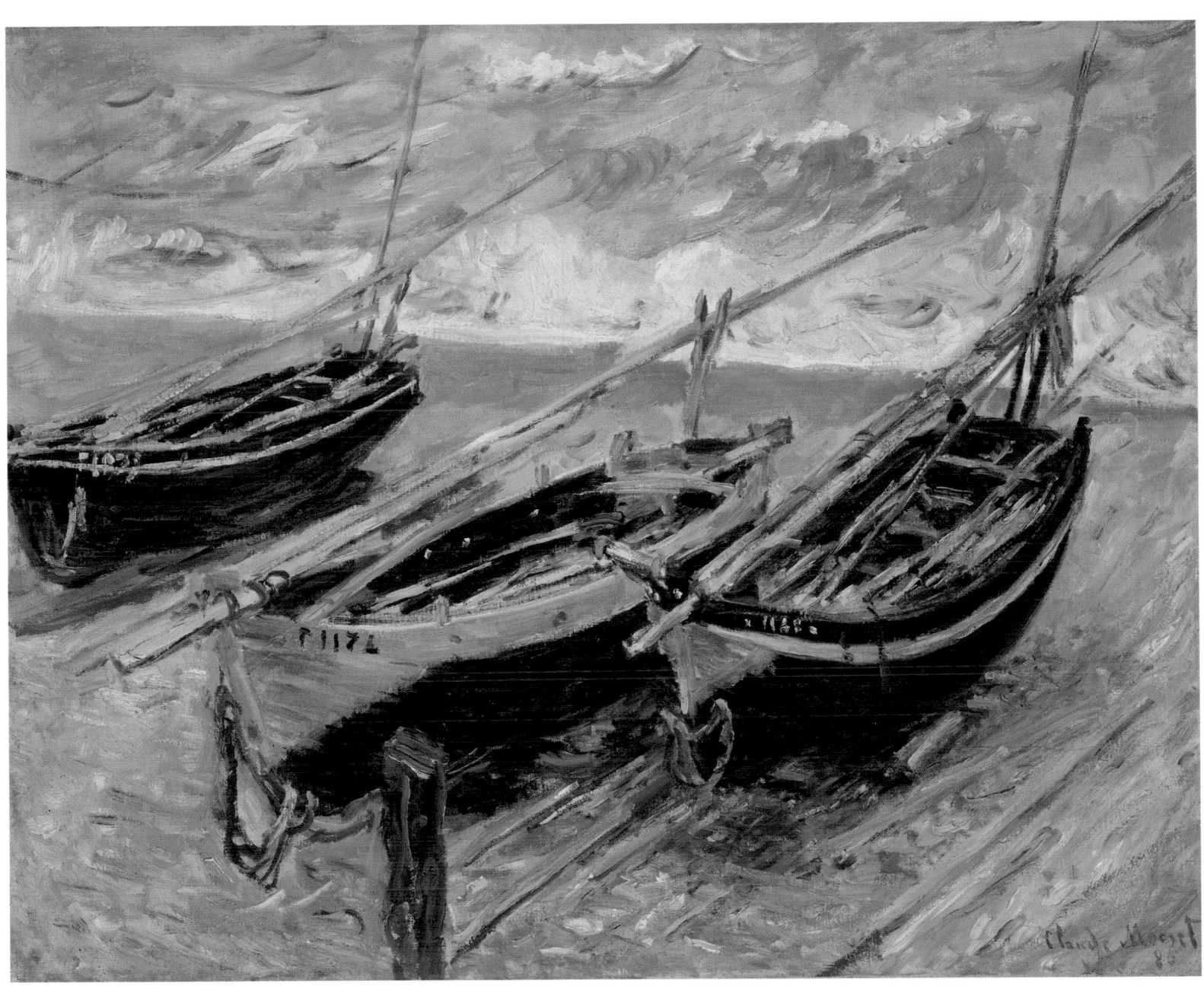

198 Claude-Oscar Monet, *Three Fishing Boats*

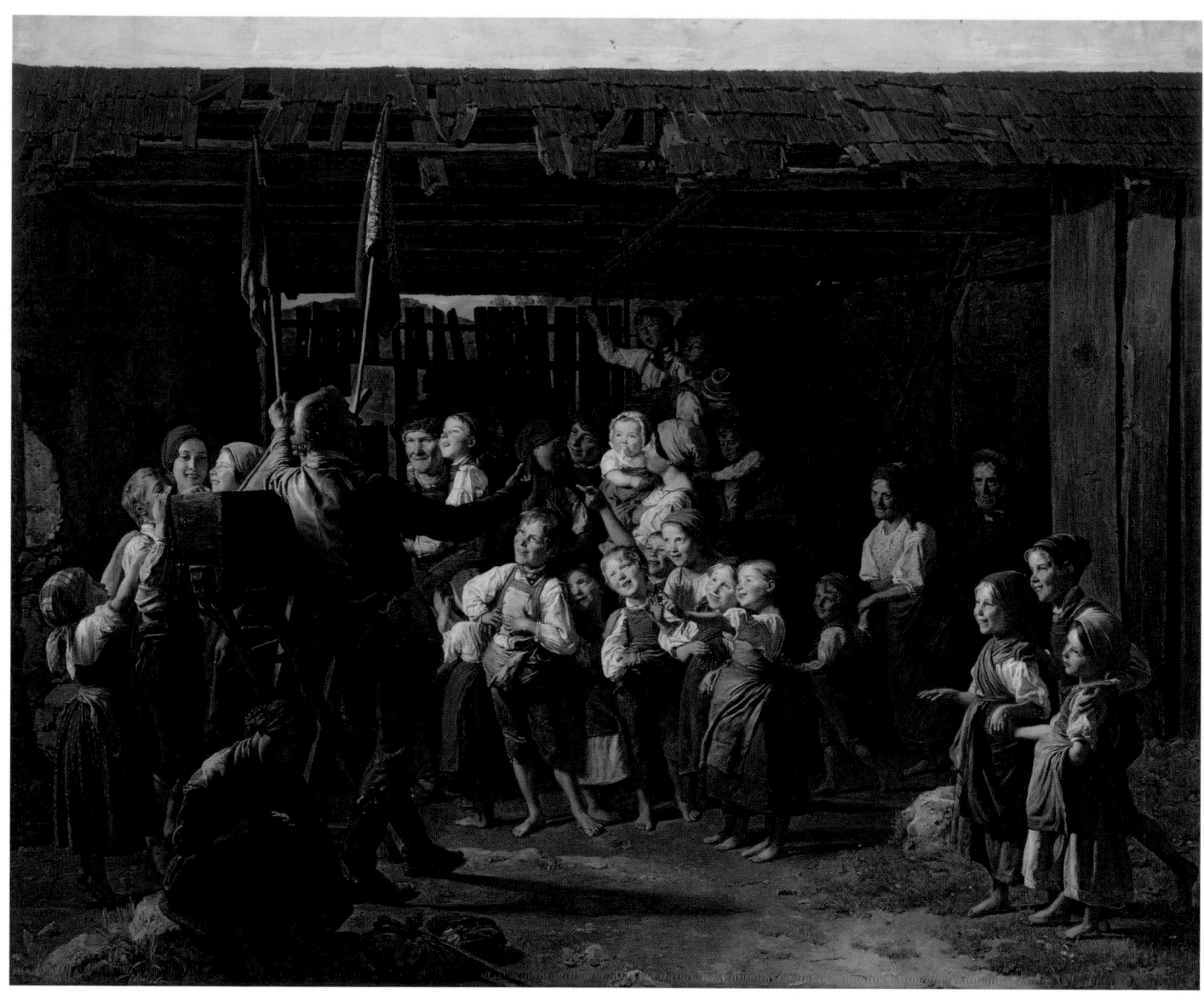

199 Ferdinand Georg Waldmüller, *Man with Magic Lantern*

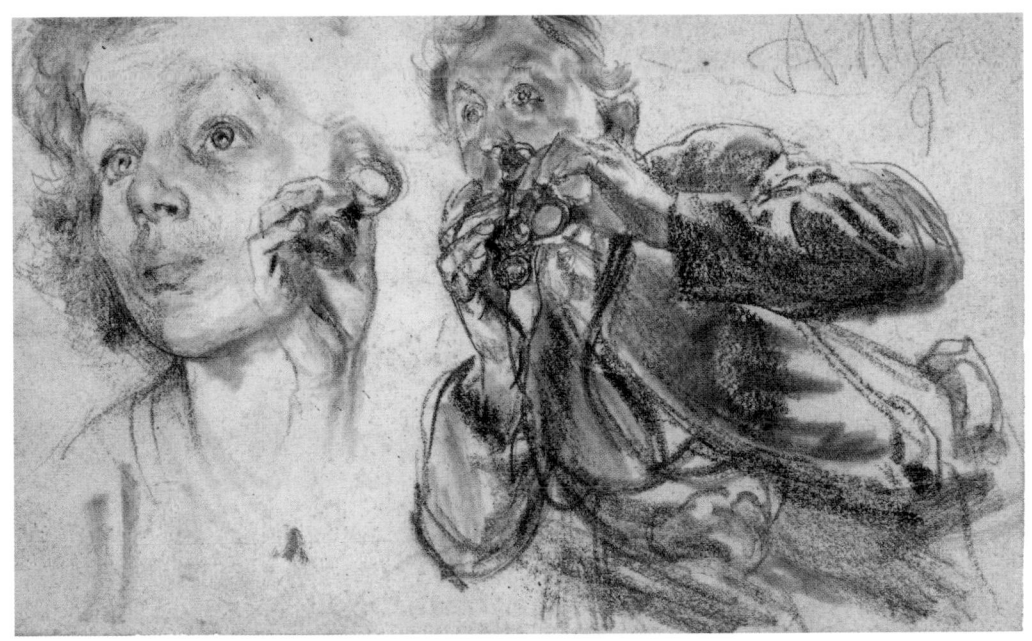

200 Adolph von Menzel, *Studies for Travelling through the Beautiful Landscape*

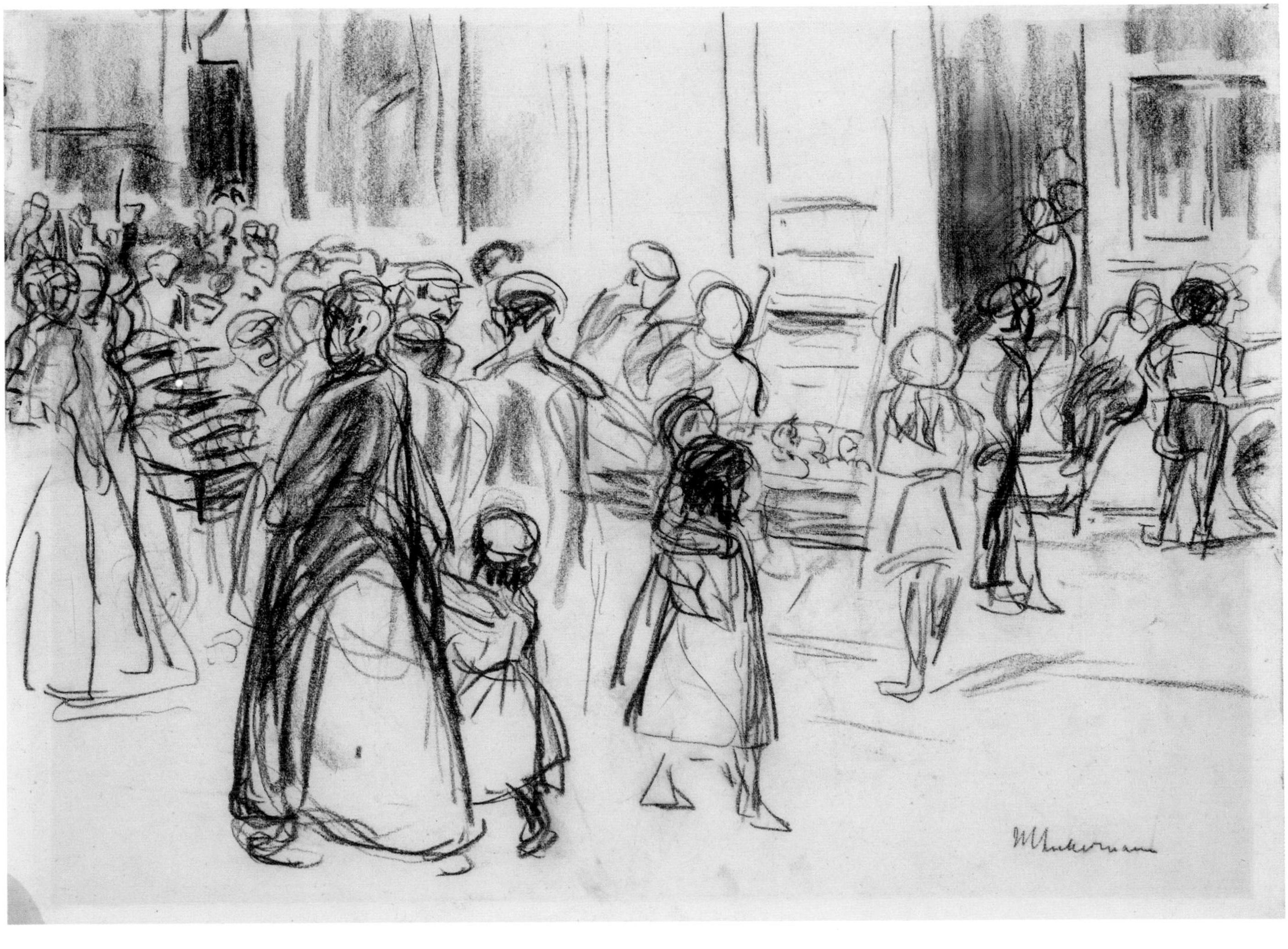

201 Max Liebermann, *Sketch of Jodenbreestraat in Amsterdam*

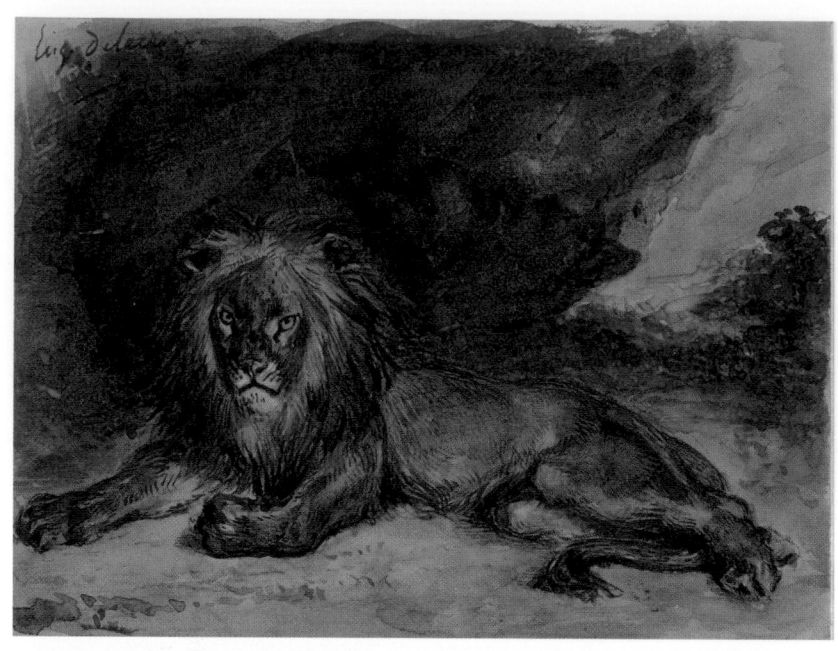

202   Eugène Delacroix, *Lion Resting*

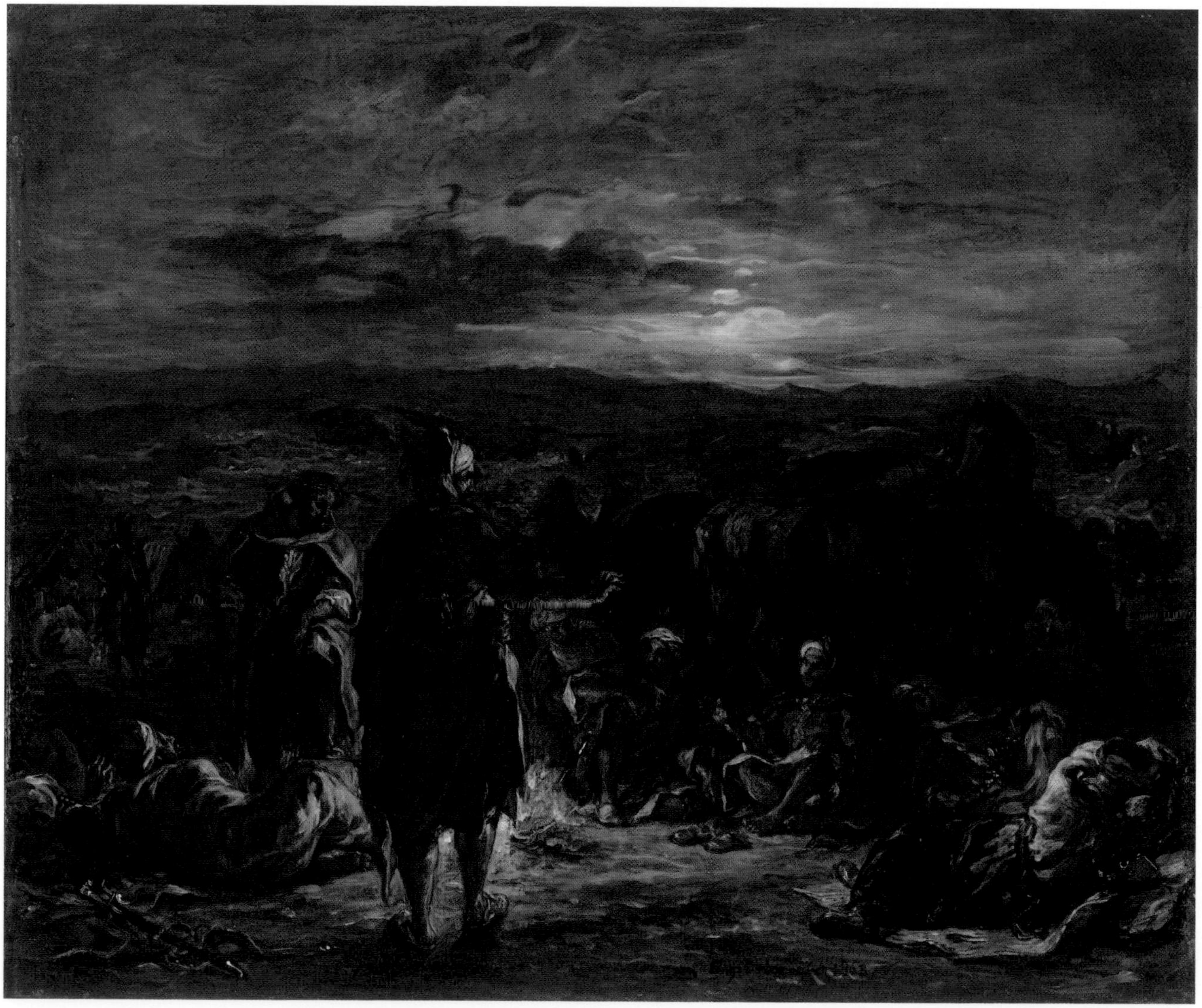

203   Eugène Delacroix, *Arab Camp at Night*

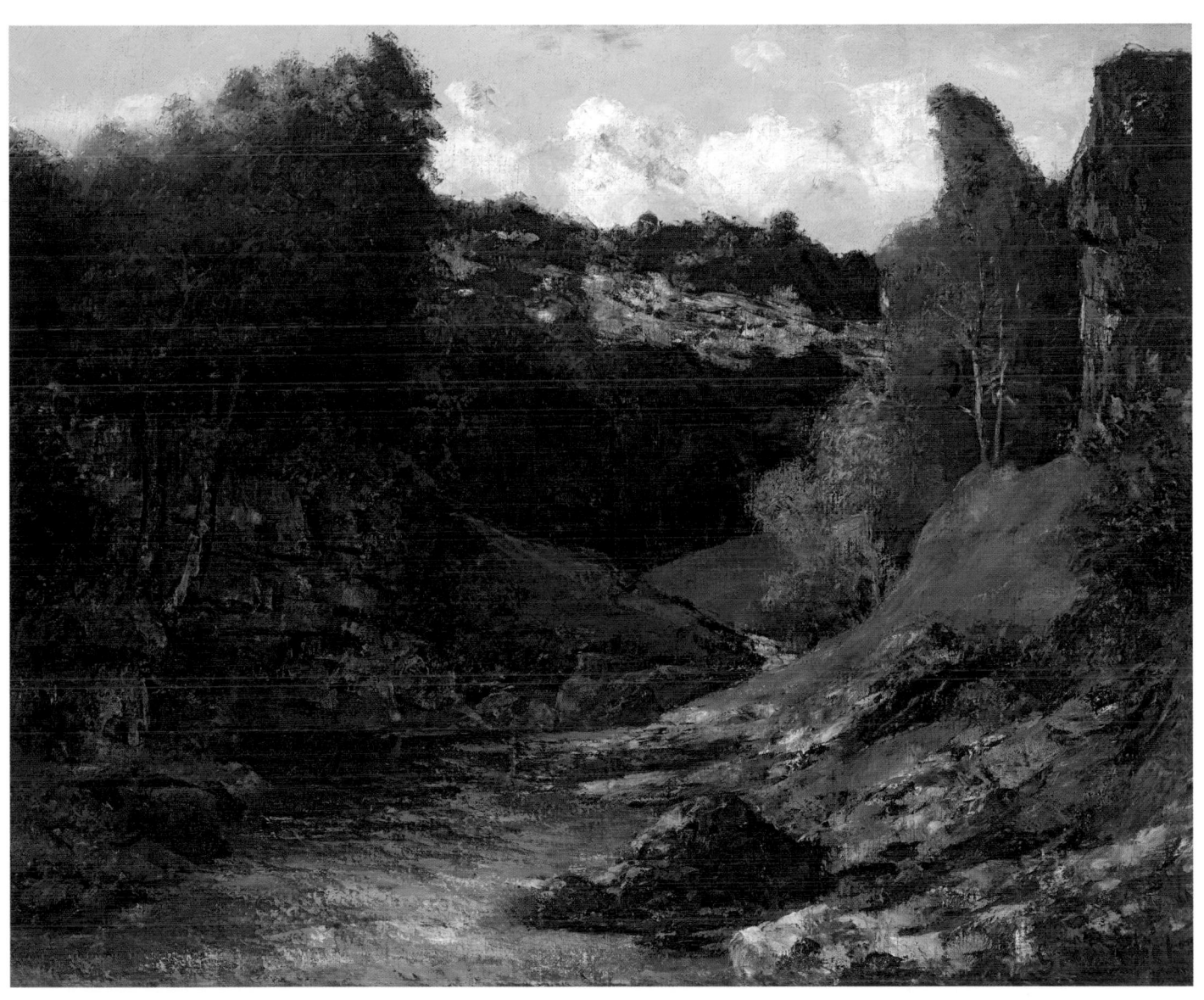

204   Gustave Courbet, *Rocky Landscape*

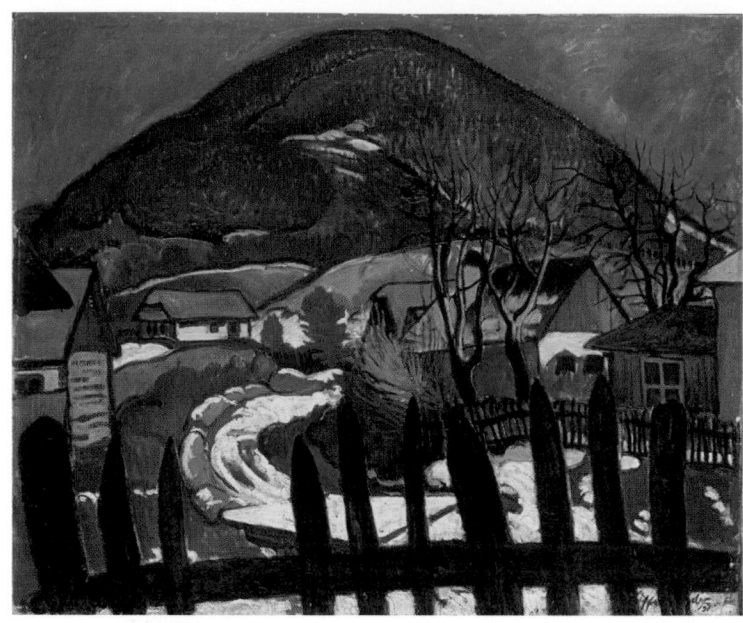

205 Sándor Ziffer, *Landscape with Fence*

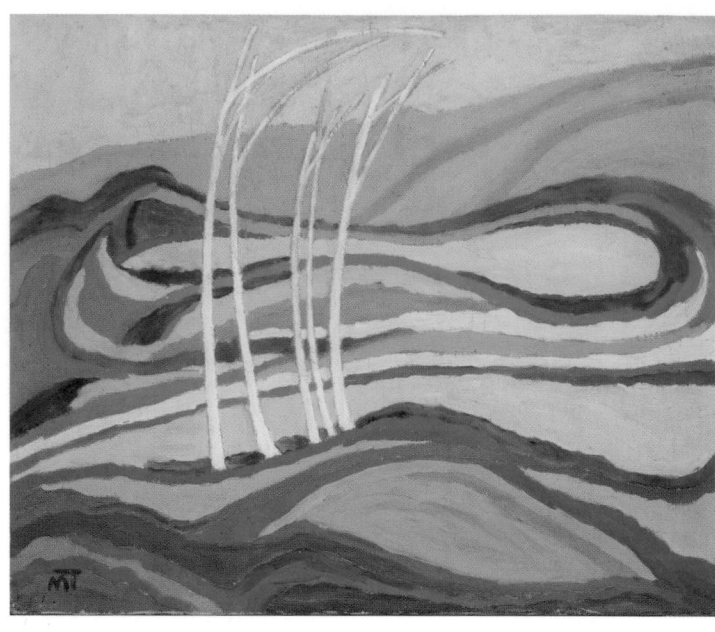

206 János Máttis Teutsch, *Landscape*

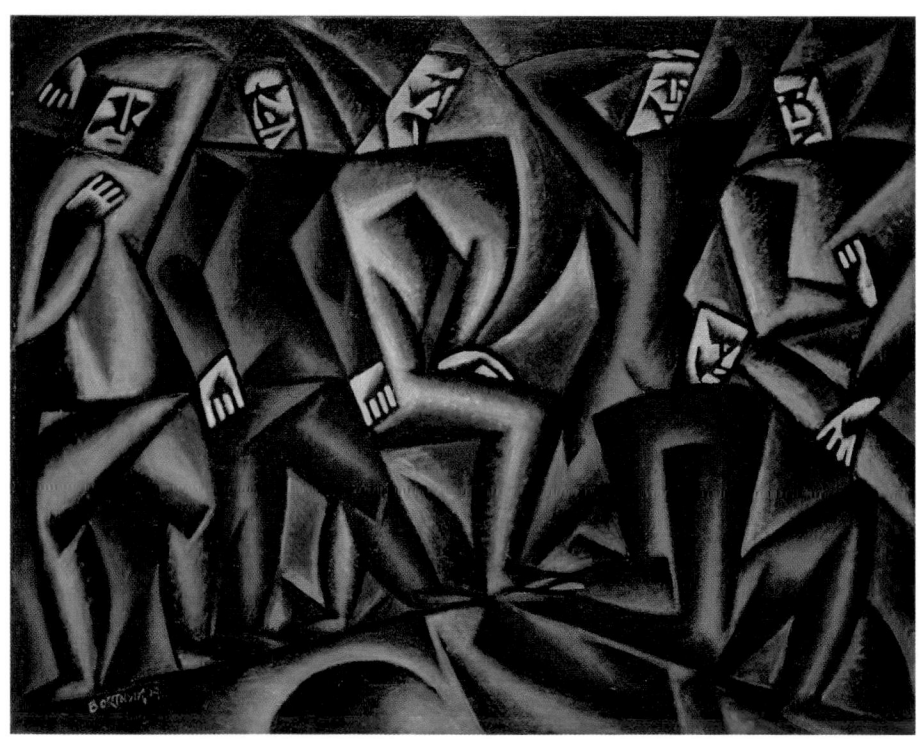

207 Sándor Bortnyik, *Composition with Six Figures*

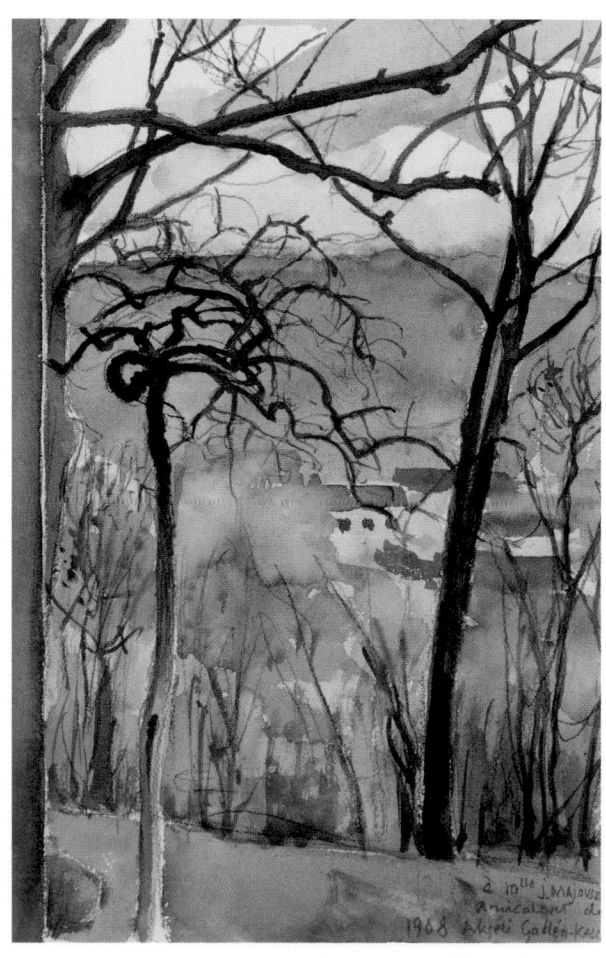

208 Akseli Gallen-Kallela, *March Evening in the Garden of the Majovszky Villa on Gellért Hill*

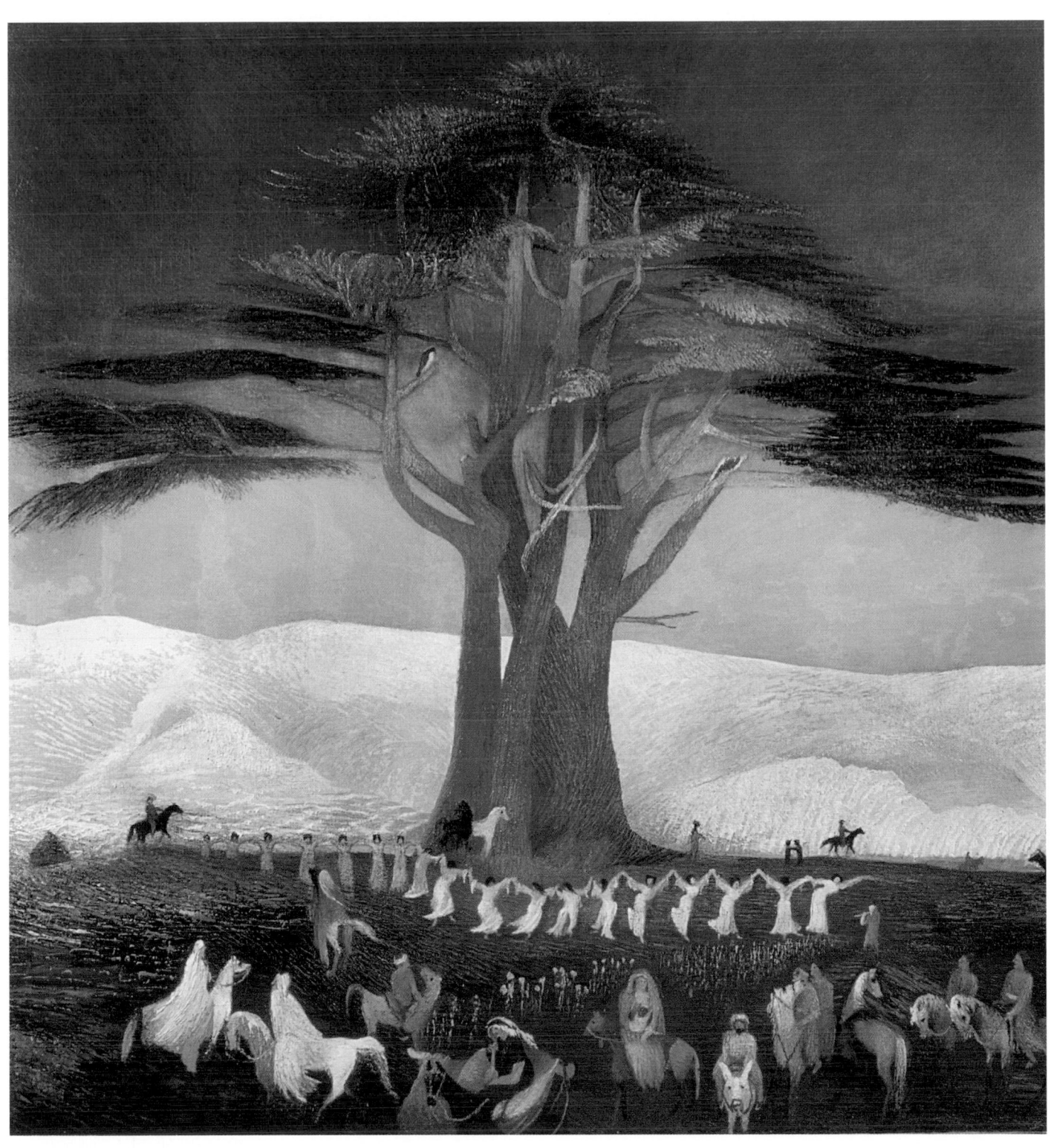

209 Tivadar Csontváry Kosztka, *Pilgrimage to the Cedars of Lebanon*

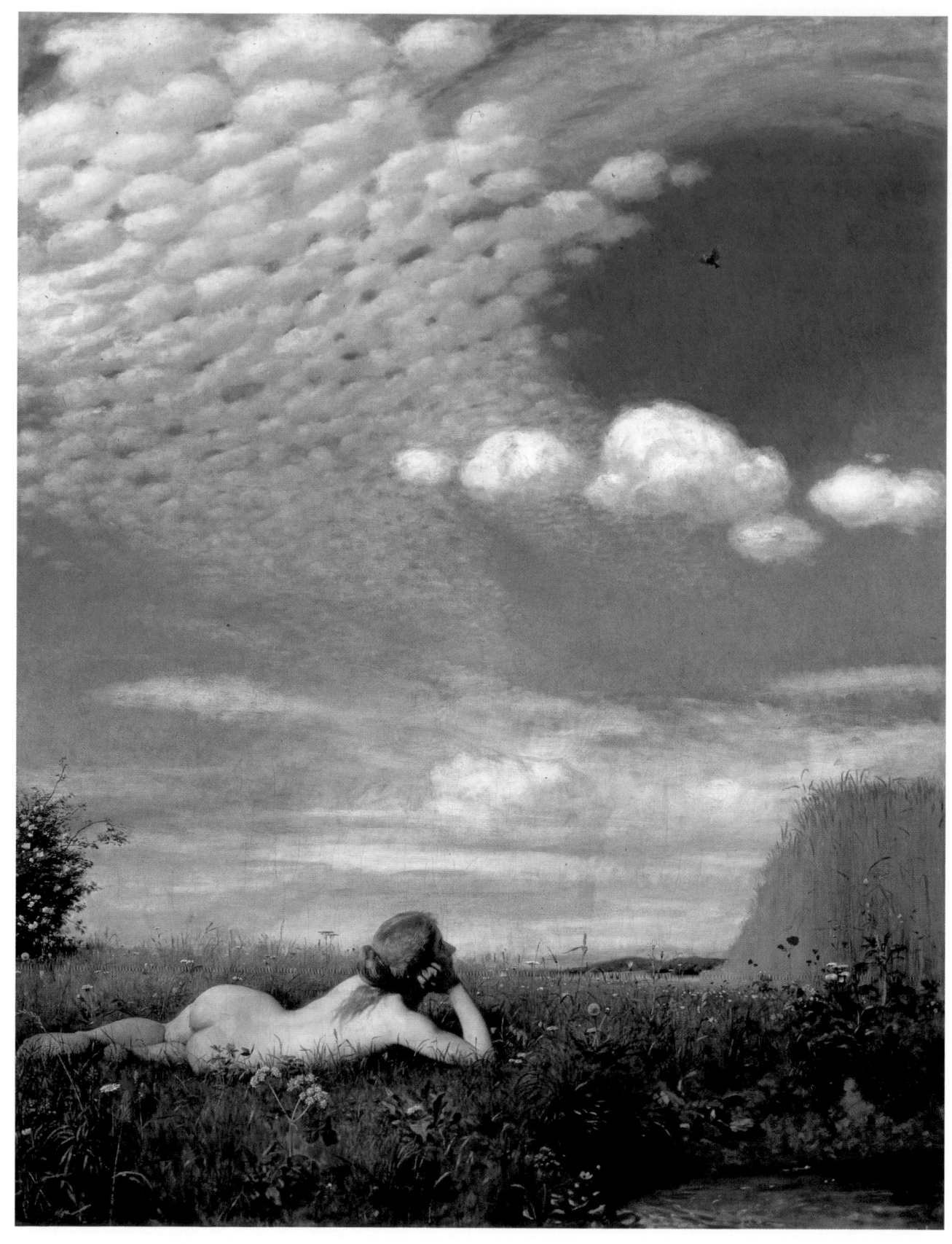

210   Pál Szinyei Merse, *Skylark*

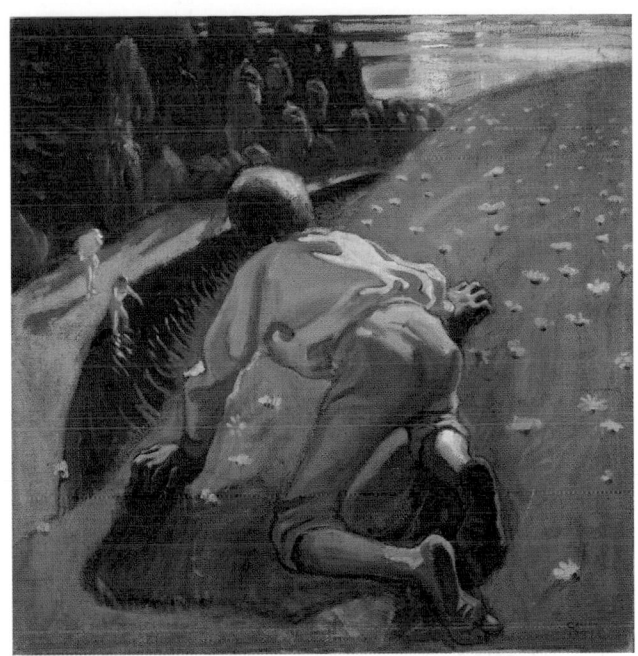

211 Akseli Gallen-Kallela, *Young Faun*

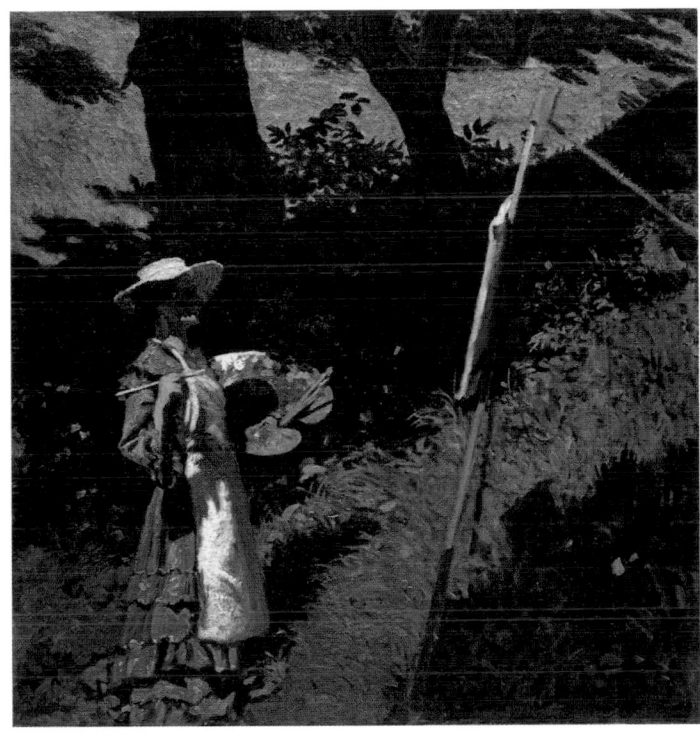

213 Károly Ferenczy, *Woman Painting*

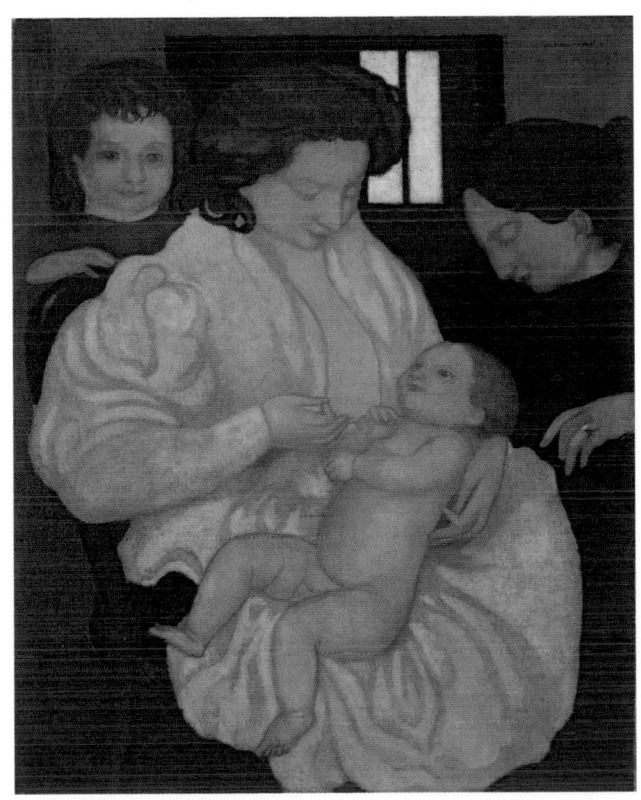

212 Maurice Denis, *Maternity*

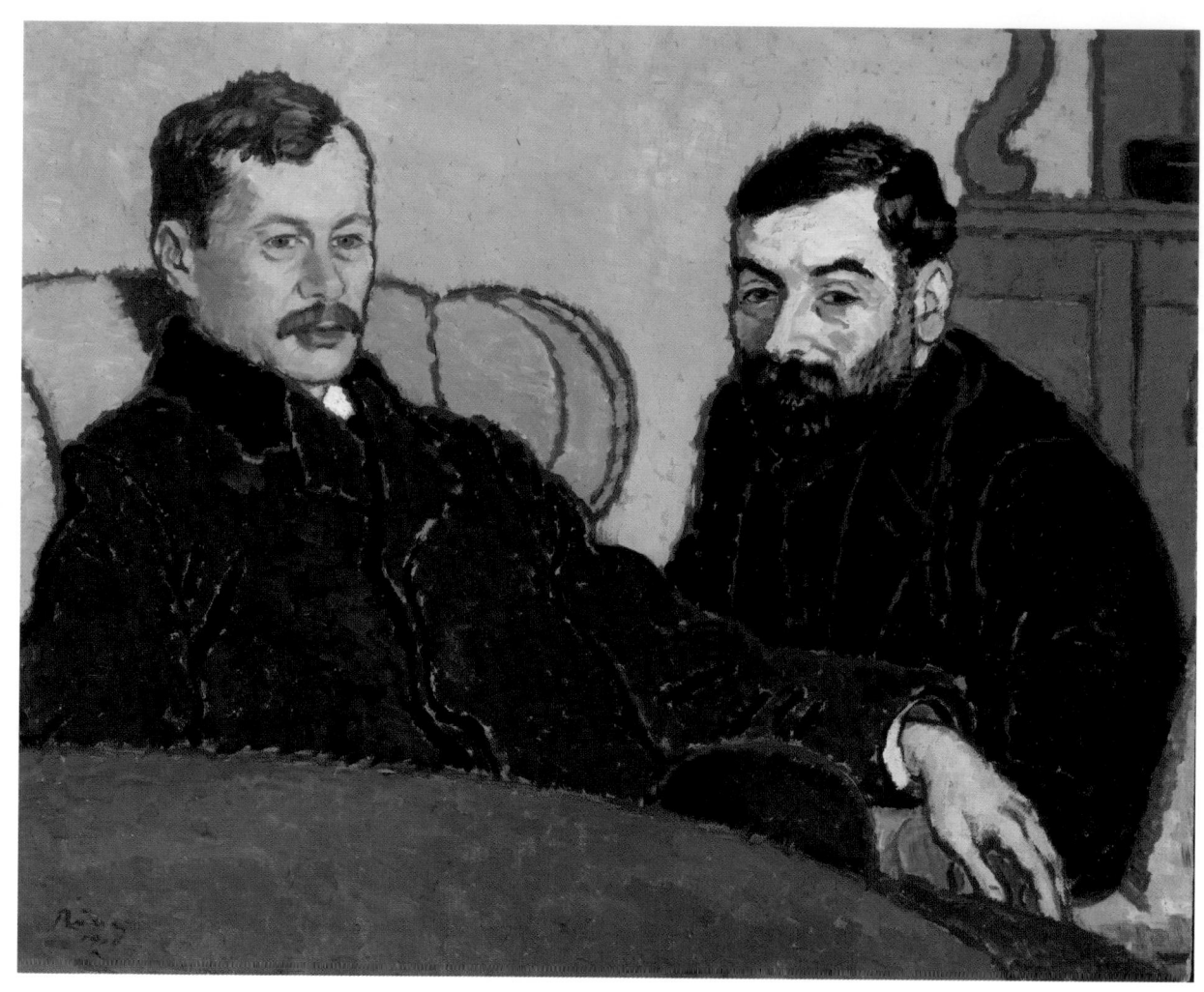

214   József Rippl-Rónai, *Portrait of Elek Petrovics and Simon Meller*

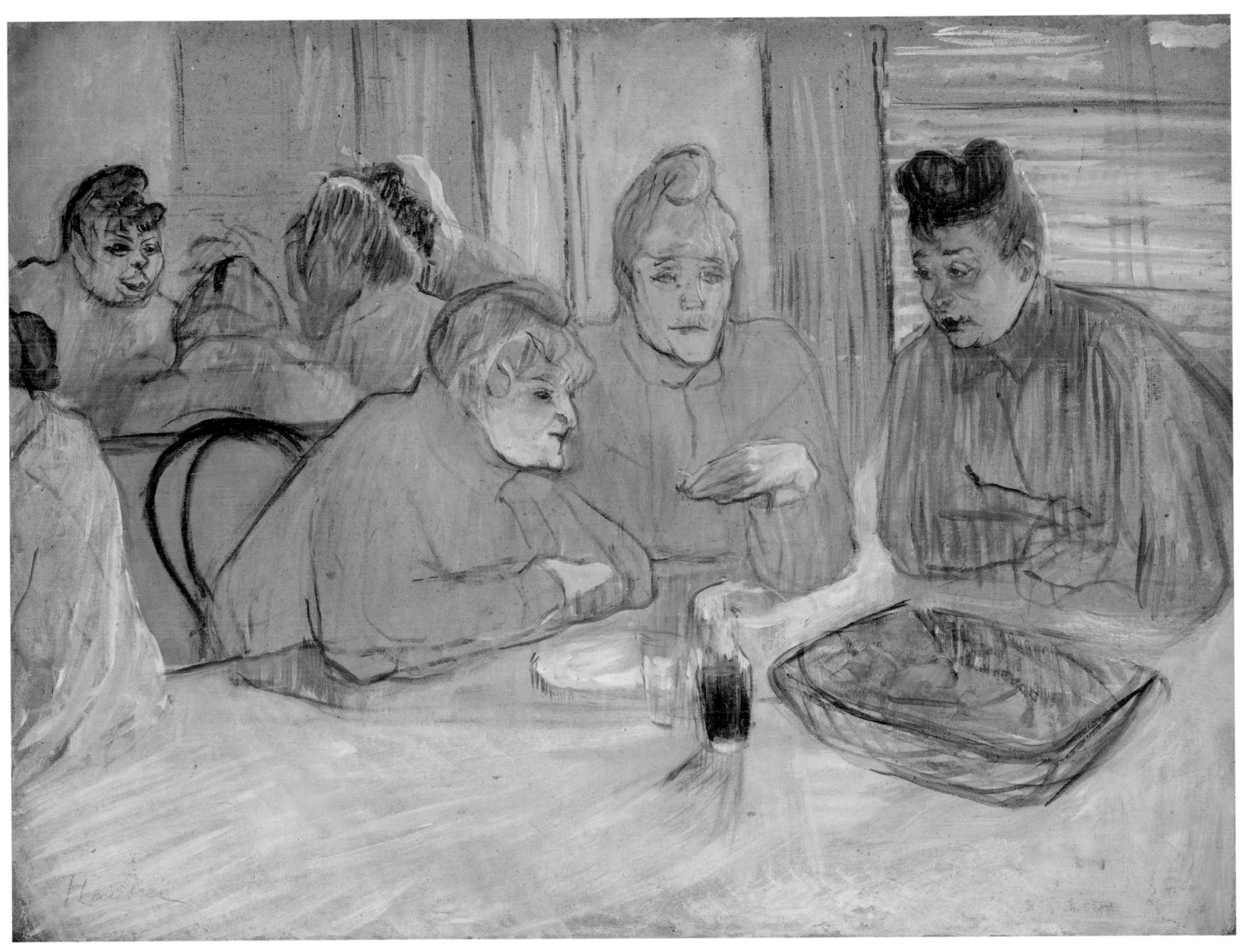

215   Henri-Marie-Raymond de Toulouse-Lautrec, *Women in the Dining Room*

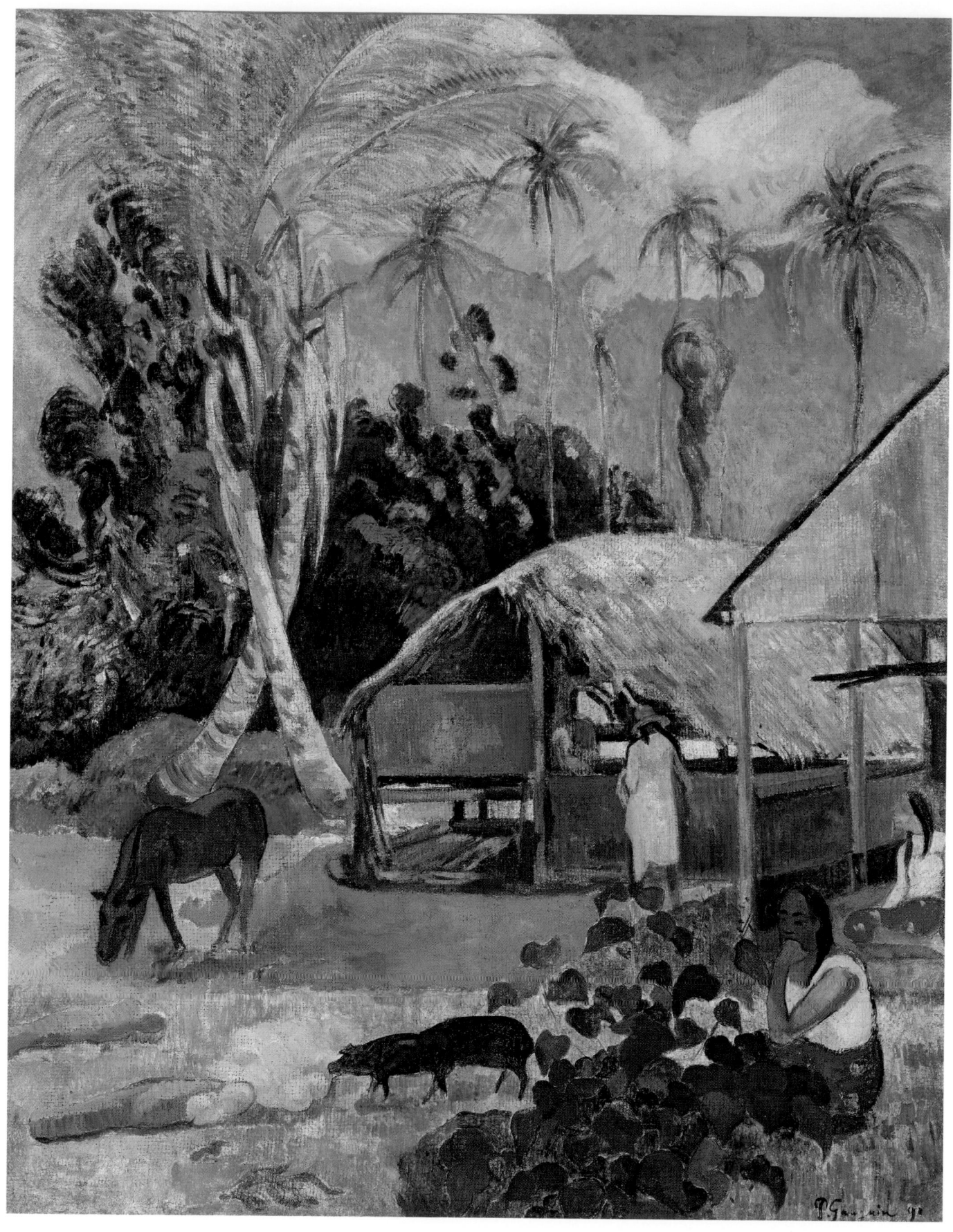

216 Paul Gauguin, *Black Pigs*

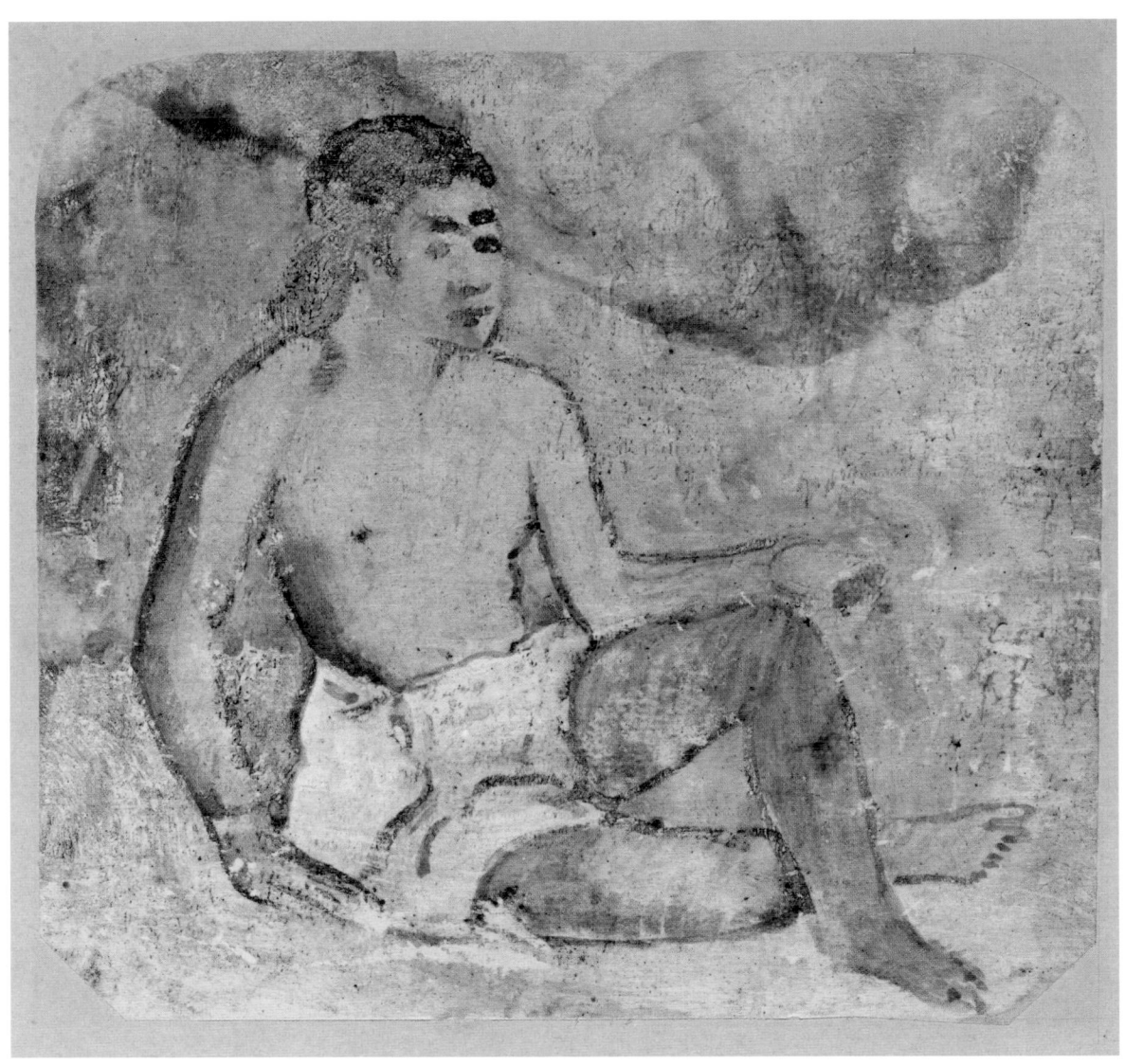

217 Paul Gauguin, *Man from the Marquesas Islands*

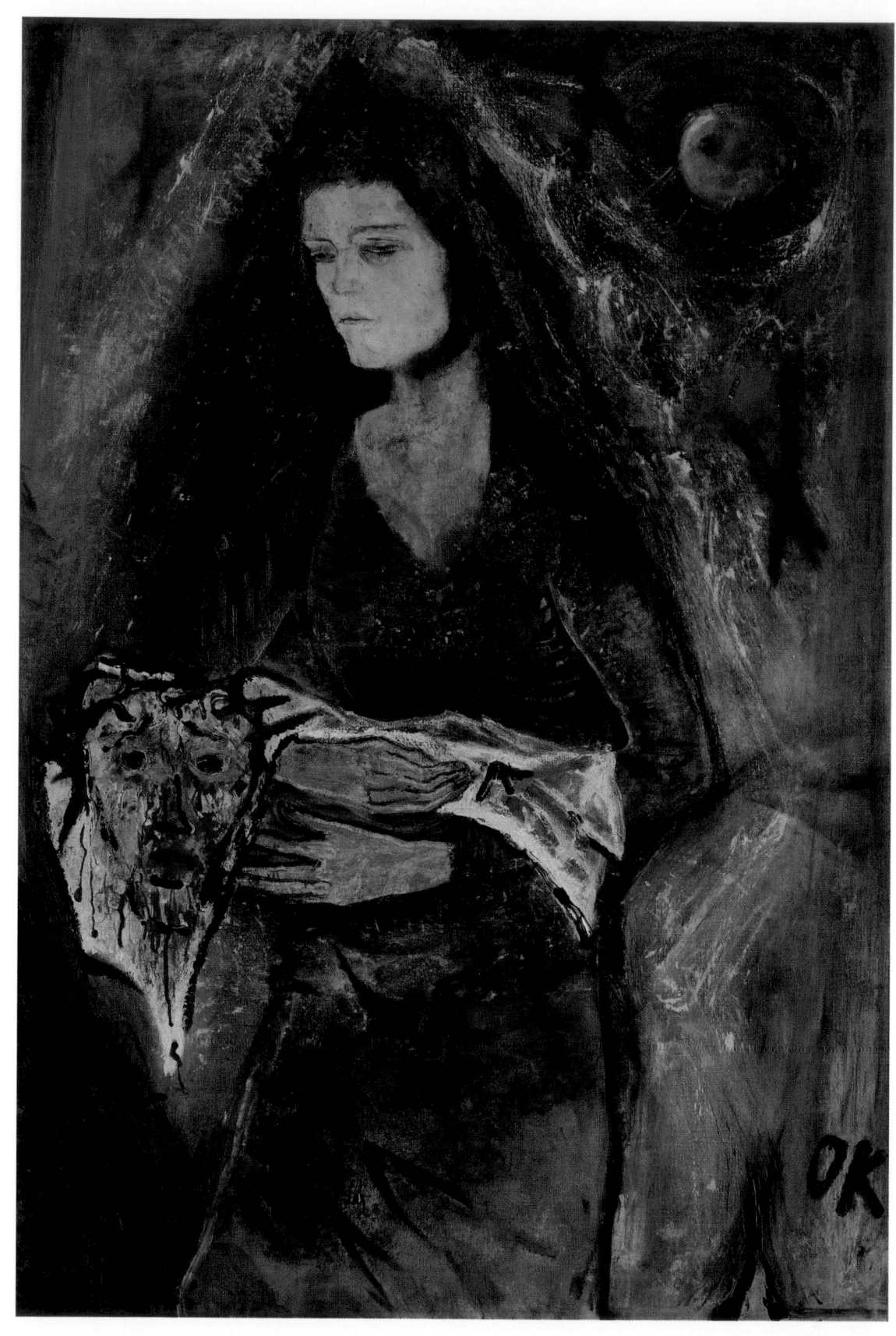

218   Oskar Kokoschka, *Veronica's Veil*

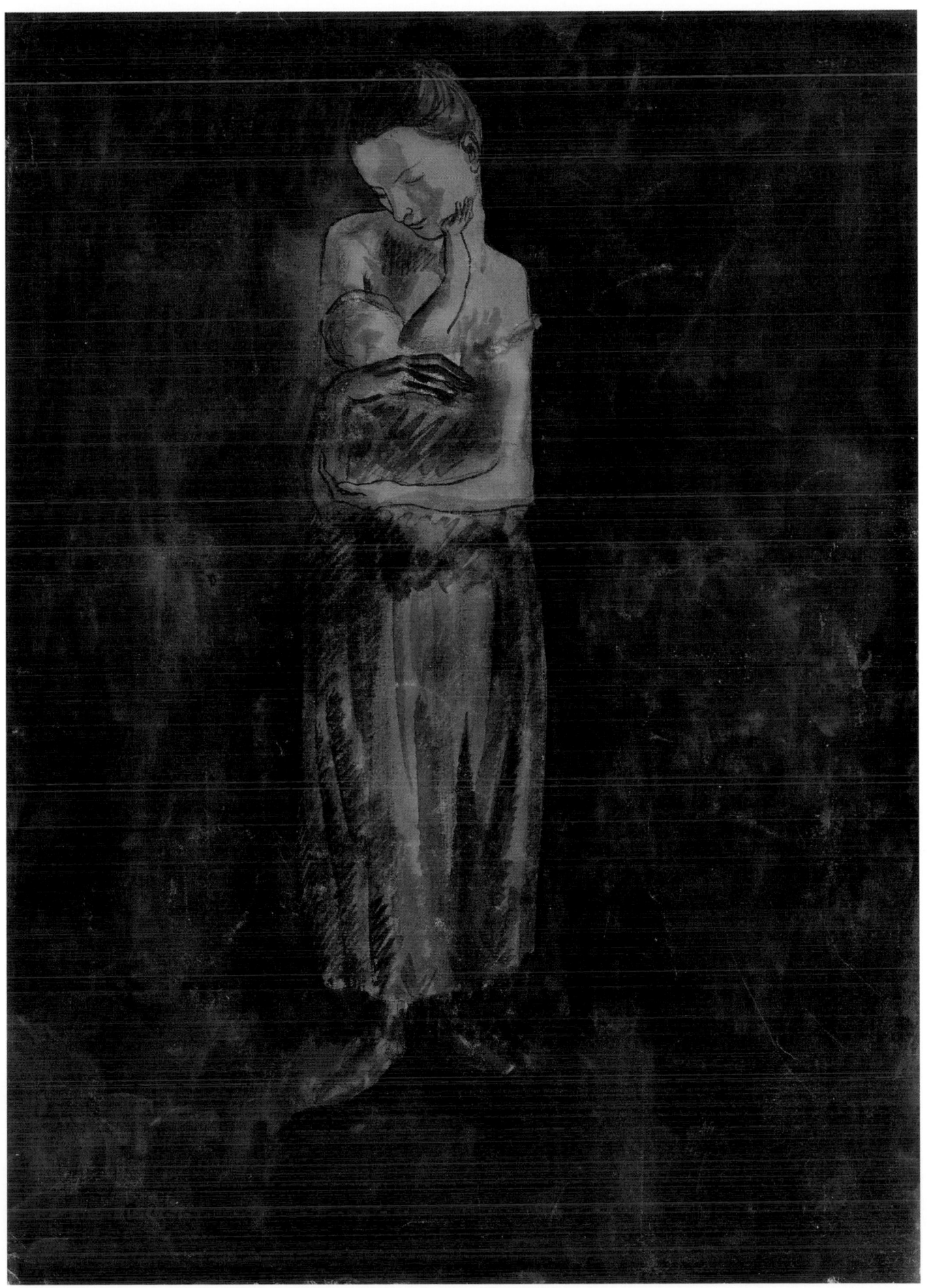

219 Pablo Picasso, *Mother and Child*

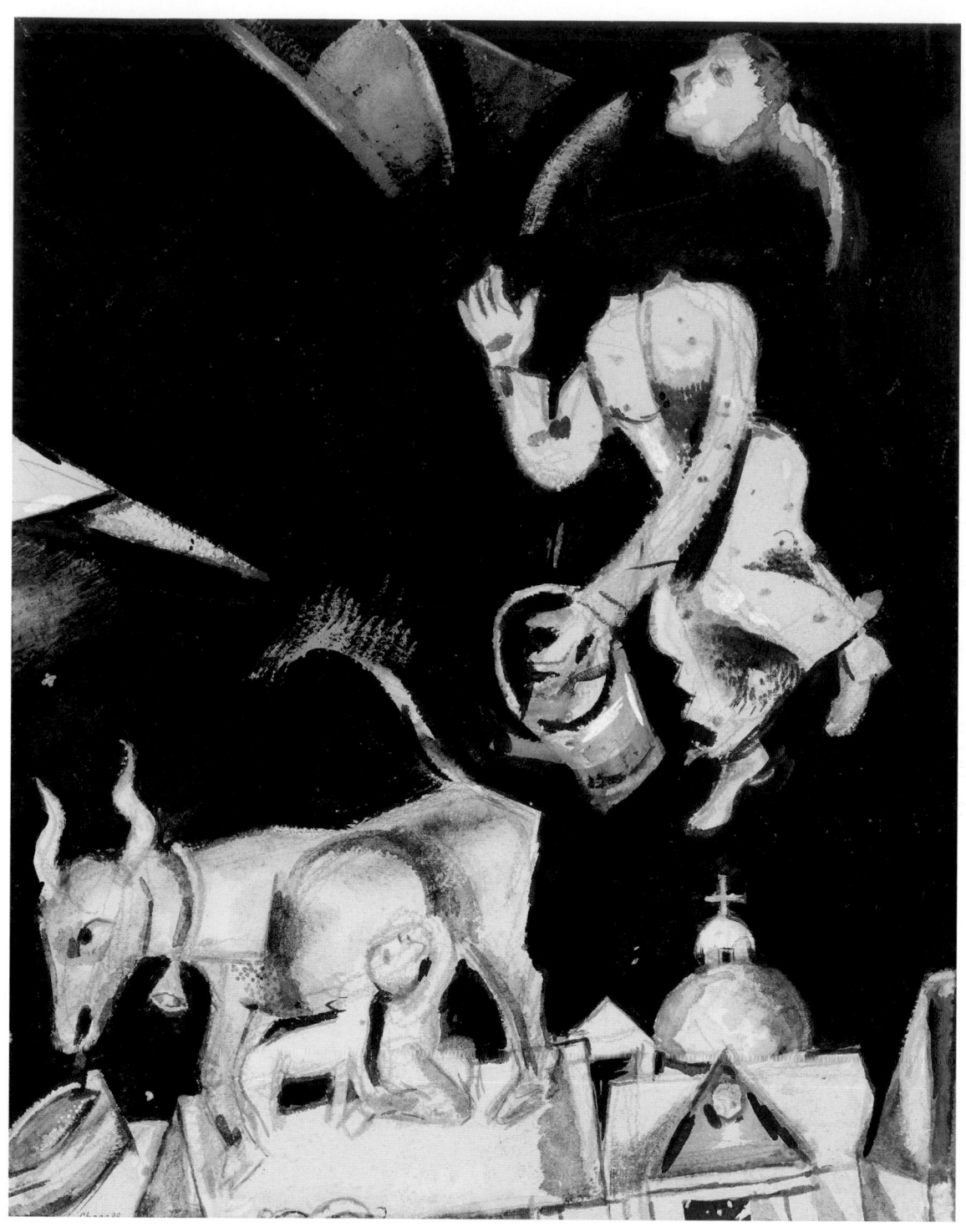

220   Marc Chagall, *Donkey on the Roof*

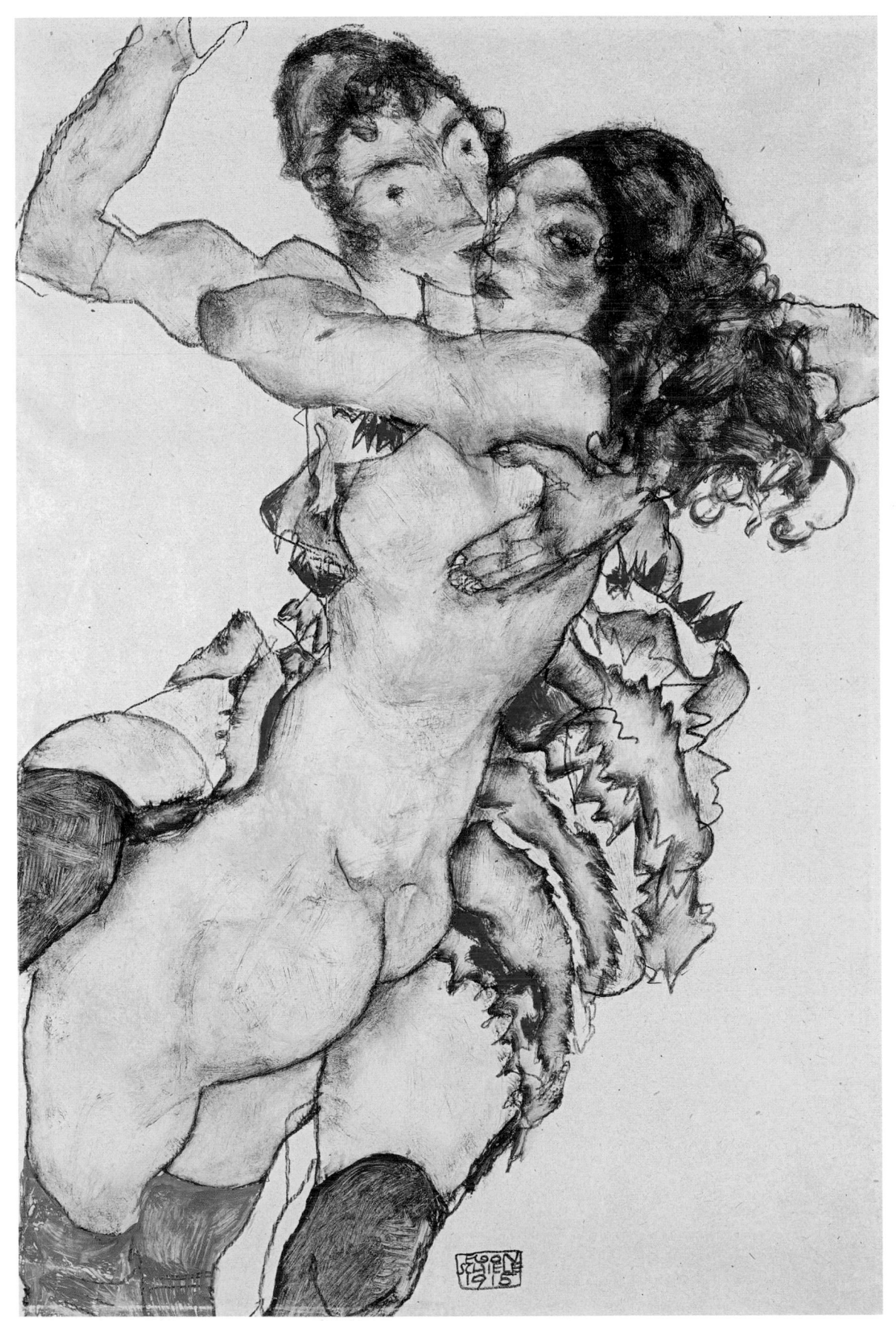

221 Egon Schiele, *Two Women Embracing*

Catalogue
entries

1

Maso di Banco doc. 1335–1350
Coronation of the Virgin, c.1335–40
Tempera on panel, 51.2 × 51.7 cm

INVENTORY NUMBER: 7793
SELECTED REFERENCES: David Wilkins, *Maso di Banco: A Florentine Artist of the Early Trecento*, New York, 1985, pp.85–92; Miklós Boskovits, *Frühe italienische Malerei: Staatliche Museen Preussischer Kulturbesitz, Gemäldegalerie Berlin, Katalog der Gemälde*, Berlin, 1987–88, pp.109–12, fig.167; Vilmos Tátrai (ed.) *Summary Catalogue 1*, London and Budapest, 1991, p.74; Ugo Feraci, 'Maso di Banco: Incoronazione della Vergine', in Angelo Tartuferi (ed.), *L'eredità di Giotto: Arte a Firenze 1340–1375*, exh.cat., Galleria degli Uffizi, Florence, 2008, pp.114–16, no.12

Maso di Banco was arguably the most faithful – although by no means the most celebrated – of all the followers of Giotto. This comparative obscurity has nothing to do with the quality of his art, but is instead explained by the fact that the number of extant works by him is so modest. His only securely attributed productions are his frescoes of the story of St Sylvester and the Emperor Constantine in the Bardi di Vernio Chapel to the left of the choir in the Basilica of Santa Croce in Florence, but their distinctively monumental figure types mean that a handful of panel paintings may also be associated with his name.

The present panel was originally part of a larger Marian complex, of which the only other surviving elements are a *Dormition of the Virgin* (Musée Condé, Chantilly), and an *Assumption of the Virgin with St Thomas Receiving Her Girdle* (Gemäldegalerie, Berlin). According to Catholic doctrine, the Virgin did not die, but instead fell into a sleep, was assumed bodily into Heaven and then crowned as its Queen. Here, unusually, Maso restricts the attendant figures around the seated Christ and his kneeling Mother to serried ranks of standing angels, accompanied by eight kneeling angel-musicians in the extensive and otherwise empty foreground space, thus creating an imposing sense of weight and volume.

This panel was a gift from Harold Harmsworth, 1st Viscount Rothermere, in 1940, at the time when his name was put forward as a possible occupant of the vacant throne of Hungary.

DAVID EKSERDJIAN

2

Artist active in Vienna early fifteenth century
Pregnant Virgin, c.1420
Oil and tempera on larchwood, 89 × 78 cm

HUNGARIAN NATIONAL GALLERY, INVENTORY NUMBER: 52.656
SELECTED REFERENCES: Zsuzsa Urbach, ' "Dominus possedit me" (Prov. 8, 22): Beitrag zur Ikonographie des Josephszweifels', *Acta Historiae Artium*, 20 (1974), pp.199–266; Gyöngyi Török, 'Neue Erkenntnisse durch Infrarot-Reflectographie zur Ikonographie der "Maria Gravida" aus Güssing (Németújvár) in der Ungarischen Nationalgalerie', *Österreichische Zeitschrift für Kunst und Denkmalpflege*, 48 (1994), pp.133–39; Jörg Oberhaidacher, 'Zur Datierung der Güssinger Maria-gravida-Tafel in der Ungarischen Nationalgalerie in Budapest', *Pantheon*, 57 (1999), pp.57–60

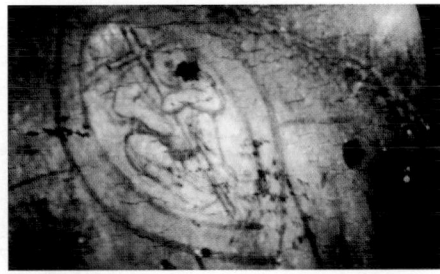

This painting belonged to a large altarpiece of the Virgin from Némétújvár (today Güssing in Austria) that included several other scenes. Originally the work had a horizontal format, but it has since been truncated on the left side. Its style is related to the Viennese Soft Style of around 1400, a connection that may be explained by its provenance in Western Hungary on the Austrian border. Until recently the painting was thought to be a fragment of a scene depicting Joseph's Doubt, but infrared reflectography taken in 1993 (see illustration) revealed the figure of the Infant Jesus with a cross, surrounded by a double mandorla, under the drapery covering the Virgin's belly. That this figure was originally painted on the Virgin's gown has been established on the basis of the underdrawing and comparisons with similar compositions; it was subsequently painted over and obliterated in the Baroque period. A response to Joseph's Doubt, this type of representation is connected to the cult of the Pregnant Virgin (*Maria Gravida*) and emerged in the late fourteenth century, eventually evolving into a distinct category of devotional picture.

GYÖNGYI TÖRÖK

3

Domenico (di Giovanni) Rosselli 1439–1497/98
Virgin and Child, end of the fifteenth century
Pietra di Cesena with traces of original paint and gilding, height 68 cm

INVENTORY NUMBER: 1160
SELECTED REFERENCES: Cornelius von Fabriczy, 'Sculture di Domenico Rosselli', *L'Arte*, 10 (1907), pp.218–22; Ulrich Middeldorf, 'Some New Works by Domenico Rosselli', *Burlington Magazine*, 62, 361 (1933), pp.165–72; Linda Pisani, 'Domenico Rosselli a Firenze e nelle Marche', *Prospettiva*, 102 (2001), pp.49–66

The figure of Domenico Rosselli, who was born in Pistoia, remains something of a mystery. His work focused primarily on ecclesiastical fittings, baptismal fonts, altarpieces, decorative ornamental carvings, friezes and fireplaces, carved in marble or stone. In the early part of his career he made these to commissions in Florence and its environs, then after 1476 in the towns of the Italian region of the Marche: Urbino, Pesaro and Fossombrone.

As was the case with most Florentine sculptors, Domenico Rosselli created reliefs of the Virgin intended for private devotion. Of these, the fifteen reliefs depicting the Virgin and Child form a distinctive group, not only because of their subject, but owing also to their mood and the attractive charm of the figure of the Virgin. It is in these works that Rosselli managed to give of his true self, bringing to perfection his own individual style. The Madonna reliefs recall the compositions of famous Florentine sculptors, particularly Antonio Rossellino and Desiderio da Settignano, but in style they are akin to the works of Agostino di Duccio and Mino da Fiesole; thus even without written documentation, they attest to the fact that Rosselli mastered the craft of sculpture in Florence.

One of the most notable features of the present relief is the shallow carving and its drawing-like idiom. The relief was carved in pietra di Cesena

stone from quarries near Pesaro, like the Madonna relief in the Kunstmuseen Krefeld, a work which, along with the Madonna relief formerly in the Kauffmann Collection in Berlin, comes closest in style to the Budapest relief.

MANGA PATTANTYÚS

4

Liberale da Verona c.1445–1527/29
Virgin and Child with an Angel, c.1468–70
Tempera on panel, 66 × 46.6 cm

INVENTORY NUMBER: 68.13
SELECTED REFERENCES: Carlo del Bravo, *Liberale da Verona*, Florence, 1967, pp.92–93; László Mravik, *North Italian Fifteenth-century Paintings*, Budapest, 1978, 1983, no.4; Vilmos Tátrai (ed.) *Summary Catalogue 1*, London and Budapest, 1991, p.64

Liberale began his career in his native Verona, but was in Siena by 1466 and remained there for a decade. After his return home, he was also documented in Venice in 1487. In addition to being a gifted painter of panels and frescoes, he was arguably the most distinguished Italian manuscript illuminator of the second half of the fifteenth century, and was responsible for a number of spectacular and fantastical miniatures in choirbooks for Siena Cathedral.

By the mid-1400s the use of a gold background was somewhat archaic, and this feature and the distinctly claustrophobic composition of this charmingly intimate Madonna indicate that the work almost certainly dates from the artist's years in Siena. The wriggling Christ Child, who is sporting a carmine-red skullcap that complements the pinker colour of his Mother's dress, is represented looking out at us and embracing the Virgin. He is shown half-kneeling on an olive-green cushion, which in its turn rests upon a stone parapet. Mary's almond-shaped eyes look down protectively to her right towards her Son, and her veiled head is topped by a substantial halo adorned with the text 'AVE GRACIA PLEN[A] DOMINVS TECV[M] BENED[ICTA]', which is adapted from the Archangel Gabriel's salutation at the Annunciation as recorded in St Luke's Gospel: 'Hail, thou that art highly favoured, the Lord is with thee: blessed art thou among women' (Luke I, 28). Over to the right but slightly further back, the insertion of a single blond, winged angel balances the composition. The thinning of the upper paint layers over time has meant that extensive underdrawing has become visible.

DAVID EKSERDJIAN

5

Michel Sittow c.1468–1525/26
Virgin and Child, c.1489–92
Oil on panel, 33.7 × 23.9 cm

INVENTORY NUMBER: 4327
SELECTED REFERENCES: Zsuzsa Urbach, *Early Netherlandish Painting*, Budapest, 1971, no.16; Jazeps Trizna, *Michel Sittow: peintre revelais de l'école brugeoise*, Brussels, 1976, pp.10–11, 98, no. 21, pl. XVII; Dirk De Vos et al., *Hans Memling*, exh.cat., Groeningemuseum, Bruges, 1994, p.165, no.44; Ildikó Ember and Zsuzsa Urbach (eds), *Summary Catalogue 2*, Budapest, 2000, p.158; Tiina Abel (ed.), *Michel Sittow, 1469–1525: The Artist Connecting Estonia with the Southern Netherlands*, Tallinn, 2001

By 1486, Michel Sittow, who was born and indeed spent much of the latter part of his career and died in Reval (now Tallinn), in Estonia, was in the third year of an apprenticeship in Bruges. In terms of his art as opposed to his nationality, he is a straightforwardly if also superbly accomplished Netherlandish painter. His extremely successful career took him to Spain, where he was in the service of Isabella, Queen of Castile and León, for a decade from 1492, and collaborated with Juan de Flandes (c.1465–1519) on an exquisite series of 47 small narrative panels of the lives of Christ and the Virgin. However, while almost all the considerable number that survive are by Juan, a mere two – in the National Gallery of Art, Washington and at Brocklesby Park, Lincolnshire – are by Sittow, and are his only secure works. He may also have been in England in 1505, if the attribution to him and identification of portraits of Catherine of Aragon (Kunsthistorisches Museum, Vienna) and Henry VII (National Portrait Gallery, London) is accepted, and he certainly travelled to Denmark to portray King Christian II.

It is often claimed that Sittow was a pupil of Hans Memling (1430/40–1494), and while there is no firm documentary evidence for this, the present panel is blatantly inspired by the Virgin and Child of the latter's *Diptych of Maarten van Nieuwenhove* (Memlingmuseum, Bruges), which is dated 1487. While the attitude of the Virgin is slightly modified, the playful but also symbolic motif of the Christ Child is identical. Cradled in a white cloth and seated on a ledge covered by an oriental carpet, he reaches out for the apple of Original Sin. Moreover, the pose of the Child has been reversed, and Sittow has also introduced the charming detail of him tweaking his own big toe.

DAVID EKSERDJIAN

6

Hungarian master   early fifteenth century

Virgin and Child from Toporc, 1410–20

Limewood with traces of paint, gilding and silver, height 139.5 cm

HUNGARIAN NATIONAL GALLERY, INVENTORY NUMBER: 57.15-M
SELECTED REFERENCES: Ernő Marosi, 'Magyarországi gótikus Madonna-faszobor a párizsi Louvre gyűjteményében', in G. Környei Attila and Katalin Szende (eds), *Tanulmányok Csatkay Endre emlékére*, Sopron, 1996, pp.89–94; Milena Bartlová, 'Madona z Toporca II, nazyvaná biela', in Dušan Buran (ed.), *Gotika: Dejiny slovenského Výtvarného Umenia*, exh.cat., Slovenská narodná galéria, Bratislava, 2003, p.700, no.4.22; Mária Verő, 'Madonne (Vierge à l'Enfant)', in Imre Takács (ed.), *Sigismundus Rex et Imperator: Kunst und Kultur zur Zeit Sigismunds von Luxemburg 1387–1437 (Art et culture à l'époque de Sigismond de Luxembourg)*, exh.cat., Museum of Fine Arts, Budapest, and Musée national d'Histoire et d'Art, Luxembourg, 2006, p.578, no.7.16

Embodying the Gothic ideal of the 1400s, this delicate statue of the Virgin comes from the church at Toporc in Upper Hungary (today Toporec, Slovakia), dedicated to SS. Philip and James. In it, form and content are melded with outstanding artistic virtuosity. The subtle S-shaped curve of the female figure that faithfully preserves the natural proportions of the body, the decorative drapery of the cloak with its dense and richly varied folds, the subtle modelling of her face and serious expression all serve to convey the young mother's emotional and intellectual poise, the purity of her soul and her beauty. The statue retains some of its original polychromy, which only adds to its presence. On the Virgin's chest can be seen a glazed silver underdress fastened with a gilded belt, over which she wears an

---

azurite-lined, burnished gold cloak. Her veil is white and her hair must originally have been gilded. Only the porcelain-coloured surfaces of her body have remained intact. The naked Child is perched on his mother's left arm, his back erect and his head tilted forward. Their glances meet on the golden orb that the Virgin – as the second Eve – holds in her right hand, alluding to the doctrine of Redemption.

The reverse of the statue is hollowed out, which suggests it originally stood in the shrine of an altarpiece or in front of a pillar or console. Stylistically the work is related to a *Madonna* now in the Louvre, various works from Szepesség (today Spiš, Slovakia), such as the *Madonna of Kislomnic* (today Lomnička, Slovakia) and a statue of *St Catherine* from Podolin (today Podolinec, Slovakia).

GYÖRGYI POSZLER

7

Jacopo del Sellaio   c.1441–1493

St John the Baptist, c.1485–90

Tempera on canvas, 157 × 79.5 cm

INVENTORY NUMBER: 5957
SELECTED REFERENCES: Miklós Boskovits, *Toskanische Frührenaissance-Tafelbilder*, Budapest, 1978, pp.42–43; Vilmos Tátrai (ed.), *Summary Catalogue 1*, London and Budapest, 1991, p.109; Nicoletta Pons, 'Jacopo del Sellaio e le confraternite', in *La Toscana al tempo di Lorenzo il Magnifico: politica, economia, cultura, arte*, Pisa, 1996, pp.287–95; Nicoletta Pons, 'Jacopo del Sellaio: Saint John the Baptist', in Dóra Sallay, Vilmos Tátrai and Axel Vécsey (eds), *Botticelli to Titian: Two Centuries of Italian Masterpieces*, exh.cat., Museum of Fine Arts, Budapest, 2009, p.140, no.11

Jacopo del Sellaio – which means 'James the saddler's son' – was a Florentine painter, mainly of small-scale devotional images and domestic furnishings. His teacher was Fra Filippo Lippi, but his mature style was even more profoundly influenced by the latter's disciple, Sandro Botticelli. At the date when the present work was executed, wood was a far more popular support than canvas for paintings, and it has therefore been plausibly suggested that this imposing image of Florence's principal patron saint, John the Baptist, was in all probability designed as a processional banner for a religious brotherhood or confraternity.

Sellaio has adapted the figure's pose and emaciated, sensitive physical type from his counterpart in Botticelli's *St Barnabas Altarpiece* of around 1485, now in the Uffizi in Florence, but the most recondite iconographic details are inspired by a painting by Lippi. Thus, although the presentation of the Baptist in what St Matthew's Gospel refers to as 'raiment of camel's hair' (Matthew III, 4), holding a reed cross and with his baptismal bowl at his feet, is all entirely conventional, as is the rocky wilderness landscape setting, the dead tree to the right is not. Ivy snakes around its gnarled trunk, but more crucially a sharply foreshortened axe is embedded close to its base, a motif inspired by the tenth verse of the same chapter of Matthew, which reads: 'And now also the axe is laid unto the root of the trees: therefore every tree which bringeth not forth good fruit is hewn down, and cast into the fire', a passage which was inevitably interpreted as alluding to heaven and hell.

DAVID EKSERDJIAN

8

Luca della Robbia   1399/1400–1482

Christ and St Thomas, 1463–65

Terracotta with traces of original paint, height 44.5 cm

INVENTORY NUMBER: 4974
SELECTED REFERENCES: Bruce Boucher, 'Luca della Robbia: Christ and St Thomas', in Bruce Boucher (ed.), *Earth and Fire: Italian Terracotta Sculpture from Donatello to Canova*, exh. cat., Museum of Fine Arts, Houston, and Victoria and Albert Museum, London, 2001, pp.120–21; Zsombor Jékely (ed.), *Verrocchio's Christ*, exh.cat., Museum of Fine Arts, Budapest, 2003, no.8

The Florentine sculptor Luca della Robbia came to fame thanks to a technical innovation: the discovery of a ceramic glaze made according to a special recipe. Luca was hailed by Leon Battista Alberti as 'worthy of admiration', no doubt because he considered his invention one of the proofs of the renaissance of Florentine art. Luca della Robbia, who was studying as a goldsmith, had in fact already shown himself to be capable of producing excellent sculptures in other materials, such as marble and bronze. He continued to fashion works in these media to the end of his life, as well as undertaking commissions for glazed terracotta.

This small terracotta statuette of Christ and St Thomas is a *modello* that Luca della Robbia made as a preparatory study for a monumental bronze group. The statue was intended for one of the niches decorating the exterior of Orsanmichele, the church of Florence's guilds, which previously contained Donatello's statue of St Louis of Toulouse. In 1463, as part of the project, Luca had made the glazed terracotta coat of arms for the patrons of the niche, the *Arte della Mercanzia*, for which he was paid separately. Subsequently, 400 gold florins' worth of bronze was purchased for the casting of the statues, but for reasons unknown the sculpture was never executed, and years later the commission passed to Andrea del Verrocchio.

Unlike Verrocchio's bronze group, in Luca della Robbia's composition the Apostle Thomas, doubting Christ's resurrection and placing his hand into the wound in Christ's side, rather than being troubled by violent emotion, humbly accepts what is incomprehensible to the human mind. The figures are motionless, and time seems momentarily to stand still. Though the head of Christ has been destroyed, and the group retains only traces of original paint, this is compensated for by the delicacy of the modelling. The features of Thomas's face and the arrangement of the folds of his clothes are reminiscent of Della Robbia's figures in relief on the bronze door of the sacristy of the Duomo in Florence, which were made at the same time as the model.

MANGA PATTANTYÚS

9

Jacopo Parisati da Montagnana   1440/50–1499

Pietà, c.1480

Tempera on panel, 76 × 50.5 cm

INVENTORY NUMBER: 1066
SELECTED REFERENCES: C. Furlan, *Dopo Mantegna: Arte a Padova e nel territorio nei secoli XV e XVI*, exh.cat., Palazzo della Ragione, Padua, 1976, pp.33–36; Vilmos Tátrai (ed.), *Summary Catalogue 1*, London and Budapest, 1991, p.79; Hans Werner Grohn, *Die italienischen Gemälde: kritischer Katalog mit Abbildungen aller Werke*, Hanover, 1995, pp.101–03; Alberta De Nicolò Salmazo and Giuliana Ericani (eds), *Jacopo da Montagnana e la pittura padovana del secondo Quattrocento*, Padua, 2002

The documentary record, taken in conjunction with the quality of his few surviving paintings, leaves no doubt that Jacopo da Montagnana was one of the leading artists active in Padua in the last decades of the fifteenth century. The key to an understanding of his work is afforded by a grandly impressive *Lamentation* in the Niedersächsisches Landesmuseum, Hanover, which reveals the extent of his dependence upon the twin examples of Andrea Mantegna and Giovanni Bellini, but at the same time underlines his own very considerable powers.

The present panel, which must date from much the same period of Jacopo's career, is similarly reliant upon Mantegna and Bellini, and ultimately on the emotional and formal lessons they both learnt from the sculpture of Donatello for the high altar of the Basilica of the Santo in Padua. It represents the Virgin's last farewell to her Son, and shows the half-length figures in the neutral grey sarcophagus and set against a green cloth of honour flanked by slivers of sky to either side. The rigid frontality and impressive musculature of Christ's pale body both project strength even in death, but in contrast the defeated expression of his foreshortened head and the elegant elongation of his fingers suggest sensitivity and frailty. By his side, the tears pour down the face of his lamenting Mother, who is clad in imperial purple. She glues her flushed cheek to his and envelops him in an unbearably final embrace.

DAVID EKSERDJIAN

10

Ambrogio da Fossano, called Bergognone   c.1453–1523

Lamentation, c.1485

Tempera and oil on panel, 64.7 × 49.3 cm

INVENTORY NUMBER: 65
SELECTED REFERENCES: László Mravik, *North Italian Fifteenth-century Paintings*, Budapest, 1983, no.44; Vilmos Tátrai (ed.), *Summary Catalogue 1*, London and Budapest, 1991, p.15; Gianni Carlo Sciolla (ed.), *Ambrogio da Fossano detto il Bergognone: un pittore per la Certosa*, exh. cat., Castello Visconteo, Pavia, 1998, pp.162–65, no.17; Edoardo Villata, 'Bergognone: The Lamentation of Christ', in Dóra Sallay, Vilmos Tátrai and Axel Vécsey (eds), *Botticelli to Titian: Two Centuries of Italian Masterpieces*, exh. cat., Museum of Fine Arts, Budapest, 2009, p.226, no.50

Bergognone was one of the most important painters active in his native Milan in the last quarter of the fifteenth century and the first quarter of the sixteenth. The major influence upon his early manner was the work of Vincenzo Foppa (1427/30–1515/16), and – unlike the vast majority of his contemporaries in Milan – he was unaffected by the more generally overpowering presence of Leonardo da Vinci. A fine painter of altarpieces (two are in the National Gallery, London) and smaller religious paintings, he was also responsible for a number of memorable frescoes at the Certosa di Pavia, including a remarkable series of illusionistic representations of Carthusian monks.

In the present panel, which is universally agreed to date from the beginning of Bergognone's career and is often thought to reveal Netherlandish influence, he represents the Lamentation over the Dead Christ as a pathos-filled crowd scene. The V-shaped figure composition is bookended by the cave where Christ will be buried and St John the Evangelist to the left, and the hill of Calvary and

St Mary Magdalene in echoing red to the right, with a detailed imaginary prospect of Jerusalem, dominated by a vast piazza, in between. At the centre is the swooning Virgin, sustained by two of the Holy Women, with the heartbreakingly frail and scarred body of her Son on her lap, his lolling head supported by St Joseph of Arimathaea. To the sides and beyond can be seen a trail of secondary figures, whose subordinate status is underlined by their lack of haloes. Both the glow of the clouds in the evening sky and on the buildings is achieved by the lavish if by now old-fashioned application of gold pigment.

DAVID EKSERDJIAN

11

Leonardo da Vinci   1452–1519

Studies for the Heads of Two Soldiers in the Battle of Anghiari, c.1504–05

Soft black chalk or charcoal, some traces of red chalk, 191 × 188 mm

12

Leonardo da Vinci

Study for the Head of a Soldier in the Battle of Anghiari, c.1504–05

Red chalk on very pale pink prepared paper, 226 × 186 mm

INVENTORY NUMBERS: 1775, 1774
SELECTED REFERENCES: Loránd Zentai, *Sixteenth-century Central Italian Drawings: An Exhibition from the Museum's Collection*, exh.cat., Museum of Fine Arts, Budapest, 1998, nos 3–4; Carmen C. Bambach (ed.), *Leonardo da Vinci: Master Draftsman*, exh.cat., Metropolitan Museum of Art, New York, 2003, nos 90–91

These magnificent head studies were produced for the ill-fated *Battle of Anghiari* mural in the Sala del Gran Consiglio (Hall of the Grand Council) of the Palazzo della Signoria (Palazzo Vecchio) in Florence. Leonardo was commissioned to decorate one of the two longer walls of the hall around the middle of 1503. His composition was to commemorate the decisive military victory in the history of the Florentine Republic, the triumph over the Milanese at Anghiari in 1440. Leonardo worked on the battle scene from October 1503 with interruptions until May 1506, when he returned to Milan, leaving the unfinished work behind once and for all. He devised an oil-based technique for the wall painting, which rapidly deteriorated, but his mural was nevertheless regarded as one of the principal sights of Florence; Giorgio Vasari obliterated its last traces during his renovation of the hall in 1563.

Although neither the wall painting nor its cartoon (a full-scale drawing used directly for copying the composition onto the wall) have survived, with the help of contemporary accounts, copies and Leonardo's extant sketches, the destroyed work can be reconstructed. Out of the complete composition Leonardo only painted the crucial episode of the battle, the Fight for the Standard, the moment when the young Florentine captain-general, Pier Giampaolo Orsini, is just about to wrench the standard from the hand of Niccolò Piccinino, the Milanese *condottiere*. Leonardo created these two masterly sheets as preliminary studies for the full-scale cartoon. The head in half profile on the black chalk

study is for the Milanese *condottiere*, while the red chalk study was executed for the horseman, Pier Giampaolo Orsini, on the right edge. The scene, in which, in the words of Vasari, 'rage, fury and revenge are perceived as much in the men as in the horses', offered a perfect opportunity for the representation of intense emotions and extreme states of mind reflected on the human face. The vitality of both of the Budapest studies results from the use of live models. The dramatic force of expression faithfully recalls the shocking horror of the brutal fighting rage of the soldiers, rushing on each other with unrestrained ferocity in the heat of battle, which Leonardo termed *pazzia bestialissima* – most bestial madness.

ZOLTÁN KÁRPÁTI

13

Attributed to Andrea Briosco, called Riccio   1470–1532

Rape of Europa, c.1505–10

Bronze, height 18.2 cm

INVENTORY NUMBER: 5363
SELECTED REFERENCES: Volker Krahn, *Bronzetti Veneziani: Die venezianischen Kleinbronzen der Renaissance aus dem Bode-Museum Berlin*, Cologne, 2003, pp.128–31; Andrea Bacchi and Luciana Giacomelli (eds), *Rinascimento e passione per l'antico: Andrea Riccio e il suo tempo*, exh. cat., Castello del Buonconsiglio, Trento, 2008, no.37

By the sixteenth century Padua had become the foremost centre of bronze casting in Italy. The leading sculptor of the Paduan school was Andrea Briosco, whose thick, curly locks earned him the sobriquet 'Riccio' (hedgehog). He maintained close relations with the humanists of the venerable University of Padua, and produced a large number of small bronzes inspired by classical antiquity. His passionate enthusiasm for the antique is equally apparent in his monumental, three-metre high bronze candlestick for the Basilica of the Santo in Padua – one of the most classically inspired works of sixteenth-century religious art.

The *Rape of Europa*, a masterly small bronze traditionally attributed to Riccio with reservations, was also inspired by classical antiquity. It shows one of the most popular scenes of Greek mythology at the time of the Renaissance: Zeus, fearing the jealousy of his wife Hera, takes the form of a bull to seduce the Phoenician princess, the beautiful Europa, who is playing at the seaside with her companions. Having been adorned by her with flowers, the bull manages to lure the girl to sit on his back and swims off with her to Crete. However, in the often-portrayed Ovidian version of the story there is no trace of the combative resistance shown in the Budapest bronze. Here instead the sculptor probably drew on an ode by Horace, which tells of Europa's desperate protest. Given the sculptor's breadth of culture, as may be inferred from his connections with Paduan humanists, it would not be surprising if he had chosen this lesser-known, unusual source for his work.

MIRIAM SZŐCS

229

14

Attributed to Leonardo da Vinci 1452–1519

Mounted Warrior, first half of the sixteenth century

Bronze, height 24.3 cm

INVENTORY NUMBER: 5362
SELECTED REFERENCES: Mária G. Agghàzy, *Leonardo's Equestrian Statuette*, Budapest, 1989; Gary M. Radke (ed.), *Leonardo da Vinci and the Art of Sculpture*, New Haven and London, 2009, pp.153, 175

The first known owner of this small bronze, the Hungarian sculptor István Ferenczy, purchased it in Rome between 1818 and 1824 as an antique Greek statuette. Only in the early twentieth century was it proposed that this might be Leonardo's sole surviving sculptural work. Although Leonardo received a number of commissions for sculptures, little trace of them remains. Both of the colossal equestrian monuments for Milan that he undertook ended in failure: the clay model for the statue of Lodovico Sforza was destroyed before casting, while its successor, for Gian Giacomo Trivulzio, was never completed. Thus, with the exception of the enthusiastic accounts of his contemporaries, a few notes in his own hand and numerous magnificent preparatory drawings, we know very little about Leonardo's sculptural activity.

The Budapest bronze can be connected with drawings of horses in motion for the ill-fated mural of *The Battle of Anghiari*, executed between 1503 and 1506 in the Palazzo della Signoria (Palazzo Vecchio) in Florence. On one of these, a sheet in the Royal Collection at Windsor, Leonardo's note refers to the fact that he has made small wax models to compose the complicated battle scenes. The Budapest bronze also reflects the use of a similar wax or clay model, which was probably enlarged and cast in bronze by one of Leonardo's pupils or followers, most likely in the early sixteenth century. While it would have been inordinately complicated to cast the small Budapest bronze on a large scale, the statuette nevertheless tackles a problem that Leonardo was unable to overcome in his abortive designs for equestrian monuments, but which evidently obsessed him – the idea of an almost upright sculptural group of a rearing horse and its rider.

MIRIAM SZŐCS

15

Marco Basaiti doc. 1496–1530

Dead Christ, c.1510

Oil on panel, 87 × 69.8 cm

INVENTORY NUMBER: 4206
SELECTED REFERENCES: László Mravik, *North Italian Fifteenth-century Paintings*, Budapest, 1983, no.37; Vilmos Tátrai (ed.), *Summary Catalogue 1*, London and Budapest, 1991, p.5; Mauro Lucco: 'A l'occasion de la redécouverte d'un tableau du musée des Beaux-Arts, nouveau regard sur l'oeuvre de Marco Basaiti', *Bulletin des musées et monuments lyonnais*, 1 (1993), pp.32–33, 37; George Keyes: 'Marco Basaiti: The Dead Christ', in István Barkóczi, George Keyes and Jane Satkowski (eds), *Treasures of Venice: Paintings from the Museum of Fine Arts Budapest*, exh.cat., High Museum of Art, Atlanta, Seattle Art Museum, and The Minneapolis Institute of Arts, 1995, pp.84–85, no.6

Giovanni Bellini is credited with having taught almost every notable Venetian painter of the succeeding generation, but the evidence for there being a genuine master–pupil relationship is usually extremely tenuous. In contrast, among his undisputed followers (who are known as the 'Belliniani'), Marco Basaiti was arguably the most talented. His finest

works, such as the altarpieces of the *Agony in the Garden* of 1510 and the *Calling of the Sons of Zebedee*, both now in the Accademia in Venice, are remarkably distinguished productions.

The present half-length representation of the dead Christ is clearly inspired by the general example of Bellini, but – unlike Basaiti's *Risen Christ* in the Pinacoteca Ambrosiana, Milan, which takes his master's Stockholm *Dead Christ* as its model – it is not based upon a specific prototype. Here Jesus is seated propped up against a beautifully observed and detailed rock formation, which is bathed in warm sunshine and covered in symbolic plants, including birchwort, pennywort, ivy and fig, offset by a glimpse of cloud-filled blue sky beyond. The overall impression is of heroic serenity, but the bloody marks of Christ's wounds, not to mention the way the fingers of his left hand in particular still seem to be clenched in a rictus of pain, ensure that we are not allowed to forget the horrific suffering of the Crucifixion. By this date, the idea of including a flagrantly unrealistic gold disc-halo must have seemed faintly ridiculous, but Basaiti has the best of both worlds, by instead including an understated cruciform arrangement of golden rays that subtly accentuates the Saviour's divinity.

DAVID EKSERDJIAN

16

Master of Portillo active first half of the sixteenth century

Mass of St Gregory, c.1500–25

Tempera on panel, 96.2 × 66.5 cm

INVENTORY NUMBER: 85.7
SELECTED REFERENCES: Vilmos Tátrai (ed.), *Summary Catalogue 1*, London and Budapest, 1991, p.149 (as follower of Pedro Berruguete); Éva Nyerges, *Obras maestras del arte español, Museo de Bellas Artes de Budapest*, exh.cat., Banco Bilbao Vizcaya, Madrid, and Museo de Bellas Artes, Bilbao, 1996, pp.55–58, no.3; Éva Nyerges, *Spanish Paintings: The Collections of the Museum of Fine Arts, Budapest*, Budapest, 2008, pp.54–55, no.20

The anonymous Master of Portillo, active around Valladolid in the first half of the sixteenth century, is a characteristic example of a Spanish master whose art was profoundly responsive to late fifteenth-century Netherlandish painting at a time when that Northern influence had not yet been overwhelmed by the long shadow of the Italian Renaissance. The work from which he derives his name was originally the high altar of the church of Sant'Esteban (Stephen) in Portillo, to the south of Valladolid (it is now in the chapel of the Archbishop's Palace there), but arguably even more impressive is another multi-compartment altarpiece, in the parish church of Fuentes de Año in the province of Ávila.

The attribution of the present panel, which is clearly inspired by a painting of the same subject by Pedro Berruguete in Burgos, to the Master of Portillo is based upon its stylistic similarity to these and other works, and it must originally have been a single element within a larger whole. The subject is the Mass of St Gregory, a crucial episode in relation to religious debates around the real presence of the body and blood of Christ in the bread and wine of the sacrament. Artists represented the story in a number of slightly different ways, but here Pope Gregory is seen celebrating Mass accompanied by

two kneeling and tonsured acolytes, a mitred bishop who is shown holding his papal tiara, and a cardinal in his traditional red attire. As the pope elevates the host, on which a miniature Christ on the cross flanked by the Virgin and St John the Evangelist is just visible, a second representation of Jesus – now as the Man of Sorrows, with blood pouring from his wounds – appears to emerge miraculously from the chalice on the altar in front of him.

DAVID EKSERDJIAN

17

Albrecht Dürer 1471–1528

Lancer on Horseback, 1502

Pen and dark brown ink, 272 × 215 mm

INVENTORY NUMBER: 75
SELECTED REFERENCES: W. L. Strauss, *The Complete Drawings of Albrecht Dürer*, 6 vols, New York, 1974, 2, p.620, no.1502/15; Teréz Gerszi, 'Albrecht Dürer: Lancer on Horseback', in Teréz Gerszi (ed.), *Dürer to Dalí: Master Drawings in the Budapest Museum of Fine Arts*, Budapest, 1999, p.100, no.42

Albrecht Dürer was the leading painter and graphic artist of the German Renaissance, and introduced the ideas and inventions of the Italian Renaissance into Northern Europe. His woodcuts and engravings, the most influential of his works, soon became universally known and admired. Throughout his life Dürer was preoccupied with art theory and wrote treatises on a number of subjects such as geometry, military fortifications and the proportions of the human body. A series of drawings reveals Dürer's passionate interest in the physiognomy of horses and the possibilities of representing them in movement.

Dated 1502 and monogrammed in Dürer's own hand, this drawing shows a horse in dynamic mid-stride, with two of its legs raised in the air, ridden by a soldier with a lance in his right hand. The elongated body of the animal reflects the forms of Gothic tradition, while the harmonious proportions of the rider follow Renaissance ideals. The animation of the horseman and the expressive eyes of the beast, its slightly raised head, its fluttering mane and the persuasive depiction of its tense musculature, all suggest that Dürer probably employed live models for the drawing. To render the representation as accurately as possible, the artist used a pair of compasses to draw the outlines of the horse's neck, belly, chest, haunches and back. The Budapest drawing, above all by virtue of the horse's similar stepping movement, seems to represent an early anticipation of the horse and rider in Dürer's renowned engraving of 1513, *Knight, Death and the Devil*.

SZILVIA BODNÁR

18

Hans Baldung Grien 1484/85–1545

Christ with the Instruments of the Passion and a Donor, c.1504

Pen and grey ink, 282 × 199 mm

INVENTORY NUMBER: 36
SELECTED REFERENCES: Katrin Achilles-Syndram, 'Hans Baldung Grien: Stehender Schmerzensmann, verehrt von Christoph Scheurl', in Katrin Achilles-Syndram et al., *Kunst des Sammelns: Das Praunsche Kabinett: Meisterwerke von Dürer bis Carracci*, exh.cat., Germanisches Nationalmuseum, Nuremberg, 1994, pp.128–30, no.10; Teréz Gerszi, 'Hans Baldung Grien: Christ with the Instruments of Torture and a Donor', in Teréz Gerszi (ed.), *Dürer to Dalí: Master Drawings in the Budapest Museum of Fine Arts*, Budapest, 1999, p.106, no.45

Born into a learned family of lawyers and doctors in Swabia, Hans Baldung Grien was active as a painter, printmaker, draughtsman and stained-glass designer. He probably received his artistic training in Strasbourg before entering Dürer's Nuremberg workshop in 1503, but by 1508 he was back in Strasbourg, where he spent most of the rest of his career, apart from a five-year sojourn in Freiburg im Breisgau (1512–17). His subjects include unusual, often eccentric themes such as witchcraft or allegories of vanity.

The present drawing was executed in Baldung's Nuremberg period either as a preliminary design for stained glass or for a devotional painting. Depictions of Christ with the Instruments of the Passion (the cross, the spear, the sponge on a reed, the scourge, the bundle of twigs and the crown of thorns) served to invite believers to contemplate Christ's sufferings with appropriate devotion. Since the donor on the left is the famous jurist, diplomat and humanist Christoph Scheurl (1481–1542), the work was presumably commissioned by him or his family in Nuremberg. Baldung shows Christ in three-quarter profile in front of a diagonally placed cross, with his right leg bent and turned outward, and his loincloth fluttering behind him. The artist later used the same *contrapposto* pose with a similar flapping cloth for his 1512 woodcut of *St Sebastian*. The late Gothic forms of the loincloth and the banderole looping above the donor add considerably to the decorative quality of the sheet.

SZILVIA BODNÁR

19

Hungarian master   early sixteenth century

St Andrew Altarpiece, 1512

Overall height 420 cm, width when open 270 cm; shrine: painted and gilded pine, 161 × 135 × 31 cm; tympanum: painted limewood with traces of gilding, height 202 cm; predella: painted pine, 48 × 200 × 40.5 cm; statue of St Andrew: gilded and painted limewood, 123 cm; statue of St Bartholomew: gilded and painted limewood, 72 cm; moveable wings: gilded and painted pine, 161 × 67.5 cm; panels 72.5 × 57.5 cm each

HUNGARIAN NATIONAL GALLERY, INVENTORY NUMBERS: 53.569.1–12
SELECTED REFERENCES: János Végh, 'Szent András oltár Liptószentandrásról', in Miklós Mojzer (ed.), *A Magyar Nemzeti Galéria régi gyűjteményei*, Budapest, 1984, p.97; Gyöngyi Török, *Gótikus szárnyasoltárok a középkori Magyarországon: Állandó kiállítás a Magyar Nemzeti Galériában*, Budapest, 2005, pp.20, 124

Almost completely intact, this altarpiece came from the church of Liptószentandrás in Upper Hungary (today Liptovský Ondrej in Slovakia), which is consecrated to the patron saint of the town. The frame separating the panels on the inner side of the moveable wings bears an inscription, which dates the work to 1512. The altarpiece was probably made at Besztercebánya (today Banská Bystrica, in Slovakia), one of the most important artistic centres in Hungary in the late Middle Ages.

In the relatively wide shrine, under subtly carved foliage and on a slightly raised pedestal stands the statue of St Andrew, a work of outstanding quality. He reads from a book held in his right hand, and holds his attribute, the saltire (diagonal) cross, in his left. His gilded cloak is richly carved with expressive folds. The back of the shrine is decorated with a gold brocade curtain ending in coloured tassels, the colour

---

enhanced by the silver of the two slender pillars. The inner sides of the wings feature two episodes each from the life of Christ and the Apostle. On the upper level the Crucifixion of Christ corresponds to the Tormenting of St Andrew, and on the lower level the Resurrection of Christ is paired with the Crucifixion of St Andrew. The figures are located within the stage-like spaces set against the uniform gold grounds. In some of the scenes elaborate background landscapes can be seen beyond the buildings or above the parapet, consisting of rocks and pine forests, with blue mountains, buildings and glimpses of water. Employing the technique of aerial perspective, the landscapes and the figures themselves, the gestures and objects, such as the crosses crudely built from tree trunks, attest to the indirect influence of the Danube School that was widespread in Hungary at the time. In the dramatic, slightly fragmented predella panel, two hovering angels open up Veronica's veil, which extends vertically almost from top to bottom; the back surfaces, not visible to the congregation, feature the outlines of ornamental carvings. Consisting of slender turrets (with the middle one tilting forward in a subtle 'S' shape) and connecting arches, the canopy, which was originally decorated with azurite and gold, holds the figure of the Apostle St Bartholomew. The heavily damaged outer wings portray male and female saints.

GYÖRGYI POSZLER

20

Master of Okolicsnó   c.1490–c.1510

Lamentation, c.1510

Tempera and gold on pine, 133 × 100 cm

HUNGARIAN NATIONAL GALLERY, INVENTORY NUMBER: 184
SELECTED REFERENCES: Gyöngyi Török, 'Farbangaben in der Unterzeichnung am Beispiel des ehemaligen Hochaltars der Franziskanerkirche in Okolicsnó (1500–1510)', in Zsuzsanna Dobos (ed.), *Ex Fumo Lucem: Baroque Studies in Honour of Klára Garas Presented on Her Eightieth Birthday*, 1, Budapest, 1999, pp.37–50; Jiri Fajt, 'Der Meister von Okoličné und die künstlerische Repräsentation der Familie Zápolya: Zum Begriff der Hofmalerei in Oberungarn unter den Jagiellonen', in Evelin Wetter (ed.), *Die Länder der Böhmischen Krone und ihre Nachbarn zur Zeit der Jagiellonenkönige (1471 1526): Kunst Kultur – Geschichte, Studia Jagellonica Lipsiensia*, 2, 2004, pp.173–95

Portraying the *Lamentation of Christ*, this panel was painted by the so-called Master of Okolicsnó, who was the head of a large workshop. The work was part of the high altar of a Franciscan church in the town of Okolicsnó (today Okoličné, Slovakia) in Upper Hungary. Dedicated to the Virgin Mary and decorated with scenes from her life and episodes from the Passion of Christ, the altar complex also included a shrine probably decorated with sculptures. The altarpiece was replaced in the eighteenth century with a new Baroque-style version and its elements ended up in various collections. The *Lamentation* was the lower panel on the outer side of the right wing, and appears on the reverse of the picture depicting the *Presentation in the Temple*, which is also today one of the Budapest National Gallery's treasures. The high altar was donated by a member of the family of István Szapolyai, Lord Lieutenant of Szepes (today Spiš, Slovakia) and Palatine of Hungary (1492–1499), possibly his widow, the Duchess Hedvig of Teschen.

Decorated with gold leaf, the composition is well balanced in the classical sense. The figures are

---

arranged in the foreground on either side of the cross as though on a stage, with the mourning women on the left and John and Mary holding the upper body of the dead Christ in their laps on the right. Painfully immersed in thought, eliciting the viewer's sympathy, the figures are impressively three-dimensional presences. The vivid reds, greens and blues of the draperies and the white of the shroud set off the dull, almost lifeless, brown and grey landscape whose barrenness befits the tragic event. Infrared reflectography has revealed that the painter first drew the details with a fine brush and added letters indicating the colours of the draperies.

GYÖRGYI POSZLER

21

Hungarian(?) master   early sixteenth century

Woman of the Apocalypse Clothed with the Sun and the Dragon, c.1520

Oil and tempera on spruce, 122.8 × 76.7 cm

HUNGARIAN NATIONAL GALLERY, INVENTORY NUMBER: 7639/b
SELECTED REFERENCE: Gyöngyi Török, 'La visione di San Giovanni a Patmos: La "Mulier amicta solis" e il drago a sette teste', in Serenella Castri (ed.), *Apocalisse: L'ultima rivelazione*, exh.cat., Musei Vaticani, Salone Sistino, Rome, 2007, pp.132, 199, no.50

This painting, once the outer side of an altarpiece wing painted on both sides, came from Károly Kornis's mansion at Szentbenedek (today Mănăstirea) in Transylvania. The inner side, now detached and also in the collection of the Hungarian National Gallery in Budapest, depicts the *Transfiguration*. The original location of the winged altarpiece is unknown. Although the powerful colour scheme, extreme animation and some technical aspects speak for its Transylvanian origin, stylistically the panel cannot be closely related to any known altarpiece from the region. The main motifs of the scene were borrowed from the corresponding woodcut from Albrecht Dürer's *Apocalypse* cycle (1496–98), which accurately illustrates the Revelation of St John the Divine (Revelation XII, 1–16). By showing St John the Evangelist, who is missing from Dürer's composition, the painter returned to an earlier iconographic treatment of the theme. He enlarged the composition by means of the inclusion of this figure and a militant angel carrying a cross in the top right-hand corner. This motif was taken from another sheet of the *Apocalypse* series, *The Beast with Two Horns like a Lamb*. The anonymous painter of this work not only adopted Dürer-inspired motifs, but also enriched his composition with exquisite painterly skill.

GYÖNGYI TÖRÖK

22

Raffaello Santi, called Raphael   1483–1520

Study for a Temporary Decoration, c.1508–09 or later

Pen and brown ink over stylus, some traces of black chalk, 199 × 153 mm

INVENTORY NUMBER: 1935
SELECTED REFERENCES: Paul Joannides, *The Drawings of Raphael*, Oxford, 1983, no.215; Loránd Zentai, *Sixteenth-century Central Italian Drawings: An Exhibition from the Museum's Collection*, exh.cat., Museum of Fine Arts, Budapest, 1998, no.7

After four years in Florence, Raphael arrived in Rome probably in late 1508 where he started his

231

unprecedented glorious career. Pope Julius II had invited the young artist to decorate the papal private rooms, the so-called *Stanze,* in the Vatican Palace. The *Stanza della Segnatura,* accommodating the pope's new private library, was the first to be frescoed. The compositions included Raphael's much admired *Disputation of the Holy Sacrament,* commonly known as the *Disputa.* It represents the image of the Church, on earth and in heaven, with the Trinity above an altar displaying the Eucharist. Many preliminary drawings preceded the fresco and no fewer than 30 sheets have survived.

The group of cherubs and an angel on the verso of the Budapest sheet, drawn in flickering pen strokes, was intended for the upper part of this renowned fresco, and represents an initial phase of the preparatory work. The puzzling drawing on the recto, probably executed slightly later than the verso, depicts a sculptural ensemble. However, no surviving documents indicate that Raphael ever received such a commission. Although it is more plausible that the drawing was produced as a study for a temporary decoration, the purpose of the composition is not clear. The trophies and the main figure generally identified as Mars suggest a decoration for a victory celebration, but the putto with the inverted torch is a common funerary symbol and therefore weakens this interpretation.

ZOLTÁN KÁRPÁTI

23

Raffaello Santi, called Raphael 1483–1520

*Esterházy Madonna, c.*1507–08

Tempera and oil on poplar panel, 29 × 21.5 cm

INVENTORY NUMBER: 71
SELECTED REFERENCES: Klára Garas, 'Sammlungsgeschichtliche Beiträge zu Raffael: Raffael-Werke in Budapest', *Bulletin du Musée Hongrois des Beaux-Arts,* 60–61 (1983), pp.41–53; Vilmos Tátrai (ed.), *Summary Catalogue 1,* London and Budapest, 1991, p.100; Jürg Meyer zur Capellen, *Raphael: A Critical Catalogue of His Paintings,* 1, Landshut, 2001, pp.254–57, no.34; Axel Vécsey, 'Raphael: Esterházy Madonna', in Monica Bietti and Annamaria Giusti (eds), *The Splendour of the Medici: Art and Life in Renaissance Florence,* exh.cat., Museum of Fine Arts, Budapest, 2008, p.180, no.93; Jürg Meyer zur Capellen, 'Raphael: Virgin and Child with the Young Saint John the Baptist (The Esterházy Madonna)', in Dóra Sallay, Vilmos Tátrai and Axel Vécsey (eds), *Botticelli to Titian: Two Centuries of Italian Masterpieces,* exh.cat., Museum of Fine Arts, Budapest, 2009, p.270, no.68

As well as being one of the greatest artists of all time, Raphael was exceptional for his ability to learn from others and to reinvent himself, with the result that the works of his first period in Umbria, of his middle years in Florence, and of his final apotheosis in Rome are all thrillingly different from each other.

The present panel, which is unfinished in parts, with the result that extensive underdrawing is visible, is almost invariably placed towards the end of Raphael's time in Florence on stylistic grounds, and not just because a geographical move would explain the abandonment of such a minute work. This dating is also supported by the existence of an all but identical full-scale preliminary drawing in pen and ink, whose figure group of the Virgin and Child with the Infant St John the Baptist was mechanically transferred to the surface of the panel. The only real differences between the two concern the centring of the figures here, the omission of the Baptist's cross, and the modification of the landscape background, ironically enough to include various ancient Roman

monuments and the medieval Torre delle Milizie in Rome. The *Esterházy Madonna* is one of a group of Leonardo-inspired pyramidal compositions executed by Raphael in Florence, in which the first impression of tender intimacy and innocence is undercut by a symbolic detail. In the drawing, the Christ Child was shown reaching out for the Baptist's cross, but here instead he points to the scroll held by his young cousin, which was customarily inscribed with the words from St John's Gospel: 'Behold the Lamb of God, which taketh away the sin of the world' (John I, 29).

DAVID EKSERDJIAN

24

Sebastiano Luciani,

called Sebastiano del Piombo 1485/86–1547

*Girl Pointing, c.*1508

Oil on panel, 52.5 × 42.8 cm

INVENTORY NUMBER: 51.2879
SELECTED REFERENCES: Michael Hirst, *Sebastiano del Piombo,* Oxford and New York, 1981, pp.4, 29, 31, 93–94, pl. 4; Vilmos Tátrai (ed.), *Summary Catalogue 1,* London and Budapest, 1991, p.97; Bernd Wolfgang Lindemann and Claudio Strinati, with Roberto Contini, *Sebastiano del Piombo: 1485-1547,* exh.cat, Palazzo di Venezia, Rome, and Gemäldegalerie, Berlin, 2008, pp.94–95, no.2

Sebastiano was part of the golden generation of painters active in Venice during the first decade of the sixteenth century. With his move to Rome in 1511, only a year after Giorgione's death in 1510, he left the way clear for Titian to establish himself as the supreme master of the Venetian school of painting. In Rome, Sebastiano attached himself to the notoriously uncompanionable Michelangelo and enjoyed a remarkably successful career that culminated in his appointment to the lucrative post of Keeper of the Papal Seal (his nickname, del Piombo, which literally means 'of the lead', refers to this office).

This strikingly immediate and intimate likeness of an alluring and attractive young woman, set against the corner of a room, hovers on the borderline between portraiture and the idealised representation of the eternal feminine. Details such as the sideways glance out of the corners of the eyes, the pearl earring and the uncovered forearm may all seem entirely innocuous today, but would almost certainly have been designed to raise the temperature of a male viewer at the time. Interestingly, in a later *Portrait of a Lady* by Bernardino Licinio (Alte Pinakothek, Munich), which is plainly modelled on this panel, the erotic charge is significantly toned down. The chronology of the mere handful of works executed by Sebastiano prior to his move to Rome is far from secure, but it is generally agreed that this exquisite painting must be among the earliest of his extant productions, although the creamy white impasto at the girl's neckline already foreshadows the bold brushwork of his organ shutters for San Bartolomeo a Rialto, now in the Accademia, Venice.

DAVID EKSERDJIAN

25

Giovan Giorgio Lascaris, called Pyrgoteles doc. 1496–1531

*Bust of a Woman, c.*1500–20

Rock crystal in original silvered copper frame, height 9.5 cm

INVENTORY NUMBER: 79.2
SELECTED REFERENCES: Anne Markham Schulz, *Giambattista and Lorenzo Bregno: Venetian Sculpture in the High Renaissance,* Cambridge and New York, 1991, pp.10–11, 43, 81, 92, 194–95; Andrea Bacchi, 'Riflessioni e novità su Pirgotele', *Nuovi Studi,* 9–10, 11 (2005), pp.105–16

Pyrgoteles was the name of a classical gem-engraver discussed by Pliny the Elder in his *Natural History* (VII.cxxv), where it is recorded that Alexander the Great had decreed that he was the only artist allowed to execute his portrait in emerald. The name was adopted as his sobriquet by Giovan Giorgio Lascaris, a sculptor of Greek origin active in Venice and Padua from the late fifteenth century until his death in 1532. A number of archival records refer to his activity as a sculptor in marble and wood, and underline the fact that he was greatly admired, but none of these documented works has survived.

There is only one signed extant sculpture by Pyrgoteles, a marble relief of the *Virgin and Child* prominently placed in the lunette over the main door on the exterior of the church of Santa Maria dei Miracoli in Venice by Pietro Lombardo (*c.*1435–1515), but around it a small body of work has recently been convincingly assembled. In view of the fact that Lascaris adopted the alias of a gem-engraver, it makes sense to wonder if he himself might have worked in this exceptionally demanding medium. On the basis of their stylistic correspondences with the Miracoli relief, two plausible candidates for such productions have been proposed. One is an exquisite *Virgin and Child* in chalcedony (J. Paul Getty Museum, Los Angeles), while the other is this stunning bust, which is made from an almost flawless piece of rock crystal, set against a silvered copper damask-patterned backdrop in its original frame. Both pieces are spectacularly impressive technical accomplishments, and the present work in particular is plainly related to the sculptures of Pietro Lombardo and his sons Tullio and Antonio.

DAVID EKSERDJIAN

26

Nicolò dell'Abate 1509/12–1571

*Bust of a Woman, c.*1550

Black chalk, pen and brown ink, heightened with white on beige prepared paper, 254 × 182 mm

INVENTORY NUMBER: K58.1183
SELECTED REFERENCE: Katrin Achilles-Syndram et al., *Kunst des Sammelns: das Praunsche Kabinett: Meisterwerke von Dürer bis Carracci,* exh.cat., Germanisches Nationalmuseum, Nuremberg, 1994, pp.85, 231, no.88
The attribution of this sheet to Nicolò dell'Abate was proposed by Aidan Weston-Lewis.

Nicolò dell'Abate was born and trained in Modena, but also worked in Bologna before moving to France and the court of King Henri II, where – alongside Francesco Primaticcio – he established himself as one of the leading artists of the so-called First School of Fontainebleau.

The attribution of the present portrait drawing from the Praun Collection is by no means straightforward, and no name has hitherto been universally accepted. Yet its arresting immediacy –

regardless of its authorship — is instantly apparent, and its association with Nicolò seems compelling. Be that as it may, it certainly gives every indication of being the work of an artist of considerable quality. Both for that reason and because it does not really fit stylistically with what is known of his draughtsmanship, a previously voiced idea that it might be by the epically obscure Giulio Molina seems unconvincing. Conversely, the facts that Molina was from Bologna, and that this sheet has so much in common with the rather fantastical ideal female heads drawn by another Bolognese artist, Bartolomeo Passerotti, are extremely suggestive. Nicolò certainly produced a number of secular frescoes that included elegantly dressed and coiffed ladies during his Bolognese period, although this particular head does not correspond to any that has survived. On the other hand, it compares particularly well with the facial type of the figure of St Catherine represented in profile in a splendid drawing in red, black and white chalks by the artist in the Uffizi, and might almost be her sister seen full face.

DAVID EKSERDJIAN

27

Baccio della Porta, called Fra Bartolommeo 1472–1517

Three Studies of Dominican Friars, c.1504–08

Black and white chalk on brown prepared paper, 262 × 268 mm

INVENTORY NUMBER: 1766
SELECTED REFERENCE: Loránd Zentai, *Sixteenth-century Central Italian Drawings: An Exhibition from the Museum's Collection*, exh.cat., Museum of Fine Arts, Budapest, 1998, no.16

Fra Bartolommeo was already a prolific painter in Florence when under the influence of Savonarola he destroyed his profane works. Shortly afterwards he completely abandoned painting and entered the city's Dominican monastery as a novice. Probably at the incentive of the cultivated prior of San Marco, Fra Bartolommeo resumed painting after a four-year hiatus, operating a prosperous workshop within the monastery. Leonardo's new painterly and compositional method found fertile ground in the religious art of Fra Bartolommeo, who responded to the great master's innovations with finesse and sensibility. He was also an innately gifted draughtsman, leaving behind an unusually extensive corpus of drawings.

This haunting image comprises two originally independent fragmentary studies, which were ingeniously joined together when they were in the famous collection of Pierre-Jean Mariette, who was responsible for the beautiful and distinctive mount. Both drawings were executed during Fra Bartolommeo's first years at San Marco in his preferred combination of media, black and white chalk. The right-hand study of a praying friar, his hands raised in the so-called *orans* position, was probably intended for the kneeling figure of St Peter Martyr in Fra Bartolommeo's *Assumption of the Virgin*. This was his first monumental altarpiece, which was painted for the Florentine Compagnia dei Contemplanti around 1508 (the work was destroyed in Berlin in 1945). The fragment to the left comprises

two studies of a second kneeling friar embracing the foot of a cross. This iconography was doubtless inspired by related motifs in the work of his great precursor at San Marco, Fra Angelico (c.1395/1400–1455). No extant painting or fresco by Fra Bartolommeo may be directly connected to these two studies. However, Fra Paolino (?1490–1547), his pupil, who inherited the direction of his workshop, painted a reversed version of the figure in his altarpiece for the church of San Domenico in Pistoia in the 1530s.

ZOLTÁN KÁRPÁTI

28

Jacopo Carucci, called Pontormo 1494–1557

Study for a Seated Youth, c.1514–16

Black chalk and charcoal, 242 × 315 mm

INVENTORY NUMBER: 2198
SELECTED REFERENCES: Janet Cox-Rearick, *The Drawings of Pontormo: A Catalogue Raisonné with Notes on the Paintings*, 2 vols, New York, 1981, 2, p.364, no.12a; Loránd Zentai, *Sixteenth-century Central Italian Drawings: An Exhibition from the Museum's Collection*, exh.cat., Museum of Fine Arts, Budapest, 1998, no.17

In his canonical *Lives of the Artists* (1550 and 1568), Giorgio Vasari introduced Pontormo as a withdrawn, neurotic artist who was a very slow worker and who had an eccentric attitude towards his patrons. Vasari's description, colourfully enriched with anecdotal elements, may have been motivated by professional rivalry with a competitor for Medici patronage. At the time when his biographies were written, the most successful and competing Florentine workshop besides Vasari's *bottega* was that of Agnolo Bronzino (1503–1572), Pontormo's closest and most talented pupil.

Parmigianino, Rosso Fiorentino and Pontormo were all highly individual painters, whose bizarre genius produced an extraordinary body of work in sixteenth-century Italy. Pontormo's *Visitation*, painted as a part of a fresco cycle in the atrium of the church of Santissima Annunziata in Florence between 1514 and 1516, clearly demonstrates his distinctive early manner, which was deeply influenced by Andrea del Sarto (1486–1530) and which combines emotional drama with classic amplitude. During the initial phase of the preparation, this splendid chalk drawing was intended as a study for the nude boy seated on the steps at the right of the composition. Pontormo altered the details repeatedly, correcting in new lines (pentimenti) in his efforts to perfect the figure. The robust forms and vitality of the youth result from the use of a live model, and like many of Pontormo's figure studies, the Budapest sheet (which has been substantially made up) may depict one of the artist's apprentices.

ZOLTÁN KÁRPÁTI

29

Albrecht Altdorfer c.1480–1538

St Barbara, 1517

Pen and black ink, heightened with white on green prepared paper, 161 × 123 mm

INVENTORY NUMBER: 23
SELECTED REFERENCES: Franz Winzinger, *Albrecht Altdorfer Zeichnungen*, Munich, 1952, p.82, no.62; Katrin Achilles-Syndram, 'Albrecht Altdorfer: Die heilige Barbara', in Katrin Achilles-Syndram et al., *Kunst des Sammelns: Das Praunsche Kabinett: Meisterwerke von Dürer bis Carracci*, exh.cat., Germanisches Nationalmuseum, Nuremberg, 1994, pp.155–56, no.34

Albrecht Altdorfer was a highly innovative artist who worked as a painter, draughtsman, architect, engraver and etcher. He also had a successful political career as a member of the Regensburg City Council. He played an important role in establishing landscape as an artistic subject in its own right in the first quarter of the sixteenth century, both with his drawings of identifiable sites and by producing the first pure landscape prints.

Altdorfer made many of his drawings, like this monogrammed *St Barbara*, on dark prepared paper (brown, reddish-brown, green or blue) using black ink, heightened with white, to create powerful chiaroscuro effects. Barbara, the female saint shown here, lived in the third century. In order to discourage her suitors she was shut in a tower by her father Dioscurus of Heliopolis. When she turned to Christianity, Dioscurus made every effort to persuade his daughter to abandon her new faith. After refusing to obey his orders, Barbara was beheaded. Altdorfer depicted the saint stepping forward holding one of her attributes, the chalice, on top of which rests the wafer of the host, since she was commonly invoked by those endangered by storm or lightning, who feared sudden death without the benefit of the last sacrament. It has been suggested that the Budapest *St Barbara* was connected to Altdorfer's altarpiece for the Abbey of St Florian in Austria, completed by 1518, but on stylistic grounds and by virtue of the figure's distinctive proportions, the composition is arguably even closer to the eleven apostle drawings in the library of the monastery of Seitenstetten, Austria, also dated to 1517. The *St Barbara*, of which what is probably an autograph replica (private collection) and a derivation in reverse (Kunstmuseum, Bern) also survive, might originally have belonged to a series of representations of saints.

SZILVIA BODNÁR

30

Hans Hoffmann c.1550–1591/92

Two Studies of Hands, c.1580

Pen and brush with black ink, heightened with white on blue prepared paper, 238 × 251 mm

INVENTORY NUMBER: 142
SELECTED REFERENCES: Szilvia Bodnár, 'Hans Hoffmann: Händestudien', in Szilvia Bodnár and Teréz Gerszi, *Meisterzeichnungen des Künstlerkreises um Kaiser Rudolf II. aus dem Museum der Schönen Künste in Budapest*, exh.cat., Salzburger Barockmuseum, Salzburg, 1987, p.50, no.25; Szilvia Bodnár, 'Hans Hoffmann, d'après Albrecht Dürer: Etude de mains', in Emmanuel Starcky (ed.), *Nicolas II Esterházy 1765–1833: Un prince hongrois collectionneur*, exh.cat., Musée national du château de Compiègne, 2007, p.162, no.64

Hans Hoffmann's faithful copies of Albrecht Dürer's drawings earned him a deservedly high reputation among his contemporaries. The artist began his career in Nuremberg and then moved to Munich where he resided for a short time. From 1586 until his death he worked as a painter and art adviser in Prague at the court of Rudolph II (1552–1612), where he helped the Emperor acquire several original works by Dürer. Hoffmann signed some of his copies with the letters 'AD', while other pieces bear his own

233

monogram. He achieved particular success with works of his own invention that mimicked Dürer's style.

In the Budapest drawing of the two pairs of hands, the model for the praying hands on the left was Dürer's famous study for the mid-section of the Heller Altarpiece, which was destroyed by fire in 1729. Dürer's drawing, now at the Albertina in Vienna, was originally on the same sheet as a study for an apostle's head, which was also linked with the altarpiece. On Hoffmann's sheet, the pair of hands on the right is a copy of a lost drawing by Dürer made in preparation for the hand of the pope in the *Feast of the Rose Garlands* (1506), a work now in the National Gallery in Prague. In its present form, the pope's hands do not resemble Hoffmann's copy because the picture, having been severely damaged, was repainted in the nineteenth century. However, a copy dating from the late sixteenth century in which the pair of hands is clearly identifiable has survived (Kunsthistorisches Museum, Vienna). Hoffmann's Budapest drawing, in which the blue ground and white heightening result in a painterly effect, is a good example of how the artist produced new compilations – presumably for sale or as gifts – based on Dürer's studies. The drawing, together with almost 60 further works by Hoffmann, originates from the Praun Collection of Nuremberg.

SZILVIA BODNÁR

31

Hans Leu the Younger *c.*1490–1531

*St Jerome, c.*1515

Pen and black ink, heightened with white on brick-red prepared paper, 171 × 235 mm

INVENTORY NUMBER: 307
SELECTED REFERENCES: Teréz Gerszi, 'Un dessin inconnu de Hans Leu le Jeune au Musée des Beaux-Arts', *Bulletin du Musée Hongrois des Beaux-Arts*, 7 (1955), pp.28–34, fig.21; Teréz Gerszi, 'Hans Leu the Younger: St Jerome', in Teréz Gerszi (ed.), *Dürer to Dalí: Master Drawings in the Budapest Museum of Fine Arts*, Budapest, 1999, p.122, no.53

Hans Leu, one of the foremost Swiss artists of the early sixteenth century, received his initial training in his father's workshop in Zurich. On his apprentice travels he must have studied with Albrecht Dürer in Nuremberg and Hans Baldung Grien in Freiburg before returning to Zurich by 1514. His style of drawing, as well as his manner of rendering nature, also reveals the influence of such Danube School masters as Albrecht Altdorfer and Wolf Huber. Due to financial difficulties brought about by a lack of commissions, he earned his living as a mercenary fighting in military campaigns. He died in the 1531 battle between the Catholics and Protestants at Gubel near Zurich.

St Jerome (342–420), one of the four Latin Fathers of the Church, retreated into the desert as a hermit for four years. He is depicted at the right edge of this composition, kneeling before a tiny crucifix at the right margin, ascetically beating his breast with a stone. He and his companion, the tame lion in the lower left corner, are shown in harmonious unity with the surrounding landscape. Nature is the main subject of the sheet, and Leu represented the striking

cliffs, with a distant view of a town in between, with broad strokes rather than aiming for flawless perspectival accuracy. The decorative foliage of the trees covering the rocky hills is rendered with great fluidity. Some of the figural and landscape motifs, such as the kneeling saint and the shape of the cliffs, are reminiscent of details in Dürer's prints. The spontaneously drawn landscape, on the other hand, together with the painterly chiaroscuro effect achieved by the white heightening on brick-red prepared paper, suggest Leu's knowledge of Altdorfer's romantically inclined works, although the Swiss artist's style is far less calligraphic.

SZILVIA BODNÁR

32

Lucas Cranach the Elder 1472–1553

*Christ and the Virgin Interceding for Humanity before God the Father, c.*1516–18

Oil and tempera on limewood panel, 74.5 × 56 cm

INVENTORY NUMBER: 128
SELECTED REFERENCES: Max J.Friedländer and Jakob Rosenberg, *Die Gemälde von Lucas Cranach*, Berlin, 1978, p.97, no.134D; Vilmos Tátrai and Zsuzsa Urbach (eds), *Renaissance Paintings from the Budapest Museum of Fine Arts*, exh.cat., Tokyo, 1994, no.49; Ildikó Ember and Imre Takács (eds), *Summary Catalogue 3*, Budapest, 2003, p.32; Bodo Brinkmann (ed.), *Cranach*, exh.cat., Städel Museum, Frankfurt, and Royal Academy, London, 2007, pp.234–35, no.58

Lucas Cranach the Elder was one of the most individual and remarkable artists of the German Renaissance. Although he is best known as a painter of slinkily alluring female nudes and as a portraitist, not least of such heroes of the Reformation as Martin Luther, he was also a very considerable religious artist.

The present panel, which dates from Cranach's Wittenberg period, is a highly original combination of the two related iconographic traditions of the Virgin of Mercy and the Double Intercession. At the top, he represents God the Father, surrounded by cherubim and armed with a drawn bow and three arrows, perhaps in reference to Psalm VII, 11–13 ('God judgeth the righteous, and God is angry with the wicked every day. If he turn not, he will whet his sword; he hath bent his bow, and made it ready. He hath also prepared for him the instruments of death; he ordaineth his arrows against the persecutors.') The object of his attention at bottom right is humankind, and not least the high and mighty of both church and state – pope, cardinal and bishop; emperor and king – here shown sheltering under Mary's red mantle, which denotes her as the Virgin of Mercy. It is the inclusion over to the left of Christ as the Man of Sorrows kneeling on a T-shaped cross and looking upwards which means that the image is equally inspired by the visual tradition of the Double Intercession, which in its turn is derived from the *Speculum Humanae Salvationis*, an anonymous text universally believed at the time to have been written by St Bernard.

DAVID EKSERDJIAN

33

Albrecht Altdorfer *c.*1480–1538

*Crucifixion, c.*1518

Oil on limewood panel, 75 × 57.5 cm

INVENTORY NUMBER: 5892
SELECTED REFERENCES: F.Ficker, *Altdorfer*, Milan, 1977, pp.94, 105, 184; Ildikó Ember and Imre Takács (eds), *Summary Catalogue 3*, Budapest, 2003, p.14; Thomas Noll, *Albrecht Altdorfer in seiner Zeit: Religiöse und profane Themen in der Kunst um 1500*, Munich, 2004, pp.204–12; Mark Leonard, Carole Namowicz and Anne Woollett, 'Albrecht Altdorfer's Crucifixion (Budapest, Museum of Fine Arts)', in *Studying Old Master Paintings – Technology and Practice*, Proceedings of The National Gallery Technical Bulletin 30th Anniversary Conference, London, forthcoming

Albrecht Altdorfer is perhaps most admired for his remarkable and pioneering landscapes, above all of the Danube valley and the Alps, in which the figures almost seem to dwindle into insignificance, but he was at the same time a major narrative painter.

The present panel stands out in Altdorfer's *oeuvre* by virtue of its archaic gold background, whose patterned decoration has been revealed by a recent restoration. The artist represents the Crucifixion as a crowded and at least superficially chaotic drama, albeit without the Good and the Bad Thief. In the left foreground, the Virgin swoons and is supported by two of the Holy Women, while beyond her an aged man engages our gaze (his stick suggests he may be Joseph, who is not normally included in the scene) and a soldier wearing steel gauntlets attempts to throttle another of the Holy Women. In the centre Mary Magdalene embraces the foot of the cross, while John the Evangelist looks upwards, and between them the earth splits to disclose Adam's skeleton, in accordance with the account in St Matthew's Gospel. Also beside the cross is an apparently kneeling man looking intently out at us, conceivably a self-portrait. In the bottom right corner, next to the artist's blood-red 'AA' monogram (whose colour matches that of Christ's halo), soldiers throw dice to determine who will claim Christ's robe, while beyond are the massed forces of evil. Above the fray, and flanked by two lamenting angels, is the lifeless but remarkably unscarred body of Christ.

DAVID EKSERDJIAN

34

Girolamo Romanino 1484/87–1560

*Men on Horseback Riding to the Right, c.*1524–25

Pen and ink on blue paper, now faded beige, 280 × 270 mm

INVENTORY NUMBER: 1990
SELECTED REFERENCES: Alessandro Nova, *Girolamo Romanino*, Turin, 1994, p.254; Alessandro Nova, 'The Drawings of Girolamo Romanino: Part I', *Burlington Magazine*, 137, 110 (1995), pp.159–68; Loránd Zentai, *Sixteenth-century Northern Italian Drawings*, exh.cat., Museum of Fine Arts, Budapest, 2003, no.2

This sheet was traditionally attributed to Titian, whose name was inscribed by a proud if misguided owner in the bottom right corner, but the muscular vigour of its boldly applied thick pen line is entirely characteristic of Girolamo Romanino's ink drawings. The wheeling group of horsemen, the foremost of whom appears to be wearing a helmet as well as a fluttering cape, is accompanied by a couple of foot soldiers. One is prominently located at bottom right, while the other is wittily reduced to a pair of disembodied legs striding behind the principal steed. These figures do not correspond with those found in any extant work by Romanino, but it has been plausibly suggested that they are related to a lost work by the artist referred to in an early source. In 1525 the Venetian connoisseur Marcantonio Michiel (1484–1552), whose manuscript notes on art in the Veneto are of inestimable value in attempting to unravel who did what in the region during the Renaissance, recorded seeing a large canvas in the celebrated collection of the Venetian patrician Taddeo Contarini (c.1466–1540). He described the painting as an 'ordinanza di cavalli' (literally 'formation of horses'), for which this sheet may well have been a first idea. The dating of the drawing to before 1525 is perfectly in accordance with what is known concerning Romanino's stylistic evolution, and it is a mark of the esteem in which he was held that the completed painting was deemed worthy to rub shoulders in Contarini's collection with such absolute masterpieces as Giovanni Bellini's *St Francis* (Frick Collection, New York) and Giorgione's *Three Philosophers* (Kunsthistorisches Museum, Vienna).

DAVID EKSERDJIAN

35

Luca Signorelli   c.1450–1523

St James the Greater with a Living and a Dead Pilgrim,
*c.*1508

Oil on panel, 34 × 26.2 cm

INVENTORY NUMBER: 1084
SELECTED REFERENCES: *Catalogo de' quadri, sculture in marmo, musaici, pietre colorate, bronzi, ed altri oggetti di belle arti esistenti nella Galleria del Sagro Monte di Pietà di Roma*, Rome, 1857, p.26, no.566 ('Francesco Signorelli. Un soggetto tratto dalle leggende di S.Giacomo Apostolo. Tavola alta cent. 33 larga cent. 26'); Robert Oertel, *Frühe italienische Malerei in Altenburg: beschreibender Katalog der Gemälde des 13. bis 16. Jahrhunderts im Staatlichen Lindenau-Museum, Altenburg*, 1961, pp.175–78; Bernard Berenson, *Italian Pictures of the Renaissance. Florentine School*, London, 1963, p.123 (as Eusebio da San Giorgio); Tom Henry and Laurence B. Kanter, *Luca Signorelli: The Complete Paintings*, London, 2002, pp.217–19
The attribution to Signorelli was independently proposed by Andrea De Marchi in letters of 28 September 1993 and 22 January 1994. The information concerning the work's early provenance was kindly supplied by Matteo Mazzalupi. I am extremely grateful to Tom Henry for discussing this painting with me.

Luca Signorelli was one of the most important and distinctive Italian painters active in the last quarter of the fifteenth century and the first of the sixteenth. As a young man, he was part of the team responsible for the fresco cycle on the walls of the Sistine Chapel in Rome, while the most remarkable achievement of his maturity was the fresco decoration of the Cappella di San Brizio in Orvieto Cathedral, which was famously much admired by Michelangelo, whose obsession with muscular male anatomy Signorelli unquestionably anticipated.

The present panel, whose scale, character and horizontal wood-grain all indicate that it must originally have formed part of a predella (the sequence of small scenes at the base of an altarpiece), has not previously been published as the work of Signorelli. Instead it has been suggested that it is by a minor Umbrian painter called Eusebio da San Giorgio or simply generically assigned to the Umbrian School, although it has recently been discovered that it was attributed to Signorelli's son, Francesco, in the 1857 catalogue of the Galleria del Sagro Monte di Pietà in Rome, where it was deposited in 1850. It was then sold in 1873 to the Florentine dealer Auguste Riblet, and subsequently purchased in Venice from the dealer Luigi Resemini in 1893 by the director of the Budapest Museum,

Károly Pulszky. Its style, height and subject-matter all suggest it may originally have belonged to the predella of a *Virgin and Child with James, Simon, Francis and Bonaventure* dated 1508 in the Pinacoteca di Brera, Milan. If so, it very probably accompanied five somewhat wider elements of what is presumed to be that altarpiece's predella in the Lindenau Museum, Altenburg, while the fact that its left edge is painted suggests it formed the base of the left pilaster of the altarpiece's frame. The rare subject depicted here, which involves the miraculous appearance of St James on horseback to a pilgrim en route to Compostela whose companion has died, is recounted in the *Golden Legend*, a best-selling compilation of sacred stories whose author is believed to have been Jacopo da Voragine, who was Archbishop of Genoa from 1292 to 1298.

DAVID EKSERDJIAN

36

Master of Frankfurt   1460–?1533

*Nativity, c.*1520

Oil on panel, 55.5 × 75 cm

INVENTORY NUMBER: 3880
SELECTED REFERENCES: Max J. Friedländer, *Early Netherlandish Painting*, 14 vols, Leiden, 7, 1971, pp.54–57; Ildikó Ember and Zsuzsa Urbach (eds), *Summary Catalogue 2*, Budapest, 2000, p.102

The reason why the anonymous artist responsible for this impressive picture has come to be known as the Master of Frankfurt is that two of his major works – an altarpiece of the *Holy Kinship* and a triptych of the *Crucifixion* were both painted for patrons in Frankfurt, and have remained there (respectively in the Historisches Museum and in the Städel). It is plain that the artist was one of the most important painters active in Antwerp in the last years of the fifteenth century and the early part of the sixteenth, and attempts have been made to identify him with one Hendrik van Wueluwe, who died in 1533, but this is far from certain. His masterpiece is a self-portrait with his wife dated 1496 in the Koninklijk Museum voor Schone Kunsten, Antwerp.

The present panel, which dates from the artist's maturity, represents the Virgin, attended by three angels – the one on the right has a depiction of the Annunciation on his cope, while he and his neighbour both have the most enormous wings – kneeling in adoration around the Christ Child, a defenceless grub-like newborn lying on the bare ground. Further back and over to the left is a doddering St Joseph, who is shown nursing a candle (this detail is mentioned in the description of St Bridget of Sweden's vision of the scene), while balancing him at the right margin is an equally aged kneeling shepherd, one of whose fellows hears the glad tidings from a swooping angel in the distance behind him, while two more – one of them with bagpipes – kneel much closer to hand. The setting is a grandiose classical ruin, but beyond it are naturalistic glimpses of more local architecture and landscape.

DAVID EKSERDJIAN

37

Girolamo Romanino   1484/87–1560

*Adoration of the Shepherds, c.*1524–25

Red chalk, 255 × 200 mm

INVENTORY NUMBER: 2224
SELECTED REFERENCES: Alessandro Nova, *Girolamo Romanino*, Turin, 1994, p.354; Alessandro Nova, 'The Drawings of Girolamo Romanino. Part 1', *Burlington Magazine*, 137, 110 (1995), pp.159–68; Loránd Zentai, *Sixteenth-century Northern Italian Drawings*, exh.cat., Museum of Fine Arts, Budapest, 2005, no.3

Girolamo Romanino, alongside such masters as Savoldo and Moretto, was a leading light of the school of Brescia in the first half of the sixteenth century, and arguably its most fearlessly original representative. Brescia was a dependency of Venice, with the result that all these artists worked in the shadow of Titian, whose spectacular polyptych of the Resurrection was painted for their home town and remains one of its greatest treasures. Yet none of them – least of all Romanino – gives the impression of having been overawed by him.

The general arrangement of the composition links it with two paintings of the *Nativity* by Romanino, which appear to date from widely different periods of the artist's career: the earlier, which is of around 1524–25, forms the central panel of his polyptych in the National Gallery, London, while the later one, of around 1545, is in the Pinacoteca Tosio-Martinengo, Brescia. In all probability, the drawing was made in the 1520s and then preserved by Romanino for potential exploitation at a later date, but in fact neither painting quite corresponds. Crucially, there are no shepherds in the London picture, while in the Brescia version they are differently positioned. On the other hand, such elements as the kneeling Virgin, shown here with her hands crossed in prayer, the unprotected Child, and the head of the ox at bottom left are common to all three compositions.

DAVID EKSERDJIAN

38

Master of the Budapest Abundance   active 1530–1540

*Abundance, c.*1530–40

Bronze, height 28 cm

INVENTORY NUMBER: 5311
SELECTED REFERENCES: Jolán Balogh, *Katalog der ausländischen Bildwerke des Museums der Bildenden Künste in Budapest*, Budapest, 1975, no.337; *Von allen seiten schön: Bronzen der Renaissance und des Barock*, exh.cat., Staatliche Museen zu Berlin und Preussischer Kulturbesitz, Berlin, 1995, p.254

Inspired by Italian small bronzes, an interest in bronze casting arose in sixteenth-century Germany, primarily in Augsburg and Nuremberg. While in the case of Italian bronzes the sculptor is usually known, in Germany at best it is the name of the caster that has come down to us. The identity of the creator of this piece is likewise shrouded in mystery, and the name by which he is known derives from the present statuette. Unlike the majority of his German contemporaries, who only rarely used a classical prototype, the works of the Master of the Budapest Abundance reveal the explicit influence of antiquity mediated by Italian models.

German sculptors made tremendous efforts to adopt the genre of the small bronze, but used a completely different technique. As a rule, they did not model their bronzes in clay or wax, as was the custom in Italy, but continued the centuries-old German tradition of woodcarving. The model for the Budapest female figure – who must have once held the cornucopia, an indispensable attribute of Plenty and Wealth – was likewise carved in wood before being cast in bronze. The bronze surface faithfully reflects the unusual material of its wooden model, the chisel marks of which can be clearly perceived. The traces of pigment show that the sculptor was even in this respect unable to shake off the tradition of German wood sculpture: instead of patina, the Budapest statuette was originally covered with a thick layer of paint. This not only disguised the irregularities of the surface, but also destroyed the typically metallic texture of the bronze.

MIRIAM SZŐCS

39
Camillo Boccaccino   1504/05–1546
*St Bernard, c.*1525
Black and white chalk on blue paper, 375 × 220 mm

INVENTORY NUMBER: K.58.213
SELECTED REFERENCES: G. Bora, 'Note cremonesi I: Camillo Boccaccino, le proposte', *Paragone*, 25, 295 (1974), pp.40–70; Mina Gregori (ed.), *I Campi e la cultura artistica cremonese del Cinquecento*, Milan, 1985, pp.275–76, no.2.5.1; Loránd Zentai, *Sixteenth-century Northern Italian Drawings*, exh.cat., Museum of Fine Arts, Budapest, 2003, no.31

Cremona, like so many Italian cities during the Renaissance, had a remarkably distinguished as well as distinctive local school of painting. Camillo Boccaccino, the son of the Ferrarese painter Boccaccio Boccaccino (*c.*1466–1525) who settled there, was arguably its greatest master, but he died relatively young, and only a handful of his works have survived. Alongside a number of altarpieces, the most notable of these are his organ shutters in Santa Maria di Campagna at Piacenza and various frescoes in the church of San Sigismondo at Cremona.

Camillo studied in Venice until 1525, when he returned to Cremona following the death of his father. The same date is inscribed on his first surviving work, the high altarpiece for the church of Santa Maria del Cistello, which is a dramatically asymmetrical *Virgin and Child with Three Saints and a Donor*, now in Prague, seemingly inspired by Titian's *Pesaro Altarpiece* for the church of the Frari in Venice (completed in 1526). The present sheet, a highly finished study on an unusually large scale for the figure of St Bernard in the altarpiece, reveals how profoundly influenced Camillo was at this time by the art of Venice. Later on, he would emulate the stylishly elongated figure canon of Parmigianino, but here it is the monumental solidity of the twisting saint that impresses. The technique, in which the blue of the paper forms a mid-tone between the black chalk used for the outlines and for shading, and the white employed for the highlights, is also entirely typical of sixteenth-century Venetian practice.

DAVID EKSERDJIAN

40
Giulio Pippi, called Giulio Romano   1492/99–1546
*Family Meal, c.*1531–34
Pen and brown ink and wash, 220 × 414 mm

INVENTORY NUMBER: 2126
SELECTED REFERENCES: Amadeo Belluzzi, Howard Burns, Kurt Forster et al., *Giulio Romano*, exh.cat., Museo Civico Palazzo Te and Palazzo Ducale, Mantua, 1989; Loránd Zentai, *Sixteenth-century Central Italian Drawings*, exh.cat., Budapest, 1998, pp.70–71, no.25; Loránd Zentai, *Sixteenth-century Northern Italian Drawings*, exh.cat., Museum of Fine Arts, Budapest, 2003, no.20

Giulio Romano was Raphael's principal assistant until his master's death in 1520, and thereafter his artistic heir. By 1524, however, after the scandal caused by his designs for a series of explicit engravings of couples engaged in sexual intercourse (*I Modi* – literally 'the ways'), he had fled Rome and settled in Mantua, where he spent the rest of his career as court artist to the Marquess, Federico Gonzaga (1500–1540), and his family. In this role, his supreme achievement was the Palazzo Te, which revealed him as one of the most boldly innovative architects of the entire Renaissance, and in connection with whose decoration he operated above all as a designer-cum-impresario, delegating the actual execution of expanses of fresco and stucco to others.

The present drawing is a fully developed idea for the central scene in the vault of the Loggia della Grotta in the Palazzo Te, a space which was frescoed around 1531–34 by Giulio's assistants. Although it has not always been regarded as an autograph study, both the changes of mind over contours and the energetic handling of the pen and wash, which creates a powerful chiaroscuro effect, support the notion that it is the work of Giulio himself. In the fresco, the poses and disposition of the figures are unchanged, but the composition is less tightly framed. Interestingly, even at this date, the two figures who flank the dining group were inspired by Roman models (both in reverse): the water-pourer by a servant in a fresco on the vault of Raphael's loggia decoration of the Villa Farnesina, and the woman with the candelabrum by Michelangelo's marble sculpture of the *Risen Christ* in Santa Maria sopra Minerva.

DAVID EKSERDJIAN

41
Giulio Campi   *c.*1508–1573
*Design for a Frieze, c.*1540–45
Pen and brown wash, heightened with white, 135 × 363 mm

INVENTORY NUMBER: 2034
SELECTED REFERENCES: Mina Gregori (ed.), *I Campi e la cultura artistica cremonese del Cinquecento*, Milan, 1985, pp.281–92; Loránd Zentai, *Sixteenth-century Northern Italian Drawings*, exh.cat., Museum of Fine Arts, Budapest, 2003, no.32

The Campi were the most talented and enduring clan of artists active in Cremona during the Renaissance. Giulio and his brothers, Antonio and Vincenzo, were the sons of the painter Galeazzo Campi (*c.*1477–1536), but oddly there is no proof that they were also related to Bernardino Campi. Giulio was equally accomplished as a painter of frescoes and of altarpieces: in his native Cremona, there are fine examples of the former in the church of Sant'Agata,

---

while his masterpiece in the latter category is the high altarpiece of San Sigismondo, a church whose highly decorated interior provides a spectacular demonstration of how impressive the local school could be.

The present, highly finished sheet is exactly the same size as a related drawing in the British Museum, and both of them are designs for decorative friezes in the manner of Giulio Romano, the only significant difference being that the chained satyr and satyress within niches in the former are replaced by manacled prisoners in the latter. Such *trompe-l'oeil* friezes, usually executed in grisaille in order to counterfeit sculptural reliefs, often featured as elements of both the exterior and the interior decoration of secular buildings, but this was probably not their *raison d'être* in this particular instance. In 1541 Giulio is known to have contributed to the adornment of the temporary triumphal arches erected for the entry of the Emperor Charles V into Cremona, and in 1545 he fulfilled a similar commission for the investiture of Pier Luigi Farnese as 1st Duke of Parma and Piacenza, so it seems logical to surmise that the drawings were designs for one of the two festivities.

DAVID EKSERDJIAN

42
Ludovico Mazzolino   *c.*1480–1528
*Christ before Pilate, c.*1520
Oil on panel, 45.3 × 38.5 cm

INVENTORY NUMBER: 4247
SELECTED REFERENCES: Silla Zamboni, *Ludovico Mazzolino*, Milan, 1968, pp.25, 39, no.13, pl. 55b; Vilmos Tátrai (ed.), *Summary Catalogue 1*, London and Budapest, 1991, p.77; Alessandro Ballarin, *Dosso Dossi: la pittura a Ferrara negli anni del ducato di Alfonso*, 2 vols, Cittadella, 1994–95, 1, p.247, no.162, fig.CXLVIII

Even more than his Ferrarese contemporary Garofalo, Ludovico Mazzolino specialised in small-scale multi-figured religious scenes. They are populated by an often grotesque cast of grimacing and gesticulating characters, who are reminiscent of the figures found in Northern – and especially German – Renaissance prints, yet it is almost impossible to identify direct quotations from any such sources in his work. Only rarely did he execute large altarpieces, such as his *Christ among the Doctors* (Gemäldegalerie, Berlin), and even then the effect is of a grossly inflated version of his customary productions.

The present panel is a richly detailed representation of the episode from the Passion when Christ is brought before Pontius Pilate, who is shown washing his hands in the hope of cleansing himself of guilt. The massive turbans worn by the twisting figure of Pilate and a number of attendant figures lend the scene an oriental feel, as do the predominantly dark complexions of the protagonists, who are mostly dressed in warm reds and greens. In contrast, the pale and bowed figure of Christ, who is wearing a cool blue-white robe, stands out. As so often with Mazzolino, the action takes place on two levels, but the exultant asymmetry of the architecture, with gigantic columns to the right but not to the left, is extremely unusual. So are the fantastical patterns of the leggings of the young soldier at top left.

A later treatment from around 1530 of the same subject (Fitzwilliam Museum, Cambridge) is once again determinedly asymmetrical, but contains considerably more figures.

DAVID EKSERDJIAN

43

Benvenuto Tisi, called Garofalo 1481–1559
Christ and the Woman Taken in Adultery, c.1540

Oil on panel, 55 × 44 cm

INVENTORY NUMBER: 165
SELECTED REFERENCES: Vilmos Tátrai, 'Une peinture peu connue de Garofalo', *Bulletin du Musée Hongrois des Beaux-Arts*, 68–69 (1987), pp.91–102; Vilmos Tátrai (ed.), *Summary Catalogue 1*, London and Budapest, 1991, p.45; Anna Maria Fioravanti Baraldi, *Il Garofalo: Benvenuto Tisi, pittore (c.1476–1559): catalogo generale*, Rimini, 1993, p.266, no.193; Vilmos Tátrai, 'Benvenuto Tisi, detto il Garofalo: Cristo e l'adultera', in Pietro C.Marani (ed.), *Il Genio e le Passioni: Leonardo e il Cenacolo*, exh.cat., Palazzo Reale, Milan, 2001, p.304, no.120; Michele Danieli, Cristo e l'adultera', in Tatiana Kustodieva and Mauro Lucco (eds), *Garofalo: Pittore della Ferrara Estense*, exh.cat., Castello Estense, Ferrara, 2008, pp.176–77, no.63

During the second half of the fifteenth century and the first half of the sixteenth, the highly distinctive local school of painting in Ferrara enjoyed a golden age. Painters such as Garofalo, Dosso Dossi and Ludovico Mazzolino absorbed the lessons of their Venetian and Roman contemporaries, and succeeded in creating their own intensely personal and highly recognisable styles of painting.

Like almost all Renaissance painters, Garofalo executed large-scale altarpieces and frescoed decorations, but was arguably at his finest when painting cabinet pictures, whose intimate format and jewelled finish invite close and prolonged contemplation. Here he represents the episode from St John's Gospel, when Jesus memorably deterred the mob ready to stone the Adultress with the words: 'He that is without sin among you, let him first cast a stone at her' (John VIII, 7). Unusually, Garofalo did not show Christ writing with his finger on the ground, but the fact that the woman's right breast is exposed leaves no doubt as to her identity. This very picture was the subject of an exceptionally eloquent eulogy by Gerolamo Baruffaldi (1697–1722), a pioneering authority on the local school of painting, when it belonged to Cardinal Tommaso Ruffo at Ferrara. He was particularly struck by the contrast between the gorgeous Adultress and the hideous man by her side, and indeed Garofalo has derived his facial type from that of Socrates, whose physical ugliness was proverbially contrasted with his beautiful mind. More generally, the knotted crowd of figures set against a coolly classical grey architectural backdrop is a telling combination of the grotesque and the idealised.

DAVID EKSERDJIAN

44

Pietro Buonaccorsi, called Perino del Vaga 1501–1547
Battle of the Lapiths and the Centaurs, c.1545–47

Pen and black ink over lead-point, 203 × 285 mm

INVENTORY NUMBER: 1868
SELECTED REFERENCES: Loránd Zentai, *Sixteenth-century Central Italian Drawings: An Exhibition from the Museum's Collection*, exh.cat., Museum of Fine Arts, Budapest, 1998, no.37; Elena Parma (ed.), *Perino del Vaga, tra Raffaello e Michelangelo*, exh.cat., Palazzo Te, Mantua, 2001, pp.302–07

The celebrated *Cassetta Farnese* (Museo e Gallerie Nazionali di Capodimonte, Naples), a spectacular silver-gilt casket made for Cardinal Alessandro Farnese, is one of the supreme masterpieces of Renaissance metalwork. It is decorated with six oval rock crystals by the eminent gem-engraver Giovanni Bernardi (1494–1553), and inset into the *Cassetta* between 1548 and 1561 by the goldsmith Manno Sbarri (1536–1576). Two of the crystals are based upon antique prototypes, whereas the designs for the other four were created by Perino del Vaga in the first half of the 1540s.

From Bernardi's biography by Giorgio Vasari, we learn that Perino made *disegni finiti*, finished studies that served as models for the gem-engraver. Three of these drawings have survived, and there would have been a fourth of the same kind for the *Battle of the Lapiths and the Centaurs*. Evidently related to the corresponding scene, the Budapest drawing nevertheless differs from the finished studies. Although it closely resembles the rock crystal, the oval composition was apparently extended at the sides to a rectangular format. Since it is unlikely to be a preparatory study connected with a hypothetical design stage that envisaged rectangular crystals, it may rather have been made after the crystal for another purpose, most probably for a bronze plaquette. The Budapest study has repeatedly been compared with another drawing by Perino of the same subject and format, today in the British Museum, which is less well preserved and bears indentations for transfer. Although the precise relation between the two sheets is not completely clear, the London study is plainly the later and more resolved of the two.

ESZTER SERES

45

Pietro Buonaccorsi, called Perino del Vaga 1501–1547
Studies for the Ceiling of the Entrance Hall in the Palazzo Doria, 1528–30

Pen and brown ink, 204 × 150 mm

INVENTORY NUMBER: 1930
SELECTED REFERENCES: Loránd Zentai, *Sixteenth-century Central Italian Drawings: An Exhibition from the Museum's Collection*, exh.cat., Museum of Fine Arts, Budapest, 1998, no.31; Elena Parma (ed.), *Perino del Vaga, tra Raffaello e Michelangelo*, exh.cat., Palazzo Te, Mantua, 2001, pp.216–19, no.107; Loránd Zentai, *Sixteenth-century Northern Italian Drawings*, exh.cat., Museum of Fine Arts, Budapest, 2003, no.25

Perino del Vaga, a painter of Florentine origin, moved to Rome around 1516. He joined Raphael's workshop and became involved in the decoration of the Vatican Loggie. Perino soon established himself as a specialist in frescoes, and besides working with Giovanni da Udine on the Sala dei Pontefici in the Vatican, he also received a variety of other commissions. In his later career he grew to be the leading decorative painter in Rome, running a busy studio approaching the complexity of that of Raphael.

From the horrors of the Sack of Rome in 1527, Perino fled to Genoa and entered the service of Andrea Doria (1466–1560), the celebrated admiral of the papal fleet. During his decade-long stay in the city, Perino decorated the renovated Palazzo Doria

---

with frescoes and stuccoes. The works celebrated Andrea Doria's political role as defender of the Genoese Republic with references to mythology and Roman history. The present sheet contains rapid sketches made in preparation for the painted spandrels of the ceiling of the atrium. The energetic figures of the verso do not yet clearly resemble mythological gods. Nevertheless, the studies of the recto, bound by lines indicating the architecture, can be identified as Neptune and Hebe at the top, and Hercules and Vesta at the bottom. These elongated figures have much in common with the elegant manner of Parmigianino and Rosso Fiorentino. The smaller groups in between them are probably early ideas for the historical scenes in the lunettes. Containing drawings on both sides, among them various studies of heads and dishes, the Budapest sheet was perhaps originally a page from a sketchbook.

ESZTER SERES

46

Girolamo Mazzola Bedoli c.1505–1569/70
Holy Family with St Francis, c.1532–35

Oil on panel, 90.5 × 65 cm

INVENTORY NUMBER: 170
SELECTED REFERENCES: Anne Rebecca Milstein, *The Paintings of Girolamo Mazzola*, New York and London, 1978, pp.136–37, fig.3; Vilmos Tátrai (ed.), *Summary Catalogue 1*, London and Budapest, 1991, p.77; Mario di Giampaolo, *Girolamo Bedoli, 1500–1569: Città di Viadana*, Florence, 1997, p.116, no.3; Mario di Giampaolo, 'Girolamo Mazzola Bedoli: Die Heilige Familie mit dem heiligen Franz von Assisi', in István Barkóczi (ed.), *Von Raffael bis Tiepolo: Italienische Kunst aus der Sammlung des Fürstenhauses Esterházy*, exh.cat., Schirn Kunsthalle, Frankfurt, 1999, p.170, no.30; Vilmos Tátrai, 'Girolamo Mazzola Bedoli: Die Heilige Familie mit dem heiligen Franziskus von Assisi', in Michael Philipp, Vilmos Tátrai and Ortrud Westheider (eds), *Sturz in die Welt: Die Kunst des Manierismus in Europa*, exh.cat., Bucerius Kunst Forum, Hamburg, 2008, p.66, no.6

Girolamo Bedoli was married to a cousin of Francesco Mazzola, called Parmigianino (1503–1540), and incorporated the latter's surname into his own name. More importantly, and for all his own considerable merits as an artist, Bedoli's style is inextricably linked with that of his precociously gifted relative by marriage.

Parmigianino moved to Rome in 1524, fled to Bologna in 1527 after the Sack of Rome that year, and only returned to his native Parma around 1530. The present work, which in all probability dates from not long after, is loosely based on Parmigianino's so-called *Madonna di San Zaccaria* (Uffizi, Florence), with the difference that the prophet seen in profile in the foreground is here replaced by St Francis, who is represented holding a wooden cross and an open book. While it is obvious that the centrally positioned Virgin looks directly out at us, and explicitly points at this book, it has not been observed that the admittedly minute red and black writing inscribed upon its open pages is perfectly legible, and consists of the beginning of the Magnificat ('My soul doth magnify the Lord'), the hymn of praise recited by Mary at the news conveyed to her at the Annunciation by the Archangel Gabriel (Luke I, 46–55). Close examination of the panel reveals not only the ravishing beauty of such still-life details as the rose at the unusually mature Christ Child's feet and the cherries in his left hand, and the dreamily romantic landscape beyond the figure group, but also subtle changes of mind, notably in the modification of St Joseph's left hand.

DAVID EKSERDJIAN

47

Lorenzo Lotto c.1480–1556
Apollo and the Muses with Fame, c.1549
Oil on canvas, 44.5 × 74 cm

INVENTORY NUMBER: 947
SELECTED REFERENCES: Andor Pigler, 'A New Picture by Lorenzo Lotto: The Sleeping Apollo', *Acta Historiae Artium Academiae Scientiarum Hungaricae*, 1 (1953), pp.165–68; Giordana Mariani Canova and Rodolfo Pallucchini, *L'opera completa del Lotto*, Milan, 1975, pp.119–20, no.248; Vilmos Tátrai (ed.), *Summary Catalogue 1*, London and Budapest, 1991, p.69; Peter Humfrey, *Lorenzo Lotto*, New Haven and London, 1997; Axel Vécsey, 'Lorenzo Lotto: Der schlafende Apollo, die entweichenden Musen und die entfliegende Fama', in Wilfried Seipel (ed.), *Vom Mythos der Antike*, exh.cat., Kunsthistorisches Museum, Vienna, 2008, pp.58–60, no.16

Lorenzo Lotto was one of the most quirkily gifted artists of the entire sixteenth century, but suffered the misfortune, as a result of the dominance of Titian, of being unable to achieve real success in metropolitan Venice. Nevertheless, from the point of view of posterity, the fact that he was reduced to working in such peripheral locations as Bergamo and the Marche is largely immaterial, and his highly individual accomplishments as a religious painter, a designer of *intarsie* (inlaid wood panels), and above all as a portraitist have probably never been more admired than they are today.

This enchanting canvas, which later belonged to George Villiers, Duke of Buckingham, must originally have been considerably wider and have had the sleeping Apollo at its centre. It is first recorded in 1549 in the account book kept by Lotto during his final years. At that point, he was trying to arrange for its sale in Venice to pay off a loan from the great architect Jacopo Sansovino, and a year later he included it in a lottery in Ancona, before unavailingly attempting to sell it in Rome in 1551. Its subject-matter is without parallel, and represents the sleeping Apollo ensconced within a wooded glade on Mount Parnassus, surrounded by the discarded garments and attributes of the nine Muses as well as his own bow, quiver, spear, violin and fiddle-bow. Over to the left, four of the Muses are sporting in the nude: they were presumably originally balanced by the remaining five on the other side, while up above flies the winged figure of Fame, brandishing two trumpets.

DAVID EKSERDJIAN

48

Paolo Caliari, called Veronese 1528–1588
Portrait of a Man, c.1555
Oil on canvas, 120 × 102 cm

INVENTORY NUMBER: 4228
SELECTED REFERENCES: Vilmos Tátrai (ed.), *Summary Catalogue 1*, London and Budapest, 1991, p.129; István Barkóczi, George Keyes and Jane Satkowski (eds), *Treasures of Venice: Paintings from the Museum of Fine Arts Budapest*, exh.cat., High Museum of Art, Atlanta, Seattle Art Museum, and The Minneapolis Institute of Arts, 1995, pp.192–93; Filippo Pedrocco and Terisio Pignatti, *Veronese*, 2 vols, Milan, 1995, 1, pp.231–32; Axel Vécsey, 'Paolo Veronese: Ritratto di uomo', in Vilmos Tátrai (ed.), *Da Raffaello a Goya: Ritratti dal Museo di Belle Arti di Budapest*, exh.cat., Palazzo Bricherasio, Turin, 2004, p.48, no.6; John Garton, *Grace and Grandeur: The Portraiture of Paolo Veronese*, London and Turnhout, 2008, pp.137–51, 191–92; Frederick Ilchman et al., *Titian, Tintoretto, Veronese: Rivals in Renaissance Venice*, exh.cat., Museum of Fine Arts, Boston, 2009, pp.202, 295, no.37; Peter Humfrey, 'Veronese: Portrait of a Man', in Dóra Sallay, Vilmos Tátrai and Axel Vécsey (eds), *Botticelli to Titian: Two Centuries of Italian Masterpieces*, exh.cat., Museum of Fine Arts, Budapest, 2009, p.366, no.111

Paolo Veronese, as his name implies, was originally from Verona, and it was there that his artistic career

began, but he soon moved to Venice, which was to remain his base until his death. Veronese was one of the most extravagantly gifted of all sixteenth-century artists, and was equally accomplished in all the genres of the age: altarpieces and other religious pictures, mythologies, allegories and histories, secular fresco decorations (most notably for Palladio's Villa Barbaro at Maser), and last but not least portraiture.

The identity of the youngish bearded man represented here at three-quarter length is not known, but it is generally agreed that this canvas dates from the earlier part of the artist's career. The subject is shown standing against a foliage-clad wall fronted by a swathe of deep red velvet, which acts as a dark foil for his centrally positioned head. The wall fills slightly more than the right half of the composition, while the left affords an enticing prospect of a landscape with a tree and a classical ruin (inspired by a print dated 1551 by Hieronymus Cock of the Baths of Caracalla in Rome), which may have some symbolic or personal significance. The virtuosity of the painting of the opulent fur edging and trim of the black satin costume reveals the fact that Veronese was already a fully established master at this juncture. He also knew how to capture a convincing likeness, and it is the penetratingly appraising gaze of his subject looking back out at us that most compels our attention.

DAVID EKSERDJIAN

49

Giovanni Battista Moroni c.1520/24–1578
Portrait of Jacopo Foscarini, 1570s
Oil on canvas, 105 × 83.5 cm

INVENTORY NUMBER: 53.501
SELECTED REFERENCES: Mina Gregori, *Giovan Battista Moroni: tutte le opere*, Bergamo, 1979, p.247, no.81, pl. 5; Klàra Garas, *Italian Renaissance Portraits*, Budapest, 1981, no.34; Vilmos Tátrai (ed.), *Summary Catalogue 1*, London and Budapest, 1991, p.80; H.K.Szépe, 'Civic and Artistic Identity in Illuminated Venetian Documents', *Bulletin du Musée Hongrois des Beaux-Arts*, 95 (2001), pp.59–64; Axel Vécsey, 'Giovanni Battista Moroni: Ritratto di Jacopo Contarini (?)', in Vilmos Tátrai (ed.), *Da Raffaello a Goya: Ritratti dal Museo di Belle Arti di Budapest*, exh.cat., Palazzo Bricherasio, Turin, 2004, p.90, no.31

In the sixteenth century, the rule of the Venetian Republic was by no means confined to Venice and its immediate environs. In consequence, the local schools of painting of such cities as Brescia and Bergamo, which are geographically much closer to Milan, were under the sway of the Venetian school of painting. This should not be taken as implying that their productions were either slavishly dependent upon the metropolis or second-rate. On the contrary, artists such as Giovanni Battista Moroni – and indeed Girolamo Romanino and Moretto – not least when it came to portraiture, were more than a match for all but the very greatest painters of the age. Furthermore, they were hugely admired in Britain in the nineteenth century, which is why the National Gallery in London boasts an unrivalled collection of Moroni portraits.

In the present work, the artist's signature and the date 157[?] (the final numeral is lost) are original, but the inscription at top right identifying the subject is a later addition. It claims he is Jacopo Contarini, who was a prominent collector, and that he was the Podestà (governor) of Padua, which he was not. In

view of the fact that an equally celebrated individual called Jacopo Foscarini held that office at the time, and that two earlier portraits of the Podestà of other Northern Italian towns by Moroni show them wearing a similar combination of pinkish-red and black attire, it seems reasonable to suppose that the name was simply mis-transcribed. The confident gaze and easy stance of this luxuriously bearded man, who rests his left hand on a stone shelf with a *dogale* (an official confirmation of such an appointment) upon it, confirm his elevated status and undoubtedly project a convincing air of authority.

DAVID EKSERDJIAN

50

Michele Tosini, called Michele di Ridolfo 1503–1577
Pietà, c.1550
Oil on poplar panel, 115 × 85.7 cm

INVENTORY NUMBER: 4242
SELECTED REFERENCES: Vilos Tátrai, *Cinquecento Paintings of Central Italy*, Budapest, 1983, no.23; Vilmos Tátrai (ed.), *Summary Catalogue 1*, London and Budapest, 1991, p.39; David Ekserdjian, 'Parmigianino and Michelangelo', in Francis Ames-Lewis and Paul Joannides (eds), *Reactions to the Master: Michelangelo's Effect on Art and Artists in the Sixteenth Century*, Aldershot, 2003, pp.53–67, especially p.58; Vilmos Tátrai, 'Michele di Ridolfo, eigentlich Michele Tosini: Pietà', in Michael Philipp, Vilmos Tátrai and Ortrud Westheider (eds), *Sturz die Welt: Die Kunst des Manierismus in Europa*, exh.cat., Bucerius Kunst Forum, Hamburg, 2008, p.104, no.23

Michele Tosini took the name by which he is commonly known from the most significant of his teachers, Ridolfo del Ghirlandaio. Never an artist of the first rank, he spent his entire career based in Florence, and was more than willing to draw inspiration from the work of others, although his highly personal facial types and colour schemes – such as the green and violet complementaries on the loincloth here – make his work very recognisable.

In this instance, and by no means for the only time in his career, his model was a work by Michelangelo: his celebrated early marble *Pietà* for St Peter's in Rome, which was begun in 1498 and completed soon after. It may have been around half a century old when Michele di Ridolfo copied it, but it was still of compelling interest to artists, and not long after was to be the subject of an engraving dated 1565 by Adamo Ghisi (Scultori). The interpretation of it here sets it against a murky rocky background, and is in the main impressively faithful to the original, but there are minor – yet at the same time telling – modifications. Michele di Ridolfo has carefully made sure that Christ's features are wholly visible and not over-dramatically foreshortened. He has also aged Michelangelo's evergreen Virgin and made her notably less serene – tears pour from her red-rimmed eyes. The scale of the present panel, which is first recorded in the mid-nineteenth century, might suggest it was made as a small altarpiece, but if so the absence of supplementary figures around the grieving Mother of God and her dead Son is highly unusual.

DAVID EKSERDJIAN

51

Maerten van Heemskerck 1498–1574
Lamentation, c.1540–45
Oil on oak panel, 78.5 × 67.5 cm

INVENTORY NUMBER: 4936
SELECTED REFERENCES: Rainald Grosshans, *Maerten van Heemskerck: die Gemälde*, Berlin, 1980, pp.154–55, no.41, fig.62; Ildikó Ember and Zsuzsa Urbach (eds), *Summary Catalogue 2*, Budapest, 2000, p.81; András Fay and Miklos Gálos, 'The Restoration of Maarten van Heemskerck's Budapest Lamentation Panel', *Bulletin du Musée Hongrois des Beaux-Arts*, 105 (2006), pp.73–92; Júlia Tátrai, 'Maarten van Heemskerck: Beweinung Christi', in Michael Philipp, Vilmos Tátrai and Ortrud Westheider (eds), *Sturz in die Welt: Die Kunst des Manierismus in Europa*, exh.cat., Bucerius Kunst Forum, Hamburg, 2008, p.102, no.22

In the first half of the sixteenth century, it became far from uncommon for Northern European artists to visit Italy, and in particular Rome, to study and admire the remains of classical antiquity and more recent achievements, above all the works of Michelangelo and Raphael. During his time in Rome from 1532 to 1536/37, Maerten van Heemskerck executed numerous detailed pen drawings of the most notable collections of ancient sculpture, and subsequently in 1553 also produced a magnificent *Self-portrait* (Fitzwilliam Museum, Cambridge), in which the foliage-encrusted remains of the Colosseum serve as a backdrop to his arresting likeness.

It may come as something of a surprise, therefore, that the present work – which was executed not long after his return from Italy – is so resolutely Northern in spirit. The body of Christ at the foot of the cross is heroically muscular but the greyish flesh-tones and the marks of the Crucifixion and of the Crown of Thorns starkly emphasise the fact that it is both broken and drained of life. Still-life elements – the Crown itself, together with an elegant gilded glass vessel with an arabesquing handle adorned with a grotesque mask – mark the transition from our world to that of the holy personages, who are deliberately crowded around their Saviour. Evidently this sense of claustrophobic enclosure displeased a previous owner, who arranged for the five heads in the upper corners, which were only recovered in 2006 when the picture was restored, to be painted over with more sky.

DAVID EKSERDJIAN

52

Nicolò dell'Abate 1509/12–1571

God the Father with Angels, c.1565–70

Pen and brush in brown ink over pencil, washed, heightened with white, 285 × 316 mm

INVENTORY NUMBER: 3015
SELECTED REFERENCES: Loránd Zentai, *Sixteenth-century Northern Italian Drawings*, exh.cat., Museum of Fine Arts, Budapest, 2003, no.39; Sylvie Béguin and Francesca Piccinini (eds), *Nicolò dell'Abate: Storie dipinte nella pittura del Cinquecento tra Modena e Fontainebleau*, exh.cat., Modena, 2005, p.435, under no.223

Nicolò dell'Abate was already a renowned painter by the time he arrived in France in 1552, summoned by King Henri II to assist Francesco Primaticcio with the decoration of the royal château of Fontainebleau, near Paris. The frescoes of the *Salle de Bal*, envisaged by François I in the 1540s and completed between about 1552 and 1556 under Henri II, marked the beginning of the long and exceptionally fruitful collaboration between the two artists, which was both mutually sustaining and determined the development of the School of Fontainebleau. Two further joint masterpieces followed: the *Galerie d'Ulysse* at Fontainebleau and the *Chapelle de Guise* in Paris. At the same time, Nicolò received commissions of his own, and – as the head of a productive workshop

– his activity also included sketches for engravings, festive events and metalwork.

This splendid *God the Father with Angels* dates from the last years of Nicolò's career and is perhaps related to his lost painting for the church of L'Assomption Saint-Honoré in Paris. Like many drawings of the artist's French period, it reflects his painterly skills: the image was created with delicate lines in pen, complemented by fluid touches of wash. The Budapest study originally constituted the upper half of a larger drawing that included the Annunciation below, the original composition of which is preserved in a copy at the Louvre. This explains the presence of the Holy Spirit in the form of a dove and other fragmentary details at the bottom of the Budapest sheet. For instance, the thin curved line to the lower left remains from the radiance of the angel, whose already incomplete figure must have been cut off at the lower left corner.

ESZTER SERES

53

Francesco Primaticcio 1504–1570

Phaeton Begging Apollo to Let Him Drive His Chariot, c.1552–56

Red chalk, heightened with white, 314 × 344 mm

INVENTORY NUMBER: 3016
SELECTED REFERENCE: Dominique Cordellier et al., *Primatice: Maître de Fontainebleau*, exh. cat., Musée du Louvre, Paris, 2004, pp.383–86, under no.215

A distinctive artistic phenomenon began to develop at Fontainebleau from around 1530. Summoned by François I, excellent Italian masters arrived to execute decorative projects at the court, thus introducing the Italian Renaissance style in France. Francesco Primaticcio, a painter from Bologna, came in 1532. At the suicide of his predecessor, Rosso Fiorentino, he took over the direction of work in 1540. Serving as court painter to four successive kings, Primaticcio's prominent position permitted him to limit his own involvement to the conception of the decorations, entrusting the execution to his fellow artists.

This was also the case in the *Salle de Bal*, the ballroom of the château. Primaticcio designed the eight mythological scenes on the spandrels between the bays, while the frescoes were carried out by Nicolò dell'Abate, his new assistant. Nicolò brilliantly fulfilled his role as interpreter, but unfortunately his works there are now heavily repainted. Thus Primaticcio's fabulous drawn models, most of which have survived, give a better idea of how the frescoes must originally have looked. A case in point is the present sheet, which displays the same delicate and vibrant chiaroscuro effects, achieved by red chalk and white heightening. Its complex composition consisting of superimposed figures that occupy the entire space must have been developed with the help of live models. Their feature seem to appear all through the study, most notably in Apollo's face.

ESZTER SERES

54

Paolo Caliari, called Veronese 1528–1588

Peter of Amiens Exhorts Doge Vitale Michiel, after 1574

Pen and brown ink with grey wash, 140 × 273 mm

INVENTORY NUMBER: 2408
SELECTED REFERENCES: Richard Cocke, *Veronese's Drawings: A Catalogue Raisonné*, London, 1984, no.97; Loránd Zentai, *Sixteenth century Northern Italian Drawings*, exh.cat., Museum of Fine Arts, Budapest, 2003, no.54

The controversy over the relative merits of *disegno* (drawing) and *colore* (colour) characterised the traditional rivalry between Central Italian and Venetian practice, which came to a head in the sixteenth century. While Tuscan and Roman theorists defined *buon disegno*, or good drawing, as the fundamental basis of art, Venetian writers upheld the superiority of colour as embodied in the paintings of Titian, Tintoretto and Paolo Veronese. However, despite the fact that Veronese was a supreme colourist and was called the 'prince of the palette' by his contemporaries, he also left an impressive drawn legacy.

This double-sided compositional sketch, with its free touches of pen and painterly use of wash, perfectly exemplifies Veronese's brilliant gifts as a draughtsman. It was made for one of the two tapestries commissioned by the Senate from the artist after the disastrous fire that ravaged the Doge's Palace in 1574. They formed part of the new decoration of the destroyed Sala del Collegio, together with Veronese's grandiose ceiling paintings, all of which were designed to celebrate the Venetian Republic. No traces of the tapestries, however, have survived; only a poor-quality oil painting – generally regarded as a workshop production – records Veronese's design for the apocryphal episode of Peter of Amiens persuading the Doge to join his crusade (Pinacoteca Nazionale, Lucca). Although its large size suggests the project went quite a long way, the canvas is not pricked for transfer and there are no records of the finished tapestries, so it seems feasible that the commission was never completed. If this hypothesis is correct, the Budapest drawing preserves the most impressive image of this ultimately abortive project.

ZOLTÁN KÁRPÁTI

55

Lelio Orsi c.1510–1587

Joseph Cast into the Pit by His Brothers, 1560s

Pen and brown and grey wash, heightened with white, on bluish-grey prepared paper, 150 × 510 mm

INVENTORY NUMBER: 2531
SELECTED REFERENCES: Elio Monducci and Massimo Pirondini (eds), *Lelio Orsi, 1511–1587: Dipinti e disegni*, exh.cat., Teatro Municipale, Reggio Emilia, 1987; Loránd Zentai, *Sixteenth-century Northern Italian Drawings*, exh.cat., Museum of Fine Arts, Budapest, 2003, no.41

Lelio Orsi was one of the most quirkily eccentric artists of the sixteenth century, and is celebrated as a superb draughtsman who forged a unique blend of the muscular heroism of Michelangelo with the graceful charm of Correggio. He was based for his entire professional career in the small town of Novellara, which was ruled by a minor branch of the Gonzaga family of Mantua. There and in nearby Reggio Emilia, he executed numerous decorative frescoes for both the exteriors and interiors of palaces, almost none of which has survived.

The unusually long and low format of the present drawing, which was formerly in the Praun Collection in Nuremberg, indicates that it must have been intended as a design for a frescoed frieze, probably for the upper part of the wall of a room. No such fresco by Orsi now exists, but the large scale of the sheet and the fact that the elaborate composition is fully resolved in every minute particular both suggest that it was a last thought as opposed to an early idea for the scene. The violent main subject, which is taken from Genesis XXXVII, precedes Joseph's brothers' sale of him to the company of Ishmaelites who take him to Egypt (of whom there is no sign), and is confined to the extreme left of the design. For the rest, Orsi conjures up an expansive landscape setting, in which the flocks tended by Joseph's brothers – including the charming detail of two butting rams – are to be seen, and adds a man ploughing with horses, one of whom has taken advantage of the interruption to graze, and a woman on a donkey, to the biblical account.

DAVID EKSERDJIAN

56

Luca Cambiaso   1527–1585

Stoning of St Stephen, early 1560s

Pen and brown wash, some traces of black chalk, 672 × 715 mm

INVENTORY NUMBER: 1799
SELECTED REFERENCES: Loránd Zentai, *Sixteenth-century Northern Italian Drawings*, exh.cat., Museum of Fine Arts, Budapest, 2003, no.29; Jonathan Bober (ed.), *Luca Cambiaso 1527–1585*, exh.cat., Blanton Museum of Art, Austin, Texas, and Palazzo Ducale, Genoa, 2006, p.82

Luca Cambiaso may not be a household name, but he was certainly one of the most important home-grown artists active in Liguria during the sixteenth century. Although the Genoese works of Perino del Vaga, Pordenone and Domenico Beccafumi had a significant impact on his formation, he probably visited Rome, where he would have experienced Michelangelo's frescoes at first hand. Cambiaso's grandiose decorations in both the churches and palaces of Genoa established narrative fresco painting in the region. Having spent almost all his career in his native Genoa, near the end of his life he was invited by Philip II of Spain to decorate the monastery church of the Escorial.

Cambiaso was an outstandingly original and prolific draughtsman, whose new method of making figure studies, in which the forms are reduced to geometrical shapes, spread rapidly among his followers. The Budapest *Stoning of St Stephen* is one of Cambiaso's most beautiful drawings, both by virtue of its extraordinary size and carefully elaborated, painterly wash, and it represents a fundamentally individual approach. Since it cannot be associated with any existing or documented work by the artist, it is assumed that Cambiaso produced it as an independent virtuoso tour de force. In the absence of a print-publishing industry in Genoa, Cambiaso's large-scale drawings were nevertheless designed to disseminate his artistic vision, much like monumental engravings produced in Rome. The ambitious composition of the Budapest drawing

explicitly quotes Giulio Romano's altarpiece of the *Martyrdom of St Stephen*, painted for the eponymous church in Genoa between 1519 and 1521. Giulio's vast altarpiece was the first work to introduce the Roman classical style into provincial Genoa, and it remained an inevitable model for any local artist aspiring to modernity.

ZOLTÁN KÁRPÁTI

57

Ferraù Fenzoni   1562–1645

Study of a Male Nude Entwined by a Serpent, 1587

Red and black chalk, some traces of dark brown wash, 400 × 275 mm

INVENTORY NUMBER: 1851
SELECTED REFERENCES: Loránd Zentai, *Sixteenth-century Central Italian Drawings: An Exhibition from the Museum's Collection*, exh.cat., Museum of Fine Arts, Budapest, 1998, no.64; Giuseppe Scavizzi and Nicolas Schwed, *Ferraù Fenzoni*, Todi, 2006, no.D35

The installation and interior decoration of the Scala Santa in Rome was one of the major artistic undertakings of the papacy of Sixtus V (1585–1590). The building housed the sacred relic of the Scala Santa (Holy Staircase), which purports to be the steps that Christ ascended when he was tried before Pontius Pilate. The Scala Santa, located next to the Basilica of St John Lateran, contains five parallel staircases that lead to a corridor and two chapels. The walls and ceilings were richly frescoed with scenes from the Old Testament and the Passion of Christ between 1587 and 1588. Cesare Nebbia (*c.*1536 –1614) and Giovanni Guerra (1544–1618) supervised the execution of the extensive fresco cycle, which involved nineteen painters, including Ferraù Fenzoni.

Nothing certain is known of Fenzoni's early years before his move to Rome during the pontificate of Gregory XIII (1572–1585). Fenzoni's activity in the Eternal City covers a relatively short period between 1589 and 1593, when he executed his first datable frescoes, including *Moses and the Brazen Serpent*, which dominates the back wall of the corridor in the Scala Santa. The composition, painted some time before 10 May 1587, is based on a design by Nebbia, which clearly reflects Michelangelo's fresco of the same subject in one of the corner spandels of the Sistine Chapel ceiling. The present drawing in red chalk is undoubtedly the most beautiful of the four surviving studies for the fresco. Drawn from the life, it is a thrilling derivation from the left-hand son of the classical Laocoön group, and represents a youth struggling to free himself from a serpent to the right of the wall painting. The dramatic realism and the perfect grasp of human anatomy of this vigorous figure study suggest that the new tendencies of the Carracci Academy may have played an important role in Fenzoni's artistic formation.

ZOLTÁN KÁRPÁTI

58

Annibale Carracci   1560–1609

Study for a Bacchante, 1597–1600

Charcoal, white chalk and brown wash on blue paper, 478 × 279 mm

INVENTORY NUMBER: 1812
SELECTED REFERENCES: John Rupert Martin, *The Farnese Gallery*, Princeton, 1965, p.255, no.64, fig.171; Andrea Czére, *L'eredità Esterházy: Disegni italiani del Seicento dal Museo di Belle Arti di Budapest*, exh.cat., Palazzo di Fontana di Trevi, Rome, 2002, no.3; Andrea Czére, *Seventeenth-century Italian Drawings in the Budapest Museum of Fine Arts: A Complete Catalogue*, Budapest, 2004, no.71

Annibale Carracci has long been regarded as the reformer of Mannerism and a pioneer of Baroque painting. He revived the geometrical compositional principles of the great Renaissance masters as well as the custom of drawing from live models to create a monumental classical style, which was followed by many Bolognese and other Italian painters in the first half of the seventeenth century.

His masterpiece is the ceiling fresco of the Galleria Farnese in Rome (1597–1600), which represents the loves of the classical gods. The different episodes in this fresco decoration are presented as though they were framed pictures, and were preceded by many composition and figure studies, including the Budapest drawing, traditionally – and rightly – attributed to Annibale. It depicts the maenad in Bacchus's retinue in the middle of the central scene representing the *Triumph of Bacchus and Ariadne*. Annibale was inspired by a similar figure in a drawing by Perino del Vaga of the same subject in the Louvre, which he probably knew from an engraving. Other compositional sketches by Annibale for the same scene are preserved in the Louvre, the Albertina in Vienna, and elsewhere. The Budapest sheet, acquired with the Esterházy Collection in 1870, presents the still incomplete figure in the last phase of its formation. The altered right arm corresponds precisely to the cartoon in the Galleria Nazionale delle Marche, Urbino, and to the painted figure in the fresco.

ANDREA CZÉRE

59

Jacopo Robusti, called Tintoretto   1519–1594

Supper at Emmaus, *c.*1542

Oil on canvas, 156 × 212 cm

INVENTORY NUMBER: 111
SELECTED REFERENCES: Rodolfo Pallucchini and Paola Rossi, *Tintoretto: L'opera completa*, 3 vols, Milan, 1990, 1, p.137, no.42, 3, pl. 50; Vilmos Tátrai (ed.), *Summary Catalogue 1*, London and Budapest, 1991, p.116; István Barkóczi, George Keyes and Jane Satkowski (eds), *Treasures of Venice: Paintings from the Museum of Fine Arts Budapest*, exh.cat., High Museum of Art, Atlanta, Seattle Art Museum, and The Minneapolis Institute of Arts, 1995, pp.90–91, no.9; Frederick Ilchman et al., *Titian, Tintoretto, Veronese: Rivals in Renaissance Venice*, exh.cat., Museum of Fine Arts, Boston, 2009, pp.67–68, 148–53, no.22; Frederick Ilchman, 'Jacopo Tintoretto: Supper at Emmaus', in Dóra Sallay, Vilmos Tátrai and Axel Vécsey (eds), *Botticelli to Titian: Two Centuries of Italian Masterpieces*, exh.cat., Museum of Fine Arts, Budapest, 2009, p.356, no.106.

Tintoretto ('the little dyer', on account of his father's profession) was the most extravagantly exciting painter of sixteenth-century Venice. It has been claimed that he programmatically aspired to combine the colour of Titian with the *disegno* (which means drawing but also design) of Michelangelo, but the truth is that he was blissfully his own man. Outrageously prolific and wildly uneven, his finest works – and above all his decoration of the Scuola di San Rocco in his native city – are both incredibly vital and profoundly moving.

The present canvas, which is one of the artist's earliest surviving works, depicts the moment in the narrative recounted in St Luke's Gospel when – shortly after the Resurrection – Christ, having walked to the village of Emmaus with two of his disciples (identified as travellers here by their staffs) who do not recognise him and have stopped there for supper, is about to break bread. Even now and in spite of his cruciform halo, they are turning away from him, but in a moment their eyes will suddenly be opened, and immediately after that he will vanish. Christ forms the still centre of an artfully spiralling assemblage of figures, and the main impression is of a humble meal in modest surroundings, although the splendid gilt auricular vessel, whose spout forms a grotesque face, being handed round by the maid is an unexpectedly luxurious touch. What is clear is that Tintoretto is already ploughing his own furrow, and the beautifully observed and hopeful cat at bottom left is only the first of many in his work.

DAVID EKSERDJIAN

60

Jacopo dal Ponte, called **Bassano**   c.1510–1592
Way to Calvary, c.1552
Oil on canvas, 94 × 114 cm

INVENTORY NUMBER: 5879
SELECTED REFERENCES: Rodolfo Pallucchini, *Bassano*, Bologna, 1982, p.30, pl. 19; Alessandro Ballarin, *Jacopo Bassano*, 2 vols, Cittadella, 1995, 1, pp.15, 32, 125, 143, 174, 87, fig. 83; 2, pp.15 209, 387, 395, fig. 34; Vilmos Tátrai (ed.), *Summary Catalogue 1*, London and Budapest, 1991, p.5; Maria Elisa Avagnina, 'Andata al Calvario', in Beverly Louise Brown and Paola Marini (eds), *Jacopo Bassano: c.1510–1592*, exh.cat., Museo Civico, Bassano del Grappa, and Kimbell Art Museum, Fort Worth, 1992, pp.302–03, no.21; Vittoria Romani, 'Jacopo Bassano: The Way to Calvary', in Dóra Sallay, Vilmos Tátrai and Axel Vecsey (eds), *Botticelli to Titian: Two Centuries of Italian Masterpieces*, exh.cat., Museum of Fine Arts, Budapest, 2009, p.350, no.103

Although he trained in the metropolis, was perfectly familiar with the works of the Venetian big three of Titian, Tintoretto and Veronese, and kept in touch with all the latest developments there, Jacopo dal Ponte is known as Bassano after the town in the Veneto where he lived and worked throughout his career. By far the most important member of a dynasty of painters, he is above all admired for his impassioned and increasingly tenebrous religious pictures and for the dazzling boldness of his brushwork, but was equally a very powerful portraitist.

The subject of the present canvas involves an amalgamation of what is recounted in the various Gospels, and represents the moment on the road to the Crucifixion when Christ collapses under the weight of his Cross, and is replaced by Simon of Cyrene, a theme that first arose in this form around 1500. To this is added here – as was often the case – the episode of St Veronica offering Jesus the Sudarium, the cloth to wipe away his sweat, which was miraculously imprinted with his features, and is one of the principal relics of St Peter's in Rome. At the same time, Jesus turns back to bid a last farewell to the Virgin Mary and the other Holy Women, while all around them is a savage, seething mass of soldiery on foot and on horseback going about their business. In particular, the focus is upon the centrally positioned soldier with the extravagantly plumed helmet towering over Christ and brandishing a flail against the cloud-streaked evening sky.

DAVID EKSERDJIAN

61

Wolf Huber   c.1480/85–1553
Landscape with Willows and a Mill, 1514
Pen and brown ink, 154 × 208 mm

INVENTORY NUMBER: 191
SELECTED REFERENCES: Franz Winzinger, *Wolf Huber: Das Gesamtwerk*, 2 vols, Munich, 1, 1979, p.83, no.23; Fritz Koreny, 'Wolf Huber: Weidenlandschaft mit Mühle', in Artur Rosenauer (ed.), *Spätmittelalter und Renaissance: Geschichte der Bildenden Kunst in Österreich*, 3, Munich, 2003, p.564, no.303

Born in Feldkirch in Vorarlberg, and later court painter to the Bishop of Passau, Wolf Huber was active as a painter, draughtsman, woodcut designer and architect. Together with Albrecht Altdorfer, he is regarded as the most influential artist of the Danube School, the painters and draughtsmen who worked in the Danube region between Regensburg and Vienna at the beginning of the sixteenth century and whose landscape 'portraits' were based on the direct observation of nature.

This virtuoso drawing representing pollard willow trees along a stream and the wooden water mill, together with a few other landscape studies of the same size, probably once made up a sketchbook that Huber used on his travels in the Lower Alps in 1514. Despite its seemingly spontaneous character, the composition is carefully constructed, with the gradually diminishing trees on either side of the central winding path leading the viewer's eye into the picture space. The short curved lines characterising the uneven ground, the wattle fence and the knobbly tree trunks contrast with the bold pen strokes of the bare branches, creating a strong calligraphic effect. A copy showing its original state (formerly Koenigs Collection, Rotterdam) demonstrates that this sheet has been cut extensively at the right edge. The many surviving sixteenth-century copies made after Huber's landscape drawings underline the considerable regard in which he was held by his fellow artists.

SZILVIA BODNÁR

62.1

Augustin Hirschvogel   1503–1553
Squirrel Hunt, c.1530–36
Pen and dark brown ink, 47 × 254 mm

62.2

Augustin Hirschvogel
Stalking Partridges into a Tunnel-net, c.1530–36
Pen and dark brown ink, 241 × 241 mm

INVENTORY NUMBERS: 111, 102
SELECTED REFERENCES: Jane S. Peters, 'Early Drawings by Augustin Hirschvogel', *Master Drawings*, 17 (1979), pp.388–89, nos 38, 46, fig.16; Katrin Achilles-Syndram, 'Augustin Hirschvogel: Rebhuhnjagd mit dem Reusennetz', in Katrin Achilles-Syndram et al., *Kunst des Sammelns: Das Praunsche Kabinett: Meisterwerke von Dürer bis Carracci*, exh.cat., Germanisches Nationalmuseum, Nuremberg, 1994, pp.178–79, no.53; Szilvia Bodnár, 'Augustin Hirschvogel: Squirrel Hunt with Crossbows', in Teréz Gerszi (ed.), *Dürer to Dalí: Master Drawings in the Budapest Museum of Fine Arts*, Budapest, 1999, p.126, no.55

Augustin Hirschvogel learned his craft in his father's stained-glass workshop. A multifaceted artist, he not only designed and produced stained-glass windows but also worked as an etcher, a cartographer and a mathematician. He was active during the tumultuous period when the city of Nuremberg embraced the Reformation. This significantly reduced the number of commissions received by the Hirschvogel

workshop, which had previously specialised in the production of monumental stained-glass windows for churches. Thus the focus shifted to smaller windows depicting secular themes.

A series of drawings by the artist in the Budapest Museum of Fine Arts, originating from the Praun Collection, comprises fifty-three sheets depicting hunting and fishing scenes. On the twenty-seven square and twenty-six round designs for stained glass, most scenes are featured at least twice: first, as sketches in square format on one or two sheets; second, as more finished designs in the round. Of the stained-glass panels produced on the basis of these Budapest drawings, nine are known today – but two of these only from reproductions, one having been destroyed and the other lost. Of these nine windows, two were produced based on the circular designs, while the others were made after the square-format drawings.

In the foreground of the *Squirrel Hunt*, the hunter raises his crossbow towards the branches of a nearby tree, but the targeted animal is invisible. In the square-format variant, however, a hunter in a similar posture points his weapon at a squirrel. Hirschvogel depicts rows of trees and fills in the spaces with parallel shading, thereby achieving the illusion of a dense forest, in which the lively motion of the hunters and their yapping dogs breaks the monotonous rhythm of the trees. The foliage, the rough surface of the tree trunks drawn in curving pen strokes and the diagonals of the branches all contribute to the decorative effect, which was a customary feature of stained-glass designs.

In the second scene from the same series, which depicts the capture of partridges, the hunter is driving the birds towards a tunnel-shaped net while concealing himself behind a board bearing the image of a bull, a trick that was noted in various hunting books from medieval times onwards. In the background is an airy view of a hilly landscape with village houses and high mountains and a duck flying across the foremost cloud. The calligraphic pen strokes used for the foliage and the style of shading are reminiscent of drawings by Albrecht Dürer. A stained-glass roundel of the same size based on this composition and produced by the Hirschvogel workshop is now at the Cloisters of the Metropolitan Museum of Art in New York.

SZILVIA BODNÁR

63.1

Master of the Budapest Sketchbook   active 1590–1600
River with Houses on either Side, 1590–1600
Pen and brown ink, 153 × 201 mm

63.2

Master of the Budapest Sketchbook
Town with Jetty, 1590–1600
Pen and brown ink, 154 × 202 mm

INVENTORY NUMBERS: 1318, 1319
SELECTED REFERENCES: Teréz Gerszi, *Netherlandish Drawings in the Budapest Museum: Sixteenth-century Drawings*, 2 vols, Amsterdam and New York, 1971, p.62, nos 151a, 151b; Teréz Gerszi, *Renaissance et maniérisme aux Pays-Bas: Dessins du musée des Beaux-Arts de Budapest*, exh.cat., Musée du Louvre, Paris, 2008, no.69

The anonymous artist responsible for these works is known as the Master of the Budapest Sketchbook because the Budapest collection holds a fragment of a sketchbook containing fourteen sheets, with twenty-seven landscapes on the respective rectos and versos. All the pages carry images of landscapes of the same countryside, in which reality is blended with fantasy. A small town also appears in the sketches, amid a hilly setting dotted with an abundance of rivers and forests. The houses – comprising numerous storeys and topped with steep roofs – are constructed with *Fachwerk* (timber framing), their individual characteristics carefully detailed by the artist. Based on print analogies we know that the architectural features are characteristic of Southern Germany.

In both of the present works a river cuts diagonally across the small town, but the two images differ significantly from each other. In *River with Houses*, the eye is drawn to bizarre-shaped rocks and a dense forest on the left riverbank. Near the mountains a group of small, modest houses to the right reveals that this part of the town lies further from the centre, which appears on the sheet entitled *Town with Jetty* with more representative, larger houses and a communal building with four corner turrets to the right, probably the town hall or a guildhall. This same building features in several of the drawings.

The trees in the foreground with their intersecting branches stylised into a decorative ornament are characteristic of the whole series of drawings. In contrast to the meticulous portrayal of the houses, the depiction of the landscape is a highly stylised web of lines; it is precisely this dualism that renders the works so memorable. The emphasis on decorative values suggests that the artist had experience in the design of tapestries. Some of the Protestant Flemish tapestry weavers who fled abroad to escape religious persecution settled in Frankfurt and the surrounding area, where they established workshops. Emigré painters then provided them with designs. Stylistic resemblances between the Budapest series dating from late 1590s and works by Gillis van Coninxloo, Antoine Mirou and Pieter Schoubroeck suggest a Frankenthal origin.

TERÉZ GERSZI

64

Alessandro Allori   1535–1607
Dead Christ with Two Angels, c.1593
Oil on copper, 45 × 39 cm

INVENTORY NUMBER: 166
SELECTED REFERENCES: Vilmos Tátrai, *Cinquecento Paintings of Central Italy*, Budapest, 1983, no.36; Simona Lecchini Giovannoni, *Alessandro Allori*, Turin, 1991, p.278, no.125, pl.303; Vilmos Tátrai (ed.), *Summary Catalogue 1*, London and Budapest, 1991, p.1; Alessandro Cecchi, 'Alessandro Allori: Der Leichnam Christi mit zwei Engeln', in István Barkóczi (ed.), *Von Raffael bis Tiepolo: Italienische Kunst aus der Sammlung des Fürstenhauses Esterházy*, exh.cat., Schirn Kunsthalle, Frankfurt, 1999, pp.156–57, no.22; Axel Vécsey, 'Alessandro Allori: Dead Christ Attended by Two Angels', in Monica Bietti and Annamaria Giusti (eds), *The Splendour of the Medici: Art and Life in Renaissance Florence*, exh.cat., Museum of Fine Arts, Budapest, 2008, p.311, no.190

Alessandro Allori belonged to a veritable dynasty of Florentine painters, since he was both the nephew and pupil of Agnolo Bronzino (1503–1572) – which is why this work is signed 'ALESSANDRO/BRONZINO/ALLORI FACEVA' – and the father of Cristofano Allori (1577–1621). A prolific painter of religious subjects,

who was also a coolly brilliant portraitist, he emulated his master both in his figure canon and in the alabastrine perfection of his technique.

The present work must be one of the three pictures of 'the dead Christ in the tomb with two angels' by Allori recorded in the wardrobe accounts of the Medici on 24 May 1593. All three were executed on copper, a support of whose smooth surface the artist took full advantage. The familiar subject is represented in a most unusual way, which is an extraordinary blend of radiant opulence and gloomy intensity. In the centre, the pale body of Christ, resting on a deep burgundy cushion which symbolises the red Stone of Unction, on which he was said to have been anointed, is tended by angels, who are equipped with the most luxurious vestments. At the point where their world ends and ours begins is a starkly beautiful still-life, comprising a shallow gilt bowl containing the Crown of Thorns and the three nails of the Crucifixion, flanked by two covered lapis-lazuli vessels. Beyond the figure group is an altar topped by a wine-filled chalice flanked by two flaming oil lamps, arranged to echo the foreground arrangement, just as the Mass is a re-enactment of the sacrifice of the Passion.

DAVID EKSERDJIAN

65

Giorgio Vasari   1511–1574
Marriage at Cana, 1566
Oil on panel, 40 × 28 cm

INVENTORY NUMBER: 172
SELECTED REFERENCES: Laura Corti, *Vasari: catalogo complete dei dipinti*, Florence, 1989, pp.114–15, no.92; Alessandro Cecchi, 'Giorgio Vasari: Die Hochzeit zu Kana', in István Barkóczi (ed.), *Von Raffael bis Tiepolo: Italienische Kunst aus der Sammlung des Fürstenhauses Esterházy*, exh.cat. Schirn Kunsthalle, Frankfurt, 1999, pp.156–60, no.24; D. Franklin, 'Giorgio Vasari's "Marriage Feast at Cana" in Budapest', *Bulletin du Musée Hongrois des Beaux-Arts*, 95 (2001), pp.79–90; Vilmos Tátrai, 'Giorgio Vasari: Marriage at Cana', in Dóra Sallay, Vilmos Tátrai and Axel Vécsey (eds), *Botticelli to Titian: Two Centuries of Italian Masterpieces*, exh.cat., Museum of Fine Arts, Budapest, 2009, p.398, no.125

Giorgio Vasari was an extremely competent and prolific painter, and a distinguished architect (he designed the Uffizi in Florence). His greatest claim to fame, however, is as the author of the *Lives of the Artists*, which has been described as the Bible of modern art history. This unprecedentedly informative yet also highly entertaining *magnum opus* exists in two editions, respectively published in 1550 and 1568.

In 1566 Vasari – with the help of assistants – executed three large canvases for the refectory of the Benedictine abbey of San Pietro in Perugia, which are now in the church there. They represented a trinity of sacred meals, whose respective protagonists were Elisha, Christ and St Benedict, and the present work – together with an equally unmodified reduction on the same scale of the scene involving Elisha, now in the Uffizi – is evidently related to this major commission. The liveliness of their execution confirms their autograph status, but it is generally agreed that they are not preliminary sketches but rather contemporary repetitions, perhaps made for Vasari's friend Vincenzo Borghini, who had helped him to obtain the commission. The elaborate and crowded composition here is focused upon Christ, flanked by

the Virgin and the abbey's patron saint, Peter, in dialogue with the standing governor of the feast, who tastes the water that has been turned into wine.

This panel was acquired by the Museum of Fine Arts with the Esterházy Collection in 1870. It disappeared amid the chaos of the Second World War, and spent the years from 1963 to 1999 in the Montreal Museum of Fine Arts before finally returning home.

DAVID EKSERDJIAN

66

Jacopo Robusti, called Tintoretto   1519–1594
Hercules Expelling Faunus from Omphale's Bed, c.1585
Oil on canvas, 112 × 106 cm

INVENTORY NUMBER: 6706
SELECTED REFERENCES: Klára Garas, 'Le tableau du Tintoret du Musée de Budapest et le cycle peint pour l'empereur Rodolphe II', *Bulletin du Musée Hongrois des Beaux-Arts*, 30 (1967), pp.29–48; Rodolfo Pallucchini and Paola Rossi, *Tintoretto: L'opera completa*, 3 vols, Milan, 1990, 2, p.228, no.447, 3, pl. 572; Vilmos Tátrai (ed.), *Summary Catalogue 1*, London and Budapest, 1991, p.117; Sylvia Ferino-Pagden, 'Jacopo Tintoretto: Herkules vertreibt Pan vom Lager der Omphale', in Ekkehard Mai (ed.), *Das Capriccio als Kunstprinzip: Zur Vorgeschichte der Moderne von Arcimboldo und Callot bis Tiepolo und Goya*, exh.cat., Wallraf-Richartz-Museum, Cologne, and Kunsthistorisches Museum, Vienna, 1996, pp.216–17, no.25; Axel Vécsey, 'Tintoretto: Herkules stösst den Faun aus dem Bett der Omphale', in Michael Philipp, Vilmos Tátrai and Ortrud Westheider (eds), *Sturz in die Welt: Die Kunst des Manierismus in Europa*, exh.cat., Bucerius Kunst Forum, Hamburg, 2008, p.124, no.32

Tintoretto was above all a painter of religious subjects and portraits, but his occasional mythologies were no less remarkable. The opportunities for nudity that such themes afforded clearly contributed to their popularity, but in the present instance Tintoretto combined the erotic with the comic. The exploits of Hercules, most celebrated of all the Greek heroes, principally but by no means exclusively by virtue of his twelve labours, were favourite subjects in Renaissance art, but the present episode is almost never represented. After committing murder in a fit of madness, Hercules was sentenced by the Delphic Oracle to be the slave of Omphale, Queen of Lydia, for a year. She humiliated him by making him do women's work and wear female clothing, which here misled Faunus into thinking he was hopping between the sheets with Omphale. Tintoretto shows an indignant Hercules literally kicking him out of bed, while a variety of servants with flaming torches and others, including two prominent female nudes, look on. The canvas is nearly square, but the composition is in effect octagonal, while the speed of the recession into depth is abnormally extreme.

This work has an exceptionally illustrious early provenance, having originally belonged to the Emperor Rudolph II in Prague, and then passed to Charles I's favourite, George Villiers, Duke of Buckingham. The painting subsequently entered the collection of the Archduke Leopold Wilhelm of Austria, which formed the basis of the imperial holdings and hence of the Kunsthistorisches Museum, Vienna, from which it was transferred as part of a larger agreement in 1932.

DAVID EKSERDJIAN

67

Annibale Carracci   1560–1609
Christ and the Woman of Samaria, c.1597
Oil on canvas, 76.5 × 63.5 cm

INVENTORY NUMBER: 3823
SELECTED REFERENCES: Gianfranco Malafarina, *L'opera completa di Annibale Carracci*, Milan, 1976, no.91; Vilmos Tátrai (ed.), *Summary Catalogue 1*, London and Budapest, 1991, p.21; Daniele Benati and Eugenio Riccòmini (eds), *Annibale Carraci*, exh.cat., Museo Civico Archeologico, Bologna, and Chiostro del Bramante, Rome, 2006, pp.280–81, no.VI.2

Annibale Carracci's fame has been overshadowed in recent times by that of Caravaggio, but this circumstance should not be allowed to affect his pivotal importance in any assessment of Italian art around 1600. In his early works in Bologna, Annibale painted low-life subjects with remarkable brio, but his style of painting was soon refined by journeys to Parma and Venice. Around 1595 Annibale moved to Rome, and it was there that he transformed his art, under the influence of the antique and Raphael, to achieve a new classicism in the Farnese Gallery and elsewhere. Annibale was the most illustrious member of a family of painters, together with his cousin Lodovico and his brother Agostino.

The model for the present canvas, which dates from his early Roman years, is a significantly larger version of the same subject executed by Annibale for the Palazzo Sampieri in Bologna (now in the Pinacoteca di Brera, Milan) around 1593–94. The attitudes of the two protagonists and even the colours of their draperies are very similar, but the poses of the attendant disciples are entirely different, while the horizontal format of the prototype is tightened here, and the overall mood is lighter and less monumental. The story, which is narrated in St John's Gospel, concerns Christ's meeting with the Samaritan woman at Jacob's well, and is the occasion when he says: 'Whosoever drinketh of this water shall thirst again: But whosoever drinketh of the water that I shall give him shall never thirst' (John IV, 13–14).

DAVID EKSERDJIAN

68

Domenikos Theotokopoulos,
called **El Greco** *c.*1541–1614
*St James the Less, c.*1595–1600
Oil on canvas, 49.5 × 42.5 cm

INVENTORY NUMBER: 9048
SELECTED REFERENCES: Tiziana Frati and Gianna Manzini, *L'opera completa del Greco*, Milan, 1969, no.93; Marianne Haraszti-Takács, *Spanish Paintings from the Primitives to Ribera*, Budapest, 1982, no.27; José Álvarez Lopera, *El Greco: estudio y catálogo*, Madrid, 2005; Vilmos Tátrai (ed.), *Summary Catalogue 1*, London and Budapest, 1991, p.154; Éva Nyerges, *Obras maestras del arte español*, *Museo de Bellas Artes de Budapest*, exh.cat., Banco Bilbao Vizcaya, Madrid, and Museo de Bellas Artes, Bilbao, 1996; José Álvarez Lopera, 'Santiago el Menor (Estudio)', in José Álvarez Lopera (ed.), *El Greco: Identidad y transformación*, exh.cat., Museo Thyssen Bornemisza, Madrid, Palacio de Exposiciones, Rome, and Pinacoteca Nacional-Museo, Athens, 1999, pp.395–96, no.55; Éva Nyerges, *Spanish Paintings: The Collections of the Museum of Fine Arts, Budapest*, Budapest, 2008, pp.72–73, no.29

El Greco (Spanish for 'the Greek') was born in Crete and his very earliest works are in the Byzantine tradition, but he soon made his way to Venice and then on to Rome, absorbing influences as he went. By 1577 he had moved to Spain and – seemingly after having failed to make the grade at the court of Philip II – was based in Toledo, where he remained for the rest of his days. An unusually learned artist, his mature style is instantly recognisable and involves a visionary approach to religious subjects inspired by the writings of Pseudo-Dionysius the Areopagite. Perhaps paradoxically, in his portraiture he displayed a remarkable gift for capturing a convincing likeness.

This splendidly animated head study, which one instinctively feels must have been based upon the

likeness of an actual individual, is traditionally and not implausibly identified as St James the Less. The reason is that a later, less compact version, which belongs to a series of the twelve apostles, generally dated to around 1600, in the collection of the Marqués de San Feliz in Oviedo, is inscribed with that apostle's name. It is also worth noting, however, that in a *Holy Family with St Anne* in the Ospedale Tavera, Toledo, which is generally dated slightly earlier (around 1595), the head of St Joseph is to all intents and purposes the same, albeit in reverse. Where the present canvas scores over the other two, however, and regardless of the man's identity or the work's purpose, is in its intense scrutiny of its subject.

DAVID EKSERDJIAN

69

Domenikos Theotokopoulos,
called **El Greco** *c.*1541–1614
*St Mary Magdalene, c.*1580
Oil on canvas, 156.5 × 121 cm

INVENTORY NUMBER: 5640
SELECTED REFERENCES: Tiziana Frati and Gianna Manzini, *L'opera completa del Greco*, Milan, 1969, no.38; Vilmos Tátrai (ed.), *Summary Catalogue 1*, London and Budapest, 1991, p.154; Éva Nyerges, *Obras maestras del arte español*, *Museo de Bellas Artes de Budapest*, exh.cat., Banco Bilbao Vizcaya, Madrid, and Museo de Bellas Artes, Bilbao, 1996, pp.67–70, no.7; Marianne Haraszti-Takács, *Spanish Paintings from the Primitives to Ribera*, Budapest, 1982, nos 24, 25; José Álvarez Lopera, *El Greco: estudio y catálogo*, Madrid, 2005; Éva Nyerges, *Spanish Paintings: The Collections of the Museum of Fine Arts, Budapest*, Budapest, 2008, pp.72–73, no.29

El Greco was by no means averse to producing copies and variants, both from his own hand and by his workshop, of his most popular inventions. Despite the fact that almost no drawings by him or his pupils are known, it seems inconceivable that, in order to do so, he did not have a well-organised stock of drawings either preparatory to or copied after the favourite items in his repertoire.

The present canvas appears to date from not long after El Greco's arrival in Spain. The three-quarter-length presentation of the penitent but beautiful Magdalene against a rocky backdrop is inspired by a much-repeated invention of Titian's, yet already the manner in which the work is painted is deeply idiosyncratic. Both the spatial organisation of the setting and the physical type of the penitent are wilfully stylised, and characteristically both the seemingly endless expanse of water to the left and the radiant azure of the sky contribute to the dramatic sense of mystical illumination. However, this tendency to abstraction is counterpointed by the earthbound realism of the still-life elements dotted around the composition: the glass ointment vase at bottom left, the skull resting on the open book, and even the trailing tendrils of ivy against the mossy rock.

DAVID EKSERDJIAN

70

Pietro Faccini *c.*1562–1602
*St Mary of Egypt, c.*1590
Pen and black ink with brown and grey wash, 280 × 429 mm

INVENTORY NUMBER: K.58.1184
SELECTED REFERENCES: Andrea Czère, *Disegni di artisti bolognesi nel museo delle Belle Arti di Budapest*, exh.cat., Bologna, 1989, pp.58–59, no.25; Emilio Negro and Nicosetta Roio, *Pietro Faccini: 1575/76–1602*, Modena, 1997, p.128, no.85a

Pietro Faccini was a relatively late starter as an artist, and only around a dozen paintings by him have survived. He studied at the Carracci Academy in Bologna, and his earliest dated work is an altarpiece of 1590 depicting the *Martyrdom of St Lawrence* in the church of San Giovanni in Monte there. Conversely, he was a prolific and enchanting draughtsman, and the Museum of Fine Arts in Budapest has a group of seven particularly fine drawings by his hand.

The present sheet, from the Praun Collection, is one of a number of studies for the same composition (others are in the Hamburg Kunsthalle and the Louvre), and is clearly inspired by a much admired lost painting on copper by Correggio, formerly in the Gemäldegalerie, Dresden, which has not been seen since the Second World War. That work represented St Mary Magdalene, and it has been universally assumed that Faccini's composition follows suit, but this is not the case. The clue to the identity of the reclining penitent here is provided by the bread rolls – two here, although more usually three in accounts of her life – at her side. The rolls are a crucial feature of the legend of St Mary of Egypt, whose only sustenance they were for the 47 years she spent in the wilderness before being discovered by the priest Zosimus, who also gave her his own habit, which she is shown wearing. The beautiful handling of the landscape, in which use of the pen is minimal and almost the entire scene is brought to life with the brush, reveals Faccini operating at the height of his powers.

DAVID EKSERDJIAN

71

Karel van Mander 1548–1606
Rape of Europa, 1589
Pen and brown ink with grey and brown washes, diameter 162 mm

INVENTORY NUMBER: 1461
SELECTED REFERENCES: Teréz Gerszi, *Netherlandish Drawings in the Budapest Museum: Sixteenth-century Drawings*, 2 vols, Amsterdam and New York, 1971, pp.59, 60, no.146; Teréz Gerszi, *Renaissance et maniérisme aux Pays-Bas: Dessins du musée des Beaux-Arts de Budapest*, exh. cat., Musée du Louvre, Paris, 2008, no.59

The Netherlandish artist, Karel van Mander, produced paintings and drawings as well as translations and a significant quantity of poetry. He achieved prominence, however, with his work *Het Schilder-Boeck* (1604) on the biographies of Antique, Italian and Netherlandish masters, which remains an important source for art historians to this day. During his stay in Italy (1573–77), he worked in Florence and Terni before spending three years in Rome, where he came into close contact with Bartholomäus Spranger. In 1583 he settled in Haarlem, founding the so-called Haarlem Academy with Hendrick Goltzius (1558–1617) and Cornelisz. van Haarlem (1562–1638). Van Mander drew alongside his associates and introduced them to Spranger's drawings, thus exerting a significant influence upon the art of Haarlem's late Mannerists.

This monogrammed and dated *Rape of Europa* is a characteristic example of the stylistic preferences of this small group of artists in the late 1580s. The

Ovidian mythological theme is presented in a crowded composition, with intertwining figures of elongated proportions. Their varied poses and strong and affected movements enliven the scene, which is set against a rocky landscape. We encounter figures of a similar type in Goltzius's *Creation* series of drawings (Prentenkabinet der Rijksuniversiteit, Leiden). The Budapest composition study for the *Rape of Europa* is connected with two other drawings (in Leiden and Dresden respectively) and with an engraving. The number of figures is reduced in Van Mander's drawing in Dresden, which seems to be the closest to the engraving produced by Zacharias Dolendo.

TERÉZ GERSZI

72

Francesco Furini   1603–1646

Venus Lamenting the Death of Adonis, c.1626–30

Oil on canvas, 233 × 190 cm

INVENTORY NUMBER: 493
SELECTED REFERENCES: Ágnes Szigethi, 'Remarques sur notre collection de la peinture Florentine du XVIIe siècle', *Bulletin du Musée Hongrois des Beaux-Arts*, 53 (1979), pp.157–69; Vilmos Tátrai (ed.), *Summary Catalogue 1*, London and Budapest, 1991, p.44; Ágnes Szigethi, 'Francesco Furini: Venus beweint Adonis', in István Barkóczi (ed.), *Von Raffael bis Tiepolo: Italienische Kunst aus der Sammlung des Fürstenhauses Esterházy*, exh.cat., Schirn Kunsthalle, Frankfurt, 1999, p.198, no.43; Mina Gregori and Rodolfo Maffeis, *Un'altra bellezza: Francesco Furini*, exh.cat., Palazzo Pitti, Florence, 2007, pp.95, 166–68, no.10

Until relatively recently, Florentine painting of the seventeenth century tended to be undervalued. In the wake of the supreme achievements of Florence over the span of the fifteenth and sixteenth centuries, and the sense of a gradual subsequent decline, set against the contrasting rise of such artistic centres as Bologna and above all Rome, the reasons for this neglect are easy to understand. Yet the truth is that Furini is only one of a number of later Florentine artists of real quality whose work deserves to be better known.

The present monumental canvas is recorded in the biography of the artist in Filippo Baldinucci's *Notizie de' Professori del Disegno…* (1681–1728), where it is placed among his early works and the patron is identified as a Florentine merchant called Giovambatista Baccelli. Its subject represents the writhing agony of Venus at the spectacle of the dead body of her young mortal lover, who has been killed while out hunting, and from whose blood the scarlet anemone at his feet has sprouted. The story is famously told by Ovid in the *Metamorphoses*, but Furini's direct and up-to-the-minute source is the treatment in Giambattista Marino's epic poem *L'Adone* (1623). The dimensions of the canvas, the top left to bottom right narrative structure, and the contrast between a waking female and a sleeping or dead male all associate it with Furini's slightly earlier *Aurora and Cephalus* (Museo de Arte de Ponce). Indeed, were the evidence of their different ownerships not incontrovertible, it would be natural to presume they were created as pendants, with the tender serenity of the one being artfully counterpointed by the emotional intensity of the other.

DAVID EKSERDJIAN

73

Giuseppe Cesari, called Cavaliere d'Arpino   1568–1640

Diana and Actaeon, c.1602–03

Oil on copper, 50 × 69 cm

INVENTORY NUMBER: 508
SELECTED REFERENCES: Vilmos Tátrai, *Cinquecento Paintings of Central Italy*, Budapest, 1983, nos 37–39; Vilmos Tátrai (ed.), *Summary Catalogue 1*, London and Budapest, 1991, p.25; Ágnes Szigethi, 'Giuseppe Cesari: Diana verwandelt Aktäon in einen Hirsch', in István Barkóczi (ed.), *Von Raffael bis Tiepolo: Italienische Kunst aus der Sammlung des Fürstenhauses Esterházy*, exh.cat., Schirn Kunsthalle, Frankfurt, 1999, p.248, no.71; Herwarth Röttgen, *Il Cavalier Giuseppe Cesari d'Arpino: un grande pittore nello splendore della fama e nell'incostanza della fortuna*, Rome, 2002, pp.346–47, no.110, fig.60

Giuseppe Cesari, who was known as the Cavaliere (knight) d'Arpino after his birthplace near Rome, was a remarkably prolific and versatile painter of both religious and secular subjects, who was hugely admired in his own day. His great misfortune, in terms of how he has come to be seen by posterity, is that he is regarded as a bastion of the dead tradition against which that troublesome genius Caravaggio, who worked in his studio on his arrival in Rome, was rebelling.

The present work, which is painted on copper, demonstrates just what a gifted and enchanting artist Arpino was at his best. Signed 'JOSEPH ARPINAS FECIT' on a rock in the lower right-hand corner, it appears to be a second – but arguably even more gorgeous – treatment of the composition on wood panel in the Louvre (a coloured drawing of the identical composition on the same scale, but in reverse, was sold at Sotheby's, London, in July 2010). To an artist such as Titian, in his version of the subject jointly owned by the National Gallery, London, and the National Gallery of Scotland, Edinburgh, the Ovidian subject of Diana and Actaeon was an occasion for sublime tragedy, but Arpino exploits it as an excuse for voyeuristic indulgence. In accordance with the myth, Diana, goddess of the hunt but also of chastity, who is singled out from her nymphs by the jewel in the shape of the crescent moon in her coiffure, splashes water on the hunter Actaeon, who has unwittingly caught them bathing, and his transformation into a stag has already begun. Soon he will be hunted down and killed by his own hounds (for all that the trio at his feet look singularly harmless), but his savage end is of no concern to Arpino, who instead delights in pert female bodies organised into an almost Eadweard Muybridge-like sequence of poses.

DAVID EKSERDJIAN

74

Joachim Wtewael   1566–1638

Judgement of Paris, c.1605–10

Oil on copper, 22.1 × 28.4 cm

INVENTORY NUMBER: 4281
SELECTED REFERENCES: Anne W. Lowenthal, *Joachim Wtewael and Dutch Mannerism*, Doornspijk, 1986, pp.105, 138, no.A-26; M. Chiarini, I. Ember and A. Gosztola, *Rembrandt, Rubens, Van Dyck e il Seicento dei Paesi Bassi*, exh.cat., Palazzo della Permanente, Milan, Sinclair-Haus, Bad Homburg, Von der Heydt-Museum, Wuppertal, 1995, no.15; Ildikó Ember and Zsuzsa Urbach (eds), *Summary Catalogue 2*, Budapest, 2000, p.187; Júlia Tátrai, 'Joachim Wtewael: Das Parisurteil', in Michael Philipp, Vilmos Tátrai and Ortrud Westheider (eds), *Sturz in die Welt: Die Kunst des Manierismus in Europa*, exh.cat., Bucerius Kunst Forum, Hamburg, 2008, p.164, no.50

Joachim Wtewael – sometimes spelled Uytewael – spent four apprentice years in Italy and France, but was otherwise based throughout his career in Utrecht. His exquisitely crafted and often almost

---

miniaturistic works, whether of religious or mythological subjects, in which both the proportions and the attitudes of the figures are wilfully elongated and distorted, are representative of the artistic current that is sometimes referred to as Haarlem Mannerism.

The Judgement of Paris, when Paris chose Venus over Juno and Pallas Athene as the fairest of the fair and presented her with the golden apple, thus ultimately setting in motion the Trojan War, was a favourite subject of Wtewael's, which he painted on no fewer than six occasions (an earlier version of 1602 is in the Cleveland Museum of Art, while a later one of 1615 is in the National Gallery, London). The present work, which is painted on copper, is indissolubly linked to a slightly smaller treatment – also on copper – at Waddesdon Manor, where the three groups of figures are on the same scale and identical in disposition. Both paintings were presumably derived from a single finished drawing or cartoon, and the major change here is that the surrounding landscape is more extensive and at the same time somewhat differently handled, all of which probably indicates that the Waddesdon picture was executed first. This unusual notion of creating an expanded repetition of a composition is not unique in Wtewael's practice: at much the same period, he also executed two versions of a *Battle between the Gods and the Titans*, now in the Art Institute of Chicago (more compact) and a private collection (less compact).

DAVID EKSERDJIAN

75

Jan Brueghel the Elder   1568–1625

Entry of the Animals into the Ark, c.1613–15

Oil on panel, 61 × 90.2 cm

INVENTORY NUMBER: 548
SELECTED REFERENCES: K. Ertz, *Jan Brueghel der Ältere (1568–1625): Die Gemälde mit kritischem Oeuvrekatalog*, Cologne, 1979, pp.236–49, no.274; Ildikó Ember and Zsuzsa Urbach (eds), *Summary Catalogue 2*, Budapest, 2000, p.29; Christine Van Mulders, 'Les Paradis terrestres de Jean Brueghel le Vieux', in Carl van de Velde (ed.), *Flemish Art in Hungary: Budapest, 12–13 May 2000*, Brussels, 2004, pp.95–100; Arianne Faber Kolb, *Jan Brueghel the Elder: The Entry of the Animals into Noah's Ark*, Los Angeles, 2005; Anne T. Woollett (ed.), *Rubens and Brueghel: A Working Friendship*, exh.cat., J. Paul Getty Museum, Los Angeles, 2006, pp.192–201

Jan Brueghel was the son of the incomparable Pieter the Elder and the brother of the woefully talentless Pieter the Younger. Above all remarkable for the exquisite detail of his landscapes and still-lifes, he was in Naples in 1590, and the next year met his fellow Northerner Paul Bril in Rome, before moving on to work in Milan for a great patron, Cardinal Federico Borromeo, whose collection is largely preserved there in the Pinacoteca Ambrosiana. By 1596 he was back in Antwerp, where he later formed an exceptionally harmonious partnership with Peter Paul Rubens, who in addition executed a memorable group portrait of Jan and his family, now in the Courtauld Gallery, London.

This is an autograph repetition – the signed and dated first version of 1613 is in the J. Paul Getty Museum, Los Angeles – of one of Jan's most successful inventions. The subject would not be immediately apparent, were it not for the great panoply of animals proceeding, two by two, from the bottom right corner under the direction of a turbaned man in red. The tiny ark is easily overlooked, and Noah, his wife, and one of his daughters-in-law in the middle distance might almost be mistaken for farmers taking a breather on their way to market. In essence, this is a celebration of the beauty of the countryside, and of the many-splendoured richness and diversity of the animal kingdom, whether exotic or homely. The snarling lions are borrowed from Rubens, in whose *Daniel in the Lions' Den* in Washington they also occupy a prominent position.

DAVID EKSERDJIAN

76

Francesco Vanni   1563–1610

Holy Family, c.1600

Oil on canvas, 97 × 83.5 cm

INVENTORY NUMBER: 473
SELECTED REFERENCES: Vilmos Tátrai, *Cinquecento Paintings of Central Italy*, Budapest, 1983, no.48; Vilmos Tátrai (ed.), *Summary Catalogue 1*, London and Budapest, 1991, p.25; Vilmos Tátrai, 'Francesco Vanni: Sainte Famille', in Emmanuel Starcky (ed.), *Nicolas II Esterházy 1765–1833: Un prince hongrois collectionneur*, exh.cat., Musée national du château de Compiègne, 2007, p.102, no.9

Francesco Vanni was the most important Sienese artist of the late sixteenth and early seventeenth centuries. He was responsible for numerous major altarpieces for his native city, and also worked for such eminent churchmen as Cardinal Cesare Baronio (1538–1602) and Cardinal Paolo Emilio Sfondrati (1560–1618) in Rome. His mature art is based upon the twin foundations of Federico Barocci and the latter's ultimate inspiration, Correggio, to see whose works Vanni visited Parma in 1595.

The present canvas demonstrates the fact that Vanni was at least as well suited to working on an intimate, domestic scale as he was to creating monumental compositions for ecclesiastical settings. As in Correggio's *Madonna del Latte* (c.1523), also in Budapest, the narrative thread appears to involve the Christ Child innocently turning away from his Mother. There he is explicitly shown spurning her milk, whereas here the emphasis is upon the apple Joseph hands him, which plainly alludes to the Original Sin of Adam and Eve (the handle of Joseph's stick is visible in his left hand). Only Christ's death on the Cross can redeem mankind, and the pure white cloth in which the Virgin seems to be about to scoop him up must be intended to anticipate the winding-sheet in which he will be buried. Similarly, the white jasmine flowers in the glass vessel to the left no doubt possess symbolic significance. Both the pastel shades of the turquoise and lilac draperies, and the vaporous subtlety of the brushwork contribute to the tender and tranquil mood, while the sharply focused lighting of the figures is contrasted with the enveloping darkness that surrounds them.

DAVID EKSERDJIAN

77

Daniele Crespi   1597/1600–1630

St Cecilia at the Organ, 1620s

Pen and brown ink with black chalk underdrawing, 276 × 378 mm

INVENTORY NUMBER: 2396
SELECTED REFERENCES: Andrea Czére, *Seventeenth-century Italian Drawings in the Budapest Museum of Fine Arts: A Complete Catalogue*, Budapest, 2004, no.129; Andrea Czére (ed.), *Museum of Fine Arts, Budapest: Masterpieces from the Collection*, Budapest, 2006, no.80

Daniele Crespi, like most Lombard painters of the early seventeenth century, was especially skilled at conveying the emotions of his subjects. He worked in Milan, an archbishopric, where religious subject-matter was in great demand. Although Crespi's career was cut short after eleven years, when he fell victim to the plague of 1630, his paintings and drawings, appreciated for their dramatic realism, represent a substantial *oeuvre*.

The Budapest drawing of *St Cecilia*, acquired with the Esterházy Collection in 1870, ranks among the artist's finest works. His estate included a painting of the same subject, to which the drawing is perhaps related. Given the subject-matter and the composition it may have been designed for the organ shutters of a Lombard church, but no related painting has survived. The drawing's attribution to Crespi is based on its distinctive style, which is similar to that of his drawing of the *Resurrection of Raimond Diocrés* in the Ambrosiana, Milan. The artist's shading in chalk and his vigorous pen strokes lend a strong plasticity and liveliness to the figures of the angel pumping the organ and the saint immersed in music-making. On the side of the organ's base is represented the Sacrifice of Isaac.

ANDREA CZÉRE

78

Giovanni Francesco Barbieri,
called Il Guercino   1591–1666

Triumph of David, 1636–37

Pen and brown ink with brown wash, 235 × 316 mm

INVENTORY NUMBER: 1917-190
SELECTED REFERENCES: Denis Mahon and Luigi Salerno, *I dipinti del Guercino*, Rome, 1986, p.254; Andrea Czére, *Seventeenth-century Italian Drawings in the Budapest Museum of Fine Arts: A Complete Catalogue*, Budapest, 2004, no.177; Andrea Czére (ed.), *Museum of Fine Arts, Budapest: Masterpieces from the Collection*, Budapest, 2006, no.86

Guercino, arguably the supreme bravura draughtsman of seventeenth-century Bologna, followed Caravaggio's dramatic realism in his early period, but gradually adopted a cooler, more classical style.

The Triumph of David, purchased from Jacques Rosenthal in 1917, features lively contrasts of light and shade and is composed of half-length figures seen close to. Its style is characteristic of Guercino's draughtsmanship, and is connected to a painting ordered by Cardinal Girolamo Colonna for his gallery in Rome. The date of the painting's execution is known from a note in the artist's account book, which records payments in 1636 and 1637. In 1847 the Marquess of Exeter purchased the work and it is now in the Burghley House Collection at Stamford, Lincolnshire.

Guercino's compositional study corresponds in most respects to the final painting; the changes concern only minor details. The theme, taken from the Old Testament, is the triumph of the Israelites over the Philistines. When Goliath, the champion Philistine, challenged the Israelites to single combat,

---

the young David defeated him by knocking down Goliath with a stone from his sling and then beheading him. The triumphal procession following David's victory was frequently represented in Italian art with an escort of women making music, appropriately enough since David was the author of the Psalms.

ANDREA CZÉRE

79

Artemisia Gentileschi   1593–1654

Jael and Sisera, 1620

Oil on canvas, 86 × 125 cm

INVENTORY NUMBER: 75.11
SELECTED REFERENCES: Agnes Szigethi, 'Quelques contributions à l'art d'Artemisia Gentileschi', *Bulletin du Musée Hongrois des Beaux-Arts*, 52 (1979), pp.35–44; Vilmos Tátrai (ed.), *Summary Catalogue 1*, London and Budapest, 1991, p.46; R. Ward Bissell, *Artemisia Gentileschi and the Authority of Art*, University Park, Pennsylvania, 1999, pp.211–13, no.11; Keith Christiansen and Judith W. Mann, *Orazio and Artemisia Gentileschi*, exh.cat., Metropolitan Museum of Art, New York, St Louis Art Museum, and Palazzo di Venezia, Rome, 2001, pp.344–45, no.61

Like a number of other women artists of the early modern period, Artemisia was the daughter of a painter. Her father Orazio Gentileschi (1563–1639) – also called Lomi, which is how Artemisia signs this canvas on the base of the classical pier beyond the figures – was one of the most original and successful associates of Caravaggio in Rome. In 1611 Artemisia was raped by Agostino Tassi, a painter-collaborator of Orazio's, who was tried and imprisoned for the crime. This circumstance, in conjunction with the absolute merits of her work, has made her something of a heroine of feminist art history.

The present work is dated 1620, which is the year when Artemisia returned to Rome after a stay in Florence, and might therefore have been painted in either city. Its brutal subject, drawn from the Old Testament Book of Judges, represents the assassination of the sleeping Canaanite general Sisera by Jael, wife of Heber the Kenite. Jael drives a tent peg into Sisera's temples, but the scene is treated here in an almost stately fashion, with the heroine shown taking careful aim. As with the thematically related and better-known story of Judith and Holofernes, the narrative offered an obvious opportunity for savagery and violence, which Artemisia resisted. The main lines of the composition are based upon a lost painting of the same story by Guercino (known in the form of a copy), with which Artemisia must have been familiar, but here the setting is a dark interior as opposed to an extensive landscape.

DAVID EKSERDJIAN

80

Nicolas Poussin   1594–1665

Holy Family with the Infant St John the Baptist and Putti, c.1627

Oil on canvas, 57 × 74 cm

INVENTORY NUMBER: 57.18
SELECTED REFERENCES: Timothy Standring, 'Some Pictures by Poussin in the Dal Pozzo Collection: Three New Inventories', *Burlington Magazine*, 130 (1988), pp.625–26; Vilmos Tátrai (ed.), *Summary Catalogue 1*, London and Budapest, 1991, p.143; Arabella Cifani and Franco Monetti, 'Un Poussin et retrouvé: Le repos pendant la fuite en Égypte de Budapest', in Gilles Chomer and Sylvain Laveissière (eds), *Autour de Poussin*, exh.cat., Musée du Louvre, Paris, 1994, pp.56–58; Denis Mahon, *Nicolas Poussin: Works from His First Years in Rome*, Rome and Jerusalem, 1999, pp.128–29, no.29; Agnes Szigethi, *Old French Painting: Sixteenth to Eighteenth Centuries (The Collections of the Museum of Fine Arts, 6)*, Budapest, 2004, pp.50–53, no.16

Although Nicolas Poussin was French, he spent his entire working life – with the exception of a brief and unhappy return to Paris – in Rome. The foundations of his art were the very different works of Titian and Raphael, to which he responded in an increasingly classical spirit. He specialised in comparatively small-scale pictures, whose frequently profound intellectual seriousness does not diminish their very considerable sensual appeal.

In recent years, Poussin's beginnings have been re-evaluated, and the attribution, sometimes doubted, of works such as the present canvas now seems absolutely plain. At the same time, it has been recognised that these early works have tended to be dated too late. In the case of this oval, there is documentary evidence indicating that it – and a now lost pendant – entered the collection of Amedeo dal Pozzo, Marchese di Voghera, a cousin of Poussin's great patron Cassiano dal Pozzo, very early on. The work is a jubilantly colourful amalgamation of two of the many apocryphal legends told around the story of the Holy Family's Rest on the Flight into Egypt, and combines a miraculous meal with the first meeting between the Christ Child and his cousin the Infant John the Baptist. On the left, putti (baby angels) collect juicy ripe apples in a basket, while on the right the Baptist proffers his cross in a blatant allusion to the Passion. Beyond the bivouac, an unusually youthful and vigorous Joseph – like all too many new fathers – keeps out of the way, and buries himself in a book.

DAVID EKSERDJIAN

81

Laurent de La Hyre   1605–1656
Theseus and Aethra, c.1635–36
Oil on canvas, 141 × 118.5 cm

INVENTORY NUMBER: 693
SELECTED REFERENCES: Pierre Rosenberg and Jacques Thuillier, *Laurent De la Hyre, 1606–1656: l'homme et l'oeuvre*, exh.cat., Musée de Grenoble, Musée des Beaux-Arts de Rennes, and Musée des Beaux-Arts de Bordeaux, 1989, pp.178–82, no.110; Vilmos Tátrai (ed.), *Summary Catalogue 1*, London and Budapest, 1991, p.141; Ágnes Szigethi, *Old French Painting: Sixteenth to Eighteenth Centuries (The Collections of the Museum of Fine Arts, 6)*, Budapest, 2004, pp.85–87, no.35

Laurent de La Hyre was one of the most poised and elegant French painters of the seventeenth century. As was the case with the majority of his contemporaries, his artistic output was divided between religious works, mythologies and allegories, but it was in the latter two categories that he excelled. His *Allegory of Grammar* of 1650 (National Gallery, London), which originally formed part of a series of canvases representing the Liberal Arts, is an outstanding example of his coolly refined late manner.

By contrast, the present work is significantly earlier in date, and altogether less austerely classical in mood. It shows Theseus, accompanied by his freakishly youthful mother Aethra – whom one might be forgiven for mistaking for his lover, and not just because her breasts are exposed – effortlessly lifting up the stone block under which his father Aegeus had hidden a sword and sandals that his son, who had been exiled at birth, was to bring to him in Athens.

Cardinal Richelieu (1585–1642) is recorded as having commissioned La Hyre to paint three mythological subjects, of which this was one, for the Salle des Gardes of his Parisian residence, the Palais Cardinal (later Palais Royal), and in all probability this is that work. However, there is another candidate in the form of a closely related but probably slightly earlier variant of much the same dimensions, in reverse, in the Musée des Beaux-Arts, Caen. That canvas is signed and dated 1634, and the absence of a signature here may reflect the fact that this one was part of a larger ensemble, not all of whose elements would have needed to be signed.

DAVID EKSERDJIAN

82

Giovanni Francesco Barbieri,
called Il Guercino   1591–1666
Landscape with Travellers
Pen and brush with brown ink, 186 × 288 mm

INVENTORY NUMBER: 2320
SELECTED REFERENCES: Andrea Czére, *L'eredità Esterházy: Disegni italiani del Seicento dal Museo di Belle Arti di Budapest*, exh.cat., Palazzo di Fontana di Trevi, Rome, 2002, no.30; Andrea Czére, *Seventeenth-century Italian Drawings in the Budapest Museum of Fine Arts: A Complete Catalogue*, Budapest, 2004, no.184

Although Guercino was mainly interested in figural subject-matter with biblical or mythological themes, he also produced landscapes throughout his life, especially in the form of drawings of spectacular brilliance. In contrast to his compositional and figure drawings, which were executed as preliminary studies for paintings, his landscape drawings were mostly made as independent works of art. They are all similar in style, which makes them exceptionally hard to date.

Landscape with Travellers, acquired with the Esterházy Collection in 1870, is one of Guercino's most impressive landscape drawings, and its attribution to the artist has never been questioned. It is a fine example of the artist's felicitous amalgamation of the Carraccesque ideal landscape tradition and northern realism, uniting decorative motifs and naturalistic details into harmonious compositions displaying virtuoso spatial illusionism. The winding path leading to the distant hill, surmounted by a building, crosses an almost symmetrically balanced composition of wind-blown trees, whose dramatic vitality is emphasised by the tiny figures of travellers. Another composition with similar motifs and drawing style, representing a man and child sitting on a hill amid trees, can be found in a sheet in the British Museum. The artist's unique system of lines, expressing tonal values through their varying thicknesses, and their emotional atmosphere makes his drawings highly distinctive. Since they were in great demand among collectors, not only in the artist's lifetime, but also in the eighteenth century, many an artist was induced to follow and imitate Guercino's style.

ANDREA CZÉRE

83

Claude Gellée, called Claude Lorrain   1600–1682
Deer Hunt, c.1645
Pen and wash in brown ink over black chalk, 233 × 329 mm

INVENTORY NUMBER: 2849
SELECTED REFERENCES: Marcel Roethlisberger, *Claude Lorrain: The Drawings*, 2 vols, Berkeley and Los Angeles, 1968, no.589; Andrea Czére, in Emmanuel Starky (ed.), *Nicolas II Esterházy 1765–1833: Un prince hongrois collectionneur*, exh.cat., Musée national du château de Compiègne, 2007, no.43

Claude Lorrain was born in France, but he chose to work in Italy; the countryside around Rome features in many of his drawings and paintings. He is regarded as the most talented and influential representative of classical ideal landscape, above all because his work is so rich in atmospheric light effects.

The present drawing, acquired with the Esterházy Collection in 1870, was mounted in the eighteenth century. An inscription on the reverse names Filippo Lauri (1623–1694) as the author of the hunters running across the centre. Although there are contemporary instances of collaboration between landscape artists and figure draughtsmen, this does not seem to be the case here, since the drawing style is unlike that of Lauri and does not significantly differ from that of other figures by Claude. The artist is known to have worked in the open air, finishing the drawings in his studio, and the Budapest piece is a typical example of this method of working. The carefully balanced composition combines horizontal and diagonal axes – the dark foreground provides a definite horizontal, whereas the castle on the upper left, identified as La Crescenza, north of Rome, with the slope in front of it reaching the trees in the right foreground, creates a transversal axis – resulting in a harmonious structure. The drawing was first sketched with black chalk, which can be seen through the brown wash in several places, contributing to the overall colour scheme.

ANDREA CZÉRE

84

Claude Gellée, called Claude Lorrain   1600–1682
Villa in the Roman Campagna, c.1646
Oil on canvas, 68.8 × 91 cm

INVENTORY NUMBER: 708
SELECTED REFERENCES: Marcel Roethlisberger, *Claude Lorrain: The Paintings*, 2 vols, London, 1961, 1, pp.270–71, no.LV 107, 2, fig.188; Ágnes Szigethi, *French Painting of the Seventeenth and Eighteenth Centuries*, Budapest, 1975, nos 17–18; Vilmos Tátrai (ed.), *Summary Catalogue 1*, London and Budapest, 1991, p.136; Ágnes Szigethi, *Old French Painting: Sixteenth to Eighteenth Centuries (The Collections of the Museum of Fine Arts, 6)*, Budapest, 2004, pp.60–62, no.22; Ágnes Szigethi: 'Claude Lorrain: Villa dans la campagne romaine', in Emmanuel Starcky (ed.), *Nicolas II Esterházy 1765–1833: Un prince hongrois collectionneur*, exh.cat., Musée national du château de Compiègne, 2007, p.134, no.39

According to Joachim von Sandrart, Claude Lorrain started out as a pastry-cook, and if so, patisserie's loss was art's gain, for he was one of the greatest landscape painters who has ever lived, and unquestionably – both by virtue of his importance for the evolution of the landscape garden and for Turner – the most influential for England. By 1630 Claude was established in Rome, and a few years later he felt obliged to begin to compile his *Liber Veritatis* (Book of Truth), now in the British Museum, as an archive of his inventions in an attempt to deter copyists and outright forgers.

Not infrequently, the drawings in the *Liber* are strikingly different from the corresponding pictures, but in the present instance the composition is essentially the same. This was one of no fewer than five works executed by Claude for Principe Camillo Pamphilj, who was among the most important patrons of art in seventeenth-century Rome. Camillo was the son of Pamphilio Pamphilj and the formidable Olimpia Maidalchini, and thus the nephew of Pope Innocent X, who made him a cardinal in 1644. However, this did not deter him from renouncing that office in 1647 to marry Olimpia Aldobrandini, with whom he lived in exile at Frascati until his death in 1666. The setting is an idealised and timeless vision of the Campagna, the countryside around Rome, warmed by the late afternoon sun and dominated by a splendid villa on the horizon. In the foreground, close to a pair of stately trees set against the subtle blues and golds of the sky, a herdsman drives his livestock across a stretch of water in which their reflections are brilliantly captured.

DAVID EKSERDJIAN

85

Jacopo Palma il Giovane   *c.*1548–1628
*Miracle of the Loaves and Fishes, c.*1614–16
Pen and brown wash, some traces of red chalk,
168 × 445 mm

INVENTORY NUMBER: K.57.1
SELECTED REFERENCES: Stefania Mason Rinaldi, *Palma il Giovane: L'opera completa*, Milan, 1984, no.D16; Loránd Zentai, *Sixteenth-century Northern Italian Drawings*, exh.cat., Museum of Fine Arts, Budapest, 2003, no.60

The fires of 1574 and 1577 in the Doge's Palace afforded new opportunities for young painters in Venice to participate in the redecoration of the destroyed interiors. Jacopo Palma il Giovane was undoubtedly the most eminent among them. He spent his formative years at the court of Urbino and in Rome, and by the time he returned to Venice in the early 1570s he was exceptionally widely travelled and familiar not only with the local tradition, but also with the Roman late Mannerism of Taddeo and Federico Zuccaro. It is not surprising that he became the most esteemed painter in Venice after the deaths of Veronese and Tintoretto.

Palma was an immensely productive artist who created over 600 paintings, most of which were made for Venetian churches and confraternities. The dramatic compositional study in Budapest is preparatory for his monumental frieze-like painting decorating the choir of the church of Santa Maria del Carmelo in Venice, executed between 1614 and 1616. The vigorous sketch of the *Pietà* on the verso is one of his countless painted and drawn treatments of that subject, and is probably connected with the altarpiece in a chapel of the church of San Trovaso in Venice, painted around 1600. The etching-like handling of the head study has been linked to Palma's activity as a printmaker. He collaborated with Odoardo Fialetti, a painter and printmaker from the Carracci circle, as well as with the Venetian publisher Giacomo Franco, to publish two treatises on drawing. These were the first publications to interpret the new concepts of the

Bolognese Academy, surprisingly appearing in colourist Venice.

ZOLTÁN KÁRPÁTI

86

Nicolas Poussin   1594–1665
*Finding of Moses, c.*1647
Pen and brush with brown ink and brown wash, 161 × 245 mm
(original fragment: 67 × 193 mm)

INVENTORY NUMBER: 2881
SELECTED REFERENCES: Louis-Antoine Prat and Pierre Rosenberg, *Nicolas Poussin 1594–1665: catalogue des dessins*, 2 vols, Milan, 1994, I, no.307; Vera Kaposy, 'The Finding of Moses', in Teréz Gerszi (ed.), *Dürer to Dalí: Master Drawings in the Budapest Museum of Fine Arts*, Budapest, 1999, no.104

Nicolas Poussin seems to have been fascinated by the Old Testament scene in which the Pharaoh's daughter and her attendants rescue the child Moses floating on the Nile in a basket (Exodus II, 1–10). He painted three versions of this subject: the earliest in 1638, during the artist's first stay in Italy, the second in 1647, after he returned to Rome from a short period in Paris, and the last one in 1651. The Budapest study relates to the second painting, which was made for one of his most important patrons, Jean Pointel, a banker from Lyons, and perhaps commenced in his presence in Rome. The painting, together with two further drawings connected with it, is now in the Louvre.

In the present study Poussin developed his compositional idea with vigorous light and shade effects. Unlike the painting, its arrangement resembles an antique bas-relief with a rhythmic and symmetrical structure: the central group of the infant Moses surrounded by tall women is supplemented to the left by an oarsman, while to the right, next to a classical river god, a fisherman bends over the water.

Only the narrow, horizontal section with the figures remains of Poussin's drawing. Possibly because the upper part of the original had been seriously damaged, the fragment was applied onto a larger sheet. Thus an ill-proportioned study, lacking any landscape background, was brilliantly transformed into an airy composition, with the mountaintop completed by a later hand. These interventions, which were in all probability the responsibility of the collector Pierre-Jean Mariette, occurred before the various collectors' marks were placed on the supplementary lower edge.

ESZTER SERES

87

Caspar Gras   1585–1674
*Mercury and Psyche, c.*1630–40
Bronze, height 40 cm

INVENTORY NUMBER: 5360
SELECTED REFERENCES: *Prag um 1600: Kunst und Kultur am Hofe Kaiser Rudolfs II*, 2 vols, exh. cat., Kunsthistorisches Museum, Vienna, 1988, no.78; Charles Avery, *Studies in Italian Sculpture*, London, 2001, p.435

The mythological story of Psyche, who was granted immortality after many trials and is taken by Mercury, the messenger of the gods, to Olympus in order that she may marry her beloved, Cupid, was popular with the Mannerist sculptors. Adriaen de

Vries (*c.*1545–1626), a talented pupil of Giambologna, made the most famous large bronze of *Mercury and Psyche* in 1593 for the Prague court of the Habsburg Emperor Rudolf II (1552–1612), which is now in the Louvre. Other bronzes on the same subject are known from the circle of Hubert Gerhard (?1540/50–?1621), a Dutch artist who also studied in Italy. Caspar Gras, a German-born Austrian sculptor, was a member of Gerhard's workshop, and followed his master an apprentice embosser at the Innsbruck court of the Habsburg archdukes. Although he never travelled to Italy, he was influenced by Giambologna at second hand thanks to his apprenticeship with Gerhard. Moreover, he was able to study his renowned Florentine predecessor's small bronzes in the ducal collection.

The Budapest *Mercury and Psyche* is an inventive derivation both of Giambologna's *Mercury in Flight* and the female figure from his *Rape of a Sabine*. The two entwined, seemingly weightless figures are characteristic of the idiom of Mannerist artists, and the sculptor was clearly untroubled at producing the scene in bronze, a medium that is hardly associated with airiness. The casting of the Budapest group is unusual: the two figures were cast separately and only soldered together after their surfaces had been chased. The same technique was used for the variant of this work in the Kunsthistorisches Museum in Vienna, and the method is characteristic of other small bronzes by Gras, reflecting a mode of production strikingly different to contemporary Italian practice.

MIRIAM SZŐCS

88

Ferdinando Tacca   1619–1686
*Venus and Adonis, c.*1650
Bronze, height 44 cm

INVENTORY NUMBER: 5352
SELECTED REFERENCES: Jolán Balogh, *Katalog der ausländischen Bildwerke des Museums der Bildenden Künste in Budapest*, Budapest, 1975, no.174; Anthony Radcliffe, 'Ferdinando Tacca: The Missing Link in Florentine Baroque Bronzes', *Kunst des Barock in der Toskana, Italienische Forschungen des Kunsthistorischen Institutes in Florenz*, 3, 9 (1976), p.15

In Florence in 1590, Grand Duke Ferdinando I allowed Giambologna to set up a workshop next to his house in Borgo Pinti. After the master's death, the workshop was inherited by Pietro Tacca, and later by his son, Ferdinando. As head of the Borgo Pinti workshop Ferdinando Tacca was responsible for organising festivities and religious ceremonial for the Medici court. He designed many ingenious machines for theatrical performances and festivities, and he was also involved in Florence's first theatre, the Teatro della Pergola. Because a large portion of his time was taken up with temporary decorations, he was long considered primarily as a stage designer, engineer and architect. Only recently has his authorship of a group of sculptures been recognised. Somewhat perplexingly, although he was the head of the grand ducal sculpture workshop and foundry in Borgo Pinti, the centre of bronze casting in Florence, centuries passed before any bronzes were attributed to him.

Today he is credited with an extensive series of small bronzes on mythological subjects, including the Budapest *Venus and Adonis*. In the story from Ovid, the goddess of love tried to protect her beautiful mortal beloved Adonis: the youth was fatally wounded by a wild boar during a hunt. This group depicts the episode – popular in both Renaissance and Baroque art – in which Venus tries desperately to restrain her love from setting out on the fatal hunt. The Budapest bronze is notable for the typically graceful figures of Ferdinando Tacca, while the refined, extremely polished working of the surfaces is an excellent example of the technical perfection achieved by bronze casters in the seventeenth century.

MIRIAM SZŐCS

89.1

Damiano Capelli   doc. 1662–1688

Rider Killing a Bull, c.1675

Bronze, height 28.5 cm

89.2

Damiano Capelli

Rider Pursuing a Boar, c.1675

Bronze, height 28 cm

INVENTORY NUMBERS: 59.4, 59.3
SELECTED REFERENCES: Nicholas Penny and Anthony Radcliffe, *Art of the Renaissance Bronze, 1500–1650: The Robert H. Smith Collection*, London, 2004, p.260; Miriam Szőcs, 'Horseman Killing a Bull and Horseman Pursuing a Boar: Two Small Bronzes by Damiano Capelli in the Museum of Fine Arts, Budapest', *Bulletin du Musée Hongrois des Beaux-Arts*, 100 (2004), pp.119–31.

The undiminished fame of the sculptor Giambologna during the sixteenth and seventeenth centuries was due mainly to the small bronzes made after his works. For generations, his pupils and followers kept the master's models, from time to time casting them in bronze. Damiano Capelli was one of those who began his career in Giambologna's former workshop in the third generation after the master's death. Little is known of his life. Filippo Baldinucci, a biographer of Italian Baroque artists, records him as an able bronze caster. Before opening his own establishment Capelli worked under Ferdinando Tacca, who followed his father Pietro in Giambologna's Borgo Pinti workshop. Only five signed works by Capelli have survived, all of them small bronzes finished to an extremely high standard; four depict hunting scenes (Alain Moatti, Paris), and two of them are variants of the small bronzes in Budapest.

Certain details of Capelli's hunting bronzes, such as the rearing and galloping horses, the boar and the stag, appear in a similar form in works by Giambologna, and later by Pietro and Ferdinando Tacca, and the idea of representing hunting scenes may have been stimulated by the hunts of which the Medici family and their circle were so fond. One of Capelli's contemporaries, the draughtsman and etcher Stefano della Bella, was commissioned by the Medici to make a unique series of prints on this theme. Yet the small bronzes reflect not only the hunts, but also the animal fights similarly popular in Florence – an indispensable part of every important public spectacle there. In these events, frightened animals, which were usually far from aggressive, were

set upon by horsemen armed with spears or swords, in an attempt to provoke them to fight. The men would sometimes don oriental-style costume to lend greater colour to these barbaric spectacles.

MIRIAM SZŐCS

90

Karel Dujardin   1626–1678

Tobias and the Angel, 1660s

Oil on canvas, 85 × 64.7 cm

INVENTORY NUMBER: 3862
SELECTED REFERENCES: Ildikó Ember, *Niederländische Malerei des 17. Jahrhunderts aus Budapest*, exh.cat., Wallraf-Richartz-Museum, Cologne, and Centraal Museum, Urecht, 1987, no.13; Ildikó Ember and Zsuzsa Urbach (eds), *Summary Catalogue 2*, Budapest, 2000, p.47; Jennifer Kilian, *The Paintings of Karel Du Jardin, 1626–1678: Catalogue Raisonné*, Amsterdam, 2005, p. 200, no.101

Karel Dujardin is above all renowned for his Italianate landscapes, but in his later years he also produced a number of important subject pictures in a Flemish-influenced classical manner inspired by the paintings executed for Amsterdam Town Hall by various other artists in the 1650s, of which the *Conversion of St Paul* of 1662 (National Gallery, London) is an outstanding example. He probably travelled to Italy in the 1640s, and appears to have been in France in 1650, and there met his wife. They were living in Amsterdam in 1652, but from 1656 to 1659 were in The Hague, before returning to Amsterdam. In 1675, he sailed to Italy, rather unexpectedly by way of Tangiers, and was to spend his final years there.

The story of Tobias and the Angel, which is narrated in the Book of Tobit in the Apocrypha, was exceptionally popular in the Italian Renaissance. Its account of the travels under the protection of an archangel of a devoted son, not forgetting his faithful dog, who returns safely home, was one with which many patrons would have wished to identify. In the present work, which is signed at bottom right, Tobias is shown with the miraculous fish from whose gall – under the guidance of the Archangel Raphael – he will manufacture an ointment to cure his father Tobit's blindness, and it is this crucial element of the plot that explains the fact that the angel is pointing to his eye. The compact half-length composition, the elegant figures of the protagonists, and the blond tonalities of the palette are all entirely characteristic of this late phase of Dujardin's career.

DAVID EKSERDJIAN

91

Joseph Heintz the Elder   1564–1609

Study of Two Nymphs, c.1595–1600

Black and red chalk, 210 × 183 mm

INVENTORY NUMBER: 83
SELECTED REFERENCES: Teréz Gerszi, 'Joseph Heintz d. Ä.: Studienblatt mit zwei Nymphen', in Szilvia Bodnár and Teréz Gerszi, *Meisterzeichnungen des Künstlerkreises um Kaiser Rudolf II. aus dem Museum der Schönen Künste in Budapest*, exh.cat., Salzburger Brockmuseum, Salzburg, 1987, p.30, no.6; Jürgen Zimmer, *Joseph Heintz der Ältere: Zeichnungen und Dokumente*, Munich, 1988, p.142, nos. 66–67, figs. 107–08

Joseph Heintz, one of the most celebrated painters and architects of his era in Northern Europe, spent his formative years in Basel at the workshop of Hans Bock the Elder (c.1550–1623). Having completed his apprenticeship, he moved to Rome to study the

works of antiquity and those of the Renaissance masters. He subsequently went to Florence and then to Venice, where he remained until 1591, when Rudolph II appointed him court painter and portraitist in Prague. In the following years Heintz travelled widely, in particular to Italy, where, besides his artistic activities, he also advised the emperor on the acquisition of artworks. He received painterly and architectural commissions from other sources, too, including clients in Graz and Augsburg.

This *Study of Two Nymphs*, an elaborate sheet in red and black chalks, bears witness to Heintz's masterful drawing skills. It was produced on a piece of paper previously used for other purposes, which, in light of the text on the verso, would seem to have come from a clockmaker's workshop. On the verso the artist drew – partly over several lines of writing – a version of the left-hand female figure on the recto, in addition to a sketch of a head. The graceful movements of the nymph combing her hair on the recto, her *contrapposto* pose and her charming expression, all evoke Correggio's works. Heintz modelled the figure, whose contours he emphasised with a continuous line, by delicately rubbing together the two colours. The figure sitting on the right is sketchier; various details, including the movement of the right arm, are still uncertain. Although none of the motifs on the sheet is identical to figures in surviving paintings by Heintz, the studies may have been made in preparation for one of these works, possibly the *Diana and Actaeon* (Kunsthistorisches Museum, Vienna).

SZILVIA BODNÁR

92

Bartholomäus Spranger   1546–1611

Diana and Her Nymphs, c.1595–1600

Oil on canvas, 129 × 199.5 cm

INVENTORY NUMBER: 351
SELECTED REFERENCES: Michael Henning, *Tafelbilder Bartholomeus Sprangers 1546–1611*, Essen, 1987, p.192, no.B 1; Thomas DaCosta Kaufmann, *The School of Prague: Painting at the Court of Rudolf II*, Chicago and London, 1988, p.269, no.20.60; Ildikó Ember and Imre Takács (eds), *Summary Catalogue 3*, Budapest, 2003, pp.127–28; Andrew John Martin, 'Bartolomäus Spranger: Diana after the Hunt', in Bernard Aikema and Beverly Louise Brown (eds), *Renaissance Venice and the North: Crosscurrents in the Time of Bellini, Dürer and Titian*, exh.cat., Palazzo Grassi, Venice, 1999, pp.626–27, no.194

Bartholomäus Spranger, who was trained in Antwerp and then enjoyed a peripatetic career in Paris, Rome and Vienna (where he worked for the Emperor Maximilian II in 1575), before finally settling in the Emperor Rudolph II's Prague, was one of the most brilliant of all the artists employed at that remarkable court. His forte was the painting of sinuously erotic mythological subjects, deeply imbued with the spirit of Correggio and Parmigianino, whose works in Parma he had studied at first hand during his Italian years.

The attribution of this imposing canvas now seems incontrovertible, but is nevertheless of relatively recent date. The reclining figure of Diana, with the identifying crescent moon on her coiffure, was in all probability inspired by a specific Venetian prototype, possibly by an artist like Paris Bordone (1500–1571), but the other elements of the composition are marked with Spranger's highly personal stamp. This is apparent above all in the extremely stylised physiognomies of the two central nymphs in attendance upon the goddess, in her hunting dog at the left edge of the picture, and perhaps even more tellingly in the inclusion of the black huntsman offering his tribute of a dead stag. In view of the fact that Diana was the goddess of chastity as well as of the chase, her companions are customarily exclusively female (indeed, Actaeon was famously hunted down and killed for gazing upon her naked form), and his presence is without precedent. Given the taste for the wonders of nature at Rudolph's court, the erudite detail of the huntsman's Native American-style feathered headdress would undoubtedly have been much admired.

DAVID EKSERDJIAN

93

Leonhard Kern 1588–1662

Three Graces, c.1625–50

Stained brown wood, height 63 cm

INVENTORY NUMBER: 6145
SELECTED REFERENCES: E. Grünenwald, *Leonhard Kern: Ein Bildhauer des Barock*, Schwäbisch Hall, 1969, pp.18–20, no.23 pl. 49; H. Siebenmorgen (ed.), *Leonhard Kern: Meisterwerke der Bildhauerei für die Kunstkammern Europas*, exh.cat., Schwäbisch Hall, 1988, pp.215–16, no.100, pl.10

Leonhard Kern is one of the most instantly recognisable sculptors of all time and a truly great original. As was customary for a Northern European artist at this period, as a young man he made a study trip to Italy (1609–13), which however most unusually included a visit to North Africa. In 1620 he settled in the town of Schwäbisch Hall, where his artistic production consisted almost exclusively of small-scale figures and reliefs, executed primarily in ivory and boxwood.

By Kern's standards, this group is an unusually monumental production, which also explains the fact that it could not be carved out of his beloved boxwood, and is composed of a number of separate pieces of wood. It is inscribed with the artist's monogram on the original wooden base, into which the figures are set, and represents the classical subject of the Three Graces. Given Kern's travels in Italy, it is perfectly possible that he knew the most celebrated ancient treatment of the theme, a marble group that has been in the Piccolomini Library attached to Siena Cathedral since the Renaissance. If so, then he gleefully failed to follow its lead, either in the way he disposed the figures – for it is extremely rare not to show the central one the other way round from her companions – or indeed in his conception of the female nude. Kern's women may justly be described as Rubensian, since he clearly admired his Flemish near-contemporary, but they are actually even less classically inspired, and instead glory in their massive-thighed amplitude in a manner which could hardly be further removed from today's supermodel norm.

DAVID EKSERDJIAN

94

Johann Liss c.1595/1600–1631

Peasant Wedding, c.1616–19

Oil on canvas, 65.5 × 81.5 cm

INVENTORY NUMBER: 3844
SELECTED REFERENCES: M. Chiarini, I. Ember and A. Gosztola, *Rembrandt, Rubens, Van Dyck e il Seicento dei Paesi Bassi*, exh.cat., Palazzo della Permanente, Milan, Sinclair-Haus, Bad Homburg, Von der Heydt-Museum, Wuppertal, 1995, p.22, no.44; Rüdiger Klessmann, *Johann Liss: eine Monographie mit kritischem Oeuvrekatalog*, Ghent, 1999, pp.163–64, no.30, pl.2; Ildikó Ember and Imre Takács (eds), *Summary Catalogue 3*, Budapest, 2003, p.80

Johann Liss was born in Germany, but he appears to have learnt his craft in the Netherlands, before moving on to France. By 1621 he had settled in Venice, where he died of the plague a decade later. Works from this final period, such as the *Fall of Phaeton* (collection of Sir Denis Mahon, on loan to the National Gallery, London) and the *Vision of St Jerome* (San Nicolò da Tolentino, Venice), reveal the full tragedy of his premature demise, since he is never less than outstanding.

The raucous exuberance of the present work, which is closely linked to a *Peasant Brawl* described as its pendant by Joachim von Sandrart in his *Teutsche Akademie* (1675–79) and known in two versions (respectively in Nuremberg and Innsbruck), indicates that it was in all probability a product of his Flemish period. The vogue for scenes of peasants making merry was already extremely widespread in Northern Europe in the sixteenth century, and while the greatest exponent of the genre was Pieter Bruegel the Elder (c.1525/30–1569), the specific details of this composition and its companion suggest that Liss was directly inspired by the prints of his fellow German, Hans Sebald Beham (1500–1550). Liss constructs the right to left movement of the composition around a witty and schematic contrast between the woozily high-kicking men and the stern profiles of their womenfolk, and is more than willing to dwell on the baser realities, with his gleefully unflinching vignette of a young man over to the left who is shown vomiting copiously onto the ground.

DAVID EKSERDJIAN

95

Gerbrandt van den Eeckhout 1621–1674

Elisha and the Shunammite Woman, 1664

Oil on canvas, 101 × 157.5 cm

INVENTORY NUMBER: 5610
SELECTED REFERENCES: Werner Sumowski, *Gemälde der Rembrandt-Schüler*, 6 vols, Landau, 1983, 2, pp.735, 803, no.440; *Im Lichte Rembrandts: Das Alte Testament im goldenen Zeitalter der niederländischen Kunst*, exh.cat., Westfälisches Landesmuseum, Münster, 1994, pp.283, 162–64, no.51; Ildikó Ember, 'Gerbrandt van den Eeckhout: Der Prophet Elischa und die Sunamitin', in Ildikó Ember and Marco Chiarini (eds), *Rembrandt, Rubens, Van Dyck: Italiensehnsucht Nordischer Barockmaler: Meisterwerke aus dem Museum der Bildenden Künste Budapest*, exh.cat., Sinclair-Haus, Bad Homburg, and Von der Heydt-Museum, Wuppertal, 1995, p.44, no.5; Ildikó Ember and Zsuzsa Urbach (eds), *Summary Catalogue 2*, Budapest, 2000, p.56

Although less well known than such artists as Nicolaes Maes (1634–1693), Govaert Flinck (1615–1660) and Ferdinand Bol (1616–1680), the Dutch painter Gerbrandt van den Eeckhout was arguably both the most unwaveringly devoted and the most talented of all Rembrandt's pupils. He is above all celebrated for his religious narratives, often drawn from the Old Testament, although he did also paint portraits, landscapes and even genre scenes, and at his best he was a remarkable draughtsman.

The present canvas, which is signed and dated 1664 at bottom right, is a characteristic work of his latter years. Its subject is taken from Chapter 4 of the Second Book of Kings, and concerns the story of Elisha and the Shunammite Woman, who was childless, and whose kindness the prophet rewarded through the birth of a son. Years later, when the child dies, she comes with her servant on an ass – the sleeping boy, who is using the animal as a pillow, is visible in the middle distance against a rolling sun-kissed landscape – and seeks out Elisha. Here she is shown kneeling before him, and lamenting with the words, 'Did I desire a son of my lord?' Elisha then commands his servant Gehazi, who is standing behind them, to take his staff – which forms such a prominent element of the foreground still-life, together with a basket containing a loaf of black bread – and use it to bring the boy back to life, although in the event he himself has to accomplish the miracle. Both the solemn reverence of the figure group and the rich, deep colours bear witness to the influence of Rembrandt, but Eeckhout's highly distinctive manner is far from being a pale imitation of his master's.

DAVID EKSERDJIAN

96

Gioacchino Assereto 1600–1649

Mocking of Job, c.1630

Oil on canvas, 121.5 × 148.5 cm

INVENTORY NUMBER: 783
SELECTED REFERENCES: G. V. Castelnovi, 'Intorno all'Assereto', *Emporium*, 110 (1954), pp.17–35; Vilmos Tátrai (ed.), *Summary Catalogue 1*, London and Budapest, 1991, p.3; Mary Newcome, *Kunst in der Republik Genua*, exh.cat., Schirn Kunsthalle, Frankfurt, 1992, nos 19–25; Agnes Szigethi, 'Gioacchino Assereto: Giobbe deriso', in Agnes Szigethi (ed.), *L'Europa della pittura nel XVII secolo: 80 capolavori dai musei ungheresi*, Milan, 1993, p.56, no.1; Mary Newcome Schleier, 'Gioacchino Assereto: Hiob wird von seinem Weib und Dämonen verhöhnt', in István Barkóczi (ed.), *Von Raffael bis Tiepolo: Italienische Kunst aus der Sammlung des Fürstenhauses Esterházy*, exh.cat., Schirn Kunsthalle, Frankfurt, 1999, p.324, no.115

During the Renaissance, indigenous artistic production in Genoa was surprisingly undistinguished, given the city's political prominence and sheer scale, with the result that the best works of art were commissioned by the likes of the great admiral Andrea Doria from outsiders such as Perino del Vaga and Bronzino. However, all this changed in the seventeenth century, with the rise of a distinguished and distinctive local school of painting, of which Gioacchino Assereto was one of the most able representatives. While both Rubens and Van Dyck executed important pictures for Genoa, where the latter was also resident for a period, these influences proved inspirational as opposed to crushing.

The Old Testament Book of Job relates how Job, in God's words 'a perfect and an upright man', has all manner of torments visited upon him by Satan, but never wholly despairs, and is ultimately redeemed. In Assereto's canvas, the emaciated old man is shown looking up in supplication to heaven, while his gruesome wife, her face contorted in fury, mocks him after he has been smitten with sore boils 'from the sole of his foot unto his crown'. She shakes her fist in his face and slips her thumb between her first two fingers in the obscene gesture – still current in Italy and elsewhere – known as making a fig. The almost monochrome tonality of the picture only adds to its sombre power, and Assereto's gifts as a painter of still-life are brilliantly expressed in the earthenware pitcher in the bottom left-hand corner of the composition.

DAVID EKSERDJIAN

97

Jusepe de Ribera   1591–1652

Martyrdom of St Andrew, 1628

Oil on canvas, 209 × 183 cm

INVENTORY NUMBER: 523
SELECTED REFERENCES: Marianne Haraszti-Takács, *Spanish Paintings from the Primitives to Ribera*, Budapest, 1982, no.47; Nicola Spinosa, *Ribera: l'opera completa*, Naples, 2003, p.270, no.A61; Vilmos Tátrai (ed.), *Summary Catalogue 1*, London and Budapest, 1991, p.158; Éva Nyerges, 'José de Ribera: Martyrium des heiligen Andreas', in István Barkóczi (ed.), *Von Raffael bis Tiepolo: Italienische Kunst aus der Sammlung des Fürstenhauses Esterházy*, exh.cat., Schirn Kunsthalle, Frankfurt, 1999, pp.296–97, no.101; Éva Nyerges, *Spanish Paintings: The Collections of the Museum of Fine Arts, Budapest*, Budapest, 2008, p.102, no.44

Ribera was born in Valencia in Spain, and may have studied there under Francisco Ribalta (1565–1628), but he was in Rome by 1615, and by the next year was established in Naples, a city then under the rule of the Spanish viceroys. The tenebrous and dramatic chiaroscuro of his early works, such as the present canvas, represents a blending of Caravaggesque influences with a quintessentially Spanish realism, although over time this gave way to a richer and more luminous palette with no loss of power or energy.

This grandiose *Martyrdom of St Andrew*, which is signed and dated 1628 on the rock at bottom right, is one of the supreme achievements of the young master (his first dated works are of 1626). It is dominated by the shrivelled body of the all but nude apostle being attached to the saltire (diagonal) cross upon which he is to be crucified by a man who is intently tightening the cords around his ankles. Andrew looks imploringly heavenwards, and ignores the taunting hooded figure – presumably intended to be a pagan priest – looming over him and holding aloft a gilt-bronze statuette of Jupiter brandishing a thunderbolt and accompanied by an eagle. The saint appears to be virtually surrounded by the agents of evil, and only in the middle distance do we glimpse a weeping figure, presumably one of his followers, seemingly being kept at bay by a soldier with a tall spear. The colour scheme is deliberately sombre, with the startling exception of the blood-red flag inscribed with the 's' of the Roman SPQR set against the lowering dark of the sky.

DAVID EKSERDJIAN

98

Giovanni Francesco Barbieri,
called Il Guercino   1591–1666

Flagellation of Christ, 1611

Oil on canvas, 351 × 176.5 cm

INVENTORY NUMBER: 4225
SELECTED REFERENCES: Maria Teresa Dirani Mistrorigo, *La chiesa e il convento di San Biagio Nuovo*, Vicenza, 1988, pp.33–37; Luigi Salerno, *I dipinti del Guercino*, Rome, 1988, p.290, no.21; Vilmos Tátrai (ed.), *Summary Catalogue 1*, London and Budapest, 1991, p.53; Ágnes Szigethi, 'Guercino: La flagellazione di Cristo', in Ágnes Szigethi (ed.), *L'Europa della pittura nel XVII secolo: 80 capolavori dai musei ungheresi*, exh.cat., Palazzo della Permanente, Milan, 1993, p.102, no.29

Il Guercino means 'the squinter', but this disability certainly did not stand in the way of his career as an artist. Born in nearby Cento, he was one of the most important Bolognese painters and draughtsmen of the seventeenth century, and enjoyed a very considerable international reputation. The stylistic turning point of the artist's career was his stay in Rome in 1621–23, when he executed an altarpiece for St Peter's and a fresco of *Aurora* for Pope Gregory XV. After his return home, the dramatically

chiaroscural Baroque style of his early period gave way to an increasingly serene and luminous classicism.

Guercino's account book records that on 12 August 1644 he received 500 *ducatoni* for this impressive altarpiece from Giovanni Locatelli acting for the Signori Beregani of Vicenza. It is first recorded in the church of San Bartolomeo there, and then appears to have been transferred to the church of San Biagio Nuovo. Christ is shown looking heavenwards in supplication and attached to a squat column, modelled on the antique porphyry column, then as now in Santa Prassede in Rome, which was believed to be the actual column of the Flagellation. The perfection of Christ's nude body is contrasted with the rough-hewn brutality of his tormentors. Oddly, he stands on a rocky base set upon the pavement where the action takes place, and another original touch is the discarded flail of prickly branches in the bottom right-hand corner. Among other preparatory drawings for the composition, there is a fine study in red chalk for the central group in the Ashmolean Museum, Oxford.

DAVID EKSERDJIAN

99

Bernardo Strozzi   1581–1644

Tribute Money, c.1631

Oil on canvas, 158 × 225 cm

INVENTORY NUMBER: 614
SELECTED REFERENCES: Vilmos Tátrai (ed.), *Summary Catalogue 1*, London and Budapest, 1991, p.114; Luisa Mortari, *Bernardo Strozzi*, Rome, 1995, pp.144–48, no.293; István Barkóczi, 'Bernardo Strozzi: Der Zinsgroschen', in István Barkóczi (ed.), *Von Raffael bis Tiepolo: Italienische Kunst aus der Sammlung des Fürstenhauses Esterházy*, exh.cat., Schirn Kunsthalle, Frankfurt, 1999, p.312, no.109

The most important Genoese painter of the seventeenth century, Bernardo Strozzi joined the Capuchin order at the age of seventeen, and hence came to be known as both 'Il Cappuccino' and 'Il Prete Genovese' (the Genoese priest). From around 1610 he was allowed to live and work outside the cloister to support his widowed mother, but when she died in 1630 he clashed with both his order and the papacy, and his refusal to return to the monastery involved him in a succession of kidnappings, disguises and escapes worthy of a picaresque novel. Only after his move to Venice in 1631 did things calm down, and he was made a monsignor in 1635.

The present work, one of a number of autograph versions of this composition, has been variously dated to the end of his Genoese and the beginning of his Venetian period. It illustrates the moment in the story of the Tribute Money related in St Matthew's Gospel, when St Peter returns with the coin after obeying Christ's command to him: 'Go thou to the sea, and cast an hook, and take up the fish that first cometh up; and when thou hast opened his mouth, thou shalt find a piece of money' (Matthew XVII, 27). Both the freedom of the brushstrokes and the richness of the colours are typical of Strozzi's best work, as is the lively characterisation of the figures, who range in age from the fashionably attired young boy at bottom left, who meets our gaze, to the bald and bearded ancients surrounding Jesus.

DAVID EKSERDJIAN

100

Antonio de Bellis   doc. 1636–1657/58

Moses Striking Water from the Rock, c.1640–45

Oil on canvas, 203 × 257.5 cm

INVENTORY NUMBER: 767
SELECTED REFERENCES: Silvia Cassani (ed.), *Civiltà del Seicento a Napoli*, 2 vols, exh.cat., Museo di Capodimonte and Museo Pignatelli, Naples, 1984, 1, pp.126–27, 234–39, nos 248–52; Nicola Spinosa, *La pittura napoletana del '600*, Milan, 1984, no.209; Vilmos Tátrai (ed.), *Summary Catalogue 1*, London and Budapest, 1991, p.32; Éva Nyerges, 'Antonio de Bellis, zugeschrieben: Mose schlägt Wasser aus dem Felsen', in István Barkóczi (ed.), *Von Raffael bis Tiepolo: Italienische Kunst aus der Sammlung des Fürstenhauses Esterházy*, exh.cat. Schirn Kunsthalle, Frankfurt, 1999, p.302, no.104

Antonio de Bellis, who may have been born around 1616, was a Neapolitan artist who was inspired by Jusepe de Ribera, but also by other leading if lesser lights of the local school of painting, such as Bernardo Cavallino (1616–1656) and Massimo Stanzione (c.1585–1656). His earliest documented works, an unfinished cycle of oil paintings for San Carlo alle Mortelle in Naples (still *in situ*) representing scenes from the life of the church's patron, San Carlo Borromeo, were commissioned and executed around 1636–39, and exhibited there in 1640. The existence of two monogrammed late works in and near Dubrovnik suggests he made a visit to what is now Croatia in the years before his early death.

The present canvas, in which the main subjects of the narrative, Moses and Aaron, are subordinated to the middle ground and pushed over to the right margin, is a real tour de force. The composition is exultantly asymmetrical, so that the most prominent figures of the kneeling mother and her child with a wooden bucket at the left edge act as a kind of introduction to the action, but are not balanced to the right, while the centre of the canvas is almost devoid of figures and instead occupied by the waters of Moses's miracle in the desert streaming towards the foreground. Behind the mother and child are a half-nude man carrying a grey earthenware vessel on his shoulders, and another man in the top left-hand corner who is looking probingly out. This mode of representation within complex narrative pictures was habitually reserved for self-portraits, so there is every reason to believe this must be a likeness of the artist.

DAVID EKSERDJIAN

101

Luca Giordano   1634–1705

Flight into Egypt, c.1684–85

Oil on canvas, 202 × 290 cm

INVENTORY NUMBER: 528
SELECTED REFERENCES: Vilmos Tátrai (ed.), *Summary Catalogue 1*, London and Budapest, 1991, p.49; Oreste Ferrari and Guiseppe Scavizzi, *Luca Giordano: l'opera completa*, Naples, 1992, pp.310–55, no.A353; Éva Nyerges, 'Luca Giordano: La fuga in Egitto con la barca', in Ágnes Szigethi (ed.), *L'Europa della pittura nel XVII secolo: 80 capolavori dai musei ungheresi*, exh.cat., Palazzo della Permanente, Milan, 1993, p.95, no.25

Luca Giordano's nickname 'Fa Presto', which may be loosely translated as 'Get a move on', supposedly arose from his father's importunate exhortations, but has had the baleful consequence that the artist is often unjustly condemned for having been over-productive. The truth is that he was not only the best painter active in Naples in the second half of the seventeenth century, but also that his finest works – such as his magnificent ceiling fresco for the Palazzo

Medici in Florence – are among the most uplifting achievements of the age.

The present canvas, of which there is a closely related variant in Madrid, represents one of the most popular subjects drawn from the infancy of Christ, for all that its visual representation had to be based upon the exceptionally telegraphic account given in the New Testament. In St Matthew's Gospel, Joseph is visited by an angel in a dream, who says: 'Arise, and take the young child and his mother, and flee into Egypt' (Matthew II, 13), and both in the Middle Ages and the Renaissance it was customary to show the Virgin and Child on a donkey, but in the seventeenth century a number of artists – among others Ludovico Carracci and Nicolas Poussin – chose to depict the Holy Family embarking upon a boat (here they have just dismounted from the ass). Giordano's frieze-like composition, with the straw-hatted Virgin and her sleeping, swaddled Child adding a genre-like touch, is set against an expansive landscape, while the bottom right corner is occupied by a muscular boatman. His pose is adapted from that of a figure in Raphael's tapestry of the *Death of Ananias* in the Vatican.

DAVID EKSERDJIAN

102

Salvator Rosa   1615–1673
Harbour with Ruins, c.1640–43
Oil on canvas, 87.5 × 111 cm

103

Salvator Rosa   1615–1673
Rocky Landscape with Waterfall, c.1640–43
Oil on canvas, 86.5 × 110.5 cm

INVENTORY NUMBERS: 535, 529
SELECTED REFERENCES: Klára Garas, 'Wiedergefundene Gemälde Salvator Rosas', *Pantheon*, 27 (1969), pp.42–47; Luigi Salerno, *L'opera completa di Salvator Rosa*, Milan, 1975, nos 46–47; Vilmos Tátrai (ed.), *Summary Catalogue 1*, London and Budapest, 1991, p.104; Éva Nyerges, 'Salvator Rosa: Paesaggio con cascata', in Ágnes Szigethi (ed.), *L'Europa della pittura nel XVII secolo: 80 capolavori dai musei ungheresi*, exh.cat., Palazzo della Permanente, Milan, 1993, pp.120–23, no.41

Salvator Rosa was a multi-faceted universal man, a poet, actor and musician as well as an artist, and the Romantic period's ideal of the creative genius. He was born and began his career in Naples, tried his luck in Rome on two occasions in the 1630s, and then spent the next decade in Florence, before finally establishing himself back in Rome. He was one of the finest landscape painters of the seventeenth century, but was also a remarkable portraitist, and painter of battles and philosophical subjects. The story of his having been a bandit is a fiction, but it is a matter of record that it was only less than a fortnight before his death that he finally married Lucrezia, his muse and the mother of his children, who had been the love of his life since 1640.

By this date, the notion of paired and consciously contrasted landscapes was already fully established. These two represent the wide-open expanse of water and shoreline of a port and a tree-dominated rocky landscape with a natural arch over to the right. The former is signed with the artist's surname on the plank at bottom centre, just to the left of a diminutive

---

self-portrait of Rosa – wearing red, gesticulating and carrying what appears to be some sort of portable artist's box – and both may be dated on stylistic grounds to Rosa's Florentine period. Unlike numerous other landscapes by Rosa, they do not tell a story, but are inhabited by everyday figures going about their business. In the case of the *Rocky Landscape*, however, the inclusion of a woman on horseback accompanied by a man on foot turns it into a secular equivalent of the Flight into Egypt.

DAVID EKSERDJIAN

104

Jacob Jordaens   1593–1678
Fall of Man, c.1630
Oil on canvas, 184.5 × 221 cm

INVENTORY NUMBER: 555
SELECTED REFERENCES: Marianne Haraszti-Takács, *Rubens and His Age*, Budapest, 1972, nos 23–24; Roger Adolf d'Hulst, *Jacob Jordaens*, London, 1982, pp.208, 359; Ildikó Ember and Zsuzsa Urbach (eds), *Summary Catalogue 2*, Budapest, 2000, p.90

After Van Dyck, Jacob Jordaens was unquestionably Peter Paul Rubens's most talented pupil. Jordaens never moved from his native Antwerp, and followed his master's example by producing a steady stream of large-scale altarpieces, mythologies, histories and allegories, as well as portraits. A particular speciality were his celebrations of the pleasures of eating and above all drinking, of which his massive bean-feast, *The King Drinks* (Musées royaux des Beaux-Arts de Belgique, Brussels), is the most famous example.

If Rubens is notorious for the generous proportions of his feminine ideal, then Jordaens – for all that he did not often paint female nudes – is more than a match for him. This is by no means his only treatment of the subject of the Fall, however: there is a smaller variation on the theme in Warsaw, while a preliminary oil sketch for the present work is in Darmstadt, and there is another large-scale treatment of the subject in the Toledo Museum of Art, Ohio. Here the monumental figures of Adam and Eve dominate the composition, and it is hard to call to mind the fact that they are in the process of accepting the serpent's offer of the apple, which will lead to their expulsion from the Garden of Eden, since Jordaens is primarily intent upon delighting in its bounty. The animals who keep them company are not the exotic creatures found in Jan Brueghel's treatments of the same subject, but instead a humble sheep, goat and cow, while at their feet is assembled a selection of gigantic vegetables which pay tribute to the superabundance of prelapsarian nature. In the distance is a splendidly romantic but at the same time carefully observed landscape.

DAVID EKSERDJIAN

105

Peter Paul Rubens   1577–1640, possibly assisted by
Anthony van Dyck   1599–1641
Mucius Scaevola before Lars Porsena, c.1618–20
Oil on canvas, 187 × 156 cm

INVENTORY NUMBER: 749
SELECTED REFERENCES: Elizabeth McGrath, *Subjects from History I, Corpus Rubenianum*, London, 1997, 2, no.46, fig.163 (as studio); Géza Galavics and Gerda Mraz (eds), *Von*

Bildern und anderen Schätzen: Die Sammlung der Fürsten Esterházy, Vienna, Cologne and Weimar, 1999, p.126, pl. 30; Ildikó Ember and Zsuzsa Urbach (eds), *Summary Catalogue 2*, Budapest, 2000, p.142; Ulrich Heinen, 'Peter Paul Rubens und Werkstatt: Mucius Scaevola vor Porsenna', in Nils Büttner and Ulrich Heinen, *Peter Paul Rubens. Barocke Leidenschaften*, exh.cat., Herzog Anton Ulrich-Museum, Braunschweig, 2004, pp.161–65, no.18; Susan J. Barnes et al., *Van Dyck: A Complete Catalogue of the Paintings*, London, 2004, pp.17, 19

Peter Paul Rubens was the most admired and successful painter of his age, a supreme master not just of religious and mythological subjects, but also of portraiture and landscape. If today he is less loved than such very different seventeenth-century artists as Rembrandt and Johannes Vermeer (1632–1675), then that is a reflection of our age's predilections and is certainly not any fault of his.

The dramatic subject of this imposing work, to which strips of canvas were added at top and bottom at some juncture, would undoubtedly have appealed to Rubens given his interest in Stoicism. It concerns the legendary exploit of the Roman, Mucius Scaevola ('left-handed'), who was brought before King Lars Porsena after having killed one of his men, whom he mistook for the king. Scaevola plunged his right hand into the flames to show his utter fearlessness at the prospect of his own sudden execution, at which the king spared his life.

Rubens's inexhaustible fertility of invention meant he had to have recourse to assistants to help him execute an endless stream of large-scale productions. In this case, the oil sketch from which the present work is derived (Pushkin Museum, Moscow) is clearly entirely by his own hand, but it is generally agreed that the finished canvas is not wholly autograph, and it has been suggested that the young Anthony Van Dyck may have been involved. It is certainly true that the soldier at the right margin – in his turn borrowed by Rubens from the similarly located executioner in Taddeo Zuccaro's fresco of the *Martyrdom of St Paul* (c.1557/58) in San Marcello al Corso, Rome – was adapted in Van Dyck's early *Christ Carrying the Cross* (1617/18) in the Sint-Pauluskerk in Antwerp.

DAVID EKSERDJIAN

106

Unidentified painter active in Rome   first half of the seventeenth century
Sleeping Girl, c.1610–20
Oil on canvas, 67.5 × 74 cm

INVENTORY NUMBER: 609
SELECTED REFERENCES: Eduard A. Šafařík, *Fetti*, Milan, 1990, p.301, no.A14; Vilmos Tátrai (ed.), *Summary Catalogue 1*, London and Budapest, 1991, p.37 (as Domenico Fetti); István Barkóczi, 'Domenico Fetti: Schlafendes Mädchen', in István Barkóczi (ed.), *Von Raffael bis Tiepolo: Italienische Kunst aus der Sammlung des Fürstenhauses Esterházy*, exh.cat., Schirn Kunsthalle, Frankfurt, 1999, pp.252–53, no.73 (as Fetti); Hilliard T. Goldfarb, 'A Mysterious Beauty and a French Attribution: The Sleeping Magdalen of Budapest', *Bulletin du Musée Hongrois des Beaux-Arts*, 98 (2003), pp.63–74 (as Claude Vignon); Vilmos Tátrai, 'Anonyme romain: Jeune Fille endormie', in Emmanuel Starcky (ed.), *Nicolas II Esterházy 1765–1833: Un prince hongrois collectionneur*, exh.cat., Musée national du château de Compiègne, 2007, p.103, no.10 (as anonymous Roman, c.1610)

Over the centuries, it is by no means uncommon for the names of artists to be forgotten. However, it is often possible on the basis of stylistic analysis to create coherent bodies of work that appear to be by the same hand, and to group them under such names as the Master of This or the Master of That. Conversely, on rare occasions major works of art stubbornly refuse to give up the secret of their authorship, and – thus far – the present work remains a particularly haunting and distinguished case in point.

In 1812, when it was first recorded, in the Esterházy Collection, it was ascribed to Paolo Veronese, which is clearly very wide of the mark, above all in terms of its date. Nowadays, it is universally agreed that it is a work of the seventeenth century, but none of the subsequent attributions – to the Italians Domenico Fetti, Sigismondo Coccapani and Bernardo Strozzi, or to the Frenchman Claude Vignon – has proved wholly convincing. Moreover, the identity of the elegantly attired sleeping girl, who clutches a lace handkerchief and whose folded arms rest upon a red and gold damask, has proved equally puzzling: is this a simple scene of everyday life, or is she Mary Magdalene? In either case, technical examination does not suggest that this captivating image was once part of a larger whole, although it is worth noting that the few centimetres of black background above the girl's head represent a later addition on a separate strip of canvas. Regardless of these mysteries, what is not in doubt is the bravura of the heavy impasto or the tender evocation of mood.

DAVID EKSERDJIAN

107

Eustache Le Sueur   1616–1655

Study of Juno Distributing Riches to Carthage, 1652–55

Black chalk and white heightening on beige paper, 282 × 395 mm

INVENTORY NUMBER: 2876
SELECTED REFERENCES: Pierre Rosenberg, 'Dessins de Le Sueur à Budapest', *Bulletin du Musée Hongrois des Beaux-Arts*, 39 (1972), pp.63–75, fig.53; Andrea Czére, in Emmanuel Starky (ed.), *Nicolas II Esterházy 1765–1833: Un prince hongrois collectionneur*, exh.cat., Musée national du château de Compiègne, 2007, no.44

Eustache Le Sueur, one of the most prominent painters of seventeenth-century France, was among the founders of the French Academy of Painting in Paris, where he passed his whole life. A pupil of Simon Vouet (1590–1649), Le Sueur died at a relatively young age and executed his most important commission not long before his death.

Between the years 1652 and 1655 the young Louis XIV (1638–1715) and his mother, Anne of Austria, had their apartments rebuilt at the royal palace of th Louvre. Seven paintings were commissioned from Le Sueur for the queen's winter quarters, the Appartement des Bains. Because of the subsequent conversions of the palace, this decoration does not survive completely, except for two allegorical paintings, for which drawings are preserved in Budapest. Both paintings represent Jupiter's wife, Juno: one of them depicts her ordering the destruction of Troy, the other – for which the present drawing is a study – shows Juno distributing riches to the city of Carthage. The subject is taken from the first book of Virgil's *Aeneid*.

The paintings are now both in Venice, in the Pinacoteca Manfrediniana at Seminario Patriarcale. The Budapest drawing, acquired with the Esterházy Collection in 1870, was executed by the artist in his usual technique for figure studies of black chalk with white heightening on beige paper. The majestic figure of Juno seated on clouds is a likeness of Anne of Austria, identifiable from the painting. The

drawing is not only a figure study but also a complete compositional study, although the putti accompanying the goddess are indicated only by a few faint lines. By contrast, the noble figure of Juno is more fully elaborated and the pleats of her robe are delineated with a masterful chalk technique.

ANDREA CZÉRE

108

Jan Fyt   1611–1661

Still-life with Dead Hare and Birds, 1640s

Oil on canvas, 62.5 × 86 cm

INVENTORY NUMBER: 729
SELECTED REFERENCES: Edith Greindl, *Les peintres flamands de nature morte au XVIIe siècle*, Brussels 1983, p.349, no.44; Ildikó Ember, *Delights for the Senses: Dutch and Flemish Still-life Paintings from Budapest*, exh.cat., Leigh Yawkey Woodson Art Museum, Wausau, 1989, no. 11; M. Chiarini, I. Ember and A. Gosztola, *Rembrandt, Rubens, Van Dyck e il Seicento dei Paesi Bassi*, exh.cat., Palazzo della Permanente, Milan, Sinclair-Haus, Bad Homburg, Von der Heydt-Museum, Wuppertal, 1995, no.52; Ildikó Ember and Zsuzsa Urbach (eds), *Summary Catalogue 2*, Budapest, 2000, p.71; Ildikó Ember, *Dutch and Flemish Seventeenth- and Eighteenth-century Still-life Paintings in the Budapest Museum of Fine Arts*, The Hague, forthcoming, pp.71–73, no.23

Jan Fyt was one of the leading Flemish still-life specialists of the seventeenth century. He was a student of Frans Snyders (1579–1657) in Antwerp, and the city remained his base throughout his career, with the exception of his extensive trips abroad between 1633 and 1641. These took him to Paris, all over Italy (he visited Venice, Genoa, Florence, Rome and Naples) and – according to Pellegrino Orlandi's *Abecedario Pittorico* of 1704 – also to Spain and England.

The present work, which is signed at bottom left but not dated, is a characteristic example of a genre in which Fyt excelled, namely the still-life with dead game. In an age as squeamish as our own, some people will doubtless find the idea of adorning one's home with such a gory image repugnant, but there is no denying the artist's masterly skill in – so to speak – bringing these dead creatures to life. The centrepiece of the composition is the dead hare, which is shown lying on a grey stone ledge, its head flopping lifelessly down, blood dripping from its mouth, and with the soft white fur of its belly exposed to view. Around it are assembled a variety of birds, including pairs of jays and green woodpeckers, and a mass of finches and sparrows skewered together at the top of the canvas, to which ominous thorns have been added at the base of the composition. The colour scheme is constructed around the contrast between muted tones and the radiant plumage of the birds, while Fyt's distinctively feathery brushstrokes capture the range of textures of his subjects.

DAVID EKSERDJIAN

109

Abraham Bloemaert   c.1565–1651

Huntsman with Dogs, 1630–45

Pen and wash in brown ink over black chalk, heightened with white, on pale green washed paper, 93 × 150 mm

INVENTORY NUMBER: 1916-74/a
SELECTED REFERENCES: Teréz Gerszi, *Netherlandish Drawings in the Budapest Museum: Sixteenth-century Drawings*, 2 vols, Amsterdam and New York, 1971, p.22, no.9; Jaap Bolten, *Abraham Bloemaert, c.1565–1651: The Drawings*, 2 vols, Leiden, 2007, p.271, no.800

Abraham Bloemaert is one of the most fascinating artists active in the decades around 1600. In both his

paintings and drawings, he produced masterpieces in every genre. During his long life he never went abroad, with the exception of three years spent in Paris in his youth. Nevertheless, working from his home in Utrecht, he reacted with sensitivity to all the major artistic developments of his era. At the same time, he managed to preserve the basic character of his artistic individuality: his attraction to balanced compositions reflecting individual solutions, to harmonic and beautiful forms, and to forceful picturesque qualities.

A typical example of this is the present drawing. The artist's son, Frederick, produced an engraving of this sheet as part of a series depicting birds and domestic animals. Invoking a few naturalistic motifs, the artist clearly indicates the scene: the huntsman, having reached the top of the ridge, unleashes his dogs so that they will be able to accomplish their task. The animals seem to quiver with excitement, pricking up their ears they listen for sounds in the distance. The precise characterisation of the dogs suggests the artist's close observation. Their slim bodies, beautiful poses and tensed muscles are indicative of the heightened tension felt before the start of the hunt. Bloemaert here achieved a perfect balance between faithfulness to reality and artistic style, a characteristic harmony that makes his drawings so attractive.

TERÉZ GERSZI

110

Herman van Swanevelt   c.1600–1655

Rocks and Trees, 1635–41

Brush and pen in brown ink, over black chalk, 262 × 384 mm

INVENTORY NUMBER: 2882
SELECTED REFERENCES: Teréz Gerszi, 'Die Zeichnungen von Herman van Swanevelt', *Bulletin du Musée Hongrois des Beaux-Arts*, 42–43 (2000), pp.95–106, fig.53; Teréz Gerszi, *Seventeenth-century Dutch and Flemish Drawings in the Budapest Museum of Fine Arts*, Budapest, 2005, pp.279–80, no.274; Anna Charlotte Steland, *Herman van Swanevelt (um 1603–1635) Gemälde und Zeichnungen*, 2 vols, St Petersburg, 2010, no.22, 16, A66.Z34

The Dutch painter Herman van Swanevelt, a member of the second generation of seventeenth-century Italianising landscapists, was one of the era's best landscape artists. He spent more than a decade in Rome (1629–41), and these years profoundly influenced the development of his art. Rome had become the centre of landscape painting in the 1620s–30s, through the work of Paul Bril, Cornelis van Poelenburgh, Bartholomeus Breenbergh, Nicolas Poussin and Claude Lorrain, whose landscapes were a source of inspiration for the young Dutchman. The 'naar het leven' (from the life) drawings produced by Swanevelt during his Roman period constitute the zenith of his *oeuvre*. Although the landscapists in Rome followed different paths, they all observed natural phenomena with unprecedented care, and did their utmost to convey effects of light and atmosphere.

In this fresh and spontaneous drawing, the forest setting, bathed in strong midday sunshine, captures the vitality of nature. The vigorous and bold brush drawing with fluctuating contrasts evokes with suggestive power the ephemerality of light and the constantly changing natural world. Particularly bold are the white patches, which almost seem to be vibrating, and the foliage of the trees, painted with the tip of the brush to evoke the motion of the leaves. Set against the resolute and summary areas of wash, the delicate and precise ink drawing of the ivy growing up the rock offers an attractive contrast. The Budapest drawing is closely related in mood to others on the same theme by Bril, Poelenburgh and Breenbergh.

TERÉZ GERSZI

III

Paulus van Vianen   *c.1570–1613*

River Landscape with Bridge, 1604–05

Pen and brown ink with blue wash, 193 × 296 mm

INVENTORY NUMBER: 1404
SELECTED REFERENCES: Teréz Gerszi, *Netherlandish Drawings in the Budapest Museum: Sixteenth-century Drawings*, 2 vols, Amsterdam and New York, 1971, p.100, nos 306a, 306b, Teréz Gerszi, *Paulus van Vianen: Handzeichnungen*, Hanau, 1982, p.206, no.52, fig.56

The Dutch artist Paulus van Vianen was not only the most prominent goldsmith of the period but also – in view of the novel realism of his drawings – arguably the greatest master of the depiction of nature active in Europe around 1600. After travelling in France, Germany and Italy, he spent two years in Salzburg (1601–03) in the service of the Prince-Bishop Wolf Dietrich von Raitenau (1559–1617). These years greatly influenced the development of his landscape art. He abandoned the traditional patterns of Mannerist landscape and depicted the beauty and diversity of what he saw with his own eyes amid the majestic Alpine surroundings – from wide and deep panoramas to landscape details drawn with almost scientific accuracy.

This sheet, one of seventeen drawings by the artist in Budapest, comes from his so-called Salzburg sketchbook – but is actually from the period after he left Salzburg. He was living in Prague, having moved there in December 1603 at the invitation of the Emperor Rudolph II (1552–1612), and he continued to use the same sketchbook there. The peasant's house and river in the present drawing, which represent the mountainous surroundings of Prague, are depicted from another angle in drawings in a Dutch private collection and the Nationalmuseum in Stockholm. However, in the Budapest drawing, which offers the spectator a distant view, the novelty of Vianen's landscape art is fully apparent; his masterful rendering of the light and atmospheric conditions brings the scene magically to life. The artist's use of short, sensitive lines coupled with a very fine brush technique produces a rich tonal effect.

TERÉZ GERSZI

II2

Pieter Stevens the Younger   *c.1567–1624*

Landscape with a Weir, 1610s

Pen and brown ink, washed in various pale watercolours, 197 × 309 mm

INVENTORY NUMBER: 1381
SELECTED REFERENCES: Teréz Gerszi, *Netherlandish Drawings in the Budapest Museum: Sixteenth-century Drawings*, 2 vols, Amsterdam and New York, 1971, p.85, no.249; Teréz Gerszi, *Renaissance et maniérisme aux Pays-Bas: Dessins du musée des Beaux-Arts de Budapest*, exh. cat. Musée du Louvre, Paris, 2008, no.57

The Flemish painter Pieter Stevens the Younger was a leading landscape artist at the turn of the seventeenth century. After studying in Italy, he became, in 1594, court painter in Prague to Emperor Rudolph II. It was there that his draughtsmanship came to fruition in a mutual exchange with his compatriots Paulus van Vianen and Roelandt Savery (1576–1639). As a result of their cooperation, Prague became both a bastion of late Mannerist figurative art and a major centre of European landscape painting. Except during the last decade of his career, Stevens remained essentially a master of idealising and decorative landscapes; in his drawings, nature was transformed into a stylised and colourful fantasy world, which, however, increasingly incorporated elements of reality.

In this drawing the enormous rock crowned with thick vegetation and the numerous stones in the foreground serve to enhance the decorative character of the Mannerist fantasy landscape. At the same time, the detailed and precise depiction of the weir indicates a sense of realism. The trees drawn with delicate lines and shrouded in the background mist are the results of the artist's observation of light and atmospheric conditions, exploiting to the full the technical possibilities of watercolour.

TERÉZ GERSZI

113

Cornelis Dusart   *1660–1704*

Peasant Counting, 1680s–90s

Black and red chalk, 294 × 202 mm

INVENTORY NUMBER: 1503
SELECTED REFERENCE: Teréz Gerszi, *Seventeenth-century Dutch and Flemish Drawings in the Budapest Museum of Fine Arts*, Budapest, 2005, p.83, no.65

Cornelis Dusart was the last and best-loved pupil of Adriaen van Ostade. He inherited the entire artistic property of his master. From the latter half of the 1670s Dusart studied and worked in Van Ostade's workshop, where he so successfully mastered the style of his mentor that he was able to complete his unfinished pictures and turn his sketches into paintings. In the process, he developed his own style of drawing, which was inspired by the achievements of his predecessors in Haarlem but accorded with the changed tastes of the late seventeenth century, which favoured greater formal and technical perfection. There was a demand for such artistic refinement among the rich and cultivated Dutch burghers, who had been influenced by French culture.

In Dusart's draughtsmanship the most evident attempt to satisfy such requirements is manifest in his chalk drawings in two or three colours and representing a single figure. The model used in *Peasant Counting* is recognisable in several other drawings, clothed and capped differently and undertaking an activity requiring some kind of characteristic movement. In each case the boy, who is rather scruffily dressed, is endowed with an almost monumental presence. The shading of these delicate chalk drawings is achieved with ultra-thin parallel hatching lines that emphasise the plastic forms of the

figure as well as the creases in the clothing, which follow the vibrant movements of the figure; indeed, the folds in the fabric are rendered palpable and realistic. In view of its accomplished elaboration, everything suggests that this drawing was not a study for a single figure in a painting, but rather an autonomous work made for a collector.

TERÉZ GERSZI

114

Adriaen van Ostade   *1610–1685*

Family Group at the Fireplace, early 1640s

Pen and brown ink with brown and grey wash on black chalk, 176 × 236 mm

INVENTORY NUMBER: 1554
SELECTED REFERENCE: Teréz Gerszi, *Seventeenth-century Dutch and Flemish Drawings in the Budapest Museum of Fine Arts*, Budapest, 2005, p.186, no.176

A painter, an etcher and a productive draughtsman, Adriaen van Ostade from Haarlem was the greatest master of depictions of peasant life in seventeenth-century Holland. His work, which spans a period of 50 years, shows the fate of Dutch peasants in the decades during and after the Dutch War of Independence (1568–1648). It was only towards the end of the 1630s that the peasants began to escape poverty; most of the figures in the earliest works by the artist are drinking, drunk or quarrelling among themselves. The topics and the technique indicate links with Adriaen Brouwer (1605/06–1638), but Van Ostade also drew inspiration from the works of such earlier masters as Pieter Bruegel, David Vinckboons, Jacob Savery and Karel van Mander.

The present drawing portrays peasants living in better conditions, in a more handsome and spacious interior. The artistic muddle of various domestic objects adds to the homely atmosphere. Light from the fireplace illuminates a rough and ready group of figures. Even so, if we examine their shapes, drawn with strong outlines and reduced to simple forms, we see that they are well nourished. The unity of the sketches of diverse motifs is maintained by a bluish-grey wash, signalling the influence of the colouring of early works by Rembrandt. In making use of the atmosphere created by light and shadow, and in emphasising the emotional content of the family idyll, the artist was inspired once again by Rembrandt. Based on the slightly incoherent lines and the cold colour tones of the wash, this compositional sketch, inscribed at bottom right, can be dated to the early 1640s, but it cannot be linked with a surviving painting.

TERÉZ GERSZI

115

Carlo Maratta   *1625–1713*

St Peter Baptises SS. Processus and Martinian in the Mamertine Prison, before 1697

Pen and brown ink with brown wash and black chalk underdrawing, heightened with white, 460 × 274 mm

INVENTORY NUMBER: 2364
SELECTED REFERENCES: István Barkóczi (ed.), *Von Raffael bis Tiepolo: Italienische Kunst aus der Sammlung Esterházy*, exh.cat., Schirn Kunsthalle, Frankfurt, 1999, no.98; Andrea Czére, *Seventeenth-century Italian Drawings in the Budapest Museum of Fine Arts: A Complete Catalogue*, Budapest, 2004, no.233

Papal support, several official posts – among them the presidency of the Academy of Fine Arts in the Accademia di San Luca, Rome – as well as an impressive number of commissions from home and abroad, indicate the leading role that Carlo Maratta played in Roman art. His style he owes much to Annibale Carracci and Guido Reni, although Maratta's drawings are not as close to nature as theirs. He preferred to move towards an ideal of beauty, his main concern being the expression of the monumentality and dignity of the human figure – whether in depictions of biblical or mythological subjects, secular themes or even portraits.

One of a pair, the Budapest drawing, from the Albani and Esterházy Collections, represents an episode from the life of St Peter drawn from Roman legend, depicting the miraculous baptism of his jailors, Processus and Martinian, in the Mamertine Prison, with water struck from the rock of the wall (here shown welling up from the ground). The painting, for which this sheet was a preparatory sketch, was intended for one of the side altarpieces in the Baptistery of St Peter's in Rome, commissioned by Pope Innocent XII, and was executed by a pupil of Maratta, Giuseppe Passeri (1654–1714), at the later date of 1714. The Budapest drawings are illustrated in a 1697 publication about the Baptistery, from which we know the approximate date of their execution. Together with its pendant, the drawing was precisely described in the 1790 inventory of the contents of the Palazzo Albani in Rome as Maratta's work, being part of the decoration of the palace, and recorded as being glazed and set in a gold frame. Passeri's oil *bozzetto* for the painting also survives and is in the Accademia di San Luca, Rome.

ANDREA CZÉRE

116

Giovanni Benedetto Castiglione   1609–1664

Allegory in Honour of the Ruling Couple of Mantua,
1652–55

Brush with brown and black ink, reddish-brown, light blue and white oil paint, on yellow prepared paper, 455 × 332 mm

INVENTORY NUMBER: 2296
SELECTED REFERENCES: Andrea Czére, *Seventeenth-century Italian Drawings in the Budapest Museum of Fine Arts: A Complete Catalogue*, Budapest, 2004, no.105; Andrea Czére (ed.), *Museum of Fine Arts, Budapest: Masterpieces from the Collection*, Budapest, 2006, no.109

Castiglione absorbed many elements of the animal-filled genre painting of his native Genoa. He also drew inspiration from the philosophical themes of Nicolas Poussin, who was active in Rome, and the brilliant technique of the oil sketches of Anthony van Dyck and Peter Paul Rubens, who also worked in Genoa. Castiglione's works are permeated with the notion of the transience of human life and with yearning for the Arcadian simplicity of a lost Golden Age. His Old Testament stories, and mythological and allegorical subjects are difficult to distinguish from simple pastoral scenes.

The same might be said of the present *Allegory*, acquired with the Esterházy Collection in 1870, and the drawings and paintings related to it (Royal Library, Windsor; Musée des Beaux-Arts, Grenoble;

Kunsthalle, Hamburg; as well as two pictures in Genoese private collections), which represent a symbolic triumph over mortality, celebrating the endurance of the dynasty through the birth of a child, in the form of a complex allegory in honour of the ruling Gonzaga dynasty in Mantua. This explains why the gazes and gestures of the protagonists are directed at the child, who guarantees the survival of the ruling family and is a symbol of the continuity of life more generally. The four figures also represent the four ages of man, according to the spirit of the condensed allegories of the Baroque.

ANDREA CZÉRE

117

Pieter Jansz. Saenredam   1597–1665

Interior of the Nieuwe Kerk at Haarlem, 1653

Oil on panel, 86 × 103 cm

INVENTORY NUMBER: 311
SELECTED REFERENCES: Rob Ruurs, *Saenredam: The Art of Perspective*, Amsterdam, 1987, p.46; Marten Jan Bok and Gary Schwartz, *Pieter Saenredam: The Painter and His Time*, Maarssen and The Hague, 1989, p.217, no.74, fig.228; Jeroen Giltaij and Guido Jansen, *Perspectives: Saenredam and the Architectural Painters of the Seventeenth Century*, exh.cat., Museum Boymans-van Beuningen, Rotterdam, 1991, no.19; Ildikó Ember and Zsuzsa Urbach (eds), *Summary Catalogue 2*, Budapest, 2000, p.154

Pieter Jansz. Saenredam, who was from Haarlem, is rightly best known for his miraculously luminous representations of the interiors of Dutch churches, although he was also a fine painter of their exteriors. His pictures build upon a meticulous campaign of preparatory drawings, which often began with a freehand sketch made *in situ*, followed up by altogether more scientific measured drawings which he subsequently transferred to the surface to be painted. On a number of occasions, the drawings were made years before he got round to painting.

In the case of the present panel, which is prominently signed and dated to the day (16 August 1653) at the foot of the pier to the right, he was portraying a church he must have known like the back of his hand. The Protestant Nieuwe Kerk was one of the supreme achievements of Jacob van Campen (1595–1657), not only the greatest architect of the age, but also a good friend of Sanraedam's, and it had been constructed in their home town between 1646 and 1649. Such is the conviction of Saenredam's masterly evocation of its light-filled, spacious interior, sparsely populated by the local citizenry and a scampering dog, that it seems almost heretical to ask whether this is what the church actually looked like. However, the reality is that Saenredam was making a work of art, and there is every reason to believe that some of the details here reflect Van Campen's original plans as opposed to the building as executed. What is more, the point of view has been ingeniously selected in order to create an effect of asymmetry in defiance of the church's centrally planned Greek-cross layout.

DAVID EKSERDJIAN

118

Andries Benedetti   doc. 1638–1649

Still-life with Fruit, Oysters and Lobsters, c.1640–45

Oil on canvas, 168 × 240 cm

INVENTORY NUMBER: 255
SELECTED REFERENCES: Ildikó Ember, *Delights for the Senses: Dutch and Flemish Still-life Paintings from Budapest*, exh.cat., Leigh Yawkey Woodson Art Museum, Wausau, 1989, p.27, no.B2; Federico Zeri (ed.), *La natura morta in Italia*, 2 vols, Milan, 1989, 1, pp.408–09, no. 486; Ildikó Ember and Zsuzsa Urbach (eds), *Summary Catalogue 2*, Budapest, 2000, p.18; Ildikó Ember, 'Andries Benedetti: Prunkstilleben mit Obst, Austern und Seekrebsen', in Wilfried Seipel (ed.), *Das flämische Stilleben 1550–1680*, exh.cat., Kunsthistorisches Museum, Vienna, and Kulturstiftung Ruhr, Essen, 2002, p.272, no.92; Ildikó Ember, *Dutch and Flemish Seventeenth- and Eighteenth-century Still-life Paintings in the Budapest Museum of Fine Arts*, The Hague, forthcoming, pp.14–18, no.4

Andries Benedetti is an unusually mysterious figure, a painter of Italian origin, possibly from Parma, who is recorded in Antwerp during the fifth decade of the seventeenth century, and is then lost from view, in all probability because he returned to his native land. His few extant works, which are all still-lifes, eloquently testify to his profound dependence upon the peerless example of the great Jan Davidsz. de Heem (1606–1684). He was obviously well thought of in his day, since one of his still-lifes (now Kunsthistorisches Museum, Vienna) – which includes fruit, a lobster and a lute – was recorded in the Archduke Leopold Wilhelm's collection in 1659. The present work, whose attribution to Benedetti is confirmed by the fact that it is signed twice, is unarguably his masterpiece. It is an example of a type known at the time as a *pronk* still-life, in which both the sheer physical scale of the picture and the exuberant excess of the display are designed to impress the viewer. Thus, plentiful supplies of drink fill a wine-cooler over to the left, while the table is laden with prawns and oysters, fruit (including the statutory peeled lemon), lobsters, a raised pie, tall drinking glasses and various items of silverware. On the right are a blue and white porcelain dish of ceps and an armchair, upon which there rests a large earthenware lidded beer-jug. The Doric architecture of the backdrop is draped in midnight blue velvet, and leads on to a glimpse of wooded landscape.

DAVID EKSERDJIAN

119

Pieter Claesz.   c.1597–1660 and   Roelof Koets   1592–1655

Still-life with a Large Rummer and Fruit, 1644

Oil on canvas, 104.5 × 146 cm

INVENTORY NUMBER: 53.478
SELECTED REFERENCES: Onno ter Kuile, *Seventeenth-century North Netherlandish Still-lifes / Rijdienst Beeldende Kunst: Catalogue of Paintings by Artists Born before 1870*, The Hague, 1985, no.VI-18a; Ildikó Ember, *Delights for the Senses: Dutch and Flemish Still-life Paintings from Budapest*, exh.cat., Leigh Yawkey Woodson Art Museum, Wausau, 1989, pp.54–55, no.7; Ildikó Ember and Zsuzsa Urbach (eds), *Summary Catalogue 2*, Budapest, 2000, p.34; Martina Brunner-Bulst, *Pieter Claesz.: Der Hauptmeister des Haarlemer Stillebens im 17. Jahrhundert*, Lingen, 2004, pp.180ff, 283, no.136; Ildikó Ember, *Dutch and Flemish Seventeenth- and Eighteenth-century Still-life Paintings in the Budapest Museum of Fine Arts*, The Hague, forthcoming, pp.44–47, no.24

Pieter Claesz., who was based in Haarlem, originally came from the Southern Netherlands (roughly modern Belgium), but was nevertheless one of the greatest of all seventeenth-century Dutch still-life painters. He specialised in tabletop still-lifes, in which the effect verges on the monochrome. On a handful of occasions, he joined forces with the incomparably less well-known but by no means negligible artist Roelof Koets, and indeed this is the only known instance of each partner in the enterprise carefully signing and dating his particular portion, unsurprisingly to the same year.

The overall impression is harmonious, but it is not hard to recognise the fact that two hands have been at work here. Comparisons with their independent productions would allow one to identify who did what, even without the clues provided in the form of the locations of their respective signatures. Pieter Claesz. executed the left third of the composition, with the gleaming white cloth, the wonderfully crumbly bread roll and knife on the pewter plate, the dish of oily green olives and the two drinking glasses – the Rummer in which there glints a mighty draught of white wine, and the foreshortened Berkemeyer on its side. In contrast, the explosion of fruit and foliage – which is restricted to vine leaves, a few plums, bunches of red and green grapes, and red and yellow apples – on the right was painted by Koets.

DAVID EKSERDJIAN

120

Rembrandt Harmensz. van Rijn   1606–1669

Saskia van Uylenburgh Sitting by a Window, 1635–38

Pen and brown ink with brown wash and black chalk, 164 × 125 mm

INVENTORY NUMBER: 1582
SELECTED REFERENCE: Teréz Gerszi, *Seventeenth-century Dutch and Flemish Drawings in the Budapest Museum of Fine Arts*, Budapest, 2005, p.209, no.201

Rembrandt is the emblematic figure of the golden age of Dutch art. He is generally considered one of the greatest draughtsmen and printmakers of all time. An independent-minded and meditative artist, he sought to portray the fullness of human life and the natural world. His greatest skill was as a chronicler of human frailties, and he tirelessly strove to capture the reality of the inner self rather than formal beauty. He never travelled to Italy, preferring to develop his art based on experiences in his own milieu and on the great Netherlandish traditions.

In the early years of his career, most of Rembrandt's studies of the human physiognomy were detailed but unadorned portraits of himself and family members. Later, in the 1630s, he often portrayed his wife, Saskia van Uylenburgh, who was to die young, in intimate and spontaneous drawings, paintings and etchings such as the present work. The motions and tender glance of the woman reading a book, suddenly looking up as her husband enters the room, capture her expression of surprise. The light streaming through the window creates space and atmosphere, and also enhances the vitality of the figure, which is drawn with quick brushstrokes. While the figure is sketch-like, the face is actually even more abbreviated, and is depicted with firm, simple lines. Even so, the glance is expressive and brisk – the drawing is the work of an accomplished master. In place of the elaborated details of his early portraits, Rembrandt's focus is now on the essence of his subjects.

TERÉZ GERSZI

121

Peter Paul Rubens   1577–1640

Portrait of Albert Rubens, Son of the Artist, in Profile, c.1619

Pen and wash in brown ink, over black and red chalks, 246 × 202 mm

INVENTORY NUMBER: 1745
SELECTED REFERENCES: Teréz Gerszi, 'Porträtzeichnungen des Kindes Albert Rubens in Budapest und Wien', *Bulletin du Musée Hongrois des Beaux-Arts*, 97 (2002), pp.77–85, fig.52; Teréz Gerszi, *Seventeenth-century Dutch and Flemish Drawings in the Budapest Museum of Fine Arts*, Budapest, 2005, p.254, no.249

Rubens's depictions of his family deserve special attention on account of the intimacy and empathy they so manifestly express. This drawing of Albert (1614–1657), the first-born son of Rubens and his first wife Isabella Brandt, is closely comparable – both in terms of its quality and the all-embracing tenderness – with other portraits of the Rubens family. The great master was able to show in a convincing manner the character of his children, as well as any momentary changes of mood. The four-year-old Albert's slightly open mouth – so often a feature of small children, if one looks closely – indicates the artist's profound knowledge of behavioural expression. Originally, Albert's portrait was done in black and red chalks, like the portrait of Clara Serena and Nicolaas (Albertina, Vienna). However, this can only be seen in bright light, owing to the brown wash applied to the hair. The most noteworthy aspect of the face is the lively glance, which enhances the vitality of the whole drawing. The infant John the Baptist has the same observing eyes in Rubens's *Virgin and Child with Saints* (Staatliche Museen, Kassel) and the artist may have painted the corresponding head in that painting on the basis of the Budapest drawing.

TERÉZ GERSZI

122

Cornelis van Poelenburgh   1594/95–1667

Children of the Elector Palatine Frederick V, King of Bohemia, 1628

Oil on panel, 37.9 × 65.3 cm

INVENTORY NUMBER: 381
SELECTED REFERENCES: N.Sluijter-Seiffert, *Cornelis van Poelenburgh*, unpublished diss., Rijksuniversiteit te Leiden, 1984, pp.108, 246, no.194; Arthur MacGregor (ed.), *The Late King's Goods: Collections, Possessions and Patronage of Charles I in the Light of the Commonwealth Sale Inventories*, London and Oxford, 1989, pp.204, 229, no.12, pl.19; Ildikó Ember and Zsuzsa Urbach (eds), *Summary Catalogue 2*, Budapest, 2000, p.135; Simon Groenveld, *De Winterkoning. Balling aan het Haagse hof*, exh.cat., Haags Historisch Museum, The Hague, and Stadtmuseum, Amberg, 2004, p.58

Cornelis van Poelenburgh, together with Bartholomeus Breenbergh (1598–1657), was one of the most refined Dutch painters of the first half of the seventeenth century; their specialities were religious and mythological subjects set in extensive Italianate landscapes. Poelenburgh in particular customarily worked on a small scale, usually on copper or panel, with the result that within the context of his practice the Budapest painting is an exceptionally substantial as well as immaculately preserved production.

In the present work, which was commissioned by King Charles I, the figure group of the seven children of Frederick V of Bohemia, best known as the Winter King, is centred conventionally enough, but is set somewhat back from the front plane of the scene. This allows the artist to add a spectacular and minutely observed still-life of dead game just above the signature and date in the bottom right-hand corner, whose presence is explained by the fact that the two eldest children play the parts of Meleager and Atalanta in the Greek myth of the Calydonian boar hunt.

On 14 February 1613, Frederick had married Elizabeth Stuart, the daughter of King James I and VI and Queen Anne of Denmark, thus indissolubly linking his family with the Stuart dynasty and the British crown. Thus, while his eldest surviving son, Charles Louis (1617–1680), followed in his footsteps as Elector Palatine in 1648, it was his fourth child (1619–1682) who took centre stage in the history of England during the Civil War as Prince Rupert of the Rhine. Arguably even more crucially, it was because he was the son of Frederick's youngest daughter, Sophia (1630–1714), that George I became monarch of the British Isles.

DAVID EKSERDJIAN

123

Jan-Erasmus Quellinus   1634–1715

Lamentation at the Foot of the Cross

Brush and dark grey, grey, brown and bluish-grey ink, heightened with white on brown paper; framing lines in dark brown ink, 298 × 247 mm

INVENTORY NUMBER: 1567
SELECTED REFERENCE: Teréz Gerszi, *Seventeenth-century Dutch and Flemish Drawings in the Budapest Museum of Fine Arts*, Budapest, 2005, p.208, no.200

At the end of the seventeenth century, the influence of Peter Paul Rubens and Anthony van Dyck was replaced by classicising endeavours within Flemish painting. The art of Jan-Erasmus Quellinus was rooted, via his father the better-known Erasmus, in that of Rubens, but he fell under the spell of Italian and especially Venetian art following a journey to Italy. With their picturesque quality and their refined forms and ingenious technical solutions, Quellinus's drawings – formally perfect but somewhat lacking in expressive power – are typical examples of around 1700.

Christ's Descent from the Cross was an extremely popular theme among Baroque artists, since it allowed them to portray strong emotions, complex movements and intense physical effort. Despite growing up in the shadow of Rubens, Quellinus was driven by other artistic ambitions, mediated to him by his father. Even the choice of motif suggests how his artistic ideas differed from the dramatic Baroque approach: rather than portray Christ's removal from the Cross, he captures the moment when the mourners surround Christ's corpse, already on the ground. The figures – including Mary, who is holding Christ's hand – appear to express inner emotion rather than outward pain. Signs of brutal torture are absent from Christ's body. Indeed, in all aspects of the work, the artist avoided creating discord or provoking shock. With their subdued movements and emotional reserve, the slim and elegant figures embody beauty and harmony. The surrounding decorative trees also serve to alleviate the tragic effect. The drawing suggests intimate knowledge of Italian art, and of the works of Paolo Veronese in particular. The hand of the kneeling woman touching the limp hand of Christ repeats a similar gesture in Veronese's *Descent from the Cross* in the Chiesa dell'Annunziata in Ostuni. After his years in Rome (c.1657–59), it was only in 1660 that Quellinus visited

Venice, and yet this visit, during which he became acquainted with the works of Veronese, had a decisive effect on his art. The Budapest work is signed at lower left in pen and grey ink: *JE Quellinus* (interlaced). Produced with a delicate brush technique, Quellinus's dated works exhibit few stylistic changes between 1660 and 1696. Thus the approximate date of his undated works – such as this sheet – can be determined only with difficulty.

TERÉZ GERSZI

124

Jacob Jordaens   1593–1678

*Holy Family with St John the Baptist, His Parents and Angels, c.*1617

Brush with brown ink and brown wash with traces of preliminary black chalk, 284 × 233 mm

INVENTORY NUMBER: 1912-684
SELECTED REFERENCE: Teréz Gerszi, *Seventeenth-century Dutch and Flemish Drawings in the Budapest Museum of Fine Arts*, Budapest, 2005, p.143, no.136

The sensual realism of the Flemish Baroque is most acutely expressed in paintings by Jacob Jordaens. The artist led a large workshop performing various activities, thus for him drawings were an essential tool in the creation of paintings or tapestries. Accordingly, compositional studies dominate Jordaens's rich draughtsmanship. His preferred drawing type was the *modello*, a meticulously executed compositional sketch that usually combined various techniques. Revealingly, he was particularly concerned with problems of colour and chiaroscuro.

This compositional drawing, produced for a painting in the Muzeum Narodowe, Warsaw, comes from the early period of Jordaens's career, when he mainly painted religious and mythological themes. The first idea for the composition – now in the Louvre, Paris – is a rough sketch executed using light strokes. Half-length figures feature in that version, and their positioning at the margins of the drawing differs from that of the painting. Jordaens established the final composition in the Budapest study: he drew the figures in a more decisive and detailed manner, and he used shading to emphasise volume, establishing a balance of darker and lighter areas for the composition as a whole. Despite its sketchiness, this drawing brings out the significance of light as well as the movements and facial expressions determining the emotional content. The rich multi-figure composition follows an established iconographical type in Italian art, known as the *Sacra Conversazione*, in which the Madonna is depicted accompanied by saints. It was principally through Rubens that Jordaens became subject to Italian influences. However, to a greater extent than his elder colleague, Jordaens adapted the influences to suit his individual taste and Flemish traditions. For his figures, he chose characteristic Flemish types, depicting them with simple gestures and intimate expressions. Both the painting and the drawing seem to have been produced around 1617. This was at the very end of Jordaens's early period, revealing that he

had already begun to develop his own style, and had stepped out of Rubens's shadow.

TERÉZ GERSZI

125

Luis Tristán de Escamilla   *c.*1585/90–1624

Adoration of the Magi, 1620

Oil on canvas, 232 × 115 cm

INVENTORY NUMBER: 6373
SELECTED REFERENCES: Jeannine Baticle and Cristina Marinas, *La Galerie espagnole de Louis-Philippe au Louvre, 1838–48*, Paris, 1981, pp.177–78; Vilmos Tátrai (ed.), *Summary Catalogue 1*, London and Budapest, 1991, p.161; Éva Nyerges, *Obras maestras del arte español, Museo de Bellas Artes de Budapest*, exh.cat., Banco Bilbao Vizcaya, Madrid, and Museo de Bellas Artes, Bilbao, 1996, pp.89–90, no.15; Alfonso Pérez Sánchez, *Luis Tristán*, Madrid, 2001, pp.199–200, no.12; Éva Nyerges, *Spanish Paintings: The Collections of the Museum of Fine Arts, Budapest*, Budapest, 2008, p.84, no.35

Luis Tristán, whose professional base was Toledo, travelled to Italy shortly after 1606, where he viewed the works of Caravaggio and his followers, as well as the Lombard school of the early seventeenth century. His mature manner represents a sometimes uneasy alliance of these strands – and the works of Carlo Saraceni in Rome and Juan Bautista del Maino in Toledo – with the dominant presence of El Greco. In 1616 he executed his masterpiece, the high altarpiece of the parish church of Yepes, Toledo.

The present canvas, together with a companion piece of the *Adoration of the Shepherds* of identical dimensions (Fitzwilliam Museum, Cambridge), also signed and dated 1620, and like it formerly in the legendary collection of Spanish pictures assembled by King Louis-Philippe of France, is very much in the same vein, and may have been executed for the church of the Jerónimas de la Reina in Toledo. The intense colours and dazzling richness of the costumes reveal Tristán's debt to El Greco and indeed to the sixteenth-century Venetian tradition that inspired him, but the boldness of the composition and the portrait-like realism of the figures are Tristán's own. Particularly arresting in this regard is the pageboy holding the eldest magus's crown in the bottom right-hand corner of the composition, who looks out almost imploringly at us, and serves to establish a link with the action beyond. From the far distance, the radiance of the guiding star projects onto the stable, and the grooms with their camels, which conveyed the wise men to Bethlehem, are picked out against the horizon.

DAVID EKSERDJIAN

126

Bartolomé Esteban Murillo   1618–1682

Virgin with the Infant Christ Distributing Bread to Pilgrims, 1678

Oil on canvas, 219 × 182 cm

INVENTORY NUMBER: 777
SELECTED REFERENCES: Diego Angulo Iñiguez, *Murillo*, 3 vols, Seville, 1981, 2, pp.144–45, no.145, 3, pl. 423; Marianne Haraszti-Takács, *Spanish Masters from Zurbarán to Goya*, Budapest, 1984, pp.24–26; Vilmos Tátrai (ed.), *Summary Catalogue 1*, London and Budapest, 1991, p.157; Maria de los Santos García Felguera, in Gary Tinterow (ed.), *Manet/ Velázquez: The French Taste for Spanish Painting*, exh.cat., Metropolitan Museum of Art, New York, 2003, no.58; Éva Nyerges, *Spanish Paintings: The Collections of the Museum of Fine Arts, Budapest*, Budapest, 2008, p.166, no.76

Bartolomé Esteban Murillo was the most distinguished representative of the Sevillian school of painting in the seventeenth century, and he remained based there throughout his long and prolific career,

with the exception of occasional visits to Madrid. Traditionally, his production is divided into three phases, beginning with the cool realism of the initial *estilo frío* (cold style), which is followed by the *estilo cálido* (hot style) of his middle years, and finally from the 1660s by the *estilo vaporoso* (vaporous style). The vast majority of Murillo's works are religious in subject, but he was also a masterly painter of genre scenes of beggar children and an extremely fine portraitist.

In 1678 the artist's friend, patron and ultimately executor Don Justino de Neve, a canon and prebendary of Seville Cathedral, commissioned this splendid canvas for the refectory of the Hospital de los Venerables Sacerdotes (House of Refuge for Aged Priests). In 1665 Murillo had executed a full-length portrait of Don Justino, now in the National Gallery, London, and it has been plausibly proposed that the foremost of the three pilgrim-priests at bottom right, one of whose companions has a staff and cowl, may be a likeness of his significantly older self. The idealised character of the heavenly apparition of the Virgin and Child with a single angel backed by a golden radiance ringed by cherubim, allied to the rich reds and blues of the Madonna's robes, is lovingly contrasted with the portrait-like presentation of the black-clad supplicants, and above all by the basket of bread rolls, of types known as *roscas* and *panecillos*, which the Infant Saviour hands out with all the solemn concentration of childhood.

DAVID EKSERDJIAN

127

Anthony van Dyck   1599–1641

*Married Couple, c.*1620

Oil on canvas, 112 × 131 cm

INVENTORY NUMBER: 754
SELECTED REFERENCES: Géza Galavics and Gerda Mraz (eds), *Von Bildern und anderen Schätzen: Die Sammlung der Fürsten Esterházy*, Vienna, Cologne and Weimar, 1999, pp.125–26, fig.11; Ildikó Ember and Zsuzsa Urbach (eds), *Summary Catalogue 2*, Budapest, 2000, p.52; Susan J. Barnes et al., *Van Dyck: A Complete Catalogue of the Paintings*, New Haven and London, 2004, pp.107–09, no.I.114; Annamária Gosztola, 'Anthonis van Dyck: Ritratto di coniugi', in Vilmos Tátrai (ed.), *Da Raffaello a Goya: Ritratti dal Museo di Belle Arti di Budapest*, exh.cat., Palazzo Bricherasio, Turin, 2004, p.150, no.69; Nora de Poorter, 'A Wedding Ring in Budapest: Reflections on the Image of Married Couples in Antwerp Portraiture (1609–1621)', in Carl Van de Velde (ed.), *Flemish Art in Hungary: Budapest, 12–13 May 2000*, Brussels, 2004, pp.25–29; Alexis Merle Du Bourg, *Antoon van Dyck: Portraits*, exh.cat., Musée Jacquemart-André, Paris, 2008, no.3

One of the most extraordinary artistic prodigies of all time, Anthony Van Dyck was already painting pictures of remarkable authority while still in his teens. He had the good fortune to be a pupil of Peter Paul Rubens in his native Antwerp, where he became a member of the Guild of St Luke in 1618, but was soon on the move. A first visit to England in 1620 was swiftly followed by six years in Italy, and he was then once again in England, where he established himself as the seemingly prescient recording angel of the doomed Charles I and his court, from 1632 until his death.

At the early date when he executed this canvas, Van Dyck could have had no idea how overwhelmingly his professional practice would be dominated by portraiture, but his supreme gifts in that direction are already impressively apparent. In Antwerp, it was customary for married couples to be represented in paired portraits, and there are only one or two instances of the unification found here from Van Dyck's first period. Although the couple in question are decidedly not in the first flush of youth – the wife in particular looks distinctly careworn – the artist has taken full advantage of the format to emphasise their physical and emotional closeness. In the ancient world the joining of right hands had legal significance, but here it is more likely simply to indicate marital constancy. The red backdrop and the gold and white accents of gloves, cuffs and ruffs all serve to enliven the predominantly sombre tonality.

DAVID EKSERDJIAN

128

Peter Paul Rubens   1577–1640

*Head of a Bearded Man, c.*1616–19

Oil on oak panel, 55 × 42 cm

INVENTORY NUMBER: 3835
SELECTED REFERENCES: Marianne Haraszti-Takács, *Rubens and His Age*, Budapest, 1972, no.3; M. Chiarini, I. Ember and A. Gosztola, *Rembrandt, Rubens, Van Dyck e il Seicento dei Paesi Bassi*, exh.cat., Palazzo della Permanente, Milan, Sinclair-Haus, Bad Homburg, Von der Heydt-Museum, Wuppertal, 1995, no.19; Ildikó Ember and Zsuzsa Urbach (eds), *Summary Catalogue 2*, Budapest, 2000, p.142; Annamária Gosztola, 'Pieter Paul Rubens: Studio di testa virile', in Vilmos Tátrai (ed.), *Da Raffaello a Goya: Ritratti dal Museo di Belle Arti di Budapest*, exh.cat., Palazzo Bricherasio, Turin, 2004, p.73, no.22

By the early sixteenth century, it had become customary – especially in Italy – to make detailed head studies, usually in red or black chalk, for the principal figures in large-scale paintings and frescoes. The idea of executing these preparations in oils must have seemed like a logical next move, and by the end of the century painters such as Federico Barocci (*c.*1535–1612) routinely produced such studies in oil on paper. Peter Paul Rubens himself, both here and in an expanded variant in the Fitzwilliam Museum in Cambridge, which includes the sitter's right hand, goes one step further still by using wood as the support. Both panels must have been preceded by an autograph sheet at Chatsworth, which comprises a series of head studies, mostly of the same model, one of which is almost identical. What is more, the intention in a case such as this does not simply seem to have been to employ the work for a particular project, but rather to retain it in the studio for repeated adaptation and re-use as a character type. Thus, for all that the present work is clearly the likeness of an actual person, it was not intended to be a portrait in the usual sense.

The sitter was evidently a favourite model of Rubens's, since his bushy beard and instantly recognisable features are repeated elsewhere, and notably in the guise of one of the wise men in the central panel of his *Adoration of the Magi* triptych in the church of St-Jean at Malines, which was commissioned in 1616 and delivered in 1619.

DAVID EKSERDJIAN

129

Jan Lievens   1607–1671

*Half-length of a Girl, c.*1630–31

Oil on panel, 61.5 × 48 cm

INVENTORY NUMBER: 51.2977
SELECTED REFERENCES: R. Ekkart and H. Schneider, *Jan Lievens: Sein Leben und seine Werke*, Amsterdam, 1973, p.142, no.215; Werner Sumowski, *Gemälde der Rembrandt-Schüler*, 6 vols,

Landau, 1983, 3, pp.1802, 1906, no.1267; Ildikó Ember and Zsuzsa Urbach (eds), *Summary Catalogue 2*, Budapest, 2000, p.96; Ildikó Ember, 'Jan Lievens: Mädchenkopf', in Ildikó Ember and Marco Chiarini (eds), *Rembrandt, Rubens, Van Dyck. Italiensehnsucht Nordischer Barockmaler: Meisterwerke aus dem Museum der Bildenden Kunste Budapest*, exh.cat., Sinclair-Haus, Bad Homburg, and Von der Heydt-Museum, Wuppertal, 1988, no.27; Dagmar Hirschfelder, *Tronie und Porträt in der niederländischen Malerei des 17. Jahrhunderts*, Berlin, 2008, p.416, no.309

Like his friend Rembrandt, Jan Lievens came from Leyden, and they both then studied in Amsterdam under Pieter Lastman (1583–1633), before returning home and sharing a studio in the late 1620s. After Rembrandt's return to Amsterdam, Lievens appears to have travelled to England in 1632, and by 1635 he was in Antwerp, where he came under the influence of Van Dyck. The classicism of his later work is worlds removed from his early, Rembrandtesque manner.

This panel, which dates from what is generally regarded as Lieven's golden period, when his art came closest to that of Rembrandt, gives every indication of being a likeness of a particular individual, but it is not a portrait. On the contrary, both the way in which the girl is shown looking intently heavenwards, and indeed the manner in which the light is concentrated upon her face, suggest that this may be intended to be a representation of the Virgin of the Annunciation. If so, one would normally expect her to be accompanied by the Archangel Gabriel, but there was a tradition – which was particularly popular in Italy – for showing the Virgin Annunciate in isolation. The most plausible other explanation for the work's appearance would be that this is a fragment of a once larger composition, but all the available technical evidence contradicts this hypothesis. Regardless of the precise meaning of this image, the muted colour scheme, the encrusted texture of particular passages of the paint surface, such as the gold necklace, and the intense contrast between the lights and the darks, are typical of Lieven's work around 1630.

DAVID EKSERDJIAN

130

Frans Hals   1581/85–1666

*Portrait of a Man, c.*1652–54

Oil on panel, 64.5 × 46.3 cm

INVENTORY NUMBER: 277
SELECTED REFERENCES: Seymour Slive, *Frans Hals*, 3 vols, London, 1970–74, 1, pp.129, 174, 189, fig.200, 2, pp.101–02, no.194, 3, pl.304; Ildikó Ember, *Niederländische Malerei des 17. Jahrhunderts aus Budapest*, exh.cat., Wallraf-Richartz-Musem, Cologne, and Centraal Museum, Utrecht, 1987, no.19; Claus Grimm, *Frans Hals: Das Gesamtwerk*, Stuttgart and Zurich, 1989, p.285; Ildikó Ember and Zsuzsa Urbach (eds), *Summary Catalogue 2*, Budapest, 2000, p.79

Frans Hals is one of the most exciting portrait painters of all time, famed for the unique blend of psychological insight and human sympathy with bravura brushwork that characterises him at his best. He spent his entire working life in Haarlem in the Netherlands, and was all but exclusively a portraitist, yet what impresses about his work is its range not its narrowness.

Hals was a master of elaborate multi-figured group portraits, but was at least as successful when it came to such intimate one-to-ones as the present panel. Here the subject is shown standing at half length against a neutral backdrop. He is clad in predominantly dark-toned garments, against which

both his left hand and the electrifying white and gold accents around his right side, his collar and the tie-string stand out. For the rest, the focus is upon his good-humoured moustachioed face, framed by unruly black hair. Although it has been unconvincingly proposed that he is the landscape painter Jan Asselijn (after 1610–1652), in fact nothing is known concerning the identity of this particular individual. In any event, it is hard to believe such information would greatly enhance our enjoyment of the work; what matters is that the sense of an unremarkable middle-aged man's presence is overpowering. Looked at close to, it is almost impossible to believe that such freely applied pigment can resolve itself into a coherent whole, yet Hals's magic consists above all in conjuring up a solid form on a flat surface out of these seemingly effortless flicks of his brush.

DAVID EKSERDJIAN

131

Bartholomeus van der Helst   *c.*1613–1670

Portrait of Gideon de Wildt, 1657

Oil on canvas, 135.8 × 119 cm

INVENTORY NUMBER: 4316
SELECTED REFERENCES: S. S. Dickey, 'Bartholomeus van der Helst and Admiral Cortenaer', *Leids Kunsthistorisch Jaarboek*, 8 (1989), p.230, figs 3, 232–33; M. Chiarini, I. Ember and A. Gosztola, *Rembrandt, Rubens, Van Dyck e il Seicento dei Paesi Bassi*, exh.cat., Palazzo della Permanente, Milan, Sinclair-Haus, Bad Homburg, Von der Heydt-Museum, Wuppertal, 1995, no.25; Ildikó Ember and Zsuzsa Urbach (eds), *Summary Catalogue 2*, Budapest, 2000, p.82; Gerlinde de Beer, *Ludolf Backhuysen (1630–1708): Sein Leben und Werk*, Zwolle, 2002, p.41

Bartholomeus van der Helst was the son of a Haarlem innkeeper, but he spent his entire professional career in Amsterdam. His earliest known work dates from 1637, and appears to confirm that he was a pupil of Nicolaes Eliasz. Pickenoy (1588–1650/56), whose smooth and polished style he was to extend and develop. Just two years later, he was already vying with Rembrandt, having been commissioned to execute a group portrait of a military company as part of the same series of canvases as the *Night Watch*. As a result of the success of his contribution, which he completed in 1642, from that date until his death Van der Helst was the favourite portrait painter of the Amsterdam élite.

Van der Helst was just as comfortable painting individuals as groups, and this portrait, which is signed and dated at bottom left, is a classic demonstration of what he offered his subjects. Gideon de Wildt (1624–1674) was a rear admiral in the Dutch navy, and an associate of such legendary figures as Maerten Tromp and Michiel de Ruyter. As the commander of his ship, the *Vrede*, he was on the losing side at the battles of the Kentish Knock (which is known as the Slag bij de Hoofden in Holland) in 1652 and Scheveningen in 1653 during the First Dutch War, but in 1657 he triumphed over the French 'pirates' at Cadiz and was rewarded with the gold chain and medallion, which he is shown wearing in the present portrait. Van der Helst presents him in all his swaggering pomp, holding his baton of command in his right hand, with ships at sea beyond, and with a splendid red fabric to his left offsetting his sombre but opulently gold-trimmed attire.

DAVID EKSERDJIAN

132

Salomon van Ruysdael *c.1600/03–1670*
Road among the Dunes with a Wagon ('After the Rain'), 1631
Oil on panel, 56 × 86.4 cm

INVENTORY NUMBER: 260
SELECTED REFERENCES: Wolfgang Stechow, *Salomon van Ruysdael*, Berlin, 1975, p.95, no. 181; Helga Möbius and Harald Olbrich, *Holländische Malerei des 17. Jahrhunderts*, Leipzig, 1990, p.215, pl.73; Ildikó Ember and Zsuzsa Urbach (eds), *Summary Catalogue 2*, Budapest, 2000, p.149; Peter C. Sutton, 'S. van Ruysdael: Road in the Dunes with a Passenger Coach', in Peter C. Sutton (ed.), *Masters of Seventeenth-century Dutch Landscape Painting*, exh.cat., Rijksmuseum, Amsterdam, Museum of Fine Arts, Boston, and Philadelphia Museum of Art, 1987, no.91; Pieter Biesboer, *De Gouden Eeuw begint in Haarlem*, exh.cat., Frans Hals Museum, Haarlem, and Kunsthalle der Hypo-Kulturstiftung, Munich, 2008, pp.48, 176

Salomon van Ruysdael, together with his brother Isaak and nephew Jacob van Ruisdael, was one of the most distinguished of a family of painters, which also included his son Jacob Salomonsz. van Ruysdael. He was a member of the Painters' Guild in his native Haarlem as early as 1623, but his first dated works are of 1627. He was a Mennonite, and enjoyed a long and successful career.

It is generally agreed that his early works, of which this panel – signed in monogram and dated at lower right – is a particularly fine example, are his greatest achievements. He shared a taste for a broadly monochrome palette and humbly realist subject-matter with his contemporaries Jan van Goyen (1596–1656) and Pieter de Molijn (1595–1661), but he is both an inherently better and a less formulaic painter than either of them. It is a tribute to the brilliance of the atmosphere Salomon conjures up that this particular painting has come to be known as *After the Rain*. The gentle zigzag of the dirt track leads the eye past the brown hogs who have been wallowing in the muddy pond over to the left and into the composition, where it comes to rest on the sturdy wagon, packed with figures and drawn by a white horse, which all but conceals its companion. Beyond are two knotted clumps of trees and a low-lying farmhouse with outbuildings, which give this quintessentially tonal landscape a structure and focus.

DAVID EKSERDJIAN

133

Aelbert Cuyp *1620–1691*
Cows in a River, c.1650
Oil on panel, 59 × 74 cm

INVENTORY NUMBER: 408
SELECTED REFERENCES: Ágnes Czobor, *Dutch Landscapes*, Budapest, 1967, nos 37–38; Ildikó Ember and Zsuzsa Urbach (eds), *Summary Catalogue 2*, Budapest, 2000, p.41; Arthur K. Wheelock (ed.), *Aelbert Cuyp*, exh.cat., National Gallery of Art, Washington DC, and National Gallery, London, 2001, pp.134–35, no.21

Aelbert Cuyp, who was from Dordrecht, is best known for his landscapes, but he was a master of a whole range of genres in an age of habitual specialisation, and painted sea-pieces, portraits and even still-lifes. Despite all his other accomplishments, however, it is as the champion of the humble cow that he richly deserves his immortality. After marrying a wealthy widow in 1658, he became a landowner and all but abandoned his brushes for the remainder of his life.

Cuyp was hugely admired in England in the eighteenth and nineteenth centuries, with the result that he is exceptionally well represented in British collections, above all in those of the National Gallery

---

and the Dulwich Picture Gallery in London. It should come as no surprise, therefore, to discover that this superb panel, which is signed at bottom left and has long been one of the artist's best-loved works, was formerly in the collections of John Barnard and Thomas Hankey in London, before entering the collections of the Museum of Fine Arts in 1871. Dordrecht had been the victim of disastrous floods in 1421, but successful land reclamation had led to prosperity, and Cuyp's cows are almost invariably shown in or near water. Their mighty bulk commands the foreground of the composition, while the rest of the scene is entirely given over to the limpid surface of the waters dotted with sailing vessels, the exceptionally low horizon, and the golden glow of the seemingly limitless expanse of the cloudy heavens. Although undated, this work may be placed around 1650 on stylistic grounds, together with related works in the Hermitage and in the collection formed by Abraham Robarts MP (1779–1858).

DAVID EKSERDJIAN

134

David Teniers the Younger *1610–1690*
Landscape with a Castle, c.1650–55
Oil on canvas, 161 × 224.5 cm

INVENTORY NUMBER: 59.13
SELECTED REFERENCES: Marianne Haraszti-Takács, *Rubens and His Age*, Budapest, 1972, no.34; Margret Klinge, *David Teniers the Younger: Paintings, Drawings*, exh.cat., Koninklijk Museum voor Schone Kunsten, Antwerp, 1991, pp.214–15, no.73; Ildikó Ember and Zsuzsa Urbach (eds), *Summary Catalogue 2*, Budapest, 2000, p.164; Ildikó Ember, 'Nouvelles attributions de paysages flamands du 17e siècle en Hongrie', in Carl van de Velde (ed.), *Flemish Art in Hungary: Budapest, 12–13 May 2000*, Brussels, 2004, p.40; Margret Klinge and Dietmar Ludke (eds), *David Teniers der Jüngere (1610–1690): Alltag und Vergnügen in Flandern*, exh.cat., Staatliche Kunsthalle, Karlsruhe, 2005, p.266, no.84

David Teniers the Younger, so called to differentiate him from his notably less talented and infinitely less prolific painter father, was one of the most successful Flemish artists of his time. He is particularly renowned for landscapes of precisely this type, but also for low-life genre scenes and so-called gallery pictures, in which he accurately recorded the holdings of leading collectors, not least those of the Archduke Leopold Wilhelm of Austria (1614–1662).

No doubt prosperous and aristocratic patrons enjoyed Teniers's rose-tinted visions of the cheerful carryings-on of peasants, and equally representations of their social peers, but they must also have understood that what set him apart from so many of his contemporaries who peddled similar subject-matter was the quality of his painting. With the exception of the elegant family group of father, mother and child over to the right in the company of an elderly rustic and his gambolling dog next to a rock bearing the artist's signature, the colour scheme of the present work is deliberately confined to neutral tones, but the evocation of light breaking through the clouds to the left is wonderfully convincing. What is more, the romantic prospect of a turret-topped castle on a lofty eminence must have been very consciously intended to entrance the original owners of the work, and to afford a delicious contrast to the unrelieved flatness of the Flemish countryside.

DAVID EKSERDJIAN

135

Donato Creti *1671–1749*
Studies of Jacob Wrestling with the Angel, c.1720
Pen and brown ink, 174 × 197 mm

INVENTORY NUMBER: 1898-897
SELECTED REFERENCES: Andrea Czére, *Disegni di Artisti Bolognesi nel Museo delle Belle Arti di Budapest*, exh.cat., San Giorgio in Poggiale, Bologna, 1989, no.72; Andrea Czére, *Italienische Barockzeichnungen*, Hanau, 1990, no.21

Lodovico Carracci's sublime lyricism and Guido Reni's rhythmic fluency were examples for Donato Creti, as were Simone Cantarini's turbulent brio and the stylish calligraphy of Parmigianino's drawings. By taking his inspiration from all these sources, he created an elegant and unique amalgam that was one of the supreme achievements of eighteenth-century Bolognese draughtsmanship.

Giovan Pietro Zanotti, the artist's biographer, states that Creti produced two paintings representing Jacob's dreams for Cardinal Davia. The present drawing (De Mestral de Saint-Saphorin; purchased from Ahim Berenfeld, Vienna, 1898) is a preparatory study for one of these paintings (now in the Casa del Clero, Bologna), which shows Jacob wrestling with the angel of the Lord, whom he refused to release until he received a blessing (Genesis XXXII, 24–29). Creti's idealised portrayal of motion in the finished work is reminiscent of the choreographed weightlessness and stylisation of ballet. The effect is even stronger in the sweeping and forceful drawings for *Jacob Wrestling with the Angel*. On the Budapest sheet, we see two versions of the interlocked figures, to which may be added another sheet in the Princeton Art Museum, with four additional versions of the scene. The angelic figures in both sketches almost seem to be flying.

ANDREA CZÉRE

136

Giambattista Tiepolo *1696–1770*
Virgin in Glory with Six Saints, c.1749–50
Oil on canvas, 72.8 × 56 cm

INVENTORY NUMBER: 651
SELECTED REFERENCES: Vilmos Tátrai (ed.), *Summary Catalogue 1*, London and Budapest, 1991, p.116; Zsuzsanna Dobos, 'Giovanni Battista Tiepolo: Madonna e Santi', in Mauro Natale (ed.), *Itinerario Veneto: Dipinti e disegni del '600 e '700 veneziano del Museo di Belle Arti di Budapest*, exh.cat., Finarte, Milan, 1991, p.68, no.21; Massimo Gemin and Filippo Pedrocco, *Giambattista Tiepolo: i dipinti: opera completa*, Venice, 1993, p.404, no.384; Fernando Moreno Cuadro, 'En torno a las fuentes iconográficas de Tiepolo para la "Visión Teresiana" del Museo de Bellas Artes de Budapest', *Archivo Español de Arte*, 82 (2009), pp.243–58

Giambattista Tiepolo was without question the last great decorative painter in the Renaissance tradition, and at the same time arguably the most admired artist of eighteenth-century Europe. In Palazzo Labia in his native Venice, the Archbishop's Palace in Würzburg, in the Palacio Réal in Madrid, and in many other places besides, his frescoes testify to his extraordinarily inventive verve and brilliance of touch.

It might therefore seem natural to assume that he could only work on a grand scale, but in fact he was a superlative, quicksilver draughtsman, while both his oil sketches and his more intimate easel pictures are equally irresistible. The present canvas, whose date is much discussed, is too polished to be a preparatory study for an altarpiece, and must instead have been created as a private commission. It represents the Virgin of the Immaculate Conception, crowned with a ring of stars and with the serpent – his tail is just visible – at her feet. She is flanked by six saints, some of whom are distinctly obscure. Reading from left to right, they have been plausibly identified as King Louis of France, Pedro da Alcantara, Teresa, Francis, Joseph and Filippo Neri, which suggests that the painting must have been commissioned by someone with a particular devotion to the Franciscans, and specifically to the reformed strand of the order. The spiralling composition is dominated by a gorgeous combination of saturated colours, yet the most prominent foreground presence is the austere figure of St Francis, who turns away from the celestial vision to point out and contemplate one of the two skulls in the picture.

DAVID EKSERDJIAN

137

Giandomenico Tiepolo   1727–1804

Head Study of St James, c.1750

Red and white chalk on blue paper, 322 × 253 mm

INVENTORY NUMBER: 1929-2164
SELECTED REFERENCES: George Knox, *Giambattista and Domenico Tiepolo: A Study and Catalogue Raisonné of the Chalk Drawings*, 2 vols, Oxford, 1980, no.M.116; Andrea Czére, *Capriccio in Time and Space: Giandomenico Tiepolo*, exh.cat., Museum of Fine Arts, Budapest, 2004, pp. 22–55, no.9, fig.14

The art of one of the most prominent painters and graphic artists of late eighteenth-century Venice, Giandomenico Tiepolo, is characterised by its lively decorative style and typically bourgeois themes. Giandomenico's works are unique in their combination of rococo and neoclassical features, and his subjects are often presented with a distinctly ironic flavour.

The present study (formerly in the Habich Collection and presented to the museum by Simon Meller in 1929), was copied by Giandomenico from his father Giambattista's painting of *St James of Compostela*, executed for the Spanish Chapel in London in 1750 and now in the Budapest Museum of Fine Arts. The drawing dates from Giandomenico's early years and is much closer in style to his father's chalk drawings than his characteristic later compositional studies in pen and brush. Nevertheless, in the *Head of St James* Giandomenico's personal touch as a draughtsman is readily apparent: instead of the plasticity and painterly tones typical of Giambattista, there is more emphasis on linear values, and the flowing hair drawn with deft lines is in piquant contrast to the solemn and triumphant expression. Since the hand holding the flag is not complete, and the blank space corresponds to the head of the horse seen in the painting, it is obvious that the drawing is not a preliminary study for it, but was made after its completion.

ANDREA CZÉRE

138

Giambattista Tiepolo   1696–1770

Figure Study, 1750–53

Red and white chalk on blue paper, 392 × 228 mm

INVENTORY NUMBER: 1923-1022
SELECTED REFERENCES: George Knox, *Giambattista and Domenico Tiepolo: A Study and Catalogue Raisonné of the Chalk Drawings*, 2 vols, Oxford, 1980, no.M.67; Andrea Czére, *Italienische Barockzeichnungen*, Hanau, 1990, no.58; Teréz Gerszi (ed.), *Dürer to Dalí: Master Drawings in the Budapest Museum of Fine Arts*, Budapest, 1999, no.32

Giambattista Tiepolo's luminous rococo creations include a series of frescoes for the Archbishop's Palace in Würzburg, to which the present drawing is related. Between 1750 and 1753 Giambattista painted in conjunction with his sons, Giandomenico and Lorenzo, the *Allegory of the Planets and Continents* with Apollo embarking on his daily course for the staircase of the Archbishop's Palace. The deities around Apollo symbolise the planets, while the allegorical figures on the cornices represent the four continents of Europe, Asia, Africa and America. The allegory can be interpreted as the glorification of the achievements of the Prince-Bishop Karl Philipp von Greiffenklau (1749–1754). The continent of Europe is symbolised by a crowd of allegorical figures representing Christianity, military power and the flowering of the arts and sciences. The artist produced preliminary studies for the figures, mainly using his preferred technique of red chalk, many of which have survived in a sketchbook in the Museo Correr, Venice. The Budapest study, presented by Gustav Nebehay in 1923, depicts Sculpture in a majestic *sotto in sù* (worm's-eye view). The model may have been the Venetian sculptor Antonio Bossi, a collaborator of the Tiepolo family.

ANDREA CZÉRE

139

Giambattista Pittoni   1687–1767

St Elizabeth of Hungary Distributing Alms, 1734

Oil on canvas, 72 × 42.5 cm

INVENTORY NUMBER: 6155
SELECTED REFERENCES: Franca Zava Boccazzi, *Pittoni*, Venice, 1979, p.122, no.37, fig.352; Vilmos Tátrai (ed.), *Summary Catalogue 1*, London and Budapest, 1991, p.97; Zsuzsanna Dobos, 'Giovanni Battista Pittoni: Elemosina di Santa Elisabetta', in Mauro Natale (ed.), *Itinerario Veneto: Dipinti e disegni del '600 e '700 veneziano del Museo di Belle Arti di Budapest*, exh.cat., Finarte, Milan, 1991, p.50, no.15; Klára Garas, 'Giovanni Battista Pittoni: Saint Elisabeth Distributing Alms', in Géza Galavics (ed.), *Crossroads: Baroque Art in Central Europe*, exh.cat., Budapesti Történeti Múzeum, Budapest, 1993, p.317, no.125

Like Giovanni Antonio Pellegrini, Giambattista Pittoni was one of the most accomplished painters of the second rank active in eighteenth-century Venice. His light and airy rococo confections were also strikingly popular with foreign patrons, and he exported a considerable body of work as far afield as Russia, Poland and Germany.

The present sketch is a finished study for the first altarpiece Pittoni executed for Germany, a lively conception representing the saintly Queen of Hungary dispensing charity in the form of bread rolls, which remains *in situ* in the Schlosskirche at Bad Mergentheim in Wurttemberg. Extensive documentation in the archives at Ludwigsburg allows the progress of the commission to be followed in considerable detail, and reveals that Clemens August, Archbishop-Elector of Cologne, set the process in motion on 10 February 1734 with an order for three

---

altarpieces for the Schlosskirche to be commissioned in Rome. In the event, there must have been a change of plan, since his agent Triva, who travelled to Italy for the purpose, evidently did not limit himself to Rome. The *St Elizabeth*, which was not actually delivered until 1736, is the only one of the three altarpieces to have survived, but – on the assumption that they were all by the same artist – the deal must have been struck in Venice, since that is where Pittoni was based. The compositional differences between this canvas and the full-scale altarpiece are minimal, but it is only in the former that it is still possible to appreciate fully the bravura of Pittoni's handling and the brilliance of his colours.

DAVID EKSERDJIAN

140

Giovanni Antonio Pellegrini   1675–1741

Christ Healing the Paralytic, 1731

Oil on canvas, 95 × 50 cm

INVENTORY NUMBER: 654
SELECTED REFERENCES: Vilmos Tátrai (ed.), *Summary Catalogue 1*, London and Budapest, 1991, p.95; Zsuzsanna Dobos, 'Giovanni Antonio Pellegrini: Cristo guarisce il paralitico', in Mauro Natale (ed.), *Itinerario Veneto: Dipinti e disegni del '600 e '700 veneziano del Museo di Belle Arti di Budapest*, exh.cat., Finarte, Milan, 1991, p.48, no.14; Klára Garas, 'Giovanni Battista Pittoni: Saint Elisabeth Distributing Alms', in Géza Galavics (ed.), *Crossroads: Baroque Art in Central Europe*, exh.cat., Budapesti Történeti Múzeum, Budapest, 1993, p.314, no.122; George Knox, *Antonio Pellegrini, 1675–1741*, Oxford and New York, 1994, p.228, no.P.31, pl.167

Giovanni Antonio Pellegrini, like his fellow-Venetians Sebastiano Ricci and Giambattista Tiepolo, enjoyed considerable international success by virtue of his secular frescoes and altarpieces, which variously appealed to important patrons all over Europe. From 1708 to 1713, he was in England, where his two greatest triumphs were his decorative cycles for Kimbolton Castle and Castle Howard, the latter sadly now largely destroyed, but he also worked in and for such centres as Paris, The Hague, Dresden, Prague and Vienna.

The present canvas is a fluidly executed sketch for a monumental altarpiece (still *in situ*) that Pellegrini painted for the Karlskirche in Vienna. This church, the masterpiece of Johann Bernard Fischer von Erlach (1656–1723), was a pet project of the Emperor Charles VI. Work began on it in 1716, and between 1725 and 1730 Johann Michael Rottmayr was engaged on the frescoing of the interior. Both Pellegrini and Ricci were awarded commissions for altarpieces in 1731, and they had presumably both delivered their works by the time of the latter's death in 1734. A comparison of the present canvas with the finished work reveals the fact that this truly was Pellegrini's last thought concerning the composition, since there were no subsequent changes of plan. As was so often the case with long-range commissions, neither artist actually visited the Austrian capital, but the luminous colour scheme here accords well with the whites, pinks and golds of the setting. Conversely, the conception is both solemn and static, with the exception of the figure of the kneeling apostle in the bottom left-hand corner who recoils in wonder at the miracle.

DAVID EKSERDJIAN

141

Philipp Jakob Straub 1706–1774

St Roch, 1757

Painted limewood, height 121 cm

142

Philipp Jakob Straub

St Sebastian, 1757

Painted limewood, height 119 cm

HUNGARIAN NATIONAL GALLERY, INVENTORY NUMBERS: 4964, 4963
INVENTORY NUMBER: Mária Aggházy, *A barokk szobrászat Magyarországon*, 3 vols, Budapest 1959, 1, pp.140–41, 282, 2, pp.52, 76, 3, figs 259–60; Mária G. Aggházy, 'Steierische Beziehungen der ungarländischen Barockkunst', *Acta Historiae Artium*, 13 (1967), pp.338–43, figs 18–19; Miklós Mojzer (ed.), *The Hungarian National Gallery: The Old Collections*, Budapest, 1984, no.175; Géza Galavics (ed.), *Barokk művészet Közép-Európában: Utak és találkozások / Baroque Art in Central Europe: Crossroads*, exh.cat., Budapest History Museum, Budapest, 1993, nos 199–200

These exquisite rococo wood statues of SS. Roch and Sebastian came to Budapest from the parish church at Egervár in Zala County, Western Hungary. In 1757 Count Ignác Széchényi, the patron of the church, commissioned a large new tabernacle for the high altar, which had been created in 1730. The two statues originally stood in the niches of the tabernacle, where now copies of them can be seen. The two saints, protectors against the plague, represent suffering and pain. Wearing a pilgrim's cloak, St Roch looks upward with a tortured expression: his lips are parted, he is about to cry out, and he points to the wound on his leg. Next to him is the dog that brought him bread when he was suffering from the plague. Tied to a tree and pierced with arrows, the martyr St Sebastian endures his agony solemnly and with resignation. His head droops onto his shoulder and tears fall from his closed eyes.

These statues are attributed to Philipp Jakob Straub on stylistic grounds. Born into a family of Württemberg sculptors, Straub moved to Vienna in 1727 with his brother, the future Munich court sculptor Johann Baptist Straub (1704–1784), and he attended the Academy in Vienna from 1730 to 1733. He eventually settled in Graz and married the widow of the sculptor Johann Jakob Schoy (1686-1733), inheriting his workshop and clientele. A sculptor in wood and stone, he received commissions from the church, the aristocracy and the bourgeoisie. The activity of his workshop extended to several towns around Egervár (among them Ercsi and Szécsisziget) in the Transdanubia region, where the patron – and indeed all of the Széchenyi family – maintained active economic and artistic ties with Graz.

The dramatic and emotionally rich South German rococo idiom of the art of Philipp Jakob Straub made a great contribution to the tradition of woodcarving in the Steier region. Straub also possessed brilliant anatomical skills, which he owed to his years in Vienna. The complex attitude of the sensual, beautiful figure of St Sebastian, the way the light slips softly over it, is a case in point. The main feature of the statue of St Roch is the virtuoso treatment of the drapery; the fluttering, deep folds of the costume reveal a tension between light and shade. Their outstanding sense of volume, delicate and subtle colouring, and the profound emotions they display,

mark these statues out as among the finest examples of Hungarian rococo sculpture.

ZSUZSANNA BODA

143

Jakob Bogdány before 1660–1724

Still-life with Fruit, Parrots and White Cockatoo, 1710s

Oil on canvas, 98 × 128.5 cm

HUNGARIAN NATIONAL GALLERY, INVENTORY NUMBER: 3681
SELECTED REFERENCE: Miklós Rajnai, *Jacob Bogdani (c.1660–1724)*, exh.cat., Richard Green, London, 1989, no.7

Jakob Bogdány left his home town of Eperjes (today Prešov, Slovakia) in the 1670s and temporarily settled in Vienna. Nothing is known about his artistic education, but he turned up in Amsterdam in 1684 as a painter of flower and fruit still-lifes. The Dutch experience would determine his career, its influence evident in the treatment of colour and subtle technical features in his still-life paintings, and the example of Melchior d'Hondecoeter (1636–1695) in the genre scenes with birds. In June 1688 Bogdány was living in London where his Dutch-style still-lifes quickly earned him a considerable reputation among the aristocracy, and he received many of his commissions from the royal family. As a token of his artistic and social standing he was naturalised in 1700, and bought an estate near London. Around then he dropped the epithet 'Hungarus' he had occasionally used before. He was active as a respected and successful painter to the end of his life, and maintained links with expatriate Hungarian and Transylvanian Protestants, especially in England.

Bogdány usually signed (here at lower right) but never dated his works. From paintings of flowers and fruit typical of his early years, he moved on around 1700 to produce pictures that mostly featured exotic birds and elements of classical architecture, a genre of which Bogdány would remain the first, and for some time the most outstanding, representative. He had the opportunity to study the exotic birds of his paintings at the Windsor aviary of one of his most important patrons, Admiral George Churchill. Lifelike and depicted with objective accuracy, his 'models' appeared in an identical setting in more than one of his paintings.

ENIKŐ BUZÁSI

144

Jan van der Heyden 1637–1712

Corner of a Room, 1712

Oil on canvas, 75 × 63.5 cm

INVENTORY NUMBER: 201
SELECTED REFERENCES: Ildikó Ember, *Delights for the Senses: Dutch and Flemish Still-life Paintings from Budapest*, exh.cat., Leigh Yawkey Woodson Art Museum, Wausau, 1989, pp. 82–83, no.21; *Leselust: Niederländische Malerei von Rembrandt bis Vermeer*, exh.cat., Schirn Kunsthalle, Frankfurt, 1993, pp.220–21, no.43; Ildikó Ember and Zsuzsa Urbach (eds), *Summary Catalogue 2*, Budapest, 2000, p.83; Ildikó Ember, in E. Mai, S.Paarlberg, G.J.M. Weber et al., *Vom Adel der Malerei: Holland um 1700*, exh.cat., Wallraf-Richartz-Museum, Cologne, Dordrechts Museum, and Museumslandschaft Hessen, Kassel 2007, no.21; Ildikó Ember, *Dutch and Flemish Seventeenth- and Eighteenth-century Still-life Paintings in the Budapest Museum of Fine Arts*, The Hague, forthcoming, pp 136–39, no.44

It would be an understatement to describe Jan van der Heyden as a man of parts. Not only was he was a superb painter, above all of radiant townscapes of his native Amsterdam, but he was also a brilliant

engineer, who designed the city's street lighting as well as a revolutionary new type of fire engine, about which he wrote a book illustrated with his own etchings (1669).

Both at the beginning and at the end of his career, he executed still-lifes, of which only a dozen or so survive. The present example must have been painted in the last year of his life, since he delightedly gives his age as 75 in an almost invisibly diminutive signature on the red damask seat of the chair. The luminous precision with which he conjures up this interior in all its richness and variety is indeed remarkable, but it is also immediately apparent that what is being represented is not merely a slice of life. In part, this is a celebration of exotica, with oriental silks and carpets, Chinese porcelain, a Japanese sword and a hanging armadillo all on display, but more importantly it is a meditation on the transitory nature of life. Heavenly and earthly globes, together with the open volume of Joan Blaeu's *Atlas Maior* (1665), underline the extent of the physical universe, but the Bible in the vernacular at bottom right is open at the Book of Ecclesiastes, whose most famous motto is 'Vanity, vanity, all is vanity'. In the same spirit, the painting of the *Death of Dido* over the fireplace (after a print by Pietro Testa) is a grim reminder of the fickleness of human love.

DAVID EKSERDJIAN

145

Jean-Baptiste Greuze 1725–1805

Portrait of Paul Randon de Boisset, 1773

Oil on canvas, 73 × 58 cm

INVENTORY NUMBER: 1345
SELECTED REFERENCES: Ágnes Szigethi, *Menschenbild in Werken Alter Meister vom 16. bis 18. Jahrhundert*, exh.cat., Gemäldegalerie im Bodemuseum, Berlin, 1987, no.5; Vilmos Tátrai (ed.), *Summary Catalogue 1*, London and Budapest, 1991, p.140; Colin B. Bailey, *Patriotic Taste: Collecting Modern Art in Pre-revolutionary Paris*, New Haven and London, 2002, pp. 26–27; Ágnes Szigethi, 'Jean-Baptiste Greuze: Ritratto di Randon de Boisset', in Flavio Caroli (ed.), *Il Gran Teatro del Mondo: L'Anima e il Volto del Settecento*, exh.cat., Palazzo Reale, Milan, 2003, p.280, no.I.102; Ágnes Szigethi, *Old French Painting: Sixteenth to Eighteenth Centuries (The Collections of the Museum of Fine Arts, 6)*, Budapest 2004, pp.191–92, no.89; Anne Leclair, 'Une vente secrète en 1765: la correspondance inédite entre Pierre Paul Louis Randon de Boisset (1709–1776) et le marquis de Voyer d'Argenson (1772–1782)', *Bulletin de la Société de l'Histoire de l'Art français*, 2006, pp.152–54

Jean-Baptiste Greuze was enormously admired in his own day, not least by the novelist, philosopher and art critic Denis Diderot. He was famed for his sentimental scenes of everyday life, such as *Marriage Contract* (now in the Louvre), which were inspired by seventeenth-century Dutch genre painting, and for his mawkishly titillating representations of half-dressed young girls. His longevity meant he had the grim fate of outlasting the taste for his art, although – perhaps unexpectedly – he was patronised by Napoleon and his circle in his latter years.

This darkly impressive portrait of one of the great art collectors of the day, the Receveur Général des Finances, Randon de Boisset (1709–1776), reveals Greuze's perhaps surprising gift for capturing a likeness, and at the same time the esteem in which he was evidently held by one of the supreme connoisseurs of the age. Very much in line with the taste of the time, the great strength of Randon de Boisset's collection was its holdings of Dutch and Flemish masterpieces. The catalogue of his paintings and drawings, which were auctioned the year after his death, referred to his collection as 'containing the rarest that Flanders and Holland have produced'. It featured such names as Dou, Murillo, Rembrandt, Rubens, Teniers and Van de Velde, but Randon de Boisset also owned French paintings of his own century and the previous one, including Nicolas Poussin's early *Bacchanalian Revel before a Term*, now in the National Gallery, London, and Jean-Antoine Watteau's *Les Plaisirs du Bal*, now in the Dulwich Picture Gallery.

DAVID EKSERDJIAN

146

Thomas Rowlandson   1756/57–1827

Gluttons, c.1800–05

Watercolour, 244 × 234 mm

INVENTORY NUMBER: 1935-2641
SELECTED REFERENCE: John Hayes, *Rowlandson: Watercolours and Drawings*, London, 1972

Thomas Rowlandson, who trained at the Royal Academy Schools in London from 1772, and exhibited at the Annual Exhibition in 1775, was the supreme master of the art of caricature – as opposed to political cartoon – of his age. He was also a very considerable topographical artist, whose prospects of town and country are invariably populated by a cast of characters who might have stepped from the pages of the novels of Laurence Sterne or Henry Fielding, both of whose works he illustrated. In spite of their frequently grotesque subject-matter, the handling of his drawings and watercolours, a good number of which achieved a wider currency as prints and through their publication in illustrated books, is unfailingly elegant.

If Rowlandson's reputation suffered as a consequence of Victorian prudery, then these days his work is more likely to be underestimated precisely because its mockery of human frailty tends to be so unfailingly good-natured and cheerful, especially when compared with the occasionally demented savagery of his contemporary, James Gillray (1756–1815). Yet the present example, which is signed in the bottom left-hand corner, shows that Rowlandson could at times be the very opposite of toothless. Here the fluttering delicacy of the pen line brings to life two hideous creatures: a woman with a foreshortened pig-like snout, sausage fingers, and a massive embonpoint, keeping company with a man whose most arresting features are his exploding drinker's nose and mighty pot belly. Rowlandson's works are not easily dated with any precision, but the treatment of the man in particular is very similar in spirit to a memorable caricature of a judge of about the same date (Tate).

DAVID EKSERDJIAN

147

Sir Joshua Reynolds PRA   1723–1792

Portrait of Admiral Sir Edward Hughes, 1786–87

Oil on canvas, in a feigned oval, 76 × 63 cm

INVENTORY NUMBER: 693
SELECTED REFERENCES: Klára Garas (ed.), *Trésors des Musées du Budapest*, exh.cat., Palais des Beaux-Arts, Bordeaux, 1972, no.76; David Mannings, *Sir Joshua Reynolds: A Complete Catalogue of His Paintings*, New Haven and London, 2000, pp.268–69, no.961, fig.1498; Ildikó Ember and Imre Takács (eds), *Summary Catalogue 3*, Budapest, 2003, p.148; Zsuzsanna Dobos, 'Sir Joshua Reynolds: Ritratto dell'ammiraglio Sir Edward Hughes', in Vilmos Tátrai (ed.), *Da Raffaello a Goya: Ritratti dal Museo di Belle Arti di Budapest*, exh.cat., Palazzo Bricherasio, Turin, 2004, p.98, no.36

Sir Joshua Reynolds was both a tremendously prolific and – at his best – inspired portrait painter, but he was also the founding father and first President of the Royal Academy of Arts, the author of *Discourses on Art* (1769–90), and last but not least a notable collector of Old Master drawings. Born in Plympton in Devon, where his father – a former fellow of Balliol College, Oxford – was the headmaster of the local grammar school, he transformed the standing of artists in Great Britain, and ended his career showered in honours, many of which (including an honorary doctorate from Oxford) would hitherto never have been awarded to a mere painter.

Reynolds kept precise records of sittings, so we know that this enchanting likeness, set within a fictive oval frame, of his near-contemporary, Sir Edward Hughes (1717 or 1720–1794), as well as a full-length in a totally different pose (now in the National Maritime Museum, Greenwich) and two untraced head-and-shoulders portraits, all date from 1786–87. The sitter is represented wearing a new type of vice admiral's full dress uniform, which was authorised in 1783 but was only to last for four years, together with the star and ribbon of the Order of the Bath. He is a splendidly rubicund and genial presence, whose white wig perfectly offsets a plump cheek the colour of rare roast beef. Hughes, who died – according to his obituary – 'full of years and honour', had been involved in a number of engagements during his naval career, and most notably under Sir Charles Saunders at the taking of Quebec in 1759.

DAVID EKSERDJIAN

148

Thomas Hudson   c.1701–1779

Portrait of a Lady, 1740s

Oil on canvas, 127.5 × 101.5 cm

INVENTORY NUMBER: 3963
SELECTED REFERENCES: Ildikó Ember and Imre Takács (eds), *Summary Catalogue 3*, Budapest, 2003, p.144 (as Hogarth); Orsolya Radványi, 'William Hogarth (?): Ritratto di donna', in Flavio Caroli (ed.), *Il Gran Teatro del Mondo: L'Anima e il Volto del Settecento*, exh.cat., Palazzo Reale, Milan, 2003, p.136, no.I.31 (as Hogarth(?)); Axel Vécsey, 'Brit gyűjtemény a Szépművészeti Múzeumban', *Artmagazin*, 6, 4 (2008), pp.87–88 (where first attributed to Thomas Hudson)

The English painter Thomas Hudson was an important link in two separate artistic chains. A portrait specialist both in the south-west of England, including its artistic capital, Bath, and after 1740 exclusively in London, he was the pupil and son-in-law of Jonathan Richardson (1665–1745), but more significantly he was the teacher of Sir Joshua Reynolds. At the same time, he was a major art collector, celebrated for having assembled distinguished holdings of drawings not only by the likes of Rubens, Van Dyck and Guercino, but also by his contemporaries. Many of these sheets were acquired by Hudson at the Richardson sale in 1747, and were to pass after his death into Reynolds's collection. It is possible to trace their genealogy as a happy consequence of the fact that since the time of Sir Peter Lely – and occasionally even nowadays – collectors have stamped their drawings with marks of ownership.

Hudson made his definitive move to London when Richardson retired, and the present portrait, which was formerly assumed to be by William Hogarth and has only recently been attributed to Hudson, may be dated to his first decade in the metropolis on grounds of style. The middle-aged sitter is anonymous and does not give the impression of having been a person of any great importance. Hudson presents her to our attention with a plain-speaking dignity that is characteristic of an unpretentious strand within English portraiture, although by the second half of the 1750s this approach was losing out to the greater ambition and bravura of his erstwhile student Reynolds. Hudson delegated the finishing of the costume in his portraits to the noted drapery painter Joseph van Aken (c.1699–1749) from 1743 to the latter's death.

DAVID EKSERDJIAN

149

Ádám Mányoki   1673–1757

Self-portrait, c.1711

Oil on canvas, 87 × 61.5 cm

HUNGARIAN NATIONAL GALLERY, INVENTORY NUMBER: 6508
SELECTED REFERENCE: Enikő Buzási, *Ádám Mányoki (1673–1757): Monographie und Oeuvrekatalog*, Budapest, 2003, pp.67–69, 270–71, no.A.92

One of the most significant painters of the Baroque era in Hungary, Ádám Mányoki began his career in Hanover and Hamburg, and at the beginning of the eighteenth century he worked in Berlin for, among others, Friedrich Wilhelm, Crown Prince of Prussia. Between 1707 and 1709 he worked in Hungary as a portrait painter at the court of Prince Ferenc Rákóczy II, who sent him to Holland in 1709 and later to Berlin. There he met Antoine Pesne, painter to the Prussian court, whose portraits had a profound influence on him. From 1713 onwards he was in the employ of Augustus II the Strong, King of Poland and Elector of Saxony, who appointed him court portrait painter in 1717.

Mányoki is remembered as a painter of Saxon rulers, but thanks to his unostentatious, intimate portraits he also received commissions from bourgeois and intellectual circles in Leipzig. After a short stay in Vienna he returned to Hungary in 1724; however, due to a lack of patrons and commissions, he finally settled in Dresden in 1731. His late works were chiefly shaped by the demands of eighteenth-century German art collectors. This agreeably direct self-portrait melds the influence of Pesne's Venetian-inspired painting with Mányoki's Northern German experience. Mányoki's biographer Christian Ludwig von Hagedorn relates how in his youth the artist trained himself by copying works in the Salzdahlum collection of Anton-Ulrich, Duke of Braunschweig-Wolfenbüttel. Familiarity with a self-portrait by Johann Heinrich Roos shines through Mányoki's own portrait, in particular in the motif of the low-cut shirt.

The painting was first recorded in 1775 in the gallery of the Bavarian electors at the Palace of

Schleissheim. It subsequently passed to the Museum of Fine Arts, Budapest in 1931 by exchange.

ENIKŐ BUZÁSI

150

Jan Kupecký   1667–1740

Self-portrait of the Artist with His Wife and Son, c.1719

Oil on canvas, 113 × 91.2 cm

INVENTORY NUMBER: 3922
SELECTED REFERENCES: E. Jackisch, *Das Budapester Familienbild des Johannes Kupezky*, diss., Frankfurt University, 1991; A. Fáy, 'Le dilemma d'une mise au jour: La restauration de l'Autoportrait de l'artiste avec sa femme et son fils par Johann Kupezky', *Bulletin du Musée Hongrois des Beaux-Arts*, 85 (1996), pp.26, 123; Eduard A.Šafařík, *Johann Kupezky 1666–1740: Ein Meister des Barockporträts*, exh.cat., Aachen, 2001, pp.43–46, no.8; Ildikó Ember and Imre Takács (eds), *Summary Catalogue 3*, Budapest, 2003, p.72; Annamária Gosztola, 'Johann Kupezky: Autoritratto con moglie e figlio', in Vilmos Tátrai (ed.), *Da Raffaello a Goya: Ritratti dal Museo di Belle Arti di Budapest*, exh.cat., Palazzo Bricherasio, Turin, 2004, p.127, no.54

Jan Kupecký was born in Bohemia, but accompanied the painter Benedikt Claus (1632/33–1707) – whose daughter he later married – to Vienna at the age of fifteen. Three years later the two artists travelled together to Italy. Kupecký settled in Rome, yet it was not until about 1700 that he fully established himself as a portraitist. Around 1709, he returned to Vienna at the invitation of Prince Johann Adam Andreas I of Liechtenstein, only to make a final move to Nuremberg in 1723, possibly to flee religious persecution (he was a member of the sect of Moravian Brothers).

Kupecký's most remarkable works are his unusually intimate portraits of himself, either alone or with various members of his immediate family. The present canvas, which may never have been satisfactorily completed (the child's anatomically impossible right arm belongs to a later and different conception, which explains its infelicitous appearance), is one of the most movingly immediate of the entire series. The beautiful description of it in the biography of the artist, published in 1758, and written by his friend, fellow-painter and executor Johann Caspar Füssli (1706–1782), the father of Henry Fuseli, deserves to be quoted in full: 'This is a piece that shines out from among his other works like a diamond. Here there are all the magical effects of light and shade in the man, and of freedom and gentleness of the brush in the woman, arranged in such a wondrous relationship that it is very hard for a painter to determine whether it is above all the spirit of Rembrandt or of Van Dyck that one most marvels at in it.'

DAVID EKSERDJIAN

151.1

Franz Xaver Messerschmidt   1736–1783

Self-portrait, Laughing, c.1780

Alabaster, diameter 9.5 cm

151.2

Franz Xaver Messerschmidt

Self-portrait, Serious, c.1780

Alabaster, diameter 8 cm

151.3

Franz Xaver Messerschmidt

Self-portrait with Wig, c.1780

Alabaster, diameter 10 cm

INVENTORY NUMBERS: 8522, 8524, 8529
SELECTED REFERENCES: Maria Pötzl-Malikova, *Franz Xaver Messerschmidt*, Vienna and Munich, 1982, nos 55–57; Michael Krapf (ed.), *Franz Xaver Messerschmidt*, exh.cat., Österreichische Galerie Belvedere, Vienna, 2003, no.60

Franz Xaver Messerschmidt is mainly known today for his unique series of character heads. Born into the Straub family of sculptors, he started carving alongside his uncles, and later continued his studies at the Vienna Academy of Art. The success of his early bronze busts of the Empress Maria Theresa and her husband Franz Stefan of Lorraine (both in the Österreichische Galerie Belvedere, Vienna) led to a whole series of further commissions. Messerschmidt soon became the imperial family's preferred sculptor, but his rapid rise to fame was halted by a mysterious illness. Although he seemed certain to secure a job as professor in the Department of Sculpture at the Vienna Academy of Art, he was denied the promotion on the grounds of mental illness, and was pensioned off when he was barely forty years old. Deeply hurt, he then moved to Pozsony (now Bratislava, Slovakia). There he spent most of his time working on his famous series of character heads.

This series of fifty-four busts depicting grimacing faces rather than conventional character studies is unique in the history of sculpture, and no fewer than three are in the Museum of Fine Arts in Budapest. Although studies of physiognomy and expression, which at the time were enjoying a new renaissance, certainly influenced them, their meaning and the artist's intentions remain a puzzle to this day. Due to the great popularity of his larger character heads, Messerschmidt's small-scale alabaster medallions tend to be overlooked. There were only a small number of them, twelve of which are extant, and seven have ended up in the Museum of Fine Arts. Though small in size, they present a faithful reflection of the artist's extravagant style, apparent also in the series of character heads; one, *Self-portrait, Laughing*, even has an equivalent among the character heads, in the bust entitled *The Artist as He Imagined Himself Laughing* (private collection). This is the only one of the character heads to depict decidedly positive feelings, but the alabaster medallions are lighter in spirit and indulge in playful evocations of the artist's changing moods. At the same time, they are reminiscent of caricatures, which were also popular at the time.

MIRIAM SZŐCS

152.1

Franz Xaver Messerschmidt   1736–1783

Archduchess Maria Christina, c.1780

Alabaster, diameter 8 cm

152.2

Franz Xaver Messerschmidt

Duke Albert of Sachsen-Teschen, c.1780

Alabaster, diameter 8 cm

INVENTORY NUMBERS: 8527, 8523
SELECTED REFERENCES: Maria Pötzl-Malikova, *Franz Xaver Messerschmidt*, Vienna and Munich, 1982, nos 58–59; Michael Krapf (ed.), *Franz Xaver Messerschmidt*, exh.cat., Österreichische Galerie Belvedere, Vienna, 2003, no.62

Franz Xaver Messerschmidt was fond of recording his friends and patrons for posterity on alabaster medallions. The German writer of the Enlightenment period, Friedrich Nicolai – a great enemy of Goethe – recounts that while he was chatting with the sculptor in his house in Pozsony (now Bratislava, in Slovakia), Messerschmidt had carved a medallion portrait of him in a couple of hours. This story well illustrates the artist's brilliant craftsmanship and skill, equally apparent in his character heads. Alabaster was also favoured for his portrait heads: although it gives the same effect as marble, it is much softer and can be scratched even with a fingernail, making it an ideal medium for the swiftly and brilliantly carved medallions.

Messerschmidt's link to the aristocracy remained unbroken in Pozsony too, and they frequently commissioned works from him after he withdrew into self-imposed exile from Vienna. One of the most important patrons of his Pozsony years, Duke Albert of Sachsen-Teschen (1738–1822), the newly appointed Habsburg governor, moved to Pozsony (then the capital of Hungary) at the same time as Messerschmidt. The duke is best known to posterity because his enormous collection of prints and drawings laid the foundation for the superlative graphic holdings at the Albertina in Vienna, which is also named after him. As well as making his portrait Messerschmidt fashioned busts of him, in marble and lead (Albertina, Vienna, and Bayerisches Nationalmuseum, Munich). The pair to this medallion portrait of the duke is that of his wife, Archduchess Maria Christina, the favourite daughter of Maria Theresa, ruler of the Habsburg Empire. Contrary to the custom of the ruling houses of the time, the marriage of the ducal couple was made not for diplomatic reasons, but for love. Later, after Maria Christina's death, Albert had a tomb made to the memory of his beloved by the neoclassical sculptor Antonio Canova (Augustinerkirche, Vienna).

MIRIAM SZŐCS

153

Angelica Kauffmann RA   1741–1807

Portrait of a Woman at Her Toilet, 1795

Oil on canvas, 131 × 103 cm

INVENTORY NUMBER: 444
SELECTED REFERENCES: Bettina Baumgärtel (ed.), *Angelika Kauffmann: Retrospektiv*, exh.cat., Kunstmuseum, Düsseldorf, Haus der Kunst, Munich, and Bündner Kunstmuseum, Chur, 1998, pp.306–07, no.166; Rainer Michaelis, 'Mrs Smith als Aphrodite bei der Toilette', in István Barkóczi (ed.), *Von Raphael bis Tiepolo aus der Sammlung des hochfürstlichen Hauses Esterházy*, exh.cat., Schirn Kunsthalle, Frankfurt, 1999, pp.406–07, no.170; Ildikó Ember and Imre Takács (eds), *Summary Catalogue 3*, Budapest, 2003, p.68

Angelica Kauffmann was born in Switzerland, but spent her professional career moving between Rome, Venice and London, where she was a great ally – or rather more – of Sir Joshua Reynolds and one of only two women who were founder members of the Royal Academy of Arts. Her greatest strength was as a portrait painter, although in England she is best known for her decorative history paintings, often inserted into ceilings, two of which are in Burlington House, London. Her second husband, the painter Antonio Zucchi (1728–1795), was a specialist in this line of work, and it has been suggested that many so-called Kauffmanns may actually be by him.

The present canvas, which is signed and dated as having been executed in Rome in 1795, appears to have been a second version of a now lost portrait of a Mrs Smith painted in May of that same year, and was commissioned in June by the Dowager Princess Esterházy, who is recorded as having paid a fee of 240 crowns for it in February 1796. There is a sketch for the composition in the Vorarlberger Landesmuseum, Bregenz, which reveals that from the outset Kauffmann determined to replicate the attitude of one of the most celebrated of all classical statues, the so-called *Callipygian Venus* ('Venus of the beautiful bottom'), which formed part of the Farnese Collection in Rome, and is now in the Museo Nazionale, Naples. To a modern eye, the idea of quoting such an attitude may seem bizarrely convoluted, especially considering the otherwise wholesome and not especially flattering treatment of the unidentified sitter and the realism of the still-life on her dressing-table.

DAVID EKSERDJIAN

154

Francisco José de Goya y Lucientes   1746–1828
Portrait of Manuela de Ceán Bermúdez, c.1790–93

Oil on canvas, 121 × 84.5 cm

INVENTORY NUMBER: 3792
SELECTED REFERENCES: Marianne Haraszti-Takács, *Spanish Masters from Zurbarán to Goya*, Budapest, 1984, nos 41–42; Vilmos Tátrai (ed.), *Summary Catalogue 1*, London and Budapest, 1991, p.153; José Luis Morales y Marín, *Goya: catálogo de la pintura*, Zaragoza, 1994, pp.226–27, no.225; Éva Nyerges, *Obras maestras del arte español, Museo de Bellas Artes de Budapest*, exh.cat., Banco Bilbao Vizcaya, Madrid, and Museo de Bellas Artes, Bilbao, 1996, pp.164–66, no.45; Manuela B. Mena Marqués: 'Francisco de Goya: Retrato de doña Manuela Camas y de las Heras (?)', in Manuel-Jesús González (ed.), *Campomanes y su tiempo*, exh.cat., Fundación Santander Central Hispano, Madrid, 2003, pp.268–69; Éva Nyerges, *Spanish Paintings: The Collections of the Museum of Fine Arts, Budapest*, Budapest, 2008, p.194, no.90

The extraordinary evolution of Francisco José de Goya's unusually long and prolific career as a painter, draughtsman and printmaker stretched from the sunlit rococo optimism of his early works to the savage independence of his late black paintings. A stunningly insightful portraitist – whether of the degenerate members of the Spanish royal family, the great and the good of the day, his intimate friends, or indeed himself – he was also the most remarkable chronicler of the political turmoil and folly of his age, and one of the most truly inimitable, if paradoxically also deeply influential, artists who has ever lived.

The present canvas is generally agreed to represent the wife of Goya's longstanding friend and supporter Juan Agustín Ceán Bermúdez (1749–1829), and to be the pendant to a portrait of closely similar dimensions in a private collection, which shows her husband sitting cross-legged at a table. Ceán Bermúdez worked at the Banco de San Carlo in Madrid, and is presumed to have assisted Goya to secure a commission to paint five of its directors in 1785. In 1800, he published his still valuable *Diccionario histórico de los más ilustres profesores de las bellas artes in España*.

Goya presents the stylishly dressed sitter looking up suddenly from her work, as if momentarily distracted

---

from her embroidery, but with the needle between the thumb and forefinger of her right hand still poised in readiness. This no doubt artfully contrived overall effect nevertheless conjures up an atmosphere of naturalness and ease, which is matched by the apparent directness of the woman's sympathetic expression.

DAVID EKSERDJIAN

155.1

Giuseppe Cades   1750–1799
Pinabello Pushes Bradamante into a Ravine, 1788

Pen and grey ink with brown wash and black chalk underdrawing, 531 × 366 mm

155.2

Giuseppe Cades
Argalia's Spirit Appears to Ferragù, 1788

Pen and grey ink with brown wash and black chalk underdrawing, 490 × 338 mm

INVENTORY NUMBERS: 2661, 2656
SELECTED REFERENCES: Andrea Czére, 'Esquisses nouvellement découvertes de Giuseppe Cades aux peintures murales à Ariccia', *Bulletin du Musée Hongrois des Beaux-Arts*, 56–57 (1981), pp.153–75, figs 103, 105; Andrea Czére, *Italienische Barockzeichnungen*, Hanau, 1990, no.37; Maria Teresa Caracciolo, *Giuseppe Cades et la Rome de son temps*, Paris, 1992, nos 105a, 105b

Although in recent decades his neoclassical paintings have been the subject of extensive research, the Roman Giuseppe Cades arguably still remains underrated as a draughtsman. After the colour and light that had characterised the rococo, the beauty of Cades's drawings lies in their accurate, steadfast and shape-defining line.

These two works, acquired with the Esterházy Collection in 1870, are part of a series of thirteen large drawings that depict various episodes taken from what is arguably the greatest poem of the Italian Renaissance, the heroic epic *Orlando Furioso* (1532) by Lodovico Ariosto (1474–1533). In the various compositions, most of which focus on just one or two figures, a lively or dramatic interpretation of events is given. The artist chose the critical moments in the heroes' destinies. On the first sheet, Pinabello is portrayed pushing Bradamante, who is searching for her lover, into a ravine. In the other scene, the spirit of Argalia, who has been killed in a duel, appears to the knight Ferragù in order to regain his helmet. The drawings were produced for a series of wall paintings at the Palazzo Chigi in Ariccia, near Rome, where two rooms were devoted to Ariosto's poetry. Cades gained inspiration for his compositions from drawings produced fifteen years earlier by Giovanni Battista Cipriani (1727–1785), which appeared in the 1773 Birmingham edition of *Orlando Furioso* in the form of prints by Francesco Bartolozzi (1727–1815). Cades used a number of motifs from these prints, but transformed the slightly saccharine scenes, endowing them with Roman grandeur. His refined taste, inspired by classical sculpture and the works of great Renaissance masters, is manifest in his figures, which are formed in accordance with classical proportions and ideals of beauty.

ANDREA CZÉRE

156

Sebastiano Ricci   1659–1734
Venus and Cupid with a Satyr, c.1716–20

Oil on canvas, 102 × 125.5 cm

INVENTORY NUMBER: 58.43
SELECTED REFERENCES: Jeffrey Daniels, *Sebastiano Ricci*, Hove, 1976, no.344; Vilmos Tátrai (ed.), *Summary Catalogue 1*, London and Budapest, 1991, p.102; Zsuzsanna Dobos, 'Sebastiano Ricci: Venere e Satiro', in Mauro Natale (ed.), *Itinerario Veneto: Dipinti e disegni del '600 e '700 veneziano del Museo di Belle Arti di Budapest*, exh.cat., Finarte, Milan, 1991, p.30, no.7; Annalisa Scarpa, *Sebastiano Ricci*, Milan, 2006, pp.168–69, no.69

Sebastiano Ricci was the first Venetian artist of real distinction since the Renaissance, and in that sense the founder of its eighteenth-century greatness, paving the way above all for Giambattista Tiepolo. His true master was Paolo Veronese (1528–1588), whose blond tonalities and light-hearted approach to mythological and historical subjects he devotedly but never slavishly emulated. He travelled far and wide, achieving a spectacular pan-European fame, as is triumphantly apparent in his commission from Lord Burlington for the staircase of Burlington House, London, for which he executed four mythologies.

The present work, which is recorded in a post-mortem inventory of the artist's possessions drawn up on 19–20 May 1734, is an entirely characteristic example of the way he looked backwards in order to move forwards. The subject of a lecherous satyr, half-man and half-beast, ogling a sleeping nude woman is found in paintings by such earlier sixteenth-century masters as Correggio and Titian (both of which have coincidentally ended up in the Louvre, Paris). However, the most probable source not only for the general arrangement of the composition, but also for the unmistakable direction of the satyr's gaze, is an engraving by Annibale Carracci of 1592, which also influenced a ravishing etching by Rembrandt. The major differences between Ricci's canvas and Annibale's print are the even more lusciously abandoned pose of the goddess of love, and the fact that here Cupid is fast asleep, whereas in the engraving he enjoins the intruder to silence by pressing his finger to his lips and thus connives in the goatish unveiling of his mother.

DAVID EKSERDJIAN

157

Giovanni Antonio Canal, called *Canaletto*   1697–1768
Lock at Dolo, c.1756

Oil on canvas, 30.5 × 44.5 cm

INVENTORY NUMBER: 78.14
SELECTED REFERENCES: W.G.Constable, revised by J.G.Links, *Canaletto: Giovanni Antonio Canal 1697–1768*, Oxford and New York, 1976, no.373; Zsuzsanna Dobos, 'Antonio Canal, detto Canaletto: Le porte del Dolo', in Mauro Natale (ed.), *Itinerario Veneto: Dipinti e disegni del '600 e '700 veneziano del Museo di Belle Arti di Budapest*, exh.cat., Finarte, Milan, 1991, pp.58–60, no.18; Vilmos Tátrai (ed.), *Summary Catalogue 1*, London and Budapest, 1991, p.18

Luca Carlevaris painted Venice before Canaletto, but being the first to do something by no means ensures one is the best. Since Canaletto, countless other artists, starting in his own lifetime with Francesco Guardi (1712–1793) and his own nephew Bernardo Bellotto, have followed his example and immortalised the Serenissima, but none – not even Turner – has surpassed him when it comes to capturing the magical quality of Venetian light. In consequence, for all that he executed views of other Italian cities, and indeed spent a decade in England, it is his views of Venice that have guaranteed his fame.

In addition to being a great painter, Canaletto was a superb draughtsman, and also a remarkable etcher. Unlike many other artists, who recycled their painted compositions in the form of prints, he not infrequently exploited his own etchings as sources of inspiration for pictures executed at a significantly later date. In this instance, the scene represented corresponds to a print that dates from the 1740s, but the present canvas was in all probability painted shortly after his return from England to Venice, where he is now known to have been by the end of 1755. The dimensions of this work correspond precisely with those of Canaletto's much admired *Torre di Marghera* (private collection) painted at much the same time, and it may well be that they were designed to go together, perhaps as elements in a series of picturesque views of the Veneto. The identification of the setting as Dolo is not in doubt.

DAVID EKSERDJIAN

158

Bernardo Bellotto   1721–1780

The Arno towards the Ponte Santa Trinita, Florence, 1742

Oil on canvas, 62 × 90 cm

INVENTORY NUMBER: 647
SELECTED REFERENCES: Ettore Camesasca, *L'Opera completa del Bellotto*, Milan, 1974, no.17; Vilmos Tátrai (ed.), *Summary Catalogue 1*, London and Budapest, 1991, p.8; Edgar Peters Bowron (ed.), *Bernardo Bellotto and the Capitals of Europe*, exh.cat., Museo Correr, Venice, and Museum of Fine Arts, Houston, 2001, pp.88–89, no.14; Bozena Anna Kowalczyk, 'The Arno towards the Ponte Santa Trinità, Florence', in Edgar Peters Bowron (ed.), *Bernardo Bellotto and the Capitals of Europe*, exh.cat., Museo Correr, Venice, and Museum of Fine Arts, Houston, 2001, pp.88–89, no.14; Gerlinde Gruber, 'Bernardo Bellotto: Florenz, Blick auf den Arno vom Ponte Vecchio Richtung Santa Trinità', in Wilfried Seipel (ed.), *Bernardo Bellotto, genannt Canaletto: Europäische Veduten*, exh.cat., Kunsthistorisches Museum, Vienna, 2005, pp.74–75, no.3; Zsuzsanna Dobos, 'Bernardo Bellotto: L'Arno à Florence', in Emmanuel Starcky (ed.), *Nicolas II Esterházy 1765–1833: Un prince hongrois collectionneur*, exh.cat., Musée national du château de Compiègne, 2007, pp.124–25, no.29

Bernardo Bellotto was Canaletto's nephew and pupil, and he too was almost exclusively a specialist painter of what the Italians term *vedute*. Although the word literally means 'views', *vedute* were never pure landscapes but rather architectural prospects, either of individual buildings or of townscapes. Historically it has been Bellotto's bad luck to live in his uncle's shadow, yet the greatest of his representations of Northern Europe are arguably more than a match for the latter's sunlit evocations of Venice and England, and are increasingly critically admired. Bellotto left Venice for good at a young age, and after spending time in and around Milan, he made his way to Dresden, where he worked for Augustus the Strong, Elector of Saxony and King of Poland. He then moved on to Vienna, before spending the final years of his career at the court of King Stanislaus Poniatowski of Poland in Warsaw.

The present early work already reveals Bellotto's darkly distinctive manner, and is one of a pair of views of Florence in Budapest (its pendant is a magnificent prospect of the Piazza della Signoria). Unsurprisingly, given his Venetian origins, Bellotto was captivated by the Arno and the higgledy-piggledy array of houses along its banks, and we may be forgiven for thinking he has turned it into a Tuscan substitute for the Grand Canal, even introducing a couple of surrogate gondolas. This view looks

upstream to the Ponte Santa Trinita and the Ponte alla Carraia beyond, while a closely related canvas in the Fitzwilliam Museum, Cambridge, concentrates on the Ponte Vecchio as seen from the embankment of the Ponte Santa Trinita.

DAVID EKSERDJIAN

159

Henry Fuseli RA   1741–1825

Portrait of the Artist's Wife, c.1790

Black pen and watercolour over black pencil, 228 × 178 mm

INVENTORY NUMBER: 1914-143
SELECTED REFERENCES: Gert Schiff, *Johann Heinrich Füssli, Oeuvrekatalog*, 2 vols, Zurich, 1973, I, p.549, no.1086; Andrea Czére (ed.), *Museum of Fine Arts, Budapest: Masterpieces from the Collection*, Budapest, 2006, p.125

Heinrich Füssli – Henry Fuseli is the anglicised form of his name – was born in Zurich, the son of the painter Johann Caspar Füssli (1706–1782). Having been ordained as a Zwinglian minister in 1761, he first visited England as early as 1764, at which point his ambitions were theological, philosophical and literary, but he was encouraged to become an artist by Sir Joshua Reynolds (1723–1792), whom he met around 1767–68. He only settled in London definitively in 1780, having spent the years from 1770 to 1778 in Italy. Always a prominent figure in literary as well as artistic circles, Fuseli was unquestionably the most daringly eccentric narrative painter and draughtsman of the age, specialising in themes from the works of such giants of the European grand tradition as Homer, Dante, Shakespeare and Milton, and achieving a unique blend of Michelangelesque muscularity and kinky gothick horror.

In 1788 Fuseli married the much younger Sophia Rawlins, who had been an amateur artist's model, and some of his most extraordinary drawings are of his new bride. Here, as so often, he portrays her sporting an extravagantly expansive and bizarre heart-shaped coiffure, in this instance complemented by enormous droplet earrings. She stares straight out at us, and her commanding presence is fully established, even though the forms of her dress tail off below the waist and the dark backdrop is not wholly finished. The use of the highly distinctive combination of pink and blue-grey washes found in the present sheet is entirely characteristic of the artist's work.

DAVID EKSERDJIAN

160

Jean-Antoine Watteau   1684–1721

Studies of Women and Drapery, c.1716–17

Black, red and white chalk on brownish paper, 242 × 337 mm

INVENTORY NUMBER: 1912-719
SELECTED REFERENCES: Louis-Antoine Prat and Pierre Rosenberg, *Antoine Watteau, 1684–1721: Catalogue raisonné des dessins*, 3 vols, Milan, 1996, no.496; Vera Kaposy, 'Studies of Women and a Drapery', in Teréz Gerszi (ed.), *Dürer to Dalí: Master Drawings in the Budapest Museum of Fine Arts*, Budapest, 1999, no.107

Jean-Antoine Watteau represented a refreshing current in French painting in contrast to official art in the era of Louis XIV (1638–1715). His works represent a radical change of taste towards a new kind of subject: the worlds of theatre and masquerade. Inspired principally

by sixteenth-century Venetian landscapes, Watteau introduced a genre known as *fêtes galantes*, in which elegant figures are gathered in a poetic landscape, dancing, playing music or acting. The originality of such scenes, on which he concentrated between 1714 and 1717, derives from the emotional interaction between the characters and their detachment from time and space.

The three studies on this sheet are unrelated to one another and were in all probability drawn at different times. Watteau seems to have considered each as a separate drawing, assembling them on a single page for reasons of economy or convenience, and only fortuitously creating a harmonious ensemble. The rapid sketches were executed in his characteristic technique, which employed three chalks, combining blacks, reds and whites. There have been attempts to identify the female figures with counterparts in two paintings of widely differing dates: the graceful walking woman has been associated with *Promenade on the Ramparts* (private collection) and the seated lady with the famous *Pilgrimage to the Island of Cythera* (Musée du Louvre, Paris). However, they do not precisely correspond to any of Watteau's painted figures. The Budapest sheet reveals the artist practising drawing for its own sake. Watteau's sketches of this kind were not intended as preparatory for specific paintings, nor did he pose models with particular figures in mind. Instead, he preserved his drawings and kept them to hand, using and re-using them in his painted compositions.

ESZTER SERES

161

Friedrich Heinrich Füger   1751–1818

Portrait of the Empress Maria Luisa, c.1790

Oil on canvas, 206 × 140 cm

INVENTORY NUMBER: 95-4
SELECTED REFERENCES: Ildikó Ember and Imre Takács (eds), *Summary Catalogue 3*, Budapest, 2003, p.43; Annamária Gosztola, 'Friedrich Heinrich Füger: L'imperatrice Maria Ludovica', in Vilmos Tátrai (ed.), *Da Raffaello a Goya: Ritratti dal Museo di Belle Arti di Budapest*, exh.cat., Palazzo Bricherasio, Turin, 2004, p.100, no.37; Robert Keil, *Heinrich Friedrich Füger (1751–1818): Nur wenigen ist es vergönnt das Licht der Wahrheit zu sehen*, Vienna, 2009, p.280, no.WV254

After a precocious start (he was already painting miniatures at the age of eight), followed by various setbacks, the decisive moment in Friedrich Heinrich Füger's career was his meeting in Dresden with the British ambassador, Sir Robert Murray Keith (1730–1795), whom he followed to Vienna in 1774. Keith set him up with various commissions at the court, and Füger was then awarded a scholarship to visit Italy, where he divided his time between Rome and Naples, and painted portraits and allegories for the Royal Palace of Caserta, finally returning to Vienna in 1783. He was appointed deputy director of the Akademie der Bildenden Künste, becoming its director in 1795, and then in 1806 took charge of the imperial gallery, the precursor of the Kunsthistorisches Museum.

The identity of the heroine of this imposing yet also affectionate unfinished portrait, which is a relatively recent addition to the collection, having been acquired in 1995, has in the past been the subject of some debate. There is a miniature on ivory of the same sitter at much the same age by Füger in the Metropolitan Museum of Art, New York, which is a portrait of the Empress Maria Luisa (1745–1792), who became the wife of the Emperor Leopold II (1747–1792) in 1765, which suggests a date around 1790. That portrait was previously thought to represent the Empress Maria Ludovika (1787–1816), who became the wife of the Emperor Franz II (1768–1835) in 1808, which would require it to be considerably later in date.

DAVID EKSERDJIAN

162

Melchior Steidl   1657–1727
Assumption of the Virgin, 1710–11
Pen and brown ink with grey wash, heightened with white on blue paper, 495 × 302 mm

INVENTORY NUMBER: 1019
SELECTED REFERENCES: Bruno Bushart, 'Melchior Steidls Entwürfe für die Fresken in der Schönenbergkirche zu Ellwangen', in Eberhard Ruhmer (ed.), *Eberhard Hanfstaengl zum 75. Geburtstag*, Munich, 1961, pp.95–111, fig.2; Viktoria Meinecke (Berg), *Die Fresken des Melchior Steidl*, diss., Munich University, 1971, p.184, no.233; Terez Gerszi (ed.), *Dürer to Dalí: Master Drawings in the Budapest Museum of Fine Arts*, Budapest, 1999, p.142, no.63; Josef Strasser, *Melchior Steidl (1657–1727): Die Zeichnungen*, exh.cat., Salzburger Barockmuseum, Salzburg, 1999, p.62, illus. on p.63, no.23

Melchior Steidl of Innsbruck served his apprenticeship under Johann Anton Gumpp (1654–1719), also originally from Innsbruck, who was court painter to Maximilian II Emanuel, Elector of Bavaria (1662–1726), in Munich. Steidl officially became a master in 1687 and worked mainly in Upper Austria and in the South German provinces. He is considered the most significant representative of the Southern German School of fresco painting and draughtsmanship around 1700. His art integrated the traditions formed in the late sixteenth-century court of Munich, with the influence of seventeenth-century Italian masters, notably Pietro da Cortona, Luca Giordano and Andrea Pozzo. Late in 1710, Steidl received a commission to paint the frescoes in the newly reconstructed church at Schönenberg near Ellwangen, a pilgrimage centre in Northern Swabia dedicated to the Madonna of Loreto.

This large sheet is a compositional study by Steidl for the ceiling fresco at Schönenberg. The painting, which occupies two vault sections in the nave and represents the Assumption and the Coronation of the Virgin, was executed in 1711. With its sweeping lines, richness of tone and ingenious sculptural effects, the drawing is a characteristic and seminal piece in Steidl's *oeuvre*. The dynamic composition echoes the altarpiece in the church of the Benedictine abbey of Göttweig (Lower Austria) painted by Johann Andreas Wolff (1652–1716) in 1694, which represents the same subject. The connection between Steidl's fresco and Wolff's altarpiece becomes obvious on closer inspection of the present study: it is not only certain dominant motifs and the arrangement of figures which are reminiscent of the Göttweig altarpiece, but also the proportions of the composition, although these underwent a slight transformation in the completed fresco. Until recently, Wolff was considered to have been Steidl's master, but this was probably not the case. Wolff and Steidl's recorded master, Johann Anton Gumpp, shared the title of court painter to the Elector of Munich. From the

1680s, when Steidl is presumed to have entered Gumpp's workshop, the two artists often collaborated. This would explain how Steidl came to be acquainted with his colleague's composition for the Göttweig altarpiece.

ANNA ECSEDY

163

Johann Georg Heintsch   1647–1712
Design for the St Francis Xavier Group on the Charles Bridge in Prague, c.1709
Pen and brown ink with grey wash, 327 × 265 mm

INVENTORY NUMBER: K.58.164
SELECTED REFERENCES: Pavel Preiss, 'J. G. Heinsch et les groupes des saints jésuites sur le Pont Charles des Prague', *Bulletin du Musée Hongrois des Beaux-Arts*, 43 (1974), pp.97–107; Vit Vlnas (ed.), *The Glory of the Baroque in Bohemia: Art, Culture and Society in the Seventeenth and Eighteenth Centuries*, exh.cat., Art Gallery of Prague Castle, St George's Convent, Wallenstein Riding School Gallery and Kinský Palace, Prague, 2001, p.421, illus. on p.422, no.II/4.43; Pavel Preiss, *Český barokní kresba / Baroque Drawing in Bohemia*, exh.cat., National Gallery, Prague, 2006, p.82, illus. on p.83

After two years' procrastination, the Jesuits of Prague decided to fill three spaces in the row of monumental statues forming a sculpture gallery on the Charles Bridge over the river Vltava. Ferdinand Maximilian Brokof (1688–1731) was commissioned in 1709 to create three groups of figures dominated by the figures of SS. Ignatius of Loyola, Francis Borgia and Francis Xavier. Contemporary practice usually relegated preliminary sketching of sculptures to painters. The present drawing by Johann Georg Heintsch, a painter much patronised by the Jesuits, represents an ideal rather than practicable conception for the Xavier group. The triangular composition is devoid of all artistic mannerism. It provides a precise, detailed depiction of figures in a traditionally structured, balanced arrangement, representing Xavier's extensive missionary work in Asia. The saint, standing tall on a pedestal at the focal point surrounded by a tableau of minor figures, wears a windswept surplice and a stole embroidered with a cross. He holds up the crucifix in the customary gesture of missionaries, to the people of Asia gathered below. In the foreground, two boys play with one of Xavier's attributes, the crab, which according to a legend restored the saint's crucifix that had been lost in sea. Two seated angels flank the pedestal, with symbols alluding to Xavier's missionary activities in their hands. One is holding a pilgrim's staff and hat, the other a rosary. It is not known what role Heintsch's sketch actually played in the planning of the St Francis Xavier group. Although the debates around the composition have, fortunately, been preserved in documents, and provide detailed information about the proposed designs and the progress of the composition, also they say nothing about Heintsch. His drawing represents a diffuse arrangement more fit for an altarpiece. It is far larger in scale than any group of statues on a column of the Charles Bridge could have been, and may only have served as inspiration for the (now lost) *modelletto* of Brokof and his work which, finished in 1711, has the dignified spirit of an ecclesiastical monument, and is now in the Lapidarium of the National Museum in Prague.

ANNA ECSEDY

164

Joseph Bergler   1753–1829
Venus Persuading Helen to Love Paris, 1799
Brown and grey ink with washes and some white heightening, 550 × 442 mm

INVENTORY NUMBER: 581
SELECTED REFERENCES: Teréz Gerszi and Zsuzsa Gonda (eds), *Nineteenth-century German, Austrian and Hungarian Drawings from Budapest*, exh.cat., Cleveland Museum of Art, University Art Museum, Berkeley, and Frick Art Museum, Pittsburgh, 1994, no.3; Roman Prahl (ed.), *Prag 1780–1830: Kunst und Kultur zwischen den Epochen und Völkern*, Prague, 2000, pp.94–95

Born in Salzburg, Joseph Bergler received his first drawing lessons from his father, and from 1776 he had a chance to spend a decade in Italy. In Rome he copied the works of Raphael and Domenichino, but he also came into contact with such representatives of neoclassicism as Angelica Kauffmann, Jacques-Louis David and Antonio Canova. In 1786, he settled in Passau, where he was soon appointed court painter. He was chosen in 1800 to head the newly founded Academy of Arts in Prague, where he served as director until his death, greatly influencing the development of Czech patriotic art.

Bergler took part in the first art competition announced in the periodical *Die Propyläen* in 1799 by Goethe and his friend Heinrich Meyer, who hoped to promote classical values in art. The episode in the third book of the *Iliad*, in which Venus leads Helen to the amorous Paris and tries to persuade her to love him, was the chosen theme of the first contest. In August 1799, Bergler wrote a letter to Goethe, attaching a sketch and noting his enthusiasm for the competition. Based on the evaluation published in *Die Propyläen* the carefully executed signed and dated Budapest drawing, containing all the elements of the final composition, would seem to have been produced between the first sketch and Bergler's oil painting, which received third place in the competition. Its significance is enhanced by the fact that – apart from the written sources – this is the only record preserving the artist's invention, which did not satisfy the strict classicist requirements of the organisers of the competition. The heavy draperies and the elaborate folds show traces of Bergler's late Baroque training. The soft faces and Paris's graceful stature most closely resemble a painting on a similar theme by Angelica Kauffmann (Hermitage, St Petersburg).

ZSUZSA GONDA

165.1

Attributed to Georg Raphael Donner   1693–1741
Venus in the Forge of Vulcan, c.1735
Tin and lead alloy, 63 × 99 cm

165.2

Attributed to Georg Raphael Donner
Judgement of Paris, c.1735
Tin and lead alloy, 63 × 99 cm

INVENTORY NUMBERS: 5379, 5380
SELECTED REFERENCE: Michael Krapf (ed.), *Georg Raphael Donner: 1693–1741*, exh.cat., Österreichische Galerie, Vienna, 1993, nos 39–40

As a sculptor and architect, Georg Raphael Donner was one of the leading personalities of the Austrian Baroque. Although he spent his formative years in Vienna in the workshop of the goldsmith Johann

Kaspar Prenner, and later worked alongside the German sculptor Balthasar Permoser in Dresden, his highly individual style was deeply influenced by Italian art. Between 1728 and 1739 Donner was in Pozsony (now Bratislava) as court sculptor and director of building works for Imre Esterházy, the Prince-Archbishop of Esztergom and Primate of Hungary, a significant patron of the period. At the court of Esterházy, Donner created his most important works, including the high altar of St Martin's Cathedral, completed in 1736.

Venus in the Forge of Vulcan represents the story told in the *Aeneid* when Venus visits Vulcan in order to ask for divine arms for Aeneas, her son by Anchises, the heroic protector of Troy. The subject normally contrasts Venus's beauty with Vulcan's ugliness, but Donner's version differs from this tradition. Every figure exemplifies his anatomical knowledge and accuracy. Donner modelled Vulcan's forge with realistic details, especially the hammers, chisels, furnace and anvil. Some scholars believe that in the figure of Vulcan the artist aimed to portray his own youthful self, and the difficulty of working metal. The pair to the relief depicts the *Judgement of Paris*. According to the myth, Juno, Minerva and Venus competed for the apple of Eris, which bore the inscription 'for the fairest one'. Paris, the handsome prince of Troy, chose the winner: he gave the apple to Venus, goddess of love, and in return he won the love of Helen the fair, and unwittingly set the Trojan War in motion.

The Budapest reliefs are made of an alloy of tin and lead, which has the disadvantage of being heavy, but is easier than bronze to work with after casting. This is perceptible in the details of Vulcan's forge as well as the capitals of the columns of the round temple in the *Judgement of Paris*.

ESZTER MOLNÁR-ACZÉL

166

Francesco Guardi   1712–1793
Campo San Zanipolo in Venice, 1760s
Pen and brown ink with brown wash and black chalk underdrawing, 350 × 581 mm

INVENTORY NUMBER: 2814
SELECTED REFERENCES: Antonio Morassi, *Guardi: I disegni*, Milan, 1984, no.594; Andrea Czére (ed.), *Museum of Fine Arts, Budapest: Masterpieces from the Collection*, Budapest, 2006, no.119

In the late seventeenth and early eighteenth centuries, cityscapes became increasingly popular in graphic art and painting, and travellers were eager to take them home from their journeys as souvenirs. Visitors were attracted to Venice by its distinctive architecture, incorporating oriental elements, and the unique prospect of the Lagoon, the main subject-matter of Francesco Guardi's art. The secret of his success was the masterly rendering of the misty atmosphere of the city and the play of light and reflection on the water. His personal style was characterised by forms broken down into patches, for which he has been regarded as a distant precursor of Impressionism.

The present view, acquired with the Esterházy Collection in 1870, is dominated by the Gothic church of the Franciscan order, San Giovanni e Paolo (or San Zanipolo in the Venetian dialect), a burial place for the great and the good of the city. To the right of it, Andrea del Verrocchio's famous equestrian statue of the military leader Bartolomeo Colleoni (*c.*1400–1475), erected in 1481, is prominently visible. The early Renaissance Scuola di San Marco, built by Pietro Lombardo (1435–1515) for a confraternity supporting the poor, and now a hospital, appears like a little jewel on the left side of the composition. Guardi based his study on a painting by Canaletto (Royal Collection) – which he would have known via an etching by Antonio Visentini – and used it as the basis for his painting of the same subject, now in the Louvre.

ANDREA CZÉRE

167

François Boucher   1703–1770
Resurrection of the Son of the Widow of Nain, c.1725–30
Red chalk, pen and brown wash, 223 × 340 mm

INVENTORY NUMBER: 1916-15
SELECTED REFERENCES: Alexandre Ananoff, *L'Oeuvre dessiné de François Boucher (1703–1770): catalogue raisonné*, Paris, 1966

François Boucher was one of the most successful French artists of the eighteenth century. Although he is celebrated – and sometimes reviled – as the definitive purveyor of titillating erotic confections of his age, he was actually a much more versatile and intelligent figure than this caricature would suggest.

The present drawing, in which the broad outlines of the composition were established in red chalk and then fluently defined in pen and wash, is a characteristic example of his early manner. The subject is a religious one, taken from the New Testament, and concerns one of Christ's miracles. In St Luke's Gospel, Christ and his disciples visit the city of Nain, and there encounter the funeral procession of the son of a widow. 'And when the Lord saw her, he had compassion on her, and said unto her, Weep not. And he came and touched the bier: and they that bare him stood still. And he said, Young man, I say unto thee, Arise. And he that was dead sat up, and began to speak. And he delivered him to his mother' (Luke VII, 13–15). Boucher's treatment is both admirably energetic and at the same time remarkably faithful to the text, but also full of wonderful incidental details, such as the genuflecting mother seen from the rear, the bowed and muscle-bound porter waiting to be allowed to proceed, and the almost Christo-like wrapped figure of the deceased rising up and returning to life.

DAVID EKSERDJIAN

168

Jacob Philipp Hackert   1737–1807
View of the Villa Patrizi from the Villa Costaguti, Rome, 1779
Pen and brown wash over pencil, 417 × 649 mm

INVENTORY NUMBER: 1914-25
SELECTED REFERENCE: Claudia Nordhoff, *Jakob Philipp Hackert, 1737–1807: Verzeichnis seiner Werke*, 2 vols, Berlin, 1994, 1, pl. 366, 2, p.311, no.757

This impressive drawing, which is inscribed '*à la Villa Costaguto à Roma 1779 Ph. Hackert f.*', is a particularly fine example of Jacob Philipp Hackert's gifts as a chronicler of the Roman scene. Despite the potential ambiguity of the wording, the building that dominates the skyline is actually the Villa Patrizi, seen from the Villa Costaguti. The present sheet was originally paired with a pendant of identical dimensions, also dated 1779, now in the Schloss at Weimar, which presents a panoramic view of the Eternal City from the Villa Patrizi, with the Porta Pia near at hand over to the left and the dome of St Peter's against the horizon to the right. In 1781 the artist returned to the Villa Patrizi and executed two further views.

From his vantage point at the Villa Costaguti, Hackert looks across a virtually empty foreground, populated by three goats and a couple of figures, which serves as an introduction to the wide horizontal expanse of the ancient Aurelian Wall. This in its turn is succeeded by the dense foliage of the park of the Villa Patrizi, above which its roof and two upper storeys can be seen. Away in the far distance, the strong, hazy light all but bleaches out the Tiburtine Hills, which are the backdrop to the prospect.

Perhaps inevitably, this part of Rome has changed out of all recognition in the intervening two centuries. The Villa Costaguti was demolished after the Second World War, while the Villa Patrizi has been swallowed up within the building complex that now houses the Roman Ministry of Transport.

DAVID EKSERDJIAN

169

Jean-Baptiste Oudry   1686–1755
Boar Hunt, c.1720–40
Oil on canvas, 81 × 101 cm

INVENTORY NUMBER: 2010.1
Previously unpublished. The attribution to Oudry was proposed, tentatively, by Fred G. Meijer in 2008.

Jean-Baptiste Oudry was a specialist in the often closely related categories of animal, hunting and still-life painting. He far surpassed his nearest rival, François Desportes (1661–1743), in the first two disciplines, and at his best – as in his legendary *White Duck* (stolen from Houghton Hall, Norfolk; present whereabouts unknown) – he is even a match for the greatest still-life painter of eighteenth-century France, Jean-Siméon Chardin (1699–1779). The esteem in which he was held was marked by his appointment as court painter to Louis XV, in which role he managed the Beauvais tapestry factory, and made designs both for it and the Gobelins factory. In addition, his work was extremely popular with a number of German princely courts, with the result that museums whose collections are descended from such holdings – such as the one at Schwerin – have exceptionally rich groups of his pictures.

The present canvas, which entered the Museum of Fine Arts on long-term loan from Mr Gyula Pintér in 2010, demonstrates the fact that the collection continues to grow. The painting is a typical example of a hunting scene, which positively delights in the savagery of 'nature red in tooth and claw', and shows the hounds surrounding their furiously struggling and extremely dangerous quarry for the kill. As if to emphasise this, the boar's eyes are blood red, and there is a pool of blood from a gored dog at bottom right. There are dated treatments of precisely the same subject by Oudry in Ansbach (1726) and in Schwerin (1734), but in each instance both the overall composition and the disposition of the individual participants is entirely novel. As a backdrop to the knotted carnage in the foreground, Oudry has effectively bisected the landscape, with a distant prospect to the left and an impenetrable thicket on the right.

DAVID EKSERDJIAN

170

Adrian Zingg   1734–1816

Landscape with Waterfall, 1796

Pen and brown ink with washes, 496 × 654 mm

INVENTORY NUMBER: 976
SELECTED REFERENCES: Teréz Gerszi and Zsuzsa Gonda (eds), *Nineteenth-century German, Austrian and Hungarian Drawings from Budapest*, exh.cat., Cleveland Museum of Art, University Art Museum, Berkeley, and Frick Art Museum, Pittsburgh, 1994, no.2

The Swiss-born Adrian Zingg played a crucial role in the development of German landscape painting in the late eighteenth century as a professor of the Dresden Academy. He and his compatriot Anton Graff (1736–1813) took frequent walks in the surrounding hills and along the banks of the river Elbe, and are regarded as the 'discoverers' of the Saxon countryside, or 'Saxon Switzerland' as they termed it. Zingg's large-scale finished drawings were elaborated in his studio by using the pencil sketches done outdoors during his excursions. He skilfully mixed realistic motifs and natural elements with *coulisses* and staffage figures. With his depictions of the landscape in the Dresden region, Zingg was to become a forerunner of German Romanticism.

This large pen and wash drawing, dated 1796, features one of the artist's favourite motifs, a cascading waterfall among huge boulders. It is not a landscape drawn directly from nature and therefore cannot be topographically located. Though rooted in the tradition of fictitious, idealised landscape, the rendering of the flora indicates that the artist studied nature in depth. The temple-like building in the middle ground was drawn on a separate piece of paper and later superimposed onto the sheet by the artist. Originally that part of the drawing featured a male figure standing next to a huge vase. Zingg was probably dissatisfied with their proportions and therefore modified his composition. The rocky hillside supplemented by the archaising structure may have been intended to counterbalance the huge pines on the right. The juxtaposition of a classical motif with the ruins of a medieval church on top of a hill appears in several works by the artist. The use of brown wash over contours drawn mostly in pen and ink creates a harmonious interplay of light and shade. The strong, decorative brushstrokes become increasingly delicate towards the background, and

---

the mountains are almost completely dissolved. Another drawing by the artist of almost identical size, *View of Amselfall in Saxony*, dated 1794 (Los Angeles County Museum of Art), closely resembles the Budapest sheet both in style and motifs.

ZSUZSA GONDA

171

Franz Kobell   1749–1822

Rocky Landscape by Moonlight, 1799

Pen and brush, brown ink with grey and brown washes, 205 × 320 mm

INVENTORY NUMBER: 708
Previously unpublished

Franz Kobell was probably the most prolific draughtsman of his time, making his living almost entirely through drawings. Over 10,000 of his sheets are known to have survived, but his contemporaries estimated the number of his drawings at 100,000. His art is rooted in the tradition of ideal and heroic landscape associated with Claude Lorrain and Nicolas Poussin. Even before his formative years in Italy (1779–84), Kobell was familiar with the seventeenth-century masters of landscape through reproductive prints.

Since he adhered to classical landscape motifs for decades and rarely dated his works, a small group of meticulously executed, signed and dated drawings by him at the Budapest Museum of Fine Arts is of special significance for an understanding of his chronology. The present drawing, which is dated 1799, derives from the artist's most significant creative period. At that time he lived in Munich with his brother Ferdinand, also a landscape artist. Franz Kobell had a small repertory of motifs, most of them visible in this drawing. He used variations of rock formations overgrown with brush and trees as dramatic landscape elements in combination with streams, waterfalls and wind-blown trees. The overwhelming dominance of landscape elements contrasts sharply with the tiny staffage figures in classical dress at the lower right corner, thus emphasising man's insignificance before nature. At the top of the hill there is a classical temple, brightly lit by the moonlight. The association with the remote past lends an emotional intensity to the sheet. The dramatic contrasts of light and shade demonstrate the artist's chief skill: his sensitivity to tonal values. He alternates washed surfaces with those made by the pointed, short strokes of his brush. Kobell continuously rearranged his favourite motifs into new compositions, which attest to his extraordinary imagination. His works, conveying the magnificence and beauty of nature, were held in high esteem: no less a figure than Goethe himself requested drawings from him.

ZSUZSA GONDA

172

John Wootton   c.1682–1764

Classical Landscape, 1720s

Oil on canvas, 103 × 127.5 cm

INVENTORY NUMBER: 1699
SELECTED REFERENCES: Éva Benkő, 'Paysage de John Wootton à Budapest', *Bulletin du Musée Hongrois des Beaux-Arts*, 68–69 (1987), pp.173–90; M. Chiarini, I. Ember and A. Gosztola (eds), *Rembrandt, Rubens, Van Dyck e il Seicento dei Paesi Bassi*, exh.cat., Milan, 1995, p. 192, no.79; Ildikó Ember and Imre Takács (eds), *Summary Catalogue 3*, Budapest, 2003, p.150

John Wootton was one of the first English artists to paint ideal landscapes in the manner of Claude Lorrain and Gaspard Dughet (sometimes known as Gaspard Poussin), and indeed his contemporary George Vertue described him as having 'perfectly entered into his [Gaspard's] manner'. A pupil of Jan Wyck, he may have visited Italy before 1710, and in a sense his works in this vein are a natural response to the English taste for such effects that not long afterwards led to the landscape gardens of Capability Brown and others. In addition to pure landscapes, he was also a prolific painter of horse portraits, hunting scenes and sporting conversation pieces, some of them on a monumental scale.

The present canvas is a particularly fine example of Wootton's classical approach, with the landscape rigorously, even schematically, divided into four distinct spatial planes, one after the other. Thus, the entire foreground is dominated by a massive tree on the left, in whose shadow diminutive pastoral figures rest with their flocks. Next comes the glassy surface of a broad river, followed by the woods and classical buildings on its far bank. Finally, beyond those structures there is a distant prospect of a range of mountains against the far horizon. The overall conception could hardly be more carefully planned, and is designed to create an effect of peaceful horizontal stasis and to suppress any precipitate progression into depth.

DAVID EKSERDJIAN

173

Jacob Philipp Hackert   1737–1807

Landscape with River, 1778

Oil on canvas, 64.5 × 88.5 cm

INVENTORY NUMBER: 1397
SELECTED REFERENCES: Claudia Nordhoff, *Jakob Philipp Hackert, 1737–1807: Verzeichnis seiner Werke*, 2 vols, Berlin, 1994, 2, p.48, no.117; Rainer Michaelis, 'Flusslandschaft', in István Barkóczi (ed.), *Von Raphael bis Tiepolo aus der Sammlung des hochfürstlichen Hauses Esterházy*, exh. cat., Schirn Kunsthalle, Frankfurt, 1999, pp.404–05, no.169; Ildikó Ember and Imre Takács (eds), *Summary Catalogue 3*, Budapest, 2003, p.60; Annamária Gosztola, 'Jacob Philipp Hackert: Paysage fluvial', in Emmanuel Starcky (ed.), *Nicolas II Esterházy 1765–1833: Un prince hongrois collectionneur*, exh.cat., Musée national du château de Compiègne, 2007, pp.169–70, no.71

Although he was German by birth, it makes more sense to regard Jacob Philipp Hackert – like his great predecessor Claude Lorrain before him – as an Italian artist. Having previously travelled to Sweden and France, he arrived in Rome in 1768, and thereafter divided his time between Rome and Naples, where he was court painter from 1786. Goethe befriended Hackert during his years in Italy, and the artist is one of the supporting players in his *Italian Journey* (1816–17) as well as the subject of a posthumous biography published by Goethe in 1811.

In the main, Hackert was a believer in the direct observation of nature, and accordingly contended that: 'A landscape painter must spend many summer months in rural districts as yet unsullied by human hands.' In consequence, the vast majority of his pictures are topographically accurate portraits of the landscape. The present canvas, which is an approximately half-size repetition of a similarly signed and dated prototype of 1776, now in a private collection, is evidently a devoutly Claudian exception to this general rule. Here, such elements of the pastoral idyll as the circular temple on the bluff over to the right, which is a cross between the body of Bramante's Tempietto and the dome of the Pantheon, and the many-spanned bridge in the hazy distance are born of the artist's imagination and not simply of his intimate knowledge of the Campagna (the countryside around Rome). Hackert signed and dated the work 1778 at bottom centre, and in addition specified that it was painted in Rome.

DAVID EKSERDJIAN

174

Mihály Munkácsy 1844–1900

Dusty Road II, after 1874

Oil on wood, 96 × 129.7 cm

HUNGARIAN NATIONAL GALLERY, INVENTORY NUMBER: 2563
SELECTED REFERENCES: Lajos Végvári, *Munkácsy Mihály élete és művei*, Budapest, 1958, p. 161; Zsuzsanna Bakó, *Munkácsy Mihály*, Budapest, 2009, p. 35

The genre paintings and landscapes of Mihály Munkácsy represent the Hungarian version of French Realism, while his portraits, the trilogy of paintings on the Life of Christ, and the painted ceiling for the Kunsthistorisches Museum in Vienna, are all outstanding examples of historicising academism.

Munkácsy made two versions of the present work, but neither is dated. According to a letter written by the artist's wife during their honeymoon in Hungary in 1874, Munkácsy painted a picture in Békéscsaba called *Dusty Road*. However, the literature refers to the painting in question as the second version, and it has been variously dated to 1874 and the 1880s. In any case, both versions are unique both in Munkácsy's work and contemporary Hungarian painting of the period. The second version of *Dusty Road* is a yellowish-pinkish vision in which the sunlight penetrating the dust stirred up by the cart becomes an atmospheric phenomenon, evocative of the mood of works by Joseph Mallord William Turner (1775–1851). The picture is unprecedented because although Munkácsy had spent the year 1873 in Barbizon, the many landscapes he painted there have more in common with the realism of Gustave Courbet – as do the pictures he produced in his folk-genre period up until the mid-1870s. *Dusty Road II* reveals Munkácsy's intense preoccupation with light phenomena and their representation in paint. In this work he came very close to *plein-air* techniques for depicting the effects of air and light, although he consciously disassociated himself from that trend. His subsequent landscapes are completely lacking in such effects, but his painterly *oeuvre* reached its peak in the 1880s, deservedly winning him a place in the pantheon of European academic art.

ZSUZSANNA BAKÓ

175

Károly Markó the Elder 1791–1860

Landscape with a Vintage Scene near Tivoli, 1846

Oil on canvas, 116 × 153.5 cm

HUNGARIAN NATIONAL GALLERY, INVENTORY NUMBER: 76.32T
SELECTED REFERENCES: Éva Bodnár, *Id. Markó Károly*, Budapest, 1982, p. 44, no. 11; Gabriella Szvoboda Dománszky, *Markó*, Budapest, 2004, p. 10, no. 39; Orsolya Hessky, *Markó*, Budapest, 2009, p. 42, no. 64

Drawing on seventeenth-century classicism, the landscape paintings of Károly Markó the Elder assumed an important role in the quest to help establish a Hungarian artistic tradition. The first collectors of Markó's works were, from the 1830s onwards, the Hungarian Academy of Sciences, the National Museum and other key advocates of a national culture. They believed his paintings possessed universal artistic values that would contribute to the long-awaited birth of Hungarian national art.

Count István Károlyi, who had generously supported the founding of the Academy of Sciences, commissioned the present painting from the artist. In 1843 Markó requested an advance payment and subsequently painted the picture on location at Tivoli near Rome, site of the ancient town of Tibur. The area was popular among artists, not least for Hadrian's Villa, the Renaissance Villa d'Este and the nearly 100-metre waterfall on the river Aniene. In Markó's painting, the figures dressed in folk costume are no less prominent than the historical and natural landmarks.

One of the key features of the most monumental paintings among Markó's late works is the disc of the setting sun, painted in broad, thick brushstrokes, a technique the artist used here for the first time. Given that his deteriorating eyesight had forced him to leave Pisa in 1843, this new method of painting the sun, which is a dominant feature of these pictures, might be regarded as a form of therapy by an artist who was losing his sight.

GÁBOR BELLÁK

176

John Constable RA 1776–1837

Celebration of the General Peace of 1814 in East Bergholt, 1814

Oil on canvas, 23 × 33.5 cm

INVENTORY NUMBER: 4624
SELECTED REFERENCES: Robert Hoozee, *L'opera completa di Constable*, Milan, 1979, p. 108, no. 216; G. Reynolds, *The Early Paintings and Drawing of John Constable*, 2 vols, New Haven and London, 1996, 1, pp. 195–96, 198, no. 14.33, 2, pl. 1181; Ildikó Ember and Imre Takács (eds), *Summary Catalogue 3*, Budapest, 2003, p. 142

John Constable, like his great rival Joseph Mallord William Turner, is that rarest of phenomena: an English painter whose work is rightly taken seriously beyond his country's shores. He was the son of a mill-owner from East Bergholt in Suffolk, and many of his most sublime and evocative landscapes were inspired by the scenes of his boyhood, with the result that the area has come to be known as 'Constable country'. Once best known for such highly resolved compositions as the *Hay Wain* and the *Cornfield* (both National Gallery, London), he is now equally admired for the almost abstract quality of his oil sketches and studies of clouds.

This vibrant little study was traditionally presumed to portray Constable's native East Bergholt on 18 June 1815 at the time of the celebration of Wellington's victory at the Battle of Waterloo, but a related drawn study instead suggests that in fact it represents the military procession held for the poor of East Bergholt to commemorate the peace treaty signed with France on 9 July 1814. The ant-like mass of humanity is dominated by the gold and red accents of the royal standard billowing out from the flagpole, and by the effigy of the defeated enemy – Napoleon – wearing his distinctive hat hanging from a gibbet by its side. It may be that Constable contemplated turning this snapshot into a grand historical record in the spirit of his *Opening of Waterloo Bridge* (Yale Center for British Art, New Haven), but if so nothing came of the scheme.

DAVID EKSERDJIAN

177

Francisco José de Goya y Lucientes 1746–1828

Knife-grinder, c. 1808–12

Oil on canvas, 68 × 52 cm

178

Francisco José de Goya y Lucientes

Water-carrier, c. 1808–12

Oil on canvas, 68 × 52 cm

INVENTORY NUMBERS: 763, 760
SELECTED REFERENCES: Marianne Haraszti-Takács, *Spanish Masters from Zurbarán to Goya*, Budapest, 1984, nos 43–45; *Summary Catalogue 1*, London and Budapest, 1991, p. 153; José Luis Morales y Marín, *Goya: catálogo de la pintura*, Zaragoza, 1994, pp. 304–05, no. 394; Manuela B. Mena Marqués, 'La aguadora – El afilador', in Peter-Klaus Schuster and Wilfried Seipel (eds), *Goya: Prophet der Moderne*, exh. cat., Alte Nationalgalerie, Berlin, and Kunsthistorisches Museum, Vienna, 2005, pp. 250–52, nos. 97–98; Éva Nyerges, *Spanish Paintings: The Collections of the Museum of Fine Arts, Budapest*, Budapest, 2008, p. 198, nos. 92–93

This pair of canvases is recorded in the inventory of goods belonging to Goya and his wife that was drawn up on 26 October 1812, where the paintings are listed under no. 13 as 'Una aguadora y su compañero' (a female water-carrier and its companion) and valued at 300 *reales*. They were probably executed not long before that date, and x-rays have revealed that – as was often his wont – Goya reused old canvases, in this case painted with bouquets of flowers.

The representation of people engaged in particular trades has a long and venerable history, and these are by no means the first examples in Goya's *oeuvre*, but it has been convincingly suggested that in this instance the ostensibly incongruous pairing reflects the political situation in Spain at the time. According to this reading, both the sustaining figure of the woman of Saragossa, a city which was twice besieged by Napoleon's forces in 1808 and 1809, and the knife-grinder, whose role in maintaining resistance was crucial given that the knife was the weapon of choice, should be interpreted as standing for the heroism of the Spanish people. Like Goya's etchings of the *Disasters of War*, which were not completed until around 1820 and only published after his death, these images were intensely private and personal. The solidly planted stance of the water-carrier, which goes back to Donatello's *St George* in Florence, was by this date emblematic of defiance, but the sombre brio of the dark overall tonality, against which the accents of yellow and white explode, is uniquely Goya's.

DAVID EKSERDJIAN

179

Friedrich Heinrich Füger 1751–1818
Christ among the Doctors, c.1805

Black chalk and brown ink, 476 × 296 mm

INVENTORY NUMBER: K.58.1186
SELECTED REFERENCES: Teréz Gerszi and Zsuzsa Gonda (eds), *Nineteenth-century German, Austrian and Hungarian Drawings from Budapest*, exh.cat., Cleveland Museum of Art, University Art Museum, Berkeley, and Frick Art Museum, Pittsburgh, 1994, no.6; Robert Keil, *Heinrich Friedrich Füger (1751–1818): Nur wenigen ist es vergönnt das Licht der Wahrheit zu sehen*, Vienna, 2009, p.373, no5.WV30

The career of the German painter Friedrich Heinrich Füger came to fruition in Vienna. As an esteemed artist he was appointed director of the Vienna Academy in 1806, and subsequently exerted a decisive influence on Austrian neoclassicism. The Budapest drawing is noteworthy because in the artist's rich *oeuvre*, religious compositions tend to be overshadowed by portraits, portrait miniatures and history paintings.

Füger's illustrations (1796–97) for *The Messiah* by Friedrich Gottlieb Klopstock (1724–1803) represented a turning point in his career and strengthened his interest in the Bible. The stylistic influence of the Messiah series is evident in his drawing of the twelve-year-old Jesus among the doctors. According to St Luke's Gospel (Luke II, 42–51), after the celebration of Passover in Jerusalem, Jesus became separated from his parents. He remained in the temple where he debated with the Jewish sages. Füger places Jesus emphatically in the centre of the composition; standing on a podium, his figure rises above the men surrounding him, symbolising his intellectual superiority. The twisted column refers to the setting: the biblical Temple of Solomon. The doctors poring over the scroll in the foreground provide a connection with Mary and Joseph, who are anxiously watching the scene from behind a balustrade. Thematically and stylistically, the drawing is closely related to an oil sketch depicting the religious debate of St Catherine of Alexandria (Akademie der Bildenden Künste, Vienna), and therefore it may be assumed that it was made at the same time, around 1805. In terms of its size, its arched top and vigorous execution, the Budapest sheet corresponds with a drawing of Jesus with his disciples (Städtische Museen, Heilbronn). Both may have been sketches for altarpieces, neither of which appears to have been executed.

ZSUZSA GONDA

180

Mihály Munkácsy 1844–1900
Portrait of Franz Liszt, 1886

Oil on canvas, 130.5 × 99.5 cm

HUNGARIAN NATIONAL GALLERY, INVENTORY NUMBER: 2820
SELECTED REFERENCES: Lajos Végvári, *Munkácsy Mihály élete és művei*, Budapest, 1958, pp.227, 334; Zsuzsanna Bakó, *Munkácsy Mihály*, Budapest, 2009, p.65

From 1872 onwards Mihály Munkácsy resided in Paris where, together with his French wife, he

enjoyed the high life in their private palace on the earnings he made as a successful artist. From the 1880s, at their famous Thursday afternoon salons, they entertained the most distinguished guests from all over Europe, including aristocrats, heads of state and artists, as well as many Hungarians such as Lajos Haynald, the Archbishop of Kalocsa (1816–1891) and Franz Liszt (1811–1886). Liszt attended a grand soirée and a concert organised by Madame Munkácsy on 23 March 1886, and another two days later on 25 March at the church of Saint Eustache where his Esztergom Mass received its premiere. During this visit Munkácsy set out to paint a portrait of Liszt, which he completed relatively quickly, in just two weeks. It is the last portrait of the composer, as Liszt died in Bayreuth in the summer of the same year. Munkácsy, who possessed a keen understanding of the human soul, created the best portrait of his life. The whiteness of the elderly maestro's hair and face is offset by the dark background and costume, which in turn not only records his features, but also brings out his character.

ZSUZSANNA BAKÓ

181

Philip de László (Fülöp Elek László) 1869–1937
Portrait of Pope Leo XIII, 1900

Oil on canvas, 110 × 94 cm

HUNGARIAN NATIONAL GALLERY, INVENTORY NUMBER: 3206
SELECTED REFERENCES: Owen Rutter, *Portrait of a Painter: The Authorized Life of Philip de László*, London, 1939, pp.184, 186, 187–93, 195–204, 233; *A Brush with Grandeur: Philip Alexius de László*, exh.cat., London, 2004, pp.18, 80

Fülöp Elek László (Philip de László after he was ennobled in 1912) was the last great Hungarian master of classical academic portrait painting. His *Portrait of Pope Leo XIII* (Giovanni Vincenzo Pecci; 1810–1903) marks one of the turning points in an extremely successful career, on which the artist embarked in 1894. The portrait of the Holy Father was commissioned by Bishop Vilmos Fraknói on behalf of the Hungarian state on the occasion of the 900th anniversary of the founding of the Christian Hungarian state and the coronation of the Holy King St Stephen. The artist arrived in Rome in March 1900 and made two portraits of his subject.

The first version did not appeal to the pope, who remarked that it resembled Voltaire. László kept the unfinished canvas until his death and left it in his will to the Vatican Museum where it remains to this day. The second portrait, however, was more successful and the artist was presented with a silk scarf and a papal gold medal as tokens of gratitude. The picture went on to win the grand gold medal at the 1900 Exposition Universelle in Paris.

This brilliant painting belongs to a great tradition of papal portraits, including those by Raphael, Titian, Velázquez and Maratta. László is known to have studied Velázquez's *Portrait of Pope Innocent X* at the Palazzo Doria-Pamphilj in Rome. He was equally impressed by Velázquez's portrait and by the human grandeur and modesty of Pope Leo XIII, not least by his positive attitude to the tiring task of sitting for his portrait.

In the same year De László married an Irishwoman, Lucy Guinness, and together with his family he settled in London in 1907.

GÁBOR BELLÁK

182

Rudolf von Alt 1812–1905
View of Budapest with the Chain Bridge and the Royal Palace, c.1880

Watercolour, 425 × 563 mm

INVENTORY NUMBER: 1950-4247
SELECTED REFERENCE: Teréz Gerszi and Zsuzsa Gonda (eds), *Nineteenth-century German, Austrian and Hungarian Drawings from Budapest*, exh.cat., Cleveland Museum of Art, University Art Museum, Berkeley, and Frick Art Museum, Pittsburgh, 1994, no.51

Urban views, landscapes and interiors by Rudolf von Alt, the most accomplished and productive exponent of nineteenth-century Austrian watercolour painting, were popular both with aristocratic clients and with publishers of prints. From a young age he worked alongside his father, the landscape painter Jakob Alt (1789–1872). He was influenced above all by his travels rather than his academic studies. Father and son worked together on a series of watercolours depicting the most beautiful scenery of the Habsburg Empire. Some of the individual works in what has become known as the *Guckkasten* (magic lantern) series (1830–49) so closely resemble each other that it is difficult to differentiate between the two artists.

On account of his commissions, Rudolf von Alt travelled throughout Europe. He came to Pest for the first time in 1844, producing watercolours of the major buildings for lithographs in a volume published by Hartleben and entitled *Buda-Pest* (1845). Compared with other *vedute* of the period, these works are notable for their naturalness and freshness. This first album already contains a depiction of the Széchenyi Chain Bridge, the first permanent link between Pest and Buda, still under construction. Spanning the river Danube, the bridge was designed by the English civil engineer William Tierney Clark, and was based on Hammersmith Bridge in London. The construction of the Chain Bridge was a prerequisite for the unification of Pest, Buda and Óbuda in 1873, establishing Budapest. The carefully elaborated, large watercolour by Rudolf von Alt was produced around 1880. Viewed from the boat station on the Pest side, it shows the structure with the Royal Palace in the background.

Until the middle of the century the waterfront had remained undeveloped. The first section of the embankment was constructed in 1853 alongside the bridgehead in Pest, where it was used as a place to dock steamboats and for loading goods. In the foreground of the watercolour, barrels and various goods can be seen amid the bustle of the market.

ZSUZSA GONDA

183

Rudolf von Alt 1812–1905
View of Budapest from Castle Hill, 1881

Watercolour, 343 × 565 mm

INVENTORY NUMBER: 1933-2390
SELECTED REFERENCES: László Beke and Emmanuel Starcky (eds), *Budapest 1869–1914: Modernité hongroise et peinture européenne*, exh.cat., Musée des Beaux-Arts de Dijon, 1995, pp. 286–87, no.149; Zsuzsa Gonda, *Travel Impressions: Austrian Artists Working in Hungary 1820–1880*, exh.cat., Museum of Fine Arts, Budapest, 2001, no.66

In the last quarter century of his life, Rudolf von Alt travelled less frequently. This watercolour, signed and dated on the side of a building at lower left, preserves the memory of his final visit to Hungary: he came to Budapest in the autumn of 1881, shortly after his wife's death.

The artist recorded the view from Castle Hill, a popular vantage point for tourists even today. The Danube, which cuts the city in two, is seen from above, with the well-known geometric structure of the Chain Bridge. The Margaret Bridge, opened in 1876, can be seen in the background. The lively boat traffic and the smoking factory chimneys indicate the dynamic industrialisation of the Hungarian capital. Elegant mansions line the riverbank on the far Pest side, and the central building of the Hungarian Academy of Sciences, in neo-Renaissance style, is visible near the Chain Bridge. In addition to accurately portraying the buildings, Alt gives a good impression of the vast expanse of the Pest side: receding into the distance, the city merges almost without interruption into the sky with its bluish-grey tones. The Austrian artist surveyed the development of Pest and Buda – latterly the unified Budapest – over some four decades, noting changes in the urban landscape. For this reason, his watercolours have significant documentary value.

Alt's paintings were highly esteemed, and the artist was ennobled. Apart from official recognition, the elderly master also enjoyed the respect of a younger generation of artists. Members of the Viennese Secession rallying around Gustav Klimt elected him as their honorary president, and at their first exhibition in 1898, a selection of the finest watercolours by Rudolf von Alt featured prominently.

ZSUZSA GONDA

184

Richard Parkes Bonington   1802–1828

View of the South Coast, 1825

Watercolour, 141 × 231 mm

INVENTORY NUMBER: 1935-2627
SELECTED REFERENCES: Andrea Czére (ed.), *Museum of Fine Arts, Budapest: Masterpieces from the Collection*, Budapest, 2006, p.127; Patrick J. Noon, *Richard Parkes Bonington: The Complete Paintings*, New Haven and London, 2008, p.152, no.99

Richard Parkes Bonington was the son of a minor artist and entrepreneur from Nottingham, who set up in business in Calais in late 1817 or early 1818. In that single, transforming year, the younger Bonington studied under Louis Francia, met Eugène Delacroix, with whom he was to visit London and share a studio in 1825, and enrolled in the Paris atelier of Baron Antoine-Jean Gros. Both his English origins and his French experiences (he exhibited not only at the Paris Salon, but also at the Royal Academy) are apparent in Bonington's art, for although his supreme gift was unarguably for watercolour landscapes, he was also an accomplished painter in oils, notably of landscapes

and historical costume pieces. An artist of real originality and astonishing precocity, he died of tuberculosis at the age of twenty-six.

The present work, which is a later repetition of an oil painting in the Wallace Collection, London (for what appears to be a preliminary study in the Yale Center for British Art, New Haven), is initialled and dated 'R P B 1825' in the bottom right-hand corner. It is a wonderfully free evocation of the experience of being in a boat that is pitching up and down on a choppy sea. The viewpoint is from low down, and the foreground plane is artfully established by the inclusion of a gull with black-tipped wings to the left balanced by a bobbing red buoy to the right. The main focus of the composition, however, is the group of boats in the middle distance, on whose decks the tiny individual figures are picked out with razor-sharp precision, while beyond are the white cliffs of the south coast of England against an unfriendly sky.

DAVID EKSERDJIAN

185

Jean-Baptiste-Camille Corot   1796–1875

Shepherd Wrestling with a Goat, 1852

Black and white chalk, charcoal and pencil on blue-grey paper, 308 × 238 mm

INVENTORY NUMBER: 1935-2681
SELECTED REFERENCES: Alfred Robaut, *L'Oeuvre de Corot: Catalogue raisonné et illustré*, 4 vols, Paris, 1905, 4, no.2881; Judit Geskó and Josef Helfenstein (eds), '*Zeichnen ist Sehen*': *Meisterwerke von Ingres bis Cézanne aus dem Museum der Bildenden Künste Budapest und aus schweizer Sammlungen*, exh.cat., Kunstmuseum Bern and Kunsthalle Hamburg, 1996, no.33

Jean-Baptiste-Camille Corot was called 'Père Corot' in his social circle, which indicates that the popular and respected master was already considered to be the forerunner of modern landscape painting by his contemporaries. During his grand tour in Italy he painted landscapes based on the observation of nature. These works, constructed with rigorous discipline on the basis of meticulous observation, renewed the vision of French landscape painting.

Shepherd Wrestling with a Goat is an autonomous drawing, which is signed at lower left and inscribed in the top left corner. In his great monograph on Corot, Alfred Robaut dates it to the year 1852 on the basis of its style. The drawings of the master executed in the 1850s differ both from the earlier studies in their use of contour lines, and from the later drawings that exploit the opposition of light and shadow to achieve more painterly solutions. In 1874 Corot also realised a *cliché-verre* (a type of etching) after the present sheet. The artist worked with black chalk on blue-grey paper, occasionally blurring the lines to create quivering, hazy smears or strengthening some lines with a lead pencil, which adds a glimmering, silvery light to the whole work. The subject of the drawing is a shepherd struggling to turn his animals homeward at the end of the day, and Corot chose his materials well to convey the atmosphere of twilight. His first painting bearing the same title was executed in 1847, and he entered it for the Salon exhibition that year. The present drawing is a new treatment of the same topic. He realised a third painting on that theme between 1855 and 1860.

In 1852 and the following years, Corot repeatedly visited his painter friend in Arras, Constant Dutilleux (1807–1860), the first owner of the drawing; it then passed into the hands of Dutilleux's son-in-law, the aforementioned Alfred Robaut, and was presented to the Museum of Fine Arts by Pál Majovszky in 1934.

JUDIT GESKÓ

186

Jean-Baptiste-Camille Corot   1796–1875

Nest-robbers (Italian Landscape), c.1830

Oil on canvas, 36.3 × 28.3 cm

INVENTORY NUMBER: 364.B
SELECTED REFERENCES: Alfred Robaut, *L'Oeuvre de Corot: Catalogue raisonné et illustré*, 4 vols, Paris, 1905, 2, p.225, no.646; Mária Illyés, *Oeuvres françaises du XIXe siècle: Les collections du Musée des Beaux-Arts Budapest*, 4, Budapest, 2001, pp.11–13, no.2

Jean-Baptiste-Camille Corot is best known as a formative influence on the Barbizon School, the group of painters who settled in the village of Barbizon, near the forest of Fontainebleau to the south-east of Paris, from the late 1830s. Working from sketches made *en plein air*, and in opposition to the academic tradition that only endorsed idealised, heroic landscapes, these artists depicted the minute, lyrical details of the landscape. In many ways they can be regarded as forerunners of Impressionism, however they did not practise the same self-reflexive techniques, remaining true to the academic pictorial tradition.

In keeping with the custom of the age, Corot went on study trips to Italy on three occasions – albeit not with the Rome Scholarship of the Paris Academy of Fine Art, but with the support of his wealthy parents. He shared the view of his master, Pierre-Henri Valenciennes, who believed that an artist had to paint 'evocations' of the landscape in his atelier. *Nest-robbers* – a part of the series made in Italy – is one such 'souvenir', inspired by a memory dating from Corot's first stay near Rome. The graphic contour that brings together the forms, the rhythmic arrangement of the progressive layers of the shady foreground and the sunny background follow the classical landscape scheme. The scene is revealed in stages, in an almost narrative manner, between the dynamic figures in the arbour in the foreground and the building in the background, San Tomasso da Villanova, creating the illusion of depth. The rigour of the composition is mitigated by a *sfumato*-like misty rendering of the surfaces, a more stylised technique than that used by the Realists, and a number of anecdotal elements that give meaning to the *veduta*.

MÁRTON OROSZ

187

Arnold Böcklin   1827–1901

Centaur at the Village Blacksmith's Shop, 1888

Oil on panel, 80 × 100 cm

INVENTORY NUMBER: 26.B
SELECTED REFERENCES: Julius Meier-Graefe, *Der Fall Böcklin und die Lehre von den Einheiten*, Stuttgart, 1905, p.243; Rolf Andree, *Arnold Böcklin: Die Gemälde*, Basel and Munich, 1977, no. 408; Brigitta Coers, 'Kentaur in der Dorfschmiede: 1888', in *Arnold Böcklin: Eine Retrospektive*, exh.cat., Kunstmuseum Basel, Musée d'Orsay, Paris, and Neue Pinakothek, Munich, 2001, p.296

Trained in the tradition of Central European Realist

landscape painting at the Academy in Düsseldorf, the Swiss artist Arnold Böcklin worked in a highly individual Symbolist style. His canvases, characterised by brilliantly rich sunlit colour schemes, exerted an immeasurable influence on the art of the German-speaking countries. Rendered in a sensual painterly manner, Böcklin's figures were the descendants of the fantastical late Romantic mythology that James Macpherson's cycle of poems *Ossian* (1761) had introduced to European public consciousness. Held in the highest esteem throughout his life, in 1850 Böcklin joined the circle of German painters in Rome known as the Tugendbund ('League of Virtue'), and his affection for Italy was also marked by his friendship with the renowned art historian Jacob Burckhardt (1818–1897) and by his marriage to an Italian woman.

He began working on *Centaur at the Village Blacksmith's Shop* in his Zurich workshop, after his return from Florence in 1885. The painting takes its theme from a work by Böcklin's writer friend Paul Heyse, *The Last Centaur* (1870), which draws a parallel between the mythical creatures of classical antiquity and the nature spirits of German folklore. The dialogue between the village blacksmith and the half-animal, half-human creature seeking to have its hooves shod is observed by an audience of peasants gathered before a landscape with a broad horizon and seen from a low viewpoint. Their expressions reflect not so much fear of the beast as curiosity. The Metaphysical painter Giorgio de Chirico (1888–1978) went so far as to note in connection with this scene that the centaur elicited sympathy in the viewer. Böcklin spent three years painting the work, excising a number of distracting anecdotal elements along the way to create his final coherent and tension-laden image.

MÁRTON OROSZ

188

Franz von Stuck   1863–1928

Kiss of the Sphinx, 1895

Oil on canvas, 160 × 144.8 cm

INVENTORY NUMBER: 124.B
SELECTED REFERENCES: Edwin Becker, 'Eros – Woman: The eternal enigma', in Sjraar van Heugten (ed.), *Franz von Stuck 1863–1928: Eros and Pathos*, exh.cat., Van Gogh Museum, Amsterdam, 1995, pp.19–22; Andrea Czére (ed.), *Museum of Fine Arts, Budapest: Masterpieces from the Collection*, Budapest, 2006, no.136; Margot T. Brandlhuber, 'Sphinx', in Margot T. Brandlhuber and Michael Buhrs (eds), *Franz von Stuck: Meisterwerke der Malerei*, exh.cat., Museum Villa Stuck, Munich, 2008, p.80

Rising from a humble background to become a professor at the Akademie der Bildenden Künste in Munich, Franz von Stuck, one of the most influential German Symbolists, had long been active as an illustrator when in 1889 he exploded on the scene with his painting *The Guardian of Paradise*. From that time his career took off, and his often erotic, dramatic paintings drew on the popular literature-inspired Symbolist themes of the age. In 1892 he was one of the founding members of the Munich Secession. His home in Munich, the Renaissance palazzo-style Villa Stuck (1899), for which the artist designed the interiors and furnishings, is a monumental *Gesamtkunstwerk* (total work of art) that encapsulates his *oeuvre*.

The Sphinx is a recurring theme that holds a special place in Stuck's art. The half-lion, half-woman monster best known from the story of Oedipus went on to become an incarnation of the *femme fatale* triumphing over men in the works of such late nineteenth-century Symbolist painters as Gustave Moreau, Fernand Khnopff and Félicien Rops. In a dramatic scene, the lion-bodied woman perched on a rock holds the powerless, limp body of a man in a deadly embrace set against a fiery red backdrop. She presses her lips tightly against those of her victim, as though sapping his vital fluids. Depicting the emblematic moment when pleasure and death unite, the painting was inspired by Heinrich Heine's poem *Die Sphinx*, which appeared in his *Buch der Lieder* (1827).

In 1896 Adolf Hengeler probably produced a copy identical to the original in size, which is today exhibited at the Museum Villa Stuck in Munich.

MÓNIKA KUMIN

189

János Vaszary   1867–1939

Golden Age, 1898

Oil on canvas, 92.5 × 156 cm

HUNGARIAN NATIONAL GALLERY, INVENTORY NUMBER: 1614
SELECTED REFERENCES: Géza Perneczky, 'Vaszary János', in *Vaszary bibliográfia*, Budapest, 1970, pp.1–13; Judit Szabadi, *Art Nouveau in Hungarian Painting, Sculpture and Graphic Arts*, Budapest, 1989, pp.24–26; Nóra Veszprémi (ed.), *János Vaszary (1867–1939) gyűjteményes kiállítása*, exh.cat., Hungarian National Gallery, Budapest, 2007; Edit Plesznivy, *Vaszary János*, Budapest, 2007, pp.16, 35–37, 172–74

János Vaszary's Secessionist painting *Golden Age* was first exhibited at the Budapest International Exhibition held at the Palace of Arts in the spring of 1898, where it was awarded the *grand prix* of the Arts Society. It went on to receive a bronze medal at the Paris Exposition Universelle in 1900. The Hungarian Museum of Fine Arts bought the picture from the artist in the year it was painted. Evocative of the subtle decadence found in works by Franz von Stuck and Gustav Klimt, this mystical painting features finely wrought details. It depicts a curious rite performed in the shimmering light of dusk filtering through the forest trees. Sacrificing a rose before a group of classical sculptures, a young couple seem to be yearning for the happiness of the long-distant past and expecting the other to provide shelter. The all-embracing, translucent veil of opaque green enhances the picture's archaic sense of decay. The exuberant vegetation creeps out onto the frame in the form of gilded floral patterns. Organically connected to the composition of the picture, the Secessionist frame was also designed by the artist. The golden motifs applied to a black background bear funereal associations, serving as a reminder of the transience of worldly life and the painful reality of bereavement. The depiction of nostalgia for the classical cultures of past eras in *fin-de-siècle* art sheds light on the weighty existential preoccupations of the age. Vaszary reveals his creative disposition by conveying artistic concepts with the sensitivity of an intellectual painter acutely aware of the Zeitgeist and with exceptional meticulousness.

MARIANN GERGELY

190

Gustave Doré   1832–1883

*Young Woman with a White Scarf, c.*1870

Oil on canvas, 125 × 95 cm

INVENTORY NUMBER: 77.3.B
SELECTED REFERENCES: Jean Favière et al., *Gustave Doré 1832–1883*, exh.cat., Musée d'Art Moderne, Strasbourg, 1983, no.85; Mária Illyés, *Oeuvres françaises du XIXe siècle. Les collections de Musée des Beaux-Arts Budapest*, 4, Budapest, 2001, no.31

Frequently referred to as an artist-journalist, Gustave Doré earned his reputation with drawings and illustrations depicting the misery of the modern industrial metropolis. He travelled on several occasions between 1868 and 1872 to London, where his graphic works enjoyed great popularity. Doré summed up his experience of the joys and horrors of modern London life in *London: A Pilgrimage* (1872), a copiously illustrated book co-authored with his friend the English journalist Blanchard Jerrold (1826–1884). Less well known is his painterly *oeuvre*, which chiefly comprised landscapes and figurative works, often on a large scale, and was frequently snubbed by critics.

Two versions of *Young Woman with a White Scarf* have come down to us, and a third is known only from a photograph at the Bibliothèque nationale de France. In the Budapest version, a woman in three-quarter view sits in the shade of a striped parasol set against the background of sunlit trees with vivid green foliage. She rests her right arm on an open book; her posture is light and her expression mild and slightly pensive. In the other extant version (reproduced as no.85 in the catalogue of the 1983 Strasbourg exhibition), the same posed and clad woman is depicted in the same setting as her counterpart, only from slightly farther away, in whole figure and in the company of two dogs, suggesting that the Budapest picture may have been cut down from a larger canvas.

During his visits to London, Doré often created portraits of members of the aristocracy, and Jerrold recalls him meeting in England a woman who went on to become the 'idol of his dreams'. It is nevertheless assumed that the young woman here is not a real person, but rather an embodiment of the feminine ideals of the age.

MÓNIKA KUMIN

191

Pierre Puvis de Chavannes   1824–1898

Magdalene, 1897

Oil on canvas, 116.5 × 89.5 cm

INVENTORY NUMBER: 389.B
SELECTED REFERENCES: Aimée Brown Price, *Pierre Puvis de Chavannes*, exh.cat., Van Gogh Museum, Amsterdam, 1994, no.145; Mária Illyés, *Oeuvres françaises du XIXe siècle: Les collections du Musée des Beaux-Arts Budapest*, 4, Budapest, 2001, pp.145–48; Aimée Brown Price, *Pierre Puvis de Chavannes*, 2 vols, New Haven and London, 2010, 2, pp.396–97, no.431

Pierre Puvis de Chavannes took up mural painting following his studies with Théodore Chassériau (1819–1856) and trips to Italy. He sought to recreate the style of Italian frescoes in his oil paintings, which are generally characterised by their muted colour schemes and a tendency to simplify forms. Puvis de Chavannes's wall paintings in public institutions attest to an affinity for the monumental. He adopted Trecento fresco tonalities by the latter half of the

1870s, which he also applied to his smaller easel paintings. Painted in 1881, his *Poor Fisherman* (Musée d'Orsay, Paris) is an outstanding proto-Symbolist work, whose allegorical simplicity and muted colour profoundly influenced a younger generation, in particular Gauguin and Seurat.

Magdalene is one of the last canvases that Puvis painted in an interval between working on his last monumental decorative cycle. Compared to two earlier representations of the Magdalene (*Noli me tangere* and *Mary Magdalene in the Desert*, 1869), it is simpler and more restrained. Neither the sculpture-like female figure nor her surroundings suggest any human presence. The picture has none of the traditional attributes of the penitent Magdalene, and Puvis de Chavannes has also omitted any individual characteristics in his idealised composition. Formal unification and mass-like modelling highlight the intimate, pantheistic harmony of landscape and figure. On account of its minimalist composition and use of colours, the painting can be regarded as summarising the artist's *oeuvre*.

FERENC TÓTH

192

József Rippl-Rónai   1861–1927
Woman with Birdcage, 1892
Oil on canvas, 185.5 × 130 cm

HUNGARIAN NATIONAL GALLERY, INVENTORY NUMBER: F.K. 1385
SELECTED REFERENCES: Mária Bernáth, *Rippl-Rónai József*, Budapest, 1998; Mária Bernáth, 'Kalitkás nő', in Mária Bernáth and Ildikó Nagy (eds), *Rippl-Rónai József gyűjteményes kiállítása*, exh.cat., Hungarian National Gallery, Budapest, 1998, pp.232–34; Mária Bernáth, 'Femme à la cage', in Agnès Delannoy, Anna Jávor and Anna Szinyei Merse (eds), *József Rippl-Rónai: Le Nabi hongrois*, exh.cat., Musée départemental Maurice Denis, Saint-Germain-en-Laye, 1999, pp.126–27; Mária Bernáth, 'Frau mit Vogelbauer', in Anna Jávor and Bettina-Martine Wolter (eds), *Ein Ungar in Paris: József Rippl-Rónai 1861 bis 1927*, exh.cat., Schirn Kunsthalle, Frankfurt, 1999, p.97

One of the most popular Hungarian painters of the twentieth century, József Rippl-Rónai arrived in Paris on a scholarship in 1887. He was to live in the city for almost a decade and a half. Exhibited at the Salon du Champ de Mars in 1894, *My Grandmother* brought him into contact with the Nabi group of artists who were closely associated with the avant-garde periodical *La Revue Blanche*. Rippl-Rónai would become a regular contributor to the Nabis' exhibitions. Known as the 'Nabi hongrois', the artist became close friends with Pierre Bonnard, Edouard Vuillard and Aristide Maillol. Siegfried Bing organised a monographic exhibition of his collected works at the Salon de l'Art Nouveau in 1897.

Rippl-Rónai referred to his low-colour phase in the 1890s as his 'black period'. The decorative works he produced in Paris at this time were characterised by their reserved, sombre colour schemes, two-dimensionality and strong outlines, reflecting in part the influence of James McNeill Whistler whose monotone, narrow-format paintings inspired Rippl-Rónai to produce numerous female figures.

An emblematic painting, *Woman with Birdcage* features an ethereal female figure dressed in dark brown and wrapped in decorative Art-Nouveau motifs. The pale, two-dimensional profile of the model and her hand holding the cage are a striking counterpoint to the dark background. The artist was

at this time creating in pastel a whole series of transcendent female faces radiating inner light. Like his other single-figure paintings, *Woman with Birdcage* features very few motifs; the idiom is simplified, focusing on the essence. Few elements refer to the external environment and only the finely curved sofa and the soft silhouette of a chair punctuate the background.

EDIT PLESZNIVY

193

Auguste Rodin   1840–1917
Sirens, 1888
Bronze, 44 × 35 × 33 cm

INVENTORY NUMBER: 1891.U
SELECTED REFERENCES: Mária Illyés, *Oeuvres françaises du XIXe siècle: Les collections de Musée des Beaux-Arts Budapest*, 4, Budapest, 2001, no.54; Judit Geskó (ed.), *Monet et ses amis*, exh. cat., Museum of Fine Arts, Budapest, 2004, no.83; Antoinette Le Normand-Romain (ed.), *The Bronzes of Rodin: Catalogue of Works in the Musée Rodin*, 2, Paris, 2007, pp.652–55

From 1864 to the early 1870s, Auguste Rodin worked in the atelier of Albert-Ernest Carrier-Belleuse (1824–1887), who was best known for his decorative sculpture. The development of Rodin's softly modelled plastic style was influenced by the sculpture of both Donatello and Michelangelo, which he encountered during his trip to Florence and Rome in 1875.

In 1880 Rodin received the commission for the bronze gates for the planned Musée des Arts Décoratifs in Paris, drawing inspiration for the *Gates of Hell* from Dante's *Divine Comedy*. Rodin worked on the sculptures for this monumental ensemble to the end of his life, yet neither the gate nor the building of the museum were ever completed.

In the present sculpture the three female figures, perched on a rock protruding from the frothing waves, are linked together like a festoon. The sirens on the left and in the centre appear in full length and can be seen from the front and the side, while the figure on the right rises from the sea with her back to the viewer. In the form of slender young women, the sirens of Homer's *Odyssey* with their magical voices are the embodiment of sensual seduction.

Rodin had originally intended the group to appear on the left side of the left panel of the *Gates of Hell*, but the sirens also featured in a plaster composition for *Death of the Poet* (c.1890) and in the second design for the statue of *Victor Hugo* (c.1898), in which the poet is depicted standing. Subsequently, however, Rodin's *oeuvre* came to feature several variants of the ensemble – which was also entitled *Nereids* or *Sea Maiden* – as independent works cast in bronze or carved out of marble in various sizes. The female figure on the left, for example, reappeared in 1889 as *Succubus*.

MÓNIKA KUMIN

194

Aristide Maillol   1861–1944
Crouching Girl with Peaked Hairknot, c.1900
Bronzed cast iron, height 16 cm

INVENTORY NUMBER: 6673
SELECTED REFERENCES: Judit Geskó, 'Le modèle antique de la "Méditerranée" de Maillol: A propos d'un dessin inconnu de l'artiste', *Bulletin du Musée Hongrois des Beaux-Arts*, 74 (1991), pp.56–57; Mária Illyés, *Oeuvres françaises du XIXe siècle: Les collections du Musée des Beaux-Arts*, 4, Budapest, 2001, no.71

The course of Aristide Maillol's career leading up to his first sculptures is complex. He only established his so-called classic style after nearly fifteen years of artistic activity. Following a series of Symbolist and smaller scale sculptures, paintings, tapestries, drawings and prints, his first monumental sculpture, *La Méditerranée* (1902–05), now in the Museum of Modern Art, New York, represented a turning point in his *oeuvre*. He here discovered the basic aesthetic principles that would underpin his later masterpieces.

During his 1908 trip to Greece, Maillol was deeply impressed by the decorative sculptures of the Temple of Zeus at Olympia: 'These forms, so beautiful in their simplicity, that is the sculpture I would have liked to do! It's strong, it's alive, it's animated … The kneeling warriors are magnificent. The central figure of Apollo, considered a masterpiece, is less beautiful than these warriors … I prefer the more primitive art of Olympia to that of the Pantheon.'

Maillol's relationship to Greek sculpture defines his position within twentieth-century sculpture. Like the Cubists, he distanced himself from later Hellenistic Greek sculptures, but he went further, rejecting all works after Phidias. The Temple of Zeus was first excavated in 1829 by a French team who took several fragments of the pediments back to Paris, where Maillol admired them in the Louvre. Later excavations, after 1875, unearthed further sculptures, which were published for the first time in 1894.

The *Crouching Girl with Peaked Hairknot*, presented to the Museum of Fine Arts by Adolf Kohner in 1934, has a number of affinities with the Olympian sculptures. The curve of the figure's left hand resembles that of the left hand touching the ground of the slave on the eastern façade of the Temple of Zeus. The *Crouching Girl* differs from it in the lower part of her right leg, as well as in her right hand, which is drawn closer to her body. Maillol's progress from the antique example to designing and realisation of *La Méditerranée* can be followed almost step by step through the observation of this small sculpture and a number of little bronze sculptures and drawings realised after 1900.

JUDIT GESKÓ

195

Edouard Manet   1832–1883
Rue Mosnier in the Rain, 1878
Lead pencil and black ink on calendered drawing paper mounted on cardboard, 190 × 360 mm

INVENTORY NUMBER: 1935-2735
SELECTED REFERENCES: Denis Rouart and Daniel Wildenstein, *Edouard Manet: Catalogue raisonné*, 2 vols, Geneva, 1975, 2, no.328; Juliet Wilson-Bareau, *Manet par lui-même*, Paris, 1991, no.179; Judit Geskó and Josef Helfenstein (eds), *'Zeichnen ist Sehen': Meisterwerke von Ingres bis Cézanne aus dem Museum der Bildenden Künste Budapest und aus schweizer Sammlungen*, exh. cat., Kunstmuseum Bern and Kunsthalle Hamburg, 1996, no.75

Although he was among the progressive painters of his day, Edouard Manet was arguably the most attached to the Old Masters. Nonetheless, in the 1870s he set out on a revolutionary path in response to Impressionism, producing works brimming with colour and light.

In this ink drawing, executed by the artist in 1878 and signed in the upper left corner, the artist first laid out his composition with a lead pencil. The drawing, which entered the Budapest collection as a gift from Pál Majovszky in 1934, shows a view of the rue Mosnier (now rue de Berne), in one of the newly developed streets in a district of Paris designed by Georges Haussmann (1809–1891). From the windows of his atelier Manet had a view straight down rue Mosnier. The paved street extends along the central axis of the drawing, cutting it into three equal parts. Hackney carriages, of which Manet realised a number of small studies, advance down the street, their hoods pulled up to protect passengers from the lashing rain and wind. A few passers-by hurry on, shielded by their umbrellas or hats. The figures carrying umbrellas proceeding in single file on the left recall the rain-sodden characters of the 1871 etching *Queue at the Butcher's Shop*.

Like the related drawing in the Art Institute of Chicago, the Budapest sheet also shows signs of the influence of Japanese brush-drawings: instead of representing shapes with precision, the patches and thick lines executed with quick brushstrokes only allude to them. This is precisely how they are able to carry the impression of instantaneous motion. The passers-by and the carriages contribute to the overall atmosphere. Instead of demarcating the silhouettes from the space surrounding them, their contours – drawn with diluted Indian ink, which softens their sharpness – connect them to the ambient atmosphere. With his brushstrokes of varied thickness and strength, Manet perfectly represented the space, air, light and mist, the plasticity of the forms and the different movements of the figures.

JUDIT GESKÓ

196

Pierre-Auguste Renoir   1841–1919

Bridge at Argenteuil, 1888

Watercolour, 173 × 230 mm

INVENTORY NUMBER: 1935-2763
SELECTED REFERENCE: Judit Geskó and Josef Helfenstein (eds), 'Zeichnen ist Sehen': Meisterwerke von Ingres bis Cézanne aus dem Museum der Bildenden Künste Budapest und aus schweizer Sammlungen, Kunstmuseum Bern and Kunsthalle Hamburg, 1996, no.105

Although Pierre-Auguste Renoir's popularity originally derived from his multi-figured Impressionist compositions and portraits, today he is particularly appreciated for the aesthetic qualities of his paintings and the complex structure of his landscapes.

The present watercolour, donated by Pál Majovszky in 1934, and signed in pencil in the lower right corner, was executed in Argenteuil and can be related to a number of works realised there. The sheet was probably created *in situ* from a carefully chosen viewpoint. The composition, depicting the banks of the river Seine, bears the marks of Paul Cézanne's influence, and is constructed according to rigorous geometrical rules: the diagonal of the line of trees on the bank complements the stretch of water running beneath the arch of Argenteuil's pillared

bridge. The dominant feature of the painting is the representation of the trees, which are endowed with a sense of volume by the use of short brushstrokes.

The village of Argenteuil, situated at a distance of 11 km from Paris on the right bank of the Seine, at the time numbered six thousand inhabitants and was a popular beauty-spot, particularly with boating parties. Train fares were relatively cheap – between 1.2 and 1.5 francs – so most inhabitants of the metropolis could afford to make the journey.

In early 1888 Renoir visited Cézanne in Aix-en-Provence for the second time, renting a house near the town. Cézanne's influence can be discerned in two pictures entitled *La Montagne Sainte-Victoire*, realised by Renoir during his stay. Both are characterised by the use of short brushstrokes in building up their structure. In relation to these images, it has been established that by the end of the 1880s Renoir was looking for new ways of shaping his landscape studies into coherent pictorial forms. The present watercolour represents one stage of this process.

JUDIT GESKÓ

197

Camille Pissarro   1830–1903

Pont Neuf, 1902

Oil on canvas, 55 × 46.5 cm

INVENTORY NUMBER: 205.B
SELECTED REFERENCES: Ferenc Tóth, 'Camille Pissarro: Le Pont-Neuf', in Ann Dumas (ed.), Impressionism: Paintings Collected by European Museums, exh.cat., High Museum of Art, Atlanta, Seattle Art Museum, and Denver Art Museum, 1999, p.197; Mária Illyés, Oeuvres françaises du XIXe siècle: Les collections du Musée des Beaux-Arts Budapest, 4, Budapest, 2001, pp. 101–02

A leading Impressionist, Camille Pissarro made a foray into Divisionism before returning, in his last years, to the unrestrained style of his earlier period, creating a synthesis of his earlier work. In the 1890s he painted a series of typical Parisian architectural ensembles, usually from a hotel room or flat specifically chosen and rented for this purpose. By this time he was suffering from a serious eye condition, which forced him to withdraw to a room rather than work outside. Pissarro painted the Pont Neuf on several occasions from the window of a flat on the Île de la Cité, presenting the same scene at different times of day.

Affording a view from above, the location reveals the façades of the houses flanking the opposite side of the river and emphasises the wide diagonal span of the bridge crossing the picture and the architectonic weight of its pillars. The vibrant motion of the bustling pedestrians is at odds with the solidity of the buildings. The artist's painting technique seems to dissolve and render immaterial their structural mass. Pissarro's cityscapes are more than just views of well-known landmarks; the focus is on minutely observed local activity. In the case of *Pont Neuf*, Pissarro appears to have been chiefly inspired by the passing traffic and busy crowds of people.

FERENC TÓTH

198

Claude-Oscar Monet   1840–1926

Three Fishing Boats, 1885

Oil on canvas, 73 × 92.5 cm

INVENTORY NUMBER: 436.B
SELECTED REFERENCES: Daniel Wildenstein, Claude Monet: Biographie et catalogue raisonné, 2, Lausanne and Paris, 1974, no.1029; Stephan Koja (ed.), Claude Monet, exh.cat., Österreichische Galerie Belvedere, Vienna, 1996, no.44; Mária Illyés, Oeuvres françaises du XIXe siècle: Les collections du Musée des Beaux-Arts Budapest, 4, Budapest, 2001, pp.94–95

One of the leading figures of Impressionism, Monet visited the coast of Normandy reguarly during the 1880s, a landscape he loved and repeatedly painted. Among his favourite spots was Etretat, a small fishing village and resort near Le Havre famous for the picturesque jagged cliffs flanking its coast. In late August 1884, and again the following year, the baritone Jean-Baptiste Fauré (1830–1914) lent his house in Etretat to the artist and his family for an extended period.

Although Monet initially painted the coast and sailing boats from his hotel he made every effort to work outdoors, even in the harshest of conditions. In the autumn of 1885 he painted for the first time the herring boats drawn up on the pebbly beach, fascinated by the formal rhythms of their graceful arcs lined up side by side. The boats in the present work, painted from the artist's window, are depicted slightly from above, with the horizon and the sky omitted. The daring angle narrows the space, creating a tense composition. Monet attached importance to rendering dynamically the frothy waves and the effects of the wind, which he accomplished with energetic, expansive brushstrokes. These expressive paintings of fishing boats had a profound effect on Vincent van Gogh, among others. When Monet returned to Giverny in December 1885, he took with him over 50 unfinished works that he later completed in his studio.

FERENC TÓTH

199

Ferdinand Georg Waldmüller   1793–1865

Man with Magic Lantern, 1847

Oil on canvas, 76 × 92.5 cm

INVENTORY NUMBER: 3.B
SELECTED REFERENCE: Rupert Feuchtmüller, Ferdinand Georg Waldmüller, 1793–1865: Leben, Schriften, Werke, Vienna and Munich, 1996, pp.169–72

The art of Ferdinand Georg Waldmüller, a leading figure of Austrian Biedermeier painting, was not characterised by religious or dramatic themes, but rather by a high degree of verisimilitude, and a unique brand of realism that explored the atmospheric effects of light and shade. Radiating eternal optimism, the sentimentality of Waldmüller's petit bourgeois-themed paintings, in particular the manifestly naturalistic style of his portraits emphasising elegance and luxury, are at stark odds with the freshness of his *plein-air* studies made for landscapes. His campaign for educational reform at the Vienna Academy of Fine Arts demonstrates his innovative views, which in many respects set him apart from established opinion.

Paintings depicting themes from rural life had become popular among city-dwellers by the 1840s. The present work belongs to Waldmüller's series of genre pictures, the so-called *Sittenbilder*. Outside a dilapidated barn stands an itinerant conjuror, whose performance is being watched with rapt attention by a group of Alpine villagers. At the centre of the show is a magic lantern (*Guckkasten*), operated by slotting painted glass negatives into the open side of the box (here facing into the picture). The projected images served as a cheap substitute for journeys to faraway exotic lands. The balanced effects of light and shade created by the late afternoon sun and the minute details captured with rapid brushstrokes give the painting a brilliantly vibrant quality. Waldmüller arranged the characters into distinctive groups. The pyramid of children, whose appreciative excitement is portrayed with acute psychological awareness, suggests that the artist had not after all broken with the classicist traditions of picture construction.

MÁRTON OROSZ

200

Adolph von Menzel   1815–1905

Studies for Travelling through the Beautiful Landscape, 1891

Carpenter's pencil with stumping, 128 × 206 mm

INVENTORY NUMBER: 1916-142
SELECTED REFERENCE: Teréz Gerszi and Zsuzsa Gonda (eds), *Nineteenth-century German, Austrian and Hungarian Drawings from Budapest*, exh.cat., Cleveland Museum of Art, University Art Museum, Berkeley, and Frick Art Museum, Pittsburgh, 1994, no.68

Adolph von Menzel, one of the most talented exponents of nineteenth-century German Realism, began his career as an illustrator and only started to paint in the 1840s. He achieved a reputation above all with his carefully researched historical paintings of the era of Frederick the Great, while the importance of his small and intimate interiors was only recognised towards the end of his life. Menzel drew incessantly throughout his career, displaying a fanatical enthusiasm for capturing the world around him. The more than 10,000 drawings in his *oeuvre* are telling evidence of this.

The Budapest study is connected with a multi-figure composition produced by the already elderly artist in 1892, the small gouache painting *Travelling through the Beautiful Landscape* (private collection, Hamburg). This work is the last in a series depicting his experiences of railway travel. Whereas a series of lithographs on a similar theme by his French contemporary Honoré Daumier (1808–1879) involve social critique, Menzel took a more psychological viewpoint. He portrayed the changing moods of the passengers in an elegant railway carriage, which varied from excited curiosity to exhaustion and fatigue. The young man in the drawing, who is leaning forward in fascination, adjusting his binoculars, is a precursor of the male figure on the right margin of the Hamburg composition. An elaborate study produced in 1892 (Schäfer Collection, Schweinfurt) corresponds exactly with the latter. The manner in which the position of the right hand is repeated once again in the centre of the sketch is typical of the artist's creative mode. The left half of

the Budapest drawing is filled with a study of a young woman's face, larger in scale, which the artist chose not to use for the painting in question. In his last decades Menzel frequently worked with a soft carpenter's pencil, rubbing the lines to produce velvety tones and painterly effects.

ZSUZSA GONDA

201

Max Liebermann   1847–1935

Sketch of Jodenbreestraat in Amsterdam, c.1908

Black chalk, 257 × 346 mm

INVENTORY NUMBER: 1915-46
SELECTED REFERENCES: Teréz Gerszi and Zsuzsa Gonda (eds), *Nineteenth-century German, Austrian and Hungarian Drawings from Budapest*, exh.cat., Cleveland Museum of Art, University Art Museum, Berkeley, and Frick Art Museum, Pittsburgh, 1994, no.95; G. Tobias Natter and Julius H. Schoeps (eds), *Max Liebermann und die französischen Impressionisten*, exh.cat., Jüdisches Museum der Stadt Wien, Vienna, 1997–98, p.187

Max Liebermann was the most admired German painter of his era. From 1899 to 1911 he led the Berlin Secession and then served as president of the Prussian Academy of Arts (1920–32). In this position he exerted considerable influence on German art. He was an enthusiast admirer of French painting; masterpieces by Edouard Manet, Edgar Degas, Camille Pissarro and Pierre-Auguste Renoir enriched his personal collection. After the dark tones and rustic portrayals of his naturalist period, from the 1890s he began producing – under the influence of French Impressionism – vivid paintings full of light and bright colours.

Liebermann's choice of themes was greatly influenced by his travels in the Netherlands. In addition to themes showing his sensitivity to social issues – net mending, orphanages and almshouses – a further recurring motif was the hustle and bustle of Amsterdam's Jewish quarter. The place appealed to him both as a Jew and as an admirer of intellectual traditions, as it had been the home of Spinoza, whom he greatly admired. Moreover, Rembrandt had also lived nearby. Liebermann made his first painting of the Jodenbreestraat, the main street in the Jewish quarter, in December 1884. During subsequent visits (1905, 1907 and 1908) he devoted several series to the same theme. As the devoutly religious Jews would not allow him to depict them, he rented rooms at several locations and observed the street activity through the windows. This drawing exemplifies his working method: he captured the view of the street which he had thoroughly examined, using quick and simple chalk lines – his intention being to reproduce the vibrating crowd and its heaving motion. Clues to the work's date are provided by the emphatic geometric elements on the right side of the composition – the flight of stairs, the dark gateway and the window frame – which are repeated in two paintings from 1908 (private collection; Jewish Historical Museum, Amsterdam) and in an etching. The Jewish-quarter theme is concluded with an oil painting produced in the Berlin workshop and shown at the eighteenth exhibition of the Berlin Secession in 1909.

ZSUZSA GONDA

202

Eugène Delacroix   1798–1863

Lion Resting, 1848–50

Pencil and watercolour, heightened with white, 152 × 200 mm

INVENTORY NUMBER: 1918-462
SELECTED REFERENCES: Lee Johnson, *The Paintings of Eugène Delacroix*, 1, Oxford, 1981, p. 35; Judit Geskó and Josef Helfenstein (eds), *Zeichnen ist Sehen*, exh.cat., Kunstmuseum Bern and Hamburger Kunsthalle, 1996, no.25

Eugène Delacroix, one of the greatest colourists among French painters, was a leading figure of the Romantic movement. While studying at the Ecole des Beaux-Arts in Paris, he improved his artistic skills by copying Old Masters at the Louvre. Paintings by Raphael, Titian, Veronese and Rubens made the strongest impression on him. Among his contemporaries Delacroix felt the closest affinity with Théodore Géricault (1791–1824), whose depictions of animals influenced him profoundly.

The strange and exotic beauty of wild animals attracted Delacroix from his earliest years. With his friend, the sculptor Antoine-Louis Barye (1796–1875), he used to visit the Jardin des Plantes, where they watched and studied the animals of the menagerie in movement and at rest. The drawings he made – on the whole directly from nature and during the early years of his career – served as a starting point for his later lithographs and historical compositions. Delacroix rarely abandoned a theme and continued to elaborate certain ideas throughout his life. His monumental painting *Lion Hunt*, commissioned for the Paris Exposition Universelle of 1855, can be regarded as the culmination of his growing interest during the 1840s and early 1850s in painting scenes with big cats. He depicted lions and tigers not only in violent action, but also devouring their prey or simply in attitudes of repose. Most of Delacroix's finished watercolours on these themes, many of which were owned by patrons or friends, were composed using his earlier studies to fulfil the growing demand for exotic scenes. He borrowed the motif of the resting lion in the Budapest sheet from his earlier oil painting *Studies of Lions* (private collection), executed around 1830. The lion's restrained character and its facial expression resembling a melancholic human face, attests to Delacroix's interest in Lavater's theory of physiognomy. The Budapest watercolour is closely related to sheets with similar representations of lions (Fogg Art Museum, Cambridge, Mass.; Musée Bonnat, Bayonne; Galerie Jan Krugier, Geneva) which can also be dated to 1848–50.

ZSUZSA GONDA

203

Eugène Delacroix   1798–1863

Arab Camp at Night, 1863

Oil on canvas, 55 × 65 cm

INVENTORY NUMBER: 72.7.B
SELECTED REFERENCES: Vincent Pomarède and Arlette Sérullaz, *Delacroix: Les dernières années*, exh.cat., Galeries nationales du Grand Palais, Paris, and Philadelphia Museum of Art, 1998, no.138; Mária Illyés, *Oeuvres françaises du XIXe siècle: Les collections du Musée des Beaux-Arts Budapest*, 4, Budapest, 2001, pp.22–23; Hermann Arnhold (ed.), *Orte der Sehnsucht: Mit Künstlern auf Reisen*, exh.cat., Westfälisches Landesmuseum, Münster, 2008, pp.223–24, no.179

The vivid colours and dynamic brushstrokes with which Eugène Delacroix treated exotic themes had a definitive influence on the avante-garde during the second half of the nineteenth century. The allegorical painting *Liberty Leading the People*, created in the wake of the revolution of July 1830, was well received and in 1832 King Louis-Philippe sent the artist to Morocco as part of a diplomatic mission. Delacroix kept a journal of his trip and created over one hundred paintings and drawings of North African people, buildings, animals and costume. The exotic oriental motifs, radiant light and brilliant colours were an inspiration that profoundly influenced his art for the rest of his career.

Time and again he would re-paint scenes from the trip, and create new themes from his memories of it. *Arab Camp at Night*, one of his last works, evokes a night spent in the desert during a ten-day caravan journey that he had made three decades earlier in the company of his Arabian escorts. The outlines of the Arabs resting by the fire dissolve into the dark landscape. Their tents and horses, barely visible, merge into the background. The flickering fire highlights only the facial contours and the hems of the figures' clothes. In this dimly lit environment the contours of the bodies, suffused with warm light, reveal the compositional choices of the elderly master, weak from illness in the last days of his life.

FERENC TÓTH

204

Gustave Courbet   1819–1877

Rocky Landscape, 1872

Oil on canvas, 73 × 92 cm

INVENTORY NUMBER: 396.B
SELECTED REFERENCES: Robert Fernier, *La vie et l'oeuvre de Gustave Courbet: Catalogue raisonné*, 2, Paris, 1977, no.832; Mária Illyés, *Oeuvres françaises du XIXe siècle: Les collections du Musée des Beaux-Arts Budapest*, 4, Budapest, 2001, pp.68–69

Gustave Courbet was the artist who defined the nineteenth-century Realist movement in France. He attacked the aesthetic ideals of academicism and the imaginative outpourings of Romanticism. His first paintings with scenes depicting the harsh realities of rural life caused shock and outrage due to their uncompromising naturalism presented on a large scale. In all genres – whether portraying people or nature – he favoured direct observation. Even so, for Courbet Realism did not mean the accurate recording of subjects. The study of individual features was often accompanied by spontaneous, raw brushstrokes. In his landscapes he liked to use a palette knife, employing rapid movements to add a thick layer of paint to a canvas, thereby enhancing the plasticity of the brushwork.

Courbet, in conjunction with the painters of the Barbizon School, highlighted the importance of *plein-air* painting, of immersing oneself in nature and perceiving the particular features of a landscape. Throughout his life the rocky terrain of his native region was a source of inspiration for his landscape art. The years immediately preceding the painting of *Rocky Landscape* were ones of torment and worry for Courbet. Arrest and imprisonment awaited him for his role in the 1871 Commune. In 1872, following the deaths of his mother and of his son, the painter

returned from Paris to his home town of Ornans. He immediately began work, having received several commissions. It was in the year of his return home that he painted the present work. The deep shadows of the landscape and the rocky crag towering above a pure spring are expressive of his emotional state at the time.

FERENC TÓTH

205

Sándor Ziffer   1880–1962

Landscape with Fence, early 1910s

Oil on canvas, 91.5 × 109 cm

HUNGARIAN NATIONAL GALLERY, INVENTORY NUMBER: 60.26 T
SELECTED REFERENCES: Mariann Gergely, 'L'influence de la peinture fauve en Hongrie', in *Le fauvisme ou "l'épreuve du feu": Éruption de la modernité en Europe*, exh.cat., Musée d'Art moderne de la Ville de Paris, 2000, pp.330, 332, 333; György Szücs, 'Landscape with Fence', in Nóra Veszprémi and Ferenc Gosztonyi (eds), *Hungarian National Gallery: The Collections*, Budapest, 2007, p.131

In 1906 Sándor Ziffer, a pupil of Simon Hollósy, met Béla Czóbel who persuaded him to go to the artists' colony at Nagybánya (today Baia Mare, Romania) and from there on to Paris. Ziffer's sudden encounter with the latest trends in art profoundly influenced his work. The Fauvist paintings at the Salon d'Automne, the Gauguin Memorial Exhibition and, it seems, the encouragement of Henri Matisse, persuaded him to diverge from the naturalist style he had developed under Hollósy. On his return to Nagybánya, between 1907 and 1908 he created his most important works, including landscapes and cityscapes, which were closer to the 'Hungarian Fauves' and the works of Lajos Tihanyi than to Czóbel's idiom.

Landscape with Fence depicts an identifiable topographical location in Nagybánya: the small street, flanked by miners' houses, which winds its way up to the foot of Kereszthegy (Cross Hill). The painting inadvertently provides a summary of Ziffer's work up to that point. In the years that followed, having married a German woman, he became more oriented towards Germany. The contrast between the cold blue contours and the burning reds, and the sharp shadows created by the oblique sunlight attest to an experiment in renewing naturalist landscape and Ziffer's understanding of the stylising, decorative concepts of the Fauves and Paul Gauguin.

GYÖRGY SZÜCS

206

János Máttis Teutsch   1884–1960

Landscape, c.1917

Oil on cardboard, 50 × 60 cm

INVENTORY NUMBER: 75.28
SELECTED REFERENCES: Steven A. Mansbach (ed.), *Standing in the Tempest: Painters of the Hungarian Avant-garde 1908–1930*, exh.cat., Santa Barbara Museum of Art, CA, 1991, no.93; Éva Bajkay et al., *Máttis Teutsch and der Blaue Reiter*, Budapest, 2001, no.P27

Born in Brassó (today Braşov, Romania), János Máttis Teutsch studied sculpture in Budapest and Munich. In 1905 he moved to Paris and spent almost three years there before returning to his native Brassó. Around the time he completed this painting, Máttis Teutsch held his first major exhibition in the editorial office of the most significant Hungarian avant-garde journal *MA* (Today) in 1917. Soon

afterwards some of his linocuts were published in Herwarth Walden's periodical *Der Sturm*, and in 1921, together with Paul Klee, he exhibited works in Walden's Der Sturm Gallery in Berlin.

Although it is not known when Máttis Teutsch took up painting, contemporary accounts suggest that he painted landscapes even during his Parisian years. In the foreground of the picture – inspired by the hilly landscape around Brassó – stands a lonely group of trees with long thin white trunks. While the naturalistic elements can be made out, the curved shapes of the roads and the slopes painted in shades of yellow, green and pink shift the work towards abstraction. Compared to the abstract works created by the artist after 1918–19, with their powerful colour schemes, evocative of whirling movement, this work is characterised by its cool, bright colours, similar to those employed by Henri Matisse in his paintings of the same period. However, on account of the motif of the rhythmically spaced tree trunks and the arabesque-like arched decorative forms, the Budapest painting has closer kinship with landscapes by the Nabis, and by Maurice Denis and Paul Sérusier in particular.

MÓNIKA KUMIN

207

Sándor Bortnyik   1893–1976

Composition with Six Figures, 1918

Oil on canvas, 76 × 95.5 cm

HUNGARIAN NATIONAL GALLERY, INVENTORY NUMBER: 75.103 T
SELECTED REFERENCES: Alfréd Kemény, 'Bortnyik képei és grafikája', *MA*, 4-7 (1919), pp.171–74; László Borbély, 'Bortnyik', Budapest, 1971; Júlia Szabó, *A magyar aktivizmus művészete 1915–1927*, Budapest, 1981, pp.74–77

Sándor Bortnyik entered Lajos Kassák's circle of young avant-garde artists in the late 1910s. After studying poster and packaging design, Bortnyik soon went on to become the leading graphic artist of *A Tett* (The Action), a magazine launched by the Activists, and after it was banned, the journal *MA* (Today). He designed covers for books of verse and literary anthologies published by *MA*, and produced highly expressive and visionary illustrations for the works of young poets. Exploiting the technical potential of reproductive graphic processes, he condensed forms into near-abstract symbols and disintegrated picture planes into surfaces, reconstructing them in a deliberately distorted and collage-like structure. His intriguing prints, made using lobed forms cut out with an etching tool, and compositions with spiky fragmented surfaces reveal his rebellious, destructive passions, as well as the innovative, creative motivations of the Activist artist. The impulsive power of Bortnyik's linocuts was in keeping with the well-defined system of monochromatic surfaces that characterise his work.

Composition with Six Figures conveys a futuristic sentiment of dynamic movement and energetic struggle. The confrontational, rhythmically repeated angular forms and the belligerent and abstract robot-like figures evoke the aggression that is prompted by the destruction of past traditions. The canvas base and thickly applied paint serve to render in a painterly way the material presence of physical force. The interactions between dynamic colour combinations (brown, blue, green) reinforce the jagged rhythms of determined struggle.

MARIANN GERGELY

208

Akseli Gallen-Kallela   1865–1931

March Evening in the Garden of the Majovszky Villa on Gellért Hill, 1908

Watercolour, 335 × 222 mm

INVENTORY NUMBER: 1935-2649
SELECTED REFERENCE: Leena Ahtola-Moorhouse and Juha Ilvas (eds), *Akseli Gallen-Kallela*, exh.cat., Finnish National Gallery Ateneum, Helsinki, 1996, no.275

Born Axel Waldemar Gallén, from 1890 the Finnish Symbolist painter had become known as Akseli Gallen-Kallela. In 1908 the Museum of Fine Arts, Budapest, organised an exhibition of his works, which were characterised by their strongly stylised decorative technique. The patrons of the exhibition were Elek Koronghi-Lippich, the chair of the Fine Arts Department of the Ministry of Education and Religion, and the renowned art collector Pál Majovszky. A close friendship developed between the three men during the artist's visit to Hungary.

After the Budapest exhibition, Majovszky – whose collection also comprised a number of important nineteenth-century drawings in the present exhibition – bought a number of drawings from the Finnish artist. The archive of the Gallen-Kallela Museum in Espoo contains a copy of the Budapest catalogue bearing the artist's own inscriptions signalling the purchases made by Majovszky and the museum. Two works by the artist are mementoes of what proved to be an enjoyable stay in Budapest, and were executed there in early 1908. One is the present work, which represents the villa of the Majovszky family, built on Gellért Hill on the Danube's right bank, and was dedicated by the artist to Irén, Majovszky's older sister. The other is a small oil painting dedicated to Pál Majovszky, probably as a souvenir of the walks and evenings spent together on the Budapest riverside promenade. Gallen-Kallela painted a number of sites in Budapest, having been issued with a permit by the head of the capital's police department on 15 March 1908.

After World War I, on 27 August 1918, Majovszky wrote to his old friend Koronghi-Lippich describing the little house and its garden, which Gallen-Kallela had painted ten years earlier, in March 1908: 'My sister and I have been staying on Gellért Hill since the beginning of July. Irén was meant to go to Szilács, but we did not get appropriate lodgings there so we have taken refuge in our little cabin up here. I cannot say we draw much pleasure from our stay. The garden is in a deplorable state, watering is prohibited, the building is in bad condition, there is nobody to be hired for the most urgent repairs, managing the household is extremely difficult, we have been unable to get even milk since the beginning of the month, but the air is still better than down town…'

The present drawing, presented to the museum by Pál Majovszky in 1934, is signed and dated at the lower left: *à Mlle I. Majovszky amicalement de Akseli Gallén-Kallela / 1908.*

JUDIT GESKÓ

209

Tivadar Csontváry Kosztka   1853–1919

Pilgrimage to the Cedars of Lebanon, 1907

Oil on canvas, 192 × 200 cm

HUNGARIAN NATIONAL GALLERY, INVENTORY NUMBER: 93.25T
SELECTED REFERENCES: Lajos Németh, 'La vie et l'art de Tivadar Csontváry', *Acta Historiae Artium*, 10 (1964), pp.125–69; Júlia Szabó, ' "Cedrus aeternitatis hieroglyphicum", Iconology of a Natural Motif', *Acta Historia Artium*, 28 (1981), pp.1–127; Hubertus Gassner, '"Wem die Fähigkeit gegeben ist, in die Sonne zu sehen": Csontváry – ein genialer Dilettant', in *Csontváry*, exh.cat., Haus der Kunst, Munich, 1994, pp.198–99

The cedar paintings of Tivadar Csontváry Kosztka – *The Lonely Cedar*, in the Csontváry Museum in Pécs, and *Pilgrimage to the Cedars of Lebanon* – are in many respects the most important works of his *oeuvre*. Csontváry invested the cedar motif with a complexity that transforms the tree into concealed self-representations, not only in his paintings, but also, frequently, in his writings. The cedar's slow-growing seed, the magnitude of its lifespan exceeding human proportions, and its association with the 2000-metre high mountains of Lebanon, are features that take on human aspects in Csontváry's world-view. Slow growth, resilience, vigour and power of resistance, as well as the perfection and beauty of the form, the perseverance of life under the harshest natural conditions, are all defining characteristics of the artist's own life and artistic ideals. He himself dedicated many years to preparing for his work as a painter, and elected to live an ascetic life so that nothing would divert his attention from his work and noble objectives. It is no accident, then, that the monumental ceremonial of *Pilgrimage* is in many ways reminiscent of the often exaggeratedly personal and nationalistic self-evaluations of Csontváry's late writings.

In the popular Hungarian tradition of Csontváry's day cedars assumed a prominent role in both ancient local cults and Magyar mythology. Symbolically identifying the thousand-year-old cedars with the thousand-year-old Hungarian people was a common feature in public discourse at the time. Csontváry's choice of theme therefore represents an idiosyncratic nationalist programme the artist would happily embrace.

GÁBOR BELLÁK

210

Pál Szinyei Merse   1845–1920

Skylark, 1882

Oil on canvas, 163 × 128 cm

HUNGARIAN NATIONAL GALLERY, INVENTORY NUMBER: 5098
SELECTED REFERENCES: Anna Szinyei Merse, *Szinyei Merse Pál: Monográfia és oeuvrekatalógus*, Budapest, 1990, pp.102–03; Gabriella Dománszky, *Szinyei Merse Pál*, Budapest, 2009, pp. 46, 59

Picnic in May (1872–73) in the Hungarian National Gallery is one of Pál Szinyei Merse's best-known Impressionist-style pictures, but it was met with incomprehension and harsh criticism by contemporary Hungarian art critics. Following what he deemed as a failure, Szinyei Merse gave up painting for a decade and retired to his estate in the north of Hungary. He ended this self-imposed exile in 1881 when he and his family moved to Vienna where he took up painting once again. After much deliberation and preliminary research he decided to address mythological themes, which he believed were always popular with audiences. Later on he painted nude studies. *Skylark*, however, lacks mythological references altogether, and simply portrays a young woman with a beautiful body, dreamily delighting alfresco in the lark's flight. The theme was a daring one, particularly at a time when the scandal of Hans Makart's nudes, suffused with eroticism, reverberated throughout Vienna. Critics did not fail to point out the provocative bizarreness and overly powerful colours of *Skylark*. However, the painting's hostile reception can be put down to the fact that Szinyei Merse's portrayal of nature reminded viewers of the artificial backgrounds used in painters' studios. The flowers are markedly separate from one another and the forms are too hard, making the nude look as though she is disconnected from her surroundings. The artist may have drifted away from the pictorial unity and atmospheric effects of *plein-air* painting, yet the highly varied rendering of the sky attests to his impressive painterly power and immense boldness.

ZSUZSANNA BAKÓ

211

Akseli Gallen-Kallela   1865–1931

Young Faun, 1904

Oil on canvas, 67 × 65.5 cm

INVENTORY NUMBER: 196.B
SELECTED REFERENCES: *Akseli Gallen-Kallela (1865–1971)*, exh.cat., Hungarian National Gallery, Budapest, 1982, no.121; Ferenc Matits, 'Die skandinavischen Gemälde der Jahrhundertwende im Museum der Bildenden Künste zu Budapest', *Konsthistorisk Tidskrift*, 2 (1994), p.122; Ferenc Matits, 'A századforduló finn festményei a budapesti Szépművészeti Múzeum gyűjteményében', in Klára Hudra, Katalin Keserü and Irene Wichmann (eds), *Finnmagyar: Az 1900-as párizsi világkiállítástól a Cranbrook Schoolig. Voimaa, elämää, ilmaisua: Suomenja Unkarin taidesuhteet 1900–1920*, exh.cat., Gallen-Kallelan Museu, Espoo, and Ernst Múzeum, Budapest, 2004, p.172

After completing his studies at the Finnish Art Society in Helsinki, Akseli Gallen-Kallela trained at the Académie Julian in Paris and attended the atelier of Fernand Cormon. His subsequent work was deeply influenced by a journey to Karelia in Finland. He won a gold and a silver medal at the 1900 Exposition Universelle in Paris, marking a breakthrough in his career. By this time the artist had established himself as a leading figure on the Finnish art scene.

Gallen-Kallela's art is highly varied both stylistically and thematically. Initially he was a follower of the naturalism of Jules Bastien-Lepage (1848–1884), and subsequently his work was characterised by the type of decorative Symbolism in which national sentiment assumes an important role. The Finnish national epic poem, the *Kalevala*, remained a key motif for the artist throughout his life, for example in his frescoes for the Pori Mausoleum (1901–03) and in his illustrations for various editions of the poem.

In *Young Faun*, a boy kneels on a hill strewn with flowers, peering at two girls about to bathe in the lake. One of them is wading into the water while the other is taking off her white dress. The blond boy wears a simple white shirt and a pair of beige breeches. The light cast from the top right corner of the picture creates a shadow on the left side of his body. The sandy shore, the grass and the soft yellows and greens of the trees, painted with broad brushstrokes, create a harmonious backdrop. A watercolour of 1888 can be regarded as a precursor to *Young Faun*. While it resembles the 1904 oil painting in many respects, it is more decorative and detailed, with both the water at the top and the flowers painted in the Secessionist style.

The Museum of Fine Arts purchased *Young Faun* at the art fair of the National Hungarian Fine Arts Society of Budapest in the winter of 1906–07, where the Finnish display was curated by Gallen-Kallela himself.

BARBARA POTZNER

212

Maurice Denis 1870–1945

Maternity, 1895

Oil on canvas, 81 × 65 cm

INVENTORY NUMBER: 401 B
SELECTED REFERENCES: Ursula Perucchi-Petri, 'Das Werk von Maurice Denis', in *Maurice Denis*, exh.cat., National Museum of Western Art, Tokyo, and Museum of Modern Art, Kyoto, 1981, p.7; Cifka Brigitta, 'Maternité', in *Budapest 1869–1914: Modernité hongroise et peinture européenne*, exh.cat., Musée des Beaux-Arts de Dijon, 1995, p.358; Mária Illyés, *Oeuvres françaises du XIXe siècle: Les collections du Musée des Beaux-Arts Budapest*, 4, Budapest, 2001, pp.152–53

Throughout his life Maurice Denis sought to achieve a renewal of religious art, in succession to the Nazarenes in Germany and the Pre-Raphaelites in England. To that end, in 1919 he established together with Georges-Olivier Desvallières (1861–1950) the Ateliers d'art sacré. Denis's style was characterised by a decorative simplification of form. Japanese woodcuts had a profound influence on his work, as did the art of Fra Angelico. He also produced some important theoretical writings, in particular as a member of the Nabis group, which was founded in 1888.

With the birth of his children, Denis repeatedly dealt with the subject of maternity. This picture portrays his first wife Marthe Meurier with their first-born son Jean-Paul, who died shortly after Denis completed the painting. Behind them are Marthe's elder sister Eva and a little girl who lived next door called Thérèse Wattilleux. The bright colours of Marthe's dress dominate the foreground, offset by the dark background lit only by a window of a similar colour to the dress. Moreover, there is a sharp contrast between the dresses of Marthe and Eva. The pinks of their skin are almost luminous, as is the ring on Eva's left hand. The work is a characteristic example of Denis's decorative style, in particular the whirling folds of the dress and the curls of Marthe's hair. The bodies have a more three-dimensional quality than those in his earlier works. A close variant of the picture is in the Josefowitz Collection; however, the Budapest version contains several parts, including the little girl's face, which are depicted in more detail.

BARBARA POTZNER

213

Károly Ferenczy 1862–1917

Woman Painting, 1903

Oil on canvas, 136 × 129 cm

INVENTORY NUMBER: 2472
SELECTED REFERENCES: György Szücs, 'Femme peintre', in *Lumières magyares: Les tendances coloristes de la peinture hongroise entre 1870 et 1914*, exh.cat., Salle Saint-Jean, Hôtel de Ville de Paris, 2001, pp.96–97; Anna Szinyei Merse, 'Pittrice', in *Alla ricerca del colore e della luce: Pittori ungheresi 1832–1914*, exh.cat., Galleria d'Arte Moderna di Palazzo Pitti, Florence, 2002, pp.160–61

After studying in Munich and Paris, around 1890 Károly Ferenczy and the co-founders of the artists' colony at Nagybánya (today Baia Mare, Romania) – Simon Hollósy, János Thorma and Béla Iványi Grünwald – embraced the 'subtle naturalism' of Jules Bastien-Lepage. But as early as the first summer of the artists' colony in 1896, Ferenczy painted *Sermon on the Mount*, influenced by *plein-air* painting, which was followed by other works based on biblical themes as well as mysterious, dreamlike scenes. While working as a professor at the Hungarian Academy of Fine Arts, Ferenczy's second Nagybánya period saw the creation of a series of sunlit landscapes.

Woman Painting is a genuinely *plein-air* composition, where the artist works out of doors to explore at first hand the relationship between colours and light. Invariably, strong sunlight will cause colours to fade and lose saturation, while deep, powerful hues can best be seen at dusk. Ferenczy has nevertheless sought to preserve both colour saturation and the effects of the sun, exploiting in this way the various shades of blue and green – a particularly difficult task. The painting brings to mind the opening lines of the catalogue for his 1903 retrospective exhibition: 'The artistic aspirations that have driven me for the past seven to eight years developed in communion with the abundant nature of Nagybánya: delight in nature fuels the desire to reproduce it. In terms of manner of expression, I seek colouristic naturalism on a synthetic basis.'

JUDIT BOROS

214

József Rippl-Rónai 1861–1927

Portrait of Elek Petrovics and Simon Meller, 1910

Oil on cardboard, 83.5 × 104 cm

On loan from a private collection
SELECTED REFERENCE: Mária Bernath and Ildikó Nagy (eds), *József Rippl-Rónai's Collected Works*, exh.cat., Hungarian National Gallery, Budapest, 1998, no.99

From the spring of 1901 onwards, József Rippl-Rónai divided his time between Paris, Budapest and Kaposvár, a small town in Transdanubia. In 1903 he moved back permanently from the French capital to Hungary and became acquainted with the great essayist Elek Petrovics (1873–1945), a lawyer by training who would later become the director of the Budapest Museum of Fine Arts. In 1906 Petrovics wrote an important analysis of Rippl-Rónai's work, which is still relevant today.

In 1907, following a highly successful exhibition, Rippl-Rónai began a new stylistic phase in parallel with the Fauves. His works from this period are characterised by large, uninterrupted planes of pure, unmixed colour. The artist described these paintings

---

as 'maize' pictures, since they are constructed from 'grain-sized' blocks of colour. The double portrait, signed and dated in the lower left corner, is one of his most successful achivements in this new style. The figures of Elek Petrovics and the art historian Simon Meller (1875–1949) – one looking to the side and the other towards the viewer, underlining the modernist concept of the isolation of the individual – are independent from each other, yet still convey solidarity. By accentuating the powerful intellect of the two experts he simultaneously emphasises not only their spiritual independence, but also their common purpose in championing modern art.

In 1911 the influential Budapest journal, *Nyugat* (West), published Rippl-Rónai's memoirs, in which the painter predicted that Petrovics would one day reorganise the rooms of the Museum of Fine Arts in such a way as to allow 'the really modern [works] to be separated from the partially modern ones…'. This prophecy came true in 1914, when Petrovics was named director of the Museum of Fine Arts. The double portrait executed four years earlier thus anticipated Petrovics's directorship by representing him together with Simon Meller, the head of the museum's Department of Prints and Drawings.

JUDIT GESKÓ

215

Henri-Marie-Raymond de
Toulouse-Lautrec 1864–1901

Women in the Dining Room, 1893

Oil on cardboard, 61 × 81 cm

INVENTORY NUMBER: 356.B
SELECTED REFERENCES: Maurice Georges Dortu, *Toulouse-Lautrec et son oeuvre: Catalogue des dessins*, 2, New York, 1971, p.499; Étienne Genthon, 'Un tableau de Toulouse-Lautrec au Musée des Beaux-Arts', *Bulletin du Musée Hongrois des Beaux-Arts*, 25 (1965), pp.47–50; Anne Roquebert, 'Ces dames au réfectoire, 1893', in Françoise Cachin and Monique Nonne (eds), *L'Europe des peintres*, exh.cat., Musée d'Orsay, Paris, 1993, p.164, no.47

Scion of the wealthy counts of Toulouse and indefatigable chronicler of the decadent Parisian scene, Toulouse-Lautrec was, on account of his eccentric, self-destructive way of life, an archetypal figure of the *fin de siècle*, an era that might be described as the apotheosis of the 'eroticism of consumption'. Disabilities and health problems throughout his childhood made him an outsider, finding consolation only in drawing and painting. As a pupil of Fernand Cormon (1845–1924) he was introduced to Edgar Degas and Vincent van Gogh, and through them to Post-Impressionism. Toulouse-Lautrec's lithographs and posters soon propelled him into the vanguard of the Art Nouveau movement. In 1885, he set up his studio in the most bohemian district of Paris, Montmartre.

Like the novelists Gustave Flaubert, Emile Zola and Guy de Maupassant, Toulouse-Lautrec frequently portrayed people on the periphery of society. His models are invariably painted with a keen sense of character in an unmoralising, dispassionately objective yet sympathetic manner. Executed in thinned-down paint using broad brushstrokes, the present work, which depicts the dining room of a brothel at 6 rue des Moulins, has the feel of a pastel drawing. Although the painting is carefully composed, the arbitrary removal of the picture edges evokes the Japanese prints popular in the period, making it equally reminiscent of a snapshot. One of the prostitutes at the table has only one arm showing, while another is presented indirectly in a mirror that expands the space within the picture. The curious spatial effect makes for a composition affording two interpretations of the women's rendezvous. It conjures up alternate, timeless symbols: the unapproachable ideal of the *femme fatale* and the off-duty world of exhausted courtesans, lost in their own thoughts.

MÁRTON OROSZ

216

Paul Gauguin   1848–1903
Black Pigs, 1891
Oil on burlap, 91 × 72 cm

INVENTORY NUMBER: 355.B
SELECTED REFERENCES: Mária Illyés, *Oeuvres françaises du XIXe siècle: Les collections de Musée des Beaux-Arts Budapest*, 4, Budapest, 2001, no.59; Andrea Czére (ed.), *Museum of Fine Arts, Budapest: Masterpieces from the Collection*, Budapest, 2006, no.146; Stephen F. Eisenman (ed.), *Paul Gauguin: Artist of Myth and Dream*, Milan, 2007, no.69

Driven by an unquenchable desire for a 'savage' life, Paul Gauguin landed on Tahiti in the summer of 1891. Initially he rented a hut in the capital Papeete, but in the autumn he moved to the district of Mataiea on the island's south-west coast.

The Black Pigs may be one of the first paintings that Gauguin produced in Tahiti, and it probably depicts a typical scene of daily life in Mataiea. On the right-hand side in the foreground and further behind on the veranda of the house, native women sit in timeless serenity, surrounded by animals. Gauguin's early Tahitian drawings, which he referred to as 'documents', and a number of paintings from 1891–92 feature similar images of buildings, pigs and horses. While Gauguin here seeks to give the figures and animals decorative planar forms, the perspective viewpoint and the meticulous carefully systemised brushstrokes are reminiscent of the painterly solutions of his earlier Pont-Aven landscapes.

The unprimed coarse canvas used for the Budapest painting was typical of this period. The approach to subject-matter and the material simplification of form can perhaps be regarded as a precursor of Gauguin's subsequent larger symbolic works, and its somewhat mystical tone and decorative quality exemplify the period's notions of the 'exotic' and the 'primitive'.

MÓNIKA KUMIN

217

Paul Gauguin   1848–1903
Man from the Marquesas Islands, 1902
Monotype, watercolour, gouache, white body-colour and starch on mechanically manufactured calendered paper, 146 × 162 mm

INVENTORY NUMBER: 1935-2715
SELECTED REFERENCES: Bernard Dorival, 'Sources of the Art of Gauguin from Java, Egypt and Ancient Greece', *Burlington Magazine*, 93, 577 (1951), p.118; Richard S. Field, *Paul Gauguin: Monotypes*, exh.cat., Philadelphia Museum of Art, 1973, no.138; Judit Geskó and Josef Helfenstein (eds), *'Zeichnen ist Sehen': Meisterwerke von Ingres bis Cézanne aus dem Museum der Bildenden Künste Budapest und aus schweizer Sammlungen*, exh.cat., Kunstmuseum Bern and Kunsthalle Hamburg, 1996, no.123

After his rejection of Impressionism in the mid-1880s, Gauguin painted decorative pictures, applying the

---

colours without blending them. However, he grew disatisfied with the confines of Parisian Symbolist circles and in 1891 he travelled to Tahiti, to which he also returned in 1895. Six years later, he was living on the Marquesas Islands, where he died in 1903.

Photographs of the ninth-century high reliefs at the Javanese temple of Borobodur served as a constant source of inspiration for Gauguin's decorative style. Between 1891 and 1902 he used images of the carvings glued onto cardboard as models for paintings, monotypes and woodcuts. In the Budapest monotype, presented to the Museum of Fine Arts by Pál Majovszky in 1934, the attitudes of the hands and feet exactly follow the composition of one of the reliefs.

The sheet was executed after Gauguin had moved from Tahiti to the Marquesas Islands in September 1901. From that time on, he realised his monotypes on mechanically manufactured calendered paper supplied by the Parisian art dealer Ambroise Vollard. Gauguin imprinted the outlines of the figure and the surface of the thighs from cardboard onto the wet paper. The colours of the background and the soil were applied in a variety of ways: the blue and pink of the background, as well as the blue-grey of the soil were printed, or possibly applied with a brush. On the upper right edge of the sheet, he pressed his palm into the fresh white body colour, and on the lower left, the edge of his hand. In some places, he used a rag. For the modelling of the body, in places he employed the brush, sometimes – as on the thighs – over printed parts. He also pressed a small piece of wood into the black hair of the figure: its grain can be clearly seen. The plasticity of the white part of the loincloth is accentuated with white body-colour. The background and the stripe of the soil of the small, picturesque monotype did not meet, so Gauguin painted the missing narrow strip with red watercolour.

JUDIT GESKÓ

218

Oskar Kokoschka   1886–1980
Veronica's Veil, 1909
Oil on canvas, 119 × 80 cm

INVENTORY NUMBER: 542.B
SELECTED REFERENCES: Éva Kovács, 'Un chief-d'oeuvre de jeunesse d'Oscar Kokoschka', *Bulletin du Musée Hongrois des Beaux-Arts*, 18 (1961), pp.95–100; Johann Winkler and Katharina Erling, *Oskar Kokoschka. Die Gemälde 1906–1929*, catalogue, Galerie Welz, Salzburg, 1995, p.13; Sylvie Aigner, 'Véronique et la sainte face / Veronika mit dem Schweisstuch', in *Vienne 1900: Klimt, Schiele, Moser, Kokoschka*, exh.cat., Galeries nationales du Grand Palais, Paris, 2006, p.150

As well as creating an *oeuvre* as a playwright, Oskar Kokoschka completed his artistic studies as a pupil of Gustav Klimt, one of the best-known figures of the Austrian Secession, at the Viennese School of Applied Arts in 1909. Diverging from earlier painterly traditions, Kokoschka was not interested in depicting the world in a realistic or natural way, but was concerned with the psychological process of suggestively portraying the inner self. His tour-de-force portraits focusing on the workings of the soul made him a leading figure of German Expressionism.

Veronica's Veil is Kokoschka's first painting with a religious theme, and remains a key work of his early

---

period. In his autobiographical book *My Life*, he refers to it as 'my favourite religious picture'.

The painting portrays Veronica, known from the Apocrypha, who wipes with her veil the blood and sweat from the face of Christ on the Way to Calvary, and miraculously the veil preserves an imprint of the Saviour's face. The work shows Veronica in three-quarter view, her slender body arranged vertically across the picture plane, slightly tilting to the left. Her white, angular face radiates melancholy. The gesture with which she tightly embraces the veil can be traced back to traditional depictions of the Virgin Mary and the iconography of the *Pièta*. Transforming the Passion into a cosmic force field, the full moon in the upper right corner is a female symbol that also appears in Kokoschka's drama *Murderer, Hope of Women* (1907–08), which was staged at the time. Some years later the full moon came to refer metaphorically to Alma Mahler, the composer Gustav Mahler's widow, with whom Kokoschka had a brief but passionate love affair. The picture may also have provided the artist with a pretext to address a profane theme: while he was painting it he recalls the windows of his studio being washed by the caretaker's daughter, also called Veronica.

MÁRTON OROSZ

219

Pablo Picasso   1881–1973
Mother and Child, 1905
Watercolour on paper, 353 × 253 mm

INVENTORY NUMBER: 1918-461
SELECTED REFERENCES: Josep Palau I. Fabre, *Picasso: Life and Work of the Early Years, 1881–1907*, Oxford, 1981, no.1022; Veronika Kaposy, 'Dessins de Picasso à Budapest', *Bulletin du Musée Hongrois des Beaux-Arts*, 58–59 (1982), pp.93–106

This watercolour depicting the intimacy of mother and child was made in 1905, at a turning point in Picasso's career. It represents one of the first works to be produced in his Rose Period, which succeeded the Blue Period, a year after the artist had moved permanently to Paris. The neighbourhood to which Picasso had recently moved, with its numerous, rather poor studios, brought new friendships and romances – among others, with Fernande Olivier, who is here portrayed in pen and ink on the verso – as well as fresh artistic themes. The beggars of the Blue Period were replaced by the somewhat brighter compositions of the Rose Period, featuring circus acrobats, harlequins and other entertainers. In place of cold blues, we find warm oranges, pinks and pale reds. Meanwhile, human relations are depicted in a more intimate and romantic manner, representing a return to the relatively unclouded creativity that preceded the more austere Blue Period. While this period drew to a close around 1906, the circus turned into a lasting love for Picasso, and the Paris Medrano Circus continued to inspire him in works such as *Harlequin* (1915) and the *Circus Series* (1939).

The broader context of *Mother and Child* becomes clearer when it is compared to a preliminary drawing (Picasso Museum, Paris) made for the 1905 etching *Harlequin Family*. The relationship between mother and child has changed in the etching, but in the drawing the woman, who is breastfeeding her child, is still being watched by a man in harlequin costume, who has his back to the viewer but whose half-profile is visible. Meanwhile a dog is nuzzling up to the woman's leg. At the bottom, the mother and child are repeated, with the detailed portrayal of the child's hand reaching for its mother's face. The closed and angular figure of the mother almost melts into the dark background, which is stained by reddish watercolour patches. Emphasis is placed on the finely contoured face and on the child reaching up to its mother's cheek, as well as on her protective hands.

KATA BODOR

220

Marc Chagall   1889–1985

Donkey on the Roof, 1911–12

Gouache on paper, 430 × 345 mm

INVENTORY NUMBER: K.69.48
SELECTED REFERENCES: Sandor Kuthy and Meret Meyer, *Marc Chagall 1907–1917*, exh.cat., Museum of Fine Arts, Berne, 1995; Teréz Gerszi (ed.), *Dürer to Dalí: Master Drawings in the Budapest Museum of Fine Arts*, Budapest, 1999, no.124

Marc Chagall was one of ten children born into a Jewish family in Vitebsk near St Petersburg. As a young man he studied painting in the former capital, but soon realised that he could learn more in the workshops of renowned painters than at the State Academy. He left Russia for the first time in 1910 when Max Winawer, a lawyer whom he had met in St Petersburg and who supported him like a father, financed a four-year scholarship to study art in Paris. He left Russia permanently in 1924.

'My art is rooted in the soil of Vitebsk, yet it needed Paris just like a tree needs water', wrote Chagall in his autobiography, explaining his dual French-Russian identity. In Paris he initially established close relationships with such poets as Guillaume Apollinaire and Blaise Cendrars. Having moved to the Montparnasse artists' colony 'La Ruche' (The Hive), he found himself in the company of Albert Gleizes, Robert Delaunay and his fellow Russian immigrants Alexis von Jawlensky, Wassily Kandinsky and Jacques Lipchitz, and thus familiarised himself with Fauvism, Cubism and Futurism. His art, as *Donkey on the Roof* demonstrates, owes much to this circle of friends: several titles were inspired by the poets, the liberated colours and the angular Cubist forms by the painters.

Nevertheless, Chagall's roots are also apparent in this image of a small town with its folk atmosphere. The floating figure, losing his head, and the pinkish-red donkey suckling the infant could be motifs from a dream or a folktale. Perhaps it was such visions that inspired Apollinaire to label Chagall's art 'Surnaturalisme'. In composition this sketch is related to Chagall's painting *To Russia, Asses and Others* of 1911 (Musée d'art moderne de la Ville de Paris); since the two works are so similar, it is unlikely that the drawing was a first idea for the canvas, but rather a version painted after it, albeit one executed in an unelaborated, sketchy style.

KATA BODOR

221

Egon Schiele   1890–1918

Two Women Embracing, 1915

Pencil, watercolour and gouache, 485 × 327 mm

INVENTORY NUMBER: 1915-933
SELECTED REFERENCES: Jane Kallir, *Egon Schiele: The Complete Works*, New York, 1990, no.1742; Klaus Albrecht Schröder, *Egon Schiele*, exh.cat., Albertina, Vienna, 2005, no.178

The year 1915 marked an important milestone in Egon Schiele's short artistic career, which spanned a mere decade. By the 1910s he had found his own individual style; initially working under the influence of Gustav Klimt (1862–1918), by 1907 he had moved beyond the decorative tendencies of his early career. The troubled, lonely and exposed figures of this period, revealing their most private instincts, received both negative and positive criticism. Nonetheless, he managed to find a few buyers, which was helpful as he had been short of money since 1910 when his uncle withdrew financial support following Schiele's break with the Academy. In 1915 he found a generous patron who supported him with monthly payments. This encouraged him to separate from his former partner and to marry the middle-class Edith Harms. Only Schiele's call-up papers clouded their idyllic relationship.

The sudden blossoming of this romantic love influenced Schiele's art. His works more frequently included couples who represent the happier and more positive side of erotic love. He portrayed himself and his wife as an intimately connected couple, but Edith also appears with her nephew in drawings that depict the intimacy of mother and child in a decidedly bizarre way, with distinctly sexual undertones. Lesbianism was not a new topic in Schiele's art, just as the frank portrayal of all manifestations of sexuality was a characteristic feature of Viennese art at the turn of the century. Such subjects were also treated in fine art photography of the period, a medium with which Schiele also experimented and whose effect can be felt in this portrait of a couple, depicted from an unusual, overhead angle. The figures, cut off at the knee, fill the whole picture field. One woman is looking at her partner without expression, while the other glances back provocatively at the viewer; together they form an embracing couple floating dynamically in space, almost like dancers. The colours are more dull and reserved in this period, and the angular contours of the earlier figures have been replaced by soft curves. Nevertheless, expressivity is still tangible in the thick, notched edges of the red dress and in the abundance of freely flowing hair.

KATA BODOR

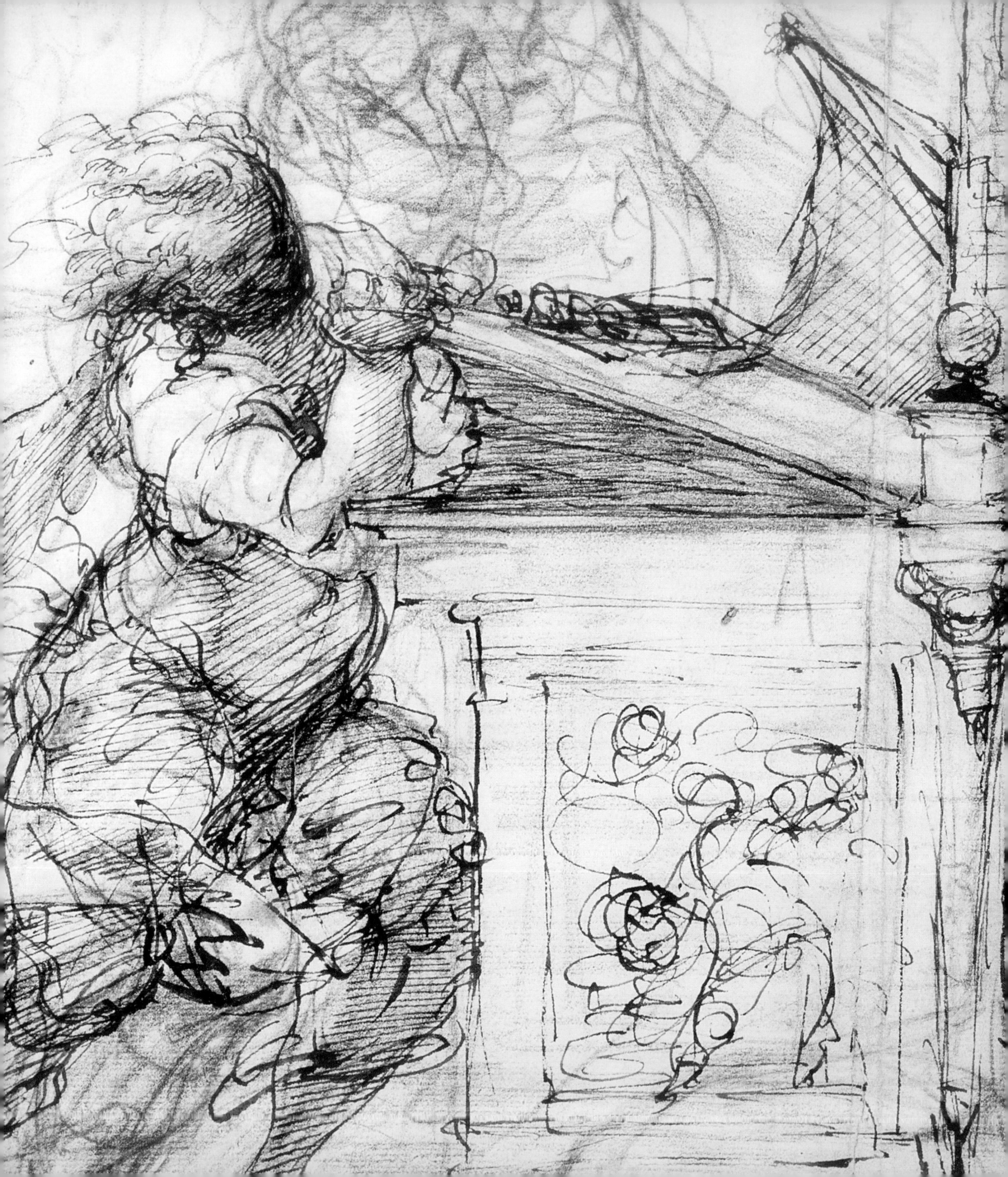

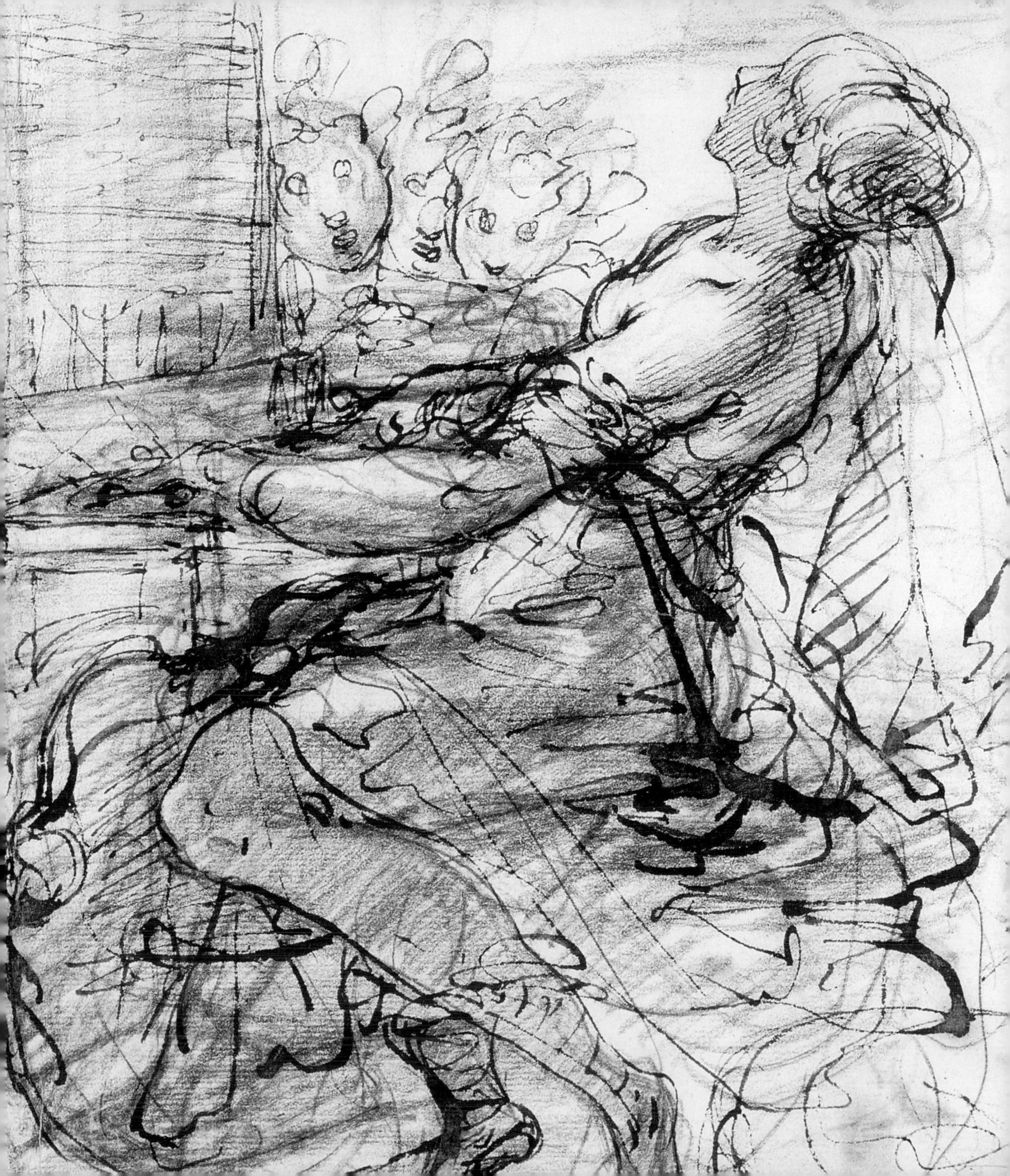

Index